NO QUARTER

THE THREE LIVES OF

JIMMY PAGE

By the same author

Hot Wired Guitar: The Life of Jeff Beck
The Life of Blur
Nailed to History: The Story of the Manic Street Preachers

NO QUARTER

THE THREE LIVES OF

JIMMY PAGE

MARTIN POWER

OVERLOOK OMNIBUS

This edition published by Omnibus Press and distributed in the United States and Canada by The Overlook Press, Peter Mayer Publishers Inc, 141 Wooster Street, New York, NY 10012. For bulk and special sales requests, please contact sales@overlookny.com or write to us at the above address.

Copyright © 2016 Omnibus Press
(A Division of Music Sales Limited)
14/15 Berners Street,
London, W1T 3LJ, UK

Cover designed by Fresh Lemon

ISBN: 978-1-4683-1214-0

Images supplied by: Alamy, Getty, Press Association, Rex Features, Channel Islands TV, Country Life, James Noble, Linda Westmore & Mona Shafer Edwards (courtroom sketch).

Every effort has been made to trace the copyright holders of the photographs in this book but one or two were unreachable. We would be grateful if the photographers concerned would contact us.

Printed in the USA

A catalogue record for this book is available from the British Library.

Cataloguing-in-Publication data is available from the Library of Congress.

Visit Omnibus Press on the web at www.omnibuspress.com

Contents

Contents

PART 1

YOUR TIME IS GONNA COME

"Music is the one thing that has been consistently there for me. It's never let me down..."

Jimmy Page

CHAPTER 1

Mama Don't Allow No Skiffle Round Here

James Patrick Page was born on January 9, 1944 at the Grove Nursing Home in Heston, a small but verdant suburb of the London borough of Hounslow, neatly situated about ten miles from Big Ben and the political centre of England's capital city. 'Owned' by King Henry VIII and his daughter Elizabeth in the 1500s, by the time of Page's arrival, Heston was perhaps best known for the aerodrome that sat imposingly on the outskirts of town, expansion of which from a small airfield to a major international airport began the year of Jimmy's birth. Originally called London Airport but renamed Heathrow in 1966, it was still known as Heston Aerodrome when British Prime Minister Neville Chamberlain flew to Munich in September 1938 for appeasement talks with Nazi leader Adolf Hitler. Some two weeks later, Chamberlain returned to Heston clutching a piece of paper in his hand that declared 'Peace in our time'. He was being a tad optimistic. Within a year, the Nazis invaded Poland and Great Britain was at war with Germany for the second time in as many decades. Soon, the rest of the world was involved too.

The war was still raging when Jimmy was taken from Grove Nursing Home to his parents' house at 26 Bulstrode Road in central Hounslow a day or so after his birth. Though the awful, nightly bombing raids that defined 'The Blitz' of 1941 had receded somewhat, London was still a very dangerous place to be as German V1 and V2 rockets soon took up where Luftwaffe planes had left off, the new 'doodlebugs' targeting the city and its citizens with ruthless efficiency and deadly accuracy. Difficult times then, especially for those raising a newborn. Thankfully, the Page family seemed to have matters in hand.

Jimmy's father, James Page – from whom Jimmy took his name – was in his mid-twenties when his son came home. Born in 1917, James could easily trace his own family history back to his paternal great-grandfather, Thomas Page, whose thriving carpentry business had employed seven men in Banbury, Oxfordshire during the 1870s. And it was in Banbury that James' own father, Herbert Miller Page, was born in 1879. A nurseryman by trade, Herbert had his fair share of ups and downs to contend with early in life. Soon after the Page clan moved north from Banbury to Bottesford, Nottinghamshire, Herbert lost the sight of one eye when he was struck by a rebounding air gun pellet fired by his brother John. A horrible thing to befall anyone, Herbert's bad luck was reported in the local paper at the time. "Such a distressing accident has evoked much sympathy for the young Mr. Page and his family." It didn't hold Herbert back either romantically or socially.[1] Marrying Florence Wilson – three years his junior and originally from Southampton, Hampshire – the couple had three children, Gladys, Norman, and then after a ten-year gap, Jimmy's own father, James.

Jimmy's mother, Patricia – whose epithet provided the inspiration for his second name, Patrick – had an equally interesting family background. Born in Croydon in 1925, Patricia's own parents were John and Edith

---

1   Herbert Miller Page was to become a pillar of the community in Bottesford. For instance, when local bride-to-be Ms. Myrtle Elmbourn needed someone to escort her to Bottesford church in the absence of her father (presumably deceased), Herbert Miller was on hand to help. "The bride was escorted... by Mr. Herbert Page," said the local paper, "and given away by her mother, who was wearing a dress of amethyst shade trimmed with ecru lace, and a black hat." However, Herbert had long moved his family – including Jimmy's father – from the area to Ewell, Surrey by the time World War II broke out.

Gaffikin, though as her father's Gaelic-sounding surname suggested, there was northern Irish blood in her veins. Indeed, tracing the Gaffikins' history back a generation or two, Patricia's father, John, two of his four brothers and his own mother, Jeanie, were born in Belfast and Donaghendry, County Tyrone, respectively.

A young couple by today's standards (though certainly not at the time), James and Patricia Elizabeth Page had been married nearly three years when Jimmy came along. They had prepared admirably well for his arrival. Like Patricia's father, John[2] – who sadly died before his daughter wed on April 22, 1941 – the studious James had found a promising office job in the local aircraft industry, working as a wages clerk. Soon, he would rise to the position of 'Industrial Personnel Manager', again an extremely respectable role. After a youthful start in the catering trade, Patricia too put her skills to excellent use, becoming a doctor's secretary after Jimmy reached school age.

Though central Hounslow was a comfortable enough spot to put down roots, proximity to family and possible work connections may have played a hand in the Pages' decision to leave the town and move further south to Feltham while James Jr. was an infant. Still nominally in the borough of Hounslow – if now on the other side of its rangy heath – Feltham was in essence much the same as Heston where Jimmy was born: similar transport links to central London, similar look, similar village feel and, again, once 'owned' by King Henry VIII. But perhaps of greater importance was the fact that Feltham was a good deal closer to James and Patricia's relatives who lived near the town, thus creating a stronger support network for all concerned. Additionally, Feltham was the base of Menzies Aviation, which like fellow employer 'The Heston Aircraft Company', may well have been useful to James Page when considering his long-term career prospects.

Another plausible reason for the Pages' move to Feltham was the fact that the Nazis had stopped bombing it, as they had indeed stopped

---

2   John Gaffikin had been a progress manager at an aircraft works in either Heston or
    Feltham before his death in 1941. Though records are sketchy on this point, it seems a
    fair bet Jimmy's father might have been employed at the same company/companies.

bombing most everywhere else by the spring of 1945. The site of Britain's second largest railway marshalling and freight yard, Feltham had been the target of repeated air strikes but now – as throughout the rest of Europe – its residents could sleep soundly in their beds once again. Nevertheless, like the rest of Europe, the onus was very much on picking up the pieces. After years of conflict and the death of millions, towns, cities and countries had to dust themselves off, clean up the rubble and start again. For Feltham, London, England and Great Britain as a whole, this meant a decade or so of avoiding falling masonry or plunging into craters left by bombs and rockets while the process of slow re-building took place. In this oppressive, grey post-war atmosphere, money was tight and food rationing abounded. Prosperity would eventually return, but Jimmy Page was unlikely to get his first proper chocolate bar for another eight years.

It could have been worse. While Page had to wait a while to discover the joys of the cocoa bean, he at least wouldn't have it snatched away by fellow siblings, as he was to remain an only child. The subject of much psychobabble, only children are meant to be many things, quite a few of them negative: slow to share, excessively private, over-protected, unduly sensitive and, sometimes, just plain odd. On the upside, however, such children were also said to have fine, positive traits including high levels of independence and academic achievement, good organisational skills and strong attention to detail. They also mature faster. In later life, Jimmy would display some, if not quite all of these. But like all only children, the biggest hurdle for him to overcome at the time was socialising with other kids.

Having no brother or sister there to help guide or influence "the rules of the game", every social skill and human interaction Page learned was by observation alone, and more often than not by watching the adults around him. Not a perfect start when entering a classroom for the first time, then. But Page didn't seem to mind. He rather liked it that way. "Until the age of five, I was totally isolated from kids my own age," he later told archivist Howard Mylett. "That early isolation probably had a lot to do with how I turned out. A lot of people can't be on their own. They get frightened. But it doesn't bother me at all. It gives me a sense of security." And as time came to show, it also gave him a formidable base of operations from which to access his own creative process.

When Jimmy was eight, the family upped sticks again and moved to Epsom, this time putting down major and more lasting roots. Again, it was the smart thing to do. Though only half an hour's drive from their former home in Feltham, the town was neatly removed from the main flight path leading into Heathrow, then at the start of its 50-year run towards becoming Europe's busiest airport. James Page might have earned his wages from the industry, but he didn't want the planes it produced ruining his Sunday afternoons. "When the airport got jets, we moved away," Jimmy recalled in 1983, "it was just so noisy." Cannily avoiding a future price crash on their house due to constant air traffic, the Pages settled at 34 Miles Road, a pleasant 'three up, two down' located in a crescent close, but not too close, to Epsom High Street. Its front room would become Jimmy's main base of operations for over a decade.

As far as the Page's new home town was concerned, there was much to commend it, with Epsom full of local history and future promise. Named for a wealthy landowner called Ebba – Epsom literally translates as 'Ebba's manor' – it was a strategic meeting place for Anglo-Saxon gentry dating back to the fifth century until the Norman invasion of 1066 called time on such activities. Meriting a mention in the Domesday book of 1086 (two churches, two mills, 38 houses and 24 acres of woodland, no less), Epsom kept mostly to itself until the 1700s, when the Georgians discovered a spring at its centre and turned it into a spa town.

Then a fashionable and, indeed, profitable enterprise, Epsom's association with spas, flowing water, healing minerals and restful slumber made it well worth a visit, the locals soon producing 'Epsom salts' for ailing souls to take home after their stay. In keeping with its spa success, Epsom's modest racecourse was duly expanded, offering residents and tourists not only the opportunity for physical restoration, but a chance to bet on the horses too.

By 1780, the now famous Epsom Derby and Oaks were off and running, their importance on the racing calendar growing exponentially over the next 100 years. Come 1910, and the Derby and Oaks were bringing over 50,000 visitors to the town for each meeting, this surge in popularity seeing off any remaining farmland in favour of shops, roads and the odd hotel. Surrounded by countryside, with a striking clock tower to mark its centre and the added oddity of having not one, but five psychiatric hospitals to confirm its borders, Epsom in the early fifties was non-threatening, more or less aircraft-free and suited the Pages well. "Most of my childhood was spent in Epsom," Jimmy later told Howard Mylett. "It was really nice there."

Enrolled in a local primary school on Pound Lane, Page set about making friends and finding things to do. One early success was reportedly sports, with the youngster showing an aptitude for hurdling that eventually led to him becoming school champion. According to local legend, he was also a keen cricketer. Jimmy's efforts with brush and canvas were duly noted too, as his teachers encouraged him to focus on art as much as English or arithmetic. Though once describing himself as "a terrible draughtsman", Page was obviously good enough to be marked out by tutors as one to watch, a useful observation on their part that would help him out of a tight spot when career troubles threatened to flare in his late teens. Away from academia, Jimmy could take full advantage of Epsom's more leafy aspects, with the local Common, Longrove Park and Mounthill Gardens all within easy reach. In due course, his fondness for walking expanded to a love of full-blown hikes, with Page gaining access to bigger outdoor spaces such as Horton Country Park and the Surrey Hills.[3]

Crucially, Jimmy was also gaining exposure to the pleasures of music, its essential mysteries coming to him from three distinct sources. First was his enrolment in the choir of St. Barnabas Church on Epsom's Temple Road. Overseen by the cadaverously named Mr. Coffin, Page could be found singing every Sunday morning to the faithful while dressed in the choir robes – a black cassock, white surplus and white ruff neck – required for the role. "Yes, I was a choir boy," he told Channel 4 some 60 years after the event, "and lots of black musicians in the States have said that their (musical inspiration) came from church. But you

---

3   One story has it that Jimmy became so adept at hiking, he actually hitched a ride to Scandinavia for a walking tour in his late teens.

know, I don't know if I could say that." Given his later interests, this seems almost certain.

Another less formal route from which music seeped into Jimmy's consciousness was the radio. With no siblings to distract him, the youngster spent most nights in the company of his parents, listening to whatever songs crackled across the airwaves. Aside from a staple diet of crooners and balladeers, Page was privy to the crash, bang and wallop of British big bands, trad-jazzers, American swing and oodles of tunes specifically aligned to dance crazes then sweeping UK ballrooms: 'The Cha Cha', 'The Bossa Nova' and, maybe on a lively night, even 'The Jitterbug'. From Ella Fitzgerald, Glenn Miller and the Andrews Sisters to Jack Parnell, Ted Heath and the silky-smooth tones of singer Dennis Lotis, Jimmy would have heard the lot. "In fifties Britain," someone once joked, "swing was king."

The third and certainly most beguiling source of potential music for Jimmy Page had been sitting around the house since he and his parents moved to Epsom. Unsure whether it had been left by the previous owners or relatives, it seemed to simply materialise one morning in the living room. "Well," Page would later maintain, a bit mysteriously, "nobody seemed to know where it had come from or quite why it was there." The object in question was a Spanish acoustic guitar; fully strung and in reasonable shape, just sitting there, staring at them all from a corner. As neither of Jimmy's parents was musical and Page himself was still a tad unsure of it, the guitar remained untouched for years. However, he always knew it was there. "Well," he later said, "a guitar kind of makes an intervention, if you like..." A little secret to be unlocked, then.

The set of keys required to do just that landed squarely in Page's lap with the arrival of the skiffle boom in 1956. A simple, some might even say crude, cocktail of American country blues and Appalachian bluegrass, skiffle relied on three central chords and a hollering vocal to make its musical point. But when performed well, as demonstrated by Lonnie Donegan, that simplicity of form could be as propulsive and emotionally involving as the finest classical symphony. "Lonnie," Page later told Charles Shaar Murray, "was the first person who was really giving it some passion that we could all relate to."

A native Scot, Anthony Donegan adopted the name Lonnie from bluesman Lonnie Johnson, and began his run at fame in the late forties, first as a member of Ken Colyer's Jazzmen and then as a part of the Chris Barber Jazz Band. Originally employed to bolster Barber's Dixieland-themed troupe on banjo, Lonnie soon found himself bashing out a "skiffle break" on guitar during the interval. Largely designed to give his fellow musicians a breather between sets, Donegan's anarchic readings of old Leadbelly and Woody Guthrie tunes nonetheless gained real traction with audiences, keeping punters away from the bar and rooted to their seats. Backed by a duo playing washboard and tea chest bass respectively, Lonnie's skiffle break might have reeked of novelty and upset some jazz purists, but it soon made him a star. After grinning his way through Leadbelly's 'Rock Island Line' on the BBC's flagship music show *6.5 Special* in 1956, he went to number eight on the UK charts, gaining the first of 31 hits both in Great Britain and the USA. "I [was] trying to sing acceptable folk music," he later said. "I wanted to widen the audience beyond the artsy-craftsy crowd and the pseudo intellectuals, but without distorting the music itself."

At the heart of Donegan's skiffle sound, of course, was the acoustic guitar. Never a showy player, he seldom strayed above the first three frets. Yet, Lonnie still managed to strum the instrument within an inch of its life, his train-like chug and almost evangelical vocal delivery pulling listeners along with him until the song finally came off the tracks. For a new generation desperately trying to find their own musical hero outside their parents' record collections, Donegan and his skiffling guitar were it. "Lonnie Donegan," said Paul McCartney, "was the man." Within weeks of Donegan's appearance on *6.5 Special*, legions of teenagers had formed their own skiffle groups.[4] After all, the tools of the trade were so simple: a tea chest, a bit of wood, a length of string and a washboard stolen from the kitchen. For those with bigger ambitions, an acoustic guitar was the essential purchase.

---

4   Some estimates put the number of UK teenagers playing skiffle in 1956/7 at between 30,000 to 50,000. One of the emerging bands, of course, was called the Quarrymen; five Liverpool lads led by John Lennon.

Jimmy Page already had one.

Like many his age, Jimmy fell hard for Lonnie Donegan. A stunned witness to the skiffle king's *6.5 Special* performance, he was thrilled by Donegan's obvious enthusiasm for his music as transmitted down the cathode tubes of the family TV set and straight into his head. But it was only when he saw a fellow pupil at Danetree secondary school, named Rod Wyatt, banging out 'Rock Island Line' on his own acoustic that the penny dropped. "I have a guitar at home," was all Jimmy said. A few words. Hardly even a sentence, really. Wyatt's reply, however, was a crucial moment for Page. "Bring it in," said Rod. "I'll tune for you..."

The Spanish guitar still residing in a corner of the family home was now quickly called into action. After Wyatt made good on his promise and tuned the thing, he showed Jimmy some rudimentary chords – enough certainly to play 'Rock Island Line', and perhaps even 'Bring A Little Water, Sylvie', another Donegan hit at the time. Page was off the mark and running. Bert Weedon's immortal *Play In A Day* instruction book for aspiring guitarists was the next box to be ticked. Bought "more out of curiosity" than anything else, Weedon's instruction book didn't appeal to Jimmy who was eager to "learn more by ear" than from the page. "The tutor [books] fell a bit flat when it came to the point of the dots," Page recalled to John Tobler, "because I was far too impatient." No doubt wanting to indulge their son's newfound interest, but also give it formal shape, Jimmy's parents reportedly sent him to a guitar teacher for lessons. Again, this was no great meeting of minds. Page wanted to learn hits. The teacher was offering more theory. But it did at least expand his chord vocabulary and picking technique, if not his ability to actually read music. Given later difficulties, he probably should have paid more attention.

Despite these early teething problems, Jimmy's dedication to the instrument was absolute, a point underlined when he parted company with his mysterious Spanish gut-string and bought a Hofner President instead. A handsome beast with a single cutaway and brunette finish, the President had a deep body to maximise volume and was a real step up the guitar ladder from the Spanish box top. Even better was the fact that Jimmy could electrify its sound by installing a small, soap bar pick-up

11

beneath the strings, giving him the chance to plug into his parents' radio or record player and hear himself back through the speaker. Having done a milk round over several months in order to save for the Hofner, the reward of finally being 'on the radio' must have been immensely pleasing. And probably quite noisy.

Armed with a basic knowledge of musical theory and a reasonable guitar to test it on, Jimmy took things to the next level by forming a band, though that might be a rather grand title for it. More a collection of skiffle enthusiasts that met weekly in the front room of his parents' house, it still constituted Page's first real commitment towards making music with others. Regrettably, the names of all but one of the quartet – drummer David Hassall – have been lost to history. But thanks to some old film footage, which we will come to soon enough, it seems clear that the bass player – who commendably built his own instrument – later joined the Royal Air Force, while the lead singer and Jimmy's fellow guitarist may have been called Anthony; small beer, perhaps, but all surely worth a mention for the purposes of posterity. Nonetheless, there was no mistaking the name of the band: 'The James Page Skiffle Group'.

Like most of his peers, Jimmy's earliest experiments with a band would probably have remained hermetically sealed forever, away from all prying eyes. But someone in or around the group – Page's mother has been mentioned as a possible candidate – came up with the bright idea of getting them on television. Whatever the case or whoever the culprit, a letter was definitely written to the BBC, which ended up in the hands of the makers of *All Your Own*. A late afternoon magazine show aimed at youngsters and hosted by the unflappable Huw Wheldon[5], *All Your Own* gave a platform for kids to display their talents and discuss their hobbies while the rest of Great Britain watched at home.

It all must have seemed a bit of a long-shot for the boys until they were actually granted an audition in the spring of 1957. Fifty-one years

5   A class act, Wheldon soon left behind children's TV, first fronting the BBC's groundbreaking arts programme *Monitor*, before moving behind the scenes and into management. By 1968, he had become managing director of the organisation.

later, Page winced at the memory. "It was in a large hall filled with children," he confirmed to *Classic Rock* in 2008. "Then, in walks Huw Wheldon who says 'All right, where are these bloody kids, then?'" Quaking in their boots, the James Page Skiffle Group still impressed Wheldon enough for him to offer them a spot on the show, thus setting in motion one of the more curious and, it has to be said, genuinely funny episodes in pop and rock folklore.

Now but an internet click away (though worth dwelling on at some length here), Jimmy Page's turn on *All Your Own* in the spring of 1957 provides a near perfect snapshot of the future rock star in his early teens. All neat hair, jumper and britches, he looks unbelievably young, fresh-faced, carefree and delightfully unaware of where the years would take him. But even from his first moments on camera, it is blindingly obvious that Page was a natural at this show business malarkey. Wearing his Hofner President with pride, the youngster smiled and strummed his way through 'Mama Don't Allow No Skiffle Round Here' with the rest of the band before breaking for a brief interview with Wheldon. Asked whether he played anything other than these skiffle tunes, Page's easy, almost eager reply "Yes, Spanish and dance", deftly set him up for further enquiry by the host. And that's when things got interesting.

Perhaps sensing some fun for himself, and indeed, older viewers, Wheldon ribbed Jimmy as to whether he wanted to take up skiffle after school. Page's deadpan reply remains justly famous. "No, I want to do biological research." Causing his host to giggle, then mumble "I do that already, as a matter of fact" under his breath, Wheldon recovered sufficiently to enquire what exactly Page meant. "Well, cancer, if it isn't discovered by then." With the presenter back on stable footing, it was now Jimmy's turn to be flummoxed. "You mean be a doctor?" asked Wheldon. "No I haven't enough brains for that, I don't think," replied Page. When Wheldon comedically gasped "No? I'm sure you have," Jimmy appeared unsure, looked around the TV studio in search of his footing and then did something truly wondrous. Saying nothing more, he smiled broadly, if flintily into the middle distance until Wheldon gave up and went on to bother another member of the group. Teenage embarrassment. Middle class modesty. Maybe just a case of the jitters.

13

But over the next five decades, whenever an interviewer's questions became trite, intrusive or potentially uncomfortable, that steely quiet and disarming smile would be employed with almost universal success.

Finishing up their set with 'The Cotton Song', during which Jimmy summoned up a feathery guitar trill as the tune's introduction, some whistles on the verse and a full-blown backing vocal for the chorus, his trial by fire on *All Your Own* was by all accounts a real nerve rattler. "I was quite nervous on that, actually," he said later. "[Being] 13 or 14, it was quite a big deal going on television." As for his pithy response regarding future career prospects, Page was again nothing but honest. "At that time, it wasn't unusual for kids at school to have an academic route too, [so] whatever I said then was probably what I was studying that week!" Even in this age of smart phones and instant uploads, there are precious few opportunities to observe celebrities at close range before the advent of fame. As such, Page's appearance on BBC's *All Your Own* should rightly be cherished. "I was just an enthusiastic 13-year-old [and] we all start out that way, don't we? Not everyone ends up with that stuff haunting them on *YouTube*, though..."

Beyond the perilous world of television interviews, skiffle actually gave Page much in the shortest of times. As with so many of his generation, it had acted as a superb primer into the joys of music and the simple fun that could be had by sharing it with others. "In England, we'd [been] separated from our folk music tradition centuries ago," said Lonnie Donegan in 1998, "and were imbued with the idea that music was for the upper classes. You had to be very clever to play music. When I came along with the old three chords, people began to think that if I could do it, so could they." As importantly, skiffle had also put a spotlight on an instrument that had thus far languished on the musical sidelines in the UK. "The great thing about the guitar when I was 12 years old was that it was portable[6]," Jimmy told *Rolling Stone*'s David

---

6   The guitar's portable nature might have appealed to Jimmy, but his teachers were less sure. When the teenager insisted on bringing the instrument to school with him every day, they soon confiscated it, only returning it to him for lunch breaks or when classes were finished.

Fricke in 2008, "[That] made music accessible to me. You could get together with your mates and before you knew it, the serious spirit of music was there."

For all its attendant charms, skiffle's time in the sun was to be relatively brief, the music soon brushed aside by a much larger, unwieldy and electrified beast recently escaped from the United States of America. Suffice to say, Jimmy Page was to be among its first victims. "When I was about 12, 13, I heard rock'n'roll," he said. "Elvis, Little Richard, Jerry Lee Lewis. It was all so... primeval. There was so much urgency conveyed in rock'n'roll that young people were instantly drawn to it. I was no exception."

CHAPTER 2

Baby Let's Play House

There are many theories about the origins of rock'n'roll. Some say it began with jump blues and boogie-woogie. Others will make a case for western swing, jazz or even gospel. There are those who swear blind it was all the work of hillbillies. But a couple of songs can lay some real claim to being rock'n'roll's errant father. On December 10, 1949, for instance, piano giant Fats Domino recorded a tune called 'The Fat Man' at Impact Studios, New Orleans that has more than a little rock'n'roll about it. Ironically, 'The Fat Man' wasn't fat at all, more a lean slice of no-frills boogie borne along by Domino's sparkling keyboard work, scatting asides and drummer Earl Palmer's metronome-like back beat.

Another worthy contender came in the spring of 1951, when Jackie Brenston and his Delta Cats cut a track named 'Rocket 88' for producer Sam Phillips at Sun Studios in Memphis, Tennessee. Actually the work of Ike Turner's Kings of Rhythm (with saxophonist Brenston pulling double duties on vocals), 'Rocket 88''s fulsome mix of swinging brass, shuffling sticks and a guitar teetering on the edge of distortion made it another strong contender for rock'n'roll's ground zero. Ike Turner wasn't so sure. "I don't think that 'Rocket 88' is rock'n'roll," he later told record producer Holger Petersen. "I think [it's] R&B, but I think [it's] the *cause* of rock'n'roll existing. [It was] the first black record to be played on a white radio station, and man, all the white kids broke out to the record shops to buy it..." Over half a million of them, to be precise.

Domino, Turner and Brenston's early experiments all pass muster as possible progenitors of the form. But it was to be a 29-year-old former country singer from Michigan that ended up popularising what we now call 'rock'n'roll'. First testing the lock in 1954 with 'Shake, Rattle & Roll', before removing the door altogether a year later with 'Rock Around The Clock', Bill Haley & his Comets took rock'n'roll from its largely black origins and made it palatable for white, middle-class America. Then a young man called Elvis Presley came along and made it dangerous all over again. Arriving on the music scene in 1955 like some visiting alien, Presley was picture-book handsome, sexually tumescent and gifted with one of the finest voices ever to grace a slab of vinyl. He also fulfilled a prophecy of sorts. According to Ike Turner, Presley's early producer, Sam Phillips, had once said, "If I get me a white boy to sound like a black boy, then I got me a gold mine." With Elvis, Phillips started counting the coins.[7]

Jimmy Page was probably first exposed to rock'n'roll at the same time as he was leading his skiffle band through their paces at Miles Road. But it wasn't long before he traded in Donegan for Presley. "[Hearing] Elvis just electrified me. It really captured me, like a fish caught in a big net. I just wanted to be a part of it." Strangely, it wasn't one of Presley's stream of 1956 UK hits on RCA – from 'Heartbreak Hotel' and 'Hound Dog' to 'Blue Suede Shoes' and 'Love Me Tender' – that bowled him for six. Instead, that honour went to a lesser known tune Elvis cut with Sam Phillips for Sun Records the year before. "The record that really made me want to play guitar was 'Baby Let's Play House'," said Jimmy. "When I heard that record, I just wanted to be part of it... the acoustic and electric guitars, the slap bass, those instruments seemed to generate so much energy."

---

7   Elvis Presley's earliest recordings were all cut at Sam Phillips' small, independent label Sun Records during 1953–1955. When Phillips sold on Presley's contract with him to industry giant RCA a year later, he reportedly pocketed a tidy $40,000.

If one were being picky, 'Baby, Let's Play House''s combination of descending acoustic bassline and bouncing drums was probably more 'rockabilly' than rock'n'roll. In the end, such distinctions were irrelevant. The instrument teasing the best out of Presley's deliciously slurred vocal and making Jimmy's ears pop as a result was Scotty Moore's guitar. Elvis's secret weapon, Moore was a man who could combine country fills, double stops and hillbilly chord twangs like the ingredients for a gourmet meal, served up on his gold Gibson ES (Electric Spanish) 295 in a way Page once described as "heart-stopping". Obviously, this whole rock'n'roll thing was to be investigated, and quickly.

Like any new follower to a cause, Jimmy's days and nights went by in a haze of discovery and growing devotion. When he wasn't listening to Radio Luxembourg or the American Forces Network (AFN)[8] under his bed sheets for all the latest releases from the States, Page could be found in the back room of his local *Rumbelows*, buying any single he could get his hands on. There were plenty to choose from. As rock'n'roll established the same foothold it had in America months before, an influx of performers followed Elvis across the ocean and into the British charts. The primal scream of Little Richard. The animal magnetism of Jerry Lee Lewis. And, of course, the rascal charms of Charles Edward Anderson Berry. "I got my guitar and pretended to be Chuck Berry," Jimmy said in 1982. "I still do!" Another enormous influence on Page, Chuck Berry's duck-walking guitar boogie was pure teenage heaven, while his lyrics created a world where having no particular place to go sounded like a great night out. "It was what Berry was singing about," Page later told *GQ*. "The stories he was telling. He was singing about hamburgers sizzling night and day. We didn't have hamburgers in England. We didn't even know what they were."

By 1957, however, Great Britain was starting to play catch up. Having now got the hang of Elvis, Jerry Lee and Chuck, British youth

---

8 While rock'n'roll made a tremendous impact on Britain's youth, British radio stations were initially reticent to give it any airtime, regarding it as a 'seditionary influence'. Therefore, for a while at least, the only place to hear new US rock'n'roll releases was either on pirate radio or via the American Forces Network.

were increasingly keen to put their own spin on America's obsession with youth, rebellion and "caveman music". Fashion, for instance, was one such quick win. Originally taking hair and style tips from US actors such as James Dean, Marlon Brando, Tony Curtis and Montgomery Clift, UK teenagers now started their very own derivation on the theme of wild ones and rebels without a cause: the Teddy Boy. A beautiful explosion of drape jackets, day-glo socks, brothel creepers and bad attitudes, Britain's Teds put the fear factor back into rock'n'roll only months after politicians stopped worrying Elvis might bring down society with a sneer.

Elsewhere, a new breed of British-born rock'n'roll singer was also emerging. Keen to mimic Stateside-based chart invaders with home-grown performers of their own, UK record companies and manager/ impresarios like Larry Parnes and Jack Good began scouring central London's then box-fresh coffee bar and club scene in search of suitable talent. There was no shortage of it waiting to be found. Marty Wilde, Tommy Steele and, latterly, Joe Brown and Billy Fury could all approximate what was being exported from the USA, though the best of this new breed was Cliff Richard. As close as Britain had yet come to producing its own Elvis, Cliff's debut single – 1958's thundering 'Move It' – was nearly as good as anything released by the King himself. "After hearing Elvis," Richard later said, "thousands of us woke up the next morning wanting to be rock'n'roll singers. I was one of them." Backed by the Shadows, crack instrumentalists who in turn produced the UK's first real guitar hero in the form of bespectacled Hank Marvin, Richard's ambitions crystallised a nation eager to embrace rock'n'roll and make it their own.

There is no doubt that Jimmy Page was aware of 'Cliff and the Shads', Marty Wilde and Billy Fury. After all, they were all regular faces on *Oh Boy!*, the slightly off-kilter *ITV* show that replaced *6.5 Special* as the only place teenagers could watch their musical idols for half an hour each week circa 1958. Yet, Jimmy's interests at the time remained firmly connected to American rock'n'roll, his investigations into its still growing retinue of performers not to be undone by British duplicates. Joining Chuck and Elvis on the family Dansette were the likes of Ricky

Nelson and Gene Vincent, whose own guitar men, the Blue Caps, again added much flavour to Page's ever-growing style.

Nelson's silken, expressive vocals were backed by the eloquent guitar excursions of James Burton. A tasteful, economic picker who never wasted a note, Burton's twanging Fender Telecaster enlivened many a Nelson classic, including 'I'm Walkin'' and 'Hello Mary Lou'. It was also from Burton that Page learned the value of replacing the wound 'G' string on his guitar for the much lighter 'B' string, or even one taken from a banjo. This simple switch meant Jimmy could now bend notes up a semi-tone, tone or wherever his fingers took him. The work of 'Blue Cap' Cliff Gallup was equally impressive to Page's ear, not least because he was pulling off similar tricks to Burton without the benefit of that lighter 'G' string. A magician armed with a Gretsch Duo Jet, Gallup's dextrous mangling of Gene Vincent's raw rockabilly songs such as 'B-I-Bickey-Bi-Bo-Bo-Go', 'Catman', 'Cruisin'' and 'Be Bop A Lula' was both futuristic and thrilling, his every trill, chromatic ascent, over-bend and discordant clang a little miracle unto itself.

From the double-barrelled charm of James Burton to the fizz and pop of Gene Vincent and his Blue Caps, Page sought to master all of it on guitar, occasionally sacrificing his source material in the effort. "I'd try and work out solos, some of which were particularly complex," he later said. "The only way to do that was by listening to the record... and moving the needle back to where the solo started again. Back and forth you'd go, so it would damage the record itself sometimes." Several sides went the way of the dodo due to Jimmy's obsession, with one wrecked Buddy Holly LP still the cause of considerable psychic pain. "It was *The Chirping Crickets...*" he groaned to *Mojo* in 2010.

When Jimmy wasn't dissecting rock'n'roll, he was chasing the guitar sounds of Les Paul. A true "sonic architect" before the phrase had been invented, Paul's mastery of swing, country and jazz styles was only eclipsed by his skills as an inventor. Contributing greatly to the development of electric guitar in the forties, Paul was also instrumental in expanding recording studio techniques such as overdubbing, phasing and echo-effects. By 1952, he was given the honour of having the world's first production-line signature model named after him, the

Gibson Les Paul 'Goldtop'. Partnered by his wife Mary Ford on vocals, Paul's hits such as 'How High The Moon', 'Tiger Rag' and 'Bye Bye Blues' might have had critics calling him 'gimmicky' for the use of multi-tracking and sped-up tape, but this was rather missing the point. Strip away Les's wildly inventive nature, and there would have been no gimmicks for them to criticise. "I loved Les Paul, precisely because he was so flamboyant [with sound]," said Jimmy. "Without him, there would be no electric guitars or multi-track recording."

By adding Les Paul to his inventory of guitarists to be studied, Page gained much pleasure, though there was also a fair amount of pain in figuring it all out. Tunes like 'How High...' and 'The World Is Waiting For A Sunrise' allowed the teenager to follow threads back in time to Paul's own formal influences, in this case, the Gypsy genius Django Reinhardt's 'The Sheik Of Araby'. Another major discovery for Jimmy, Reinhardt's inimitable prowess on guitar was surely to be marvelled at. However, unlike hillbilly rebels and chord kings such as Scotty Moore and Buddy Holly, whose work was clever but now within his overall grasp, the technical proficiency displayed by Reinhardt and other fifties jazzers like Tal Farlow or Johnny Smith could be intimidating in the extreme. "Those people left me standing," Page later laughed. "Their technical prowess alone made me think 'Aw, leave that alone!'"

If learning the intricacies of jazz guitar was still a step too far for the young Page, then at least he could try his hand at emulating another of Les Paul's abiding interests: studio wizardry. In this pursuit, he had to seek approval from his parents. Having already commandeered the front room of Miles Road for skiffle practice, Jimmy wanted to expand his base of operations by turning it into a make-shift studio. Showing admirable foresight, the Pages acquiesced to their son's request, while also funding his request for a tape recorder and better record player. According to Jimmy's friend John Gibb, an early witness to this Aladdin's cave and later to pursue his own musical interests, this collection only grew over time. "In most homes, the front room is usually a family room, but Pagey's parents had turned it over to Jimmy," Gibb said. "There were records everywhere, a tape recorder... guitars, other instruments plus a really good hi-fi system. Jimmy's mum usually just stayed in the kitchen brewing tea for everybody." Singles and LPs strewn across the furniture. A guitar in one corner. A stereo in the other. This was no passing fancy. "Les Paul, rockabilly, pure rock'n'roll," Page later said, "I had a voracious appetite for all of it."

Things moved quickly now.

CHAPTER 3

Be Bop A Lula

Having skiffled his way into the nation's living rooms via the wonder of TV and learnt every lick, riff and available chord from an ever-expanding record collection, it was inevitable that Page's next steps would lead him to the concert stage. In fact, a tentative toe or two had been poked in that general area already. Jimmy's skiffle combo had banged out a few tunes in front of a small audience at nearby Tolworth Hall before their brush with Huw Wheldon, while he also made a solo appearance as part of a talent show held in St. Martin's parish church, a long stone's throw from his parents' house on Miles Road. On that occasion, Page was content to entertain the crowd by strumming his guitar while sitting on the edge of a raised platform. His next moves proved bolder in scale.

By 1959, Jimmy had begun to attend local dance clubs, with venues like Ebisham Hall and Purley's Orchid Room offering both live music and the rare opportunity to meet girls without their parents or teachers inspecting the cut of his jib. That said, it was the weekend concerts held at Epsom Baths that most caught Page's attention. Here, he could watch up close and personal a talented young singer called Chris Farlowe raise merry hell with his band, the Thunderbirds. "Yep, I knew Jim when he was nobody!" Farlowe laughed. "In fact, I first met him when we were playing at the Epsom Baths. This young dude used to come and stand at the side of the stage, and just listen... I mean *really* listen. We had a guitar player called Bobby Taylor and Jim absolutely loved him. He'd just stand there and watch what he was playing. And one night, he came up and introduced himself. You know the sort of thing, 'My name's Jimmy Page, I'm a guitarist and I think your band's great'. That's how I got to know Jimmy."

Born John Henry Deighton in Islington, north London, Farlowe's early exploration of his mother's 78s brought about an abiding love of American pop and jazz vocalists such as Doris Day, Anita O'Day and Sarah Vaughan. But it was the bump of skiffle, the grind of blues and a swift name change at the age of 18 that set him on a career in music. "[Listening to] Howlin' Wolf and Memphis Slim, that's really how I first started to learn my craft as a singer. Then I joined a skiffle group and sort of brought that blues influence into it." By the time Jimmy Page stood watching intently from the wings at Epsom Baths, Farlowe and his band the Thunderbirds had been selling their versions of blues, jazz and rock'n'roll standards into the clubs for almost a year. "In my estimation," Page later said, "Chris Farlowe and the Thunderbirds were the best band in the south..."

As the story goes, there were only two Fender Stratocasters in Great Britain at the end of the fifties. One – the now famous 'Fiesta Red' – was purchased by Cliff Richard for the princely sum of 145 guineas for his right-hand guitar man, Hank Marvin. The Thunderbirds' Bobby Taylor had the other. Suffice to say, Jimmy Page was entranced with both Taylor and his Strat. "Ah, that's guitar players though," said Farlowe. "And it's the same with all guitar players. They all know each other, they all lean on each other. That's all they want to talk about really, guitars. Who played this, who played that. Singers aren't interesting enough for them! Guitar players, they're like a little community all to themselves." Nevertheless, Chris didn't think Page rude or given to ignoring the rest of the band while striking up guitar talk with Bobby Taylor. Quite the opposite, in fact. "Oh no, at the time, Jimmy was quite the reserved young gentleman. Very sweet, mild mannered and polite to us all. Very quiet, in fact. You wouldn't know [meeting him] back then what was going to happen later..."

While Page and Farlowe's paths would cross often in the future, with collaborations coming thick and fast across several decades[9], the principal benefit in Page seeing bands like the Thunderbirds was to again underline just how much he wanted to be a part of the game. "By then, rock'n'roll put me in a stranglehold," he said. "It had seduced me and the damage was done."

Putting the skiffle combo well behind him, Jimmy also put down the Hofner President that had sustained his musical explorations until now, purchasing instead his first real electric guitar. While not quite in the same league as Bobby Taylor's glorious Fender Stratocaster, Jimmy's Czech-made 1949 Grazioso Futurama was still a serviceable enough copy of the real thing. It was also covered in buttons. "Well, I got it from Bell's in Surbiton," he later told Charles Shaar Murray, "And they used to mainly sell accordions!"

Page soon put the Grazioso to work on the stages of Epsom, joining several semi-amateur bands throughout the area, the most notable of which was the Paramounts, with whom he briefly threw in his lot. In this guise, Jimmy found himself occasionally supporting acts already on route to fame, including a pre-'Bits And Pieces' Dave Clark Five. Unfortunately, while these spots earned him further notoriety around the neighbourhood, they paid little or nothing. As was often the way in Page's early career trajectory, another's keen eye for prospective talent remedied that easily enough.

In this case, the man who spotted Jimmy's early financial promise was Chris Tidmarsh, then working as a road manager for rock'n'roll bluffers Red E Lewis & the Red Caps. Comprised of vocalist Red E Lewis (aka William Stubbs), drummer Jimmy Evans and lead guitarist Bobby Oats, Red's motley crew had gained something of a reputation on the dance

---

9   The first of Page's collaborations with Chris Farlowe wasn't long in coming. "1961," Chris confirmed. "I took the Thunderbirds into the studio and cut a 12-track album, which has never been released. Jimmy's on that. Jazz stuff, rock'n'roll, it's all over the musical shop. And he loved it because we were playing stuff back then that nobody else was touching. Jim actually called me (in early 2015) and said that he's interested in putting the album out. Let's see what happens..."

circuit, their loose brand of rockabilly covers and Chuck Berry tunes going over well with Saturday night crowds across London and the Home Counties. But soon after John 'Jumbo' Spicer joined the act on rhythm guitar in the spring of 1959, Oats announced his intention to take up a place at drama school, leaving Red, his Red Caps, and their manager Tidmarsh a man down. Already impressed by Page, who he had seen performing in various pick-up bands in Epsom, Chris decided to offer the youngster an audition. It went well. "He asked me whether I'd like to play in London," said Jimmy. "[Well], of course I did."

There was one serious issue to attend to before Page could take up arms. He was only 15 years old. A smooth operator, Tidmarsh solved the age problem by going directly to those most likely to raise an objection: Jimmy's parents. "I went to his father and said 'If I promise to pay £15 a week, would you consider him playing in the group?'" Though a good wage in 1959, James Page had reservations about the offer and reportedly declined on his son's behalf. But when it became clear almost all the gigs would take place at the weekend, and the ever-courteous Tidmarsh assured him that he would drive Jimmy home after each concert, Page Sr. cautiously gave his consent. "You know," Jimmy later told Q, "my parents were very encouraging... [at least] to the extent that they weren't dismissive of my obsession. They might not have understood a lot of what I was doing, but... they had the confidence that I knew what I was doing."

Joining up with the Redcaps brought its share of problems for the young guitarist. The group were based in and around east London's Shoreditch, a long trek for the Epsom-based Page when it came to rehearsals. Moreover, the district had yet to gain the gentrified status it would later command in the New Labour-led nineties, with pockets here and there conveying a distinct edge to those visiting from outside the smoke. "Unlike now, they were really unfashionable areas back then," said Page. "In fact, they were still printing papers there at that time." There was also the fact that, despite his undoubted promise on guitar, Jimmy was only a matter of years out of primary school. Traipsing up and down various motorways at all hours of the day and night was going to severely test both his body and soul. "Sleeping in a van, breaking down on the M1," he later told *NME*'s Nick Kent, "eventually that will knock you out." But not quite yet.

Fortified by Page's arrival, further enhanced by Jumbo Spicer's somewhat inevitable move from rhythm guitar to bass and benefiting greatly from the presence of Jimmy 'Tornado' Evans – a former army drum major whose percussive skills Page still rates highly to this day – Red E Lewis & the Red Caps now looked a much more stable proposition. In line with 'Red', 'Jumbo' and 'Tornado', Jimmy was even given his own stage name – 'Nelson Storm' – a ludicrous tag presumably coined to invoke magnificent images of the legendary English admiral. But despite all the daft nom de plumes and Americanised notions of gang bonhomie, the line-up lasted only a matter of months before cracks in their collective armour emerged. While the group itself was sturdy enough, their singer Red E struggled to gel with his new colleagues and the responsibilities of road life. Again, Chris Tidmarsh proved an astute problem solver. When Red finally flew the coup in early 1960, Tidmarsh stepped up to the plate and assumed the role of the band's new vocalist. One swift name change later, Chris Tidmarsh became 'Neil Christian' and the Red Caps became 'the Crusaders'.

Freed from their irksome origins – in honest terms, Red E's boys were nothing more than a Gene Vincent & the Blue Caps knock-off, albeit with a change of primary colours – Christian and the Crusaders now had a chance to prove their worth as a different type of proposition. But the band's decision to continue drawing from a familiar well of Gene Vincent, Johnny Burnette and Bo Diddley songs for their live shows saw them at odds with a rapid change occurring in musical tastes of the time. Then as now, pop music had already moved on at high speed since the heady days of 1957/8, with teenagers growing bored of what they deemed indispensable only two years before. In short, rock'n'roll was now distinctly passé, or as one critic aptly put it, "New kids were looking for new kicks."

The first wave of rock'n'roll performers had helped derail its progress as much as the short attention spans of the adolescents actually listening to them. Wobble number one occurred in October 1957, when a treacherous flight over the Australian outback scared Little Richard so much he turned his back on making the devil's music (once removed), and set about reinventing himself as a preacher. Seven months later, it was Jerry Lee Lewis's turn to shake the tree. While on a brief UK tour, journalists discovered Lewis had recently married his 13-year-old cousin, Myra Gayle Brown. This might have been perfectly reasonable behaviour in Ferriday, Louisiana, but it didn't travel well outside of Lewis's homestead. All but torn to shreds by the press – first in Great Britain and then at home – 'The Killer''s career was killed stone dead for the best part of two decades. Chuck Berry's fall from grace was equally ignominious, his transportation across State lines of a 14-year-old waitress bringing the combined weight of the Mann Act, two local police forces and the US media down upon his pompadoured head.

It wasn't all spiritual crises or questionable relationship choices that were contributing to rock'n'roll's ever more perilous state. When a plane fell from the skies over Iowa on February 3, 1959, the world lost not one but three early pioneers of the form, with The Big Bopper, Ritchie Valens and the magnificent Buddy Holly all killed in the resulting crash. By early 1960, Eddie 'Summertime Blues' Cochran was gone too, a car accident in the UK permanently ending his career at the age of just 21. But the writing was truly on the wall for rock'n'roll in March 1960, when its potential saviour Elvis Presley returned to civilian life after a near two-year stretch in the US army. Instead of firing up those rotating hips and reactivating that trademark sneer, however, Presley released two dreamy ballads in rapid succession ('It's Now Or Never' and 'Are You Lonesome Tonight?'), again stirring up his interest in an acting career. By the time Chubby Checker turned every teenager into a dancing fool with 'The Twist' in September 1960, it was obvious to all what record companies had already known for a year. Heroes had fallen, musical tastes had softened and rock'n'roll, if not quite dead, was looking very queasy indeed.

In this more anodyne, dance-craze driven and ballad-friendly era, Neil Christian & the Crusaders were at risk of setting themselves up as yesterday's men. They knew it too. "In the group," Page later said, "playing Chuck Berry and Bo Diddley songs, well, nothing was happening at all. Nobody wanted to hear those numbers [anymore], but that's all we wanted to do." A fitful compromise was struck. The band would continue to perform the music they loved while also making the odd concession to the demands of a new audience. To counterbalance the seismic blasts of 'Maybelline', 'Be Bop A Lula' and 'Honey Hush', the likes of Santo & Johnny's silken 'Sleep Walk', the Shadows' lilting 'Apache' and – if reports are correct – faithful renditions of 'Summertime' and 'Hava Nagila' were all duly dispensed from the stage. Corn-fed rock'n'roll, Top 20 hits, lush instrumentals, hoary jazz standards and Israeli folk songs. If nothing else, it made for an interesting night's entertainment.

Establishing a punishing schedule of club, dance hall and occasional "cinema gigs", Neil Christian & the Crusaders played most everywhere that would have them over the next two years. From supporting the newly tamed Cliff Richard & the Shadows[10] at east London's Edmonton Odeon to quick-fire visits to old stomping grounds like Epsom Baths, the band became consummate road warriors, with Jimmy Page dragging his ever-reducing frame across the hills and dales of south-east England and beyond. Driving themselves between gigs in a former council ambulance (large, rangy and a snip at £100), the Crusaders even managed to squeeze in a concert at the women's prison on London's Holloway Road. "The girls went mad," Christian told *Disc* in November 1961, "[and] we hope to make a return visit very soon!" Page later confirmed the story in an interview with *Classic Rock*. "Yes, we played Holloway Prison. Heavens knows how that happened." Under strict orders not to reveal what they saw inside at the time, Jimmy's memory of events was less about potential security issues, and more given to what the inmates were wearing. "[They] wore cotton print dresses in four different colours," he said in 2008. "The garment's shades were faded by frequent washing. It really was quite... erotic."

---

10 Like his hero Elvis, Cliff Richard had largely strayed from rock'n'roll by 1960, with a string of hits such as 'Living Doll', 'Travellin' Light' and 'Fall In Love With You' defining a new, more romantic sound. A year or so later, he and the Shadows would again follow Presley's example and seek their fortune in movies, cannily repositioning themselves as family entertainers in the process.

Not every concert held such charms. As evidenced, the band's admirable, but marginalising decision to use rock'n'roll songs as the backbone of their set still led to lukewarm receptions at certain venues, while other gigs were sometimes stopped when fights broke out in the crowd. "The first guy to hit the floor lost," Jimmy said, laughing. In addition to those seeking an alcohol-assisted break from the rigours of their working week or just a good old-fashioned punch-up, there was now another type of visitor coming to the shows. Fellow musicians.

Since Jimmy first joined the Redcaps in 1959, word had been steadily building among local players of his talent. But quiet whispers ceded to raised voices by the time the band morphed into Neil Christian & the Crusaders. An early witness to Page's skills as a guitarist was John Hawken, then a promising young keyboardist about to make his own first steps into the music business with the Nashville Teens. "I first saw Jimmy at Weybridge Village Hall. Back then, he was this super-thin little fellow onstage of about 15, 16 years old wearing a sweaty grey suit, doing these Shadows-like dance steps with the rest of the band." Hawken was in no doubt that Page had something very special indeed. "His playing was just stunning. Believe me, Jimmy with the Crusaders was stunningly brilliant on guitar. Incredibly gifted and completely immersed in the music. Watching him was just a treat."

There were obvious reasons aside from innate talent that enabled Page's gifts. The dedication he had shown music for the last three years was starting to truly manifest itself, all those nights learning and re-learning solos by the likes of Scotty Moore, James Burton and Chuck Berry now seeping through his own hands and onto the neck of his guitar. According to Neil Christian, this dedication was only reinforced when he joined the band. Jimmy, it seemed, was seldom if ever parted from six strings. "Every time you saw him," Christian laughed, "he had a bloody guitar around his neck." Like so many of his ilk, Page found a curious joy in repetition, the mastery of chords and lead lines coming easily only after he had practised them to the point of abstraction. This, of course, brought its own rewards. When the basics were mastered, he could then begin taking the original idea in new directions, building his own particular style in the process. "Oh, Jimmy got really good, really early on," said Chris Farlowe. "He was locked into finding his own thing." Now able to play songs and sets with his eyes closed, Page was able to introduce another aspect to his performance. "Indeed," said John Hawken, "Jimmy was quite the showman."

In fact, Page's gift for showmanship often matched his prowess as a guitarist. Whether mimicking Chuck Berry's comedic duck walk, aping the Shadows' forwards/backwards step routine or mock-falling to his knees while taking on a tricky solo, Jimmy was a fine onstage foil for the charismatic Neil Christian – every bit his equal, and for some at least, the real star of the show. "Remember, Neil Christian was up there every night," confirmed Hawken, "and Neil was a great frontman with a bloody good voice and a real way with a crowd. But I just remember Jimmy standing stage right. Honestly, Jimmy stood out head and shoulders above everybody else on that stage."

Sometimes, Page's flair for the dramatic could be over-shadowed by the tools of his trade. Thanks to his gig with the Crusaders and the financial rewards it brought, Jimmy had now graduated to a different class of instrument from his sturdy, if unremarkable Grazioso. With regular earnings came the opportunity to finally buy a Fender Stratocaster all his own. But it was the purchase of a Gretsch Country Gentleman that threatened to steal the limelight. Gloriously large and exceedingly orange, this fluorescent battleship of a guitar completely dwarfed its whippet-like owner. "I went to see Jimmy with Neil Christian in 1961, 1962," said a new acquaintance of Page's, then content to lurk in the background at the odd Crusaders gig. "It was a lunchtime gig at The Boathouse in Kew Bridge. All I saw was this human beanpole with a Gretsch. It was four times bigger than he was..."

When he wasn't doing battle with the Gretsch, Jimmy was gaining his first experience of the recording studio, with the Crusaders cutting their first single, 'The Road To Love', soon after Neil Christian took over as vocalist. Like so many tunes of the era, 'The Road...' was no more than a jaunty novelty item covered in brass stabs and floating xylophones, its failure to chart when eventually released in late 1962 coming as no great surprise to anyone. Nonetheless, the song did allow

Page the opportunity to work with rising production star and arch-eccentric Joe Meek, then about to have his first international number one with the queasily electronic 'Telstar'. "I'd listen to Joe Meek's productions and try and work out where the echo and reverb were coming from," Jimmy later told Nick Kent. "I was [also] fixated with all Sam Phillips's Sun productions. They were truly revolutionary."

New guitars. Studio dates. Regular wages. Even some national coverage in *Disc* magazine. So far, so good. But there were serious issues also lurking on the periphery for Jimmy Page, not least of which was what life on the road was doing to his health. Soon after joining the Crusaders, Page had begun falling victim to regular bouts of influenza, the virus slowly but surely chipping away at his immune system. "It was actually quite soul-destroying rushing all over the place," he later said. "[We were] doing quite a physical set, and then jumping back into the van in ice cold weather. I was getting ill all the time." Things got worse when the group started touring outside their south-eastern comfort zone, with bookings now taking them up to 200 miles away from home. While the cash was good, such dates often came with all-night stopovers, the band sleeping on top of their amps or at the back of dance halls. Wobbly hygiene. Even wobblier service station food. After a few months of it, Page began to slowly unravel.

The writing on the wall came after a concert in Sheffield. "I remember one night walking outside a gig," he told *NME*, "and the next point waking up... lying on the floor of some kind of dressing room." As Page's condition continued to worsen, doctors got involved. The news wasn't good. The guitarist was diagnosed with glandular fever (Mono), a condition exemplified by a persistent sore throat, crushing fatigue, hot spells, cold sweats and painful swelling in the glands of the neck. Worse still, without a proper spell of rest, the fever could easily recur. Worn out, spectrally thin and wrestling with the added guilt of letting his fellow band mates down, Jimmy had to make a decision. "I'd been travelling around in a bus... for two years, [and] I was starting to get really good money, but I was getting ill all the time. As dedicated as I was to the guitar, I knew doing it that way was going to do me in forever. I just needed to get my strength [back] up..." With the words

"I need a change," Page handed in his cards, resigning from the group in mid-1962.

A consummate professional, Neil Christian kept his Crusaders on the road for several more years, with Jimmy even returning to their ranks for the odd studio date until 1964. At the time, Page's immediate replacement was guitarist Paul Brett, with future country rock wizard Albert Lee, eventual Jethro Tull guitarist Mick Abrahams and a moody young gun by the name of Ritchie Blackmore (later of Deep Purple) all soon to follow. Though Christian's Crusaders managed to secure a record deal with British label Strike and release several sides, major success always eluded them. Brief compensation came for Neil as a solo artist in 1966, when his single 'That's Nice' reached number 16 in the UK charts. But even after putting together a new version of the Crusaders to promote it, '... Nice' remained his only hit. Christian remained philosophical. "I wouldn't change anything," he once said. "The musicians were incredible and it was an amazing time. I couldn't have done it at any other time."

Having resigned from the Crusaders, Jimmy Page now had to deal with the aftermath. Uppermost, of course, was the recovery of his health. Beyond that, the not inconsiderable issue of what exactly to do with the rest of his life. Thankfully, Page had not fully abandoned his studies while in the band, giving the 18-year-old some much needed options. Having gained a respectable five GCSEs before leaving school two years before, he could contemplate higher education as an antidote to packed halls, cold sweats and fainting fits. "Well, I was tailored in the way to do what all young lads do," he said, "which was to go to school and pass exams." After some thought and, no doubt, the encouragement of his parents, Page decided to commit to fine art, an interest nurtured by teachers in childhood and now providing a useful route for him back into higher learning. Offered places at Croydon College and Sutton Art College respectively, Jimmy chose the latter, starting his new course in September 1962.

On the face of it, Page's choice was a commendable one. High-minded, but eminently logical, his studies gave him ample opportunity to indulge his artistic nature while also allowing time to whittle away at the guitar. Better still, Sutton Art College was a mere 10-minute bus ride from his parents' home, where Jimmy continued to live. This was surely better than driving 204 miles to Sheffield's Locarno ballroom to play 'Train Kept A Rollin'' when all the audience really wanted to hear was 'The Twist'. The fact that several of his friends were already studying at Sutton was another added bonus. But the main thrust of it was that after a two-year spell of riot, Page now appeared genuinely interested in pursuing a career in the arts. "I was sincere in that aim so I went back to art college," he later told Chris Welch. "I really wanted to be a fine art painter." He really did. But once again the world, or more specifically, the blues came calling.

CHAPTER 4

Killing Floor

The British arts scene was enjoying the first rays of what promised to be an extended holiday in the sun when Jimmy Page arrived at Sutton College during the autumn of 1962. Truth be told, it had taken a while to find its way to the beach. Having already lost ground to European Surrealists and Art Deco types before World War II, the dizzying rise of America's Abstract Expressionists in the early fifties had again threatened to make the UK's artistic landscape appear old, even antiquated. Blighty might well have given the world the likes of Constable and Turner, but the new action paintings of Jackson Pollock and colour fields of Mark Rothko looked fearfully ambitious and thoroughly modern when compared with the austere grey canvasses of post-war Britain.

The fight-back had begun with Richard Hamilton's *This Is Tomorrow*, a 1956 exhibition that turned heads in the direction of the new UK 'Pop Art' movement. Happily challenging engrained attitudes of what constituted high art, Hamilton and his peers sought out the miraculous in the mundane. Instead of images of tranquil landscapes and blurry sea ports, his canvasses juxtaposed musclemen and burlesque girls against Hoovers and coffee tables. Bucking conventional notions of beauty, mass-produced consumer products were now presented as glamorous, sought-after things. After years of rationing, penny-pinching and low expectations, British art had finally gone to the shops.

This notion of dispossessing art from the hands of the critical elite, or claiming access to items previously available only to the rich or entitled, was being mirrored elsewhere in the UK. Staid traditions surrounding ownership of the written word, for instance, also came under attack. With the advent of the 'Angry Young Men' of the late fifties, the novel, play and literary critique were all ripe for an ideological kicking, as Kingsley Amis, John Osbourne and Colin Wilson fought to mould new ideas from old sentences. Knives sharpened, these hardy souls seemed intent on declaring war on a class system that had existed in Great Britain since the Norman invasion of 1066. Drawing support from fellow writers such as John Braine and Iris Murdoch, among others, the 'Angry''s depictions of bemused young academics, morally bereft social climbers and contempt-driven intellectuals captured both the mood and temperature of a country trying to reinvent its societal mores after all those bombs. Even British film was in on the act, as *This Sporting Life*, *The Loneliness Of The Long Distance Runner* and *Room At The Top* made anti-heroes of the feckless and socially stymied.

These were changing times, with the artistic health of a nation now potentially in the hands of its young painters, authors and film directors. Curiously, only the UK music scene showed no great interest in joining the fun, with singers and bands seemingly more content to revel in lovey-dovey ballads and daft dance crazes than take on the heavy lifting of affecting social change. This was to be expected. Thus far, a 'pop' musician's brief had always been about entertaining society, not trying to alter it. But storms were now brewing in Liverpool, Dartford, Surrey and London that would arguably do more for shaking up the status quo than all those pots, brushes, pens and cameras put together.

Page was no doubt aware of this artistic kerfuffling when he started at Sutton Art College. After all, the very notion of art schools walked hand in hand with such things. A relatively new type of enterprise, places like Sutton had been recently introduced to the British education system as an enabler not only for sculptors and the like, but also those yet to find their way in more traditional academia. Little nests of innovation, such schools pooled would-be fashion designers with trainee graphic artists and wannabe advertisers, creating a wonderfully irreverent atmosphere of creative play where ideas exploded like firecrackers. "It was somewhere you just spent all your time painting, arguing [and] learning how to weld," said former Under-Secretary of State for Education (and art school graduate) Kim Howells. "Looking back on it, it was a perfect time, a perfect place, and a perfect education." Destined to become the revving engine of sixties British counter-culture, art schools also had a disproportionately high number of musicians making up their ranks, many of whom would soon spill out of the doors and into the charts.

Jimmy Page wasn't keen to promote himself as any kind of musician at Sutton. Even his previous habit of bringing a guitar to school every day was dropped. No visible distractions, no lapses of concentration, just a firm engagement with matters at hand. "I kept very quiet," he later said, "or else they'd expect me to play at lunch hour." Such model behaviour might give the impression that Page's days as a guitarist were over. Indeed, he had entered Sutton College with art very much in mind. But away from class, Page was just getting started on a new kind of musical love affair. Though still entranced by the power and immediacy of rock'n'roll, his tastes had now expanded far beyond the thrills of double stops and slash chords. The journey might have begun with skiffle, then taken a slip road towards Memphis, Tennessee, yet he was now in much deeper terrain, seeking the very roots of the music very probably behind it all. "Blues had a baby and they called it rock'n'roll," Muddy Waters once sang. Page had set off in search of the parents.

At first, it was a case of simple detective work, with Jimmy following various clues laid down in the music of Elvis Presley. "Well, I accessed early rock'n'roll before I accessed the blues," he later said. "It was purely what was available to be heard in those days. [But] Elvis was doing a lot of blues, and he was doing it his way, which was brilliant." Tracing the origin of tracks like 'Milk Cow Blues', 'That's All Right (Mama)' and 'Mystery Train' to performers such as Sleepy John Estes, Arthur Crudup and Junior Parker, Page was able to cast his pail into a much larger well of seamless talent and otherworldly sounds. From the original country blues of twenties pioneers like Tampa Red, Charley Patton and Son

House to the newfangled electric revolutionaries of Chicago, it was all up for grabs. "Hearing the [old] blues, then [people] like Howlin' Wolf, Buddy Guy, Freddie King... it knocked me sideways again."

Page's discoveries were not made in isolation. Part of a groundswell of like-minded souls pursuing what they felt to be a purer, more authentic music, young blues enthusiasts were popping up across the UK in their droves, and some just around the corner from Page. "I was really lucky because this guy lived down the road and I heard Muddy Waters' album at his place," he told *Mojo*'s Phil Alexander in 2009. "Then I bought my own copy." The album in question, probably 1958's *The Best Of Muddy Waters*, was a wise purchase for Jimmy, not only introducing him to the sound of prime Chicago blues, but also Water's deft use of alternative tunings on songs like 'I Can't Be Satisfied'.

There were other benefits too, as the LP allowed the young guitarist to hear up close and personal one of the blues' most beguiling sleights of hand. On 'Standing Around Crying', Muddy's harmonica player, the temperamental but insanely talented Little Walter, was dragging notes to pitch rather than landing them precisely as a classical flautist might. Sometimes Walter didn't even bother landing those notes at all, creating a gorgeous dissonance over the supporting chords underneath. This delicious melodic impropriety was at the very heart of the blues, defining its separation from more conventional European sounds. Suffice to say, Jimmy ate it up: "This was just amazing stuff."[11]

Another bluesman who spoke to Page on an even more profound level was Howlin' Wolf. Peer, rival and occasional nemesis of Waters on the fifties Chicago scene, Wolf's subterranean growl and wailing harp-play on 'Evil', 'Spoonful', 'Killing Floor' and 'Smokestack Lightning' was almost primal in its intensity. "I'd have to say my main blues influence was Howlin' Wolf," said Jimmy. "His stuff wasn't just straight groove, playing on the beat. I loved his voice and the sheer intensity of the music. I was also always impressed with [Wolf's guitarist] Hubert

---

11   Entranced by the sound of blues harmonica, Page would buy one of his own, soon gaining an admirable command of the instrument that he put to good use on several later recordings.

Sumlin. His style matched Wolf's (voice) perfectly. They were a great inspiration and influence on my (later) work." By finding Wolf, Jimmy Page had found Hubert Sumlin. And in finding Muddy, he had also connected with Water's army of guitar players. Jimmy Rogers, Pat Hare, Luther Tucker and, perhaps the best of them all, Earl Hooker. In time, Page would become familiar with each and every rough, tinny note they played. It wouldn't stop there. BB King, Buddy Guy, Otis Rush, Elmore James. These – and many more besides – would be captured, indexed and subsequently assimilated into Page's own style.

Ever the keen host, Jimmy held listening parties in the front room of his parents' home every Sunday night as a way of indulging his newest passion. Here, fellow local blues acolytes could gather among the amps and guitars, pulling brand new sides from crisp cardboard sleeves, all recently flown in from the USA before being snapped up from a specialist dealer on Streatham High Street. Jimmy wasn't limiting his activities to just Epsom. He was also taking the train into London to convene with musicians who were actually playing this music on a proper stage. "I used to go and jam at the main blues club in town, the Marquee." As one might expect, these blues nights at London's Marquee club did not pop into existence like some miraculous parallel universe during the summer months of 1962. That said, their origins were also far from mundane, involving various convergences, synchronicities and a dollop or two of good luck to get things finally off and running.

When interest in skiffle had started to cool, American blues was there to take its place in the UK, gaining strong momentum as a cult – one might even say elitist – alternative to mainstream rock'n'roll, first in the clubs of London's Soho district, then further afield. Respected British jazz trombonist and band leader Chris Barber was a very early champion. Arranging inaugural British tours for icons like Big Bill Broonzy and Brownie McGhee in the early fifties, Barber was also the first to introduce Muddy Waters to UK audiences at the end of the decade. Due to various post-war restrictions, however, there were only a limited number of American artists that could visit at any one time. To slake their thirst, British blues fans began seeking out alternatives closer to home.

They found them in the unlikely form of a balding builder's son from Denham and a wiry-haired, chain-smoking charmer from Paris. Despite origins of birth and their geographical distance from Clarksdale or Issaquena county, Mississippi, harmonica player Cyril Davies and guitarist Alexis Korner's passion for the blues could never be doubted. Graduates of Chris Barber's Jazz Band, where they performed a brief R&B/skiffle interlude during their boss's set in the mid-fifties, Davies and Korner soon began operating under their own steam, opening the London Blues and Barrelhouse Club as a meeting house for like-minded blues madmen.

Come 1962 and the pair had long dropped any notion of skiffle, electrified their sound and expanded their ambitions by forming Blues Incorporated. Best described as a "revolving door of a band", Davies and Korner's new enterprise was all Chicago blues covers, hot-rodded Delta standards and grudgingly played occasional rock'n'roll tunes performed by a fluid mix of promising musicians as drawn to the music as they were. Taking up a residency at London's Marquee club on Thursday nights, Blues Incorporated also operated an 'open mike' between sets where anyone with the requisite courage could join in the fun. For Jimmy Page, the temptation was simply too much. "Yes, I used to jam at the Marquee with Cyril Davies," he said. "Cyril Davies was the real father of city blues in Britain... [and] a lot of groups owe a lot to Cyril."

Indeed they did. By setting up shop at the Marquee, Davies and Korner provided every aspiring young blues musician in London and beyond with a chance to congregate under one roof for a few sweaty hours each week. Perhaps even more crucially, Blues Incorporated gigs also allowed alliances to form both within and around the band. In addition to Page, a *Who's Who* of future rock and pop royalty were part of the Blues Incorporated scene, with names such as Ginger Baker, Jack Bruce, Danny Thompson, Long John Baldry and Graham Bond all onstage at one time or another. "There was this great, big blues thing going on," Jimmy told Howard Mylett, "a real city blues. Everybody playing with [Blues Incorporated]... had all come from rock'n'roll roots as well... but [for me] blues was something I was really getting into."

Unfortunately, Davies and Korner's "Marquee paradise" didn't last too long. When the pair began arguing about choice of material[12] and the use of horns – Alexis wanted them, Cyril didn't – Davies left Blues Incorporated and immediately formed his own group: the All Stars. As canny a talent spotter as Neil Christian before him, Cyril approached Jimmy Page about joining up. Still trying to make the best of art school and mindful of the damage done to his health following two years of road life with the Crusaders, Jimmy was unsure. "I just thought it would be awful to go with him, really start enjoying it and then get ill all over again." In the end, Davies' offer was politely declined, though Page did step up for the occasional gig.

While Alexis Korner gamely soldiered on, keeping both the name Blues Incorporated and taking up a new residency at Soho's lively Flamingo Club, the seeds that he and Davies[13] had sown at the Marquee started to flourish elsewhere. In Twickenham, established trad-jazz venue Eel Pie Island now expanded its musical perimeters to include R&B-themed acts from both home and abroad. Joining established US names such as Howlin' Wolf, Jesse Fuller and Buddy Guy, weekend crowds were also treated to local acts like the Dave Hunt R&B Band, the Tridents and many an up-and-coming group soon to be mentioned in the pages of this book. Over in north London, the Haringey Jazz Club and Muswell Hill's Clissold Arms were doing much the same thing, with blues nights a regular feature of their weekly roster.

The real epicentre for young British blues-based activity in early 1963 was to be found at Richmond's Crawdaddy Club. Recently opened by

---

12 While Alexis Korner was happy enough to throw the occasional rock'n'roll song into Blues Incorporated's set and placate the less elitist elements of their audience, Cyril Davies was much more purist. Frowning on anything other than real blues, Davies' reticence to perform Chuck Berry or Bo Diddley tunes led to increasing, then irreparable friction between he and Korner.

13 A gifted musician who did much to popularise the electric harmonica in the UK, Cyril Davies's life was considerably foreshortened by the demands of touring. After falling victim to pleurisy, he began drinking heavily in an effort to numb the pain. Weakened by alcohol, but still constantly gigging, Davies's heart valves became enflamed and he died in January 1964. He was 31.

Georgian émigré, occasional film editor and full-time R&B/jazz nut Giorgio Gomelsky, the Crawdaddy was a cramped, sweaty little space tucked neatly behind a pub on Kew Road, opposite the train station. Nothing special then, but for the fact that a new and rather exciting blues/R&B combo called the Rolling Stones were the Crawdaddy's house band. "Well, that's when things changed a bit," said Chris Farlowe, with no small understatement.

Practically born under the noses of Korner and Davies at the Marquee several months earlier, where founding members Mick Jagger, guitarists Keith Richards and Brian Jones and drummer Charlie Watts had all sat in with Blues Incorporated, the Stones were a younger, snottier take on the now blossoming British blues scene. Unlike their elders, they also weren't afraid of offending blues snobs by chucking the occasional Chuck Berry tune into their set when the situation demanded it. Again, Jimmy Page was in the midst of it all, watching. "I used to see the Stones in the really early days, when people hadn't actually caught on to how good they actually were," he later told *Mojo*. "I'd see Brian Jones jamming with Alexis Korner... and I think I first saw the Stones in Sutton. It was fantastic when they started doing that Chuck Berry stuff. They did 'Carol' and it sounded as raw as fuck. They were really spitting it out. 'Carol' was the sort of thing we'd been listening to for a number of years, and all of a sudden, there's a band of guys doing it in your own living room."

If Page had really wanted to, he might have made a greater play of becoming involved with this younger British blues scene growing up around him at the Marquee, Eel Pie Island and The Crawdaddy. He was, after all, the right age, lived close to many of the venues and had actually stamped his credentials as a guitarist at several of them. He was also genuinely obsessed with the music. But aside from establishing a casual friendship with Jagger and Richards[14], while also admiring Brian

---

14 Jimmy, Mick and Keith first met in the back of a crowded van on the way to Birmingham for a screening of the now seminal 1963 documentary *Folk Festival Of The Blues*. Exchanging pleasantries on the 250-mile round trip, Page vividly recalls Richards telling him that he played guitar while Jagger "played the harp". Months later, Jimmy was watching their new band in Sutton.

Jones' skills on guitar – "Brian's slide playing was really clean and very authentic sounding" – Jimmy didn't really push it. Even when the Stones gained escape velocity, rising up from the banks of what was soon to be called "the Surrey Delta" for a head-on collision with international fame, he stood back, watching the tale unfold from a respectful distance. "It was just a good scene," he told Howard Mylett, "because everyone had the same upbringing and had been locked away with their records. There was something new to offer. But..."

But not for Page, it seemed. Wary of a return to the road and determined to see out his classes at Sutton Art College, the thought of joining, or even pulling together his own band, held no great appeal. At least, not at this juncture. Besides, by frequenting the likes of the Marquee, he could still keep his hand in and enjoy the festivities without getting burnt in the process. Again, no insane commitments. Just the occasional musical fling whenever he felt the need. Nonetheless, try as he might, Jimmy Page couldn't quite extricate himself from the music business. It just kept coming after him.

CHAPTER 5

Diamonds

While Jimmy Page was learning how to play the blues and south-east England was busy transforming itself into a more temperate version of the Mississippi Delta, the Beatles were planning their own raid on the world 230 miles to the north. Four "lovable mop tops from Liverpool" who, like Page, had been raised on a musical diet of skiffle, rock'n'roll and R&B, the Beatles had learned their trade in the clubs of Hamburg and the caverns of their hometown before being discovered by manager Brian Epstein in December 1961. By the early summer of the following year, they had also been rejected by one record company (Decca) and embraced by another (EMI Parlophone).

Teamed with George Martin, a studio producer then best known for comedy records, the Beatles cut their first single 'Love Me Do' in 15 takes. Released in October 1962, it reached number 17 on the UK charts. The follow-up, 'Please Please Me', reached number two three months later. Three months after that, the Beatles had their first number one with 'From Me To You'. All three of these tunes were penned by the group's song-writing team of John Lennon and Paul McCartney. All three tunes were utterly brilliant. And perhaps most importantly, the creative dry spell that hung over British music for so long was now well and truly over.

Ever the keen observer, Jimmy Page had seen the Beatles up close and personal just before their rocket took off in earnest, attending a London show by the band in early 1963, probably on March 9 at the Granada Cinema in East Ham. So close, in fact, was Page to the action, that he overheard John Lennon spitting the words "Fuck these London audiences" to no one in particular when crowd response to his group's charms proved more tepid than he hoped. By then used to seeing punters literally hanging from the light fixtures in Liverpool's Cavern club every time the Beatles played, Lennon's distaste for the capital's notoriously "snooty" concert-goers was perhaps understandable. But like Lennon, Page knew the Beatles were onto something huge. "The R&B revival had restored my faith in music and the Stones were playing a lot of Muddy Waters numbers," he later told Chris Welch. "Then the Beatles came along." Impressed not only by the soon-to-be Fab Four's melding of rock'n'roll grit with Everly Brothers-like vocal harmonies, Jimmy was also deeply admiring of their ability to take tunes by US girl-groups and make them their own. "Yes," he said, "They were actually doing things by the Marvelettes and the Shirelles!"

While it was still too early to officially announce the birth of the 'Swinging Sixties' or confirm the 'Angry Young Men''s vision of a Great Britain where class was no disabler to artistic or cultural potential, the Beatles' impact on the music scene was both profound and immediate. By virtue of "Looking different, sounding different, being different," the band's resounding success opened a door for others to quickly walk through, ushering in a wave of guitar-led British pop from all points across the country. Following hot on their heels from Liverpool came Gerry & the Pacemakers, the Searchers and Cilla Black, while Manchester offered up Freddie & the Dreamers, Herman's Hermits and the Hollies. Not to be outdone, the south gladly provided "the Anti-Beatles" in the lank-haired shape of the Rolling Stones, their growling sound and sullen attitude the perfect antithesis to the charm and cheek of Lennon and his boys. All these groups were snapped up by the record companies. All were spewing out hits within months.

In this brave new frontier of 'Merseybeat' and the 'Thames Delta', Jimmy Page potentially offered much. Right age. Right disposition.

Right skills. Right there. For reasons of health and the fulfilment of other artistic aspirations, however, it still didn't seem quite the time to try his luck. But, as evidenced, Jimmy couldn't quite avoid the pull of the musical riptide either. By showing up at gigs, playing every Thursday night with the interlude band at the Marquee and twisting shapes with the likes of Cyril Davies and Alexis Korner, Page had not only been enjoying himself. He had been noticed. "Well, I was concentrating more on my blues playing, just enjoying jamming really. Then someone came up to me and said, 'Would you like to play on a record?' I said, 'Why not?'"

Why not, indeed. In industry parlance, what Page had been offered was a 'session'. A paid gig of an agreed duration, he was required to enter a recording studio and provide guitar backing – lead, rhythm, perhaps both – on a tune which would later be released to the market as a single, album track or "other". For his efforts, Page would receive a flat fee, but no royalty or residual. In short, a straight-up, no frills, business transaction. His guitar expertise in exchange for money. By agreeing to participate, Jimmy was about to make his story over the next three years as much about those he worked with as himself.

Setting a precedent for much of Page's subsequent session career, there is some confusion as to which track actually marked this official 'paid' debut. Obviously, there had been previous studio dates with both Chris Farlowe & the Thunderbirds and Neil Christian & the Crusaders sometime in 1961. Another blurry account has Jimmy cutting a tune or two with Cyril Davies's All Stars a year later. Page himself vividly remembers backing a promising bassist/singer called Teddy Whadmore on a song entitled 'Feeling The Groove', though as he later told *Guitarist*:"I don't even know if that was released." To further stir the pot, Jimmy's old friend from Epsom, vocalist John Gibb – now trading under the nom de plume Brian Howard & the Silhouettes – clearly remembers him playing a few chords on his single 'The Worrying Kind'/'Come To Me'. But as it didn't hit the shops until July 1963, and exact recording dates are sketchy, verifying this as Page's first real session remains difficult. Therefore, the best place to start remains Jimmy's involvement with ex-Shadows Tony Meehan and Jet Harris on 'Diamonds' during the late autumn of 1962.

Since his escape from Cliff Richard & the Shadows in the autumn of 1961, drummer Tony Meehan had built up a strong portfolio alongside Joe 'Telstar' Meek as a musician/arranger before accepting a full-time producer's position with Decca records. So, when his former colleague Jet Harris also left Cliff behind for a solo career in April 1962, Meehan was well placed to provide assistance. After overseeing bassist Harris' debut 45 'Besame Mucho'/'The Man With The Golden Arm', Meehan suggested forming a duo for the next release. Turning to composer Jerry Lordan for suitable material (Lordan had written the gorgeous 'Apache' and 'Wonderful Land' for the Shads), the two settled on another popping instrumental named 'Diamonds'. Driven by Jet's detuned Fender Jaguar and full of clever major/minor chord changes, all the track needed was a guitar or two to sprinkle some fairy dust on top.

Enter Glyn Johns. Destined for great things, but then working as an assistant engineer at London's IPC Studios, Johns was 20 years old, brim-full of confidence and – crucially, for the purposes of this story – Epsom born and bred. In fact, Johns was witness to one of Jimmy's earliest performances at St. Martin's parish church when the 12-year-old Page sat playing tunes on guitar with his legs dangling off the stage. "I thought he was fantastic *then*," Johns later told Barney Hoskyns. Striking up a loose friendship with Page that later solidified over a shared love of the blues, the two had recently bumped into each other again at a Stones session at IPC. Possibly eager to make his mark with producer Tony Meehan, Glyn suggested he give Jimmy a try on 'Diamonds'. Meehan agreed. Game on.

By all accounts, Jimmy's first proper session was not as successful as he might have hoped. Though the recording of 'Diamonds' caused him no problems at all (it was really just a matter of strumming along), the B-side, '(Doing The) Hully Gully', was another matter entirely. Expected to provide the track's lead guitar line, Page was handed a wad of sheet music. He couldn't make heads or tails of it. "I didn't have a clue what it was all about," he later confirmed. "I could read chords but not dots at the time. I'd never bothered to learn." Truth be told, the offending melody was so simple, Jimmy could have played it in his sleep. But there was no chance to pick it up by ear as he might have with the Crusaders. Nor any extra time to reconsider reading Bert Weedon's *Play In A Day*. "All I saw," Page said, "were crows on telegraph poles." The game was potentially over before it had really begun.

Thankfully, producer Tony Meehan was in a giving mood. "I knew right away Jimmy was faking it," Meehan recalled. "He couldn't read the music I'd written for him. But he was doing well enough, [so] I switched him from lead to rhythm guitar and all went well." Providing standard bedding chords on an acoustic, Jimmy made it through the rest of the session intact, but a valuable lesson was learnt. "The other [lead guitarist] came and... played this simple sort of riff," he told Stuart Grundy in 1983, "I could have done it so easily... [and] I felt so stupid." If the recording of 'Diamonds' was a matter of dented pride for Page, he could at least take heart from the song's eventual chart position. By January 1963, 'Diamonds' was number one in the UK and Jimmy had a hit – albeit someone else's – under his belt.

If Page thought his underwhelming performance on '... Hully Gully' had ended any future chance at session work, he was sorely mistaken. Within a month or so of playing on 'Diamonds', another offer of a session presented itself, this time via a pair of ambitious tunesmiths called John Carter and Ken Lewis or, as they were then better known, Carter-Lewis & the Southerners. Tin Pan Alley through and through, the Birmingham-born Carter and Lewis[15] had dreamed of a musical career since first seeing Chris Barber's jazz band at their local town hall in the mid/late fifties. Following an increasingly familiar route, it was then just a hop, skip and jump towards rock'n'roll. Carter: "When Gene Vincent and Buddy Holly started doing UK shows, that was it. No turning back. Oh, and the film *The Girl Can't Help It*. All that Technicolour, the bands and that guitar theme tune. It was like something from another planet." Possessed with the spirit of it all, and now armed with guitars and a few songs of their own, John and Ken made a decision. "We said 'We've got to be in the music business'."

---

15   While John Carter graciously agreed to be interviewed for this book in the spring
     of 2015, sadly, Ken Lewis was unwell and could not participate.

Taking a bus to London in early 1960, the duo headed straight to Soho's famous Tin Pan Alley in search of a publishing contract. They got one within hours. "We came down to London on a coach trip. No appointments made, just Ken, me and our guitars. We toured round Denmark Street, got thrown out of most places, but Terry Kennedy at Noel Gay Music said 'OK, we'll give it a listen. Come back in an hour and the bosses will hear you'. We did, played three of our songs and a few days later, they sent us a contract through the post. Because we were still under age, it had to be countersigned by our parents. My dad said 'No way!', but my mother said 'Don't be silly, I'll sign it!', and she did. It really was that simple."

Their shin up the show business drainpipe was equally quick. Penning/arranging tunes while also doing the odd session, Carter and Lewis first scored big when vocalist Mike Sarne recorded their song 'Will I What?' and took it to number 18 in the UK charts in September 1962. By then, they were also regularly appearing on BBC light entertainment shows such as *Easy Beat*, *Saturday Club* and *Twisting Time*, performing a combination of their own material and various hits of the day. With the advent of the Beatles, Merseybeat and the rapidly expanding UK pop bubble, the duo decided to swell their ranks to band-sized proportions, using various sessioneers to provide musical backing on TV and record. Calling themselves Carter-Lewis & the Southerners, the Birmingham duo were not only a song-writing team, but now a group of sorts too. "And you know, why not?" said John. "It gave Ken and I a great opportunity to promote our songs and the records that we had coming out at the time." One such tune was 'Sweet And Tender Romance'.

John Carter recalls first meeting Jimmy Page at London's Decca Studios in West Hampstead, though he is unsure of the exact date. An educated guess might be early 1963. What remains important is that an invitation for some recording work from esteemed producer/arranger Mike Leander at the Carter-Lewis camp was later extended to Page, which he gratefully accepted. According to Jimmy, what happened next was vital in re-establishing his confidence after the wobbles of '... Hully Gully'. "The pivotal record I played on was by two staff writers for Southern Music, John Carter and Ken Lewis, who were working in

Tin Pan Alley on Denmark Street," he told *Mojo* in December 2013. "I think it was [called] 'Sweet And Tender Romance'. It was right in the early stages, lost in the annals of rock history, the foggy department! But I was allowed to have a crack and do what I wanted playing wise."

Again, without benefit of a time machine, confirming Jimmy's appearance on 'Sweet And Tender Romance' is nigh on impossible. But John Carter remembers it slightly differently. "'Sweet And Tender Romance'? Our version? No, Jimmy wasn't on that," he said. "However, we did another version with two Scottish sisters called the McKinleys and he was on that. No, Jimmy definitely wasn't on ours. I think his memory's going there!" In Carter's mind, a much safer bet in tracking Page's debut with the Southerners would be 'Your Mama's Out Of Town'. "Yes," he said, "Jimmy is definitely on 'Your Mama's Out Of Town'. There's no great call for a solo on it, but he's playing away. '... Out Of Town' was a Mitch Murray[16] song. We actually wanted to do one of our own, but Mitch was such a great character and made me laugh so much, we said 'OK, we'll do it.'"

Carter, for one, never had any doubts about Page's abilities. "Jimmy was a quiet guy, but you know, a nice guy. If you went to the pub for a drink, he'd have a chat and a pint, but he was never wandering around saying 'I'm the greatest'. He was a reserved man, but also very intelligent. And, of course, he was very good at playing the guitar." Page would maintain his association with the Southerners for a good while yet, playing on various tracks and even posing as a member of the group for publicity purposes. "Well, [Carter-Lewis] weren't a 'band' per se," he later said. "They were specifically designed to record." From now on, so was Jimmy. Following his good work with Carter-Lewis, word began to spread that the young guitarist had discipline, chops and genuine talent – a talent that could be utilised by a slew of other

---

16 Destined to win two Ivor Novello awards for his song-writing skills, Mitch Murray's hits included Gerry & the Pacemakers' 'How Do You Do It?', 'I Like It' and, perhaps most notably, Tony Christie's wonderful 'Avenues And Alleyways'. A natural comedian, Murray also wrote books (his *How To Write A Hit Song* inspired a 12-year-old Sting to take up song-writing) and after-dinner speeches.

producers, artists and groups who needed some six-string fire power on their own recordings. "It was the right place at the right time, really," he later said.

How right he was. The world Page had entered was an odd, but interesting place, and in lieu of recent events, one re-shaping its boundaries to cope with a new and musically leaner age. Of course, there had always been session players on the UK scene. ITV's flagship youth programme *Oh Boy*, for instance, had relied on them heavily, the likes of sax players Red Price and Benny Greene stepping away from their day job with Ted Heath's swing band to provide backing for singers or visiting groups. Led by arranger Harry Robertson and fronted by pianist Cherie Wainer, the *Oh Boy* troupe had even formed a band of their own – 'Lord Rockingham's XI' – scoring a number one hit with the Saltire-baiting 'Hoots Mon' in 1958. But times, as they say, were changing.

Since the advent of rock'n'roll, demand for larger session ensembles had steadily dropped. Now, with the arrival of the Beatles, the Rolling Stones and all that came in their wake, that trend only escalated. Really, it was just a matter of economics. Smaller session units were more cost effective than bigger ones: easier to record, cheaper to book. That there would always be a need for orchestras with brass and string sections to provide sweep and power was a given. Yet, "Smaller sounds meant smaller fees." To those dealing with the new order, Jimmy Page was an ideal fit. Polite, enthusiastic and still only 19 years old, Page could not only play admirably well, but was also from the same generation as the upstarts now starting to dominate the UK charts. "I," he once said, laughing "was the new pick on the block."

That pick was put to regular use on a wide variety of singles, jingles and assorted album tracks throughout 1963. In keeping with the diverse nature of the session trade, this might mean laying down a Chuck Berry-like solo on Wayne Fontana & the Mindbenders' 'Hello Josephine' one afternoon while strumming gently behind easy-listening queen Kathy Kirby the next. Whether it was backing Everly Brothers-soundalikes the Brook Brothers (whom Page greatly liked) on 'Trouble Is My Middle Name' or providing some tasty acoustic fills on the Marauders' beat-friendly 'That's What I Want' (again written by Carter-Lewis), he proved up to the task.

Jimmy was also careful not to make any more mistakes when it came to music theory. "When I first started I could read chord charts but not 'the dots'," he later said. "I soon got to it, though." The expansion in his musical vocabulary was no doubt aided by a return to guitar lessons, this time with a young flamenco/jazz player named John McLaughlin. Recently arrived in London from his native Doncaster, McLaughlin had been quick in making a name for himself on the gigging circuit with Alexis Korner and Georgie Fame & the Blue Flames, his playing shockingly good by anyone's standards. He also did occasional sessions. "John taught me about chord progressions," Jimmy told *Musician* in 1990. "He was fabulous, just so fluent and so far ahead. I learned a hell of a lot." Like Page, McLaughlin would not stay anonymous for long.

Another guitarist Jimmy could learn a thing or two from was his session colleague, 'Big' Jim Sullivan. A former member of Marty Wilde's Wildcats, with whom he had backed the likes of Gene Vincent and Eddie Cochran, Sullivan had been introduced to the world of sessions in 1961 by *Oh Boy*'s producer Jack Good. Already able to approximate most any musical style, he took to studio life like a duck to water, soon becoming "the go-to guy" on the London recording scene. In fact, Big Jim's session resumé by the time Jimmy Page arrived on the circuit was already bulging at the seams, his Gibson 345 having graced countless recordings by any number of artists. Indeed, it was Sullivan who actually took over on lead guitar when Jimmy fluffed his lines on '.... Hully Gully'. However, Jim laboured under no misapprehensions about how this session business really operated. "You'd give your heart, do a great solo, and the band would be really tight," he later said, "Then, you'd get this voice from the [recording] box saying, 'Yeah lads... that was kind of all right. Can you do another one?' Take 39 it is."

One might think that Big Jim Sullivan would have seen Jimmy Page as stiff competition when he first started popping up on studio dates in 1963. After all, Page was three years younger than him, a little hipper to be sure, and already on first name terms with the likes of Mick Jagger and Keith Richards. "Actually, I can tell you a quick story about some of that," said John Carter. "I went to a lunchtime show Ken Colyer put on with the Stones in 1963, and backstage, Mick Jagger came up to me. He said 'Here, your song, 'Sweet And Tender Romance'. Keith says it's Jimmy Page on guitar, I say it's Big Jim Sullivan. Who is it?' I said, 'You're right. It's Big Jim.' Mystery solved."

Sullivan, however, actually seemed to embrace Page on his arrival, seeing him less as a potential competitor and more a valuable addition to the overall session scene. "I was a better country player than Jimmy," he said. "I could play all that bendy stuff, but then, he could play the rock stuff and the blues. So, really, we hit a real happy medium in the studio. Whenever there was a country session, I'd do it and whenever there was a rock session, he would." Carter heartily agreed. "Big Jim and Jimmy just stood out back then. They could have been rivals. But they had two completely different styles; Big Jim used this wonderful Chet Atkins-like finger-picking, while Jimmy was always a real rock'n'roller. But they were both great, great players and would always try and do their best for you. It's also worth remembering that in the early sixties at least, there were very few players around who were that good." One problem that did need to be ironed out, however, was that Page and Sullivan shared the same forename, a fact that could lead to occasional confusion with bookings. The solution was obvious. Jimmy Page got his own nickname. "Yes, Jimmy became known as 'Little Jim'," said Carter. "It was 'Big Jim' and 'Little Jim'. Quite funny, really. Well, it was at the time."

Though Sullivan and Page had two distinct styles that could be utilised separately by various artists, the pair also enjoyed working together as and when the situation demanded it. This was nowhere more apparent than their association with singer Dave Berry, an intriguing new prospect Decca records signed in early 1963. Sheffield born and bred, Berry was another of those performers who had raised himself on a staple diet of rock'n'roll before discovering blues in his late teens. "I'd started listening to the Buddy Hollys and Eddie Cochrans of this world, but like the Stones, I soon wanted to learn where this music came from," said Berry. "So I went in search of it. Soon, I found Muddy Waters, Howlin' Wolf, Bo Diddley and Chuck Berry, the very roots of rock'n'roll." For Dave, there was no greater demi-god than the man who gave the world 'Johnny B. Goode'. "Chuck Berry. My absolute hero back in the day. No one wrote lyrics like Chuck Berry. Just listen to the words of 'Promised Land'. Marvellous."

Forming his own band, the Cruisers, in 1960, Dave Berry had worked the clubs and dancehalls tirelessly until attracting the interest of Decca. But after Top 20 success with his debut single – a faithful cover of Chuck Berry's 'Memphis, Tennessee' – it became apparent the Cruisers weren't cutting the mustard in a studio environment. "Unfortunately, after I signed with Decca, [the first recordings] didn't really work with the Cruisers," he confirmed. "I'd been used to the rough and tumble of road bands, but I don't think some of the road bands worked too well in the studio because you needed discipline. I think that was true of my band. The Cruisers were a terrific live group for sure, but they couldn't read music." What Berry required was something more controlled, reflexive and professional. "A session team, well, that suited my way of working. I wanted to go in to the studio and know the track was being put down, that everything was in hand. Then, I could put my voice over the top after the session guys had finished."

Alongside the likes of drummer Bobby Graham, bassist Alan Niven and, on occasion, legendary big band trombonist Don Lusher, Jimmy Page and Big Jim Sullivan helped form the crack team that Dave Berry had dreamed of. By the autumn of 1963, some of them had also cut Berry's own favourite of all his studio recordings, a sterling cover of Elvis' 'My Baby Left Me'. "Yep, that's the one I'd like to be known for," he said "Nothing like the Arthur Crudup original, nothing like Elvis, just our own version of the song. Jimmy Page on lead guitar, Alan Niven on slap bass – there were actually two basses on that, you know. But yes, a good song. I'm happy with that and really glad Jimmy was on it." Page was actually all over it. Providing a master class in snappy riffs and clattering chords throughout the verse and chorus before letting fly with a quite superb solo, Jimmy took Berry's already spirited reading of 'My Baby Left Me' to another level. "I remember the great solo that Jimmy did on that session," Sullivan later recalled. "It's one of the best-constructed rock solos on record."

Another prime example of how good British rock'n'roll could be in the right hands, 'My Baby Left Me' was only a modest hit for Dave Berry when released as a single in January 1964. But he soon followed it up with the song that came to define him, even if he had to be pushed into recording it by Page and Sullivan. "Being honest, at the time I wasn't all that keen on 'The Crying Game'. It was a ways away from the bluesy, R&B flavour of the early recordings and I really wanted to be a rock singer more than do ballads. But Jimmy and Big Jim had heard it from [writer/producer] Geoff Stephens, and I remember them saying to me, 'No Dave, this is a really good song'. Big Jim and Jimmy actively encouraged me to record it."

A timeless gem and featuring a fine, knowing vocal from Berry, 'The Crying Game'[17] went straight into the UK Top Five in July 1964. Unsurprisingly, it also captured some class work from both Big and Little Jim. Reversing roles this time around, Sullivan's tearful-sounding lead guitar swells (courtesy of a borrowed DeArmond 610 Tone/ Volume pedal) added depth and sensitivity to the melody, while Page's sympathetic acoustic backing held the overall track in place. "No one back then would imagine that 50 years later people would want to know who played on what, or who was bouncing off what," said Berry of the 'The Crying Game' session. "But my memory was Big Jim was the main guitarist, I suppose, with Jimmy... well, not secondary to him, that wouldn't be right... but the younger guitarist, I suppose. The way it worked was that they'd just bounce ideas off each other. Clearly, Berry was extremely keen to point out that Page was never "secondary" to Big Jim Sullivan. Just different. "You know, Jimmy was only 19 at the time, but he really knew his stuff. He could read the parts, improvise, and take – or make – suggestions with the other players. So, yes, Jimmy was way ahead of the game at that time."

Outside of his commitments with Dave Berry, the work was really starting to pile up for Page. There was breezy pop to pick on Chris

---

17 Written by Geoff Stephens in 1963, 'The Crying Game' has had an impressive shelf life. Re-recorded by Boy George in 1992 for Neil Jordan's film of the same name, the track was again a hit, this time reaching number 22 in the UK charts.

Sandford's 'Not Too Little, Not Too Much', teen idols to attend with Gregory Phillips's 'Please Believe Me', and a return to Joe Meek's pint-sized studio in London's Holloway Road for recording sessions with bottle-blond crooner Heinz and madcap country outfit Houston Wells & the Marksmen. "We absolutely loved Joe Meek's studio on Holloway Road," said John Carter. "It was such a tiny place and a little weird too. But then, Joe was a bit weird..." Yet, every studio date Jimmy accepted meant one less appearance at Sutton Art College, where he was still meant to be a pupil. When his non-attendance began to be questioned by tutors and talk turned to his student grant being revoked due to extracurricular earnings, Page had to make a decision whether to stick or twist. This time, he threw in his academic cards for life as a full-time musician. The choice was fully supported by his parents. "My parents weren't musical," he later told *Guitar Player*'s Steve Rosen, "no, not at all. But they didn't mind me getting into it. I think they were quite relieved to see something being done instead of art work, which they thought was a loser's game."

The decision to quit higher education and concentrate on studio work must have been tremendously liberating for Page. After the disappointing end to his time with Neil Christian, he seemed to accept that fine art and not music would define his future. But sessions had opened a new path, one that made fewer demands on his health yet offered financial stability. Joining a crack squad of musicians that included the likes of Sullivan, the wonderfully named Vic Flick, Bobby Graham, Bryan Bennett and Clem Cattini among others, Page was now officially "London's youngest studio ace". All in all, it was going swimmingly well. And in the unlikely event that gold turned to dust, Jimmy had a back-up plan in place. "I always thought I could return to painting," he later confirmed to *International Musician*. "But you know, I don't think I ever picked up a paint brush again..."

CHAPTER 6

She Just Satisfies

Jimmy Page's session diary in the mid-sixties must have been quite the read. While he had gamely avoided the harsh rigours of touring by pursuing a more sedentary life in the recording studio, Page's daily schedule still put most runners and cycle couriers to shame. A blur of train journeys, lifts from fellow musicians, cab rides and brisk walks from one part of London to another, the guitarist's working hours were mapped out in almost fractal detail, with little or no time to spare. Typically working in three-hour blocks – two hours on the A-side of a single, one hour on the B-side – Jimmy could find himself doing up to 15 sessions a week, with extra dates sometimes pencilled in for Saturday mornings too.

The job also required vast amounts of discipline and concentration. With producers watching the clock on the record company's behalf, any major errors during the recording process were heavily frowned upon and potentially costly. Therefore, musicians had to be accurate in their playing, sympathetic to the overall arrangement and creative in their endeavours – all with little or no preparation. "The music business is a very pressured business," said John Carter. "You have to have discipline, otherwise you won't last. I knew guys who didn't. But yes, if you wanted to succeed, you had to be serious about it. Jimmy was serious."

On occasion, Page was allowed to kick about in the sandpit. Decca records' musical director Mike Leander, for instance, often allowed his players real latitude during studio dates, giving the likes of Jimmy and Big Jim Sullivan room to improvise with their solos and rhythmic backing. Ivor Raymonde, too, would make room for "some fun between the dots", the sheer strength of his arrangements on Dusty Springfield's 'I Only Want To Be With You' or Billy Fury's 'I Will' (on which Jimmy appeared in 1964) unlikely to be undone by one stray experimental flourish. But others ran a much tighter ship. In the case of producer Charles Blackwell, any deviation from sheet music was considered a mortal sin, if not quite punishable by death.

Then again, when the song, arrangement and performance were followed to the tee, miracles could happen. A notable case in point was the session for 'Goldfinger' in August 1964. Riding atop a wave of precision-drilled strings, brass, percussion and guitars, Welsh singer Shirley Bassey was able to unleash hell, her uncanny vocal helping create the best known and perhaps best loved of all the James Bond movie title themes. Page certainly thought so. "That was a phenomenal session," he said. "[Arranger] John Barry had been rehearsing this massive orchestra waiting for Shirley Bassey. She arrived, took off her coat and went straight in. John counted (us) in, she sang and at the end, just collapsed on the floor. Watching from the orchestra, that was just astonishing."

Obviously, not every session Jimmy was involved in at the time produced an immortal song or monster hit. Though as upbeat and tuneful as they come, few are likely to remember Bobby Shafto's 'She's My Girl' from April 1964 or Page's chiming lead line on it. Similarly, the thumping garage-pop of Jean & the Statesides' 'Putty In My Hands' might also draw a blank for most, despite Jimmy's best James Burton impressions throughout. Still, his efforts on these lesser known gems were well worth seeking out. Jackie Lynton's bold cover of Lennon & McCartney's 'Little Child', for instance, featured a wonderful burst of choppy guitar from Page, while his harmonica work on Mickey Finn & the Blue Men's cover of Chuck Berry's 'Reelin' And Rockin'' would have made Little Walter proud.

And if one wanted to hear Jimmy playing with his favourite new toy, then Carter-Lewis & the Southerners' 'Skinnie Minnie' was certainly worth a listen. "Yep, 'Skinny Minnie''s all Jimmy," said John Carter. "We cut that at Olympic Studios, I think. We had no real parts worked out beforehand, so we said to him 'Just go for it'. And did he! Bo Diddley rhythm, crashing chords... absolutely brilliant. But then, if you wanted the song to be rocky or funky, you got in Little Jim. And don't forget that fuzz box solo..." The "fuzz box" Carter referred to was still a relatively new device in the UK during 1964, its primeval tone viewed more as a novelty than an essential part of the guitarist's kit bag. But like so many things at the time, that was about to change.

Since the guitar had become electrified, pervading wisdom had dictated that the signal from the instrument's pick-ups[18] be as clean as possible, thus aping its acoustic origins. This worked just fine for the majority of jazz and country music where the onus was on bell-like clarity. But with the advent of rock'n'roll, things had started to get a little dirty in the sound department. One of the first examples of this sonic griminess was on 'Rocket 88'. Legend has it that while driving to the studio, Willie Kizart's amplifier fell from the back of his car and was badly damaged. Keen not to abandon the session, Kizart padded the amp's cone with newspaper to hold it in place. The solution worked, but in doing so, he had created a mildly distorted tone. Liking the overall effect, producer Sam Phillips recorded the sound "as was", thus pricking the ears of many a guitarist on the release of 'Rocket 88' in 1951.

By the end of the decade, such gritty tones were very much on trend, as blues players like Buddy Guy and rock'n'roll types such as Link Wray began either hot-wiring their pick-ups or injuring their amps in search of "that magic noise". Come 1961, and said noise made it into the charts, with US session ace Grady Martin's faulty amp-driven guitar grumbles pushing Marty Robbins' otherwise respectable country ballad 'Don't Worry' to number three on the Hot 100. When in the same

18 Guitar pick-ups basically act as a transducer, capturing the string's mechanical vibrations and converting them to an electrical signal to be either amplified or recorded.

year, Martin recorded his own single and called it 'The Fuzz', the sound effect had its name. Soon enough, instrumental surf band the Ventures climbed on the band wagon, getting guitarist/inventor 'Red' Rhodes to recreate Grady's growl in the shape of an effects device he christened 'the fuzz box'. The device was then put to good use on the Ventures' Top 10 hit '2,000 Pound Bee'. Seizing a business opportunity (and putting the final piece of the fuzz puzzle in place by doing so), Gibson guitars put the little box into production in 1962, re-naming it the 'Maestro Fuzztone FZ-1'.

Always alert to sonic innovations, Jimmy Page was aware of both '2,000 Pound Bee' and the Maestro Fuzztone. But he knew someone who might improve on the effect. "I'd met a chap called Roger Mayer," Jimmy later recalled to *Mojo*. "He was working at the Admiralty [at the time]. I think he was in the 'hush-hush' department. Anyway, he'd seen me playing with someone around Tolworth or Kingston and said, 'I want to do something with guitars, would you help?' I said 'Absolutely'. So he came round and I played him some records with overdriven guitar because the players had bad amps. He listened, then went away and developed this little pedal that I started to use."

Actually working for the Navy in their 'Acoustical Analysis' division, Roger Mayer had known Page for a little while before they set about reinventing the sound of the fuzz box. "I grew up near Epsom, near Kingston and Jimmy was always playing in local bands at youth clubs. This was 1962, 1963," said Mayer. "Then, we'd be around at his house listening to various records, and there'd be a focus on these guitar players from the American scene. He'd be really listening to James Burton from Ricky Nelson's band." As the friendship developed, both turned their ears towards the blues. "Yeah, Pagey [was getting] slightly more blues-influenced in his playing. We'd listen to Freddie King and other blues guys, and he was after these new sounds."

Obviously, Page saw the Fuzztone as a way of gaining further dominion over these sounds and bringing them with him on the session trail. But there were problems to be resolved. Mayer was there to help. "The Ventures had done '2,000 Pound Bee' and... one or two of the music stores in London's Charing Cross Road had the new Maestro fuzz box. That's when I first became aware of the possibilities of heavy transistorised distortion. Obviously, there had been American records before that had [got that sound] by turning the amplifier up, but this was different. So, Jimmy came to me when he got the Maestro and said, 'It's good, but it doesn't have enough sustain... it's a bit staccato.' I said, 'Well, we can improve on that.' And that conversation spurred me on to design my first fuzz box."

Through a process of trial, error and using the Maestro as a rough guide for his own design – "There had to be similarities. After all, there were only three terminals to work from" – Roger finally completed his task. "Yeah, I did. I managed to build a fuzz that had much more sustain." Page and Mayer's association was beneficial for both parties. Jimmy got a custom-made fuzz box that he could put to good use in the studio, while Roger got a taste for building effects pedals. By 1967, he was doing precisely that for another promising young guitarist named Jimi Hendrix. "Ah, Jimi," said Mayer, "we can have a chat about him a bit later..."

Thus far, Page had gained invaluable experience working with the likes of artists such as Tony Meehan, Jet Harris, Dave Berry and many others. Equally, he was a careful observer of some of the best arrangers and producers of the day, taking silent note as Mike Leander, Joe Meek and John Barry went about their business. "Yes, Jimmy was always a studious fellow during sessions, keeping an eye on how things worked," said John Carter. "He was an intelligent man who took things in, with one eye on how things might be useful in future. Jimmy was always controlled. You never saw him drunk. Never." While this approach paid dividends, building him a solid reputation as a reliable studio presence, Page must also have been champing at the bit to get involved with some of the new breed at the cutting edge of the pop market – those bands, singers and characters that would come to define the 'Swinging Sixties'. He got his chance, and then some, with producer Shel Talmy.

Born and raised in Chicago, Talmy was one of those kids that was instinctively drawn as much to music as he was technology. On graduating high school in the late fifties, he set off to prove it, securing a job as a trainee recording engineer at Conway Studios in Los Angeles.

Actively encouraged to experiment with the tools of his trade by the owner, Shel used any downtime in schedules to help improve existing guitar and drum sounds or better isolate the vocal booth with carpets and cardboard. "There were no precedents then," he confirmed. "All this stuff was totally new." Promoted to producer, Talmy cut various sides with the likes of surf group the Markells and R&B all-rounder Robert 'Bumps' Blackwell, before deciding a quick change of scene was in order. "I intended to come to Europe for maybe six or seven weeks before returning to LA," he said. "I went for the usual reason most 20 [year olds] do... to expand my horizons and see some of the world before it passed me by!"

Talmy might have been expecting great things upon his arrival in London, but it took a little while to locate them. "Actually, I found the Brit music scene predictable, boring and old-fashioned," he said. "But things got better quickly. My locating [to] the Kings Road in Chelsea made me aware that 'bubbling under' was an imminent eruption. [It] was exciting and stimulating." At first, Shel had no real plans to work in London. But when a suitable position arose at Decca records, he chased after it. Enthusiasm, experience (and some borrowed acetates) got him the job, albeit not exactly the one he wanted. "One of my favorite fantasies [is that] I arrived in London three months earlier and was at Decca when Brian Epstein came in with his Beatles demos. But..." As history records, George Martin got that particular gig, but Talmy didn't do too badly either. Easing himself into the producer's seat with Irish easy-listening act the Bachelors, he soon turned his hand to a promising band from Muswell Hill, north London, then trading as the Ravens. Helping to secure them a deal with Pye records, Shel watched as the group's first two singles failed to chart. Even their funky new name – the Kinks – had done little to captivate audiences. Then came single number three.

Much has been written about 'You Really Got Me'. "The song birthed hard rock and heavy metal." "The first true punk anthem." Surely one of the better descriptions of its charms comes from writer Jon Savage. "What Shel Talmy and the Kinks did... was to concoct the perfect medium for expression of the adolescent white aggression that has been at the heart of white popular music. 'You Really Got Me' is that rare thing: a record that cuts popular music in half." Penned by Kinks leader Ray Davies, propelled into the stratosphere by his brother Ray's brutal, distorted guitar riff and produced with a minimum of fuss by Talmy, 'You Really Got Me' really was, as Savage confirmed, the break point for a new type of British pop rock: artful, aggressive, shockingly novel, but still catchy as hell. All in all, precisely the type of tune on which Jimmy Page would love to have played a fiery solo. Except, of course, he very much didn't.

A matter of heated debate for over 50 years, much of the confusion over whether Jimmy struck a single note on 'You Really Got Me' is based largely around the fact that he was present at its recording. This was at the behest of Shel Talmy, who had been using Page on various sessions for a while before, and indeed might well have had him contribute to the Kinks' first single, a cover of Little Richard's 'Long Tall Sally'. "Jimmy was a very nice, very talented kid. No mystery. I just hired him, paid him a session fee and knew he'd perform perfectly for what I needed. I guess you could call Jimmy my 'security blanket'." It was in fulfilling this role that Page turned up at IBC Studios in July 1964. But he didn't feel very wanted at all. "I know that Ray didn't really approve of my presence," he said eight years later. "The Kinks just didn't want me around when they were recording. [But] it was Shel's idea."

Whether Ray Davies felt irked because Talmy had brought Jimmy in as insurance remains unclear. Perhaps he was unhappy that his band hadn't been fully trusted to deliver. Maybe he just didn't like Page's attitude.[19] But as rumours began to fly after the event that Jimmy had a strong hand in how '… Got Me' finally turned out, Ray wasn't backward in coming

---

19   There is good reason to believe that Ray Davies was genuinely annoyed at Page during the session. In his autobiography, 1995's *X-Ray*, he writes: "[Jimmy] cringed as it came to Dave's solo. Perhaps [he] was put out about not being asked to play on the track. We were slightly embarrassed by the amount of jealousy shown by the eminent guitarist. Perhaps he thought Dave's solo was inferior to anything he could have played, but Dave not only invented a sound, but also had every right to play whatever solo he felt fitted the track."

forward as to who played what. "[My brother] Dave did all those solos," he confirmed to Ritchie Yorke in 1976. "The [version] of 'You Really Got Me' that was actually released was the third [recording]. There was a demo thing with Dave playing lead, a second cut which may have had Jimmy on it – and which Pye Records still have in their vaults – and a third which definitely had Dave on it. I know because I was standing right next to him when he played on it. And that's the one which was released. But Jimmy Page did play tambourine on our first album. It's very good tambourine and he's a very good musician. I'd use him if I was producing a recording."

Understandably, Jimmy wasn't overwhelmed with joy by Davies' remarks, especially as they focused less on his guitar playing and more on his skills with a minor percussive instrument. "I never played tambourine on the damned record," he growled in 1977. "I played guitar. But I didn't play on 'You Really Got Me' and that's what pisses [Ray] off." One year later, and Page had cooled a bit, though he now seemed to imply that he had contributed at least something to the session. "Looking back at it in retrospect, my presence there was to probably enable Ray Davies to walk around and virtually control everything... because he really was producing those records as much as Shel Talmy," he told Nick Kent. "A lot more so, actually, because he was directing it and everything. At one point, there were three guitars playing the same riff."

Without a video camera perched on the wall during the recording of 'You Really Got Me', it is unlikely that anyone will ever truly know precisely what happened. Suffice to say, the single proved a huge hit both for the Kinks and Talmy, reaching number one in the UK on its release in August 1964 and also breaking at number seven in the USA a year later. The first in a succession of world-beating 45s with Talmy – 'All Day And All Of The Night', 'Tired Of Waiting For You', 'Dedicated Follower Of Fashion' and the astounding 'Waterloo Sunset' all followed in fairly short order – '... Got Me''s explosive energy made international stars of the Kinks. "But what really makes a star?" said Shel. "Talent, fire in the belly, persistence. And a lot of luck." And in the case of Ray Davies, a fair bit of pith too.

Sadly, Page's rocky experience with the Kinks wasn't an isolated event. As more and more bands emerged in the wake of the Beatles and Rolling Stones' success, more and more record companies and producers sought insurance on their investment, keeping a steady roster of session players on hand to step in when youthful inexperience threatened to derail the final product. In fact, just two months after 'You Really Got Me', Jimmy again found himself potentially in the wars, this time with the Who. A sickeningly talented west London quartet led by the pugnacious but hyper-intelligent Pete Townshend, the Who were then at the start of their own climb towards stardom. Just as good as the Kinks, they were also just as protective of their songs.

Hence, when Page was again asked by Talmy to hover in the background while the band recorded their debut single 'I Can't Explain', guitarist/songwriter Townshend might well have been ready for war. "Jimmy had obvious competence," reiterated Shel. "Everything he played on was tasteful and fitted with a particular track." Mercifully, however, Page's presence brought no face-off with Pete. Instead they bonded over matters of the heart. "Well, Jimmy was already a friend of mine," Townshend later told *Guitar World*. "We had a mutual girlfriend. I was going out with her around the time we made that record. She'd gone out with Jimmy before and she was still kind of hooked on him... for a little longer than I was comfortable with. Anyway, she was much older than us. We were 19, 20 and she was nearly 30 years old. And a fucking sexy woman. She'd obviously fucked him to death, and then proceeded to fuck me to death. We had her in common. We were both cross-eyed with this woman. So, when Jimmy showed up at the studio, we started to talk about what we always talked about. 'How's Anya? What's she going through? Has she called you? Has she called me?' Then I said to Jimmy 'What are you doing here?' and he said 'I'm just here to add some weight to the guitar. I'm going to double the rhythm guitar on the overdubs'. And I said 'Oh, great.' Then he said, 'What are you going to play?' I told him [I was using] a Rickenbacker 12. He said 'OK, I'll play a... whatever it was!'" In the end, Page was not actually required on 'I Can't Explain', but Pete graciously allowed him to contribute a short, noodling solo on the B-side 'Bald Headed Woman', a track reportedly written in honour of the very woman with whom they had both been besotted. "Actually," concluded Townshend, "it was all very congenial..."

The same could not be said when Jimmy was asked along to a recording by another young, hard-edged blues band, this one from Northern Ireland. Formed by then upcoming singer-songwriter Van Morrison, Them were only a matter of months old when Page met them, the group having made their debut onstage at Belfast's Maritime Hotel on April 14, 1964 before being quickly snapped up by Decca records. Flown to London to cut their first 45 three months later, Them's 'Don't Start Crying Now' was a raw but spirited affair, its main highlight being Morrison's uncanny ability to mimic the throaty growl of his hero, Howlin' Wolf. On that occasion, the band had reportedly been supplemented by two session musicians, with Bobby Graham on second drum kit. But according to Page, the number of jobbing professionals employed on Them's second single, a cover of Big Joe Williams' rumbling 'Baby, Please Don't Go', markedly increased. It made for an absolutely poisonous atmosphere. "Very embarrassing," Jimmy later told journalist Dave Schulps. "As each number passed, another member of the group would be substituted by a session musician. It was horrifying. Talk about daggers." Despite a supposed revolving door of musicians, Van Morrison and Them got their break-out single, with 'Baby, Please Don't Go', reaching the UK Top 10 in November 1964.

Then a fantastic tune, now a timeless classic, Them's 'Baby, Please Don't Go' again highlights later difficulties in attributing "who exactly played what" on so many of rock'n'roll and pop's landmark recordings. In '... Don't Go"s case, Page only ever claimed to provide acoustic backing, with Them's own guitarist Billy Harrison left very much in charge of the track's signature riff. "The riff on 'Baby, Please Don't Go' was my riff. I created it," Harrison later said. "We'd been playing the song like that all over Northern Ireland... before it went on record." Yet, despite such obvious confirmations, stubborn rumours persist that Page's presence on '... Don't Go' was much more substantial – those shimmering asides and half-formed lead lines in the background not just 'ghost tracks' or 'warm-ups', but noises definitely oozing from the neck of Jimmy's guitar.

It is not just 'Baby, Please Don't Go', 'I Can't Explain' or 'You Really Got Me' where such controversy exists. Page is often credited with an appearance on Chris Ravel & the Ravers' 1963 single 'I Do'/'Don't You Dig This Kinda Beat'. But according to Chris Ravel (aka Chris Andrews[20]), that's unlikely. "Jimmy did play on several recordings of mine... to be honest, I can't remember all of them! [But] Jimmy did not play 'I Do' or 'Don't You Dig This Kinda Beat'. It was played by Johnny Kelly, unless [Jimmy] played over it at a later date."

These were not the only bumps in the road. Back in 1960, John Hawken had marvelled at Jimmy Page's guitar skills with the Crusaders from the audience at Weybridge Town Hall. By June 1964, he was playing keyboards in a fine band of his own, the Nashville Teens[21], now about to release a stoked-up treatment of country rocker John D. Loudermilk's 'Tobacco Road' as their first single on Decca Records. Subsequently a huge hit both in the UK and USA, Page has been credited as appearing on the track but, as with others, it's become a matter of some dispute. "It was [our guitarist] John Allen all the way," said Hawken. "Not Jimmy, I'm afraid." Similarly, the guitar part on the Teens' follow-up single 'Google Eye' was also attributed to Page. Hawken's response was empathic. "Sorry. No, not Jimmy."

From Tom Jones and 'It's Not Unusual' to Ian Whitcomb and 'Nervous', the list of tracks on which Page may – or may not – have featured goes on and on and there are myriad reasons for such disparities. By its very nature, the recording process allows for multiple takes, with

---

20 A greatly underrated singer, Andrews went on to have several hits under his real name, including the 1965 reggae-friendly hit 'Yesterday Man', which Jimmy definitely did play on.

21 Aside from being an excellent band in their own right, the Nashville Teens have several other claims to fame. Not only did they draw fine reviews when backing the likes of Chuck Berry and Carl Perkins onstage and on record in the early sixties, but they also provided a wonderful musical backdrop for Jerry Lee Lewis to bounce off at Hamburg's Star Club on April 5, 1964. The resulting album, *Live At The Star Club*, has been called "The purest, hardest rock & roll ever committed to record," by music critic Stephen Thomas Erlewine, and is also listed in the book *1001 Albums You Must Hear Before You Die*.

tracks being cut at one session, before being added to (or subtracted from) at another. In fact, according to drummer Bobby Graham – who, like Page, featured on thousands of such tunes – it was not unusual for session players to come in 'after the fact' and re-record certain parts, often without the knowledge of the band. "A lot of the artists didn't realise that after they'd gone, me, Big Jim and Jimmy were often called in to overdub what they'd done," he told journalist Leslie Baldock. "There are one or two groups who will remain nameless... that still say to this day that it was them playing on their records and didn't realise it was us. [For instance], their drums were still there, but now buried (underneath)."

No one in their right mind could blame Jimmy Page or his fellow musicians for this confusion over such credits. He has frequently stated over the years that remembering every studio date or recording session in which he participated from late 1962 onwards would be simply impossible. Up to his eyes and ears in singles, album tracks, advertising ditties and library music each and every day for months and years, the fact that he can recall any of it at all – especially after his subsequent career – is commendable in the extreme. "Actually, I met Jimmy again at the National Portrait Gallery a couple of years ago at an exhibition of recording artists," said Dave Berry, by way of explanation. "We were talking about the B-side of 'The Crying Game'. It's a track called 'Don't Gimme No Lip, Child', which was famously later covered by the Sex Pistols. Well, the original's actually got Jimmy playing harmonica on it. Then, we [started] trying to remember exactly what else he was [playing harp] on at the time. But, you know, we didn't think in 50 years' time, we'd all be sitting down analysing it for the purposes of history!"

Berry's observation cut to the very heart of the argument. Practically no one – including Page – had the slightest inkling back in the sixties that the tracks they were recording then would have such an extensive cultural afterlife, or mean so much to so many after the event. Neither, of course, could anyone have dreamed that Jimmy Page's work as a session musician would come under the microscope as a result of his elevation to guitar hero status in the seventies. If they had, then they would surely have taken better notes. "Well, everything was just so new back then," said John Carter. "We were inventing it all as we went along. Everything, *everything*, was up for grabs."

Perhaps the best way to draw a veil over such minor infelicities is by celebrating the very best of Jimmy's work during this period about which there is no question as to its provenance. Aside from his light-fingered excursions on Dave Berry's 'My Baby Left Me' and Carter-Lewis' 'Skinnie Minnie', Page's performance on First Gear's 'Leave My Kitten Alone' must surely rank as one of the finer guitar solos of the sixties. Signed to Pye records and managed/produced by Shel Talmy, First Gear were at the time tipped for big things, their north-eastern cocktail of Elvis-style rock'n'roll and Mersey-approved beat pop as gritty, energetic and potentially promising as Van Morrison's Them. With Talmy at the helm, the band entered the studio in the autumn of 1964 to record a single version of Ernie K-Doe's 'A Certain Girl'. In itself no slouch, 'A Certain Girl' motored along nicely on the back of lead singer Dave Walton's behind-the-beat falsetto, some pleasing female backing vocals and Jimmy's countrified string bends.

But it was when First Gear and Page ran through the B-side, a cover of Little Willie John's 'Leave My Kitten Alone', that Shel Talmy's interest was truly piqued. "Jimmy was about 18, 19 at the time, with bushy black hair, and very quiet," Dave Wilton recalled to the BBC. "But then he did this off-the-cuff, lightning guitar break on 'Leave My Kitten…'. Well, Shel came racing down from the control room and said, 'What did you just do to get that!' So, he [told] Jimmy he was going to take it again. First take, Jimmy played it note-for-note perfectly." The resultant solo really was a thing of beauty. All twists, turns and racing-speed pick work, Page's contribution to 'Leave My Kitten…' distilled all he had learnt from James Burton, Scotty Moore and Buddy Guy into just 23 seconds. Yet, there was also something else that was utterly distinctive and unique. At the start of his solo intrusion, Page's guitar actually sounded like it was riding a wave of electricity. No distinct notes per se, more a wash of undulating sound. Quite unlike anything Jimmy (or anybody else) had recorded up to that point, it was the first real pointer to where Page's muse would take him in later years.

A glorious confection of super-charged rock'n'roll licks and avant-garde experimentation, Jimmy's solo flight on 'Leave My Kitten...' was no doubt cut on the latest addition to his six-string arsenal: a 1960 Gibson Les Paul Custom or, to give it its proper name, 'The Black Beauty'. Put into production by Gibson in 1953 when Paul asked the company for a guitar that "looked like a tuxedo", the Black Beauty was 100% class from neck to toe, sporting a heavy mahogany body, a plush rosewood fingerboard and striking, pearl-block inlays. Replacing Jimmy's previous giant beast, his orange Gretsch Country Gentleman, the Black Beauty had cost a not insubstantial £185. "It was," he later recalled, "the most magnificent guitar I'd ever seen." Given the nickname 'The Fretless Wonder' due to its smooth playing action (the result of each fret being substantially filed down), Page further modified his new love by rewiring its electrical circuitry and adding a Bigsby tremolo for shimmers and bends. "It sounded so pure," he said, "so... wonderful."

Away from his duties with First Gear[22], there were other sessions for Jimmy Page throughout 1964 and early 1965. Countless dozens on them, in fact. An orchestral date with easy listening legend Burt Bacharach where Jimmy got to play on the likes 'Walk On By' was by all accounts a pleasure for both composer and guitarist, while Page also enjoyed contributing to Petula Clark's glorious single 'Downtown', then and now, a pure pop classic. Even a brief spot on Val Doonican's 'Walk Tall' must have held some comedic charm, with Jimmy watching as the likable Irish crooner tried to make himself heard above a cacophony of chirping female backing vocalists.

There was also the occasional oddity to contend with, though Page already had some form in that area. Indeed, back in 1961, he had provided

---

22 Despite being a cracking little single, 'A Certain Girl'/'Leave My Kitten Alone' didn't break open the charts for First Gear, nor did 'The In Crowd' in early 1965, a track that also featured Jimmy on guitar. Sadly, First Gear came undone soon after, when an argument over a car parking space improbably led to the break-up of the group. In 2014, singer Dave Wilton revealed plans to relaunch First Gear with brand new musicians.

acoustic backing while "erstwhile Beat Poet" (and future travel writer) Royston Ellis read passages from his book *Jiving To Gyp* onstage at London's Mermaid Theatre. But joining a full blown "guitar orchestra" was an altogether new sensation. Pulled together at the behest of Mike Leander, the always interesting arranger had booked Decca's prestigious Studio 1 at West Hampstead to see whether he could simulate the full lustre of a classical string section with a nest of guitarists instead. Joining another session legend – Joe Moretti, who froze the blood with his string work on Vince Taylor's 1960 classic 'Brand New Cadillac' and the Pirates' 'Shaking All Over' – Jimmy and at least four other players gave the experiment their best shot, replicating violin and cello parts with their own instruments of choice. Bold stuff for the time, and surely worth a listen. Regrettably, no official recording of the piece has ever come to light.

There was more. An album date with Lulu – *Something To Shout About* – saw the pint-sized, but formidable Glaswegian blues-pop shouter view Page's new fuzz box with profound suspicion. "[It] made a weird farting sound," she recalled. "The fuzz box that is, not Jimmy Page." Another mind-warping solo on the Brooks' 'Once In A While' found Jimmy's high-wire screams elevating an otherwise inoffensive tune. And he was also there to lend a hand when fellow sessioneer Bobby Graham stepped out of the shadows for a brief moment in the sun with his one of his own rare solo singles, the clattering instrumental 'Skin Deep'. "Jimmy, me, Big Jim Sullivan, Alan Wyle and Eric Ford on bass, we were the 'musical stuntmen'," Graham later laughed. "We got called in to do all the dangerous bits!"

Perhaps it was seeing Bobby Graham chancing an arm as a performer in his own right that finally persuaded Page to contemplate cutting a single of his own. As he has largely kept his counsel on the matter, we are unlikely to ever know. But on February 26, 1965, Jimmy temporarily put aside his session status and released a 45 on Fontana records. Called 'She Just Satisfies', it featured Page covering all instrumental parts bar drums, which unsurprisingly were provided by his old pal Graham. Somewhat more surprising – given their recent butting of heads – was that the song bore a keen resemblance to a Kinks tune called 'Revenge', which Jimmy had reportedly assisted on the previous year. Jaunty, but not offensively so, 'She Just Satisfies' wasn't a bad stab at the pop market, scuttling along as it did on some gritty rhythm guitar and thumping percussion. Making his vocal debut, Page was also no better or worse a singer than many of those he had backed in recent years, his semi-shouted delivery falling somewhere between a well-mannered Ray Davies and an off-colour Van Morrison. However, '... Satisfies' lacked for a real killer chorus, something no self-respecting hit could do without at the time.

Written by Page (his first such credit) with lyrics by Barry Mason (the man later behind Tom Jones' 'Delilah' and Engelbert Humperdinck's 'The Last Waltz'), 'She Just Satisfies' really was far too tepid to launch Jimmy as an artist in his own right, but it did have a mighty fine harmonica solo. In and out before you knew what had really hit you, Page's short, wheezy harp interjection confirmed what many of his fellow musicians then knew as fact: given the right song, Jimmy could play the harmonica almost as well as he could guitar. "Oh yes," said the Nashville Teens' John Hawken. "Jimmy used to have an advert in the early *Melody Makers* and maybe even the *NME* advertising his availability for sessions. But what instrument was he advertising? Harmonica. I think the blurb read 'Jimmy Page: The Finest Harmonica Player in England'. The memory can play tricks, of course, but I'm pretty sure that's what it said." For those seeking definitive proof of his skills, the B-side of 'She Just Satisfies', the bluesy part-instrumental 'Keep Moving', should suffice, with Page providing both tasty six-string fills and octave-splitting harmonica blasts over a nicely insistent beat.

Despite being given a half-hearted push by Fontana – Jimmy made promotional appearances on BBC radio's *Saturday Club* and BBC Two's early evening pop show *The Beat Room* to support its chances – 'She Just Satisfies' did not fare well in the charts, and plans to follow up its release with a cover of the Beatles' 'Every Little Thing' were soon nixed. Given his later remarks, one sensed Page was not heartbroken by the single's failure. "[The record company] probably were hoping for a lot more than they got," Page said to *Creem*, laughing. "I played all the instruments on it except for the drums and sang on it too, which is quite, uh... unique. It was all very tongue in cheek though, and better forgotten." Truthfully, he had several other things on his mind at the time, the most pressing of which was the backing singer who provided some wild whoops and hollers on the backing track to 'Keep Moving'.

Born in Kentucky, 23 years old, but already on her fourth stage name, Jackie DeShannon had been on the periphery of stardom since 1956, when she began appearing regularly as a teenager on US TV and radio shows. Nominally a country and western singer, though equally adept at rockabilly, folk, gospel and, when the mood took her, blues, DeShannon also wrote songs on guitar, scoring her first minor hit with 1963's self-penned 'When You Walk In The Room'[23]. Following this near miss, she secured a support slot touring with the Beatles on their 1964 US tour, which as one might expect perked her interest in the flourishing British music scene, and by the autumn of that year she was recording at Abbey Road in north London. Looking for an acoustic picker to help flesh out some demos, including the comely 'Don't Turn Your Back On Me, Babe', DeShannon was given Jimmy Page's name. It went from there. "He came over," she later told *Huffington Post*. "And I knew right then he had an amazing talent." Page was equally smitten. "Jackie really knew how to write a song." Within days, the two were an item.

What followed was an intense and, by all accounts, extremely earthy transatlantic romance that also involved bouts of sporadic co-writing among all the hearts, flowers and ruffled sheets.[24] For his part, Page took a trip or three to America to see Jackie (who had soon returned to the USA after Abbey Road), with the additional benefit of meeting aspiring songwriters like Randy Newman and Warner Brothers' suave A&R man Lenny Waronker while there. Crucially, he also played on

23 A number three UK hit for the Searchers in September 1964, 'When You Walk…' has been covered by many artists over the years including, in what many now cite as the definitive version, by Agnetha Fältskog, formerly of Abba, on her 2004 album *My Colouring Book*.

24 Jackie DeShannon was not Jimmy's first girlfriend. Far from it. Having fallen "truly in love" for the first time in his mid-teens, Page's romantic life was subsequently marked by a steady procession of relationships/liaisons during his tenure with the Crusaders and then as a session man. "Jimmy was quite the charmer," confirmed one of his recording colleagues. "Yes indeed, the girls really liked Jimmy…"

several sessions, as well as gaining some production credits in LA, thus ever widening his experience of the overall recording game. When Jackie and Jimmy weren't jetting around the States, they were penning tunes. According to Page, as well as the backing vocals she provided for 'Keep Moving', DeShannon had helped frame the melody of 'She Just Satisfies', enabling him to "salvage" an otherwise ordinary enterprise.

But it was the new songs they wrote together that provided more lasting gains. One of the duo's first successes was 'Come And Stay With Me'. A winsome, countrified ballad immediately gifted to Mick Jagger's singer-girlfriend Marianne Faithfull, it took Jimmy, Jackie and Marianne into the UK Top 10 and US Top Five in February 1965. Other subsequent efforts from Page and DeShannon included 'Don't Turn Your Back On Me...' and 'Dream Boy', later recorded by the likes of R&B vocalist Esther Phillips and others. "Writing with [Jackie] gave me the opportunity to bring on certain aspects of my song-writing," Page told *Mojo*, "It gave me a lot of confidence." It also gave him some royalties. "That was... unusual for me at the time," he said, laughing, in 2012.

Page and DeShannon did not last. With literally an ocean between them and work schedules so all-consuming they would shame a trainee doctor, the two parted company within a year or so. However, neither did at all badly from their temporary liaison[25], with Jimmy's newfound confidence as a writer and occasional producer kitting him out nicely for the next phase in his ever-blossoming resumé. Once again, there was a connection to all those nights spent in the Thames Delta, and once again the Rolling Stones were involved. But this time around, there was to be no channelling the rich history of the blues at the Crawdaddy or Marquee. Instead, the onus was to be very much on "the here and now".

25 Boosted by the success of 'Don't Turn Your Back...' and 'Come And Stay With Me', Jackie DeShannon continued to perform and write, with her version of Burt Bacharach and Hal David's 'What The World Needs Now Is Love' hitting number seven on the US charts in late 1965. Four years later, DeShannon's own 'Put A Little Love In Your Heart' sold a million singles, while an album of the same name went Gold. But it was 1981 that brought Jackie her biggest success when, 'Bette Davis Eyes' (this time co-written by DeShannon with Donna Weiss) went to number one in several countries and won a Grammy for 'Best Song'.

CHAPTER 7

Out Of Time

1965, and the Beatles now ruled the musical roost. Having already taken the UK and Europe by storm, the Liverpool quartet's debut appearance on *The Ed Sullivan Show* a year before ensured the USA fell too, their renditions of 'All My Loving', 'Till There Was You' and 'She Loves You' officially marking the beginning of 'The British Invasion'. Holding the door to the States wide open, John, Paul, George and Ringo now ushered a plethora of other UK acts into the hearts and pockets of teenage America, with the Animals, Dave Clark Five, Kinks and a bakers' dozen more all benefiting from their kindness. "We were all on this ship in the sixties, our generation," said a poetic-sounding Lennon, "a ship going to discover the New World. And the Beatles were in the crow's nest of that ship."

Scowling somewhere on the upper decks were the Rolling Stones. The nearest thing the Beatles had to real competition – though in all honesty, no one was in the same commercial ball park as the Fab Four at the time – the Stones had still come a long way from their early days in Richmond. First making the UK Top 20 with 'I Wanna Be Your Man' (somewhat ironically written by Lennon and McCartney) in November 1963, the group scored big with several subsequent hits, including 'Not Fade Away' and 'It's All Over Now'. But it was their delicious cover of Willie Dixon/Howlin' Wolf's 'Little Red Rooster' that made good on their promise of bringing real blues to the masses. A "slow-burning sex anthem" brought to life by Mick Jagger's lascivious vocal and Brian Jones' crowing slide guitar, the fact that '... Rooster' topped the British charts in 1964 was an astounding achievement then and simply inconceivable now. Following the Beatles overseas and into the American market, Mick and Keith's newfound abilities as songwriters were quickly rewarded when the generation-defining '(I Can't Get No) Satisfaction' and truculent 'Get Off My Cloud' both peaked at number one.

When it came to Lennon and McCartney and Jagger and Richards, Jimmy Page didn't really play favourites. In his session guise, he had already contributed to the incidental music of the Beatles' 1964 film *A Hard Day's Night* while also cutting a short solo for a demo version of Mick and Keith's 'Heart Of Stone'[26] during the same year. However, as a self-employed business man, his interest was suitably piqued when the Stones' manager and "teenage wunderkind" Andrew Loog Oldham approached him with an interesting proposition in the early spring of 1965.

Former publicist for producer Joe Meek, town crier for Bob Dylan's first UK tour and "press conduit" to the Beatles in their earliest incarnation, Loog Oldham had packed quite a lot into his first 20 years on Earth. But he really hit his stride in mid-1963 when alongside business partner Eric Easton, Andrew slyly liberated the Rolling Stones from their informal representative Giorgio Gomelsky at the Crawdaddy Club and took over management of the band. A true media terrorist, it was Loog Oldham who cultivated the Stones' "bad boy" image, his feeder headline 'Would you let your daughter marry a Rolling Stone?' setting the group up as a suitably dangerous alternative to the cheerier Fab Four. The fact that the Beatles' off-camera behaviour was probably

---

26 An insular, dramatic ballad, 'Heart Of Stone' was later recorded with Keith Richards on lead guitar in November 1964. It reached number 19 in the US charts. The demo version of the song featuring Jimmy's contributions finally surfaced in 1975 on the compilation album *Metamorphosis*. Page was not credited on the sleeve.

as bad, if not worse, than their south-east counterparts was deemed completely irrelevant.

As clever with contracts as he was with sloganeering, Andrew had also set up a deal that allowed the Stones to lease their master tapes to Decca when they signed with the company. By retaining control of their product, he had not only given his charges greater artistic freedom but better long-term financial rewards. In an equally brazen act of empire-building, Loog Oldham then installed himself as the group's de-facto producer, though he had never operated a fader switch in his life. The methods might have been shocking, but given the Stones' undoubted success, one really had to admire the results. Having thus far beaten the record companies at their own game, Andrew now decided to start up one of his own. Dragging in former Beatles promotion man Tony Calder as co-owner (Calder, not so coincidentally, had produced Marianne Faithfull's 'Come And Stay...'), Immediate Records was launched in August 1965 as the UK's first 'truly independent label'.

Ostensibly created to spotlight young R&B and blues-based talent, Immediate's manifesto was something of a two-fingered salute to existing record industry practice, whose "old and tired, slow and staid" approach to making music infuriated and exasperated Calder and Oldham. In opposition to their snail-like practices, 'Immediate' records would be just that: Immediate. Spot the talent. Get them in the studio. Produce the record. Market it effectively. Watch it head up the charts and – if Tony and Andrew had anything to do with it – make enormous profits while doing so. This was, after all, a company run by two men barely out of their teens, and there was simply no room for dithering. "To hell with those who are too old to understand," said Andrew Loog Oldham. At the time, he probably even meant it.

Not yet 22, but with an abundance of session experience already under his belt, Jimmy Page was an ideal recruit for Immediate. Formally introduced to Loog Oldham by Charlie Katz, who was then working as a "music fixer" at the new label, the young Page made a quick and decisive impact on the Stones' spin doctor. "Well, we offered [Jimmy] a job as an in-house producer because we were so fed up with the old farts that you'd gravitate towards people your own age," Andrew told *Uncut* in 2009. "It was all in the nod, the look in the eye. I saw that in Jimmy. He knew that, too." As well as in-house production, Jimmy's responsibilities also included some A&R duties and obviously, session contributions as and when required. As importantly, he could also continue working on other records outside the Immediate bubble. All in all, not a bad deal, but according to Tony Calder, it was well earned. "Jimmy was very shy, softly spoken and polite. [But] I liked the fact this guy could say what he wanted to say in 30 seconds. And he had the patience and discipline to be able to say it."

Page's time at Immediate would be invaluable to him. While in LA, he had limited access to the producer's chair. Now, he could sit in it at his leisure. That said, in 1965, the tools of his trade were still severely limited, with only three or four tracks available to capture singer, band and, where necessary, string section or full orchestra. Yet, there was still a kind of magic in firing up those tapes. And better still, Jimmy was joining a very elite club who resided "behind the recording desk" rather than in front of it. "Probably a good analogy is comparing a Model-T Ford to a new Ferrari," Shel Talmy said of Page's new role. "The Model-T drivers knew they had the best available [technology] and just revelled in it. Three/four track machines and studio boards were the best [items] at the time, and a quantum leap ahead of 'wire-recorders', so we worked with what we had and enjoyed it. Little did we know that in future what took us an hour to do, could be done in seconds."

One of Page's first production credits with Immediate was 'Moondreams', the debut single by an interesting new band from Southampton called Les Fleur De Lys. Progenitors of 'freakbeat' (where traditional beat pop started taking on a more pharmaceutically assisted tinge), the Fleur's 'Moondreams' was, as its title suggested, a dreamy little number that made the best of stacked vocal harmonies and a floating Hammond organ. The B-side, too, was also mildly compelling. Written by Jimmy, 'Wait For Me' had a distinct Beatles flavour to it, with Page ably approximating George Harrison's twanging tones on 'Help'. Rumour has it, however, that Les Fleur De Lys did not actually play on either tune, their members replaced by several of Page's session friends.

Nonetheless, the band did contribute musically to the follow-up 'Circles'. Co-produced by Page and old mate Glyn Johns, 'Circles' was a mass of snarled vocals, looping drums and clipped power chords. No great surprise, as the song was actually written by the Who's Pete Townshend for his own band.[27] But unlike the Who's version, 'Circles' came with some very wigged-out guitar interjections, notes splashing in every direction throughout the track. Some say that this was all Jimmy's handiwork. Others point to the Fleurs' own Chris Sawyer as the man behind the solo. Whoever it was certainly knew their way around a fretboard. Unsurprisingly, however, neither 'Moondreams' nor 'Circles' were hits for Les Fleur De Lys. Frankly, their experimental nature and the lack of stylistic thread between both singles probably had many a DJ shaking their head in confusion. But they did at least land the Fleurs another deal with Polydor records after their option at Immediate expired. "I always thought Jimmy was very good as a producer," Andrew Loog Oldham later quipped. "What he went on to do kind of proves it, doesn't it?"

Page was kept busy at Immediate throughout 1965 and early 1966, his lush-sounding 12-string acoustic guitar part on the Factotums' criminally overlooked 'Can't Go Home Anymore, My Love' just one of dozens of sessions in which he involved himself. "I'll tell you what," he later said, "I had an album by a guy called Dick Rosmini, called *Adventures For 12-String, 6-String & Banjo*, and it had the best-recorded acoustic guitar sound I'd ever heard up until that point. Jackie DeShannon knew Dick Rosmini and asked him how he recorded it and he said, 'You need an RCA limiter'. It took quite a while [for me] to get one, but... after that things sort of changed." Another date saw him using the same instrument to back the Baroque pop duo Twice As

27 'Circles' was the song that brought the simmering antagonism between the Who and Shel Talmy to its head. Originally produced by Talmy, the Who stuck it on the B-side of their next single 'Substitute' which, breaking their contract with Talmy, they took to Reaction for release. Talmy threatened legal action so the Who changed its title to 'Instant Party'. Either way, Talmy's threat resulted in an out-of-court settlement that cost the Who dearly.

Much on the bittersweet Jagger/Richards composition 'Sittin' On A Fence'.

Elsewhere, Jimmy took on a much wider remit, producing young German chanteuse Nico's first single, 'I'm Not Sayin'', while also writing its B-side, 'The Last Mile', with Andrew Loog Oldham. "Actually," Andrew quipped, "it might have been better than the A-side..." In the end, neither side proved popular with audiences, though it mattered little to Nico. Signed by Loog Oldham in an effort to emulate Marianne Faithfull's success, she was already heading for New York to join an upcoming little group called the Velvet Underground by the time 'The Last Mile' hit the bargain bins. Still, with each session, co-writer and producer's credit, Jimmy's overall experience was growing. "I was pulled in and absorbed everything around me [at Immediate]," he said later, "and recording techniques were something I paid particular attention to." For Page, sound was always king. "It was all part of this apprenticeship of listening and learning," he told *Guitarist*, "and bit by bit I was getting all these production ideas..."

If Immediate records had a defining moment during Page's tenure at the label, it was surely Chris Farlowe's 'Out Of Time'. Like Jimmy, Farlowe had pressed steadily on since the two first met in Epping in 1960. Several singles with Columbia/EMI and an astounding cover of T-Bone Walker's 'Stormy Monday Blues' under the pseudonym Little Joe Cook had given Chris some public profile, but it was only when he hooked up with Immediate in 1966 that proper success came. "[The Thunderbirds] were the resident band at The Flamingo Club in Soho, alongside Georgie Fame & the Blue Flames," he said. "We had such a good band at that time with Albert Lee on guitar. All the rock people would come and see us – the Stones, the Beatles – and tell us they loved what we did. We were becoming a world class group at the time. Then Andrew Loog Oldham spotted it." Offering Farlowe a deal with his label, all Loog Oldham required now was a perfect song to fit the singer. Being the manager of the Rolling Stones, he knew where he could find one.

"Mick Jagger had written some good things for me before, such as 'Think', and a couple of others," said Farlowe. "Then he rang me up and said, 'I've got a new song for you. Come along and have a listen.' I went over to his place on Harley Street, Harley House actually, and he played me 'Out Of Time' on his guitar. My first thought really was, 'I'm not sure I like this. I'm not sure I like this sort of stuff'. But Mick said, 'Bear with it. It'll sound great once it's all arranged and put together'. So, when I turned up at the studio [a few weeks later] and saw all the cellos, the whole orchestra, I thought 'Ah'. Well, they started playing, and as they say, it was history in the making..."

The manner in which 'Out Of Time' was recorded is, in many ways, the ultimate encapsulation of how the sixties session scene operated. At the helm were Loog Oldham and Jagger, there to oversee production of the song from a booth above the musicians. In charge of the orchestra below was Arthur Greenslade, an esteemed British conductor with a wealth of previous arrangement credits under his belt. At the microphone was Chris Farlowe, about to make some serious noise. And in among all the violins, flutes and oboes was young Jimmy Page on guitar. "Always nice to see Jimmy," Farlowe laughed. "He'd started as a session guitarist and he was as good then as he is now. Think about it. All those appearances on all those records, and so, so young too. You know, he had to be good to survive it."

Also gathered among the throng for 'Out of Time' was John Carter, nominally there to assist on backing vocals, but also a reliable witness to what followed. "Arthur Greenslade had done the arrangement, came into the studio, ran it over with the musicians, then counted them in," said Carter. "But at the first verse and chorus, Mick Jagger came down from the sound booth and said, 'No, it's all wrong, it's all wrong.' He just took it over. Sad for Arthur, of course... a great, great arranger, but he'd obviously done the wrong thing for that song. Mick wanted it to be more funky than it was, and less like a ballad, I guess. Then, Mick came back again and said to us [backing singers], 'Hey, I'll come and sing with you', and so he did. I remember Jimmy just watching on, smiling. But again, he didn't have much to do on 'Out Of Time', really..."

An epic tune with a fantastic vocal from Chris Farlowe, 'Out Of Time' was Immediate records' first number one in the UK, reaching the top of the charts in May 1966. "A perfect little moment," said Chris. But by then, Jimmy Page was already planning his escape from both Immediate and "studio life" in general. Over the course of six years, he had gone from gigging guitarist to session ace to fledgling record producer, and each stage of the game had served him well. Page was now ready to take on another fresh challenge: one that would involve old friends, foreign climes and more than a little madness on the way. It would also take him one step closer to the big prize.

CHAPTER 8

Muzak

All in all, the session scene had been very good to Jimmy Page. For one, it had made him financially comfortable, with those three-hour stints 10 or 12 times a week for the best part of four years mounting up to a goodly amount of cash by 1966. Always a careful fellow with his money, Page's decision to stay put at the family home in Epsom while making daily trips to London might have made for a tiring, sometimes awkward lifestyle. Imagine Jackie DeShannon's delight every time she came to town. But it also enabled him to save up enough for a deposit on a home which he spent wisely and well on an alluring, 19th-century residential boathouse in Pangbourne, Berkshire.

Parked on the leafy banks of the River Thames, the dwelling was all windy passages and mysterious, angular rooms, leading to a quite beautiful lower level where a boat was moored, ready for instant take-off. "You wouldn't have believed the scene when I moved in," he later told *Melody Maker*. "The previous owner had great garlands of plastic flowers everywhere. She even had a barrow in the corner decorated with plastic flowers. It was like a Norseman's funeral when we threw all the flowers in the river." Liberated from 'the plastic flower lady' in 1967 for the then princely sum of £6,000, Pangbourne became Page's home away from home until the early seventies.

Away from the cash and boats, Jimmy had also met and worked with many of the singers and groups that would help shape the musical brickwork of the coming decade. Sometimes, as with the Stones, Immediate Records and the Who, it had gone well. On other occasions, such as his experience with Them and the Kinks, considerably less so. And once or twice more, Page had no clue he was even working with a future megastar at all. "When I was a baby," said one David Bowie, "I did a session with one of the bands, one of the millions of bands that I had in the sixties... the Mannish Boys, that's what it was. Anyway, the session guitar player doing the solo was this young kid who'd just come out of art school and was already a top session man, Jimmy Page. He had just gotten a fuzz box and he used that for the song. He was wildly excited about it."

Improbably, Page had also negotiated four years in a highly pressurised environment without ever appearing anything other than polite, helpful and eager to please. The delightful Ian Whitcomb[28], then enjoying several US hits with the likes of 'Nervous' and 'Good Hard Rock' as well as also doing the odd session, was quick to confirm Jimmy's professionalism, even when things were going out the artistic window. "Jimmy was so helpful, nice and friendly. A warm man, a good guitarist and so easy to work with," he said. "In fact, [we were once] hired to play a session for one of the Beatles' manager Brian Epstein's acts, a chap called Tommy Quickly[29]. We ended up recording 'Right Said Fred', which had previously been a hit for [actor/comedian] Bernard Cribbins.

---

28 Teenage blues fanatic, graduate of Trinity College, Dublin and briefly a US pop star, Ian Whitcomb cut an unusual path during the sixties, his combination of traditional music hall and edgy rock'n'roll perhaps at odds with the times, but none the worse for it. "I wasn't too bothered, though," he laughed. "I've always gone my own way." In later years, Whitcomb would become an acclaimed producer, respected author, ragtime expert and fine ukulele player, with his 1997 CD *Titanic: Music As Heard On The Fateful Voyage* also nominated for a Grammy.

29 It didn't get much better for Tommy Quickly. After four flop singles, he had finally scored a Top 40 hit with 'Wild Side Of Life' in 1964. But ongoing personal problems caused him to completely withdraw from the music industry soon after his session with Epstein, Page and Whitcomb.

I played piano, Jimmy was on guitar and Georgie Fame's band, the Blue Flames, were backing us. A very difficult arrangement, I seem to remember. I found the chords hard to read, so Jimmy stepped in to help me. He simplified the chords for me. Then, Tommy came down to record his voice, but he was very drunk and it was taking ages. Brian Epstein rushed out of the control room, and snatched the bottle from his hand!"

Sure enough, the session life had given Jimmy his fair share of highs. The stunned mass silence that greeted Shirley Bassey as she fell to the floor after recording the vocal to 'Goldfinger'. His inspired, occasionally mad solo flights on 'My Baby Left Me', 'Skinnie Minnie' and 'Leave My Kitten Alone'. Even hearing 'She Just Satisfies' on the radio must have been a bit of a thrill for him. More recently, there was further cause to celebrate. Jimmy's association with Immediate had done as much for enhancing his production skills as it had for his pocket, with offers of work showing no signs of slowing down. The trouble was that Page was now heartily sick of it. "I'd just become a hired hand," he later said, "a phantom musician, if you like..."

Page's feelings in the late spring of 1966 were no temporary blip, more an overall feeling of dissatisfaction that had been growing for some time. Moving to the producer's chair had helped stave off some of the boredom but, his bread and butter occupation still the provision of guitar backing for other artists, he still felt more jobbing witness than active participant to what was happening around him. "[It] just became completely stifling," he later told Chris Welch. "Never being involved with the artist, it was just like being a computer. When I started, only Big Jim Sullivan was around. If Jim wasn't available... then the work escalated for me, [but] there was no individuality involved. The arranger said, 'This is what you play', and that's what I played. I got fed up. It became a pain in the neck."

If Page had spent all his days in the company of quality bands such as the Who or singers like Shirley Bassey, picking up generous cheques while altering the history of pop music as he went, one might have felt a little sympathy for his predicament. But a goodly proportion of Jimmy's time was actually spent in dingy studios with dirty carpets and walls covered in egg boxes playing along to charts for radio jingles and advertising slogans. This, as one noted player of the time said, was "the shit end of the stick", a world where hired musicians planned their retirements while picking at the melody line of a soap advert. For a young man like Page, it must have been thoroughly depressing. "The great attraction about using people like Jimmy [for me] was that they were like the new [blood]," said Dave Berry. "They weren't the old-style session players. Sometimes [at recordings], you'd see the brass section or violinist on a session reading a paperback when they weren't playing. But Jimmy and Big Jim were always really interested in what was taking place, what was going on with the track. They'd actually put suggestions forward, and were always contributing ideas. I found that very, very inspiring."

According to Page, the new production habit of using brass as opposed to guitar for solos on pop tunes also didn't much help his cause. "At [a] particular point, all the sessions... were really good ones and I was doing the solos, really constructive work," he told *Creem* in 1978. "Then, about two years later, guitars were almost becoming out of vogue... people were always trying to do something new, using sax sections and all that, and we were just playing doodles on guitar." In the end, it was a horrendous date for a 'muzak' recording that finally did for him. "It was fun in the beginning, when they said 'Just do what you want'. But then 80, 90% of the time, I didn't know what session I was going in on. So, there was a horrific muzak session where you just keep reading music and you don't stop, like those things you hear in lifts. I just thought, 'That's it, I'm finished, I'm out.'" Creatively stifled, bored or terrified depending on what studio date he was turning up to, and recently relegated to backing saxophone solos, it was small wonder Page was ready to close the door on the session world. Yet, he had to replace his day job with something else, and a return to Sutton Art College wasn't going to cut it.

The solution to Jimmy's woes had been brewing a while. As such, it was a story worth telling.

When the Stones handed in their resignation as house band at the Crawdaddy in exchange for a new, possibly Satanic contract guaranteeing a lifetime of international fame – and in Keith Richards' case, possibly everlasting life itself – the Yardbirds were quick to take up where "Mick and the boys" left off. Formed in and around the suburbs of south-west London in May 1963 when bassist Paul Samwell-Smith and singer Keith Relf quit the Metropolis Blues Quartet in favour of joining up with drummer Jim McCarty, lead guitarist Anthony 'Top' Topham and rhythm guitarist Chris Dreja, the Yardbirds' choice of name was indicative not only of their reading preferences, but also the road that lay ahead. A phrase stolen from American Beat novelist Jack Kerouac, who used it to describe US drifters jumping freight trains from station to station while secretly yearning for home, 'the Yardbirds' would do much the same over the course of their musical career – straying far from the blues that originally electrified them into strange, new melodic lands, yet somehow always finding their way back to the Delta. "Well, it was more the Surrey Delta in our case," McCarty laughed, "but I take your point..."

A rum bunch, the Yardbirds were full of character, and indeed, characters. Pulled together by a mutual love of Muddy Waters, Jimmy Reed, Bo Diddley and Howlin' Wolf, each member of the band also brought his own particular foibles to the table. In Paul Samwell-Smith, the Yardbirds had a prodigiously gifted, if sometimes temperamental, bass player, whose cut-glass vowels and impeccable manners craftily disguised a flair for the rebellious and a genius for song arrangements. Conversely, vocalist Keith Relf was the beatnik of the group, a man who could balance a book and beer bottle over almost any terrain, his excellent harmonica skills only occasionally undone by the chronic asthma that had afflicted him since childhood. Anthony 'Top' Topham, on the other hand, was barely out of childhood. A fine guitarist, he was only 15 years old, and was often dragged out of Yardbirds rehearsals by his parents.

In their other guitarist, Chris Dreja, and drummer, Jim McCarty, the Yardbirds had their jokers in the pack. Dry as toast, yet quick with a quip – "I mean, what's a Howlin' Wolf when you've been brought up in Surbiton?" – Dreja's wit was a sharp as it was droll. McCarty was just plain funny. A class percussionist, who would grow into a very classy songwriter, Jim could find the humour in almost anything. He was going to need it. "I was in the Boy's Brigade when I was about 16, you know," he said. "It interested me and I got the drumming bug. Then it was an easy route to Buddy Holly, the Everly Brothers and skiffle. It was all part of a more generalised movement, I suppose. That led me to joining a band, and then in turn, playing school dances. Then came the Yardbirds. Argh, slippery slope!"

Like the Stones before them, the Yardbirds wasted no time in establishing their reputation as a sterling live act. Cutting their stage teeth at Eel Pie Island and Soho's Studio 51, their ascension to house band at the Crawdaddy in the autumn of 1963 was as quick as it was inevitable. After all, they had watched Jagger and co. do the same thing only months before. "Exciting times," confirmed Jim. "This scene just started to grow when blues began making its way to England on an underground level. And of course, we started to see the Stones. We were all from the Richmond area, so it was a great place to meet and hear this music. Also, it was no longer just blues like Big Bill Broonzy. This was blues but with a rock right through it." Having lost the Stones to Andrew Loog Oldham[30], Crawdaddy club-runner and potential band manager Giorgio Gomelsky wasn't going to let another quality outfit slip through his fingers. He signed the Yardbirds almost immediately. "I didn't want a copycat Stones, though," he said. "The element that was missing from the Stones was instrumental improvisation. I needed a group and guitarist that could do solos. Brilliant solos."

It wasn't going to be 'Top' Topham. Unlike Jimmy Page, whose parents had shown great patience (and no little forbearance) in allowing their son to travel far and wide with the Crusaders, Topham's mother and father were having none of it. "I was only 15, three or four years

---

30 How Andrew Loog Oldham 'liberated' the Stones from Giorgio Gomelsky in 1963 makes for uncomfortable reading, though once again, it enhances his reputation as a sharp player. If reports are correct, Loog Oldham actually waited until Gomelsky journeyed to Switzerland to attend his father's funeral before approaching the Stones with an offer of management. By the time Giorgio returned, the band had signed with Andrew.

younger than the rest," Top later said, "and there was no way my parents would let me go out five or six nights a week to play music, even though I was already bringing home double what my father was earning. I was going on to art school [by then] and they wanted me to take it seriously." As Topham's parents temporarily closed the door on their son's musical ambitions[31], another guitarist quickly came knocking.

The illegitimate son of a young Surrey woman and a piano-playing Canadian soldier posted from Montreal to England during World War II, Eric Clapton was exactly what the Yardbirds were looking for. At least for a while. Born in Ripley, Surrey in 1944, Clapton was actually raised by his grandparents, unaware until he was a teenager that the woman he knew as an older sister was in fact his biological mother. "Life was soured... [when] I found out about my origins," he said later, "The result was that I began to withdraw into myself." Learning the real facts surrounding his birth might have been a bitter pill to swallow, but it had another, much more beneficial effect. It opened Eric's ears to the blues.

"The only way to survive was with dignity, pride and courage, and I heard that in the blues," he later told *Rolling Stone*. "One man... a guitar [and] no option but to play and ease his pain. That echoed what I felt." Throwing himself into the music – first via Big Bill Broonzy and Josh White, then through the peerless Robert Johnson ("At first, I couldn't listen to him because he scared me so much"), Clapton became obsessive about translating what he heard on record onto the neck of a guitar. His first instrument, a cheap, steel-string Hoyer acoustic, was almost impossible to play – "I could hardly press the strings down, they were so high" – but he persisted. Soon, it came. "Small phrases, the odd melody, then chords..."

---

31 It didn't turn out badly for Top Topham. On leaving art school, he became a well respected session musician, playing alongside the likes of Fleetwood Mac's Peter Green and Christine McVie. A solo album and various guest spots followed before Topham once again formed a band with Jim McCarty in the late eighties. By 2000, Top was back with a newly reformed Yardbirds, on lead guitar. He continues to make music.

By 1962, Eric Clapton was very good indeed. After trying his luck at busking around Richmond, Kingston and London's West End, he joined a local R&B band named the Roosters for several months before again moving on to Casey Jones & the Engineers. Another blues-based combo that allowed Eric to practise his new guitar hero Freddie King's lines to his heart's content, he lasted all of seven gigs before Yardbirds singer Keith Relf made him an offer he couldn't refuse in October 1963. "He asked me to come down and listen to them at the Crawdaddy," Eric recalled in his autobiography. When Topham made his exit, Clapton was in. His enthusiasm was palpable. "They were a good band, a little rough and ready, and I had nothing better to do at the time." Jim McCarty was equally enthused at the prospect of Eric signing up. "He seemed very cocksure of himself," said the drummer. "Eric was very strong when he first played with us. To be honest, I took an instant dislike to him." And so it went for the next 18 months.

At first, the Yardbirds with Eric Clapton was a match made in heaven. They loved the blues, he worshipped it like a god and both sides of the camp coalesced magnificently over their shared obsession. A record deal with Epic/Columbia was brokered by Giorgio Gomelsky in early 1964, and the group's second single, 'Good Morning Little Schoolgirl', featuring a furnace-hot blast of what would soon become Eric's signature lead guitar sound, reached number 44 in the UK charts. There was more. A memorable, early UK club tour alongside irascible harp-player Sonny Boy Williamson at the Crawdaddy found the Yardbirds well up to the task of sharing the same stage with one of their idols[32], while the band's watershed appearance at the Royal Albert Hall in December 1964 provided Eric with a venue to return to every time he visited London over the next five decades. Again, it was in this live environment that the Yardbirds really made their mark.

As evidenced superbly well on their debut LP *Five Live Yardbirds* – recorded at Soho's Marquee club and released in late 1964 – the

32 The Yardbirds/Williamson double bill was caught on tape at the Crawdaddy on December 8, 1963. The resultant album, *Sonny Boy Williamson And The Yardbirds*, was released in late 1965.

'Birds were perhaps eclipsed only by the Rolling Stones as England's pre-eminent blues experience. A mixture of Keith Relf's wheezy harp squeals, Jim McCarty, Chris Dreja and Paul Samwell-Smith's canny rhythmic interplay and Clapton's combustible solo outbursts, on tracks such as 'Smokestack Lightning', 'I'm A Man' and 'Who Do You Love?', they had taken an old musical form and given it a vigorous, youthful shaking. They had also created 'the rave-up', a mid-song interlude that saw the band reduce the volume (and sometimes tempo) only to build it back up into an orgiastic, instrumental climax. It was all their own invention. Or perhaps not.

"Well, the 'rave-up', I have to admit, was down to Paul Samwell-Smith," said McCarty. "We all used to go and see Cyril Davies, a great blues harp player who then had the Savages backing him, and Cyril's bass player was a guy called Ricky Benson. Now, Paul loved Ricky's style, and it became an influence. So, I don't know whether Paul figured out this 'rising to a crescendo' thing from Ricky, but one day he came into rehearsal and presented it to us, this slow-quiet build-up that rose and rose into a storm of sound. Anyway, whatever the case, it became an instant show-stopper."

This was a good band, potentially a great one. But there were divisions not easily resolved over a pie and a pint. Perhaps still carrying a measure of psychic detritus around the circumstances of his birth, Eric Clapton might have brought the Yardbirds undoubted firepower in the guitar department, but by his own admission he wasn't always the easiest chap to get along with. "I wasn't a likeable guy back then," he admitted later. "Actually, I was a nasty piece of work. Unreliable. Dogmatic. Anti-social. A fly in the ointment." Again, Jim McCarty wasn't in a hurry to disagree. "The thing with Eric had been rumbling on for a while," he said. "There was discontent there and he'd started to distance himself from us. Little things at first. We'd be travelling to gigs and he'd sit at the other end of the van. Then, there were the moods. And after a while, I just thought 'I'd rather not have this atmosphere. I'd rather play with someone who's happy'. That was towards the end..."

The end came in January 1965. Though blues fanatics to a man, the Yardbirds and their manager Giorgio Gomelsky were also commercially ambitious and musically inquisitive. Or in laymen's terms, they all wanted a hit and didn't mind temporarily putting aside "the 12 bar" to get it. "At that point, we were a blues band, but 'Thames Delta' rather than 'Mississippi Delta'," Dreja explained in 2010. "We weren't the real thing, and we really needed to start making our own music, creating our own identity." A plausible solution was offered by 'For Your Love', a catchy pop tune written by Graham Gouldman (later of 10cc), and brought to the group's attention via music publisher Ronnie Beck. In its original form, 'For Your Love' was sparsely arranged, with just guitar, vocals and minimal percussion, all the better to draw attention to its emotive, major/minor chord structure. Paul Samwell-Smith heard things more expansively. Now de facto 'musical director' of the group, he suggested adding a harpsichord to further augment the chords and a bowed, acoustic bass for added atmosphere. Their trademark 'rave-up' would be limited to 20 or so seconds mid-track. Four long-haired heads nodded in approval. One didn't. "Ah Eric. Back then, everyone was growing their hair. He got a crew cut."

For a dyed-in-the-wool blues purist like Eric Clapton, a world where harpsichords and bowed basses took precedence over John Lee Hooker and Howlin' Wolf covers was not one he wished to inhabit. Grudgingly providing a quick, spiteful riff or two over 'For Your Love''s middle eight, he left the Yardbirds soon after the song was recorded. "For me," he said, "that was the end." But not for Chris Dreja. "Eric was steeped in the blues. No bad thing. But when he left, he actually did us a favour because it enabled the band to follow its own instincts. It freed us up to do all the things we wanted." Having just about invented the modern British guitar hero during his time with the Yardbirds, Clapton temporarily ran off to the countryside to contemplate a possible future in antiques restoration before sanity prevailed. By mid-1965, he would return – wiser and even bluesier – to the musical fray. In February of that year, however, the Yardbirds had an imminent single release on their hands, and no lead guitarist to promote it.

Re-enter Jimmy Page.

On paper, Page and the Yardbirds went hand in glove. Like Eric, Jimmy's heart was in the blues. But it wasn't his only mistress. Page could also claim rock'n'roll, country and even orchestral easy listening among his conquests. Moreover, while still only 21, he had gained huge experience on the session scene, his reputation as a gifted, dependable and creative fellow as rock solid as his guitar playing. Pop star handsome and exceedingly polite, he was unlikely to throw any hissy fits about musical direction either. Plus – and it was a big plus – the Yardbirds really wanted him. "Jimmy had actually turned up at a show we played in the West End with Jackie DeShannon," McCarty remembered. "We thought 'Ah, this is a special night', and he really seemed to like the band. Now [when Eric left], Giorgio already knew Jimmy well, they were friendly, and we liked him too. So yes, he seemed the obvious choice to replace Eric. And let's not forget, Jimmy was one of the best guitar players around." There was a slight hitch. While the Yardbirds liked Jimmy, Jimmy was quite fond of Eric Clapton.

According to legend, Page and Clapton first met when Jimmy was "dusting his broom" at the Marquee with Alexis Korner and Cyril Davies as part of Thursday night's interval band, probably in late 1962. Page was onstage, playing. Eric was in the audience, watching. When Jimmy stepped down, Clapton stepped up, complimenting Page on his Matt Murphy-like lead style. Given few souls were familiar with Memphis Slim at that point, let alone his guitarist Murphy, Jimmy was taken aback by Eric's astute observation. "I'd been listening to Matt Murphy a lot at that point, so I was impressed by Clapton spotting that." A respectful friendship ensued, with the two meeting up for an occasional meal every now and then. "We got on pretty well," Jimmy later remembered. "We'd go out, eat and just talk about everything." Over the course of months, Page was also introduced to some of Eric's other friends, including one with a real taste for the obscure side of the blues. "Once," said Jimmy, "he took me around to this guy's place who had tapes of obscure musicians like Poppa Hop[33]. Eric was really getting into that."

---

33 A hidden diamond, Poppa Hop and his Orchestra's version of 'My Woman Has A Black Cat Bone' is well worth seeking out, the track's slide guitar solo surely as lyrical, svelte and life-affirming as anything cut by Elmore James or Earl Hooker.

If not exactly kindred spirits, Page and Clapton certainly appreciated the sincerity and devotion with which the other approached music. That in turn had led to mutual respect. And it was for this reason, though not for this reason alone, that Jimmy was unsure about taking the Yardbirds up on their offer to join the band in February 1965. "After my experience with Neil Christian," he later said, "I was still nervous about getting ill. Also, I was doing quite well money wise with the sessions. And honestly, I wasn't quite sure what the politics were with Eric because we were friendly." It was a familiar tale for Page. Still not ready to re-engage with the road, making a bundle from sessions and reticent to get drawn into a potentially sticky battle over alliances, Jimmy turned the Yardbirds down. But then, he had an idea. "I recommended the guy I'd been friends with for years. I told them about Jeff..."

Bingo.

CHAPTER 9

Shapes Of Things

The friendship between Jimmy Page and Jeff Beck has proved one for the ages. Sometimes it's been like family, with Page referring to the pair as "blood brothers". On other occasions, the path has been rocky. "I saw the show and I thought they were filth," Beck once remarked to Steve Rosen of Jimmy's best-known band. But like any buddy movie worth its salt, while the arguments are usually many, there was always likely to be a happy ending by the time the credits rolled. "Jim was very secretive about certain things," Jeff said in 2007. "That's what I found attractive. I still do. He's just got this mystery about him."

Both Page and Beck have stated in times past that they first met around the age of 13. On the evidence, that's improbable. Given that Jimmy appeared to be attending art school at the time of the encounter, they were more likely to be 18 years old apiece. What is sure, however, is that Jeff's older sister, Annetta, was a major player in their introduction. "My sister went to [Sutton Art College]," Jeff told *Uncut*. "She never spoke to me until she met Jimmy, this other crazy person who had a strange-shaped guitar. She knew where he lived, so we both went over on the bus to Epsom."

It wasn't a long journey. Jeff and Annetta lived in Wallington, only a half-hour's drive away. Like Jimmy, they too came from a respectable

background – Dad an accountant, mum now a housewife after a brief
fling working with chocolates. Nice house. Shared driveway. Good car,
not too flashy. But none of these commonalities were important to
Beck. He just wanted to meet Jimmy and see that guitar. Page didn't
disappoint. "He sang us a Buddy Holly song," Jeff later remembered.
"And his mum made us a cup of tea."

When Jeff turned up at 34 Miles Road with his own rough and
tumble, homemade electric six-string guitar, Jimmy Page must have
realised he was slightly ahead of curve in comparison to Beck. By then
the proud owner of the Grazioso (and very possibly the titanic-sized
Gretsch Country Gentleman as well), he was already a veteran of the
road wars with Neil Christian & the Crusaders. Given the circumstances,
Page could easily have cocked a snoot at the slightly younger man and his
'Frankenstein' guitar and sent him packing back to Wallington. There
were three reasons he didn't. First, Jimmy was far too polite to even
consider it an option. Second, he genuinely liked Beck. "Jeff's always
had a great sense of humour." Third, Jeff – despite his Frankenstein
guitar – could really play.

"I lived in Epsom, Jeff lived in Wallington, two towns not that far
apart," Page later recalled. "Anyway, people sort of knew I was playing
guitar, and I was friendly with a record collector [Barry Matthews] who
knew Jeff's sister. She was a little older than Jeff, who in turn was a little
younger than me [Beck was born on June 24, 1944, a fellow war baby].
The thought was 'Maybe we should get these two guys together.'"

What they played probably defined their core musical interests. Aside
from crooning his way through something from *The Chirping Crickets*,
Page could proudly display his mastery of Scotty Moore's slippery solo
on 'Baby Let's Play House'. Perhaps he also showed Beck his way around
Ricky Nelson's 'I'm Walkin'' or furtively ran through the trickier
aspects of Muddy Waters' 'I Can't Be Satisfied'. A confirmed rockabilly
nut, Jeff no doubt returned the favour, pulling off his best Cliff Gallup
impersonation on Gene Vincent's 'Catman' or a novel approximation
of Paul Burlinson's two-octave chug through 'Train Kept A Rollin''.
All supposition, of course. But given the fact the jam took place in the
Page family's front room, Beck must have surely marvelled at Jimmy's

home recording equipment. Even Page's recent discovery that if he put a microphone under a cushion and tapped it repeatedly, he could fake the sound of a bass drum would have sent the percussion-loving Jeff into spasms of delight. "Christ," he later admitted, "Jimmy was so much more advanced than me. He knew all the Buddy Holly stuff. And he was an only child... his mum had bought him all the goodies!" For Page, the greatest discovery was that only eight miles down the road there was another madman as in love with guitars as he was. "In our area, there weren't many guitarists. We were the only two. We just used to go mad..."

Their friendship firmly established, Page and Beck kept tabs on each other throughout the early sixties, their individual journeys criss-crossing at regular intervals. When, for instance, Neil Christian lost yet another Crusaders guitarist and contacted Jimmy about finding a possible replacement, Page recommended Jeff. An audition was held. According to Christian, Beck wasn't quite ready for the gig, but he still gave him money for a taxi home. After Page started his session career, it was Jeff's turn to lend a hand. "I used to drive Jimmy to the studio," he quipped. More seriously, whenever Page had more session offers than his diary could hold, he tried to put the work Beck's way. As a result, Jeff ended up contributing chord cover and the occasional lead for the likes of Fitz & Startz and the Johnny Howard Band. He also made a brief, but telling appearance on loveable British eccentric Screaming Lord Sutch's insane, but immensely entertaining 1964 single 'Dracula's Daughter'. In time, Jimmy would also inadvertently contribute to the good Lord's work. Again, the end result was entertaining.

Outside of Page's orbit, Beck tried hard to fight his own way onto the blossoming pop and blues scene then extending its tendrils into the British charts, though it was mostly a case of nil returns. Like Jimmy, he put in the hours as a teenager with various rock'n'roll outfits like the Deltones and the Crescents. No luck there. "Gene Vincent-alikes," Jeff later said, laughing. Then he found the blues at Eel Pie Island, joining a promising R&B act named the Nightshift in 1963. A marginally better proposition, Jeff's stint with the Nightshift at least allowed him to whittle away his nights crow-barring Buddy Guy licks into Howling Wolf covers at Twickenham's "premier blues nuthouse". Then, it was a few hours' sleep before going back to his day job in a car repair shop. No bad thing for Beck, though. An absolute hot-rod fanatic, the pleasure of spending hours and hours with his head stuck under a bonnet ran rings around his first brush with full-time employment. "I used to drive a tractor around a golf course," Beck later told *Record Collector*. "The golfers were a right bunch of snooty bastards. They'd shout 'Fore!' after they'd hit the ball and then it'd go bouncing off my bloody tractor..."

Again, the Nightshift provided no long-term gains for Jeff. But his next group, the Tridents, was a significant key change for the better. An incendiary little blues band led by brothers Paul and John Lucas, the Tridents cemented a strong local following around the south-east and wanted to up their game to the next level. When Beck expressed an interest in joining the party, their then current guitarist Mike Jopp graciously made his way to the nearest exit. "The guys called me up and said 'Look, Jeff wants to join'," he confirmed in 2010. "I said 'OK, you've got to have him, because he was just absolutely incredible'." Some might find this statement a little fanciful. Yet, according to many at the time, Jopp was simply stating the facts as they were. The sky is blue. The Pope is Catholic. And "Jeff was uniquely talented," said Mike. "Really. He was the most gifted guitarist I'd ever heard or seen."

Coming on in planet-sized leaps and bounds since his first encounter with Jimmy Page, Beck was, circa 1965, probably the finest unsigned guitarist in Great Britain. An astounding contradiction of rockabilly chops, cod-jazz noodles, rock'n'roll flash and Shadows-style vibrato, the recent acquisition of a Binson Echorec unit had only added to his box of tricks, Jeff's sonic vocabulary now extending into realms that might even worry Les Paul. "The crowds didn't always want straight blues," he later said. "They wanted sci-fi noises. That was all right by me." Multiple echo repeats, crashing reverbs – Beck was even de-tuning strings onstage for fun. No wonder, then, that the Tridents were drawing crowds of over 800 at Eel Pie Island or turning them away at the door of London's 100 Club.

Jimmy Page had also been watching Beck's progress carefully, and knew he was ready for more. When the Yardbirds made their approach regarding his services following the departure of Eric Clapton, Jimmy was able to deflect attention away from himself and shine a light on his friend. The trouble was, no one was quite sure who Jeff was. "Well no," said Chris Dreja, "we'd never heard of Jeff or the Tridents, to be honest."

While the Yardbirds were carrying out their own investigations into this intriguing guitar hopeful, Page was busy lining up Beck for a possible audition. Inviting him over for a drink, Jimmy played to Jeff Clapton's pan-sizzling solo on Eddie Boyd's 'Five Long Years' from *Five Live Yardbirds* before asking the question, "Would you be interested in joining them?" Loyal to the Tridents, but also recently married and permanently strapped for cash, it wasn't much of a decision. "I loved the Tridents, they were a great band[34]," Beck later said. But the Yardbirds were signed to Columbia, and they were pretty good too. No-brainer. Finally meeting up with the band at the Marquee in late February 1965[35] to try each other on for size, the two factions clicked in double-quick time. "Keith asked Jeff who his favourite guitar player was," Dreja recalled. "I think he replied 'Buddy Guy' and that was it." McCarty concurred. "I'd never seen Jeff before. So when he turned up, it was a bit of a surprise. He was a bit rough looking to be honest, a real greaser. I can't exactly remember what he was wearing, but it was probably a black leather jacket, dirty old jeans covered in oil and this shoulder length hair. But then he played. Bang."

'Bang' does quite nicely when describing Jeff Beck's impact on the Yardbirds. Before, they were a blues band trading in strident homages to the Delta, both Mississippi and Surrey branches. After Eric Clapton's departure and Beck's subsequent arrival, they became something else

---

34 They were indeed. A fine group who deserved a better shot at fame, the Tridents sadly called it a day in 1966. However, for those seeking to hear them at their best, three of their tunes are available on *Beckology*, a CD box-set retrospective covering Jeff's career up to 1991. 'Nursery Rhyme', featuring Beck on the musical warpath, is especially pleasing.

35 Jeff has said in the past that he was only one of several potential guitarists the Yardbirds auditioned at the Marquee in February 1965. Jim McCarty was keen to refute the claim. "There's all this bullshit that Jeff was one of 20 guitar players who'd turned up to audition for the band. Actually, he was on his own. Giorgio Gomelsky and his assistant Hamish Grimes had already gone ahead on Jimmy's recommendation to watch Jeff with the Tridents at Eel Pie Island, then simply asked him if he'd be interested." End of story, then.

entirely. "When Jeff came into the group," said Dreja, "we recognised a talent, a man, who could work with new ideas without getting all uptight about it." They got off to a good commercial start. Released in March 1965, 'For Your Love''s harpsichord-led flourishes propelled the Yardbirds to number three and number six in the UK and US charts, making them not only pop successes on home turf, but part of the British Invasion of the States, too. They revelled in it. "I shared a room with Jeff on our first tour of the USA," said McCarty, "and we were on something like the 40th floor in this huge New York hotel. He was looking out the window saying 'Just look at those cars, all those American... cars'. He was transfixed. Well, we both were, really." The West Coast was even better. "Endless sunshine, Beach Boys songs on the radio, Hollywood women walking up and down Sunset Strip. It was another world, but in Technicolor... like something from a movie we'd watched at home. But now we were in it."

1965 really was something of a dream year for the Yardbirds, both in and around the band. Finding themselves smack in the middle of the 'Swinging Sixties', the candle that gently illuminated artist Richard Hamilton and the 'Angry Young Men' a decade before was now a giant-sized electrical appliance beaming images of Great Britain across the world, and Jeff and co. were very much a part of the show. Joining ranks with the Beatles, Stones, Kinks and Animals, and so, so many others, the Yardbirds' responsibility was obviously holding up the musical end at home and abroad. But there was also a much bigger cultural offensive going on around them. Once mocked by its own as 'Dreary Old Blighty', the UK had become a nation of super spies (James Bond) and Supermodels (Jean Shrimpton and Twiggy). John, Paul, George and Ringo were getting gongs from the Queen at Buckingham Palace, while Terry and Julie were meeting at Waterloo Station. With class no longer an impediment to social mobility (ask Michael Caine and David Bailey) and money back in most peoples' pockets, waving the Union Jack for all to see now actually made sense. This, someone said, was "The new audacity." Good or bad, the old rule book had been abandoned and they were writing a new one as they went.

In such a heady atmosphere, some groups might have lost their footing, but the Yardbirds held firm and prospered, hitting a rich creative streak that defines the group to this day. After the resounding success of 'For Your Love' came 'Heart Full Of Soul', a second, melancholy gem from the pen of Graham Gouldman. When an Indian sitar player hired to provide the tune's main riff failed to gel on the session, Jeff borrowed Jimmy Page's fuzz box and emulated the sound of the instrument in a matter of minutes. The result was magical. "The sitar was another one of Giorgio's mad ideas," said Jim McCarty. "It was fine in principle, but it just wasn't up front enough... the sitar just didn't cut through. So Jeff said 'Well, hold on, I could do that sound on the guitar'. He got the fuzz and that was it. This great sounding riff just emerged..." Obviously a good day at the office, 'Heart Full Of Soul' gave the Yardbirds yet another hit, this taking them back into the UK and US charts at numbers two and nine respectively in the summer of 1965. "We'd suddenly taken a 90-degree detour from the blues," said McCarty. "We just couldn't get a big hit doing straight blues, then 'Heart...' took off and so did we."

By the autumn, they were at it again with 'Evil Hearted You', a Spaghetti Western of a song featuring Jeff doing his best impression of Hank Marvin, albeit using a steel slide rather than a vibrato arm to enhance Keith Relf's eerie vocal. Moody, magnificent and again written by Graham Gouldman, it took them back into the UK charts at number three. A second trip to America provided the opportunity to work with Elvis' producer Sam Phillips at Sun Records in Memphis, and while the recording session went badly for Relf – Sam didn't much like his voice, Keith got drunk, Jeff scowled in support of his friend – the end more than justified the means. Rattling the nails in Phillips' tiny studio ("It was the size of a kitchen," said Dreja, "but the sound was magnificent!"), the Yardbirds' feral take on Johnny Burnette's 'Train Kept A Rollin'' was as close as the band had yet come to harnessing the power of their live performance.

They would go one better, though. Marking a near perfect end to a near perfect year, the Yardbirds entered Chess Records' studio in Chicago for a second time on December 21, 1965 to complete work on a batch of songs they had begun recording some three months before. Holy ground to them all, Chess was the very place where Muddy Waters, Howlin' Wolf and Chuck Berry had created the soundtrack to their teenage years on the Surrey Delta. Now, they were semi-regular visitors. "We were a high-energy live band, a lot of power, a lot of audience interaction, but we just couldn't get that sound on tape, at least not in England," said Chris Dreja. "But the Americans were geared up for recording and our manager Giorgio got us into Chess, a proper studio. All of a sudden we're hanging around with heroes like Bo Diddley, who's up a ladder painting things, because Chess had them all working on a string." Chess Records' distribution of wealth might have been suspect in the extreme, but their studio sound couldn't be faulted. "When we heard the playback, we went berserk," Beck later told *Guitar Player*. "The bass drum shook the foundations of the building!"

Emerging from 2120 South Michigan Avenue just in time for Christmas, the Yardbirds had not one but two fantastic singles in their hands. In the case of 'I'm A Man', they had taken Bo Diddley's creamy hymn to his libido and given it a proper Brit-Invasion polish, with Jeff again providing an inspired solo flight courtesy of his 1954 Fender Esquire while Keith Relf's harp chased him around during the rave-up section. No surprise, then, when 'I'm A Man' reached number 17 in the US charts. 'Shapes Of Things', however, was in a different class entirely. Written by Relf, McCarty and Paul Samwell-Smith, 'Shapes...''s anti-war, pro-environmental theme was not only ahead of its time lyrically but the song was also the first true example of what was soon to be called 'psychedelic rock'. Filled with crashing chords, questing vocals and militaristic percussion, the addition of Beck's Raga-infused lead lines and pioneering use of controlled feedback[36] really did summon

---

36 Essentially a loop created when an electric guitar's pick-up captures sound from an amplifier speaker and then regenerates the signal back through the amp, feedback's main characteristic is a high-pitched, often screaming whistle, which in the hands of the right user can then be manipulated into a drone, pulse or even tune. Much controversy surrounds who experimented with it first in a concert setting. Fifties blues players Albert Collins and Guitar Slim are two likely candidates. However, the Beatles' John Lennon and the Who's Pete Townshend can also lay claim to its early recorded use on tracks such as 'I Feel Fine' (1964) and 'My Generation' (1965). Whatever the case, Beck's manipulation of feedback on 'The Nazz Are Blue' and 'Shapes Of Things' remain pioneering examples of "harnessing the banshee's wail."

new worlds of musical possibility. "Nothing was 'named'," said Dreja. "There were no road maps. We were kind of making it all up as we went along. There were fewer boundaries, it seemed. Things happened. You left a guitar alongside an amp, it fed back... first an awful sound, then a beautiful sound, which we'd then incorporate." A monument of a tune, 'Shapes Of Things' fell two places shy of the UK number one spot on its release in February 1966. Frankly, they were robbed.

'Still I'm Sad', 'Mister, You're A Better Man Than I' and, lest we forget, the completely off-kilter 'Over, Under, Sideways, Down'[37], single by single and song by song, the Yardbirds were creating their own unique space in a pop scene already brimming with innovation. But these valiant efforts to create "something truly new" were not coming without cost, especially when it came to Jeff Beck. Despite all the scowls, sneers and greaser bravado, Beck was in fact a fairly shy chap who was still trying to find his place within the band. "We were all very close, really," Dreja continued. "Various reasons. We went to the same schools, had history together and it was quite difficult for Jeff [to fit in] at first. He was very shy, and a bit of a rough diamond. He... really just communicated through his guitar... and used to play these wonderful passages that were like speech."

This 'man apart' aspect to Jeff's nature expressly manifested itself in the studio environment, where he would often add his guitar parts after the Yardbirds had finished work on basic tracks. "Yes, I suppose we did use Jeff as a weapon in the studio," said McCarty. "He could give a song real electricity, a boost of power, and we were really aware of that. So yes, we'd use that quality." It may have suited the group's working practices, and the results were often spectacular, but the expectation for

---

37 "'Over...' actually started with Jeff playing bass," said Jim McCarty. "He and I did the backing track like that and then we gradually layered it, bringing in various lines. Then, out of nowhere, he started playing what became the main riff. I'll be honest, I just stopped. I thought, 'What bloody planet is this coming from?' At the start, it sounded quite mad, but once you got used to it, you knew it was perfect for the track. In a nutshell, that was Jeff. Genius.' 'Over, Under, Sideways, Down' reached numbers 10 and 13 in the UK and US charts in May 1966.

Beck to simply walk in off the street and sprinkle shards of genius all over a song was beginning to weigh heavily on those already moody shoulders. On occasion, it was also making him quite angry. "I'd be twiddling my thumbs, waiting for my chance to get in and rip it in half," he later told *Guitar World*. "They (were watching) the flame build." Last man in – both in a personal and professional sense – and expected to go off "like a fucking rocket" whenever the situation demanded it, Jeff Beck was probably feeling more than a little isolated in mid-1966. No great surprise, then, when he decided to phone a friend.

As evidenced, Jimmy Page was facing his own set of exam questions at exactly the same time Beck began feeling the burn. Bored by sessions and still wondering what to do about it, when Jeff called inviting him along to a Yardbirds' gig at Oxford University's annual May Ball in mid-1966, the relief must have been palpable. A "high-class, black tie event" staged to celebrate the end of the students' academic year, it was quite a coup for the band, and would be quite a night for Page. In addition to a generous fee, both food and booze were laid on thick and – even better – completely free of charge. For some of the group, this was a chance to "gently unwind in a genteel environment". For Jimmy, it was a chance to see Jeff batter the hell out of his new sunburst Gibson Les Paul. For singer Keith Relf, it was an opportunity to get absolutely smashed. "Yes," said Dreja, "Keith was always a drinker, but he also had lots of medical problems [with asthma]. Good God, he lost part of a lung at one point!"

As might be expected, it took a while for Keith Relf to reach ramming speed at the May Ball. Consequently, the Yardbirds' first set went by without major incident. But as the night progressed, so did Relf's drinking. "There was some underlying aggro going on at the May Ball. A build-up of pressure, really," said McCarty. "We had to play something like three sets and you're just dog tired, which doesn't help. And of course, there's an element of boredom between sets, which can lead to drinking. In Keith's case, it did." Now sailing close to the point of no return, Relf decided to amuse himself with a demonstration of competitive sports. Bad idea. "Keith started a karate competition backstage with the Hollies' Alan Clarke," Jim continued. "Clarke was saying, 'Keith, Keith, can you break this chair?' And by then, Keith genuinely believed he could. So, he tried it and broke his hand, though he didn't know it at the time. [Suffice to say], as the night continued, he just started to lose it and by the end, he was so pissed he couldn't really perform onstage."

Keith Relf was many things, a spirited, unusual singer, a fine, fine harp player and, when on top form, a sharp and wonderfully insightful lyricist, but during the third set of the Yardbirds' appearance at Oxford University on June 18, 1966, he was just very drunk. In front of several hundred students, support group the Hollies and a visiting Mama Cass (from US dream folk-popsters the Mamas & the Papas), Relf lost the plot and then some. Forgetting the lyrics to most every song, he filled in by either blowing raspberries or "taking the piss out of all these hurrah Henrys in the audience" before capping it all with a pratfall off the stage. For Jeff Beck and the band, set three became one endless guitar solo. "At one point," Chris Dreja laughed, "we almost had to tie Keith to the microphone stand. Of course, this didn't sit well with Paul."

Like Jeff Beck, bassist Paul-Samwell Smith had also been wrestling with his own difficulties within the Yardbirds. The band's musical leader in all but name, Samwell-Smith had nonetheless grown increasingly tired of tight schedules, long tours and TV appearances and now longed to concentrate on straight record production. Thus far, he had managed to contain his growing dissatisfaction. But Relf's conduct at the May Ball proved the straw that broke the bass player's back. After reading Keith the riot act backstage[38], he stormed out into the Oxford night. "Paul was a lovely man, but a square peg in a round hole in the world of rock'n'roll, a world he didn't think was particularly civilised," said Dreja. "Paul felt it was important to act stiff in front of all these academic

---

38 Though Samwell-Smith's dressing down of Relf achieved little on the night, Keith Relf was much more contrite after the event. He was also in considerable pain. "Well, he broke three fingers trying to smash up six trays and didn't feel it until two days later," said Chris Dreja. "But he did at least have the good grace to apologise to us."

types, so in his mind Keith let him down, and that was it, really. He left the band on the spot."

Coming from the disciplined world of sessions, one might be forgiven for thinking that Jimmy Page would have been appalled by Relf's behaviour. Instead, he was rapt with delight from the word go. "I went backstage and there was a huge argument going on with Paul leaving the group," he later said, "but I thought it was all absolutely brilliant!" Man by man, the other band members began to notice Page's glee. "Yes, Jimmy was watching it all," said McCarty. "It was funny how he took to it all, he absolutely loved it. It was like he thought we were like the Sex Pistols or something!" Chris Dreja also saw the funny side. "What a wonderful gig for Jimmy to come to. And it was wonderful. Like Johnny Rotten meeting the Queen. Pure theatre, pure punk. Then, Jimmy put his hand up and said 'I want a piece of this'..."

Jeff Beck later called it "A dream come true." On the night, it must have been an incredible surprise. "Jimmy was so keen, he was like a little boy!" McCarty laughed. "He was like 'Yeah, I'll play bass if you like, I'll play tambourine if you want!'" But Page's simple statement "I'll play bass if you like" backstage at the May Ball was potentially a Godsend to the Yardbirds. Not only did it offer Jeff a new, much-needed playmate and strong potential ally within the band, it also solved a gaping and very talented hole in their line-up following the departure of Paul Samwell-Smith. "I'd been going to gigs at Eel Pie," said Jimmy. "I'd been going to gigs at The Marquee and I could see it all happening. Also, I was so brassed off at studio life by that point that, yes, I wanted in." Suffice to say, there were no long discussions before the Yardbirds reached an accord. "He was keen and we were keen!" With Samwell-Smith gone, Jimmy Page was in. "Well," McCarty continued, "there was the matter of him playing bass. That was going to be a bit of a change of tune..."

And not the only one, either.

CHAPTER 10

Stroll On

Despite all the chaos and calamities of the Oxford Ball, the band to which Jimmy Page had hitched his mast in June 1966 was still very much on a roll, with four UK Top 10 singles over the last year, and four more Top 20 hits in the States during the same period. Indeed, the Yardbirds' last 'US only' album, a cobbled together collection of old live tracks and new studio cuts entitled *Having A Rave Up...*, may well have confused fans by featuring both Jeff Beck and Eric Clapton on guitar.[39]

Nevertheless, it still did semi-respectable business across the Atlantic, peaking at number 53 in January 1966. Better still, the group's follow-up LP, *Yardbirds* – or to give it its proper 'cult' title, *Roger The Engineer* – was by far the best thing they had ever recorded, at home or abroad. Mixing straight ahead Chicago blues ('Rack My Mind'), nascent world music oddities ('Hot House Of Omagarashid') and, in the case of 'Jeff's Boogie', a three-minute master class in six-string hooliganism, *Roger...*'s

---

39 A quick-fire collection aimed at the US market, *Having A Rave Up With The Yardbirds* collected new recordings by the band with Jeff Beck alongside several cuts from their previous LP, 1965's *Five Live Yardbirds*. As a result, Eric Clapton is present, correct and on fire for 'Smokestack Lightning', 'Respectable', 'I'm A Man' and 'Here 'Tis'.

showy wares saw them leap into the UK and US album charts at number 20 and number 52 shortly after Page's arrival. A good omen, then, of stronger things to come.

On the live front, however, a few eggs had fallen out of the basket along the way. Manager and "one-man ideas machine" Giorgio Gomelsky might well have scored the Yardbirds a record deal, inadvertently dreamed up the cod-sitar-starring 'Heart Full Of Soul' and got the group through the door of both Sun and Chess Studios, but there had been misfires alongside the magic. An ill-advised booking at the stuffy San Remo Festival in January 1966 ensured the Yardbirds another dinner date with the "black-tie and bejewelled brigade". Yet again, it did nothing to enhance their reputation as a cutting edge alternative to the Kinks or the Who. Worse, the festival organisers' demand that they perform the quite awful Italian pop tune 'Paff... Bum' as part of their set led to a Beck solo so loud and offensive the audience were left hiding behind their mink stoles. Proto-punk in action, perhaps. Or, just as probably, another good reason to question the overall commercial direction Giorgio had in mind for his clients.

While the Yardbirds could more or less tolerate Gomelsky's mad-cap notions as part of his overall charm, Giorgio's reported inability to balance the books were becoming a far more pressing matter for the band. Despite high-flying record sales and strong shows to packed houses, everyone appeared to be broke. "All these American tours," said Dreja, "and we were coming back with nothing. We just weren't making any money." Nominating the then still very much present Paul Samwell-Smith to act as hatchet man, the Yardbirds dispensed with their manager before any more financial harm could be done. Giorgio, however, wasn't going without a few trinkets. "I had a contract with them," he later said. "And I wanted the rights to all the songs I had produced." Fairly sure that no one would be listening to their back catalogue in two years, let alone five decades, the group acquiesced to his demand. "Bad idea," Chris laughed. As the Yardbirds legend subsequently grew over time, Giorgio found more and more innovative ways to re-package their early songs, leading to a few houses' worth of lost royalties for Dreja and co.[40]

The man brought in to redress the Yardbirds' fortunes was Simon Napier-Bell. Sharp as a whip and born to hustle, 31-year-old Napier-Bell's habit of smoking cigars behind the wheel of a brand-new Ford Thunderbird had already marked him as "a showbiz face around town". Coming to attention as a music editor on 1965's screwball comedy *What's New Pussycat?*, it was actually Simon's skills as a lyricist that inadvertently brought him into the management game. Approached by British chanteuse Dusty Springfield to write English words for an Italian tune she had heard at the San Remo festival, the resulting 'You Don't Have To Say You Love Me' (co-written with Vicky Wickham) gave Springfield her first UK number one and Napier-Bell a taste for the pop life.

Consequently, when Paul Samwell-Smith's sister – then working as Simon's secretary – suggested he might make a good replacement for the departing Gomelsky to both her sibling and employer, all the pieces fell neatly into place. "I didn't know much about management at that time," Napier-Bell said in 2010, "but I did see it as a test of my bravery." A lunch date for band and potential manager was swiftly arranged. It went well. "I was expecting them to be bloody monsters like the Rolling Stones, but instead, I got these gentle souls with good manners." Deal signed, Simon immediately got the Yardbirds a lump sum of £25,000 by renegotiating an advance against royalties from their record company. At long last, the group had some real money. "We were a top-down, on-the-road band... a little cynical by then, and

40 Despite the undoubted bad blood generated by his sacking, Gomelsky and the Yardbirds, would resolve their differences and reactivate their friendship in subsequent years. "There was no 'one moment' with Giorgio, really," confirmed Jim McCarty. "It all just built up." Chris Dreja was also gracious about their original manager's contribution. "The thing about Giorgio was that, above all else, he was a creative man. He was the sixth member – the sixth artist – in the band. And it's not such a good thing to have an artist in a strict management role. That said, he had such wonderful ideas. Now, we might not have benefited financially from him, but we did benefit from some of the directions he took us."

Simon couldn't really relate to us personally," said Chris Dreja. "But he was a lovely man, who did several good things for us. He renegotiated our publishing contract, [and] secured our rights."

Following nearly three years of steady studio dates, endless tours, manager swapping, financial meltdowns and the recent loss of their 'musical director', by June 1966 the Yardbirds were due a break, and the events of the May Ball surely proved it. The arrival of Jimmy Page in the ranks seemed to re-energise them and they pressed on accordingly. Just as well. They were booked "back-to-back and on and on" for the next four months or so, with yet another round of dates across the UK, Europe and the States seeing them well into Christmas. Whether Page himself felt ready to take on the pressures of the road again after the excesses of the Crusaders was now a moot point. He had committed to the cause. "Fate," he later said, "just intervened."

Jimmy might have put it down to the Kindly Ones. But there were others that couldn't quite believe that he was willing to leave behind the uniformity of the studio for the uncertainty of the motorway. "Yes, I suppose I was a bit surprised when Jimmy joined the Yardbirds," said Dave Berry. "I thought given the broadness of his session life and the number of recordings he worked on, he might have pursued a career more similar to Big Jim Sullivan. Still doing sessions, but maybe sitting in with the likes of James Last and Tom Jones. I thought he might have followed that path, but Jimmy obviously had other ideas!" Page's old friend John Carter was less shaken by the news. "No, I wasn't too surprised when Jimmy joined the Yardbirds," he said. "He'd done his initiation through the session scene and I guess he wanted to progress into a group situation. I think we [studio musicians] all did, in a way."

Page got his baptism of fire on June 21, 1966 when the Yardbirds returned to one of their favourite haunts, London's Marquee Club. Supported by the Clayton Squares, the band reportedly excelled on the night, with Jimmy holding down the bottom end of their sound extremely well for a man just days into the job. Not everyone was sure, though. "Paul Samwell-Smith was the backbone of the band," Jeff Beck later told Malcolm Gerrie. "He gave the Yardbirds such depth by playing these four-string chords and letting them ring [out and] on. It sounded like an earthquake." According to Beck, Jimmy did not sound like an earthquake, more a stuttering exhaust. "Absolute disaster. He couldn't play the bass for toffee. He was running all over the neck. Four fat strings instead of six thin ones." Manager Simon Napier-Bell was also cynical about Page covering bass, but for very different reasons. "I knew Jimmy from my days organising sessions," he said. "He was a really good guitarist, but even though I didn't know him character wise, my instinct said 'No'. I just couldn't see it from an ego point of view. It meant Jeff would have an equal with him in the group. But they all kept saying, 'No, no, no, Jimmy's just going to play bass.' Well, that wasn't going to happen, was it?"

While the world and his wife could guess what was coming next, the Yardbirds soldiered on a little longer with Page on bass guitar. After all, with a new single, a much-coveted film appearance and several months of concert dates on the horizon, making any changes to the line-up would have been counter-productive. "It was," joked Chris Dreja, "all hands to the pump..."

Let us take the single first. Since the sallow Gregorian chants of 'Still I'm Sad' and the ungodly guitar drones that shaped the melody of 'Shapes Of Things', the Yardbirds had been peering down the rabbit hole. 'Happening Ten Years Time Ago' now found them diving all the way in. By their own admission "a total head fuck of a song", the rough sketch that finally became 'Happening...' was pieced together by Jim McCarty and Keith Relf at the latter's flat in the late spring of 1966. Featuring another fine lyric – this time playing with notions of déjà vu, temporal anomalies and altered psychological states ("The sounds I heard, the sights I saw, was it real... I need to know what it all means") – 'Happening...' was already full of paranoia and unease. But by the time the Yardbirds had finished recording it at IBC Studios in early August 1966, it had become the aural equivalent of a fever dream. Smattered with odd sound effects including crashing cars and loud explosions, the song's middle-section also featured a spoken word interlude from Beck possibly based around the band's experiences with an intrusive doctor at a VD clinic: "Pop group, are you?" intoned a weasly Jeff as the world fell away behind him. "Bet you're pulling the crumpet..."

111

With its mad, meandering solo guitars, irregular shunts in rhythm and a central riff that sounded like it was collapsing in on itself, 'Happening Ten Years Time Ago' was the first evidence that the Beck-Page interface could produce something potentially extraordinary. Further, alongside a recent brace of tunes that included the Beatles' 'Tomorrow Never Knows', the Stones' 'Paint It Black' and, of course, the Yardbirds' own 'Shapes Of Things', 'Happening Ten Years Time Ago' was yet another pointer towards the 'Psychedelic' movement about to envelope UK and US culture. "Funny song, 'Happening...'" said Jim McCarty. "That mix of Jimmy and Jeff, that extra twist. I really think it was years ahead of its time, or certainly ahead of what people understood at that time. Now though, it's become a cult item, the birth of 'Psychedelia' or something. All very odd."

All very odd, and for the general public, a little too odd for its own good. Not quite ready to have their senses bombarded by a strange melange of found sounds and shuffling, unpredictable time-signatures, 'Happening...' stalled in the British charts, coming to rest at a lowly number 43 in mid-October 1966. As such, it was the Yardbirds' first real misfire. "The first Yardbirds track that didn't really chart!" Page said, laughing, to *Mojo* in 2014. "But you can really tell how well we were playing. It's a shame."[41]

If 'Happening Ten Years Time Ago' was a trifle touched, then *Blow Up* was utterly bonkers. The work of Michelangelo Antonioni, whose previous films *Il Deserto Rosso* and *L'eclisse* had made a substantial impact on the European arthouse circuit, *Blow Up* was the Italian director's first

---

41 With the benefit of hindsight, if they were looking for a hit, perhaps the Yardbirds should have released 'Happening...'s B-side, 'Psycho Daisies', instead. A pleasing, if slight Beach Boys/Chuck Berry pastiche sung by Jeff with a lyric extolling the virtues of California sunshine, easy living and his then new girlfriend, US actress Mary Hughes, 'Psycho Daisies' was certainly easier to assimilate than 'Happening' on first hearing. However, needling guitar solo aside, it remains the lesser tune. "Jeff, like the rest of us, had come from black and white, and California was in full on Technicolor," said Chris Dreja. "And Mary Hughes, well, she was all the colours of the rainbow. A lovely, vivacious, blonde woman. A mini-Bridget Bardot. I think she blew his mind. Well. She'd blow most peoples' minds, actually. You can't blame Jeff for that."

foray into English-language movie making. Its plot, however, was "a bit of a head scratcher". Following the fortunes of a hip London photographer – based on David Bailey, though played with a certain doe-eyed charm by actor David Hemmings – *Blow Up* combined the metaphysical with the macabre, its central themes of personal observation versus consensus reality hung loosely around a (possible) murder inadvertently caught on camera by Hemmings' character, Thomas. In between attempts to solve the mystery at hand, Thomas spends a great deal of the film's running time bedding models, playing with cameras or looking distracted. As a snapshot of 'swinging' London it was certainly authentic, not least because at one point in the action Thomas visits a trendy nightclub to watch a band perform, their act climaxing with one of its members turning his guitar into matchwood as an emotionless audience watch on. "Hmmm," said Jim McCarty of what is now regarded by film critics as Antonioni's enigmatic masterpiece.

Antonioni had obviously become aware of the Who as part of his research into London's 'Swinging Sixties' scene. By now a popular concert draw and icons of the mod movement, Pete Townshend's group had turned the destruction of their stage gear into something approximating an art form. It came as no great surprise, then, that the director wanted them for his film. Entreaties regarding their availability were made to the Who's flamboyant co-manager Kit Lambert and a meeting between both camps was arranged. It was at this point that Simon Napier-Bell stepped into the picture to cleverly subvert the Who's chances and promote his own interests.

"Kit Lambert told me over dinner that Antonioni was coming into town to make this great art film with David Hemmings," he said. "Well, I knew this already because of my connections to the film business. Anyway, Antonioni wanted the Who to star in it because they had the reputation as great amp smashers, and he loved all that destruction. I was incredibly jealous of this, of course. So, when Kit asked me what sort of money he should ask for, I said, 'A minimum of £10,000 and absolute control of the film edit'. Of course, I knew he wouldn't get it." He didn't. Confronted by Lambert's unreasonable demands, Antonioni walked away and sought out another group to fit the bill. After vain entreaties to both the In Crowd and the Velvet Underground, Napier-Bell made his move. "I called him soon afterwards and said, 'The Yardbirds are much better at smashing equipment than the Who'." On seeing the band perform a short set at London's Royal Albert Hall on September 23, 1966, Antonioni agreed. They were in.

With the notable exception of Pete Townshend, Michelangelo Antonioni couldn't really have found himself a better equipment smasher than Jeff Beck. After all, he had been practising for some time. "Jeff didn't smash anything up as part of 'an act', though," cautioned Chris Dreja. "He smashed up amps because they were pissing him off." A habit born sometime in early 1966, when a Vox AC 30 amplifier refused to play ball onstage and Beck solved its stutters by bashing it repeatedly with his guitar, he had recently escalated his efforts to alarming proportions, with amps now being thrown out of open windows when they displeased him. "There was an incredibly hot gig [in Phoenix, Arizona] and we were on the first floor, with a window just by the stage," said McCarty. "Anyway, we had these Jordan amps, I think – Simon might have got a deal on renting them – and I gather they were pretty crap. Of course, Jeff didn't take to them and the next thing you know, the amp's gone out the window. Thank God there was nobody below."[42]

As Beck's amp-wrecking efforts intensified, so did Napier-Bell's efforts to find replacements. But according to the Yardbirds' manager, the amplifiers had to be Marshalls, and Jimmy Page was now calling the shots. "We arrived in New York, and all the airlines were on strike, so we had to do the tour on a charter plane. The first night, in Boston I think, Beck smashed his amp, which left him with nothing. So I was phoning all over the place trying to find a Marshall amp. And it was very difficult, with suppliers refusing to provide Marshalls. The band were saying, 'Well, we could use something else,' but Jimmy had really begun testing me at that point. He said, 'No, it absolutely has to be a

---

42 According to Jeff, it was a locking plug that saved the good residents of Phoenix from 'death by amplifier'. "I just went crazy," he said. "I smashed the amp, pushed it over and the top went through the window. It was dangling outside, swinging about. The thing that saved someone's life below was that it had a locking cannon plug."

Marshall. Simon's our manager, it's up to him to sort it out.' Well, I finally found a bloody Marshall amp, but the only way to get it to the next gig was to charter a plane. I mean, this was ridiculous. Chartering a plane was going to cost five times as much as buying a new amp. But I did it. Then, of course, Jeff broke it again."

In the end, Beck wasn't required to smash amps for *Blow Up*. Just guitars. And lots of them.

Arriving on set at Elstree film studios just north of London in Borehamwood, the Yardbirds were flabbergasted to find that Antonioni had lovingly recreated the inside of Windsor's Ricky Tick club to film their scene. "Literally, brick by brick," McCarty laughed. While Jim and the others were more than familiar with the setting – they had played the Ricky Tick many a time – Page had never seen it. "I'd never actually been there," he later recalled, "but the other lads said it was just identical to the Ricky, brick for brick, cobweb for cobweb." Over the course of the next few days, they would all get used to this faithful, if false, setting, as Michelangelo Antonioni and his assistants filmed the band over and over again in an effort to capture the perfect performance. "All very strange," said Jim. "Exciting to be in a movie, yes, but that short scene took a bloody week to film. We were staying in a hotel in Knightsbridge, and every morning at eight, we'd drive off to the set in Borehamwood to spend all day hanging around for a [set-up] that would last a few minutes. Boring and bizarre at the same time."

Seldom far from boredom perhaps, but there were some genuinely comedic moments along the way that helped raise spirits. At first, Antonioni had tried to persuade Jeff to smash his new Gibson Les Paul for the scene. Beck's response was as understandable as it was expected. "No. Fucking. Way." To assuage this misunderstanding between the star and his director, a box of cheap Hofner guitars was ordered in. Jeff was suitably appeased. "They were made to be smashed." But after a few days of being on set, even the thrill of breaking the unfortunate Hofners into little pieces began to lose its lustre for Beck. "I'd have broken the bloody guitars even if it wasn't in the script."

More, the original decision to perform Howlin' Wolf's 'Smokestack Lightning' for the cameras was soon jettisoned when Antonioni decided the song was too slow-paced for the emotions he wanted to convey. The Yardbirds raised few objections. They were too busy being spooked by the dozens of film extras the director had hired to stare at them. "The extras just stood there, looking at us," said McCarty. "I guess Antonioni wanted them to look mesmerised. Or drugged. I can tell you now that never happened at a Yardbirds gig. At a Pink Floyd gig, maybe, but not at one of ours..."[43]

Looking at the finished product from 50-odd years distance, Antonioni certainly caught something of the Yardbirds' gift for mixing creativity and chaos in *Blow Up*. Performing their version of 'Train Kept A Rollin'' – re-christened 'Stroll On' for copyright purposes in the film – the band gave the Johnny Burnette Trio's stout rockabilly anthem a real Surrey Delta shake-up, with Beck's fizzy solo interjections spilling every which way across the track. Jimmy, on the other hand, was all smiles for the big screen, his features still more like those of a teenager than a man now approaching his mid-twenties. But when it came to holding down 'Train...''s all-important rhythmic bounce, Page was right there in the midst of things, crashing chords against Dreja and McCarty while Keith Relf's harp howled at the moon. As for the destruction of equipment, again, Jeff did a bang-up job, bashing guitar and amp with vim and vigour as the camera zoomed uncomfortably close to his nether regions. "I had a fucking hard on, man," he later laughed. "I took my mother to the film and there it was, this horrible, sinister thing hanging down the side of the screen." The Yardbirds. Bluesy, experimental, destructive, and when required, priapic. "Bottom line on *Blow Up*?" said Jim McCarty. "Actually, I'm pleased we did a film like that rather than some 'pop caper' movie. Or *Summer Holiday!*"

It didn't hold together much longer.

Amid the recording of 'Happening Ten Years Time Ago' and on-set adventures of *Blow Up*, the Yardbirds had continued to gig with few or no breaks throughout 1966. Given Jimmy Page's history with glandular fever, and his recent, sedentary existence in the world of London's

---

43 Among the extras, seen dancing in yellow and red pants, was future media personality Janet Street-Porter.

studios, it would have come as no great surprise if he had wilted like a flower among all this frenzied activity. Not a chance. According to Chris Dreja, Page was a man reborn. "Jimmy was wonderfully professional," he confirmed in 2010. "He'd come from a background where if you were five minutes late, you were fined. He understood the finer points of contracts, music publishing, in short, the mechanics of the music industry were already under his belt. Jimmy was also very fresh [in 1966], whereas we'd been touring for years. He stepped up to the plate." Unfortunately, Jeff Beck was dropping plates left, right and centre. Weakened by a persistent throat infection he couldn't shake off and moody as hell as a result, the Yardbirds' torrid schedule throughout the autumn of 1966 was soon to push Beck towards breaking point. "I had this throat thing come on," he later said. "Inflamed tonsils, inflamed brain, inflamed cock."

The downward spiral had actually begun during August, when Beck's throat problems flared up mid-way through the Yardbirds' first prolonged US tour. Following a memorable concert at Catalina Island – where in the words of Simon Napier-Bell, "Jeff's playing... was really one of the greatest things I'd ever seen" – the guitarist collapsed in a heap soon after. With no alternative but to temporarily press on without him, Jimmy took up the slack at San Francisco's Carousel Ballroom on August 25. It was to be a game-changing night. "Well, Jeff couldn't make it so I took over lead [guitar]," he later confirmed. "Yes, it was really nerve-wracking because this was at the height of the Yardbirds' concert reputation and I wasn't exactly ready to roar off on lead guitar. But after that night, we stayed that way. When Jeff recovered, it was two lead guitars from then on."[44]

On Beck's recovery, Jeff and Jimmy worked hard and fast at melding their two guitars together. Using downtime between gigs to tighten up arrangements, with each apportioning the other clear melodic

---

44 The making of *Blow Up* has already been covered in the pages of this book, but it's worth noting that the Yardbirds' appearance was not actually filmed until the week commencing October 12, 1966. As evidenced above, and seen in the movie, Jimmy Page had switched to lead guitar by that time.

responsibilities, the duo soon had the bones of a playable set, though one often as not based on 'a joint unison attack'. "[The idea]," Jimmy later told *Rolling Stone*'s David Fricke, "was playing the riffs in harmony. The approach was almost like a big band with brass, the power of that applied to guitars." In this regard, Page probably had the advantage. Having spent the previous four years in a session environment, he had grown used to playing "for the song". Riffs and chords were not chess pieces to be moved around a board for strategic or tactical advantage. Instead, they were more like little cogs in a greater machine, each spun sequentially to make the clock tick. For Jimmy, only the solo really provided a chance to leave the machinery behind and follow his own muse. "Pagey was actually a gentle soul," said McCarty. "He was polite, well-meaning and very easy to work with, which I think was a knock-on from his session days. He actually wanted to do something that pleased you." Dreja heartily agreed. "Jimmy brought his beautiful skills with riffs and chords. He was also ambitious, disciplined and fresh. He brought all of that to us."

Beck, on the other hand, was more instinctive and, as a result, more unpredictable. Used to having his own way within a song structure, the demands of fitting in alongside another guitarist would be trickier to negotiate, both for him and the band. "It was always difficult with Jeff," said Jim. "Of course, he added so much to the music, huge amounts actually, but you just didn't know how he was going to be." Again, Chris Dreja concurred. "Jeff might have been quiet offstage, but onstage, he was King. Nobody had ever got in his space. I tried to enhance everything he did as best as I could, that was my role. But when Jimmy came along, well, Jeff knew how good Jimmy was. It was like someone had stepped into his underpants."

While Page and Beck were still gleeful at the prospect of bringing their two-guitar army to America, there remained the potentially thorny issue of who was taking Jimmy's place on bass. Thankfully for all, Dreja proved an accommodating soul. "The show had to go on," he said. "And for me, it was a case of 'They've given me the bass guitar. I can play these huge deep notes. Bloody wonderful.'" On the face of it, then, the Yardbirds had just come one step closer to sonic nirvana. Jeff was happy. Jimmy was happy. Chris was happy. Everyone was happy. "Jeff and I had [often] spoken about what two lead guitars could do," Page later said. "Working [it] like a big band... this huge, huge, two-guitar attack." Nonetheless, Napier-Bell's gut feeling that two lead guitarists rather than one might undo all the band's hard work was to prove eerily prophetic. "Indeed," said Dreja. "We'd entered the age of the gunslinger."

On a good night, the Yardbirds with Page and Beck on guitar were world-beaters, a crack team who could make the likes of 'I'm A Man', 'I Ain't Got You', 'Good Morning Little Schoolgirl' and 'Smokestack Lightning' bristle with energy or pop like a cork. "For me, it was absolutely nerve-wracking," said McCarty, "but also marvellous, [when] these two guitars started playing in perfect unison. It was just fantastic." Taking things to a new level of musical complexity, when Jimmy and Jeff got it right, the results could be astounding; swooping riffs, intertwining harmonies and breathtaking solo flights that soared away into the ether before returning to the song. But as the saying goes, "Where resides harmony also resides discord", and the proof of it arrived all too quickly. "[It was] pure dynamite onstage – good and bad – but always on the edge," said Chris. "I think if we're honest though, people like bands that are on the edge. Sadly, then it all started to go wrong."

As the American tour progressed, Jeff's health continued to deteriorate, resulting in more bad moods and more smashed amps. "God, I collapsed everywhere, didn't I?" he later joked. Things didn't pick up when the Yardbirds returned to Great Britain, either. Joining their old mates the Rolling Stones for a 12-date tour in the early autumn of 1966 should have been a cause for celebration. And indeed, the reception accorded the band at London's Royal Albert Hall on September 23 was ecstatic. "They play all Jeff's original solos in unison," marvelled Napier-Bell. "It was just amazing to watch, given that there were no proper mixing desks in those days." But a sour review from *NME* calling Beck "a guitar gymnast" only served to intensify his woes and make him wary of the music press for several years to come.

Even more worrying than Jeff's health or snippy copy was the fact that the Yardbirds' guitar dream team were starting to show definite signs of creative wear and tear. "Yeah, they just started competing with each other," said Jim. "Jeff had his style, he'd never play the same thing twice, while Jimmy was an experienced session musician who was used to playing what people wanted, playing the right part." The issue wasn't lost on Page. "I was doing what I was supposed to," he later told *Guitar Player*, "while something completely different would be coming from Jeff. That was fine for improvisation, but there were other parts where it just didn't work."

Beck's bouts of indiscipline were also causing Jimmy grave concern. "Jeff had discipline occasionally, in that when he's on, he probably the best there is," he continued. "But at the time, he had no respect for audiences. When I joined, he supposedly wasn't going to walk off any more. Well..." Watching his predictions come horribly true in the wings was Simon Napier-Bell. "These were Jeff's original solos, [but] Jimmy was getting the applause on them," he said. "And, of course, Jimmy had no particular feeling of triumph, because he was playing Jeff's stuff. It was a no-win situation. But then, most creativity comes from conflict, not resolution. The best music comes from war."

In the end, there would be no war. Just one smashed guitar and a litany of regrets. Following their excursions around the UK with the Stones, the Yardbirds again returned to the States. This time they were to be part of *American Bandstand* host Dick Clark's 'Caravan of Stars', a roving treasure trove of talent that would descend like "stardust" on various US cities during October and November of 1966. Joining a bill that included show-biz types such as Sam The Sham & the Pharaohs, Gary Lewis & the Playboys and Brian 'Sealed With A Kiss' Hyland, the tour might have looked good on paper, but in reality, it was hell on wheels.

"I understood the train of thought behind it," said McCarty. "I mean, the tour would get the band across to the maximum number of people, but really, we were just unsuited to the overall line-up. There were acts like Sam The Sham, Gary Lewis, just straighter pop acts. Next to them, we were like something from *The Outer Limits*. Then when you add the intensity of it, everyone crammed together on a Greyhound bus travelling hundreds of miles between shows to do one, maybe two sets a night, it was just so full on." Jimmy Page was reading from the same script. "It was the worst tour I've done as far as fatigue is concerned," he later told journalist Pete Frame. "Living on a bus, driving hundreds of miles, doing double gigs every day for four weeks. We didn't know whether we were coming or going."

After months of searing highs, crashing lows and near-continual illness, Dick Clark's rickety caravan journey across America proved too much for Jeff Beck. "Stuffed like an animal on a bus with 50 other people," he told *Mojo*. "[Then], it's like 'Come out, here's a few biscuits, come and play.'" After one final exhibition of random amplifier destruction in Worcester, Massachusetts on October 21, Beck officially ended his association with the Yardbirds backstage at the Memorial Coliseum in Corpus Christi, Texas some nine days later. He did so in some style. "The night before Jeff left, we finished the gig, came offstage and he completely lost it," said McCarty. "He just smashed up his guitar – I think it was his Les Paul, just a beautiful guitar – into little bits. Then, according to Jimmy, he walked up to him later and said, 'Well, you could have stopped me doing that.' There was just no way we could have done anything. He'd gone fucking crazy!" Beck was gone by morning.

With nearly 50 years of dust settled, the reasons behind Jeff Beck's departure from the Yardbirds now seem blindingly obvious. In all honesty, they probably did at the time. But for both Jeff and Jimmy, there was no bad blood or recriminations involved on either side because of it, just a sense of lost horizons. "The idea of having Jim and me on guitar was a great one," Beck told *Guitar World*'s Alan di Perna in 1999, "but it was also fraught with potential disaster because sooner or later, one of us would be cramped, style wise. I don't know. Maybe we could have worked something out."

Page felt the same. "[It was] like a kettle boiling with a cork stuck in it," he said. "There was history with the other guys... but I was really enjoying playing with Jeff. I didn't feel we were working competitively. I certainly wasn't. In fact, I'm still convinced it would have been great if he stayed. You know," he concluded, "we had some really great plans for what we could do with the two lead guitars..."

In 1961 or thereabouts, Jeff Beck had watched admiringly from the audience while a young Jimmy Page wrestled with a giant orange guitar onstage at The Boathouse on Kew Bridge. Five years later, they were sharing the boards together and making giant plans for a guitar army. Now all of that was over. "I woke up the next morning and thought 'I'm not a Yardbird anymore'," Beck later said. "'I wonder if there's any scraps left for me?' I think that was the lowest point in my life." Of course, Jeff would pull through, as would Jimmy. And as time came to show, they weren't quite done with each other yet.

Jimmy, with Carter Lewis & the Southerners, London, 1963; from top: Ken Lewis, Viv Prince and John Carter, with Jimmy leaning against the lamp stand. Carter: "Jimmy was a quiet guy, but you know, a nice guy. If you went to the pub for a drink, he'd have a chat and a pint, but he was never wandering around saying

Jimmy, top right, poses with the obscure UK band Mickey Finn & the Blue Men to whose cover of Chuck Berry's 'Reelin' And Rockin'' he contributed harmonica in 1964. Finn, whose real name was Micky Waller, went on to play guitar with Sam Gopal and the Heavy Metal Kids.

PLATFORM

4

Perhaps inspired by their appearance in the movie *Blow Up*, four Yardbirds pose with cameras to photograph Jimmy. Left to right: Chris Dreja, Jeff Beck, Jim McCarty and Keith Relf, with Jimmy a bemused subject.

The five-man Yardbirds, featuring the dual talents and mutual admiration society of Jeff Beck and Jimmy Page. At first Jimmy Page played bass: "Absolute disaster," said Beck. "He couldn't play the bass for toffee." Matters were rectified when Chris Dreja took over on bass, leaving Jimmy to duet with Beck.

The four-man Yardbirds, left to right, Chris Dreja, Jim McCarty, Jimmy Page and Keith Relf. McCarty.
Dreja: "Jimmy brought his beautiful skills with riffs and chords. He was also ambitious, disciplined and fresh.
He brought all of that to us."

CHAPTER 11

White Summer

There were no long discussions among the Yardbirds about replacing Jeff Beck. Everyone knew what had to be done. "We became a four-piece," Jim McCarty laughed. And so it went. However, there was one thing Beck did leave behind that would serve as a gentle, if very loud reminder of his departure from the group.

When Jimmy Page first joined the Yardbirds after the mad events of the Oxford Ball, Jeff had given his friend a 1959 Fender Telecaster. Purchased in 1961 for £107 from John Owen (a former colleague of Jeff's from his days in the Deltones), Beck had used the instrument as a back-up for his own trusty Fender Esquire. But being a generous soul and no doubt mindful of who actually recommended him to the group in the first place, Jeff passed it on to Jimmy to mark his arrival within the ranks. For a while, Page was content to leave the Telecaster with its original white finish. But as time progressed, it became a testing ground for several of his own artistic – and perhaps even arcane – experiments. First, he attached mirrors to the guitar's body so it might catch the light onstage: a simple trick, but effective nonetheless. In turn, these mirrors were removed in favour of a metallic pick guard and new bold, paint job that covered the axe with red, yellow and green psychedelic splashes. Now resembling some mythical beast as much as a guitar, the

'Dragon Telecaster' was born and Jimmy would play the hell out of it, not only in the Yardbirds but also well into the next phase of his own musical career.

Back in 1966, however, while Jeff might have left a fine memento for Page to remember him by, the Yardbirds still had to fulfil their obligations with Dick Clark's 'Caravan of Stars'. To a man, it almost killed them. "Thirty-three dates in all, I think," Jimmy later remembered, "and 25 of those double [engagements]. You'd think a double would be played in the same town, but it wasn't. It was two different towns. The show was in two halves. When the first half finished and there was an interval, the [performers] would get on the coach driving to the next town, while the second half carried on [behind]. Then, they in turn carried on to the next place, where the first lot had already finished." These were round robins from hell. "Human beings stuck in a rat hole, actually," said Chris Dreja. "It was a bit like being sectioned. You don't know why you're there, because you're actually sane, and yet there you are. Clever man, though, that Dick Clark. You have to give him that."

The pace was relentless. When the band finally fought their way free of Dick Clark's unholy caravan in late November 1966, they went straight back on the road in Europe, first for a date at Paris' Locomotive club in early December before returning to the UK for a spell of university shows in Bristol, Hull and Aberystwyth. Then, it was home to families, wives and girlfriends for Christmas, after which yet another trip to the States saw their dairies filled into the New Year. It wasn't over by a long shot. After the US leg of their never-ending journey, the Yardbirds were back at the airport and on another plane, this time to Denmark, then Australia, New Zealand and South-East Asia in support of the great Roy Orbison and the Walker Brothers. If there was a plan, somebody had lost it along the way. "At that time though," reasoned Jim McCarty, "we earned our money on the road and not from record sales. So, there was just no way we could take a break."

As the Yardbirds battled to keep their senses on an even keel, many others were busy gearing up to befuddle them. A movement born among the beatniks and hipsters of New York's Greenwich Village and San Francisco's Haight-Ashbury district near the start of the decade, the 'hippies' were gaining serious international traction by early 1967. Experimentally inclined, intellectually inquisitive and certainly sexually liberated, the hippie ethos of breaking free of societal norms in favour of a more altruistic and peaceful existence obviously held great appeal after years of cold war uncertainty and the escalating threat of nuclear conflict. Hippies also brought with them some serious hallucinogenics. Whereas only 10 years before the standard drug of choice in London had been a pint of warm beer, the 'Swinging Sixties' had seen the rise of amphetamines and marijuana as preferable alternatives for adjusting the senses. Now, the advent of LSD (or acid) offered an even more mind-altering choice, these 'little tabs of heaven' coming with the supposed promise of seeing the world in a new and wonderful way. In short, consciousness was realigned, the doors of perception prised opened and the 'Summer of Love' was on the horizon. "No road maps, fewer boundaries, I suppose," said Chris Dreja of the overall mood.

Suffice to say, the musical community had not been shy when it came to the use of mind-altering chemicals and redirecting the results into their songs. The Beatles' 'Tomorrow Never Knows' acted as something of a primer in this regard, its opening lines "Turn off your mind, relax and float downstream" lifted directly from the pages of LSD guru Timothy Leary's 1964 tome *The Psychedelic Experience*[45] by John Lennon to signpost his own recent experiments with the drug. The Stones, too, were in on the game early, as Brian Jones' sitar part on 'Paint It Black' and baroque use of harpsichord on 'Ruby Tuesday' both boldly pointed to a world far beyond pint pots.

Across the Atlantic where the hippies were born, it was much the same story. San Francisco's Jefferson Airplane were gearing up for the release of the trippy 'White Rabbit', the Byrds were already 'Eight Miles High' and LA quartet the Doors were readying themselves to give the overall scene a very dark underbelly. In this febrile stew of backwards

---

45 Leary's book – *The Psychedelic Experience: A Manual Based On The Tibetan Book Of The Dead* – was essentially an instruction manual for those using consciousness-altering drugs such as LSD, mescaline or peyote. Ralph Metzner and Richard Alpert also contributed to the finished manuscript.

loops, odd effects and cosmic-leaning lyricism, the Yardbirds – with or without the aid of drugs – had strong, previous form. From 'Still I'm Sad' and 'Shapes Of Things' to 'Evil Hearted You' and 'Happening Ten Years Ago', the band were proven innovators in both sound and word.

Further, their recent meandering tour across the globe had seen them experimenting even more with the extremities of the blues, as old standards like 'I'm A Man' became new training grounds for extended instrumental improvisation and trance-like rhythms. Though Beck was gone, the group was still evidently very much in touch with the "weird and wonderful" and, as such, well-placed to kick on to even greater things. So, as the Beatles made preparations for the release of their latest LP *Sgt. Pepper's Lonely Heart's Club Band* with producer George Martin at the helm, the Yardbirds entered London's Olympic Studios on March 5, 1967 to cut *Little Games* with producer Mickie Most. The end results would vary.

A "one-man *X Factor*", Mickie Most was the son of an army sergeant who had left behind his native Aldershot at the age of 15 to work as a singing waiter in Soho's most famous show-biz coffee bar, the 2is. Unfortunately, his plan to position himself at the heart of London's record industry during the British rock'n'roll boom yielded no great success, and it was only when he emigrated to South Africa with his wife in 1959 that his musical career really took off. Scoring 11 straight number ones, Mickie Most & his Playboys were, for a year or so, the biggest act in the country.

It wasn't quite enough for him. Returning to England in early 1962, Most again tried his luck as singer. Again, he was to be frustrated. Signing a deal with Columbia, Mickie's single 'Mr. Porter' was only a moderate hit, clipping the UK charts at number 45 in July 1963. Two subsequent releases also failed to ignite the public's imagination, and growing tired of grimy package tours and club appearances, Most decided to chance his arm behind the mixing desk instead of in front of it. Landing a producer's job at Columbia, he quickly developed a Midas touch for the label. The Animals' 'House Of The Rising Sun', a global smash, was recorded in one take, and was followed in fairly quick succession by the Nashville Teens' 'Tobacco Road', Herman's Hermits'

'I'm Into Something Good' and the Moody Blues' 'Go Now'. All these, and many more besides, bore Mickie Most's golden stamp of approval.

Jimmy Page had known Most for some years before the making of the Yardbirds' *Little Games*. In fact, the pair had recorded together back in the summer of 1963 when Page cut some tasty guitar fills for Mickie's single 'The Feminine Look'. Jimmy was also there for Most's follow-up 45s, lending two hands and a Gibson Black Beauty on 1964's 'Sea Cruise' and 'Money Honey'. More recently, Page had again struck a few pre-Yardbirds chords alongside fellow guitarist Eric Ford on Donovan's mega-hit 'Sunshine Superman'[46], a track Most had produced for the "Scottish Bob Dylan" in 1966. In basic terms then, they both knew, liked and respected each other. Sadly, the recording of *Little Games* would test that respect to the nth degree. "I'm not putting Mickie down," Jimmy told Charles Shaar Murray in 2004, "but he wasn't right for the Yardbirds."

In defence of Most, there was a lot of artistic and commercial juggling going on behind the scenes with the Yardbirds during the run-up to *Little Games*, and it wouldn't make his job any easier. On one hand, Page and the band were well aware of the recent rise of interest among music fans in the LP. Like everyone else, they had listened to the Beach Boys' *Pet Sounds* and the Beatles' *Revolver* with jaws slightly agape. More,

---

46   A staggered single release that reached numbers two and number one in the US and UK charts respectively in July and December 1966, Donovan's 'Sunshine Superman' is another one of those songs that can lay some claim to stealing a jump on the musical form soon to be known as 'Psychedelia'. In subsequent years, Jimmy Page's name would also be linked to Donovan's 1968 hit 'Hurdy Gurdy Man'. However, Page's participation on this track has been hotly contested, with sessioneer Alan Parker put forward as a strong alternative candidate for providing 'Hurdy...'s distinctive guitar flourishes. That said, in a 2009 interview with *Uncut*, Donovan seemed happy to confirm it was Jimmy who played on the song. "Mickie Most suggested Jimmy (and musical director) John Cameron told him, 'All you've got to do is listen to Donovan's guitar. Although it's acoustic, the way he's hitting it is the way the power-chords would go.' Rather than plug in, I was hitting driving chords on the acoustic in such a way that they buzz. So I guess Page listened. Jimmy added power and pagan rock. To this day, everyone wants that sound."

rumours were escaping from Abbey Road Studios that the Fab Four's new album might well be something truly extraordinary. Always keen on innovation, the Yardbirds were probably champing at the bit to capture the wilder excesses of their new stage act on tape. "In a way," said McCarty, "the future was calling." But the group's success thus far had strongly depended on their abilities to sell a single into the European and US charts and then tour behind it. Having watched 'Happening Ten Years Time Ago' crash land outside the Top 40, now was not the time to deviate too wildly from a winning formula. "The market at that time was still mostly about hit singles," continued Jim, "and Mickie was the master of the hit single." Sadly, he had little interest when it came to albums.

In the end, *Little Games* was the sound of the Yardbirds balancing uncomfortably between two stools, though falling from neither. In the case of the title track (written by jobbing UK songwriters Harold Spiro and Phil Wainman) and 'No Excess Baggage' (composed by American team Roger Atkins and Carl D'Errico[47]), the onus was very much on the type of snappy pop rock the Who had recently made their own. Equipped with trim choruses, quick, punchy solos and lean, no-frills arrangements, both songs worked well enough, but didn't really test any new boundaries. The group's collective composition 'Smile On Me' was also a bit hit or miss. Harking back to a time when the Yardbirds had traded on well-worn blues licks and galloping mid-section rave-ups, 'Smile...' flew by amiably enough, even if its overall construction was a little too close to *Roger The Engineer*'s 'Rack My Mind'[48] for its own good. Still, the tune did benefit from a top-notch solo from Page, with Jimmy fire-bombing its final moments with a fuzzy demonstration of manic overbends and trebly trills.

---

47 Based at New York's Brill Building – where the likes of Leiber & Stoller, Goffin & King and Greenfield & Sedaka wrote so many hits of the fifties and sixties – composers Atkins & D'Errico previously scored a Top 40 hit for The Animals in 1965 with 'It's My Life'.

48 One might argue that the Yardbirds' 'Rack My Mind' was in itself simply a rework of Howlin' Wolf's own 'Shake For Me', the title phrase of which will return with some force later on in this story.

Likewise, 'Drinking Muddy Water' – again credited to the Yardbirds collectively, but really no more than a brisk rework of Muddy Waters' 'Rollin' And Tumblin'' – had a vintage tint to it, though this time, revisiting the past had much better-informed their present. A proper showcase for frontman Keith Relf's crackling harp, McCarty and Dreja were also very much at the races, riding 'Drinking...' home like a pair of demented jockeys. Jimmy, too, was on point, his expressive slide guitar slyly tracking Relf's vocal line before revealing itself more fully as the track progressed. Subtle, yet effective, it would be a trick Page would repeat with even greater success in years to come. Conversely, 'Stealing, Stealing' was full of comedic contrast, its rag-time piano, drunken cod-trumpet and wobbling harmonica a fine homage to the New Orleans and Memphis jug bands of the twenties.

As ever, it was the more adventurous side of the Yardbirds that made *Little Games* worth a listen. With 'Glimpses' the band had turned yet another corner in their musical development, it's floating structure and drifting chants much more Haight-Ashbury hippie than Surrey Delta blues boy. A five minute 'sound poem' featuring children's voices, old newsreel clips, train station noises and, at its finale, a treated vocal intoning sombre mediations on the nature of space and time, 'Glimpses' was breaking pavement-sized slabs of new ground for the group. "Actually, 'Glimpses' was kind of easy to pull together," said Jim McCarty. "It's all in the same key and we just experimented over the top... newsreels, various tapes, bits Jimmy put in there on guitar. The usual Yardbirds cocktail!" The "bits Jimmy put in there" were certainly notable, with Page's recent purchase of a wah-wah[49] adding a novel dimension to things, with the effects pedal's ability to mimic the human voice allowing him to blend whispery notes and chords into Relf and McCarty's baritone, Gregorian rumbles.

'Tinker, Tailor, Soldier, Sailor' brought even more innovation from Jimmy. Written by Page and Jim McCarty, 'Tailor...''s mod-ish 12-string strut was pleasing enough, even if its overall construction again

49 New to the market in 1966, the wah pedal would soon become a 'go-to' device in every guitar hero's arsenal. At the time, Page favoured Vox's 'Grey' model.

faintly echoed the Who. But the tune's middle-section was where the real action could be found. Seemingly out of nowhere, Jimmy's guitar appeared to be sawing itself in half. "Ah," said McCarty, "that was the violin bow. Haven't got a clue where he got the idea for that, but the bow was pure Page. He was always looking for something new."

In fact, Jimmy had stumbled upon using a bow with his guitar while still working in sessions. Striking up casual conversation on a studio date with the Royal Philharmonic Orchestra's principal first violinist, David McCallum[50], the older man asked Page a fateful question. "String players usually kept to themselves, but [David] was quite friendly," Jimmy later told *Rolling Stone*. "He said to me one day – we'd just finished a session – 'Have you ever tried bowing the guitar?' I said it wouldn't work because the strings aren't arched over the guitar the way they are over a violin. [But] he said 'Have a go'. So I tried it, and realised there might be something in it. I don't remember if I used it on any sessions, but I certainly used it the minute I was in the Yardbirds."

No exaggeration there. Using 'I'm A Man' and occasionally 'Smokestack Lightning' as an onstage testing ground for his bow/guitar combination, Page was producing some truly strange noises by the end of 1966, with low moans, high squeals, shivery chords and unsettling drones all fighting for dominance. As ever with emerging technology, there were issues to resolve. If the concert hall was humid (and they often were), the bow worked less well if Jimmy wanted to voice full chords. But as he came to discover, regularly covering its strings with resin helped alleviate the problem. One might wonder, of course, what the hell any of this had to do with keeping the spirit of the blues intact on the likes of '... Man' and '... Lightning'. But, as intimated, both Page and the Yardbirds were now as much committed to the 'shock of the new' as they were the championing of old heroes. More, by taking bow

---

50 A revered classical violinist and orchestral leader, David McCallum was one of 40 musicians who contributed to the astounding 'string climb' featured on the Beatles' ground-breaking 'A Day In The Life' in 1967. McCallum's son, David Jr., also achieved notoriety as an actor, his best-known role being secret agent Illya Kuryakin in the hit sixties US TV series *The Man From Uncle*.

to guitar, Jimmy was simply honouring yet another influence that had marked his development as a musician.

As far back as Sutton Art College, Page had reportedly immersed himself in the work of Polish composer Krzysztof Penderecki, whose *Threnody To The Victims Of Hiroshima* shook the world of classical music when first performed in 1960. Both lamentation and tribute to the 140,000 people who lost their lives in the world's first nuclear strike, Penderecki had abandoned standard chromaticism for *Threnody...*, instead applying quarter-tones, microtones and waves of dissonance to evoke the devastation wrought upon the Japanese city on August 6, 1945. The musical results were as terrifying as they were hypnotic, and surely came to Jimmy's mind when he began applying bow to guitar onstage with the Yardbirds.[51] "I was trying a lot of new ideas in the Yardbirds that hadn't actually been done by Eric or Jeff," he later said. "All the colours were really starting to show in the palette."

Another colour emerging from Page was the sound of folk and he was more than happy to bring it with him to the making of *Little Games*. As with skiffle, rock'n'roll and the blues, Jimmy had fallen hard for folk, though truthfully he was only a recent convert to the cause. Obviously aware of the form as a teenager, but probably choosing to ignore it in favour of the electrified thrills provided by Scotty Moore, Link Wray and James Burton, all that had changed for Page in April 1965 when he heard Bert Jansch's self-titled debut album. "Bert's first album had a great effect on me," he said in 2000. "That's what got me into playing acoustic."

Arriving in London from his native Glasgow some two years before, Bert Jansch had quickly set about wresting the acoustic guitar from the strummers and 'cupped ear brigade', and establishing it as an instrument of astounding possibility in its own right. With nary an amp to help

51 As with so many things concerning Jimmy Page, there is some dispute as to whether he was the first guitarist to put a bow to use with the instrument. In fact, Eddie Phillips may well have that honour. A fine player in his own right, Phillips was certainly experimenting with bow and guitar by the mid-sixties as part of mod bands the Mark Four and the Creation, the latter of whom scored hits with the Shel Talmy-produced singles 'Making Time' and 'Painter Man'.

him, Jansch's debut was a subtle and sometimes brutal realignment of what folk had then come to represent, with tracks such as 'Needle Of Death', 'Strolling Down The Highway' and 'Running From Home' confirming both the modernity of his approach and the virtuosity of his playing. "I saw him at a folk club," Jimmy continued, "and it was like seeing a classical guitarist."

Resuming his role of musical detective, Page set about finding others like Bert Jansch. Though few and far between, there were some who could provide similar thrills. Jansch's close friend John Renbourn was one such discovery, with the dazzling intricacies of his 'folk baroque' style again seducing Jimmy's ear. Another supremely gifted acoustic guitarist – and another Bert Jansch connection – was Davey Graham, whose composition 'Angie' Jansch had covered as the closing track on his own memorable debut LP. And it was via Graham that Page very probably came across the traditional Irish folk standard 'She Moved Through The Fair', which he cannily adapted for his own purposes on *Little Games'* stand-out moment, the haunting 'White Summer'.

While there still remains something of a Celtic slant to 'White Summer', Jimmy's use of the alternate folk tuning 'D-A-D-G-A-D' also helped re-position the instrumental somewhere between Marrakech and Mumbai. With said tuning creating a delicious drone effect that allowed the strings to resonate like those of a sitar or oud, the addition of Australian drummer Chris Karan on tabla and (a sadly unidentified) oboe player shadowing '... Summer''s melody line only enhanced the sense of a magic carpet ride across three melting terrains. "It's [in] a modal tuning, a sitar tuning, in fact," Page told writer Steve Rosen in 1977. "[I call it] the C.I.A. tuning – Celtic-Indian-Arabic – because that's what it is." A regular feature of the Yardbirds' live set, where Jimmy would perform the tune on his 1961 Danelectro 3021[52], 'White

---

52 With its simple white and black appearance and inexpensive construction, Page's Danelectro 3021 might have looked ordinary. Indeed, it was actually rumoured to be the sum of two guitars, with the neck taken from one model, the body from another. Yet, it is perhaps the most underappreciated of all his electric axes, covering the majority of his open/modified-tuning work from the mid-sixties onwards.

Summer' was yet more indication of where Page would find himself travelling soon. "'White Summer' was all Jimmy's thing," said McCarty. "It showed his love of the acoustic guitar, and I used to love listening to him playing it. That folk thing, it's a side of his nature that deserves more celebration."

Completed by Keith Relf's own folky think-piece 'Only The Black Rose' – which again featured Jimmy strumming away on an acoustic guitar, though perhaps less forcefully than on the whirlwind sections of '... Summer' – *Little Games* wasn't a bad LP. But it wasn't a great one either. "In the main, I actually enjoyed making *Little Games*," said McCarty. "It was good fun. We wrote some good songs for it and we had a laugh. It's not quite as good as *Roger The Engineer*, sure, but it's not that bad. I don't think Mickie was around much during recording, [because] it was cut on a budget, really. There wasn't that much money around for [anything] too lavish."

Jim McCarty was perhaps kindly understating how ramshackle the making of *Little Games* actually was. No sooner had the Yardbirds arrived at Olympic Studios with Mickie Most on March 5, 1967 to begin work on the album than they were turfed out again, reconvening over a month later at Soho's De Lane Lea complex. Given just three extra days to complete the LP, the band was subjected to a "conveyor belt mentality" by Most that drove the ever-professional Page to distraction. "Bloody fast pace," he later told *NME*'s Nick Kent. "We weren't even allowed to hear overdubs." There were no special rules for guests, either. When the Stone's road manager/occasional pianist Ian Stewart dropped by to provide some tinkling fills for 'Drinking Muddy Water', only seconds after he completed work, Most said 'Next. Next number,' and literally removed the piano stool from under him. So rattled was Jimmy by this display of brutal time management towards his lantern-jawed friend, that he stopped recording and demanded to hear a playback. "It was about creating pockets of resistance wherever we could," Page later told *Mojo*.

At risk of banging a familiar drum, it would be all too easy to lay all of the blame at Mickie Most's feet here. Obviously employed to provide the band with a hit single, his method of working was old school to say the least: Wheel 'em in, get the track on tape, wheel 'em out again. Yet, only a year or so before, Jimmy Page was a willing practitioner in the same dark arts. Twelve months, however, was a lifetime in pop and, as mentioned, things were again changing at lightning speed. By August 1967, the Beatles' *Sgt. Pepper...* would lay the foundations that made the single secondary to the album in terms of artistic and commercial importance, and this time there would be no real way back. Ever watchful, Page knew what was coming, even if Most didn't. "But I didn't go, 'I've got to be in the Yardbirds. I'm going to make a calculating move here,'" he told David Fricke. "I really believed in the conclusions I'd come to. And for me, the way was not going to be bloody hit singles."

Worse, despite everyone's best efforts, there were to be no more hit singles, nor indeed a hit album for the band. When released as a 45 in the States during April 1967, 'Little Games' stumbled to number 51 on the charts before fading into oblivion, the only redeeming feature being its flip side 'Puzzles', which trammelled along like a poppy version of the Byrds before Page sent it flying into space with a typically rocketing solo. "We were doing these singles, but also trying to put a reflection of what we were really doing on the B-sides," Jimmy told Fricke at *Rolling Stone*.

Still trying to stop the rot, another US single – 'Ha Ha Said The Clown' – soon followed. Written by upcoming tunesmith Tony Hazzard and already recorded by Manfred Mann, 'Ha Ha...' was sold to the group by Most with the words, "Just try it and if you don't like it, we won't release it." When they passed, Mickie had a backing track cut by American session players and then stuck a reluctant Keith Relf on top at a later date. Harmless pop, but criminally lacking in any real input from the Yardbirds themselves, 'Ha Ha...' somehow managed to get to number 45 in the States on its release in June 1967. "All those singles sessions that we did with Mickie Most..." said McCarty. "Sadly, he got session musicians in to play parts on some of them and that really went against the whole ethos of the band."

Preceded by two sloppy singles and no great push from their label, the album *Little Games* proved in its own way to be the anti-*Sgt. Pepper's*

Lonely Hearts Club Band. Released on June 1, 1967, the Beatles' new LP had gone straight to number one in the UK, where it would stay for the next 22 weeks. It was a similar story in the USA. Number one again, with 15 weeks at the top of the *Billboard* chart. On the other hand, *Little Games* failed to even secure a release in Great Britain, with the Yardbirds having to make do with a desultory number 80 position in the States when the LP hit record stores in mid-August, a disappointing outcome to say the least. However, a greatest hits package that did escape four months earlier had entered the US Top 30, confirming there was still a market for the Yardbirds where the stars and stripes flew. "I knew America was the place to be," Jimmy later admitted. "[With] the San Francisco scene, ears were alive. They weren't just getting pissed, talking, jumping up and down. It was a listening generation."

So the Yardbirds went back to America, this time under the wing of a new, ambitious and road-hardened tour manager. As experienced in the underhand ways of the music business as he was fearless in the face of adversity, Peter Grant would bring big and lasting changes not only to the Yardbirds' business dealings but to the rock industry as a whole – and in him Jimmy Page found the perfect ally to turn his musical vision into a pirate's treasure.

CHAPTER 12

Dazed And Confused

The behind-the-scenes shuffle that led to the appointment of Peter Grant as manager of the Yardbirds actually happened back in late November 1966, when the music press was informed that Jeff Beck had officially left the group and Jimmy Page would be taking over as sole lead guitarist. In a decision that would have profound ramifications for all concerned, Simon Napier-Bell chose to back Beck. "The band were looking at the possibility of going in a much more commercial direction," he confirmed in 2011, "so I took them to Mickie Most and said, 'Do you want to take them on?" He said, 'OK'. But then Mickie's associate Peter – who he shared an office with – said 'I'll manage them.' I said, 'Fine. You have the Yardbirds and I'll have Jeff." Watching it all unfold from the sidelines was Jim McCarty. "Well, we just saw less and less of Simon for some reason," he laughed. "At that time, there seemed to be a lot going on, and we didn't really know the whole truth of what was going on with him. Anyway, one day we had a meeting and Simon brings along Peter Grant. He then says, 'Peter and I are going to share your management'. OK. [But] after that, we didn't see Simon anymore! [Within days] Peter called us up to he and Mickie's office in Oxford Street and said, 'Simon's no longer your manager. I'm your manager now'. That was that."

There were other reasons for Napier-Bell's swift departure, some of them possibly to do with his worsening relationship with Jimmy Page. "Well, I thought I'd made the right choice [going with Jeff], certainly at that time," he said. "[Also], I found Jimmy very narky and difficult."

Obviously, Page saw things from a somewhat different perspective. "Troublemaker? Bloody right," he told Simon Godwin in 2003. "We did four weeks with the Rolling Stones and then an American tour and all we got was £112 each!" Whatever the truth of it, Napier-Bell was glad to go. "Jimmy thought I was an inexperienced manager, and that he knew more than I did. Well, he was probably right!" As Simon Napier-Bell braced himself for the Herculean task of turning Jeff Beck's musical career around, Peter Grant eased slowly but surely into the Yardbirds' managerial hot seat.

There was no missing Grant, even in the most crowded of rooms. Standing well over six feet tall and weighing in at impressive 122 kilos, he was a formidable sight to behold. Born on April 5, 1935, Peter was raised by his mother Dorothy (a secretary) in South Norwood and Battersea before World War II saw him evacuated alongside thousands of other children to escape the Blitz. Escaping inner London for the Surrey countryside, Grant made Godalming his temporary home until he returned to the city when the bombs stopped dropping. "Peter never talked much about his childhood," Mickie Most later revealed to writer Chris Welch. "He was illegitimate, which he didn't deny. He just didn't want to discuss it."

Leaving school aged just 13, Grant could never be described as workshy. His first job was at a sheet metal factory. Then he became a courier for the news agency Reuters but soon jacked that in to work as a stage hand at Croydon Theatre. From there it was two years of national service in the Royal Army Ordnance Corps where he rose to the rank of corporal and put his theatrical experience to good use as a stage manager for shows put on by the NAAFI, the service organisation that provided entertainment for the troops. He'd evidently been bitten by the show-biz bug for after hanging up his uniform, a vacancy as an entertainment manager took him to a hotel in Jersey, while yet another opportunity saw him back in London and working as a bouncer/

doorman at Soho's 2is coffee bar. It was fortuitous timing, enabling Peter to observe Larry Parnes, Cliff Richard, Adam Faith and Tommy Steele writing the rulebook for the British rock'n'roll boom of the late fifties. It was also at the 2is that Grant befriended singing waiter Mickie Most, the beginning of a very rewarding friendship.

When 2is manager Paul Lincoln took an interest in Grant, Peter's career trajectory changed again. A part-time wrestler as well as full-time coffee bar overseer, Lincoln's suggestion that Grant join him for a few rounds eventually led to Peter fighting under his own steam, using the name tags 'The Masked Marauder', 'Count Massimo' and the wonderfully grand 'His Highness Count Bruno Alassio of Milan' to further intimidate anyone stupid enough to get in the ring with him. Showing a flare for the theatrical, it was off to the movies next, with Peter taking bit-parts as an actor, body double (to rotund thespian Robert Morley) and stuntman in various British films. Saving money from these occasional roles and skirmishes to fund his own show-biz transport firm, it was in this world that Grant finally began to settle.

At the start, Peter was content to chauffeur the stars around, with groups like the Shadows enjoying the comforts of his carriage, but when promoter/impresario Don Arden offered Grant the chance to join his organisation as a road manager, he sensibly snapped it up. Soon Peter was ensuring the likes of Gene Vincent, the Everly Brothers and Bo Diddley got to gigs "bang on time" every time they toured the UK. One tale even had Grant wrapping a temperamental Little Richard in a hotel rug, before throwing him in the back of a car and driving the helpless singer to London's Lyceum for a concert appearance. Now, of course, Grant would have been sacked for his actions. But these were different days, and given Peter's boss was Don Arden – whose reputation for tough tactics was already well-established – Grant was probably given a silver star for his decisiveness. The Nashville Teens' John Hawken, who was also managed by Arden during his band's heyday, confirmed just how fearsome Don could be.

"We were owed a lot of money [by Don]," said Hawken. "We'd often work seven nights a week, but the only time we'd put money in our pockets would be... cash at the gig. That was split six ways there and then, but the rest of the money went back to Don. So, after a while, we asked for it. Well, we agreed with Don there'd be a cheque for £120 waiting for me [at his office]. So, our roadie and I... went in and sat at reception. And we waited. And waited. And waited for over two hours. He obviously didn't want to see us. Then finally, his secretary said, 'You can go in now, John'. Don was sitting at his desk, he didn't say anything, but slid this check across the table. I picked it up, and it was [made out] for £20, not £120. I said 'What's...' Well, I never finished the sentence.

"By the time the first word was out of my mouth, Don was out of his chair and holding me up against a wall. He was almost foaming at the mouth. He said, 'John, I've got the strength of 10 men in me right now.' And I was thinking, 'Well, of course you have, you're nuts!' He then started moving us both towards the window, a big paned thing, and worse, it was open. He put me in over the lower bar and I'm looking down backwards at Carnaby Street spinning around below me. He said, 'You're going down, John, you're going down...' I really thought he was going to do it. But then he relaxed his hands and brought me back into the room. Well, I picked up the £20 cheque, and thought, 'Well, I suppose it's better than nothing.'" After a visit to a local police station failed to yield any great results, Hawken let the matter slide. "God. You know, I hate to speak ill of the dead. But in this case I'll make an exception..."[53]

With the wrestling, the bouncing and the tutelage of Don Arden, Peter Grant had no doubt picked up a pointer or two on how to take care of business and handle sticky situations. But as time would tell, while Don Arden was sometimes just fierce Grant was fiercely protective, often treating those in his charge like his children. Loyal as a Labrador and equipped with a brain for deal-making so large it blocked light from the sun, when Grant offered to act as the Yardbirds' manager, the group was assuredly in very safe hands. "Yes," confirmed Jim McCarty. "Peter was down to earth, very straightforward and really tried to look

---

53 A fearsome man, but also a sometimes brilliant manager who oversaw the careers of Small Faces, Black Sabbath and ELO, Arden died in 2007.

after the band rather than get as much out of us as he could. He was so loyal and definitely on our side." John Hawken concurred. "I knew Peter quite well when he was working with Don Arden. He sort of co-managed the Nashville Teens on the way. I found him a terrific guy, straight up, reliable, not a bad word to say about Peter, actually. He was incredibly loyal, knew the business side of things so well, and being an ex-wrestler, could handle himself too. In my book, Peter Grant was the ideal manager."

From the off, Page liked Grant and Peter liked Jimmy. Some have even likened them to "two peas in a pod". In truth, theirs was an odd combination. Page was slight, handsome, charming, polite and resolutely middle-class. Conversely, Grant was physically intimidating, bluntly spoken, familiar with the harsher realities of show business and had worked his way up from relative poverty. But the two saw something in each other that acted like an odd mirror. "Jimmy and Peter really hit it off right away," said Jim McCarty. "They were both 'into' and 'of' the business. And of course, Jimmy and Peter were very keen to carry on with band." Unlike Mickie Most, Grant also knew where the future was headed. "When I started managing the Yardbirds," he told music critic Ian Fortnum, "they weren't getting the hit singles, but [they] were on the college circuit and underground scene in America. Instead of trying to get played on Top 40 radio, I realised that there was another, emerging market. The scene," Peter concluded, "was changing."

It certainly was. As the Yardbirds readied themselves for another trip to the States during 1967's long 'Summer of Love', the genie was well and truly out of the bottle as the psychedelic movement and rock music at last joined hands in public. With debut LPs and sophomore efforts surfacing from the likes of the Grateful Dead, Jefferson Airplane and Janis Joplin, the West Coast hippie ethos was now well represented in the album charts, while elsewhere, the Doors and New York's Velvet Underground (to whom we shall return in due course) were making darker, perhaps more socially realistic noises in the background. However, the icing on the cake – for fans of guitar, at least – was the return of Eric Clapton and the arrival of Jimi Hendrix.

When Clapton walked out of the Yardbirds after cutting a few sniffy riffs on 'For Your Love' in early 1965, it brought something of an existential crisis upon him. "Through the Yardbirds, I [started] to feel very lost and very alone," he told *Guitar Player*'s Dan Forte in 1985. "I was being made to feel I was a freak, and I started wondering whether I was a freak. They all wanted the simple things of success and the [record] charts, and what was wrong with that? [I felt like] 'What's the matter with you? Why don't you want this?'" The solution proved simple. Eric followed his heart and stuck with the music he loved. Joining up with John Mayall's Bluesbreakers in April of the same year, the resulting LP – *Blues Breakers: John Mayall with Eric Clapton*, or, as it came to be known, 'The Beano Album' – was a true revelation. By combining a 1960 Les Paul Standard with a Marshall combo, Clapton created the 'Woman Tone', a creamy, warm and sustaining sound that would soon become synonymous with the phrase 'rock guitar'. Otis Rush and Willie Dixon's 'All Your Love', Freddie King's 'Hideaway' and Robert Johnson's 'Ramblin' On My Mind' were all electrifying covers of material written by some of blues' finest icons, and all bearing the smooth/sour trademark of Eric's 'Woman Tone'. Within weeks of the LP's release in July 1966, some clever wag spray-painted 'Clapton is God' on the wall of Islington Underground station and his life as a 'living legend' began. For one music fan who witnessed an early Bluesbreakers gig in Newcastle, Clapton was, if not quite 'God', then certainly one of his archangels. "He started playing," said Jim Taggart, "and we were just helpless…"

With remarkable timing, Jimmy Page bumped into Eric Clapton soon after musicians, critics and punters began discussing the exact nature of his divinity. Having turned down the Yardbirds' first offer to join the band because of their friendship – "I liked Eric quite a bit and didn't want him to think I'd done something behind his back" – Page was obviously in Clapton's good books as the two again bonded at a Bluesbreakers gig in Putney. Unfortunately, an innocent jam afterwards at Jimmy's parents' house had unexpected consequences. "I had a Simon tape recorder that you could DI [direct input] into, so the two guitars went into the machine and I just did these tapes of Eric and myself playing,"

Page later explained to *Guitarist*'s Neville Marten. "It so happened that a short time after that I was asked to produce some tracks for John Mayall's Bluesbreakers. I was working with Immediate... so I did one session [which resulted in] 'I'm Your Witchdoctor', 'Telephone Blues', 'Sitting On Top Of The World' and 'Double Crossing Time'. [Then], I told them about the stuff I'd done with Eric. [Immediate] said that Eric was under contract and that the stuff belonged to them. I played it to them... I was really championing Eric, as you would, and they wanted to put it out. I said, 'You can't do that', but in the end, the other instruments were put on by members of the Stones, and it went out"[54]. Andrew Loog Oldham and Tony Calder had struck again.

Eric Clapton didn't outstay his welcome with John Mayall's Bluesbreakers. Again finding his position confining and, perhaps like Page, sensing the music scene was on the cusp of profound change, Clapton left the band after a year and laid new plans for what was to become the first 'supergroup'. Joining former Graham Bond Organisation drummer Ginger Baker and bassist Jack Bruce, Eric formed the trio Cream, so named because, in practical terms, he, Baker and Bruce were among the finest young musicians in Great Britain. "The so-called cream of the crop," Clapton later laughed. Making their debut at Manchester's Twisted Wheel nightclub on July 29, 1966, success came soon, the band's debut album *Fresh Cream* reaching number six in the UK charts just four months after their formation. Though America would take a little longer to crack, like Page and co., Cream were up for the challenge. Mounting a heavy touring campaign, they were frequent visitors to Uncle Sam's table during 1967. As with

---

54 These instrumental tapes – featuring Page and Clapton on 'Choker', 'Freight Loader', 'Tribute To Elmore', 'Draggin' My Tail' and 'Miles Road' (named for the Page family home in which it was recorded) – were indeed put out by Immediate Records in 1968/1969 as part of a compilation series called *Blues Anytime: An Anthology Of British Blues*. Other musicians featured on the LPs include Mick Jagger and Bill Wyman, as well as Jeff Beck, Fleetwood Mac's Jeremy Spencer, singer Rod Stewart and several other young British blues notables. Re-packaged countless times on various collections over the years, these tapes are, if nothing else, a vaguely interesting artefact of two of rock's more formidable guitarists at play.

the Yardbirds, Cream's penchant for lengthy improvised, instrumental passages and breathtaking individual solo flights made old blues standards like Howlin' Wolf's 'Spoonful', Skip James 'I'm So Glad' and Muddy Waters' 'Rollin' And Tumblin'' sound fresh all over again. But if Cream saw their mission as re-shaping the blues, Jimi Hendrix's plan was to send it into outer space.

Jimmy Page would later remark that Hendrix came "crashing onto the scene like an express train", his rise to international prominence even more immediate than that of Cream, though in reality he had been waiting a while for his chance to shine. Born in Seattle in the Pacific North-West state of Washington on November 27, 1942, Jimi first learned guitar as a teenager by listening to Elvis, Chuck Berry and various R&B and rock'n'roll songs on the radio. By 19, he was a soldier, spending an uncomfortable year with the 101st Airborne Division before he got sick of the army and it got sick of him. Discharged after breaking his ankle in a parachute jump, Hendrix went to work on the notoriously hard Chitlin Circuit, backing the likes of vocalists Jackie Wilson and Sam Cooke in clubs and bars across America's Deep South and West Coast. Growing tired of all the travelling, Jimi relocated to New York, first taking up arms with Little Richard, then the Isley Brothers, before briefly fronting his own band Jimmy James & the Blue Flames. When bookings proved few, he aligned himself with soul singer Curtis Knight, and it was in this incarnation that Hendrix was spotted by Rolling Stone Keith Richards' then paramour Linda Keith at Manhattan's Cheetah Club. "He just... mesmerised me."

Linda mentioned her find to Animals' bass player Chas Chandler who, having grown disenchanted with playing in a band, was now looking to break into management. Chandler went to see what all the fuss was about and came away sufficiently impressed to offer the 23-year-old guitarist a production and management deal alongside ex-Animals manager Mike Jeffrey. By September 23, 1966 Jimi was in London. Two weeks later, he had a backing band comprising drummer Mitch Mitchell and bassist Noel Redding. Just three months after that, the Jimi Hendrix Experience was number six in the UK charts with 'Hey Joe'. "Hey, we did things fast back then," Keith Richards once said while laughing, though he really wasn't joking.

Eric Clapton knew precisely how good Jimi Hendrix was at playing guitar. In fact, one of the first things Jimi did when he got to London was to sit in with Cream for an informal jam on Howlin' Wolf's 'Killing Floor'. "He absolutely terrified me," Eric later said. By May 1967 terror had been replaced by wonder, as Hendrix's live shows and debut LP *Are You Experienced* illustrated the sheer depth of the guitarist's abilities. Whether creating choppy rhythms, lush bedding chords, angelic melody lines or screaming leads, Jimi Hendrix was unsurpassable. For Roger Mayer, soon to become as valuable at creating sound effects for Hendrix as he had been when building a fuzz box for Jimmy Page, there was no greater player. "Not only was Jimi a great guitarist, he was also an extraordinary showman and singer. Maybe that combination was a bit strong for some. But Jimi was a courteous guy, very giving to other players. He didn't want 'being Jimi Hendrix' to get in the way. For him and me [when building his effects], it was all about imagining new sounds and capturing the emotion. Jimi's was a very free form artistic approach. He really just wanted to play."[55]

With Hendrix having literally set light to the Monterey Festival in California in June and Cream also targeting American concert halls with some force, the Yardbirds had stiff competition on the road in America during the summer of 1967. But it seemed to get the band's creative juices flowing nicely as they took their live shows to even more experimental heights. Forgoing recent singles to instead concentrate on extended meditations of older hits and blues covers, their live shows were now an intriguing and sometimes disturbing night's entertainment. By using tapes of horns recorded while on the Staten Island Ferry, old speeches made by Adolf Hitler and various

---

55 Unlike Eric Clapton or Jeff Beck (who famously said "Right, I'll become a postman," after witnessing Hendrix live), Jimmy Page never got the opportunity to meet or jam with Jimi Hendrix because of his touring commitments with the Yardbirds and elsewhere. However, their paths did cross once at New York's Salvation Club. Keen to introduce himself, but seeing that Jimi was a bit 'under the weather', Jimmy "left it" for another time. Regrettably, with Hendrix passing away on September 18, 1970, said time never came.

other found sounds, the band were testing not only themselves, but the audience too. "Yes," said Page. "[It was] arts lab stuff, really. Quite avant garde..."

There was also new material to be found among all of the madness. One such addition to the band's set was a faithful cover of Velvet Underground's now iconic ode to drug-dealers, 'I'm Waiting For The Man'. "Actually, I'd heard [the Velvets'] first album when I was touring the States with the Yardbirds," Page told *The Quietus* in 2014. "It's an incredible album, it really is, [and] it still sounds marvellous. We used to cover 'I'm Waiting For My Man' a lot. We used to drop it into the middle of [our own] 'I'm A Man'. In fact, I'm pretty certain we were the first people to cover the Velvet Underground." The association didn't end there. When Jimmy met the Velvet's patron Andy Warhol at a party in New York, the artist/filmmaker asked Page to do a screen test for him. Indeed, Warhol – who used to travel regularly with Velvet Underground when they toured – might well have been present when the group supported the Yardbirds on several dates in the winter of 1966, including one particular gig at Michigan State Fairgrounds. "I remember Jimmy walking out onstage with his violin bow," Velvets viola player John Cale later recalled. "I thought 'Fuck. He's really stolen a march on me.'"

Another new tune that took on far greater significance, not only for the Yardbirds but for all Jimmy Page's future endeavours, was 'Dazed And Confused'. "By then, the change in style was down to a combination of things," Jim McCarty said by way of explanation. "Part of it was getting a bit bored with playing our songs in a particular way, and also not writing as many new songs, so we sought out other things. 'Dazed And Confused' was one in particular."

According to McCarty, the Yardbirds first came upon 'Dazed...' when they appeared alongside folk singer/guitarist Jake Holmes at New York's Village Theater on August 25, 1967. "Yes, 'Dazed...' came from Jake Holmes, who we'd played with in New York," McCarty continued. "He was playing a folky kind of act, which was still a bit unusual at that time. Again, we were a bit short of [new] material, and I heard this descending riff Jake was playing, and thought, 'Ah, that sounds good, exciting, mysterious'. So I went and bought his album, we learnt the song and did our version of it."[56]

Knowing a good tune when they heard one, but also wanting to make it their own, the Yardbirds substantially reworked Holmes' original composition, with Relf writing new lyrics, Page performing major guitar surgery throughout, and the whole band helping modify its arrangement. The end result was a doom-laden, brooding tune that had Relf sounding haunted and unsure while Jimmy plagued him further with a procession of demonic wails courtesy of his Fender 'Dragon' Telecaster and violin bow. "Give me a clue as to where I am at," sang the troubled Keith. "I feel like a mouse and you act like a cat..." By the time 'Dazed...' hit its middle-section, the Yardbirds hit their stride, with McCarty providing icy snare-drum blasts, Dreja long, sustained bass notes and Page a torrent of solo guitar, his notes cutting like shards of glass. "Jimmy's strength," reasoned Chris Dreja, "was off-the-wall chording, riffs and abrasive solos... riffs and constructions, the whole attitude."[57]

The atmospheric and ominous qualities of 'Dazed And Confused' were also well suited to the types of venue in which the Yardbirds now found themselves appearing. Having left the likes of the Crawdaddy and Oxford Ball far, far behind, they had recently come face to face with the best, brightest and weirdest that America's East and West Coast had to offer. From New York's Village Theater and Rocky Point Park in Rhode Island to the Santa Rosa Fairgrounds and Algonquin's New Place, the Yardbirds had turned left, right and sometimes stood in between in pursuit of their audience. However, it was at San Francisco's Fillmore West where they met with America's true counter-

---

56 In another version of the story, Jimmy Page actually bought the LP – *"The Above Ground Sound" Of Jake Holmes* – on the same day as Jim McCarty.

57 Though 'Dazed And Confused' became a highlight of their shows, the Yardbirds never actually recorded the song in the studio. However, two in-concert versions did make it onto vinyl and CD: one, entitled 'I'm Confused' (and featuring no writer's credit on the sleeve) appeared on 1971's *Live Yardbirds* (more of that later), while another take can be found on 2000's live collection *Cumular Limit*. As time would tell, neither Jimmy Page nor Jake Holmes were done with the song quite yet.

culture. Originally called the Carousel, when it had hosted concerts by predominantly blues and R&B acts from the Chitlin Circuit, a recent change of hands saw the newly named hall falling into the collective ownership of the Grateful Dead, Jefferson Airplane and Quicksilver Messenger Service before upcoming promoter Bill Graham took it over for his own purposes. Throughout 1967 and 1968, the Yardbirds would visit often, with Jimmy Page particularly enjoying his stays. "We were playing places like the Fillmore," Chris Dreja told *Uncut* in 2009, "and there was some very strange stuff going on there. Jimmy slipped into it a bit. That was the seed of... [what] came later. He liked strange liaisons with strange women. Jimmy," concluded Dreja, "was different. He was like an Oscar Wilde character. Not quite Dorian Gray, but..."

As Page began to build a reputation that journalists, fans and other interested parties would mull over at their leisure in subsequent decades, Peter Grant kept an eye on the money. Unlike other show-biz managers who were content to oversee their charges from the comfort of their offices and living rooms, Grant was more hands-on than an enthusiastic masseuse. Travelling as often as not with the band, he was fastidious when it came to pre- and post-concert arrangements, and always ensured all costs were closely monitored. Dealing directly with promoters like Bill Graham, he always noted the numbers present, never left a gig without the night's fee, and then made sure the band received their share as soon as the money was counted. He was also extraordinarily protective of those in his care. When, for instance, Page's stage gear – Confederate cap coupled with jodhpurs, boots and various ironic badges – threatened to see him undone by unwelcoming locals, Grant was there to see them off in turn. "Peter took care of us," said McCarty, "Well, somebody had to!"

Unfortunately, while the Yardbirds were doing well in the concert halls and by their manager, their singles still weren't selling. In October 1967, another 45 entitled 'Ten Little Indians' was released in the USA to prove the point. Possibly the nadir of the band's recorded career, '... Indians' was written by American singer Harry Nilsson for his second album *Pandemonium Shadow Show*. Always a novel tunesmith, Nilsson had imbued '... Indians' with a nursery rhyme-like lyrical structure loosely based around The Bible's Ten Commandments. Perhaps with a stronger melody, his satirical re-examination of ancient value systems might well have chimed more sympathetically with the then current mood of America and put the Yardbirds back in the Top 20. But as Jimmy Page later confirmed to *Uncut*, "I don't even have to tell you what 'Ten Little Indians' was like. You can just tell by the title." Drilling along on a militaristic drum pattern, frequent brass stabs and key changes occurring every 20 seconds or so, '... Indians' sounded more like a Broadway show tune than a psychedelic classic. Earning a place in heaven for his fiery vocal, Keith Relf gave the song his best shot, and Page's use of feedback at the finale was a nice touch. Yet, even they couldn't save a dud. Produced by Mickie Most, 'Ten Little Indians' limped to number 96 on the US charts before being consigned to the bargain bins. Jim McCarty and Chris Dreja hadn't even bothered to turn up for its recording.

There was one beam of glistening sunlight, however. Though Most had produced the majority of '... Indians' at his usual blistering pace, there had been time enough during takes for Page to try out a very clever idea. "'Ten Little Indians' was an extremely silly song that featured a truly awful brass arrangement," he later told *Guitar World*. "In fact, the whole track sounded terrible. In a desperate attempt to salvage it, I hit on an idea. I said, 'Look, turn the tape over and employ the echo for the brass on a spare track. Then, turn it back over and we'll get the echo preceding the signal.' The result was very interesting – it made the track sound like it was going backwards." No more than a few hours work at the time, the technique was destined to become standard recording practice by the end of the decade, with the Rolling Stones among others quick to copy Page's lead and use the effect – now known as 'reverse' or 'backwards echo'[58] – on their own recordings.

Back on the road, the Yardbirds kept at it. Pushing on through a fifth, then sixth American tour that found them venturing from

---

58 More potential controversy. According to some sources, backwards echo was actually first used by producer Curt Boettcher on Lee Mallory's 1966 single, 'That's The Way It's Gonna Be'. The song reached number 86 on the US charts.

Nantucket to Orlando before sliding back up to New York for another brace of engagements at New York's Village Theater in November 1967, the band's schedule was relentless as ever, though their general appearance had started to fundamentally change. There were now moustaches and beards among the ranks, with Relf and McCarty resembling riverboat gamblers and mountain men instead of the shiny pop stars who had promoted 'For Your Love' two years before. Page, too, was slowly transforming himself. The hair was longer, the jackets wilder, the shirts more ruffled. By early 1968, he looked for all the world like a wayward Regency prince, a mop of black Irish hair permanently covering one eye or the other. It was a far cry from the teenager in his jacket and skinny tie smiling into the camera alongside Carter-Lewis & the Southerners in 1963. "Ah," said Carter, "but [by then], Jimmy was growing into something else, something that would get much bigger..."

There would be one more crack at the US singles chart before it all went pear-shaped. Released in March 1968, 'Goodnight Sweet Josephine' was inoffensive enough, its big chorus and rousing beat ticking the usual pop boxes. But again, the tune wasn't a patch on previous glories such as 'Shapes Of Things' or 'Still I'm Sad', and consequently became another flop for the band. Failing to chart in the States at all, 'Goodnight...' slipped into history without so much as a kiss or a dance. Again, Chris Dreja and Jim McCarty were not present at its recording, with session musicians taking their place.

Chris and Jim were very much present when it came to cutting an impressive B-side for 'Goodnight...'. Recorded at Soho's De Lane Lea Studios, 'Think About It' captured the band as hardened road warriors, its bump and grind much more in keeping with their wild sets at San Francisco's Fillmore theatre and Detroit's Grande Ballroom than the fey pop of 'Ha Ha Said The Clown'. Dark and cantankerous with a sluggish, dragging beat and typically oblique lyrics – "Circles of life an infinite plane, that which is now will be again, who can decide who is insane?" – 'Think About It' also benefited from a sharp central riff and flying solo courtesy of Page. "Yeah, 'Think About It' is a good song, isn't it?" said McCarty. "Bit of a showcase for Jimmy that one, and quite a lively tune too."[59] In fact, so good was Jimmy's bad-tempered solo interjection, he decided to bank the bones of it for use again in the coming months.

Unfortunately, 'Think About It' would not see much more action with the Yardbirds. Having spent nearly five years living their lives at top speed, both Jim McCarty and Keith Relf were dreaming of a different, more comfortable reality, and by April 1968 they were determined to do something about it. "We were very tired, worn out by the stress of it all," said Jim. "We'd been carrying ourselves on that merry-go-round for years. Also, the chemistry wasn't quite right in the band. Keith and I used to share a hotel room on tour and we kept talking about doing something else... band ideas, song ideas. I think we just wanted to do something very, very different."

Though Page was no doubt aware of minor dissatisfactions within the band, Relf and McCarty's decision to walk away still came as a profound shock when he heard the news on tour in Los Angeles. "They just didn't want to be in the Yardbirds anymore," he later told *Mojo* editor Phil Alexander. "That was hard to understand because I thought what we were doing was amazing. I told them I'd do whatever they wanted. They loved that song 'Happy Together' by the Turtles, and told me that was the direction they wanted to go in. My jaw dropped." Despite Page's best efforts at compromise, Keith and Jim were resolute. "Well, no, Jimmy didn't want to stop," said McCarty. "But Keith and I... we'd had enough. It was time for something new."

Though rocked by their decision, Jimmy was also mindful of the events of the previous day when he had visited a palm reader on Sunset Boulevard. The reader's predictions for him were interesting. "The key phrase [I was told] was, 'You're going to make a decision in a very short

---

59 Now something of a cult tune, 'Think About It' was covered with considerable vigour by Aerosmith on their 1979 album *Night In The Ruts*. Revving up the original's pace and once again featuring a world-class solo, this time from lead guitarist Joe Perry, Jim McCarty was quite impressed by the Boston band's efforts at emulating the Yardbirds' bad-tempered original. "Oh yeah," he laughed. "Aerosmith's cover of 'Think About It' is pretty good. Now, that version is lively!"

period of time that's going to change your life.'" While there are those who may not share Page's belief in precognition, there was little doubt that on this occasion, the palm reader would be proved right.

The end was not immediate. A string of US concert dates, including three nights at the Fillmore West and one plum show at LA's Shrine Exposition Hall, had already been booked in advance and the band were obligated to appear. The Yardbirds duly trekked on in the States until early June before returning to the UK for one last rave-up on July 7, in the unlikely setting of Luton Technical College. "To be honest, the band ending was a relief for me," said McCarty. "The last tour was actually quite enjoyable I suppose because I knew it was going to be the last tour! There was no animosity among us. We all got on. But remember, Jimmy wanted to carry on. He was still [relatively] new to it all and was still energised."

For a time, it looked as if Chris Dreja was also reluctant to let the band go. "Jimmy and Chris got on very well on an intellectual level," ex-manager Simon Napier-Bell later said. "[Together], they were great planners." Initially keen to forge ahead with replacements for Relf and McCarty, various names were bandied around between Page and Dreja. One such was session drummer Clem Cattini, a superb technician and "all round good egg" who had played on the band's last few singles when Jim McCarty was found to be unavailable.

As things progressed, however, Chris began to doubt the wisdom of carrying on. After several meetings with Jimmy and Peter Grant, a swift trip to McCarty's house to see what he and Keith might be up to and a brief flirtation with the idea of pulling together a country rock group, Dreja instead decided to pursue a more left field choice of career. Always a keen amateur photographer[60], the bassist now made his

---

60 For an early example of Dreja's photographic talent, one need look no further than a striking, psychedelically tinged image he took of Jimmy Page that was used to promote the Yardbirds' appearances at Detroit's Grande Ballroom on May 3 & 4, 1968. The picture can be found in Page's own photographic autobiography – *Jimmy Page By Jimmy Page* – published by Genesis in 2010 and 2014, and mentioned later in this book.

interest professional. "It was suggested to me while at art school, 'Dreja, you're doing fine art, perhaps you'd be better off doing photography'," he said in 2010. "So I gravitated towards the camera, and it eventually became as kind to me as music had been." This, again, was typical Dreja understatement. Within months of leaving the Yardbirds, Chris was well on his way to becoming a highly respected photographer, his images as deft and imaginative as his bass and rhythm guitar fills.

For Keith Relf and Jim McCarty, the way forward remained musical. Increasingly drawn to the gentler textures of folk and classical, the duo swiftly formed Together and released one single ('Henry's Coming Home') on Columbia records in late 1968. When it wasn't a hit, they set about rethinking their strategy. As before, a band seemed to be the best way to go. They called it Renaissance. "Yes, Renaissance came out of Keith and I," said Jim. "We had these song ideas that were all a bit soft and gentle, and we'd [already] done some recordings of them at Abbey Road Studios. Anyway, to cut a long story short, we began working with Paul Samwell-Smith again as our producer, got in a manager and basically the best thing to do at that point was form another band to present that material. We didn't really know what was going to happen, but, you know, we were going to give it a go." Helping them along the way was now former Nashville Teen keyboardist John Hawken. "I got a phone call from Keith, saying that he and Jim were putting together a band with a 'classical thing' and would I like to audition? It was at Keith's sister's place... Jane's house in Thames Ditton, about four or five miles from where I was living in Weybridge, so no problems. I said, 'Sure, I'd be happy to', and off I went. There I found Keith, Jim, bassist Louis Cerrano, Jane and BJ Cole. In the corner was an upright piano. So, I just got stuck in."

While steel guitar player BJ Cole didn't quite work out – "BJ was a truly stunning player, but not quite what Jim and Keith were looking for" – everything else about the band felt right. There was even a place at the table for Jane Relf. "Well, Jane was always at rehearsals or thereabouts, and one day Keith just said, 'Why don't you try singing this one,'" Hawken continued. "It was a track called 'Island'. The next day, she's being fitted for stage wear. No previous experience, Jane, but it didn't matter. Her voice was beautiful." A supremely underrated outfit,

Renaissance would eventually cut two albums with McCarty and Relf at the helm for Chris Blackwell's then recently formed Island Records before it was all change again.[61] "We made some lovely music, and the musicianship itself was great [on those two LPs]," Hawken concluded. "Jim was, is, such a terrific drummer and a fine man... so very underrated. And Keith. Well, one of Keith's lungs was working way below capacity, so to do what he did was a miracle in itself. He and Jim were really creative writers and Keith's harmonica playing was absolutely brilliant. Another master of 'less is more'. The way he'd bend those notes... just magic. I look back on Renaissance with a lot of affection. Everyone was stretching out, trying different things. Sometimes it worked, sometimes it didn't, but it was always fun trying."[62]

At around the point McCarty, Relf and Dreja were making up their minds as to what to do next, Jimmy Page was cutting the odd session. Returning to his old day job in an effort to exercise his fingers and earn some extra cash while making simultaneous plans for the future, during 1968, Page contributed chords and leads to the work of female soul act the Staples Singers, Mike Heron of the Incredible String Band and folk troubadour Al Stewart's debut LP, *Love Chronicles*. Somehow, he had also found time while still on the road with his now defunct band to add some beautiful acoustic layers to *The Maureeny Wishful Album*[63], a

---

61 A separate book would be required to track Renaissance's various line-ups, album releases and live shows. Suffice to say, Keith Relf and Jim McCarty's major contributions to Renaissance occurred between 1969 and 1971 on the band's self-titled LP and follow-up *Illusion*. After that, they both took a backseat role, with McCarty occasionally writing songs for use by later line-ups of the band.

62 Another thoroughly 'good egg', John Hawken went on to play with several fine groups after leaving Renaissance in 1970, including Illusion, proto-punk trio Third World War and, most notably, the Strawbs.

63 An album Page is justly proud of, 1968's *The Maureeny Wishful Album* actually featured Jimmy on sitar (an instrument we will return to in due course) as well as acoustic guitar. Page's old mate Big Jim Sullivan and sixties guitar legend Vic 'James Bond Theme' Flick were also said to have made contributions. By all accounts, only 300 copies of the LP were ever made, making ...*Maureeny* one of the rarest items of Page ephemera. Thankfully, while the physical album may be almost impossible to find, it can be heard easily enough via the internet.

dreamy, wistful LP cut under the leadership of John Williams, whose long-standing connection to Page came about through session work.

Another, more strident application of Page's talents came in mid-1968 with Joe Cocker's superlative cover of the Beatles' 'With A Little Help From My Friends'. A grand singer comfortable with any musical style, Jimmy had known Cocker for years, having appeared on his 1964 debut single 'I'll Cry Instead' (again written by John Lennon and Paul McCartney). Since then, Joe's career had spluttered along in fits and starts before finally getting back on track with this single. Featuring a titanic gravel-throated vocal, 'With A Little Help From My Friends' also found Jimmy at the height of his powers, contributing a quite superb guitar part, soulful yet steeped in melodrama, that further magnified the song's inherent power. Reaching number one in the UK singles chart on its release in September 1968, Page contributed to five more cuts on Cocker's concurrent album, prompting Joe to enquire whether he and Jimmy might like to join forces. "I asked Jimmy if he'd join us in 1968," Cocker later told *Classic Rock*, "but he said, 'You know Joe, I've got something a little heavier to do...'"

Though Page could continue to distract himself with sessions until doomsday, he also knew they were small beer in comparison to the blood and thunder he had experienced on the American road. Having seen Cream, Jimi Hendrix and more recently another old friend from the Yardbirds (whom, again, we shall return to soon) make spectacular progress in the States, he was keen to rejoin the party. "[When] the Yardbirds said they didn't want to continue, I was disappointed," he later told *Rolling Stone*. "What we had going I was willing to do with them, whatever it was. I can understand how disillusioned they were, but I could also see the trajectory. FM radio was happening. I knew what that meant to underground bands. I wanted an underground band, but one that would come through and make a real difference."

What Jimmy Page now wanted was a band that combined light and shade with mystery and power, a band that sounded like a giant guitar army one second and a willowing stream the next. Lofty ambitions all, but he had already heard precedents of it: Savoy Brown's 'I Tried', Ten Years After's treatment of Howlin' Wolf's 'Spoonful' and Taste's debut single 'Born On The Wrong Side Of Time'. Iron Butterfly and Blue Cheer represented one side of this equation, Bert Jansch and Davey Graham the other. Even Texan blues maestro Johnny Winter might have captured something of the sound inside Jimmy's head. All had elements of the blues, folk or pyschedelia. All were 'heavy' in their own way. But after nine years in the game, from Neil Christian & the Crusaders to the last gasp of the Yardbirds, and with hundreds of session dates in between, Jimmy Page felt he could do it better than anyone. And by the summer of 1968 he thought he knew how.

"I said to Jimmy, 'What are you going to do?'" Peter Grant later recalled. "'Keep it together? Get some more Yardbirds together? I mean, what are you really going to do?' Then Jimmy said, 'Well, I've got this idea for a band...'"

PART 2

DANCING DAYS

"I gave everything I had. I wasn't holding back. Everything I had I put into Led Zeppelin. Rightly or wrongly, that's how it was."

Jimmy Page

CHAPTER 13

Babe, I'm Gonna Leave You

When Jimmy Page told Peter Grant he wanted to form a new group, it was no idle thought or undeveloped idea on his part. In fact, since joining the Yardbirds in June 1966, Page had long been dwelling on exactly what made the perfect group. He had tried to find it, even make it a solid entity, alongside Keith Relf, Jim McCarty, Chris Dreja and, all too briefly, Jeff Beck. And there had been times when the Yardbirds had almost captured it; the opaque, haunted quality of 'Dazed And Confused', the galloping pace and instrumental theatrics of 'Drinking Muddy Water' and 'Think About It'. These were signs and sigils of something potentially remarkable bubbling beneath the surface of the Yardbirds, but a brace of misfiring singles, divergent musical interests and the crushing tiredness that only five-odd years on the road can bring to brain and bone had ended their run before it was ever properly committed to vinyl.

Jimmy, on the other hand, wasn't tired at all. Last man in, he was still raring to go and, more than ever, he knew what that perfect group might sound like. "I wanted to do the type of work that I managed to expand around the Yardbirds' material," he later told *Guitar World*'s Brad Tolinski. "A lot of riffs of my own... passages and movements. I wanted a marriage of hard rock, blues and acoustic music, topped with heavy choruses." It was an ambitious manifesto to fulfil, requiring musicians of exceptional calibre, broad musical range and fierce creativity. He would also need a vocalist capable of fighting his own corner amid all this magnificent noise, bringing Page's wish for "light and shade" to life while still being able to deliver the heavy choruses so important for ensuring radio play in the States and at home. The focal point of any act, the singer had to be "bloody good" and, if possible, easy on the eye, too. Jimmy thought he had found his man in Terry Reid.

Page had first seen Terry Reid when he fronted Norwich act Peter & the Jaywalkers as a teenager in 1966. "Well, I wanted to get Terry in the band," Jimmy later remembered. "I'd seen him in Ipswich when he was just 16 or so, and was really impressed." Quite right, too. Even at such a tender age, Reid had precisely the qualities Page was after, his voice warm, expressive and clear, his abilities to climb to the scales or dig deep into the blues marking him out as one to watch. "I thought," said Jimmy, "'That's exactly what I'm looking for'." By 1968, Terry Reid had struck out on his own, his first solo single 'Better By Far' a radio favourite if not quite a chart hit, and a tour supporting Cream garnering positive reviews in the USA. To enable his ambitions, however, Reid had recently signed a management deal with Mickie Most, and was unsure about joining another band, even a potentially great one. Consequently, when Page came knocking, Terry played for time. "When Jimmy asked me to be the singer," Reid later said, "I was very impressed. I said 'I'd love to, [but] can you hold that thought?' Jimmy said, 'If you're not in now, you're out'." Reid chose out. But he did recommend another vocalist who might fit the bill. "Terry immediately recommended Robert Plant," said Jimmy. "So off I went to see Obbstweedle..."

Born on August 20, 1948 in West Bromwich, at the heart of England's Black Country, Robert Anthony Plant was named for his father, Robert senior, a civil engineer who had served in the RAF. His mother Annie, a housewife, gave her son an interesting cultural heritage, coming as she did from rare 'Romanichal' stock, a sub-group of the Romani people who in turn had originated from northern India. Moving to nearby Kidderminster as a child, Plant was by all accounts a gifted student but an even better Elvis impersonator, the 10-year-old reportedly finding a sweet spot between the curtains and French windows of his parents' front room where his voice resonated just like the King of Rock'n'Roll himself. "I used to try and be Elvis," he told Nigel Williamson of *Uncut* in 2005. "I didn't know anything about sexuality or innuendo. I just recognised the pleading in that voice... the confidence and assertion." One year later and Robert was in grammar school, but the music kept calling, this time in the form of soul legend Smokey Robinson. "Smokey's voice [on 1960's 'Shop Around'] just destroyed me," he later said. "The whole black experience was there... the Sunday morning prayer meeting, Detroit on fire and Parchman Farm... all those things."

Opened up "like a can" to the purity and wonder of soul, Plant's next discovery was to be even more profound. He fell head over heels for the blues. "There was a fellow called Terry Foster... and he was an incredible eight-string guitarist," he later told *Melody Maker*'s Richard Williams. "Instead of playing it the normal way, he used to play like Big Joe Williams, with it half on his lap. He was a horrible bloke at times, but he was a real white bluesman, and I, when I was 15, immediately fell under his spell. My dad used to drop me off at the Seven Stars Blues Club in Stourbridge and we used to wail on [Muddy Waters'] 'Got My Mojo Working'."

Having now left school to attend art college, Robert fell into the company of fellow blues enthusiasts who met during lunch breaks and after class would swap singles, albums and stories about "The Devil's Music". His appetite insatiable, Plant was soon delving deep into the back catalogues of Peetie Wheatstraw, Gerry Miller, Robert Johnson and Skip James, while singing his nights away at the Seven Stars. "John Lee, Memphis Slim, Jimmy Reed, I was always chasing that blue note."

There were sacrifices to be made. After college, Robert worked in a succession of jobs to feed his nocturnal blues habit. A blink and you'll miss it appearance at a chartered accountants was followed by a slightly longer spell laying tarmac for Wimpey before he left the motorways behind to work at his local Woolworths. All the while Plant kept singing, his luck in the music business as patchy as his employment history.

There were groups – the Crawling King Snakes and Band Of Joy being two early examples we shall return to in due course – and a short-lived singles deal with CBS records that saw three 45s released in his name, though with no success to speak of. But it was when Robert threw in his lot with a pick-up 'hippie-blues-folk' outfit called Obbstweedle that the gods finally smiled on him. While Plant was rehearsing with his new group, Terry Reid told him that Jimmy Page and Peter Grant were interested in hearing him sing. Both flattered and intrigued, Robert invited the duo to travel up from London to a college in Birmingham and see him perform. If first impressions counted, he might well still be there. Arriving at the venue, Grant asked where he might find "Mr. Robert Plant". "Right here," replied the vocalist. "Oh," said a nonplussed Peter. "I thought you were the roadie."

It got better, and quickly. Though Obbstweedle were reportedly a shade underwhelming, with perfunctory or overplayed cover versions of Buffalo Springfield's 'Mr. Soul' and 'Rock'n'Roll Woman', Page's interest piqued exponentially when the band launched into Jefferson Airplane's 'Somebody To Love' and Plant started singing. "I immediately thought there must be something wrong with him personality-wise or that he had to be impossible to work with," Page later recalled to *Trouser Press*, "because I just could not understand why, after he told me he'd been singing for a few years already, he hadn't become a big name yet." Equal parts astounded and bewildered, Jimmy decided to test Plant's mettle closer to home. "I asked him down to my house [in Pangbourne], just to check him out..."

A few days later, Robert took up Jimmy's invitation to visit him in Pangbourne, walking the last mile past elegant houses that bordered the River Thames, the bright blue summer sky reflected in its shimmering surface. The contrast with the noisy, crowded streets of Wolverhampton, with its traffic and multicultural mix of Indian, Pakistani and British families, was profound; this was Middle England at its most charmingly pastoral, the setting for Jerome K. Jerome's *Three Men In A Boat*, an idyll where geese sashayed across the water and garden birds twittered in the trees. This was a land where cows munched in fields and rabbits bustled in hedgerows as the endless river flowed gently past pubs with mock Tudor beams and names like The Swan or The Jolly Angler. Sadly, despite its verdant setting and chocolate box scenery, Pangbourne didn't take well to hippies. Soon after Plant exited the train station, he was scolded by a pensioner about his scruffy appearance. "Desperation scene, man," he later told writer Simon Godwin, "but I had nowhere else to go."

Legend has it that Robert brought with him LPs by Robert Johnson, the Incredible String Band, Howlin' Wolf and Joan Baez, the latter so as to make Jimmy aware of a traditional song he liked called 'Babe I'm Gonna Leave You'. Arriving at the house, his knock was answered by Jimmy's girlfriend. "The door opened and suddenly I saw 'America'," he told Williamson. "There was this beautiful woman clad in a 1920s shawl with the light behind her. She was very charming. Then Jimmy came back from somewhere and I realised that this guy had a lifestyle I could only imagine. He had quietness... a maturity. Then we sat down and talked about music."

The reality was that by the summer of 1968 Jimmy Page was a sophisticated man of the world, while in comparison Robert Plant was a cultural neophyte. Having travelled far and wide with the Yardbirds, Page had even found time for a solo trip to India, then an exotic location for Westerners. In addition, he had developed a taste for fine art and antiques that cluttered up his Pangbourne home. According to *MM*'s Chris Welch, who would visit there to interview Page, the house contained valuable paintings, records, model trains and many books. "A large white telescope has pride of place in the living room," wrote Welch. "Copies of *Man, Myth, and Magic* lay around and a huge volume of the works of mystic Aleister Crowley. In one room was a Mutoscope, a hand-cranked seaside peepshow featuring 'a gentleman's downfall', involving a lissome lass wearing not unsexy 1926 underwear and a healthy smile."

Robert Plant, on the other hand, had travelled not much further than the West Midlands, even if he did resemble a refugee from Haight-Ashbury, San Francisco with his gym pumps and skinny bell-bottomed jeans. Still, there were real possibilities here. He was a tall, handsome young man with bushy blond hair that curled over his ears, and a wide, welcoming smile that lit up his friendly face; all assets in a potential vocalist. But Plant was also well aware that he had some cultural catching up to do with the more seasoned, urbane Page. "You can smell when people have travelled, had their doors opened a little wider than most, and I could feel that was the deal with Jimmy," Plant told Williamson. "His ability to absorb things and the way he carried himself was far more cerebral than anything I'd come across. I was very impressed."

The purpose of the visit, of course, was to share music, establish compatibility within it and, hopefully, establish a friendship, and to this end 'Babe, I'm Gonna Leave You' turned out to be the key link. Jimmy, too, loved the song and had intended playing it to Robert, a symbiotic concurrence that helped Robert pass this audition – if that was what it was – with flying colours. "I'm not sure Robert knew too much about the Yardbirds, but I started playing things like 'Dazed And Confused' and 'Babe, I'm Gonna Leave You',"[64] said Page. "I'm not entirely sure he knew what to make of it all, but he did stick with it..." He was also impressed with Robert's harmonica playing . "A big plus!"

In real terms, the pair bonding over 'Babe, I'm Gonna Leave You' was incredibly important to all future progress. For Jimmy, the song exactly represented all that he wanted to achieve with his new group, its undulating structure providing the opportunity to weave between moments of musical calm and savage bursts of instrumental power ("scream to a sigh and back again," said one critic). Equally, the song gave Robert a chance to demonstrate both his vocal range and gift for inhabiting a lyric – in this case, switching the protagonist's gender to add an extra emotional dimension. Consequently, for a short time at least, 'Babe, I'm Gonna Leave You' became a pivotal moment in the fledgling band's live show, its soft/hard qualities counterbalancing their ability to amp it up, as with new material such as 'Communication Breakdown' and 'How

---

64 In some tellings of the tale, Robert did not arrive at Pangbourne with Joan Baez's 'Babe...' at all, leaving Jimmy to alert the singer to the song. Whatever the case, it remains obvious that Page and Plant's love for the tune was crucial in taking things forward between them.

Many More Times', or dial it down with 'Your Time Is Gonna Come' and 'I Can't Quit You Baby', but all in the space of just one tune.

At last, Page had found his man. Plant was in.

With the recruitment of Robert Plant, Jimmy Page had found a vocalist of something approximating nuclear power. But the unlikely discovery of such enormous talent in the centre of the Black Country didn't end there. On learning that Page was still looking for a suitably gifted drummer to fill that gap in his new group, Robert mentioned that he knew someone who might fit the bill – subject, of course – to the right financial offer. Whether Plant wanted to establish an ally within the ranks of this still hypothetical group or, more realistically, was simply keen to do his friend a favour, remains a matter for him. But by calling John Bonham into the equation, Robert was about to do he and Jimmy a world-class favour.

Born to parents Joan and John Snr. (aka 'Jack') on May 31, 1948 in Redditch, Worcestershire, John Henry Bonham had been obsessed with making percussive noises since early childhood, his habit of bashing away on biscuit tins, pots and pans in the family kitchen already well-established by the age of five. Initially drawn to soul music, though his tastes would later evolve to swing and jazz idols such as Buddy Rich, Max Roach and especially Gene Krupa, John's mother had bought him his first snare drum when he was 10, with a full, albeit second-hand kit arriving (courtesy of his father) five years after that. "Most of it," he later said, "was rust." Though Bonham took occasional advice from fellow percussionists in Redditch, he did not enhance it with formal lessons, preferring instead to learn directly from records or by watching drummers on TV and film.

By age 15, John had transferred his percussive interests from the Bonham home in Redditch to the local clubs, playing in various amateur outfits before stumbling on regular gigs with semi-professional acts such as the Blue Star Trio and Terry Webb & the Spiders. At this point the real juggling began, as Bonham left Lodge Farm Secondary School to work in his father's building firm as a trainee carpenter by day, while sitting behind the drums with Webb and a succession of other groups, including soul/mod hopefuls the Senators[65] and Steve Brett & the Mavericks at night. "When I left school I went into the trade with my Dad," he later told his brother, author Mick Bonham. "He had a business, and I used to like it. But drumming was the only thing I was any good at, and I stuck at that for three or four years. If things got bad I could always go back to building."

In small increments and steady steps, John began to establish himself on the professional circuit. Come 1966 and he had joined local heroes Way Of Life, with whom he would stay for some 18 months before throwing his hat into the ring with the gruff-voiced American folk singer Tim Rose. Now with a young wife (Pat) and infant son (Jason), it was imperative that Bonham kept his financial affairs in order. Rose's concert-pulling power – built on the foundations of strong cover material such as 'Hey Joe' and 'Morning Dew' – ensured just that, giving the drummer both a steady income as well as a creative escape route when required. "I swore to Pat that I'd give up drumming when we got married," he said. "But every night I'd come home and just sit down at the drums. I'd be miserable if I didn't."

Robert Plant had known John Bonham for some time before mentioning his name to Jimmy Page, the two having first met when the drummer temporarily joined Plant's blues band, the Crawling King Snakes, in early 1967. "I thought he was a bit too pleased with himself," Robert later confirmed to *Uncut*, "And expensive. He wanted the same ... £8 gig [that] I was getting. I wasn't having any of that!" Nonetheless, singer and drummer eventually bonded, with John linking up with another of Plant's outfits, the happily titled Band Of Joy. Noteworthy

---

65 It was with the Senators that John Bonham recorded his first single, 1964's 'She's A Mod'. Another outfit that John played with at around this time – the Nicky James Movement – included future members of the Move (Roy Wood and Bev Bevan) and the Moody Blues (Mike Pinder). "Nicky was an incredible lead singer," Bonham later told *Melody Maker*, "but we had so much equipment of hire purchase, we'd get stopped (after) a gig and they'd take back all the PA system..." By the eighties, Roy Wood and Bev Bevan had added Wizzard, ELO and Black Sabbath to their own band resumés. Sadly for Nicky James, despite a fine voice and several singles/album releases, he remained a cult artist rather than major star, until his death in 2007.

for the stage-diving antics of bassist Paul Lockey and the occasional lapse of good taste – several musicians covered their faces with make-up as part of the act – the Band Of Joy were still a reasonable draw on the Birmingham concert circuit, their mix of covers (again, 'Hey Joe') and originals (Bonham and Plant's own 'Memory Lane') going over well with the local longhairs. "It was debatable whether [John would] join," Robert remembered, "because it was a long way to go and pick him up. [Also], we didn't know whether we would have the petrol money to get over to Redditch and back! [But it] turned out to be a really good group."

In reality, Page might well have been sceptical about Plant's championing of Bonham. After all, as a session musician, he had played alongside some of the very best in the trade, with Clem Cattini and Aynsley Dunbar just two names Jimmy had dabbled with when thinking about who might make a suitable candidate for his vacant drum seat. Indeed, Page had already spent some time investigating whether Procol Harum's BJ Wilson might be interested in joining his latest enterprise. However, despite the fact he had no real information on Bonham other than Robert's word, Jimmy was willing to at least see him in action. And so it was that he and Peter Grant travelled to a club in north London's affluent Hampstead to watch Bonham perform with Tim Rose. Within seconds, Page was left stupefied.

"I'd been checking out other drummers," he later said, "but that was before I saw Bonzo." A veritable explosion of a man, who could be heard several streets away without benefit of a PA, John dominated his Ludwig kit in a way Jimmy had never seen before. Shoulders hunched, arms extended, but with all the power of his body somehow channelled into his wrists and feet, Bonham was in complete control of every cymbal, snare, tom and bass drum. "Bonzo," Page said without exaggeration, "was superhuman."

In the course of the next few days, Jimmy and Peter Grant pursued John Bonham like a besotted lover. When they discovered the drummer had no phone at home, some 30 telegrams were sent to his local pub – Walsall's Three Men In A Boat – in an effort to woo him into the group. Bonzo, however, remained unsure. At around the same time that Page, Plant and Grant were trying to procure his services, he had also received offers from Chris Farlowe and Joe Cocker to join up with them. Moreover, Farlowe and Cocker both had record deals, whereas Jimmy and co. as yet did not. A young father still fretting about where the next paycheck was coming from, he could not afford to make any mistakes on his own behalf, let alone that of his family. Negotiating hard, Bonham reportedly asked Grant for a good wage rate per gig (in excess of £40 per week, to beat his gig with Tim Rose), an additional retainer's fee and an extra £30 for driving the band's Transit van. Only when most (if not exactly all) of his demands were met did John finally sign on the dotted line. "Well," he later said, laughing, "I decided I liked the music better than Cocker's or Farlowe's..."[66]

As time would tell, Robert Plant and John Bonham were to be remarkable additions to Jimmy Page's cause, both helping complete a giant-sized puzzle the guitarist had been working on since the Yardbirds' dissolution some months before. Nonetheless, neither Plant nor Bonham could claim 'first recruit' status in Jimmy's grand plan. That honour belonged instead to a quietly-spoken, methodical, but again, humungous talent named John Paul Jones.

Born John Baldwin on January 3, 1946 in Sidcup, Kent, Jones came from a musical family, his father, Joe, a pianist and arranger for precisely the type of big bands that dominated British radio during the post-war years. John's mother was also in the business; a teenage interest in song and dance subsequently developed to a professional level. Combining their individual skills, Baldwin's parents formed a musical comedy act, finding regular work on the UK's then thriving vaudeville circuit. So busy in fact was their schedule that John – an only child ("A spoiled brat, actually") – was shipped off to boarding school at Christ's College in Blackheath, south London. It was here that genetic predisposition kicked in and John showed his first real interest in the secrets of the keyboard. "Well," he

---

66 Another possible factor in John Bonham joining up was Jimmy Page's impressive knowledge of drummers. When Bonham asked the guitarist to name the type of sound and percussionist he was after, Page listed the rockabilly wallop of Lonnie Mack's 'On The Move' and James Brown's own sticksman, the redoubtable Earl Palmer, among his examples. Both cut the necessary mustard with Bonzo.

later told BBC Radio 3, "I couldn't rival [my father] as a pianist, so I went and learnt the church organ." By the age of 14, he had learnt so well that Jones was both organist and choirmaster at his local church.

Baldwin's interests in sacred music temporarily dipped in 1961 when he heard the Phil Upchurch Combo's funk-laden 'You Can't Sit Down'. Enraptured by Upchurch's mid-section four-string solo, John immediately approached his father for the money for a bass guitar. Joe Baldwin told him if he wanted to make a living from music, he was better off buying a saxophone. Jones persisted and soon enough he not only had a bass, but was also playing it (and some keyboards) in his father's dance band. Picking up various other gigs with local groups such as the Deltas and the Jett Blacks (featuring jazz supremo and Page's future guitar tutor John McLaughlin), John toured US air force bases, halls and clubs before taking things up a notch or two with Jet Harris and Tony Meehan. Missing Jimmy's uneven performance on 'Diamonds'/ '... Hully Gully' by a cat's whisker, Jones found regular road work with the former Shadows for nearly two years before Meehan suggested he try breaking into sessions in 1964.

For the next four years, John Paul Jones found himself at the very heart of London studio life, working as a bassist and arranger for hire. Forging an early alliance with Decca Records, Jones would also take up arms with Andrew Loog Oldham, becoming his 'musical director' at Immediate when the label launched in 1965. In fact, it was Loog Oldham that originally suggested changing John's name from Baldwin to the much more striking John Paul Jones when the bassist was offered a single deal with Pye a year before they worked together at Immediate. The resulting 45 – 'Baja'/'A Foggy Day In Vietnam' – might not have set the charts afire, but Jones' new appellation stuck[67].

---

67 While conducting business in France, Andrew Loog Oldham had spotted a poster for the 1959 US bio-pic *John Paul Jones*, itself a slight tale doing scant justice to the real Jones' rise from ordinary Scottish sailor to 'Father of the early American Navy' during the 1700s. Oblivious to the film's lack of merit – Andrew just liked the name – he logged it in his memory bank, before later suggesting it as a suitable nom de plume for Baldwin/Jones.

If solo success eluded him, then John Paul Jones could at least console himself with the sheer number of requests for his skills on the session scene. From Nico, PP Arnold and Mike Berry to Twice As Much, Lionel Bart and the Outlaws, his studio diary was as musically diverse as it was full. The workload only increased when he began "directing musical traffic" for producers Mickie Most and Robert Stigwood, with Jones picking up additional arrangement credits for Herman's Hermits, Lulu and Françoise Hardy, among others. Outside of his work with Most, Stigwood and Loog Oldham, he worked as an independent contractor, his roster of artists including Tom Jones, Cat Stevens, Shirley Bassey, Dusty Springfield, Burt Bacharach and countless more, all of whom benefited from his musical touch. "I played on hundreds, thousands of songs," he once said. "Thousands, thousands..."

In the small, darkly lit world of studios, sessions and arranging, it was inevitable that John Paul Jones would come across Jimmy Page. But then, Jones had been aware of the guitarist several years before he even met him. "I can remember people saying 'You've got to go and listen to Neil Christian & the Crusaders,'" he later told Canadian music writer Ritchie Yorke. "'They've got this unbelievable young guitar player.'" While neither man can precisely remember when they first exchanged pleasantries – "Maybe 1964... at Decca Studios, or somewhere like that," said John – the first time was certainly not the last time, as the pair continued to bump into each other on various recording dates throughout the mid- to late sixties. When Donovan, for instance, required both six strings and an orchestral arrangement for 'Sunshine Superman', Jimmy and John Paul were on hand to help. Further, when Page and Mickie Most needed someone to gather their musical thoughts and provide bass for an absent Chris Dreja on the Yardbirds 'Little Games' and 'Ten Little Indians', Jones was again on hand to offer necessary back-up. But it was a notable session that took place at London's IBC Studios on May 16 and 17, 1966 that properly planted the seeds for future collaboration between them.

As we have seen, 1966 was not Jeff Beck's finest year. Habitually ill and permanently exhausted, the guitarist had also started to bemoan his musical lot with the Yardbirds. Increasingly used by the band as explosive fairy dust to be sprinkled on a tune whenever the situation demanded it, Jeff's woes were steadily growing as large as his diseased tonsils. Manager Simon Napier-Bell felt something – "anything, actually" – had to be done, and fast. Eager to keep the peace and ease the tension, he suggested Beck take on a side-project to keep him occupied.[68] "I was causing trouble by being awkward and not turning up because I wasn't happy with what was going on," Jeff told *Guitar*'s Vic Garbarini in 2001. "So Simon said, 'Give Jeff an instrumental cut. You and Jimmy Page go and write the track, or Jeff, you go over to Jimmy's and start another project that'll keep you happy'. So, I went over to Jimmy's and he had this 12-string electric Fender. [Then] he started strumming this pulsating E chord..."

Clearly referencing the slow, steady rhythmic pulse of classical composer Maurice Ravel's best-known composition – 1928's *Bolero* – a beguiling melody line was placed on top of Page's bedding chords, giving he and Beck something potentially very promising indeed to take with them to the recording studio. Now, it was simply a matter of finding the right musicians to cut the tune. Having heard rumours that the Who's John Entwistle and resident "loveable lunatic" Keith Moon were unhappy with their lot[69], Jeff and (a pre-Yardbirds) Jimmy were eager to steal the bassist and drummer away from their erstwhile leader Pete Townshend and form a new group. "I just couldn't get enough

---

68 Beck was not the only one experiencing dissatisfaction within the Yardbirds at the time. Displaying an early example of the musical restlessness that would eventually see him leaving the band for good in 1968, singer Keith Relf was also keen to explore a solo project of his own. The result was 'Mr. Zero', a wonderfully dark slice of baroque pop in the mould of Jacques Brel and early Scott Walker. Written by Bob Lind and produced by Paul Samwell-Smith and Simon Napier-Bell, 'Mr. Zero' reached number 50 on the UK charts in the autumn of 1966. File under 'Lost Classic'.

69 Entwistle and Moon's dissatisfaction was probably financial. As the Who's principal songwriter Pete Townshend was growing ever richer with each hit single, his colleagues – who were not known for their compositional abilities – languished far behind. After a time, the situation started to grate and the rhythm section began casting their net wide – albeit half-heartedly – for other job offers.

of Moonie," Jeff later told writer Alan di Perna. "A day would go by in half an hour when you were with him. Just complete lunacy and genuine organic humour. Your jaw would ache from laughing."

Ultimately, Page and Beck's clever plan turned out to be less a well orchestrated raid on the Who's rhythm section and more a mad British farce. At first, both Entwistle and Moon were happy to participate in the recording. However, because they were worried Townshend might sack them for their disloyalty, the two arranged to travel to the session in disguise. In the end, an already nervous Entwistle saw sense and backed out at the last minute, leaving Moon to arrive at IBC Studios dressed like a stray villain from a James Bond movie. "Keith got out of the bloody cab wearing dark glasses and a Cossack hat," Beck later giggled. Obviously thrilled to see Moon, but now without a bassist, Page made a phone call. Arriving soon after with his trademark Fender Jazz bass was John Paul Jones.

Beautifully arranged (by Jones), wonderfully augmented by pianist Nicky Hopkins, and featuring Page on 12-string electric[70] and Beck on lead guitar, '... Bolero' turned out to be a little masterpiece. With a majestic, soaring slide melody from Jeff, a hypnotic, pulsating beat and a mid-section guitar freak-out that some believe to be the true birth of heavy metal, the track certainly captured those who contributed to it in peak form. This was none more true than in the case of Keith Moon, who became so animated during the instrumental's 'rave-up' section that he accidentally smashed a $250 microphone with one of his sticks, thus silencing the majority of his kit for the rest of the recording. A costly mistake, perhaps, but so lively was Moon's performance that all those present began to dream of a supergroup with the drummer as its beating heart.

"Keith was just brilliant," John Paul Jones later said. "He was the life and soul of the party at all times. Plenty dangerous to go and party with, but never, ever dull." Never, ever dull, but never less than capricious,

---

70 Still prized by Page today, the 1965 Fender Electric XII was almost certainly used again on the Yardbirds' 'Little Games', as well as several key future recordings by Jimmy's most famous band.

either. Once done with the tune, Moon smiled his mad-eyed smile, shook everyone's hand and then ran straight back into the collective arms of the Who, never to return again. For the band's co-manager Chris Stamp, this was all in a day's work when dealing with 'Moon The Loon'. "Oh, but that was Keith," he later said. "He was always looking for other options. Keith always thought he was going to be the Beach Boys' drummer, the Beatles' drummer, the Stones' fucking drummer…"

While 'Beck's Bolero' would eventually take on a life of its own, with the instrumental becoming mired in various issues concerning authorship and production over subsequent years[71], there was no doubting that the musicians who cut the track had a blast. "We all thought for about half an hour [after recording it]," said John Paul Jones, "that it would be brilliant to take this line-up on the road." In 1966, Jones was obviously denied that opportunity by Keith Moon's swift exit. But when his wife Maureen (aka 'Mo') read in *Disc & Music Echo* that Jimmy Page was seeking a bassist for his brand-new band some two years later, John's interest in working with the guitarist was again piqued. "I was moping around one day and my missus said to me, 'Why don't you stop moping around the house and join a band or something?'" he later recalled. "She said, 'Jimmy Page is forming a group… why don't you give him a ring?' I thought 'Hmmm…'" Now as sick of session life as Page had been before joining the Yardbirds – "20 sessions a week, 40 arrangements a month… I just couldn't stand it any longer," said the bass player – Jones didn't take much persuasion to pick up the phone. His call to Page was met with a sympathetic ear. "Well," Jimmy later remembered, "[John Paul] didn't need me for a job, but he did feel the need to express himself. [We] figured we could do that together…"

Of course, there was no doubt that John Paul Jones, Robert Plant and John Bonham were all men of outstanding musical calibre. But Jimmy Page was not collecting individual musicians for his own amusement. He was putting together a band, and if the players concerned did not gel, then he was back to square one. Taking the view that the 'proof

---

71 Creating a veritable minefield of opposing opinions and disparate viewpoints, 'Beck's Bolero' will be returned to again in the course of this book.

of the pudding was in the eating', Page and Peter Grant arranged an afternoon rehearsal for all parties at a basement in Gerard Street, deep in the bowels of London's Chinatown in mid-August 1968.[72] Not ones for waste, Jimmy and his manager allocated exactly two hours to figure out whether the grand experiment would work. "Time," the guitarist laughed, "was money..."

On the day, there were nerves and plenty of them. Though Robert was 'a relaxed type of fellow' and seldom given to the jitters, he was also painfully aware that anything other than a stellar performance might see him straight back on the train to Wolverhampton. Bonham was also at sixes and sevens. A quiet man made all the quieter by the fact that Page was already "a big star", the drummer kept his head down and his conversation brisk, preferring instead to concentrate on matters at hand. Only the more seasoned Jones was reportedly a sea of calm, nearly five years in the studio game having imbued him with the confidence that if it all went wrong, he could at least return to sessions the following morning.

At first there was some confusion over what to play. In one reading of the story, Robert Plant suggested a song he and Bonham had covered while with Band Of Joy. "We did a Garnet Mimms thing, 'As Long As I Have You'," he later said. "That was the first number Jimmy, Bonzo, Jonesy and I ever rehearsed." However, the broader consensus is that Page suggested 'Train Kept A Rollin'', a rollicking, high-energy tune he had been on intimate terms with since 1957 and most recently performed with the Yardbirds. At the time, his choice drew appreciative nods from Plant and Bonham. Not much of a rockabilly fan, Jones professed ignorance of the chords. Jimmy dutifully showed him. Then he counted them all in, at which point "The bloody roof came off." After two more hours of restructuring the architecture of their basement space, Page was in no doubt that he had found his men. "We [all] knew how good it sounded," he later told *Mojo*. "We were really roaring. It was almost like this whole thing where the gods are looking down, and then they start helping you out, moving you through..."

---

72 Though the exact date and time of the meeting has been lost to history, given subsequent events, a reasonable bet might be 14.00 on Monday, August 18, 1968.

There was no time for back-slapping or hearty self-congratulation. While the Yardbirds were still a going concern, Peter Grant had booked a series of dates for them in Scandinavia during early September, and he and Jimmy were determined that the new outfit make good on previous obligations. With only a matter of weeks before the first scheduled date at the Brondby Pop Club on September 7, operations were swiftly relocated to Page's riverside house in Pangbourne, where the quartet began a frantic period of rehearsal, composition and beer drinking.

Though timescales were tight, progress proved little short of astounding. Working furiously throughout late August and early September, both a live set and, indeed, the base components of the group's first album were plucked from the musical ether. Robert Plant's suggestion of covering Garnett Mimms' 'As Long As I Have You' now took on a bold new shape and form, the original's swinging horns and soul inflections replaced by a much more brutal and direct approach, with Jimmy's cutting guitar riffs very much at the centre of the sonic storm. 'Flames' by Elmer Gantry's Velvet Opera was also given a swift run-through, its rock/blues structure and middle-section instrumental breakdown allowing the band to improvise to their heart's content. Elsewhere, little bits of history were being written: the crushing down-stokes, off-kilter pace and furious soloing that would become 'Communication Breakdown', the slow, pleading treatment of Willie Dixon's 'I Can't Quit You Baby', replete with a powerhouse vocal from Plant, the resurrection of 'Dazed And Confused', soon destined to become something much mightier and more brooding than Page might have ever thought possible. And last but not least, the breathless pull and punch of 'How Many More Times', its sinuous, yet free-flowing qualities perfectly suited to closing both concert and debut LP. Yet, despite these volcanic rumblings, high-volume shenanigans and Jimmy's house being literally across the water from Pangbourne's most popular pub, The Swan, not one local resident complained. "I actually think they quite liked it, you know," Robert later said, laughing.

While the new group put itself through its paces, Peter Grant continued to plan on their behalf. Having seen first-hand the possibilities available on the American concert circuit and the lucrative rewards therein, he was keen to get Page, Plant, Jones and Bonham there as quickly as possible. Peter was also painfully aware that his charges be properly tended to while he went about the business of maximising their earnings. In this regard Grant turned to a man of his acquaintance who would become his right hand for the next decade, and whose reputation for fearless devotion to duty would soon become second only to his own. Defining the term 'colourful character', Richard Cole had already packed plenty of incident into his 22 years before teaming up with Grant; dairy-factory hand, sheet metal worker, scaffolder, amateur drummer, clothes-mad mod and, if legend is to be believed, designer of Ringo Starr and John Lennon's fetching shirts for the cover of *Revolver.*

In 1965 Cole finally discovered his true calling when he became a road manager, firstly for pop hopefuls Unit 4+2, then with the Who both domestically and abroad, his efforts to curb Keith Moon's mischief on the road testing both his mettle and sanity. Finding the States more to his liking – and possibly keen to escape from Moon The Loon – Cole moved there in 1967, hooking up with operatic rockers Vanilla Fudge as a sound engineer. A year later, he heard that the Yardbirds were coming to the USA, and the group now had Grant as their manager. Having encountered 'Big Gee' in 1966 doing a stint for another of his acts, the New Vaudeville Band, Richard offered his services, which Grant gratefully accepted. Now, Cole was back in the frame, ready to provide service, succour and, on occasion, services well beyond the call of ordinary men for Jimmy and Peter's latest enterprise. Hard-working, hard-living, tough as leather and, for a time at least, Peter Grant's most trusted on-the-road asset, Richard Cole fitted perfectly into the new regime. "Most of us had left school before 16," he later told *Classic Rock.* "I was a scaffolder, John Bonham had been a bricklayer, Robert Plant had worked with asphalt on the road. Jimmy Page and John Paul Jones were session musicians – when they tell you to be there for 10 a.m., you're there. These were coveted jobs so they didn't mess around. [But] all of us, all of us had that work ethic."

With the upcoming dates in Scandinavia and a handful of gigs in the UK before setting off to the USA for a proper tour just before New Year, there was little time for anything other than work for Jimmy Page and his new recruits. Moreover, the quartet had to find space in their diary for the recording of their critically important first album. But as John Paul Jones was now finding out, when it came to balancing art and commerce, Page and Grant had become a symbiotic mechanism. "Peter trusted Jimmy's vision completely [for the band]," said Jones, "and when Peter trusted you, he didn't question you... he was just going to put all his resources behind you."

Just before the trip to Denmark, however, there were two other matters to attend to. The first, a paid favour for an old friend; the second, a minor detail, but an important one nonetheless.

Since 1964, PJ Proby had seduced and terrorised the good folk of Great Britain, with the Houston-born, huge-lunged singer scoring a slew of pop hits, including 'Hold Me', 'Together', 'Maria' and 'Somewhere' before fate – or poor tailoring – brought a halt to his gallop. While onstage in Croydon in 1965 (and again, a few days later in Luton), Proby's trousers unfortunately split, causing the British press to blow a gasket, morals campaigner Mary Whitehouse to take aim and the ABC Theatre chain to fire, with PJ subsequently banned from all their venues for decades. Given the fact that it was only his knees ("and a little bit above that") that were exposed, it all sounds faintly ridiculous now. But even at the height of the 'Swinging Sixties', such a display was potentially career-ending.[73] "The minute the pants split, Mary Whitehouse had the headlines ready and off they went," he said. "'Ruining our children', 'Disgusting man', 'Deport him now', that type of thing. Whitehouse also got MPs' wives complaining. If it happened today, I'd raise my price! Iggy Pop goes onstage near butt naked, and nothing ever happens."

---

73 PJ Proby has long contended that the real reason he was drummed off his tour with singer Cilla Black in 1965 had little to do with split trousers and more to do with backstage politics. "You know, I wasn't thrown off the tour, I was bought off it, and it had nothing to do with the pants splitting. [Promoter] Gordon Mills wanted Tom Jones on that tour and he wanted me thrown off. [However], they did keep warning me, saying, 'Well, if the pants split again...' But I thought [my] fans would win out. They were so much behind me. But [in the end], it was the politics of show business. I didn't even know there were any politics in show business."

While the hits continued (albeit more sporadically), by 1968, PJ Proby was giving serious thought to reinventing both his music and image. Enlisting the help of producer and friend Steve Rowland[74], he decided country, blues and even rock might well be the way forward. "I'd been doing these big songs with 100-piece orchestras, singing these Broadway-type tunes, and I just said to Steve, 'Could you find me some stuff that's more connected to today's music?' And he found me five, six, maybe seven demos, and we worked through them. I then said, 'Could you get me a good group together – no violins or anything – just a good group? Well, he said, 'OK, I think I can do that, and he set the session up. I went down there and there in front of me were Jimmy, Robert, Jonesy and Bonham."

Jimmy Page had known PJ Proby since he played rhythm guitar on the singer's first hit 'Hold Me' in 1964. "Well, Big Jim Sullivan was actually on lead guitar on the 'Hold Me' session," Proby recalled. "But yes, that's when I met little Jimmy Page. He was about 14, 15 years old, then. He was 19, you say? Well, he looked about 12..." Baby-faced he might have been, but Page continued to back PJ on several subsequent tunes, with the singer coming to see the guitarist's real value as time went on. "Yeah, Jimmy was on all my records, and I got on with him just great. [But] you know, I didn't see anything outstanding about Jimmy [at the start] because they didn't let him take over on lead guitar, at least at that point. But Jimmy wasn't pushy. He wasn't a bragger, in your face about his talent. You might say he was almost too nice a guy to even be in the industry! So I genuinely didn't know just how good a guitar player he was until we started recording."

How exactly Page, Plant and co. ended up backing PJ Proby for some of the songs on his comeback LP *Three Week Hero*[75] remains a

---

74 Actor, writer, singer and producer, Steve Rowland is perhaps best known in the UK for overseeing 13 top hits for pop sextet Dave, Dee, Dozy, Beaky, Mick & Tich during the sixties.

75 While Page, Plant, Jones and Bonham appear on several tracks, *Three Week Hero* also features musical contributions from the likes of drummer Clem Cattini, guitarists Amory Kane and Alan Parker, and percussionists Stan Barrett and Dennis Lopez, among others.

little mystery, though one source has it that John Paul Jones was owed several studio credits and thus brought his new colleagues along for the ride. Whatever the mechanics of it, the immensely likable Texan was unwittingly about to get one of the 20th century's great rock bands for a knock-down price. "Ha!" he laughed. "Now, we had a great session. They smoked all their shit and I did all my drinking, and we just went for it." Creating a whirlwind pace, Proby and his charges cut several songs in as many hours, with Robert Plant more than happy to contribute harmonica fills here and there while PJ took care of lead vocals. In fact, so quick were the musicians' efforts, that there was even time for a little improvisation at the end. "Well, it went so well and we did the songs so fast we had an hour or so left," recalled PJ. "So, Steve Rowland says to me, 'What are we going to do? We got all this time left.' I turned to Jimmy and said, 'Hey, can you and the boys start playing some down home New Orleans blues and I'll just make up the words as we go?' So, the boys started playing and I started singing, making it up as I went, and we got 45 minutes of great music that turned out to be 'Jim's Blues', 'Mary Hopkins Never Had Days Like These'[76] and 'George Wallace (Is Rollin' In This Morning)'."

In his own words, "a fine, fine night", so impressed was Proby with Page's band he was reluctant to let them go without asking a final question. "They were such a great, great group," he said, "so, when the session came to an end, [at about] three, four in the morning, I said, 'Listen, I've got some tours coming up, but I don't have a band. Would you boys like to back me?' And they replied, 'Sure, we'd love to, but we've got some dates of our own coming up in Europe and the States we're contracted to'. I asked where and they said, 'San Francisco, The Fillmore'. I said, 'Jesus. You're playing there? Lava lamps, dope and hippies. Well, I better shake your hands now, because boys, once you've played there and they see how good you are, you're never coming back. And, you know what, they never really did…'"

---

76 Although cut for this session, 'Mary Hopkins…' did not make it onto 1969's *Three Week Hero*. However, it does appear as the B-side to Proby's single 'The Day That Lorraine Came Down', a great tune that again features Page and co.

With the sessions for *Three Week Hero* behind them, Scandinavia beckoned like Ulysses' sirens for Jimmy Page, Robert Plant, John Paul Jones and John Bonham, but there was one other small but important matter to attend to before their departure: finding a proper name for the band. For obvious and, indeed, legal reasons, they could not strike out as the Yardbirds, while the New Yardbirds, too, offered only a short-term fix for their upcoming European dates. Quite awful alternatives such as 'Whoopee Cushion' and 'Mad Dogs' were also toyed with before being rightly discarded. Jimmy, however, had already banked an alternative name for his new outfit as far back as May 1966. During those animated, if doomed, sessions for 'Beck's Bolero', Keith Moon had joked to his fellow musicians that in the unlikely event that they did manage to get out of the studio and onto the road, their nascent supergroup would go down like "a lead Zeppelin".

While Moon was fond of the phrase, and often used it among friends to denote a shoddy enterprise or bad idea, Page had never heard it before. But it stuck. "Well, I thought that it was a really amusing name for a group," he later said. "I mean, if you start off on that foot, you just can't get any worse!" There was one amendment to be made. The word 'lead' had two separate meanings – one 'lumpen and metallic', the other denoting 'leading others from the front'. Concerned this might confuse audiences, a revision was to be made: 'lead' would be deliberately misspelled as 'Led'. 'Zeppelin', however, would stay exactly as it was – a giant airship sailing ever-upward into the sky.

Led Zeppelin it was.

CHAPTER 14

You Shook Me

It was a characteristically shrewd move on Jimmy Page's part to launch his new group away from prying eyes and in this regard the series of Yardbirds' shows booked for Scandinavia were ideal; small gigs where mistakes could be made, kinks ironed out and songs routined without the music world at large knowing much about it. With the benefit of hindsight, fulfilling those Yardbirds gigs in the lands of midnight sun was the first of many such astute tactics that he and his canny manager would adopt as the wheels began to turn.

So it was that the first show by the group that would become Led Zeppelin took place on September 7, 1968, at the Teen Club, a gymnasium complex in Gladsaxe, about six miles north-east of the Danish capital of Copenhagen. Billed as the Yardbirds, when they took the stage after a couple of local bands, the 1,200 or so Danes present were probably expecting to see Keith Relf on vocals and hear a few Yardbirds hits. As it was they only got 'For Your Love', along with a number of songs Jimmy's new group had been rehearsing, among them 'Train Kept A-Rollin', 'Dazed And Confused', 'White Summer'/'Black Mountain Side', 'Communication Breakdown', 'I Can't Quit You Baby, 'You Shook Me', 'Babe, I'm Gonna Leave You', 'How Many More Times' and 'As Long As I Have You', a cover of old Garnett Mimms' tune.

By serendipitous chance, 17-year-old Jorgen Angel was on hand to take photographs for the Teen Club magazine, thus not only capturing the moment but becoming the first man in the world to take photos of Led Zeppelin onstage. "When they went onstage it was something very special and different and spectacular," he recalled. "They were full of energy and they were different. I had no idea they were going to be big." From the remarkably impressive pictures Jorgen took using his mother's camera we can assume that Jimmy was keen to promote a visual image for his new group. His Telecaster slung low, his mop of dark curls falling over his forehead, Jimmy chose an all-white outfit to step out with Led Zeppelin for the first time, his ruffled shirt buttoned up to the neck over well-cut trousers, though he would add a little contrast later in the tour by wearing a black leather biker jacket. Plant and Bonham both wore floral-themed shirts or blousons, Plant's slashed to the waist, his hair now starting a relentless descent to his shoulders where it would set up home for the next 12 years. Jones wore a fetching long coat in satin and matching trousers.

"We were pretty green," Plant would tell *Q*'s Mat Snow in 1990. "It was very early days and we were tiptoeing with each other. We didn't have half the recklessness that became for me the whole joy of Led Zeppelin. It was a tentative start." Page was also anxious. "They don't cheer too madly there, you know?" he said. "We were really scared, because we only had about 15 hours to practice together. It was sort of an experimental concert to see if we were any good, I guess."

Peter Grant felt differently. He watched the whole show from the side of the stage. "They were onto something. There was chemistry there..."

After a second gig the same evening at the Brondby Pop Club in Nørregårdsskolen, and three further shows performed the following day, they enjoyed a three-day break before heading to Sweden for five more dates, including shows in Stockholm, mostly at outdoor amusement parks, Gothenburg and a concluding date at Malmo's gloriously named Club Bongo on September 18. "We left them stomping the floors after every show," said Page. Clearly things progressed for the better as the shows went on.

Back in the UK, some dates were played under the name the Yardbirds, some as the New Yardbirds, then as Led Zeppelin. Their first gig on British soil was on October 4 at Newcastle's Mayfair ballroom as the New Yardbirds, supported by local act the Junco Partners, and on October 18 they were at London's Marquee Club, billed as the Yardbirds, where Peter Grant negotiated 50% of the door takings, minus £15 for support act the Bakerloo Blues Line.

Just before the Marquee date Jimmy took it on himself to visit *Melody Maker*'s offices in Fleet Street and talk to Chris Welch about his new group and hopes for the future. "We're starting work on an LP and we're going to the States in early November," he said. "I'm hoping the Marquee will be a good scene. Robert can get up and sing against anybody. I thought I'd never get a band together. It's refreshing to know that today you can go out and form a group to play the music you like and people will listen. It's what musicians have been waiting for for 20 years," he added.

Chris Welch would become an ardent supporter of Led Zeppelin, seeing them for the first time at the Marquee that night. "They still weren't very well known at this point, but the club was still quite full, mainly with drummers who'd all come along to see John Bonham," said Welch. "I was actually standing next to Mark Ashton that night, who drummed in Rare Bird. And he said 'God, what a fantastic player that guy is. I'm giving up'. And he actually did. Ashton became a singer after that. The sheer power was quite extraordinary. No one knew what Robert and John were capable of, but then we saw it that night with our own eyes. The thing about Zeppelin was that it was apparent immediately there were no weak links. Everything was strong, arranged, disciplined. It all just gelled. This was a group with a masterplan, a very powerful manager and it was obvious from the start they were going places."

On October 19 the group played their last show as the Yardbirds and six days later their first show as Led Zeppelin at the University of Surrey, in Battersea, and further dates followed in Bristol, Hartlepool, Hull and Sheffield. On November 9 they were at the Roundhouse, the old railway engine shed in Camden town, a gig that doubled as Robert's wedding reception when he had married Maureen Wilson the previous day. Other notable dates included a return to Epsom for Page at Ewell Technical College on October 26 and Richmond's Crawdaddy Club on November 29. There was another Marquee show on December 10 before concerts in Canterbury, Bath and Exeter, and a final flourish at Wood Green's Fishmongers Arms on December 20.

This handful of shows in the UK during the final months of 1968 was really a warm-up for the bigger prize. From the outset Peter Grant and Jimmy Page had their eyes fixed firmly on America and to this end they would become the first ever British rock group to concentrate on the US *before* they'd become stars back home. The first of many US tours began in Denver on December 26, 1968, which meant they had to fly out over Christmas; not for a second did they hesitate to do so.

This first US tour was set up by Peter Grant with Premier Talent, the booking agency headed by Frank Barsalona who, like Grant and a handful of others, had recognised the potential of rock to become a multi-million dollar entertainment business. The first talent agency to focus exclusively on rock, Premier had already signed up the Who and Jimi Hendrix, and Barsalona was fast becoming an important figure in the emerging music business. He'd set up 28 US dates for Led Zeppelin, and in subsequent interviews Jimmy admitted he was nervous about whether his grand experiment would work: "It was on our shoulders... it was really up to us," he said.

Led Zeppelin were a last minute addition to the bill for the December 26 show at Denver's Auditorium Arena, which also featured Vanilla Fudge and Spirit. It was one of the few dates Peter Grant did not witness: "I had to ask them to fly out over Christmas and I felt bad about it. But they never queried it at all. They just knew it had to be done. Jimmy was really itching to get there." They earned $750 for their support slot and local promoter Barry Fey felt sorry for Spirit, who had to step onstage after them. "[There was] a smattering of polite applause, then Robert Plant let it rip and everybody in the audience was stunned. Frankly, I don't know how Spirit went on after that. You didn't have to be a genius to know that Zeppelin were going to be a smash," Fey wrote in his autobiography *Backstage Past*. "Oh my God! People were going crazy."

The tour would roll on into mid-February, with the majority of the dates supporting Vanilla Fudge or Iron Butterfly, who headlined some dates but occasionally refused to follow Zeppelin. There were frequent misspellings of their new name along the way with them billed as 'Led Zeppilen featuring Jimmy Page' at Portland's Civic Auditorium on December 29 and, even worse, 'Len Lefflin' in Spokane the following night. They travelled from gig to gig by station wagon and were paid $700–$750 per show. Plant often controlled the PA from the stage and John Bonham's drums sometimes went un-miked. Indeed, the drummer had been so loud in early rehearsals that Page took to stacking the Vox Super Beatle amps that he'd inherited from the Yardbirds on top of each other in an effort to compete with the volume.

On January 2 they opened a four-night run at the Whisky A Go-Go in Los Angeles, supported by Alice Cooper, but their debut appearance in the city that would soon embrace them like no other in America was ill-starred after Jimmy caught a fever. "We got to Los Angeles and I was really, really ill," he said. "In fact, the doctor said I was insane to do the set. The first night I did it I had a temperature of over 104, but he'd given me all the shots and things so I was able to make it. We managed to finish the whole engagement without letting the guy down, but of course he docked us money because we only did one long set each night, we couldn't do two. It's not the greatest paying job in the world anyway, and when he knocked money off, we were all really down about that, as you can imagine. That was our first set of dates."

From Los Angeles it was but a 400-mile drive up to San Francisco to appear at Bill Graham's Fillmore West. Like Frank Barsalona, Graham was another tough, far-sighted businessman with an eye on the future of rock and, aware of this, Peter Grant flew over in time for their dates at the old Carousel Ballroom at the intersection of Fillmore Street and Geary Boulevard. He was very pleased with their progress. "I told them to go over there and make every performance something to remember and that's exactly what they were doing," he said.

What he saw was a rapidly developing act that varied slightly but generally opened with their cover of Ben E. King's 'We're Gonna Groove', and though a version of the song was recorded at the time, it would not see the light of day until 1982. The rest of the set comprised songs recorded for their first album, in addition to versions of Otis Redding's 'Shake' and a section from Spirit's 'Fresh Garbage'. At the Fillmore they actually played two sets each night, the first including 'Train Kept A-Rollin'', 'I Can't Quit You Baby', 'As Long As I Have You' (incorporating 'Fresh Garbage'), 'Dazed And Confused' and 'How Many More Times', the second 'White Summer'/'Black Mountain Side', 'Killing Floor', 'You Shook Me', 'Pat's Delight'[77], 'Babe, I'm Gonna Leave You', 'Communication Breakdown' and 'For Your Love'. The 'How Many More Times' finale was extended and they even threw in a version of the Yardbirds' 'For Your Love' when crowds began to call them back for more. "Iron Butterfly were very despondent about following us onstage," observed Grant. "I knew that we had got a foothold – we were making an impression."

By now Page, for whom creature comforts were fast becoming a necessity, was dreaming of flying between gigs: "You have to go about [America] the right way," he said. "It's so vast, the only way to travel without knocking yourself out is by plane." Still, while the others shared accommodation, Page had his own room. Also, he often sought out Grant's company above the band, manager and band leader spending their afternoons wandering around vintage antique shops pretending to be dealers.

Everyone who was there now believes that Led Zeppelin found their dancing feet over four nights between January 23 and 26 at the Tea Party, a venue in Boston where according to witnesses they "blew the crowd into the Charles river". "At the Boston Tea Party, we had an hour and a half act by then, and played for four and a half hours," recalled John Paul Jones. "We played the set twice, then we did Beatles, Stones and Who numbers. Everything that anybody

---

77 Bonham's drum solo, so named in honour of his wife, Pat, was already a key feature of the set. Crucially, it filled space in lieu of other material.

knew. I think we did some Everly Brothers and Elvis stuff. If you knew more than four bars, you started..." Jones was referring to the now legendary fourth night at the Tea Party in front of an audience who had returned for more after seeing an earlier show, so that it became a giant celebration, band and audience now so familiar with each other that all barriers came down. "There were kids actually bashing their heads against the stage," added Jones. "I've never seen that at a gig before or since. Peter was absolutely ecstatic. He was crying and hugging us all. You know... with this huge grizzly bear hug. I suppose it was then that we realised just what Led Zeppelin was going to become."

From Boston, band and entourage drove 220 miles down to New York to play at Bill Graham's East Coast Fillmore on January 31 and February 1. Graham introduced them and two encores later, headliners Iron Butterfly were left to pick up the pieces, waiting a full 45 minutes before doing so. "The audience was still going 'Zeppelin, Zeppelin...' when Iron Butterfly had started their set!" said Grant. "Good band, not a bad band... but no match for Zeppelin." The following night someone in the audience yelled out, "To hell with the Butterfly!", a sentiment shared by many in attendance.

Fred Kirby, reporting for *Billboard* magazine, America's principal trade paper, was impressed: "Led Zeppelin landed at Fillmore East and in the first of four weekend shows," he wrote, "the British quartet showed it could develop into the next big super group. Page, a former member of the Yardbirds, ranks with the top pop guitarists in the world and his performance substantiated his reputation. Plant is a blues–style screamer and wailer, whose vocalizing was wild. Iron Butterfly had a tough assignment in following Led Zeppelin."

Though quietly confident from the outset that his vision was on the money, there can be no question that Jimmy Page's Led Zeppelin was blossoming beyond even his wildest expectations. Onstage the group began to exude new levels of confidence with each passing gig. 'Dazed And Confused' and 'How Many More Times' were particularly effective vehicles in which to transport his sonic ideas, both songs rising and falling on the band's collective energy, each seldom climaxing per se but happy to stew in its own simmering juices until a tumble from the drums and a lurch from Jones' bass moved it forward into another phase. "It allowed us to expand and go on these strange meanderings," said Plant later. "That's where Led Zeppelin really began."

Though they only had about an hour's worth of material to work with they were able to stretch things out according to the mood of the audience, taking the punters with them on this strange psychedelic trip through free-form blues, full tilt rock'n'roll and buzz-saw effects. Only occasionally did they need to rely on covers like the Isley Brothers' 'It's Your Thing' or Spirit's 'Fresh Garbage', and if all else failed, Plant would start singing, Page would play a supporting chord to establish a rhythm and they'd simply "wing it".

On the closing night at the Fillmore East an epic battle took place between Page and Plant during the call and response climax to 'You Shook Me'. "Jimmy was a vicious little bastard," Plant would tell *Rolling Stone* in 1978, long after the dust had settled on Led Zeppelin. "We used to look at each other, and he'd go higher and higher up the frets until he was around top E. I could see his fingers going further and further up [the neck], and I'd be going 'No, don't do this to me!'"

On a diversion to Toronto on February 2 they made an important ally in local music writer Ritchie York who in the *Globe & Mail* wrote: "It was Page's night. One visual image easily stood out. It was the sight of Led Zeppelin's hero-worshipped guitarist, resplendent in avocado velvet suit, bent over as if in agony to the audience, his fingers working like a touch-typist's, his foot thumping like a kangaroo's tail." Then they were back in the US, with two nights at Chicago's Kinetic Playground and at Miami's Thee Image Club before the electrifying first US tour closed at Baltimore's Civic Center on February 16.

All in all it had been a resounding success, acting as an eye-opener to the charms of American road life for Plant, Jones and Bonham, and setting the band up for future raids on US territory. Jimmy Page was vindicated, even though the airship came down with a bump when it landed back in England. "It was just a joke in England," he would say later. "We really had a bad time, they just wouldn't accept anything new. It had to be the New Yardbirds, not Led Zeppelin. We were actually given a chance in America."

Led Zeppelin's first album was released on January 12, 1969 in America and on March 31 in the UK. In the States, Atlantic had the good sense to release it while the band were on tour, and although it would reach no higher than tenth position in the *Billboard* charts it would stay on those charts for 50 weeks straight, a more rewarding performance in the long term than those albums that shoot up the charts and disappear again within a week. In the UK the album was held back until April 12 to coincide with a spring tour but in reality this was just a series of fairly low-key club dates, with home fans less inclined to give the benefit of the doubt to Jimmy Page's new group than those on the other side of the Atlantic. Nevertheless, *Led Zeppelin* – or *Led Zeppelin 1*, as it is generally referred to – did reach number six in the charts and hang around for 79 weeks.

The album had been recorded in October at Olympic Studios in Barnes, just across Hammersmith Bridge in south-west London, a studio favoured by the Rolling Stones and Jimi Hendrix, the sessions taking place immediately after the group returned from their trip to Scandinavia. It says much for Page's confidence, optimism and commitment that this was accomplished at their own expense before they had even signed a record contract – Page and Grant picked up the £1,782 studio bill – and that Grant took it on himself to offer it to record labels as an inflexible package. "It was a question of take it or leave it," wrote Chris Charlesworth, who as a writer on *Melody Maker* during the seventies would study Led Zeppelin's methods closer than most. "In this way Page and Grant imposed the message that Led Zeppelin was self-sufficient every step of the way, in absolute control of its destiny from the very outset, and required a record company merely to efficiently promote, market and distribute their work."

In the event, Grant secured a deal for the group with Atlantic Records in New York, specifically a five-album package for a reported advance of $200,000. The arrangement ceded control to the group and their manager on all artistic issues, not just the music but the packaging, too. "They were fortunate that in Ahmet Ertegun, the head of Atlantic Records, they found a label boss who not only recognised the commercial potential of their music but was sympathetic to their methods," adds Charlesworth. "Few other label bosses would have been as far-sighted or accommodating."

Under the direction of Page, now a seasoned studio professional, and engineer Glyn Johns, it took a mere 30 hours to record *Led Zeppelin* in Olympic. Expensive studio time was not wasted and, in any case, the songs had been well rehearsed in Denmark and Sweden, the gigs there having offered an opportunity to thoroughly familiarise themselves with the songs they would lay down. For the cover of the album Page picked out a black on white illustration of the *Hindenburg* airship in flames, plummeting to the ground, as Keith Moon had put it, like a 'lead' Zeppelin. The back cover photo, taken by former Yardbird Chris Dreja, was a simple two-by-two group shot over which the song titles were superimposed, none of the four smiling and Jimmy in the bottom left corner looking especially solemn.

The UK press welcomed the album, an uncredited review in *Melody Maker* – probably written by Chris Welch – declaring: "Jimmy Page triumphs!" and going on to state: "Now, with his own group, the legend comes to life, and his work on guitar, acoustic, electric, and pedal steel varieties can be studied. He proves to be technical, tasteful, turbulent and torrid... This Zeppelin is really in a gas new bag!"

Felix Dennis, who would one day become one of the wealthiest magazine publishers in the world, presciently informed readers of the underground magazine *Oz* that Led Zeppelin's debut LP represented a sea change in rock music. "Few rock musicians in the world could hope to parallel the degree of technical assurance and gutsy emotion [Page] displays throughout these nine tracks," he wrote. "Exactly 84 seconds after the beginning of 'Good Times Bad Times', the first cut, side one, Page does things with an electric guitar that might feebly be described as bewildering. From then on it only gets better." Dennis also correctly predicted that the group would soon be lost to America.

These levels of enthusiasm were not shared by reviewers in America, however. In his review for *Rolling Stone*, writer John Mendelsohn slated the record mercilessly, taking Page to task both as composer and producer. After grudgingly acknowledging Jimmy's skills on guitar he wrote: "Unfortunately, he is a very limited producer and a writer of weak, unimaginative songs, and the Zeppelin album suffers from him having produced and written most of it (alone or in combination with his accomplices in the group)." Mendelsohn's conclusion was equally blunt. "It would seem that if [Led Zeppelin] are to help fill the void created by the demise of Cream, they will have to find a producer (and editor) and some material worthy of their collective attention."

The review in *Rolling Stone* would create a stormfront between Zep and America's foremost rock magazine that rumbled on until at least the mid-seventies. Not only that, it created within Led Zeppelin – and Page in particular – a touchy attitude towards the media, a suspicion that the music press was antagonistic towards him and them, hostile and negative, which coloured his and their relationship with the press from the day that Mendelsohn's review hit the streets.

If Mendelson's sour review in *Rolling Stone* injured Page, he did not show it. As ever, there was a job to be done, and Jimmy was committed to it. However, one of Mendelson's remarks must have given him real pause, pointing as it did to an uncomfortable similarity between Led Zeppelin's debut LP and another band trying to win over America at around the same time. "[*Led Zeppelin I*]," said the critic pointedly, "[offers] little that its twin, the Jeff Beck Group, didn't say as well or better three months ago..."

As the twin-headed 45 'Hi Ho Silver Lining'/'Beck's Bolero' indicated, Jeff Beck did not roll over and die when he left the Yardbirds, though his career trajectory did become a little hard to follow at times. Scoring a huge hit with 'Hi Ho...' in March 1967, one of Great Britain's pre-eminent guitarists had entered the 'Summer of Love' as a legitimate pop star, with two follow-up singles 'Tallyman' and the (quite woeful) instrumental 'Love Is Blue' soon entering the UK Top 30 to consolidate that status. On the face of it, one might have thought Jeff would be grateful to producer Mickie Most for raising his profile and keeping him in the charts. In actuality, Beck was near suicidal, with his recent, fey output a million miles away from the type of music he longed to make.

191

"Singing on 'Hi Ho Silver Lining'," he later told *Making Music*, "was a humiliating experience. I sounded like a boy scout and I hated every fucking minute of it." What Jeff very much did want to do was form a band the equal of, or even superior to, Cream or the Jimi Hendrix Experience – an outfit willing to stretch the blues or anything they turned their hand to to its logical melodic conclusion. 'Hi Ho...' had put him back in the charts sure enough, but his heart was with 'Bolero' 100% of the way.

As it turned out, a series of linked events allowed Beck to make that transition, though the journey was a little bumpy along the way. While churning out chart-friendly releases under the careful tutelage of Most, Jeff had also been busy forming a group that took up exactly where 'Bolero' left off. Come the time of 'Hi Ho...', he even had the bones of it, with two relatively raw recruits in singer Rod Stewart and bass player Ronnie Wood signing up for the ride. In both cases, Beck struck gold. The son of a Scottish builder raised on north London's busy Archway Road in the late forties, Stewart had juggled football and silk-screen printing as two potential career choices while in his teens before making the choice to sing for his supper instead. Briefly hooking up with fellow N10 resident Ray Davies in a pre-Kinks blues quartet, Rod subsequently moved on to a succession of other choice outfits, his rasping but still honeyed voice put to good use in Jimmy Powell & the Dimensions, Long John Baldry's Steampacket and future Fleetwood Mac guitarist Peter Green's Shotgun Express before heeding Jeff's call to arms over a pint at the Cromwellian in South Kensington. "I just thought 'There's the guy'," Beck later remembered. "'The one guy I want to sing in my band...'"

With Ronnie Wood, it was really more a case of "the face fitting". Cheeky, incredibly affable and a deceptively fine musician, Wood had known Beck since his own teenage band the Birds (featuring brother Art) supported the Tridents at London's evergreen 100 Club in late 1964. A year or so later and Wood was back again, now offering to play harmonica when a bout of asthma temporarily derailed the Yardbirds' Keith Relf, this time onstage at The Marquee. Nominally a guitarist – though more than happy to back Beck on bass guitar when everyone else proved unsuitable – Hillingdon-born "Ronnie the Water Gypsy" was another fine catch for Jeff, his keen sense of humour a Godsend in the difficult months to come. "Some people thought 'Oh, you can't go to bass, it's an inferior instrument if you're a guitarist'," Ronnie later told *Guitar Player*. "But Jeff and I had a nice feel between us, so there was never any competition."

Best described as a period of "musical multiple personality disorder" for Beck, the splenetic guitar player continued to forge ahead with his new 'Jeff Beck Group' while, as evidenced above, simultaneously cutting 45s for the pop market with Mickie Most. Recruiting a succession of unsuitable drummers before settling (at least temporarily) on jazz sticksman Mickey Waller, Jeff's band spent their nights performing a mutant form of blues rock to increasingly impressed crowds around the UK and their days trying to persuade Most that albums, not singles, were the way forward. When Simon Napier-Bell – who had originally elected to manage Beck in favour of the Yardbirds – walked briskly into the sunset rather than face the increasing lunacy of the situation,[78] Mickie's business partner and then current Yardbirds manager Peter Grant stepped in to take charge. It was a good move for Beck. "Peter recognised experimental blues [rock] was going to take off in America," said Jeff. And Beck would take off with it.

Exercising his trademark professionalism, Grant made short work of sticking the 'JBG' on a plane to the States where he and Beck felt their true audience could be found. They were proved right. Fortune smiled almost immediately, with *New York Times'* Robert Shelton championing the group's debut show at the Fillmore East on June 14, 1968 in the most strident terms. "Jeff Beck and his band deal in blues,

---

78 Though Napier-Bell initially tried to steady the ship, Beck's early, near-constant revision of personnel for his band saw the manager simply give up on the whole enterprise. "They'd done about five rehearsals, and at each one, Beck had used different musicians," he said in 2011. "The only constants were Jeff and Ronnie. I sort of gave up. I didn't call because I couldn't stand the arguments and because I was reasonably new to management. I really didn't know [at that time] how to deal with difficult people. So," he concluded, "I just ran away and left Jeff to it."

mainly," reasoned the critic, "but with an urgency and sweep that's hard to resist. Wild and visionary... lean and laconic, [the Jeff Beck Group] brings the big beat of the English rock school forward." Sharp as a pin, Peter Grant sent a hot copy of Shelton's review directly to Epic Records, which in turn finally sanctioned an album release from the band. "Peter managed... to save us from almost certain death," said Jeff. Ronnie Wood was just as succinct. "That one gig," said the rooster-haired bassist, "built our reputation."

Cut in a procession of fits and starts with producer Mickie Most and rising star/engineer Ken Scott at the helm, the Jeff Beck Group's debut album *Truth* turned out to be one of the defining musical works of the late sixties. Full of raw Brit-blues swagger ('Rock My Plimsoul' and 'Blues Deluxe'), evocative balladry ('Morning Dew') and cutting-edge experimentalism ('Beck's Bolero' and an astoundingly reworked version of the Yardbirds' 'Shapes Of Things'), Most's production might have been perfunctory, but it couldn't detract from the sheer depth of talent on display. Aside from Beck, who was on revelatory form throughout – his wah-wah work on 'I Ain't Superstitious' still sounds light years ahead of the game – *Truth* also established Rod Stewart's credentials as a world-class vocalist, his soulful tones as at home on brutal cuts such as 'Shapes...' as it was on the mossy sentimentalism of 'Morning Dew'. An album for the ages that plugged straight into the Jeff Beck Group's ever-growing following on the US concert circuit, *Truth* debuted at number 15 on the *Billboard* LP listing on its release in August 1968.

Really, it should have been a rum time for Jeff Beck. After the trials and tribulations of recent years, he had been justly vindicated in his belief that there was more to life than "pop pap" and random appearances in teen photo magazines with his pet dog. Instead, a meeting with Peter Grant at New York's Americana hotel in early 1969 cut Jeff's celebrations short. "I was mortified when Peter Grant played me the acetate," he told *Guitar*'s Vic Garbarini in 2001. "Peter said 'You better come over and listen to this'. He was thrilled to bits because it was another act he managed that was about to break through and they even had a blond-haired singer like Rod in Robert Plant. This isn't a sour grapes statement or anything – it's just a fact. At the time, me, Rod and Ronnie Wood were about to make the big time, and people were really starting to take notice of us. [So], when Grant first played me Led Zeppelin's version of 'You Shook Me', I thought 'Oh great, this is a great tribute to us'. I asked 'OK, now where's the album?' And he said, 'This is the fucking album, you're listening to it.' I said 'You're joking. We've done that song just three months ago on *Truth*'. And Peter said 'Yeah, but Jimmy loves this version and Robert sings it differently'..." And so began a debate that still rages on some 50 years later.

There is no doubt that both Page and Beck were on more than nodding terms with Muddy Waters' 'You Shook Me' before they each recorded it for their debut LPs with Led Zeppelin and the JBG respectively. In fact, both have clear remembrances as to when they first properly became acquainted with the song. According to Jeff, it appeared on a Muddy EP he purchased at Dobell's records shop on London's Charing Cross Road, exact date unknown. Jimmy, on the other hand, recalled hearing the same EP at the Small Faces' house in Bayswater, with Beck in possible attendance. Given that Steve Marriott's mod-ish four piece formed in 1965, that at least provides some sense of timeline. Circumstantially at least, it also gives a sense of authenticity to why both Jimmy and Jeff ended up covering the same tune. "You've got to understand that Beck and I came from the same sorts of roots," he later told *Guitar Player*. "If you've got things you enjoy, then you want to do them... to the horrifying point where we'd done our first LP with 'You Shook Me', and then I heard Jeff [had also done it]. I was terrified that they'd be the same. But I hadn't known he'd done it and he hadn't known we had."

In reality, Beck and Page's versions of 'You Shook Me' were similar, but by no means identical. With the JBG, the emphasis was all about rolling blues, the inestimable Nicky Hopkin's tinkling piano fills adding an almost mischievous air to proceedings as Rod and Jeff wailed and riffed their way into the stratosphere. Zep's version, however, turned Muddy's lusty tale of adulterous sex into something much darker, with Robert Plant's protagonist sounding mournful rather than joyous about his extra-marital affair. Page's arrangement only added to the sense of mounting regret, those ever-ascending slide guitar lines driving Plant's voice to the point of distraction.[79] Joyous sexual abandon vs. post–coital guilt, then. While Zep and JBG's takes on 'You Shook Me' may have metaphorically risen from the same stream, they had pursued markedly different moral and musical directions thereafter.

What was a little harder to explain away from Zep's point of view was that John Paul Jones had actually appeared on both tracks, adding organ fills to *Truth*'s '... Shook Me' (as well as JBG's version of 'Old Man River') while still working as a session player. "I really didn't know that," Jimmy told writer Charles Shaar Murray when the fact was brought to his attention in 2004. "When we did our [version] he didn't say anything about it! He probably didn't know it was the same number because the two versions were so different." Page's point was plausible. In his guise as a sessioneer, John Paul Jones was often called to two or three studio dates on any working day. As such, it is unlikely he stored JBG's version of 'You Shook Me' in his memory banks with a red flag next to it in case of future use by Led Zeppelin. More, as Jimmy contended, if Jones was not listening carefully to the song's lyric, he may not have made any real connection between the two versions due to the difference in their overall arrangement.

Nonetheless, there were larger issues at play than two bands covering the same tune in close proximity. For Jeff at least, the very idea of Led Zeppelin was uncomfortably close to the original template for his own musical grand plan. "I realised [Jimmy had] completely ripped me off... used all my ideas," he later told *Guitarist*. "[When] Led Zeppelin came out, it dawned on me that I'd been pipped at the post." Beck's contention was partly based on similarities of style. After all, both groups traded on a strong blues influence. Both also had a similar core line-up, with heavy emphasis placed on guitar and vocal interplay. And, of course, both had striking lead singers with tremendous range and undoubted charisma. But Jeff was also uncomfortable with the fact that his friend had witnessed the JBG in action while they were on the

79 The unison slide guitar line that shadowed Robert Plant's voice so brilliantly on 'You Shook Me' was a trick Page first employed on the Yardbirds' 'Drinking Muddy Water' in 1967.

road in America, and may well have been taking notes. "We'd just embarked on our second US tour, and we were playing the Spectrum in Philadelphia," Beck recalled to Malcolm Gerrie in 2013. "And Peter had told Jimmy 'Watch Jeff's group, they're really taking off over there', and Jim's not going to sit back without an investigation. So, he turned up at the Spectrum and we were on fire that night. Anyway, several weeks later, I was at the Americana hotel [with Peter Grant] and there was that little record player..."[80]

It would be easy to side with Beck here. Indeed, some of his contentions make for uncomfortable reading. Yet, it is also worth noting that since Jeff's departure from the Yardbirds in 1966, Page had been increasingly trading on a heavy blues format within the constraints of a four-piece, using extended arrangements and improvisation as key tools. More, with tracks such as 'Dazed And Confused', 'Drinking Muddy Water' and 'Think About It', he was already venturing into the type of material that would inform Zeppelin's sound and style. True, some of these tunes did fall into the general timeframe when Page had seen Beck at work in America. But again, the JBG and the Yardbirds were then also sharing the same stages, with appearances at the Fillmore East and West regular fixtures for each act. Old friends. Homogenous influences and interchangeable record collections. They had even worked in the same band for a while. The notion, then, that each might come up with something broadly similar when left to their own devices was surely not beyond the realms of possibility.

As a consequence of 'You Shook Me' and all it entailed, there were gruff voices raised by both guitarists in years to come, with Beck occasionally pecking at the subject – and indeed, Jimmy and Led Zeppelin – in the music press as and when the mood took him. "I'm sorry, I can't help you there," he later said of Page and his band to writer Steve Rosen. "I wouldn't be fair to myself if I made any excuse for him. I saw the show... and it sounded like somebody paralysed his

---

80 This was not the only time Jeff remarked on Page's attendance at JBG gigs. In an interview with *NME*'s Billy Altham in 1976, he covered similar ground. "Jimmy was going from city to city with us, taking things in..."

arms." Jimmy, on the other hand, seemed content to take a higher road, though irritation was also clearly bubbling under the surface of his remarks. "[Jeff] plays things of sheer genius," he told *Guitarist*'s Richard Mann, "and I defy anyone to show me anything I've said against Beck in the press." True enough, but their relationship remained difficult and increasingly competitive over time before things were once again restored to an even keel. "Jeff and I were very close," said Jimmy. "[Then], this strange sort of professional jealousy came between us and I really don't understand why."

As Beck later conceded, perhaps the seed of the 'You Shook Me' dispute was less about who came up with what and when, and more about just how brilliantly Page had realised his vision of "the perfect group". "[Zep] had a better looking singer... golden, curly hair, and the girls loved him," he confirmed. "They also had Bonzo creating all kinds of pandemonium. It was just a much better package that what I had." Of course, whether Jeff was right about the superiority of Led Zeppelin over JBG was a matter of taste. But one thing was sure: while Beck's band would sink in a sea of acrimony before fulfilling their promise, Page's would continue to lay waste all before it with the steadfastness of Julius Caesar's assault on Gaul and Grand Britannica. Part two of their campaign for world domination came in December 1969, with the release of *Led Zeppelin II*.

CHAPTER 15

Whole Lotta Love

If the sixties belonged to the Beatles then the seventies would belong to Led Zeppelin. On January 30, 1969, while Richard Cole was chauffeuring his charges 80 miles up Highway 95 from Philadelphia to New York to appear at the Fillmore East, over in London, Beatles roadie Mal Evans was setting up guitars and amps on the Apple rooftop in Savile Row for the last public performance his charges would ever give. "I'd like to say thank you on behalf of the group and ourselves and I hope we've passed the audition," John Lennon announced before the group he created bowed out, thereafter to implode amid unseemly squabbling. The creator of the band that succeeded them rarely spoke onstage, letting his guitar do the talking and deferring to the singer to introduce songs. This reticence to address audiences imbued in Jimmy Page an aura of mystery that would cling to him like morning mist over a Scottish loch, but the twinkle in his eye conveyed his true feelings as 1969 became Led Zeppelin's 'magic year', the success of their debut LP on both sides of the Atlantic serving to confirm his essential "rightness" about the band he had put together the previous year.

"I can't see the heavy thing going out," Page told *New Musical Express'* Nick Logan at the time. "Ever since the underground thing happened a couple of years ago, peoples' tastes have been broadening. You can have a group... who are into a light, folky thing on the one hand, and us on the other. The whole scene is broad enough to take us all in, and I don't see why that situation shouldn't continue." That sense of 'continuance' for Page and Led Zeppelin meant only one thing: turning a mere band into a continent-eating war machine.

To that end, Led Zeppelin would perform almost 170 shows throughout 1969, taking in America, Europe and the UK, a territory that they were keen not to ignore despite their clear-sighted focus on the States. To this end, they performed at a slew of smallish Brit venues like the Cooks Ferry Inn in Edmonton and Nottingham Boat Club in March and April, before graduating to larger venues like Birmingham Town Hall, Newcastle's City Hall and Portsmouth Guildhall by June. In between there was another visit to Scandinavia and a second American tour that opened in New York before they jetted over to California for a series of shows in San Francisco and Los Angeles. Next they flew halfway across the Pacific to Hawaii for a show in Honolulu then returned via the northern states to the East Coast for another three concerts at the Boston Tea Party and four more at the Fillmore East in New York. Further emphasising their growing stature at home, Led Zeppelin played a key date at London's prestigious Royal Albert Hall on June 29, the grandeur of the Victorian dome alongside Hyde Park in no way intimidating a group intent on battering both venue and audience into breathless submission.

Though still trading largely on the same selection of songs that saw them through their first months on the road, the likes of 'Dazed And Confused', 'How Many More Times' and 'You Shook Me' had now taken on lives of their own. Increasingly elaborate set pieces for the group and major highlights of the show for their audience, Page's bowed guitar work and Plant's vocal gymnastics were as thrilling to watch as they were complex to perform. As ever, there was a sense that the group was committed not only to entertaining their fans but also to testing the limits of each other's individual skills. Boundaries were being pushed left, right and centre, with all four discovering more about their own abilities as a result. "Oh, absolutely," said Page when writers commented on this aspect of their shows. "My playing was going up a notch... several notches, actually!"

This was certainly evident at the Albert Hall Pop Proms, film footage of which finally saw the light of day in 2003. Having by now swapped his beloved Fender Telecaster for a recently acquired Gibson Les Paul (to which we will return in due course), Jimmy Page was in his element, swooping across the stage, his hair longer than ever, his fretwork electrifying. Still, the seas were calmed for 'White Summer'/'Black Mountain Side', which found Page sitting on a chair to skim the neck of his detuned Danelectro. After that, the band were back onstage for an ominous 'Dazed And Confused', before again altering the mood of the hall with rip-snorting, almost comedic covers of Eddie Cochran's 'C'mon Everybody' and 'Something Else'.

Nick Logan, reviewing the concert for *NME*, reported that the crowd refused to leave after the encore. Following a prolonged bout of foot stomping, Led Zeppelin finally returned to the stage, only to find that the power had been switched off. Plant demanded it be turned on again, after which he launched the band into the evergreen 'Long Tall Sally', once given the full-tilt treatment by the Beatles. "The audience was on its feet dancing in the aisles and in the boxes and there was incredible mayhem happening on and around the stage," recounted Logan. "The stage became thick with paper aeroplanes [symbolically] thrown from the boxes along with a tickertape reception of handbills and balloons and petals of the flowers from the foot of the stage."

Commenting astutely on Page's interaction with Plant, Logan wrote: "In one way, they appear to be fighting each other for dominance, in another they become as one but in the final analysis they serve to haul each other onto greater and greater heights. Plant, with shoulder length blond curls, employs his voice as a fourth instrument. Page, a contrast with shoulder length black hair, evens the score by using his instrument as an extra voice. The result at low key is fascinating; at its high devastating."

Though from the outset Led Zeppelin and Grant had decided to concentrate the thrust of their promotional push on albums rather than singles[81], they were not averse to using other media to get their evangelical message across, at least at this stage in their development. This manifested itself when the quartet appeared not once, but twice on BBC radio during June.

The first was a promo spot on *Chris Grant's Tasty Pop Sundae*, recorded between gigging commitments at the Aeolian Hall on London's Bond Street on June 16. It was originally scheduled for *Symonds On Sunday*, a Sunday morning show hosted by hip DJ Dave Symonds, but during June he was replaced by banal stand-in Chris Grant, the show renamed *Tasty Pop Sundae*. Utterly unfamiliar with the modus operandi or pedigree of Led Zeppelin, Grant asked a series of ham-fisted questions that on another day might have prompted his namesake Peter to string him up. Then again, Led Zeppelin risked a ban from 'wonderful Radio One' when Plant suggested someone might "squeeze my lemon just a little bit" during 'Communication Breakdown'. They were evidently in an experimental frame of mind at the session, throwing two new tunes and a super-charged cover version of an established classic into their four-song set. In the case of 'The Girl I Love (She Got Long Black Wavy Hair)', it was riff-rock all the way, with Page loosely adapting Sleepy John Estes' 1929 recording '... She Got Long Curly Hair' into a three-minute excuse to play the hell out of his guitar while Bonham followed suit on his drum kit.[82] After a corking take on Eddie Cochran's 'Something Else' and now old favourite 'Communication Breakdown', the group then treated listeners to a tune hot off the press, 'What Is And What Should Never Be' marking its official debut some five months before it was to become a highlight of what was fast becoming rock music's most anticipated sophomore LP.

---

81 Though a variety of singles by Led Zeppelin were released in other territories, not until 1997 was a single released in the UK, this a version of 'Whole Lotta Love' recorded at the BBC to promote the band's *BBC Sessions* album.

82 Strangely, Led Zeppelin would perform 'The Girl I Love (She Got Long Black Wavy Hair)' only once in their entire career, though snippets of the riff would sometimes emerge in other forms and during assorted medleys up to 1971.

Only two days after this was transmitted on June 22, Zep was back at the Beeb for another appearance on radio, this time the more suitable DJ John Peel's *Top Gear* show. Once more, there was a heavy emphasis on promoting new material with 'What Is...' brought back for a somewhat friskier run-through, though this time it was joined by a marvellously big-boned version of Robert Johnson's 'Travelling Riverside Blues'. Played with a sense of sass and swing by the band – Bonham's triplet fills on the bass drum simply have to be heard to be believed – and featuring Page opening up the tune nicely with some deft slide guitar, 'Travelling...' was yet more confirmation of the growing simpatico between the four musicians.

"Oh yes," Page confirmed to *Mojo* in 2014, "we'd begun to realise by then just how good the band really was. There was real alchemy involved because we were playing the whole time. There were four strong musicians with strong identities who also had the intellect to really stretch things out and make things come together." Thought cut on the fly – and none the worse for it – both the *Tasty Sundae* and *Top Gear* sessions were destined to become valuable artefacts in future days, waiting patiently in the archives for nearly 20 years before being granted an official release.

There would be no let-up in the unrelenting pace during 1969. While the band was writing new songs for their forthcoming second LP, Peter Grant was booking new venues for concerts. In addition to their European touring, Led Zeppelin made no fewer than four trips to the States in 1969, each visit picking up where the previous one left off. While the tempo might have been unyielding, the reward was a steady, ever-increasing sense of momentum, a gradual desertion of the clubs that hosted their early shows for the more spacious and financially rewarding environment of concert halls, arenas and even a few festivals like the one at Shepton Mallet near Bath on June 18 that drew a crowd of 12,000. "The whole music business was exploding at that point and Zeppelin were exploding with it," said Chris Welch. "Every week, there was a good new band to see, but in Zep's case, it was almost like riding a wave. They started playing universities and small clubs like The Marquee, then in a very short time, progressed to large halls, especially in America."

This back-to-back, business-focused, continent-jumping mentality was illustrated in the boldest terms when after receiving the highest ever fee for a one-off concert at London's Lyceum on October 12, Led Zeppelin leapt on a plane for New York for a date at the prestigious Carnegie Hall just five days later. Again, Chris Welch was an impressed witness to Page's masterplan at work. "By the Lyceum, they had a huge following," he recalled. "I did a review of the show for *Melody Maker* in which I described them like the Zeppelins that had bombed London. Then I actually discovered that the Zeppelins had actually bombed the Lyceum in 1916. Peter Grant loved that!"

Having charmed Grant with his rhetoric, Welch was given the honour of flying with the band to New York. The intensity of Zep's American audience stays with him even today. "They were to be the first rock band to play that venue in years[83]," he says. "I remember meeting Robert and John before the flight at Euston train station. They were quite late, having come down from Birmingham, but we all got to the airport on time to meet Jimmy, John Paul and Peter. Then it was on to the Boeing 707 and into first class. From The Marquee to a sold-out gig at Carnegie Hall in less than a year. Quite impressive."

Impressive and, indeed, intense. "It was like a scene from *West Side Story* when they opened the doors to Carnegie Hall," he remembered. "Thousands of teenagers running in, chasing towards the front of the stage. No one sat down, they just all stood together, whooping and hollering, shaking hands with Jimmy and Robert. Well, we weren't used to this. At The Marquee, you watched a band while drinking a pint and eating a bag of crisps. This American thing," Welch dryly concluded, "was very different indeed..."

Given their vertiginous climb in popularity, today's prevailing wisdom might suggest that Led Zeppelin should have withdrawn from the market

83 Led Zeppelin were not the first pop/rock band to play New York's prestigious Carnegie Hall. That honour had already gone to the Beatles in February 1964, followed by the Rolling Stones in June of the same year. Unfortunately, so riotous was the Stones' audience that the venue's management team banned all future performances by 'popular beat groups' until Zep were allowed through the doors some five years later.

in late 1969 to relish their victories, re-group their energies and develop new ideas before returning again refreshed and triumphant a year or so later. This, however, was not the way bands or record labels went about their business at the time. Autumn was a traditionally a strong market in which to release new product and Atlantic was keen to get something from the group and into the stores before Christmas. That said, Page wasn't complaining too strenuously about such stringent deadlines. "We were on fire," he later said. "We didn't want to stop, we wanted to keep going!" In fact, so confident was Jimmy of Led Zeppelin's collective talent, his goal was not about playing safe or even sustaining the band's position, but actually surpassing it as soon as possible.

To this end, Led Zeppelin had been in and out of various recording facilities in the UK, USA and Canada since the start of the year, cutting new songs for their second LP. Snatching time as and when they could between shows, the band made flying visits to London's Olympic and Morgan Studios, Los Angeles' A&M, Mystic, Quantum and Sound Recorder complexes, as well as stopping off in Memphis (Ardent) and New York (Mayfair, Juggy Sound & Groove). Some venues had yielded particularly impressive results, with the small, but perfectly formed space at Mirror Sound in Hollywood giving Page what in his role as producer he considered "the perfect sound for [Bonzo's] drums". Having previously played host to the likes of fifties rock'n'roll giants such as Ritchie Valens, Chan Romero and Bobby Fuller, Mirror's spare but warm qualities were right up Jimmy's alley. "When you listen to those fifties records, you could tell it was a small room," he later said. "But the energy of it came right through."

Other facilities proved less useful to the band. While already legendary for providing Phil Spector with his 'wall of sound', LA's Gold Star Studios were reportedly something of a disappointment for Page, the recording desk's poor rotary pots and overall vibe not conducive to forward progress.[84] Similarly, an idea to record some tunes at Sam

---

84 According to Page, "something" was indeed recorded at Gold Star Studios but has been subsequently lost in the shuffle of time. "(And) we don't want people searching for it, do we?" he told *Mojo* in August 2014.

Phillips' immortal Sun Studios in Memphis was also nixed. "Well," said Jimmy, "by the time of our second album, it wasn't the original Sun Studios [anymore]." However, despite its lack of proper headphones and generally archaic set-up, a small "hut in Vancouver" provided just what the band was after, with several valuable harp fills captured in the course of a night's work. In this febrile atmosphere, where overdubs were cut "on the fly", ideas literally pulled from the stage before being committed to tape and "hotel room riffs" becoming fully realised songs in just a matter of days, it was entirely unsurprising that Page was riddled with flu and the band at the point of exhaustion by the time final mixing of the LP took place, over a single weekend in New York during mid-August 1969.

There were obvious concerns here, of course. With Led Zeppelin having thrown themselves into the song-writing process while still on the road, there was a real risk that the quality of the material might suffer as a result, with tunes sounding uneven or half-baked. Of equal worry was the scattergun approach they had taken to actually getting their ideas down on tape. Having recorded vocal, guitar, bass and drum parts here, there and everywhere in a mad effort to get the LP across the commercial line by the late autumn of 1969, if recording levels were uneven or takes mismatched, the end result could potentially be dull or trebly, woolen or shrill. Having come so far in such a short space of time, to have it all fall away for the sake of speed or market forces would be a bitter pill to swallow. "It was crazy, really," Plant said in 1997. "We were writing the numbers in hotels, then [doing] rhythm tracks in London, adding vocals in New York [and] overdubbing harmonica parts in Vancouver..."

In the end, *Led Zeppelin II* turned out damn near perfect. Sometimes fevered and priapic, sometimes warm and woozy, the LP was arguably even better than its predecessor, capturing as it did both the blood and thunder of road life, coupled with occasional moments of post-concert calm. "I wanted *II* to be quite extreme," Jimmy later said. "That's what I was going for, something that showed all the peaks of what we could do." And peaks there certainly were. With 'What Is And What Shall Never Be', for instance, Robert Plant finally shed his initial shyness (and contractual difficulties with CBS[85]), and stepped forward as a writer/lyricist of real promise, his juxtaposing of dreamlike imagery with more salty wordplay suiting the track's lurches between soothing calm and brazen musical violence. "Catch the wind, see us spin, sail away, leave today," he howled amid a barrage of guitars and tom-toms. Having written the totality of lyrics for the first LP, Plant's arrival as a wordsmith was not a moment too soon in coming for Jimmy Page. "Yeah, I wanted to get to a point [quickly] where Robert was doing all the lyrics," he told *Musician* in 1990, "because I really wasn't very happy with mine!"

Plant was also on top form throughout 'Ramble On', though this time he really did share honours with the rest of the group. Shoehorning his growing interest in the fantasy works of author JRR Tolkien into the song's lyrical structure, Robert's tales of roaming youths in fictional lands beset by imaginary creatures was supported by a world-class bass line from John Paul Johns, a rhythmic masterclass from John Bonham and Jimmy's deft combination of swooning harmony lines and cut-throat riffing. "'Ramble On'," wrote one critic, "defined Zep's gift for light and shade." 'Thank You', on the other hand, featured hardly any shade at all, with Plant content to extol the virtues of his wife Maureen over Jones' melting, church-like Hammond organ and Page's Vox 12-string guitar. Regrettably, *Led Zeppelin II*'s only real misfire, 'Living Loving Maid (She's Just A Woman)'[86] had neither the instrumental heroics of 'Ramble On' or the charm and deportment of 'Thank You'. Essentially an amiable pop tune that had inexplicably managed to sneak itself onto a classic rock album, Page's reported dislike of '... (She's Just A Woman)' was understandable.

---

85 Due to contractual issues arising from his previous deal with CBS Records, Plant's name was missing from the writing credits for *Led Zeppelin I*. Grant rectified the situation by the time of the band's second release.

86 Given the working title 'Living Loving Wreck', '... (She's Just A Woman)' was allegedly written in honour of a 'malingering' groupie that attached herself to the band while they were on tour in the USA.

A much more carnal affair, 'The Lemon Song' was awash (both literally and figuratively) with sexual innuendo, as Robert temporarily set aside his caring husband persona to instead inhabit a beleaguered lover, working all hours before coming home to his fickle mistress for a few fleeting moments of pleasure. "The way you squeeze my lemon," he sang, "I'm gonna fall right out of bed..." Opening up with a grinding, two-octave climb from Jimmy, before re-doubling its pace for the middle-section, 'The Lemon Song' bore more than a passing musical resemblance – and, indeed, borrowed a line or two from – Howlin' Wolf's own 'Killing Floor'. Yet, as the record label denoted, the tune was credited only to the band. As with several other Zeppelin tracks, this omission of proper writing credits would come back to haunt them in times to come. 'Bring It On Home' also borrowed liberally from another blues veteran, its creaky opening and concluding bars the very 'spit' of Sonny Boy Williamson's original cover of Willie Dixon's own 'Bring It On Home'. However, the three-minute bit in the middle was all Led Zeppelin, as the group galloped off on the back of another classic riff from Page. Destined to be used as the basis of a spirited onstage guitar/drum battle between Jimmy and John Bonham, 'Bring It On Home''s lusty swagger was another highlight on an album already full of them.

Strangely, Bonham's own particular moment in the sun – the clattering 'Moby Dick' – failed to fully transfer his roaring energy and peerless technique from concert hall to tape. An instrumental that had been slowly evolving for some months since it was known as 'Pat's Delight'[87], 'Moby Dick' represented an ideal opportunity for Page, Plant and Jones to leave the stage in the capable hands of their drummer. A solo showpiece – which featured Bonzo cajoling, stroking, battering and pummelling every inch of his kit with both sticks and hands – the

---

87 'Pat's Delight'/'Moby Dicks'' signature riff was largely commandeered from Zep's own take on 'The Girl I Love (She Got Long Black Wavy Hair)'. However, it may have also drawn some inspiration from several other sources, including the Beatles' 'I Feel Fine' and Bobby Parker's 'Watch Your Step', which in turn were indebted to Dizzy Gillespie's 'Manteca' and Ray Charles' wonderful 'What'd I Say'.

track had put the fear of God into any percussionist that saw it. But the version of 'Moby Dick' that appeared on *Led Zeppelin II* seemed to lack a little sparkle, sounding a tad damp and muted in comparison to the almighty racket Bonham was regularly producing night after night on tour. Still, for John Paul Jones, the sheer pleasure gleaned from working alongside 'God's own drummer' was immeasurable. "Bass players and drummers tend to grow together. It's kind of like a marriage," he later told *Guitar World*'s Alan di Perna. "[But] Bonzo was one of the finest drummers I've ever come across. A joy to play with. I hope I inspired him a bit [as well]."

If 'Moby Dick' lacked a bit of bite, the two tracks that opened side one and two of Led Zeppelin's sophomore LP certainly did not. Taking the latter tune first, 'Heartbreaker' was yet another example of Jimmy Page easing into his future role as 'King of the Riffs', the guitarist's ability to fashion magical properties from a procession of random notes then, as now, unrivalled. "My influences were the riff-based blues coming out of Chicago in the fifties, Muddy, Wolf, Billy Boy Arnold records," he told *Rolling Stone* by way of explanation in 2008. "Oh, and 'Boogie Chillun'" by John Lee Hooker. That is a riff! But you take it, absorb it, apply it to your character, [and] it comes out another way." Not content with gifting Zeppelin with another gargantuan-sized riff on 'Heartbreaker', Jimmy also threw in a frantic, unaccompanied guitar solo mid-track. Sometimes forsaking pure technique for raw passion, Jimmy's display of manic overbends, straddling blues scales, fretboard tapping and percussive stops and starts might have been a tad wild in places, but it still packed a tremendous emotional punch. "Ah, [but] I always leave the mistakes in," he later said, laughing. "I've always been a bit unconventional as far as that goes, I suppose. [I'm] also a bit sloppy, unfortunately, which is my style. But I guess out of all that mish-mash, something happens. I don't know where it comes from, but it just does..."

Enabling Page to capture this peculiar magic on tape over several cuts was engineer Eddie Kramer. Brought in to replace Glyn Johns when Jimmy's old friend from Epsom had reportedly pushed too far for a co-producer's credit on Led Zeppelin's debut album[88], Kramer was already a dab hand at the studio game, having recorded with the Kinks, Petula Clark and Sammy Davis Jr. in London during the early sixties. Soon, he had added the Beatles ('All You Need Is Love'), the Stones and Small Faces to his CV, though some of Eddie's best work was done after he relocated to New York and met Jimi Hendrix, the duo subsequently combining their talents for the Seattle guitarist's superlative 1968 release, *Electric Ladyland*.

A fan of that LP and an acquaintance of Kramer's since they had both frequented Pye Studios at the birth of British pop, Page contacted Eddie when he required a safe pair of hands while recording tracks in America. "Eddie was always very, very good," Jimmy said, "and I got along well with him." Kramer was equally complimentary of Page. "Jimmy was an excellent producer... [who] had a very definite picture of what he wanted to capture on tape," he later told journalist John McDermott. "He was very demanding, but at the same time, completely open to suggestions. Jimmy's biggest asset," Kramer sagely concluded, "was he knew how to draw the best performances out of the band." Nonetheless, the engineer was surprised when Page chose to keep his madcap, unaccompanied solo for 'Heartbreaker' intact, feeling that while the spirit was certainly there, there were fundamental flaws in the finished product. "I have a hard time listening to [the 'Heartbreaker' solo], actually, because I think we did a shitty edit," he later said. "The difference in noise levels is pretty outrageous. But I don't think Jimmy cared. He was more interested in capturing an idea, and on that level, he succeeded."

---

88 As already evidenced, Glyn John's request for a joint production credit on *Led Zeppelin I* was given short shrift by Page. "A bit of an attitude problem (there)," Jimmy later told *Guitar World*. "(Besides), I wanted people to know it was (all) me." However, there seemed to be no real hard feelings between the two men, a fact underlined when Glyn's younger brother, Andy, was drafted in by Jimmy to help engineer two tracks on *Led Zeppelin II* ('Living Loving Maid...' and 'Thank You'). Glyn also made a contribution of sorts to *Led Zeppelin II*, though as a later footnote describes, probably not the one he might have had in mind.

Capturing *Led Zeppelin II*'s flagship tune both spiritually and technically, however, was a prerequisite for all concerned. Conceived by Page at his home in Pangbourne in 1968 and first played to the group during rehearsals for their debut album, 'Whole Lotta Love' was destined to become one of rock music's true cornerstones, its primal intensity and pioneering experimental spirit shocking to behold, then as now. "I suppose my early love for big intros by rockabilly guitarists was an inspiration [for 'Whole Lotta Love']," Jimmy later told *Wall Street Journal*, "but as soon as I developed the riff, I knew it was strong enough to drive the entire song, not just open it. When I played the riff for the band in my living room... the excitement was immediate and collective. We felt the riff was addictive, like a forbidden thing."

Understanding its true value, but not wanting to run before he could walk, Page allowed 'Whole Lotta Love' to gestate for some months until he was finally ready to reveal his "avant-garde masterplan". Broken in by the band during rehearsals and subsequently debuted at their live shows[89], Jimmy was finally ready to record the tune at London's Olympic Studios in April 1969. "Well," John Paul Jones later said, "'Whole Lotta Love' is when Jimmy really began coming into his own as producer..."

Assisted at Olympic by a young engineer called George Chkiantz (who had impressed Page with his contributions to Jimi Hendrix's second disc, *Axis: Bold As Love*), band, producer and sound man went to work. At the heart of the attack was John Bonham. "For the song to work as this panoramic audio experience," Jimmy again told *Wall Street Journal* in 2015, "I needed Bonzo to really stand out, so that every stick stroke sounded clear and you could really feel them. If the drums were recorded just right, we could lay in everything else." To this purpose, Chkiantz built an artificial platform under Bonham's kit, while various experiments were also conducted with ambient miking. When it came to vocals, Robert Plant was first recorded live on the studio floor before being moved to an isolation booth to better catch each vowel,

---

89 'Whole Lotta Love' was also recorded for John Peel's *BBC* radio show *Top Gear* on June 24, 1969. Its broadcast date – (29/06/69) – preceded the release of *Led Zeppelin II* by nearly four months.

howl, grunt and sibilant. Egging him on every step of the way was Jimmy. "Robert kept gaining confidence during the session and gave it everything he had. His vocals, like my solos, were about performance. He was pushing to see what he could get out of his voice. We were performing for each other, almost competitively."

To achieve the middle-section meltdown in 'Whole Lotta Love', Page threw almost everything he had at it. Employing a Theremin[90] to create eerie, otherworldly noises, the producer also used sirens, demolition effects and even de-tuned his guitar and pulled on its strings to replicate what sounded like the death-throes of a crashing motorcycle. From orgasmic squeals courtesy of Plant to blackboard-like scrapes and metal slides covered in the same backwards echo technique Page had introduced on the Yardbirds' 'Ten Little Indians' two-odd years before, the overall result was, as one critic succinctly put it, "a complete headfuck from start to finish."

Then, after an apocalyptic drum roll from Bonham, came the guitar solo. Using a half-cocked wah pedal to create his waspish lead tone, Jimmy let loose with a short, sharp barrage of notes before Plant again rose from the ashes to bring 'Whole Lotta Love' home with a series of sexually charged lyrics and inhuman wails. The only thing left to do now was mix the thing. Turning again to Eddie Kramer for assistance, Jimmy and his engineer tried frantically to control the aural storm with just eight fingers, two thumbs and a bagful of willpower. "The famous 'Whole Lotta Love' mix, where everything is going bananas," Kramer later said, "[was] a combination of Jimmy and myself just flying around on a small console twiddling every knob known to man."

90 Named for its Russian inventor Leon Theremin, who patented the device in 1928, a Theremin is an electronic instrument consisting of two metal antennae that sense the relative position of the performer's hands. One hand controls its frequency oscillators while the other controls its volume. The electric signals from the Theremin are then amplified and sent to a loudspeaker. At no point does the performer actually need to touch the Theremin. Instead, by simply waving one's hands around the device at various angles, all sorts of strange and wonderful sounds can be produced.

An LP pulled together at a plethora of recording studios against a relentless backdrop of European and US tours, *Led Zeppelin II* could have been "a bloody disaster". Instead, it proved to be a proper monument to the band, its heady confection of hard blues, electrifying rock, soft folk textures and inspired sound effects defining the depth of Page's ambitions for Led Zeppelin while also underlining his ability to deliver them. "[*Led Zeppelin II*] captured the energy of being on the road," Jimmy later told *Classic Rock*. "That's what I really like about it. [Also], you could really hear the character of these [various] studios on the recordings." Plant felt much the same. "It was still blues-based," he said of the album, "but with a much more carnal approach to the music."

Housed within a lavish, gatefold sleeve designed by David Juniper, its front cover cleverly doctored to depict the band as members of the German Luftwaffe's elite 'Jasta Division'[91], *Led Zeppelin II* was released on October 22, 1969. With advance sales of over 400,000 in the States alone, there was little doubt the album would be successful whatever its contents. However, when positive word of mouth started to build, and the band's ever-expanding tour campaign took the new songs from the LP and into the arenas, sales began to snowball. Entering the *Billboard* Hot 100 at number 15 in November, by year end *Led Zeppelin II* had dislodged the Beatles' *Abbey Road* from the top of the US charts, staying there for a further seven weeks. This rampant success was surely aided by the release of an edited version of 'Whole Lotta Love' as a 'primer'

---

91 In keeping with the overall, frantic pace of making *Led Zeppelin II*, designer David Juniper (a friend of Jimmy's from his days at Sutton Art College) was given only days to complete the album's sleeve. Keen to find an image that "made people think", he procured an old photograph of the 'Jagdstaffel 11' (aka 'Jasta' Division, a famed World War I bombing crew) before swapping the faces of the pilots with those of Page, Plant, Jones and Bonham. On Jimmy's suggestion, the features of manager Peter Grant, tour manager Richard Cole, blues guitar hero Blind Willie Johnson and actress Glynis Johns were also added to the forged photo. In using Glynis Johns, Page was being mischievous, since the actress' name was extremely similar to that of recently disengaged engineer Glyn Johns. Further, Davis' decision to tint the LP's sleeve in ruddy, almost sepia-like tones led to the album being nicknamed 'The Brown Bomber' by Atlantic Records.

single in America, with Page's almighty riff reaching number four under its own steam.[92]

Led Zeppelin II's performance in Great Britain was just as impressive. Hitting the number one spot in early February 1970, on the back of yet another domestic tour, the album subsequently made a nest for itself in the UK charts, remaining perched in the Top 30 (or thereabouts) for a whopping 98 weeks. Again, the appearance of 'Whole Lotta Love' as a single probably didn't hurt, even if it actually wasn't Led Zeppelin's version of the tune that became a hit. Sticking rigidly to their 'No 45s' policy on home soil (even if Peter Grant practically had to kidnap the UK branch of Atlantic Records to get his way), Page and the band had absolutely no intention of 'Whole Lotta Love' being removed from its natural album setting. But an acquaintance of Jimmy's from his nights jamming at The Marquee in 1962 had other ideas. Still happily bobbing about on the British music scene, Alexis Korner's latest band CCS (or 'Collective Consciousness Society') recorded 'Whole Lotta Love' as the instrumental theme tune for the BBC's premier chart show *Top Of The Pops*. Inveigling its way into the public's consciousness on a weekly basis, CCS' take on '... Love' was duly released as a 7", taking Korner to number 13 in mid-1970. Ironically, after nearly 20 years in the business, it was the wily old bluesman's first real hit.

Given his reputation for sound financial management[93], Jimmy Page was probably glad of the repeat royalties for 'Whole Lotta Love' from both *Top Of The Pops* and CCS, but even he might have had trouble spotting them on the band's account ledger in the aftermath of *Led Zeppelin II*. With the album selling over three million copies in the USA by April 1970, and the *Financial Times* announcing the

---

92 When 'Whole Lotta Love' started to go down the charts, US disc jockeys simply flipped the single and started playing its B-side, the more poppy, if inessential 'Living Loving Maid' instead. As a result, 'Living...' made it to number 65 Stateside on its own merits.

93 Page's reputation for keeping an eye on the pennies is well-established. In fact, Peter Grant once joked the easiest way to kill the guitarist was to throw some coins in front of a bus.

band's Stateside profits as "in excess of $5 million", when one added various tour revenues, UK and European record sales and additional merchandising, Led Zeppelin were now seriously rich. Little wonder, then, that Memphis collectively marked the group's position as "one of the world's top live attractions" by handing over the keys to their city when the band appeared there in the spring of 1970.

But as rich as Page and Led Zeppelin were now becoming, they still had to doff their caps to European aristocracy. Thus far, despite partially naming themselves after the illustrious airship inventor Ferdinand von Zeppelin and, indeed, using a facsimiled photograph of the doomed *Hindenburg*[94] exploding in flames as the front cover of their debut album, no contact had been made between the band and von Zeppelin's family. That all changed, however, when Led Zep were due to perform a special, one-off date at Denmark's KP Hallen. Having learned that the group had honoured her ancestor by taking his name, Countess Eva von Zeppelin was initially flattered and eager to meet Page and co. Unfortunately, when she saw a picture of said *Hindenburg* on the cover of their LP, all hell broke loose. "We'd actually invited her backstage to meet us, to see how we were nice young lads," Jimmy later told *Melody Maker*. "But on leaving the studio, she spotted our LP cover of an airship in flames and exploded! I had to run and hide. She just blew her top." So incensed, in fact, was the good countess that she threatened to sue Led Zeppelin should they use her family's appellation while in Denmark. "They may be world-famous," said von Zeppelin. "But a couple of shrieking monkeys are not going to use a privileged family name without permission."

Over $5 million in the bank. At least three million record sales and counting. The adoration of thousands of screaming fans every night of the week. Even the keys to a whole city soon to hang from their collective hand. Yet, when Led Zeppelin finally appeared onstage in

---

94 The world's most famous airship, the *Hindenburg* exploded into flames while trying to dock at a US naval air station on May 6, 1937. A total of 36 people (35 of them passengers) died as a result of the accident.

Denmark on February 28, 1970, for fear of legal action they had to do so under another name. "We called ourselves 'The Nobs'," said Page.

It didn't happen again.

CHAPTER 16

Bron-Yr-Aur

By the spring of 1970, Led Zeppelin were just about the biggest rock band on the planet. With the Beatles having slipped into the abyss following the public announcement by Paul McCartney that he no longer wished to record with them, and the Rolling Stones on the run from the combined horrors of Altamont[95] and the British tax system, their only real competitors to speak of were the Who, now riding high thanks to *Tommy* and the imminent *Live At Leeds*. For a while, Cream, the Jimi Hendrix Experience and even the Jeff Beck Group had all threatened to challenge the crown. But bitter interpersonal arguments, chaotic management practices and record company shenanigans had either undone their progress or forced them to start all over again. "Zeppelin just didn't make the same mistakes as the other bands," writer Chris Welch confirmed in 2015. "Unlike Jimi Hendrix, who could have been so, so much bigger, Zep had strong

---

95 A free festival held in northern California on December 6, 1969 before an estimated audience of 300,000, Altamont was billed as a 'West Coast Woodstock'. Unfortunately, it turned into an unmitigated disaster, with four deaths on site during the course of the festival, including Meredith Hunter, who was killed in a scuffle with security during the Stones performance.

management. And unlike Cream who imploded on itself, they were a tight, disciplined unit."

Of course, Peter Grant could take real credit for much of Led Zeppelin's burgeoning success. By creating an impenetrable wall around the band, Grant had allowed their creative talents to blossom without the need to worry about anything else. A superb business mind, he also ensured that the lion's share of Led Zeppelin's huge earnings was paid directly to them rather than concert promoters, booking agents or record company accountants. In this, he was surely aided by his physical size and blunt, occasionally intimidating rhetoric. But it still took enormous nous to build, consolidate and extend an operation like Led Zeppelin from fledging club act to potential world-beaters in the space of 20-odd months. "Though Peter Grant was a terrifying figure – lest we forget, he was an all-in wrestler and came up in an era of Soho doormen and all that meant – I think a lot of it was just an act," Welch continued. "There was genuine menace there, sure, but he could be completely lovely... a lovely guy. And lest we forget, a brilliant, brilliant manager. "

However, when it came to initial design, creative make-up, musical architecture and final delivery, the buck started and stopped with Jimmy Page. Hatching his "perfect band" from the ashes of the Yardbirds, Page had grown his idea into a multi-million selling reality, with Led Zeppelin now more resembling an ever-growing black hole, pulling America and the rest of the world into its maw, than a quartet trading on rock guitars, long hair and blues hollering. This was nowhere more apparent than the recent victories of *Led Zeppelin II*. Birthed by necessity, recorded on the run, yet delivered on time and to budget, Page's dogged persistence and vice-like grip on the album's songs, production and final mix had resulted in a commercial breakthrough few bands could dream of. "[But] it didn't seem as a producer, Jimmy was a separate entity," Robert Plant later confessed to *Uncut*. "It felt like he was the guy around whom the band had been created. It was his band, his call. And just as well, really."

An enormous undertaking, the creation of *Led Zeppelin II* and the incessant touring that accompanied it had not been achieved without some sacrifice to life and limb. According to engineer Eddie Kramer, Page had persistent stomach problems around the time of making the album, and Peter Grant had shielded him heavily as a result. It wasn't just Jimmy; all members of the band had been in the wars at one time or another, with various colds, flus and several dozen hangovers gradually wearing down their bodies, if not quite their spirits. However, their recent influx of riches now ensured that Led Zeppelin would never have to repeat the insanities of 1969 again. Before making their next album, the group could take some well-deserved time off to rest, recuperate or, in Jimmy and Robert's case, pack their bags and head off to rural Wales on a song-writing expedition.

Set on the outskirts of Machynlleth (or 'Mach', to give it its local name) within the ceremonial county of Powys, Bron-Yr-Aur[96] was a private cottage used by Plant's family as a holiday home during the mid–late fifties. Loving the serenity of the location and its relative distance from the nearest town, Robert was keen to return there following Led Zeppelin's latest, gruelling trek across the USA in March/April 1970.[97] On hearing of his singer's idea, Page jumped in with both feet, packing a bag, acoustic guitar and two roadies (Sandy MacGregor and Clive Coulson) for the trip. Also accompanying the duo into the Welsh hills were Plant's wife, Maureen, and their 18-month-old daughter, Carmen, the infant girl born only months after Robert had joined Zep in the summer of 1968.

The last place was taken by Jimmy's new girlfriend, Charlotte Martin. A successful French model whose comely face had adorned the pages of Brit-style magazines such as *Petticoat*, Martin was also something of a counter-cultural 'It Girl', her interests in art, film and literature bringing her into close proximity with London's music scene of the mid-sixties. In fact, it was at Soho's Speakeasy club in 1966 that she had met Eric Clapton, then in the process of forming his new band Cream. "I was smitten with Charlotte from the very first moment I set eyes on her," revealed the guitarist in his autobiography. A relationship followed,

---

96 'Bron-Yr-Aur' literally translates as 'golden breast' in Welsh.
97 Zeppelin's break from the US concert circuit was extremely well-timed. As they had spent close to six months of the year already touring Stateside, they were running the legal risk of being drafted as soldiers to fight in the Vietnam War.

with the pair staying together until 1968, when Clapton fell in turn for Beatle George Harrison's then wife, Pattie Boyd. That said, Martin and Clapton had long broken up by the time Jimmy was introduced to her by the Who's Roger Daltrey and his then girlfriend Heather Taylor, soon to be his wife, on Page's 26th birthday. Immediately taken with the other, Charlotte moved into Jimmy's house at Pangbourne within a matter of weeks. "Charlotte was the type of girl who you couldn't look at just once," Zeppelin's tour manager Richard Cole later said. "Tall. Thin. Blonde. Perfect features. You have to glance a second time..."

If anyone was expecting Bron-Yr-Aur to provide them with palatial splendour, they were in for a real surprise. The cottage had neither running water nor an electricity supply. More, with no shops nearby, provisions had to be shipped in by car. Candlelight, wood fires, several crates of beer and absolutely no telephones. For Page, that meant just one thing. "Wonderful countryside, panoramic views and having the guitars," he later told Nigel Williamson. "It was just an automatic thing to be playing. So, we started writing."

As ever, progress on songs was sure and swift. In the case of 'Bron-Y-Aur Stomp', Robert had written a simple, but good-natured ode in honour of his Merle dog 'Strider'[98]. Full of images of wood-walking, winding country lanes and happy, blue-eyed canines, Plant's bounding lyric sat beautifully atop Jimmy's country-folk chords and hoedown chorus. Despite its seemingly innocuous title, 'Friends' was a more intriguing proposition. On the face of it, Robert's words seem to extol the value of helping those in need. Nonetheless, there were other, obvious stress lines here, too, with Plant's protagonist left to contemplate "bright lights" and "black nights" as he lamented the end of another relationship. This sense of mounting unease was magnified by Jimmy's use of an open B6 guitar tuning, its resultant drone more akin to brewing Eastern sandstorms than the bucolic Welsh countryside. The fact that Page was reported to have had a blazing row with Charlotte Martin just

---

98 'Strider' was the nickname given to the fictional character Aragorn in Tolkien's *Lord Of The Rings* series.

before writing 'Friends' might also have been a factor in establishing its dark mood.

'That's The Way' too held its fair share of intrigue. Originally called 'The Boy Next Door', it was actually written by Jimmy and Robert after a long day's hike up hill and down dale. "It was one of those days after a long walk and we were setting back to the cottage," Page later confirmed. "We had a guitar with us. It was a tiring walk coming down a ravine and we stopped and sat down. I played the tune and Robert sang the first verse straight off. We had a tape recorder with us and we got the tune down." Again, the canny lyric to 'That's The Way' belied its relative musical simplicity. On first hearing, Plant appeared to be singing about the end of another love affair. But digging a little deeper, the song revealed itself to be as much about environmental concerns as any notion of star-crossed lovers. "And all the fish that lay in the dirty water dying, have they got you hypnotised?"

A creative interlude that not only recharged Page and Plant's batteries but also produced a glut of new material that would pop up on subsequent albums[99], the visit to Bron-Yr-Aur had two other beneficial, long-term effects. Until mid-1970, though Jimmy and Robert had toured the world together, they remained colleagues rather than real friends. Their sojourn at the Welsh cottage changed all that and, moreover, taught both a valuable lesson about travel as a useful tool in the creative process. "[It was the] first time I really came to know Robert," Page later told writer/filmmaker Cameron Crowe, "actually living together at Bron-Yr-Aur, as opposed to occupying nearby hotel rooms. The songs took us into areas that changed the band. It established a standard of travelling for inspiration... which is the best thing a musician can do." Chris Welch was also in no doubt that Jimmy and Robert's journey to Bron-Yr-Aur had a lasting impact on all that came next. "Of course,

---

99 As well as 'Bron-Y-Aur Stomp', 'Friends' and 'That's The Way', at least seven further tracks were written (or at least started) during Page and Plant's cottage holiday. While many of these songs will pop up throughout the course of this book, two tunes – 'I Wanna Be Her Man' and 'Another Way To Wales' – have never been officially released by the band.

they grew very close when they started writing songs together, when they went away to Wales," he said. "But I think Jimmy was always very fond of Robert, right from the moment they first met up and played each other records... when they first established their musical tastes. Jimmy knew what he'd found in Robert and that he was the right man [for the job]."

Refreshed by their break, Page and Plant rejoined John Paul Jones and John Bonham in the early summer of 1970 to run through songs for their third album and, after several Bron-Yr-Aur songs were tried on for size, they were ready to begin recording. They reportedly did so at two principal locations.[100] The swish settings of brand new London's Island studios and the more familiar hunting grounds of Olympic.

While recording and mixing of the group's new disc was to carry on into August[101], Led Zeppelin continued to gig sporadically throughout the summer. Though for financial reasons that will soon become apparent, the band were becoming increasingly selective as to when and where they would appear, the lure of a one-off gig in Iceland was simply too much to resist. Heading to Reykjavik's Laugardalshöll Sports Centre on June 22, Led Zeppelin found themselves performing at a venue where two years later American Bobby Fischer would meet Russian Boris Spassky in the 20th century's most celebrated World Chess Championship. Though the group's concert was part of a cultural

---

100 The Hampshire mansion house Headley Grange has long been listed in previous articles, features and books as one of the sites at which *Led Zeppelin III* was recorded. Indeed, on the original CD re-release of the album (Atlantic 7567 826 782) and 1993's *The Complete Studio Recordings Box Set*, six of the LP's 10 tracks carry the statement "Recorded in 1970 at Headley Grange, Hampshire." However, in a 2014 interview with *Mojo*, Page emphatically stated this was not the case. "You're not the first person to mention Headley Grange in connection with *III*," he told Chris Dreja. "It's complete rubbish. I should know, I was there!" When Dreja pointed out that it was Zep's own record company that had published the information, Page said "We shall have to blame Atlantic!"

101 The band were again joined by Andy Johns on their latest project. Eddie Kramer also made a brief return to the Zeppelin camp, helping out on mixing 'Gallows Pole' while Page and co. were in New York.

exchange package organised by the British government, there can be little doubt that it was a far less cerebral affair than watching Fischer's endless mind games with his noble, if doomed, opponent. However, Zep's trip to the land of the midnight sun was not entirely bereft of cultural benefit, inspiring Robert to write a lusty lyric about ice, snow, fearless warriors and mighty long ships. When Jimmy picked up on Plant's phrase 'the hammer of the gods' and attached it to a mighty staccato riff, Led Zeppelin had a new, relentless steam hammer of a song on their hands, one that at just two minutes and 27 seconds duration was also remarkably brief by their standards.

Six days later, back in the UK, Led Zeppelin played to the biggest crowd of their career thus far, opening their set with the self-same tune, now titled 'Immigrant Song'. For any other group this would have been a reckless display of bravado, but for Jimmy Page and his men it was simply another heroic demonstration of the gargantuan self-assurance they felt in the first summer of the decade they would make their own.

The Bath Festival of Blues & Progressive Music at Shepton Mallet, 18 miles south-west of the British city best known for its Roman baths and Georgian architecture, took place over the weekend of June 26–28. Doubtless because Led Zeppelin were headlining on the final night, upwards of 150,000 had paid their £2 10s to gather on the gentle incline that sloped down towards a stage that had already seen performances by the Mothers of Invention, Pink Floyd, Fairport Convention, Santana and many more by the time the sun set on Sunday evening. Realistically, Led Zeppelin's performance at Bath's West Showground was another carefully planned strategic move by Peter Grant, mindful that his charges needed a high profile UK appearance and who consequently turned down $200,000 for two US appearances over the same weekend, accepting just £20,000 from Bath promoter Freddy Bannister instead.

Allowing nothing to chance, Grant visited the concert site beforehand: "Unbeknownst to Freddy, I went down to the site and found out from the Meteorological Office what time the sun was setting. It was going down right behind the stage. By [the band] going on at sunset, I was able to bring up the stage lights a bit at a time. It was vital we went on stage at the right time. That's why I made sure the previous band, Flock – or whoever they were – got off on time."

To this end he and Richard Cole marshalled the Zep road crew to brutally hasten Flock's departure before Robert could mount the stage on the stroke of 8.30 p.m. and ad-lib the lyrics of 'Immigrant Song', the other three falling in behind him like a well-drilled fighter squadron. All bar Jones, who arrived by helicopter, were now sporting fashionably untidy Viking beards of their own. Jimmy, fearing it might be cold on the night, wore an old double-breasted greatcoat and scarecrow's hat, which, not inappropriately, made him look more like a cider-quaffing Somerset yokel than some random Norseman intent on a night's pillage.

Few who attended the Bath Festival in June 1970 came away in any doubt as to who stole the show. Chris Charlesworth, then newly recruited to *Melody Maker*, recalled Led Zeppelin's impact: "They played just as the sun was setting behind the stage, and mighty impressive they were too, even though my view was restricted by being too close to the high stage and having to crane my neck to see what was going on up there. But I could certainly hear them. Good grief! They opened their set with the hitherto unreleased 'Immigrant Song', which they attacked with all the ferocity of the marauding Vikings Robert was singing about. Drums and bass reverberated like cannon fire, and Page's guitar cut through the twilight like a broadsword. Every other band on the bill sounded decidedly limp dick compared to this onslaught. The reception was phenomenal, and they returned to the stage for multiple encores."

Perhaps sensing that this was the most crucial date of their career thus far, Page and his men played as if their very lives depended on it, delivering a set that lasted almost three hours, and climaxed with a fifties medley that included 'Long Tall Sally', 'Johnny B. Goode' and 'That's Alright Mama', Elvis' first recording for Sun Records from 1954, and still a firm favourite with Page. The following week's *Melody Maker* carried Led Zep's storming of Bath as its front page story, a joint effort written by Charlesworth and his more experienced colleague Chris Welch, and headlined 'Five Encores For Zeppelin': "Led Zeppelin stormed to huge success at the Bath Festival. About 150,000 fans rose to give them an ovation. They played for over three hours – blues, rock and roll and pure Zeppelin. Jimmy Page, in a yokel hat to suit the Somerset scene, screamed into attack on guitar, John Paul Jones came into his own on organ as well as bass, and John Bonham exploded his drums in a sensational solo. And the crowd went wild demanding encore after encore... a total of five!" Not a bad night's work for £20,000. "We knew it was an important gig for us," Jimmy later said, "so we needed to deliver."

Job done on the home front, Led Zeppelin again turned their attentions to the USA, embarking on their sixth tour in under two years. By August 1970, the clubs and small halls that marked their earliest visits were now but a distant memory, with the band graduating to large arenas designed for indoor sports such as the Los Angeles Forum and New York's hallowed Madison Square Garden, where nearly 20,000 fans helped them gross $100,000 from a single performance; a moderate sum for a major act now perhaps, but a truly humungous fee at the time. Bizarrely, though Zep made no effort to disguise the vastness of their earnings – indeed, Peter Grant seemed to positively revel in announcing the figures to the press – the group themselves were still treated like some special cult by their faithful. "It was a strange dichotomy with Zeppelin," said Chris Welch. "On the one hand, they were perceived as an underground group with all that meant. On the other, they were being actively promoted with the strength of Atlantic Records. But it worked."

In the UK, the story was the same, a fact confirmed in September when Page and his fellow band members won 'Top Group' in *Melody Maker*'s annual readers' poll, finally ousting the Beatles from the number one spot after an eight-year reign. All bar Jones turned up to receive their award from *MM* editor Ray Coleman during a ceremony held at the Savoy Hotel on The Strand. Afterwards they were photographed outside the plush venue with Sandy Denny of Fairport Convention, winner of *MM*'s 'Girl Singer' category and soon to be the first and, indeed, only guest vocalist on one of their recordings. "Onwards and upwards!" Jimmy laughed. While Led Zeppelin might have just deposed the Fab Four from the top of the tree, in order to create a long-term dynasty of their own, the group still had to write new, and if possible, even better songs than ever before. The opportunity to see if they had managed it came on October 5, 1970 with the release of their third disc, *Led Zeppelin III*.

An album that revealed its charms in slow, steady waves, *Led Zeppelin III* was still something of a divided soul in comparison to its predecessors. Never allowing the audience to truly settle, its contents swung between brutal hard rock, contemplative folk tunes, country hoedowns and sad-eyed blues. At times, this leaping between musical genres – no matter how marvellously accomplished – could feel jarring or uneven, especially on the first side of the LP.

However, *Led Zeppelin III* remains one of the band's more interesting artefacts, that very sense of listlessness and exploration crucial in creating new pathways for the four musicians to explore at their leisure in subsequent years. Opening proceedings with a bang, 'Immigrant Song' made its transition from the Bath Festival to black vinyl completely intact, with Page's crunching, two-octave riff and Plant's banshee wails conjoining to strike fear into the heart of anyone brave enough to listen. 'Friends'[102] too survived the journey down from Wales to Headley Grange without major incident, the addition of John Paul Jones' genius-level string arrangement compounding the song's sense of overall unease, despite Robert's occasional Samaritan-like pleas. "I'm telling you now," he advised, "the greatest thing you can do now, is trade a smile with someone who's blue now..." An odd, but wonderful tune, 'Friends'' troubling, almost schizophrenic nature ensured it stayed on the periphery of the Zeppelin canon for over three decades[103] until its creators rightly chose to bring it back into the light.

Led Zeppelin III's next track, the rambunctious 'Celebration Day', almost didn't make it onto the LP at all, the song's intro accidentally

---

102 Within seconds of 'Friends' opening, manager Peter Grant can be heard saying 'Fuck'. Fortunately, the expletive was not picked up by radio programmers, allowing the tune free reign over the airwaves and Zep fans a private joke for many a decade.

103 'Friends' was performed live by Led Zeppelin only once, at Osaka's Festival Hall on September 29, 1971.

damaged on the master tape, thus making it difficult to thread through the spool. Some quick thinking snatched victory from the jaws of defeat as John Paul Jones segued a descending Moog keyboard line from the acoustic finale of 'Friends' into the electrified opening bars of 'Celebration Day', thus rescuing it from the scrapheap. Just as well, as 'Celebration Day' was a right little belter from start to finish, its loose feel and joyous delivery creating an immediate uplift after the high drama of 'Friends'. The track was also something of a showcase for Jimmy, with at least four guitar parts (including a slide line tuned to open A) piling up over the course of the tune.

Conversely, 'Since I've Been Loving You' was funereally paced, but masterfully rendered. A midnight blues full of longing and regret, '... Loving You' had actually been a nightmare for the band to get right, with multiple takes failing to capture either the right mood or feel. "[But] Playing the blues is actually the most challenging thing you can do," Jimmy later told *Guitar World*. "It's very hard to play something original. 'Since I've Been Loving You' is a prime example. That [and 'Immigrant Song'] was the only song on the album that we had played live prior to our sessions, yet it was the hardest to record. We had several tries at that one. The final version is a live take[104] with John Paul Jones playing organ and foot bass pedals at the same time." Their persistence paid off. Building slowly but surely to a magnificent climax courtesy of Jones' Hammond organ, Led Zeppelin were on fire by the end of '... Loving You', with Plant's emotive roars and guttural protests topped only by Page's outstanding guitar accompaniment, his almost classically tinged solo also among the finest of his career.

'Out On The Tiles' was all about John Bonham. Inspired by a drinking song the drummer was humming (or very possibly shouting) to himself while in the studio, Bonham's self-accompanying beat proved

---

104 Page's comments about 'Since I've Been Loving You' being cut live are borne out at the one-minute mark, when stray amp buzz cuts across the track. However, like 'Heartbreaker' before it, his decision not to remove the offending noise is another good example of Jimmy's penchant for capturing the spirit of a performance rather than the "sterility of a perfect take".

just the catalyst needed by his fellow musicians to begin work on what would become '... Tiles'. "John Bonham used to do a lot of, sort of, rap stuff. He would just get drunk and start singing things," said Jimmy. "He would stomp his feet and his fingers would get going. I think he originally had some lyrics about drinking pints of bitter, you know, 'Now I'm feeling better because I'm out on the tiles...'" The final result was another prime example of how confident Led Zeppelin had become as a collective unit. Existing at the borders of musical stability as instruments and vocals wibbled and wobbled around Bonham's drums like drunken sailors, the whole band teetered on the brink of some magnificent musical collapse throughout 'Out On The Tiles'. Yet, somehow Zep managed to get away with it, the band's unified disdain for playing it straight or sitting exactly on the beat granting them wings to rise above it. Tight, but loose indeed.

The track that opened side two of the album was no less lively, though this time centuries-old English folk music was the inspiration rather than wire-walking hard rock. Entitled 'Gallows Pole', the song's history was interesting and complex. Originally known as 'The Maid Freed From The Gallows'[105] or 'Gallows Line', Louisiana folk-blues legend Leadbelly had picked up the tune in 1939 and made it his own, even giving it a new name: 'The Gallis Pole'. Inspired by Leadbelly's take on the old traditional standard[106], guitarist and luthier Fred Gerlach was next to grab the reins, gifting 'Gallis...' a novel arrangement, a modified spelling and making it the centrepiece of his 1962 debut LP, *Twelve String Guitar*. In turn, it was this version – now called 'Gallows Pole' – that Jackie DeShannon stumbled on and subsequently played to her then boyfriend Jimmy Page.

"I first heard ['Gallows Pole'] on an old *Folkways* LP by Fred Gerlach," Jimmy later said, "who was, I believe, the first white [man] to play the 12-string [guitar]. I used his version [of the song] as a basis [for

---

105 The tale of a condemned woman pleading for money so she can buy her life before being executed, 'The Maid Freed From The Gallows' dates back several centuries.

106 Both pioneers of 12-string acoustic guitar, Gerlach and Leadbelly had actually roomed together for a time.

our version] and completely changed the arrangement." Page wasn't exaggerating. Inhabiting a completely different postcode from either Leadbelly or Gerlach's treatment of the tune, Led Zeppelin stamped their own authority on 'Gallows Pole', the group starting slow before boiling up like a kettle over the course of five delirious minutes. Featuring John Paul Jones on mandolin, Jimmy on banjo[107] and Robert screaming for mercy from the hangman's noose, by the time Page brought things to a close with another inspired, fiddle-like solo, both band and listener were left sated, if a trifle exhausted.

For better or worse, *Led Zeppelin III*'s remaining songs were far less energetic and far more sedate. With 'Tangerine', Page returned to the mid-sixties for inspiration, resurrecting a tune he had written while dating DeShannon and tried out when still in the Yardbirds (albeit with a modified chorus). Replete with false start, lilting vocal from Robert and some sympathetic pedal steel work from Jimmy, 'Tangerine' was a drowsy alternative to the manic energy and frantic pace of 'Gallows Pole'. Subtly enhanced, but essentially unaffected representations of the two songs Plant and Page had worked on in Wales, both 'That's The Way' and 'Bron-Y-Aur Stomp' continued to carry themselves well, one gentle and lilting, the other certainly more celebratory in tone, but again, never in danger of scaring the horses.

Retaining this acoustic mood, but adding echo-chambered blues hollers and sharp slide guitar to pack a bit more wallop (if no great tune to speak of), the album ended with 'Hats Off To (Roy) Harper'[108], a tribute of sorts to an eccentric but always interesting musician who had meandered on the fringes of stardom since the mid-sixties. Former RAF trainee – at least until he feigned insanity to gain a medical discharge

---

107 'Gallows Pole' was the first time Page had played banjo on record.

108 Recorded during a late-night stint at London's Olympic Studios, 'Hats Off To (Roy) Harper' was loosely based on 'Shake 'Em On Down' by blues singer/guitarist Bukka White. Another of the gravel-voiced White's songs, 'Fixin' To Die', was also reportedly cut the same night, as were 'That's All Right Mama', 'Keys To The Highway and Big Bill Broonzy's 'Trouble In Mind'. The latter two tracks would make an appearance on the companion disc for the 'Deluxe Edition' of *Led Zeppelin III*, released in 2014.

– seasoned busker and traditional folk/music hall lover, Harper's first LP 1966's *Sophisticated Beggar* and its follow-ups, the Shel Talmy produced *Come Out Fighting Genghis Khan* (1968) and *Folkjokeopus* (1969) all showed undoubted promise. But despite some quality songs and spirited vocals, Roy had proved difficult to market, his resolutely anti-commercial stance and occasional habit of penning extended compositions ('McGoogan's Blues' came in at a whopping 17 minutes) rubbing managers, record companies and radio programmers up the wrong way. Still, when Harper parted company with Liberty records in 1969, EMI's subsidiary label Harvest had enough faith in his talents to offer a new deal.

Though Led Zeppelin had known of Roy Harper for a little while ("I'd heard his first album," Page later said), it was not until the Bath Festival in June 1970 that their mutual appreciation society was properly cemented. "I'd actually seen Robert a couple of years earlier at one of my gigs at Mothers in Birmingham," Roy told *Mojo*'s Martin Aston in 2013. "He was only 17 or so, but had an aura about him even then. Tall, elegant, with a girl on each arm. Anyway, at Bath, this [other] guy came up to me and asked if I could play my instrumental 'Blackpool', so I did. We shook hands and he said he was Jimmy Page. Later on there's this band onstage and I recognise it's Jimmy. I was blown away when I [also] realised who the singer was. They then turned up to see me at Birmingham Town Hall [and] we got really stoned. They couldn't believe I did the show that gone."

With friendships duly established – Plant took to calling Roy 'Merlin', Harper returned the favour by nicknaming Robert 'Arthur' – and the whole band admiring of Roy's dogged individualism ("He just went his own road," said Plant), the doffing of hats on *Led Zeppelin III* to 'Mr. H' was the first example of what became a beneficial and long-term association between the two parties.

Feisty and energetic, sedentary and sometimes somnambulant, *Led Zeppelin III* was a fine, if occasionally flawed album that found the band indulging itself in a wide number of musical and emotional moods. This was no doubt a by-product of shifting responsibilities within Led Zeppelin itself. Unlike either of its predecessors, where

Jimmy Page had maintained tight artistic control over both content and execution, the group's latest disc was a much more collaborative effort with Jones, Bonham and especially Plant now regularly listed among the song-writing credits. Though Page remained firmly in place as producer and principal architect of Zep's overall sound, the loosening of his grip in other areas not only helped his fellow band members financially, but also built a wider pool from which to fish new melodic ideas.

More, by stepping away from the blunt attack of hard blues rock and further embracing the softer side of their nature, Led Zeppelin were creating more space for themselves to grow. Author Dave Lewis, a teenager at the time of *III*'s release but destined to become an important champion of the band and its legacy, saw the album as a critical step forward for all concerned. "*Zep III* was such a watershed moment because people finally understood it wasn't just about loud amplifiers," he said in 2015. "Jimmy had a vision that Zep could be anything he or the others wanted it to be. It could be about folk, rock, blues... just anything. *III* opened up a whole new world, a whole spectrum of alternative colours. The album took them away from everything that was contemporary or even competing against them at that time. You didn't really get that breath and variety elsewhere."

As Lewis correctly deduced, with *Led Zeppelin III* the doors had again been opened a little wider. But at the time the general public was not quite ready for such deliberate expansion. Despite the fact that both *Led Zeppelin I* and *II* had already dabbled with acoustic textures and expressly demonstrated Page's wish for "light and shade", the fact that the second side of the band's new LP was all but free of electrical appliances seemed to confuse, even disappoint their audience. Further, with nothing quite as immediate as 'Whole Lotta Love' or 'Communication Breakdown' on offer, radio, too, struggled to find a flagship track to really get behind. As a result, when *III* was released on October 5, 1970, though it hit the number one spots in both the US and UK (staying at the top for four and three weeks respectively), after an initial surge, sales flagged rapidly. "*Led Zeppelin III* was not one of the best sellers in the catalogue because the audience turned round and said 'What are we supposed to do with this?'" Plant later said. "[It was like] 'Where's our "Whole Lotta Love Part Two"'?"

Critical response was surely another factor in *Led Zeppelin III*'s inability to top the sales of its illustrious predecessor. While *Record Mirror*, for instance, was still keen to champion the band – "An excellent return... [that] happily brands their third [LP] as a masterpiece of original musical strategy" – *Disc & Music Echo* was less sure. "[It's] here after a year of eager expectation, and it's disappointing. More acoustic, [*III*]... lacks that funky, exciting live feeling they captured before. The album lacks sparkle. Don't Zeppelin care anymore?"

After the mauling they gave the group's first LP, one might have thought *Rolling Stone* was ready to extend an olive branch in Led Zeppelin's general direction, or at least cut them some slack for trying something different. But *Rolling Stone*'s esteemed critic Lester Bangs was not ringing any great changes on behalf of the publication. "I keep nursing this love-hate attitude toward Led Zeppelin," he wrote. "Partly from genuine interest and mostly indefensible hopes, in part from the conviction that nobody *that* crass could be all that bad, I turn to each fresh album expecting – what? Certainly not subtle echoes of the monolithic Yardbirds, or authentic blues experiments, or even much variety. Maybe it's just that they seem like the ultimate Seventies Calf of Gold."

Though Bangs confessed a liking for 'That's The Way' ("Son of a gun, it's beautiful") and made a point of highlighting the record's production values ("You *can* hear all the parts, which is more than you can say for many of their peers..."), his final verdict remained one of disappointment. "Their third album deviates little from the track laid by the first two, even though they go acoustic on several numbers," he concluded. "Most of the acoustic stuff sounds like standard Zep graded down decibel-wise, and the heavy blitzes could've been outtakes from *Zeppelin II*. In fact, when I first heard the album my main impression was the consistent anonymity of most of the songs – no one could mistake the band, but no gimmicks stand out with any special outrageousness, as did the great, gleefully absurd Orangutang Plant-*cum*-wheezing guitar freak-out that made 'Whole Lotta Love' such a pulp classic."

With its references to a 'Calf of God', clear admissions of a 'love-hate' relationship with the band's music and a general dismissal of their approach – "Their albums refine the crude public tools of all dull white blues bands into something awesome in its very insensitive grossness" – it was hard not to feel that Bangs was only consolidating *Rolling Stone*'s original viewpoint of Led Zeppelin: blunt-edged, money-grabbing bruisers in hot pursuit of the Yankee dollar. Chris Charlesworth was certainly of that opinion. "I always thought that the only strategic mistake that Led Zeppelin made in the first phase of their career was to authorise the mail-out of a press release revealing that Atlantic Records had given them a $200,000 advance, unusually high for the time," he said. "Clearly they thought this would enhance their reputation but in an era when 'breadheads' were despised by the alternative culture to which they aspired to find their market, it was both unnecessary and imprudent. They should have kept it to themselves. The repercussion was that a number of US critics immediately assumed they were only in it for the money, which explains the terrible relationship they had with *Rolling Stone* magazine – the counter-culture's biggest flag wavers – that lasted for years."

There were other jibes circulating, and not all of them from *Rolling Stone*. With a fresh wave of 'roots rock' and folk performers such as the Band, James Taylor, Joni Mitchell and Crosby, Stills, Nash & Young either now firmly established or on the rise, the feeling that Led Zeppelin's latest musical turn might be less about a genuine love of acoustic song and more about bandwagon jumping was also prevalent. This general snippiness towards the group's output, and the fact that some reviewers were ignoring Zep's previous form in the area of gentle guitars and rural folksiness genuinely angered Cameron Crowe. "When the third LP came out and got its reviews, Crosby, Stills & Nash had [only] just formed," he later said. "That LP had just come out and because acoustic guitars had come to the forefront all of a sudden, [it was] 'Led Zeppelin go acoustic'! I thought, 'Christ, where are their heads and ears?' There were three acoustic songs on the first album and two on the second!" Only 13 years old when the record was released, Crowe would soon have his say about Led Zeppelin, ironically becoming *Rolling Stone*'s youngest ever contributor by 1972, his subsequent articles doing much to repair bridges between band and magazine.

In 2008, Jimmy Page expressed his opinion regarding the wave of negative reviews that surrounded Led Zeppelin's third album and, indeed, the two that preceded it. "Well, the press didn't 'get' any of the albums, really," he told *Classic Rock*'s Paul Elliot. "With *III*, they didn't really understand why we were doing acoustic music. [But], it was [already] all over the first album. I just wondered, 'Where are these people coming from?'" While Jimmy might have chosen his words carefully, his anger towards the press – and *Rolling Stone* in particular – was palpable. "I've said in the past [that] I'll give it the benefit of the doubt that maybe reviewers only had a short time to review the album, because it went totally over their heads. [But] there were definite hatchet jobs. The *Rolling Stone* review was a definite hatchet job. We were told that. But it didn't matter. We had a bigger circulation than *Rolling Stone*."

Indeed. But back in 1970, Zeppelin's relationship with the likes of *Rolling Stone* remained distinctly rocky, with Page in particular now beginning to distance himself from the music papers and instead letting Robert Plant do much of the talking on the band's behalf. For Chris Charlesworth, this new strategy of "staggered media withdrawal" marked the beginnings of the overall sense of mystique that would soon envelop Led Zeppelin, and in particular their lead guitarist. "But you know, Zep weren't particularly press friendly anyway," he said. "In fact, they were always incredibly touchy about bad reviews, even from the start. Odd, really. Take the Rolling Stones. If they got a bad review, well, they didn't give a shit. They were the Rolling Stones. To their credit, the Who took bad reviews in good heart but they were always very media friendly, especially Pete and Keith. But Zep, no, they really took against bad reviews, especially Jimmy and Peter Grant. Christ, if you said anything bad about Zep to Peter Grant, the bricks came tumbling down. Robert was the most at home with the press, always very open and affable, sincere too, but Bonzo could be a bit daunting if you accidentally rubbed him up the wrong way. John Paul Jones didn't seem to care one way or another. He just went his own way, slightly apart from everyone else, stayed out of it for the most part."

For some less hardy groups, the critical sniffs accorded *Led Zeppelin III* might have brought a return to the drawing board or, worse still, forced them to pander to popular opinion and re-write 'Whole Lotta Love' for the rest of their musical career. But Page and Led Zeppelin were not for turning. Sure of their vision and, thanks to recent press coverage, more determined than ever to pursue whatever musical road they damn well pleased, the band lit the candles, drew up the drawbridge and hunkered down to produce one of the finest albums of the rock era.

CHAPTER 17

Stairway To Heaven

Though some considered *Led Zeppelin III* as something of a critical misfire after the sheer wonder of previous albums, the overall sales figures still made for impressive reading. Number one on both sides of the Atlantic and with steady Top Five placings in Japan and across the majority of Europe, Zep's third LP would soon go to sell over four million units worldwide, a combined tally many groups could only dream of. Furthermore, despite not being as immediately catchy as 'Whole Lotta Love', 'Immigrant Song' made a good account of itself as a single in the USA, reaching a respectable number 16 on the charts in January 1971. Yet, despite these obvious successes, there remained a sense of anticlimax around Led Zeppelin's latest effort. Having come so far so fast, it appeared that anything other than uniform excellence was unacceptable from the quartet. No errors, no miscalculations or, if *Disc & Music Echo* had its way, no folk-orientated deviations from purpose either. Jimmy Page was having none of it. "We knew what we had and we'd kept improving all the time," he later told *Guitar World*. "Also, we were playing all the music live and people were responding to what we were doing. That [was] the ultimate test."

Nevertheless, Led Zeppelin may have learnt a lesson or two from recent concerns in the US. Their imprudent tendency to dangle financial gains before the American press having led to accusations of avarice, they were no doubt anxious to discourage anything similar at home. To this end and, no doubt, to genuinely acknowledge the continued support of UK fans, Peter Grant announced his charges would return for a brief tour of the same clubs and small halls that marked their British first dates in the autumn of 1968. Additionally, if concert promoters agreed to charge the same admission fee as they had that year, then Led Zeppelin would also appear for their original 1968 fee. "The boys came to me just after Christmas and talked about the next tour," Grant told *Melody Maker* at the time. "We decided let's do the clubs and forget about the bread and the big concert halls. We're going to play the universities and the clubs and restrict prices to about 12 bob."

For some venues, the prospect of Led Zeppelin coming home for a cut-price fee was all too much. "When I rang the manager of The Marquee," Grant continued, "he refused to believe it was me offering Led Zeppelin, so he had to call me back to be convinced!" Part 'Thank you' to the faithful, part helping hand to smaller venues ("A lot of small clubs have disappeared because bands have charged too much in the past," said Peter) and very possibly part public relations exercise too, whatever the reason, Zep sounded genuinely excited at the prospect of stepping back in time, if only for a few weeks. "It'll be great because the atmosphere [in clubs] is always much, much better than in a big place like the Albert Hall," said John Bonham. "We wanted to do a tour where the greatest number possible could come and see us at the places that made us when we started out."

In the end, Led Zeppelin's 14-date hop around the British Isles during March 1970 was as much about combining ecstasy with endurance as anything else, as countless numbers of fans tried to squeeze themselves into venues so small, the band could have easily packed them out for weeks. Opening at Belfast's Ulster Hall on March 5, before taking in (or taking on) the likes of Southampton's Old Refectory, Newcastle's Mayfair Ballroom and Nottingham's Boat Club, Zep returned to the old haunts that marked their original passage from relative unknowns to budding stardom. Drawing from a set that mixed and matched now familiar gems such as 'Dazed And Confused' and 'Communication Breakdown' with more recent additions like 'Heartbreaker' and 'Immigrant Song', there was also room for some brand new material, as 'Going To California', 'Black Dog' and an ambitious but promising little number to which we will return in due course all made their concert debuts along the way.

On March 23, Jimmy Page again found himself back on wholly familiar turf as Led Zeppelin visited London's Marquee for an extremely sweaty night's entertainment. For Chris Charlesworth, who was bumping elbows and knees with everyone else there that night, Zep's glorious return to their roots might have been well-meaning but it was also ill-conceived. "Yes, I saw them on the 'Back to the Clubs' tour at the Marquee but, being honest, I was a bit sniffy about it. The whole thing was ridiculous. A lovely gesture perhaps, but misplaced, I felt. They could have done a month at The Marquee, let alone one or two nights and in the end, the gig was hot, sticky, packed and uncomfortable. Not the most pleasant experience for the audience or the band, really."

With near perfect timing, only a day after Led Zeppelin concluded their jury-splitting 'Back to the Clubs' jaunt, Jimmy Page became the father of a baby girl. Christened Scarlet Lilith Eleida, she was – according to Robert Plant – conceived "about half an hour" after Page and he wrote 'That's The Way' while staying in Bron-Yr-Aur. The lucky recipient of her mother Charlotte Martin's distinctive eyes and Jimmy's pale colouring, Scarlet spent her early childhood at Plumpton Place, a Grade II listed Elizabethan manor house about five miles north-east of Lewes in East Sussex that Page purchased some months after her birth. Replacing Pangbourne as his main base of operations, Plumpton Place was really "a dream house" both for Jimmy and his new family, comprised as it was of six bedrooms, a large library space and a 48ft-long sitting room. Surrounded by a moat and lakes, the opulent main residence was imposingly baronial with the property also boasting two small cottages close by as well as a three-bedroom mill house with its own working water wheel. Dating back to the 16th century, benefiting from several improvements courtesy of renowned British architect Sir Edwin Luytens and set on 62 acres of land, Plumpton Place and its surrounds would prove an idyllic setting for Page and Martin to bring up their young daughter.

A less welcome arrival for Led Zeppelin's erstwhile leader came in the summer of 1971 with the posthumous release of *Live Yardbirds: Featuring Jimmy Page*. Popularly known throughout the music industry as a 'cash-in', *Live Yardbirds...* had been recorded at New York's Anderson Theatre on March 30, 1968 during one of the band's last American shows before they officially threw in the towel some four months later. With proper tools and more careful management, the album could have been an entertaining, even valuable document of one of the sixties better pop-rock acts, its contents even including the Yardbirds' eerie version of 'Dazed And Confused', a tune they had made their own before the advent of Led Zeppelin, but had never found time to commit to vinyl. However, due to the sound engineer's lack of experience in recording rock shows (a single microphone was hung over Jim McCarty's drum kit, rendering some of his work inaudible), *Live Yardbirds...* lacked both thump and fizz, the end result more sonic travesty than buried treasure. "It had been recorded at a particularly bad gig, engineered by some character strictly into muzak," Jimmy later told *NME*'s Nick Kent. "[But], we had the right to state whether... it was to be released or not." Understandably, Page threatened to sue Epic records for releasing the LP without necessary permissions and it was quickly withdrawn.[109]

It was not the first time that Jimmy's name had been linked to a project that was probably best kept in a darkened vault gathering dust. Just a year or so before *Live Yardbirds...* made its swift appearance and even swifter exit, another old friend from sixties session days released an album with contributions from Page and several others that ended up causing more ructions and reported legal threats. Still keen to break onto the international music scene despite a procession of failed singles, grand British eccentric Screaming Lord Sutch had marshalled together a

---

109 Parent company CBS (Special Products) tried their luck with a re-release of the album in 1976, but Jimmy again stepped forward with threats of legal action, causing the record label to withdraw it. A studio-enhanced version of *Live Yardbirds...* was finally released by Mooreland Street Records in 2000. All versions erroneously refer to 'Dazed And Confused' as 'I'm Confused' on both label and sleeve.

coterie of talent at Los Angeles' Mystic Studios to cut some tunes with a view to drumming up record company interest.

Drawing on former core members of his band the Savages such as the Jimi Hendrix Experience's Noel Redding and esteemed session drummer Carlo Little, Sutch had also invited Jeff Beck, pianist Nicky Hopkins, John Bonham and Jimmy himself along for the ride. Essentially an excuse for a beer "and a laugh," Page ended up producing what he thought would be some harmless demos for the good Lord. But in February 1970, the tapes were released as *Lord Sutch And Heavy Friends* by Cotillion Records. Suffice to say, Jimmy was incensed. "I just went down to have a laugh, playing some old rock'n'roll, a bit of a send-up," he told *Melody Maker* at the time. "[Then], the whole joke sort of reversed itself and became ugly." A collection of sub-standard jams, tuneless ditties and meandering guitar solos, ...*Heavy Friends* was subsequently named 'Worst album of all time' in a 1998 BBC poll, with the LP's release leading to some serious words between Sutch and Page.[110] Regrettably, it would not be the last time unauthorised releases from the guitarist's former musical life reared their ugly head.

There were more than a few ugly heads reared at Milan's Vigorelli Velodrome on July 5, 1971, when Led Zeppelin found themselves in the midst of a full-scale riot. An all-day, government-backed event staged at Milan's pre-eminent outdoor stadium, the Velodrome gig was to be the band's first real concert appearance since their 'Back to the Clubs' UK tour some two months before. With a supporting bill comprising harmless Italian pop stars Mauro Lusini, Milva and all-round entertainer/actor Gianni Morandi, the line-up might have been a tad eclectic, but there was nothing on paper to suggest the slightest concern for either the performers or their audience. However, soon after the event began,

---

110 Perhaps sensing his future did not lie in music, Screaming Lord Sutch later chose to pursue another of his teenage interests: politics. Forming the 'Official Monster Raving Loony Party' in 1983, Sutch and his colleagues sought election to various councils and British Parliament, even winning a seat on Ashburton Town Council in 1987. A lovable eccentric, Sutch committed suicide following the death of his mother in 1999.

Lusini, Milva and the others found themselves being heckled and pelted with rubbish by sections of the 15,000-strong crowd. "It could have been predicted," Morandi later said. "They were all waiting for Led Zeppelin."

When the group did finally appear on the dot of 8.30, things went from bad to worse, as groups of political agitators clashed with equally bellicose local police. Having noticed the strong riot patrol presence when he arrived at the Velodrome, Page was already concerned, but as tear-gas canisters started flying near the stage, concern was subsumed by genuine panic. "The promoters ran on stage [and asked] if we could tell the crowd to stop lighting fires," Jimmy later told writer Stuart Grundy. "So, Robert asked them and suddenly there was smoke by the front of the stage and it was actually tear gas. It was just pandemonium with nowhere immune from this blasted tear gas, including us."

Remarkably, Page and Led Zeppelin kept their composure for a while longer, trying the best they could to complete their set. But when a bottle was hurled at police close to the band all hell broke loose, with the crowd now being forced onto the actual stage itself in order to get away from the fighting below. "It was just war," said John Paul Jones. With Zep's roadies desperately trying to save the group's equipment and Jimmy and co. having to take refuge in a small room backstage while angry fans, various political factions and 2,000 police did battle with each other just metres away, the escort back to their hotel couldn't come fast enough. "I was terribly upset afterwards," Page later confirmed. "I couldn't believe we'd been used as the instrument for a political demonstration like that."

America had always been a safe haven for Led Zeppelin, and so it proved again after the events of Milan when they returned for yet another tour of the States in August 1971. Previously, US critics had made great play of the band pursuing 'cash over class' while peddling their wares, but when faced with the reality of Zeppelin's ceaseless work ethic, such accusations now appeared increasingly daft. Already well-known for the duration of their live shows, the group's performances showed no signs of letting up on their latest trip across the Atlantic, with three-hour sets commonplace. In addition to heavily extended treatments of 'Dazed

And Confused' and a four-song medley incorporated into 'Whole Lotta Love', both John Bonham and John Paul Jones were also taking solo spots, with JPJ anointing 'Thank You' with a brief but gorgeous organ solo while Bonzo continued to raise roofs with his prolonged outbursts during 'Moby Dick'.

More, the pastoral textures that had so divided fans on *Led Zeppelin III* were now transferred to the concert stage, with the front line pulling up stools and offering a break from the 'sturm und drang' of 'Immigrant Song' and 'Heartbreaker'. With Page on acoustic guitar, Jones on mandolin and Plant sat between them, they regaled audiences with the gentle strains of 'That's The Way', a box-fresh, breezy sounding new song called 'Going To California', as yet unrecorded, and a lively 'Bron-Y-Aur Stomp', for which Bonzo joined in the fun on tambourine. "This was a brave move," wrote Chris Charlesworth, "because audiences, especially in the USA, expected full-tilt rock from their Zeppelin and were often intolerant of their quieter side, much to the group's frustration." Nevertheless, the acoustic interludes would gainsay early criticisms that the quartet had commandeered folk music purely for financial gain, and in time they became a much loved part of Led Zeppelin concerts.

Acoustic guitars were also very much at the heart of 'The Same Old Rock', the centre piece of Roy Harper's latest album *Stormcock* and a track that greatly benefited from the presence of Jimmy Page. Released at around the time Zep were again storming the States and full of the same types of songs that so beguiled Harper's cult following but frustrated DJs and his record company (only one track came in at under eight minutes), *Stormcock* was never destined for a million sales. "[Harvest] hated *Stormcock*," Roy later told *The Guardian*. "No singles. No way of promoting it on the radio. They said there wasn't any money to market it. [So], *Stormcock* just dribbled out."

Despite its selective appeal, the LP was still worthy of investigation with Harper's long, involved compositions not unlike mini-folk symphonies, as stacked vocals and chiming six-strings underpinned his sometimes wise, sometimes sad lyricism. 'The Same Old Rock' certainly ticked all these boxes and more. "A contrarian's dream," built on images of ancient chivalry and modern disappointments, Roy's weary-sounding voice was both soothed and cajoled by Jimmy's guitar for 12-odd minutes before Page finally spun out of the track on a brisk, Flamenco-like flourish.

"I think he initially presented '... Same Old Rock' as one piece to me and I just listened to it as it went from one movement to another," Jimmy later told *Mojo*. "I actually thought, 'I hope he doesn't think I've got a photographic memory!'" Billed as 'S. Flavius Mercurius' so as not to alert Atlantic records to his presence on *Stormcock*, Page would be backing Harper again within no time at all.[111] "Those guys and I grew up together," Roy said of his continuing relationship with Jimmy and his band. "We were all playing the same places. I was playing The Marquee at the same time as [Jimmy was in] the Yardbirds. That means there's this whole population of people who went on to be really famous who at one time or another had come to see me as one of the lads."

Of course, while tours and various guest appearances were always genuinely enthralling for fans, allowing them to see and hear their idols up close and personal or, in the case of Milan, running for their very lives, there was also the hankering for a more permanent record of Led Zeppelin. The band knew it too, and had been hard at work for several months recording songs for their next album. In fact, Zep had actually begun their labours as far back as the winter of 1970/71 at Island's now "almost brand-new" studios in London's Notting Hill. But it was only when they relocated to East Hampshire's Headley Grange with the Rolling Stones' mobile studio in January 1971 that things began to head towards the finish line. A solid, three-storey high building that once

---

111 Following his disguised appearance on *Stormcock*, Page again teamed up with Harper on February 14, 1972 for a song or two at London's Rainbow theatre (the Who's Keith Moon and the Faces' Ronnie Lane were also in attendance). The night was captured on tape by Roy and later released in 1974 as the live album *Flashes From The Archives Of Oblivion*. Sadly, the LP's cover – which featured Harper naked but for a pair of football socks – so offended female workers at EMI's pressing factory in Hayes that a brief strike was called. Meanwhile, back in 1973, Jimmy contributed guitar parts to 'Bank Of The Dead' and the 23-minute long 'The Lord's Prayer', two cuts from Harper's sixth album *Lifemask*.

served as a poorhouse before being converted to a private residence by local builder Thomas Kemp, Headley Grange had been around nearly 200 years before Led Zeppelin arrived. It was now about to enter the musical history books. "We needed the sort of facilities where we could have a cup of tea and wander around the garden, and then go in and do what we had to do," Page later said. "That was the key to the fourth album. It was residential."

Given all that was to follow, Headley Grange has taken on an almost mythical status in the tale of Jimmy Page and Led Zeppelin. A place of secret corners and sky-high ceilings where miracles were conceived and legends were born. True enough. Yet, at the time, it also served a very practical purpose. Keen to create a "concentrated and relaxed environment" for recording, Jimmy and Peter Grant had originally struck on the idea of hiring the Stones' mobile studio and settling in at Mick Jagger's palatial manor house, Stargroves, in East Woodhay, Hampshire. But when Jagger reportedly asked too much money for renting his property to Zep, the cost-efficient Page signed up for the studio but had it driven to Headley Grange instead. In the end it proved a brilliant decision, though back in January of 1971, not everyone was happy with the new choice of venue. "I hated Headley Grange," John Paul Jones told Q. "The huge main room sounded great but the place itself was awful... damp and cold. The fact I couldn't wait to get out probably had something to do with the speed with which the album was made!"

With its yellow walls, peeling paper and a huge, unheated basement that ran under the entire length of the 10-bedroom house, Jones made a good point about Headley Grange's basic lack of amenities. However, for Andy Johns – returning to assist Jimmy Page at the engineer's desk for the third time – the rambling pile still offered its fair share of charms. "It was somewhat seedy," he later told writer Barney Hoskyns. "There was stuffing coming out of the couch and springs coming out of the bed. But it wasn't a bad place. It had a nice fireplace and I was bonking the cook."

Whether driven on by a surge of creativity or, in JPJ's case, a simple wish to exit the building as quickly as possible, Led Zeppelin's time at Headley Grange proved extremely productive. Working in quick and dirty bursts, if a tune or arrangement wasn't playing ball immediately, the band would simply park it and move on to something else so as not to lose time. With many ideas already well-rehearsed before the arrival of the mobile studio, the process of finally committing songs to tape could also be achieved "in just a handful of takes".

As ever, this desire for immediacy and improvisation did not stop with song-writing alone. Disappointed by the drum sound he was getting in Headley's drawing room, Andy Johns suggested John Bonham move his Ludwig kit into the hallway where "the ceiling was at least 25 feet high". Setting up two double-ribbon microphones at the top of the stairwell so as to capture a more ambient, yet still fulsome racket, the end result delighted Zep's resident stick-twiddler so much he kept his kit there for the duration of his stay at the house.

There appeared little separation between work and play while Led Zeppelin were in residence at Headley Grange. When done recording for the day, the band and their entourage (which included Johns and omnipresent tour manager Richard Cole) would either walk to the local pub or crack into a crate or two of beer or cider purloined earlier in the day from the off-licence. Given that much of the building was distressingly cold, more often than not they would find themselves gathered around the enormous fireplace at the heart of the house. Being musical types, this in turn led to instruments being played and, as result, even more song ideas generated. "Headley Grange was... just a wonderful place, and very imposing," Jimmy later told journalist Paul Elliot. "I liked the idea of the band being in the same place, working. It was in the countryside, so I knew there were going to be no noise problems or problems with neighbours. Headley Grange," he concluded, "seemed ideal."

After their semi-rural retreat, Led Zeppelin returned to Island Studios for further recording and overdubs, working up those tracks they couldn't quite nail in Hampshire while also adding small but still critically important elements to songs. Again, progress was quick, with one particular performance captured at Island during this time destined to carve out its own substantial niche in musical history. So far, so good. But just as Atlantic began gearing up for a late summer release for the band's new album, both group and record company hit a snag.

When finished at Island, Page, Andy Johns and Peter Grant flew to Los Angeles' Sunset Sound to complete final mixing on the LP. For Johns, who had personally recommended Sunset, the trip was doubly fortuitous. Not only did it give him an opportunity to revisit a recording complex he knew, liked and respected, but its location also offered the chance to hook up with yet another girlfriend. Or, in this case, two. "I was seeing this bird, Jeannie," he later told *Classic Rock*, "not to mention her friend, Jackie." Unfortunately, Andy was so excited at the prospect of what lay ahead after touching down in LA, he left two tapes containing Zep's latest efforts on the plane. It got worse. While Johns struggled to retrieve the reels before they were flown back to the UK, a strong aftershock from a recent earthquake in the San Fernando Valley wobbled the airport.[112] Not the greatest of omens, then, for the task ahead.

Thankfully, there were no further incidents to speak of while Jimmy Page and Andy Johns were in Los Angeles. Having given themselves a week to mix down the LP, producer and engineer laboured away at Sunset Sound until they were broadly satisfied with the results. Yet on their return to London, Page found their efforts to have been in vain. When he played the tapes through the speakers at Olympic Studios to Plant, Bonham and Jones, Jimmy was greeted with frowns. "It sounded all right to me [at Sunset], but the speakers were lying," he later told Barney Hoskyns. "It wasn't actually the balance, it was the actual sound that was on the tape. The monitoring system [at Sunset] was just very bright... and it wasn't the true sound." With the exception of just one song – albeit a good one – the album would have to be mixed again. Right or wrong, there was to be but one fall guy. "The sound of the

---

112 Page, Grant and Johns arrived in LA soon after the San Fernando (or 'Sylmar') earthquake of February 9, 1971. Measuring 6.5 to 6.7 on the 'moment magnitude' scale, the event resulted in the death of 64 people as well as causing severe damage to several buildings and various transport links. Aftershocks from the earthquake continued to rock LA for some time. "You actually could feel the bed shaking," Page later said. Somewhat ironically, Jimmy had arrived in LA with the tapes for 'Going To California', a song which contained the lyric "tremble and shake", in reference to the mountains and canyons that surrounded the city.

mixing room that Andy Johns took Jimmy to was really duff," Plant later told *Disc*, "so [he] had to start mixing all over again." Page went a little further. "Basically, Andy Johns should be hung, drawn and quartered for the fiascos he's played." After the events of Los Angeles and Olympic Studios, Johns did not work with the band again.[113]

With issues over mixing and resultant delays, the release of Led Zeppelin's fourth LP was pushed back by Atlantic Records until the late autumn of 1971. Nor were Page and the band about to make their job any easier. Still seething about the negative press coverage afforded to their last album and continuing accusations that the group were built on little more than hype, Jimmy was in no mind to play nice with the media or anyone else who felt Led Zeppelin were trading on name alone. Nevertheless, no one could have expected the lengths he was willing to go in order to make his point.

In what now appears to be an inspired piece of marketing on Led Zeppelin's part – though in 1971, it reportedly brought Atlantic's senior management team to their knees – Page decreed there would be no album title, band photo or, indeed, any mention at all of the group's name on the cover sleeve of the LP. At first, his demand was thought to be a practical joke by the label, yet when Page and Peter Grant met with Altantic's co-founder Ahmet Ertegun at their New York office in September 1971, neither was wearing clown suits. Pleading with the duo that such a move by even the most successful of bands would be commercial suicide, Ertegun begged them to reconsider. But Page was adamant and Grant was more than willing to fight his cause. "Jimmy wasn't a shouter. He left all that to Peter," said Chris Welch. "But while Jimmy was quite gentle he always got his point across. Jimmy Page was

---

113 Andy Johns went on record in 2001 to explain his version of events regarding the original mix of *Led Zeppelin IV*. "The room I'd worked in [at Sunset Sound] had been completely changed, so we used another room," he told Mick Wall. "But when we came back and played it... at Olympic, it sounded terrible." Though he did not work with Zep again, Johns continued to forge a strong and varied career as both an engineer and producer, with the Rolling Stones' *Exile On Main Street*, Television's *Marquee Moon* and Van Halen's *For Unlawful Carnal Knowledge* among his more notable successes. He died aged 62 in April 2013.

Led Zeppelin's leader, a leader of men, and the band and Peter Grant always deferred to him."

In fact, so confident was Grant in Page's singular vision that when it was put to him by Atlantic an unnamed album by an unnamed group would just sit gathering dust on the shelves, his response was both comedic and prophetic. "Listen," he said, "this record would shift units if we put it in a fucking brown paper bag." With Led Zeppelin responsible for at least 20% of Atlantic's combined sales, and the label still ravenous for yet more, Page and Grant got their way. No title. No band name. No compromise.[114] "After all we'd accomplished, the press was still calling us a 'hype', so that's why the fourth album was untitled," Jimmy later told Steve Rosen. "It was a meaningless protest, really. But we wanted to prove that people were not buying us for the name."

Though stripped of several of their traditional marketing tools, Atlantic Records did the best with what they had when attempting to trail the LP. In the weeks leading up to the album hitting shops, a series of teaser advertisements featuring a particular symbol or sign alongside the sleeve of a previous Zep release began to appear in various publications. Again the brainchild of Jimmy Page, these symbols each carried significant meaning and import. "At first I wanted just one symbol," he told *Trouser Press*. "But since it was the fourth album and there were four of us, we each chose our own. I designed mine and everybody else had their own reasons for using the symbol [they] selected."

Robert Plant chose a feather enclosed within a circle, its design reportedly based on the ancient 'crest' of the Mu civilisation[115] and signifying truth and courage. "[It's] a symbol on which all philosophies have been based," he said. "For instance, [the feather] represents courage

---

114 Well, perhaps just a little compromise. For legal reasons, both Led Zeppelin's name and the Atlantic records logo did appear on the cover sticker of the actual LP itself.

115 Mu was the name suggested by Victorian explorer Augustus Le Plongeon (and later popularised by James Churchward) for a lost continent that supposedly sank or was destroyed countless thousands of years ago. Claims have been made that the survivors of Mu consequently settled in ancient Mesoamerica and Egypt. The existence of Mu has been dismissed by most modern scholars as having little or no basis in fact.

to many red Indian tribes. I like people to lay down the truth. No bullshit. That's what the feather in the circle is all about."[116] For John Bonham, the onus was on family, his symbol of three interlinked (or 'borromean') circles denoting man, woman and child.[117] John Paul Jones' sign, on the other hand, was a more complex creation, with three distinct, but still intersecting almond shapes (or 'versica piscis') atop another, larger circle. "John Paul's symbol was found in a book of runes and was said to represent a person who is both confident and competent," Jimmy later told *Guitar World*. All in all, this was an extremely apt representation for Jones. But according to the bassist, the selection process around picking his sign carried other, less pleasing, connotations. "Jimmy got the idea not to give the album a name, jut to use four symbols," he later told *Q*. "We all had to choose one from Rudolf Koch's *Book Of Signs*. [But] much later, Bonzo and I discovered that Jimmy and Robert had their symbols specifically designed. Typical, really..."

As confirmed by Jones, like the enclosed feather of Robert Plant, Jimmy Page's own symbol had been uniquely rendered. Unlike the others, however, it did not have circles per se at its heart. Instead, Page's signifier more resembled a word, though he would state empathetically that despite the presence of what appeared to be four distinct characters – Z, O, S and O – it certainly was not. And that, really, was all Jimmy would state. Giving no clues as to the symbol's origins or meaning, the guitarist sealed its inherent power with a vow of silence. Nevertheless, as time would tell, fans, critics and those with an interest in such things would spend many an hour trying to work out the significance of 'ZoSo' and, equally importantly, what it meant to Page.

The release of 'Four Symbols' into the public domain served only to deepen the air of mystery that had been bubbling at the edges of Page and Led Zeppelin since their formation in 1968. It was therefore inevitable that the cover of the band's fourth LP would also draw its fair share of

---

116 Plant's feather is also said to signify a link to Ma'at, the Egyptian goddess of fairness and justice.

117 Many noticed that Bonham's three-circle sign also heavily resembled the logo of his favourite American beer, *Ballantine*.

speculation, more especially because it was bereft of a title or even the band's name. "It was like we were being given an exquisite set of clues to work out!" Dave Lewis laughed. In essence a gatefold sleeve in four distinct parts, the front cover featured an oil painting of a man carrying a bale of heavy sticks on his back that Plant had found in an antique shop in Reading. This painting was in turn fixed to the crumbling wall of a demolished house behind which, when the sleeve was opened out and front and back viewed together, were trees, rows of tenement houses and a block of high-rise flats[118]. Ostensibly designed to illustrate the circle of nature – "The imagery there is the old making way for the new," said Jimmy – not everyone was a fan. "The picture of the old man was Robert's," Richard Cole later told *Classic Rock*. "None of us could figure out why he wanted that old bit of rubbish on the cover."

On the inside of the gatefold sleeve, more visual treasures were revealed, though this time they were chosen by Jimmy Page alone. In pole position was a finely wrought illustration in pencil and gold paint of a bearded old man atop a rocky hill, one hand clutching a staff, the other holding out a lamp to better see the village below. The work of artist Barrington Colby Mom, 'The Hermit'[119] was part-based on a tarot card of the same name designed in 1910 by Victorian illustrator Pamela Colman-Smith under the guidance of poet/mystic Arthur Edward Waite[120]. "['The Hermit']," said Jimmy in 1993, "represents self-reliance and wisdom."

A friend of Page and something of an enigma himself, Colby Mom[121] was also responsible for another aspect of the album's symbolic tissue,

---

118   The tower block in question was in Dudley's Eve Hill district. It was demolished in 1990.

119   The illustration is also known as '*View in Half or Varying Light*' and was reportedly sold at auction with that name to an American buyer in 1981.

120   'The Hermit' was just one illustration by Colman-Smith in a much larger collection known as the 'Rider-Waite' tarot deck. First published in 1910, it still remains one of the most popular tarot decks in use today.

121   Despite his work being lauded at the time, Barrington Colby Mom seemed to literally disappear from the face of the Earth after the release of *Led Zeppelin IV*, leading to several wild theories and much speculation regarding his fate. However, popular opinion now has it the artist simply moved to Switzerland.

Dressed all in black with astrological and mystical symbols of moons, stars and dragons sewn into his clothing, Jimmy's summoning of the four winds with his violin bow before the assembled throngs was pure theatre, these larger than life gestures a winking precursor to the atonal maelstrom of screaming planes,

Carrying his dry-cleaning and purchases from Tower Records, Jimmy alights from an airport coach at Seattle, September 1, 1970, closely followed by Zeppelin manager Peter Grant. "Jimmy and Peter really hit it off right away," said Jim McCarty. "They were both 'into' and 'of' the business."

Jimmy, Robert Plant and John Bonham at the Savoy Hotel in London on September 16, 1970, there to receive their 'Top Group' award in *Melody Maker*'s annual readers' poll, finally ousting the Beatles from the number one spot after an eight year reign.

mmy on stage with Led Zeppelin in 1972. Weighing approximately 13lb, Jimmy's Gibson EDS 1275
ouble-necked guitar was as stunning as it was pragmatic, its acquisition empathically solving the problem
how to bring 'Stairway To Heaven' out of the studio and onto the concert stage. "I'd recorded the thing and
en wondered how I was going to do it," he said later, "so I got the double-neck specifically for doing
tairway To Heaven' live."

Boleskine,
Loch Ness
was once t
the occulti
abiding inte
interesting
to go wher
up by the c

Plumpton Place, the 16th century Grade II listed Elizabethan manor
near Lewes in East Sussex that Page purchased in 1971. With six b
a large library and a 48ft long sitting room, it was set in 62 acres o
and surrounded by a moat and lakes, with improvements courtesy
British architect Sir Edwin Luytens.

The Tower House in London's Holland Park was designed and built to the exact specifications of architect William Burges between 1875 and 1881. Its illustrious owners before Jimmy included archaeologist Richard Popplewell-Pullan, Poet Laureate Sir John Betjeman, Lady Jane Turnbull and Irish actor and all round hellraiser Richard Harris who sold it to Jimmy in 1972 for £350,000 in the face of competition from David Bowie.

Deanery Garden, in Sonning near Reading, also designed by renowned Victorian architect Edwin Lutyens, was built between 1899 and 1901 for Edward Hudson (founder of *Country Life* magazine) as a show home, and was once open to the public.

Charlotte Martin (above left), the mother of Jimmy's first daughter Scarlet, was Jimmy's partner throughout the seventies. Scarlet, pictured with her father at the 2005 Q Awards, became a mother in 2007, thus making Jimmy a grandfather.

Lori Mattix (with Jimmy, above left) and 'Miss Pamela' Des Barres, nee Miller (above right), were among Jimmy's romantic partners in California during Led Zeppelin's pomp in the early seventies

Jemena Gomez-Paratcha, whom Jimmy met in Rio de Janeiro while promoting *No Quarter*. After marrying they would have two children together, Jade (born in 1997) and Ashen Josan (1999).

mmy, with girlfriend Scarlet Sabet in Kensington High Street, photographed in March 2015. poet and actress, she became Jimmy's companion after they reportedly met at a reading of r verse at the Chelsea Arts Club the previous year.

Led Zeppelin's last stand. Jimmy on stage during his group's final tour of Europe during the summer of 1980. A far cry from the three-hour plus displays of the mid-seventies, their set was now shaved down to a more manageable 120 minutes, with the bloated arrangements and extreme displays of technical virtuosity left well behind. Guitar heroics were clipped, drum solos cut back and keyboard explorations mostly absent.

though again the artist had taken his cue from Jimmy. When leafing through an old back issue of the Victorian arts and crafts magazine *Studio*, Page had chanced across some ornate, illustrative lettering. Taken with what he saw, Jimmy asked Colby Mom to design a full alphabet in the same style. When completed, this 'typeface' was used for a set of song lyrics that appeared in pride of place within the album's gatefold sleeve. "There's a lady who's sure all that glitters is gold..." ran the somewhat curious opening line. Soon enough, every man and his dog would be singing it.

A laborious process that had seen the band through myriad recording sessions, botched mixes, screeds of intriguing artwork and the odd stand-off with their record company, Led Zeppelin's fourth album was finally released on November 8, 1971. For some, it was/is/always will be their masterpiece. For Jimmy Page, it was simply vindication. "The fourth album was a commitment," he told writer David Fricke in 2014. "We were living in a house with a recording truck, eating and sleeping music together. We could push everything we were doing to the point of total extremes. People now say that *IV* was a milestone album. Well yes," he concluded, "it honestly was."

Like all its predecessors, *Led Zeppelin IV*, or to give its alternative names – 'Four Symbols', 'Untitled', 'The Runes', 'ZoSo' and 'The Hermit' – opened not so much with a bang but with a deafening explosion. Fizzing into life on the back of an ominous electrical hum (actually Jimmy's guitar "waking up"), 'Black Dog' was an almost mutant blues, its call and response structure snaking around a hellishly complex guitar riff written by John Paul Jones on a train ride home from Pangbourne. "It's very common in Indian music, and you [also] hear it, slowed down, in a lot of Greek rhythms," JPJ said of 'Black Dog''s original 3/16 time signature. "I actually find bars of 3/16 or 7/4 quite natural. Why just limit yourself to 4/4 when there are so many different feels? It's like eating the same food every day..."

While the complexities of '3/16' might have been a simple dish to concoct for Jones, the rest of Led Zeppelin proved less adept chefs. In fact, on their first run-through of the tune, Page and Bonham collapsed in a fit of giggles at their inability to nail the undulating time signature.

Yet, with a few minor adjustments (Jones told Bonzo to keep playing four to the bar as the riff would eventually turn around on itself), they got there – or thereabouts – in the end. It was then down to Page to add a few stray flavours of his own. "'Black Dog' was my riff," John Paul later told *Guitar World*. "I brought it in and Page wrote [the] chordy bits. Basically with Zeppelin, anything that was notey and melodic was mine and anything that was lurchy and chordal was Page's. And a lot of times, the two things were in the same song… playing them in unison, that gave the riff lots of power."

With the Frankenstein of all rock riffs now properly bolted together, it was left to Robert Plant to find a suitable subject for the song's title. His creative gaze fell on an old, black male Labrador that roamed the grounds of Headley Grange. "We didn't know his name," Jimmy later said. "We just called him 'black dog'." Prone to disappearing at night, the pooch would return tired and bleary-eyed the next morning, only to start the cycle all over again at sunset. For Robert, there was but one explanation as to where he was going and what he had been up to. "He used to go see this old lady [dog] quite regularly," he explained to an audience in 1972, "but after he'd 'boogied' and everything else, he couldn't get back. [So] we used to carry him back."

In the end, 'Black Dog' turned out to be as horny as the canine it was named for. Another peerless Led Zeppelin anthem celebrating the power of sex and the perils of a "big legged woman", 'Black Dog' was a combustible pile-up of racing four and six-strings, off-the-wall drumming and a series of libidinous, a capella howls courtesy of Plant. Featuring no less than four multi-tracked guitars from Jimmy to help create its meaty tone – "We put my Les Paul through a direct box, and from there into a mike channel. [Then], we used the mike amp of the mixing board to get the distortion" – the song was immediately embraced by American FM radio programmers. Despite its lurching structure and distinctly salty lyrics, 'Black Dog' subsequently gifted Zep a number 15 placing when released as a single in the USA in February 1972. "[It was] the perfect image for the riff, really," concluded a justly proud John Paul Jones.

In comparison to 'Black Dog''s Labyrinthine musical complexities, 'Rock And Roll' was positively Neanderthal. The result of a loose jam between Zep and visiting Rolling Stones tour manager/keyboard player Ian 'Stu' Stewart at Headley Grange in December 1970, the tune was birthed when Bonzo launched into the cymbal-friendly introduction to Little Richard's gloriously irreverent 'Keep A Knockin'' and Stu followed suit with a Jerry Lee Lewis-inspired stride piano riff of his own. On it like a bicycle, Page joined in with a few blasts of rockabilly-style guitar before the whole thing collapsed in a heap several seconds later. Thankfully for all concerned, the studio tapes had been running. "It all ground to a halt after 12 bars," Jimmy said, "but we knew we had something. Robert then came in with the lyrics and within 15 minutes, it was virtually complete." When Plant added his whimsical, but nonetheless entertaining, take on the glories of doing "the stroll" while being carried back from whence he came, Zep had an instant crowd pleaser on their hands, the tune becoming a mainstay of the band's live shows, where it was introduced as an encore before being promoted to the opening number of their set. Whether played first or last, however, 'Rock And Roll' always provided a rampant excuse for Jimmy's best Chuck Berry impersonation, the guitarist duck walking across the stage like a man possessed.

There was more jollity to be had from 'Misty Mountain Hop'. A real bouncy castle of a song with Plant's mischievous, multi-tracked lyric taking a good-natured swipe at reactionary attitudes towards dope smoking, '... Hop''s real triumph was just how interconnected Led Zeppelin sounded as a band. With John Bonham swinging like a drunken prize-fighter, John Paul Jones positively dainty on electric piano and Jimmy either crunching chords or launching harmony lines, there was always an inherent danger that things might fall apart at any moment. But as with 'Out On The Tiles', all these disparate elements gelled together magnificently, creating a real gem of a tune.

Interconnectivity was also central to the success of 'Four Sticks'. One of the more challenging compositions Led Zeppelin attempted, the track found Bonzo employing the four sticks of the title to create a hypnotic rhythmic pattern around which all the other band members danced.

An exhaustive undertaking for the drummer – "It was done in two takes [at Olympic Studios]," Page later remembered, "because it was physically impossible for him to do another"[122] – Bonham's technical skills were little short of astounding. But the guitars were also worth a listen. Flowing, then falling away, changing tone, then timbre, Jimmy's dream of building an orchestral legion of six-string soldiers took definite shape on 'Four Sticks'. "Building up harmonies, orchestrating the guitar like an army," he later told *Guitar Player*. "I'm talking about actual orchestration in the same way you'd orchestrate a classical piece. That's where it is for me."

Unlike 'Four Sticks', 'Going To California' had no world-class drum patterns nor perfectly intertwining guitars, but it was none the worse for it. A genuine wisp of a song, its lyric and melody line undoubtedly in thrall to the work of Joni Mitchell and the larger Marin County, West Coast folk blues scene, 'Going To California' had Robert seeking "a girl out there with love in her eyes and flowers in her hair" while Page gently matched the singer's mood with a few spare chords and a delicate descending run to set up each verse. Already well-established as part of Zep's live acoustic set, '... California' took on an even more intimate quality on record, its hushed tones almost stroking the ear of the listener. Another example of Led Zeppelin sticking to their collective guns after the glum response to their earlier experiments with "rustic music", 'Going To California' may have calmed the nerves and soothed the heart, but it also poked a rather big stick in the eye of the critics. "In Led Zeppelin, we hardly ever listened to other rock bands," said John Paul Jones of Zep's taste for musical eclecticism. "On tour, we'd listen to Joni Mitchell, James Brown, Eastern music, lots of folk, all of which percolated through what we did."

'The Battle Of Evermore' was different again. Born around the fireplace at Headley Grange, Andy Johns watched with jaw agape as Led

---

122 As physically taxing as it was musically complex, 'Four Sticks' was only performed live once by Led Zeppelin at a concert in Copenhagen, during their 1971 European tour. However, both Jimmy Page and Robert Plant would return to the track over the coming years.

Zeppelin literally plucked the song from the air above them. "I'd watch them come up with ideas out of nowhere and 'The Battle Of Evermore' was a great example of that," he told *Guitar World* in 1993. "The band were just sitting in Headley having some tea when Jimmy picked up [John Paul Jones'] mandolin and started playing. I put a microphone on him... Robert started singing and we had this amazing track out of nothing." On completing his lyrics, which were part-inspired by a book he was reading about the history of the Scots/Anglo wars[123], Plant hit on a fine idea. "After I'd written the words," he said in 1972, "I realised I needed another completely different voice... to give the song its full impact." Led Zeppelin called in Sandy Denny.

Vocalist, songwriter and all-round force of nature, Alexandra 'Sandy' Denny was one of the most respected faces on the British folk scene, her credentials well-established during her stint fronting Britain's pre-eminent folk band Fairport Convention, with whom she recorded 1969's groundbreaking *Liege And Lief*. A huge fan of Fairport[124], *Liege...* and a friend of Denny's since the two first met while she was attending Kingston Art College in the mid-sixties, Jimmy Page was as keen as Robert Plant to bring Sandy on board. Having left Fairport and recently folded her own band Fotheringay to pursue a career as a solo artist, the publicity generated by linking with one of the world's biggest bands was probably quite appealing to Denny, too.

Playing the part of a "town crier urging people to throw down their weapons" in Robert's epic, Celtic-tinged tale of dark lords, flaming dragons and the "Angels of Avalon", Sandy Denny's performance on 'The Battle Of Evermore' was a delight. Perfectly complimenting Plant's role

---

123 The lyrics to 'The Battle Of Evermore' were also influenced by the work of Scottish author/folklorist Lewis Spence and the English author/poet Robert Graves.

124 In fact, Led Zeppelin and Fairport Convention had established something of a mutual admiration society by the time of 'The Battle Of Evermore'. In addition to both bands appearing at 1970's Bath Festival and Zep dropping in on one of their gigs in Los Angeles in the same year, Fairport's bassist Dave Pegg had known John Bonham since their days together in the Birmingham band Way Of Life. As will become evident in the pages of this book, the bond between Page, Zep and Fairport would only grow in time.

of 'narrator' within the song, Denny's nightingale-like voice provided an airy, almost ethereal quality among all the clashing broadswords and braying horses. "To sing with Sandy Denny was great," Robert told *Uncut* in 2005. "We were... friends and it was the most obvious thing to ask her to sing on 'The Battle Of Evermore'. If [the lyric] suffered from a certain naiveté and tweeness – I was only 23! – it more than makes up for it in the cohesion of the voices and the playing."

For Page, who had never played a mandolin let alone written a tune on one before '... Evermore', the lush textures Led Zeppelin achieved on the track were ample proof of the band's continuing desire to test their boundaries or, wherever possible, eradicate them completely. "With the likes of 'Going To California' and 'The Battle Of Evermore'," he later told writer Paul Elliott, "we were moving the acoustic aspect of what we'd done on *III* into these even more intimate areas." The first and, indeed, one of only two guests to appear on a Zep album, Sandy Denny was rewarded with the ultimate accolade: a symbol of her very own. Appearing alongside 'The Battle Of Evermore''s title on the inner sleeve of the LP, Denny's sign – three triangles joined at one fixed point – denoted an old Christian image for the Trinity or Godhead, its meaning approximately translated as "Beyond that nothing is known about it". Nonetheless, according to Fairport Convention drummer Dave Mattacks – with whom Jimmy would work closely in times to come – the symbol might have been all that Sandy got. "Ha!" he laughed, "I remember her saying 'Those bastards still haven't paid me!'"

With material as strong, simple and musically diverse as 'Black Dog', 'Rock And Roll' and 'The Battle Of Evermore', one might have forgiven Led Zeppelin for resting on their laurels and simply padding out the remainder of their fourth album with a few lively jams or a hoary old rocker. Of course, this was not their way. Instead, the band again exceeded all reasonable expectations by providing the world with two of the finest songs ever committed to tape. One a hypnotic, time-travelling blues, the other "an anthem for the ages..."

In early 1927, the Mississippi river broke its banks and caused extensive flooding to the surrounding regions. As a result, homes were upended, farms and their produce destroyed and many thousands of residents forced to flee to nearby cities such as Chicago in search of work. Two years later at a recording studio in New York, the husband and wife team of Kansas Joe McCoy and Memphis Minnie commemorated the event in song with 'When The Levee Breaks'. Centred around a steely, revolving guitar figure, and telling the story of evacuees seeking sanctuary from the rising waters on the high grounds above Greenville, Mississippi, the tune's almost jolly swagger was at complete odds with its bleak lyricism. "Oh cryin' won't help you," sang McCoy, "and prayin' won't do no good..." Released on the Columbia label in the summer of 1929, 'When The Levee Breaks' proved both a moderate hit as well as a social memento of a time many might have rightly preferred to forget. But not Jimmy Page.

Having recently rediscovered the tune, Page loved it so much he was keen for Led Zeppelin to turn it into something very much their own. Early attempts to nail 'When The Levee Breaks' at Island Studios proved unsuccessful but when John Bonham's factory-fresh Ludwig drum kit was moved out of the drawing room and into the hallway of Headley Grange by Andy Johns, things took a dramatic upturn. With a couple of Beyerdynamic M160 ribbons dangling above his head in the minstrel's gallery and Bonzo going at it hell for leather some 20-odd feet below, Johns compressed the resulting drum pattern through two further channels of the Rolling Stones' mobile studio. When he added a little echo from Jimmy's Binson Echorec Two effects unit for good measure, '... Levee Breaks' had its rhythmic pulse and Bonham had the most coveted and, indeed, most sampled drum sound in rock history. "Of course, John was also a fabulous technician," Page later confirmed. "He knew how to tune his drums and he had incredible balance. John's playing was so intense... he'd be able to just do a bass drum beat that went right through you."

With John Bonham's monstrous drums at the epicentre of 'When The Levee Breaks', Jimmy Page was now free to sprinkle magic on the rest of the band's performance. Slowing down the backing track to further add to the song's overall air of intensity, Page also used backwards echo on Robert Plant's swooping harmonica fills to create yet more sonic uneasiness. Not done by a long shot, Jimmy then heavily phased and flanged the space around Plant's forlorn-sounding vocals (which, unlike the backing track, was kept at normal speed), while subtly tweaking the levels as each verse progressed. Meanwhile, his own bottleneck guitar part remained as constant and fearful as Bonham's drums and Jones' monotonous, eerie bass, the three working in parallel to drive the tune towards it sluggish, ever-fading finale. Full of odd angles, clever panning effects, trance-like rhythms and undulating instrumentation, 'When The Levee Breaks' attained an almost majestic darkness or, as one critic had it, "the definition of primal blues". As such, it remains arguably Jimmy Page's finest work as a producer. "The whole work ethic was absolutely superb so we could – did – arrive at things like 'When The Levee Breaks', which is so ominous," he told *The Quietus* in 2014. "It's so dark... so dark that there really isn't a colour to describe it..."

Unlike 'When The Levee Breaks', the fourth track on side one of *Led Zeppelin IV* probably represented every colour of the rainbow, though it also did its best to defy traditional methods of description. Part ballad, part rock song, the tune in question broke one of the cardinal rules of pop music by speeding up its tempo after a slow, sublime start. More, at over eight minutes, it cocked a snoot at conventional wisdom that decreed how tracks this long were unlikely to be played on the radio. Since the whole band didn't come in until the sixth verse, there was also the distinct possibility it might confuse listeners. Even the normally reliable Jimmy Page had difficulty explaining the song to journalists a year before its release. "Well, it's an idea for a really long track," he said. "You know how 'Dazed And Confused' and songs like that were broken into sections? Well, we now want to try something new with the organ and acoustic guitar building up and building up, and then the electric part starts..."

Page had been working on the idea of "a really long track" for some time before talking with *Melody Maker* in November 1970. In fact, the bones of it had actually come to him some six months before when he was holidaying with Robert Plant at Bron-Yr-Aur. "How it came about was just tinkering on the guitar," Jimmy told writer Sian Edwards in 2009. "You're just playing [or] you might have just tuned up. One minute you have nothing or just a couple of chords and the next thing, you're coming up with some new... well, it's new to you anyway. Some new vision on it."

What is certain is that the song – like so many others – began life on Page's favourite acoustic guitar, his beloved Harmony Sovereign H-1260. "I always went back to my original Harmony," Jimmy later told *Guitar International*. "I had it from the third Led Zeppelin album [and] I wrote everything back then on it. On the first two albums, I was using a Gibson J-200, which belonged to Mickey Most [and] I borrowed it from him because it was such a great instrument. Unfortunately, it was stolen, so I went back to the Harmony because... it had a good recording sound."

Over time, Page began to further develop the track's three distinct parts, its gentle finger-picked intro gradually falling away to a more strident 12-string middle-section before letting loose the explosion of electricity that was to mark the finale. "I had these pieces, these guitar pieces, that I really wanted to put together," he said. "I had a whole idea of a piece of music that I really wanted to... present to everybody." To this end, Jimmy reportedly tried various experiments with the developing tune at Pangbourne, where he had recently installed an eight-track studio. Here, he was free to indulge mistakes and make necessary improvements before finalising the arrangement with his colleagues. When Page was sure he had the goods, he brought the song to the band at Headley Grange. "I literally heard it in front of a roaring fire in a country manor house!" John Paul Jones later told Chris Welch. "I picked up a bass recorder and played a run-down riff that gave us an intro, then I moved into a piano for the next section, dubbing on the guitars."

With Jones cannily adding a Renaissance-style recorder part at the song's introduction and further aiding Page with the arrangement, one member of Led Zeppelin was now on board. However, for the track to really work, John Bonham had to be deployed at precisely the right moment. "I wanted it to build towards a climax," Jimmy told Barney Hoskyns, "with John coming in at a later point to give it that extra kick." Though Bonzo initially had some difficulty with the 12-string build-up that led to the guitar solo and subsequent climax – "For some unknown reason, he couldn't get the timing right [on that bit]" – after a run-through or two, all the musicians had their parts in place. "It actually flowed very quickly," said Page.

But probably not so quickly as the lyrics to Jimmy's tune, which seemed to come to Robert Plant in the form of automatic writing. "I was sitting next to Jimmy in front of the fire... at Headley Grange," Plant later told *Guitar World*. "He'd written this chord sequence and was playing it to me. I was holding a pencil and paper and suddenly my hand is writing the words 'There's a lady who's sure all that glitters is gold....' I sat there, looked at the words and almost leaped out from my seat. Looking back, I suppose I sat down at the right moment." Page's recollection of events was similar. "I remember Robert sitting in the room, just writing and writing," he said. "So, at the point when he came to [first] sing it, he had a major percentage of the lyrics already done." There was even a title. "Ah yes," Plant laughed. "It was a little old thing called 'Stairway To Heaven'."

With rehearsals and run-throughs completed at Headley Grange, recording for 'Stairway To Heaven' commenced at Island Studios in January 1971. Having already cut 'Since I've Been Loving You' and 'That's The Way' at Island, Led Zeppelin were completely familiar with the studio's huge layout, its floor space large enough to accommodate a 70-piece orchestra. But the real trick that lay ahead of the band was making that space feel intimate and warm, a place where eye contact could be maintained and opinions exchanged without use of walkie-talkies. Setting up close together among the baffle boards, wires and microphones, Led Zeppelin went for it. "Together," Jimmy Page once said, "I felt we were capable of doing anything."

They almost nailed it on the first take. Negotiating their way through 'Stairway...''s three interlinking sections with a minimum of fuss but a maximum of effort, Page, Jones and Bonham made no real mistakes to speak of and were keen to hear the playback. Having done so, both Bonzo and JPJ were satisfied they had conquered the song. Page wasn't so sure. He asked them to go again. An old session hand, Jones calmly accepted the decision and strolled back onto the studio floor. Bonham, on the other hand, was less happy at the prospect of giving

'Stairway...' another try. "I can still see him sitting there... seething," assistant engineer Digby Smith later told *Classic Rock*. Seething, but inspired. Whacking "the beejesus" out of his kit, John Bonham not only handled the complex build of the song without error, but also made the speeded-up run towards the song's finish line feel entirely natural. "I wanted 'Stairway...' to [feel] like an adrenaline flow," Jimmy later said, "... to reach a sort of crescendo." With take two, the job was done.

Capturing the necessary "sense of urgency" that Page was looking for on the backing track, Led Zeppelin now turned their hand to overdubs. John Paul Jones was first up, his three recorder lines at the start of the tune subtly enhancing Jimmy's descending finger-picked chords while also adding an almost Elizabethan or "court-like atmosphere" to proceedings. The piano part that so beautifully hung together the song's middle-section was also dispatched by JPJ in a matter of minutes. Robert Plant again wasted no time. With the lyric now subtly softened from its original tale of a selfish "girl who's used to getting what she wants" to something far more ambiguous and bittersweet, Plant landed one of rock music's famous vocals in "two takes, [with] one punch in".

Of course, there was also the matter of Jimmy's guitar solo. Since the recording of *Led Zeppelin II*, Page had almost exclusively used a 1959 (or possibly early 1960 sunburst Gibson Les Paul for both studio and live work. The instrument, christened 'No. 1' (Page's fabled 'No. 2' Les Paul will also be covered in due course), had been sold to him by the James Gang's Joe Walsh for the not unreasonable sum of $1,200 in April 1969. Lacking a serial number on its headstock due to previous repairs, it also didn't have much in the way of the precious 'tiger top flame maple' effect so coveted by serious Gibson collectors. But it was precisely this guitar – in conjunction with a Marshall 1959 Superlead stack – that now roared out the intro to 'Whole Lotta Love', clattered heads on 'Immigrant Song' and warmed the cockles of audiences' hearts during 'Since I've Loving You'. "As soon as I played the Les Paul I fell in love," he later said. "Not that the Tele [wasn't] user friendly, but the Les Paul was gorgeous and easy to play. It just seemed like a good touring guitar. It was more of a fight... [but] the Gibson's got all that... sustain, [and] I do like sustain. It relates to bowed instruments. Sustain," he smiled, "speaks for itself."

On this occasion, however, Jimmy elected to put the Gibson down and return instead to the 'Dragon' Telecaster given to him by Jeff Beck when he first joined the Yardbirds in 1966. Plugging it into his small, 15 watt Supro amp[125], he was ready for take-off. "[I hadn't] structured it at all," he later told writer David Fricke. "I had a start, and I knew where and how I was going to begin. So I thought 'OK, take a deep breath, and play...' According to engineer Andy Johns, at first, there was trouble in paradise. "I remember sitting in the control room with Jimmy. He was standing there next to me and he'd done quite a few passes and it wasn't going anywhere," he later told *Classic Rock*. "I could see he was getting a bit paranoid and so I was getting paranoid. I turned around and said 'You're making me paranoid!' And he said, 'No, you're making me paranoid!' It was a silly circle of paranoia. Then bang!" Making three flights over the solo section, Page, Johns and Digby Smith then pulled the best bits from each and 'Stairway To Heaven' was done. "In the end," Jimmy laughed, "I winged it!"

With the recording of the song completed, Led Zeppelin now took it on the road with them. Making its live debut alongside other fellow debutantes 'Black Dog' and 'Going To California' at Belfast's Ulster Hall on March 5, 1971, audiences did not immediately genuflect before the tune. Perhaps understandably, they were more interested in just hearing the hits. "[But] there was always some resistance to new material," John Paul Jones later said. "The first time we played 'Stairway...' the audience were like 'Why aren't they playing 'Whole Lotta Love?'" Indeed, when the band performed it live at London's Paris Cinema on April 1 for a later BBC broadcast, again there was no speaking in tongues among the crowd, just some enthusiastic clapping and a few stray whoops. But by the time Led Zeppelin got to America in the autumn of 1971, things were starting to pick up. "I'm not saying the whole audience gave us

---

125 While Jimmy was probably plugged into his Supro Thunderbolt for recording the solo on 'Stairway To Heaven', he has said that a Marshall amp may have also been used during the session. "It could have been a Marshall, but I can't remember." Page also had a fondness for using Hiwatt 50/100 and Vox UL4120 amps around this time, though mainly for stage work.

a standing ovation, but there was this sizable standing ovation there," Page said of the crowd's reaction to 'Stairway...' at LA's Forum on August 21 and 22. "I thought 'This is incredible, because no one's heard this number yet. This is the first time they're hearing it!' It obviously touched them, you know. And that was at the LA Forum, so I knew we were onto something with that one."

In truth, 'Stairway To Heaven''s legendary status only began to take proper shape with the release of *Led Zeppelin IV* on November 8, 1971. Obviously "the jewel in the crown" of their fourth album, with the song's lyrics proudly displayed for all to see in arcane font on the inner sleeve, it didn't take long for fans to realise that the band were pointing attention to what they felt was a real milestone in their musical career. "We hadn't included lyrics on any album prior to that," Page later told Mick Wall, "but we knew it was special. You could say 'When The Levee Breaks' was a milestone too. But 'Stairway...' was something that was really crafted. Yes, it was certainly a milestone along one of the many avenues of Led Zeppelin."

Debuting at number 10 in the UK charts, *Led Zeppelin IV* had risen to the top by the following week. The story was much the same in the USA, where the album entered the *Billboard Top 100* at number two, a place behind Sly Stone's hellacious *There's A Riot Going On*.[126] But unlike its predecessor, Zep's latest release did not fall away after a month or two on the charts. Buoyed by the strength of its contents, further lifted by positive word of mouth and drilled home by another round of touring by the band, *Led Zeppelin IV* continued to sell in droves. Somewhat improbably, even previous detractors *Rolling Stone* seemed to like it. "Led Zeppelin have had a lot of imitators over the past few years, but it takes cuts like ['When The Levee Breaks'] to show that most have only picked up on the style [and] lacked any real knowledge of the meat

---

126 In fact, *Led Zeppelin IV* would never make it to number one in the US charts, with Carole King's multi-million selling *Tapestry* holding the LP off the top spot for much of the following year. That said, it still holds the record as the biggest ever-selling album not to actually top the US charts.

underneath," said journalist Lenny Kaye. "Not bad for a pack of Limey lemon squeezers."

'When The Levee Breaks'. 'Black Dog'. 'The Battle Of Evermore'. Fine cuts all and surely able contributors to the selling power of the LP. But it was really 'Stairway To Heaven' that was pushing sales of *Led Zeppelin IV* through the roof. Spurred on by endless requests from listeners, American radio had set aside its usual draconian format regarding song length and starting spinning the tune on a daily basis. And the more they played it, the more listeners wanted to own it. But these were not just rabid fans of Led Zeppelin. In fact, some of them had probably never heard the band before. With just one song, Zep achieved the mother of all rock ambitions. They had become a 'crossover' act.

But despite a new, broader audience keen to take 'Stairway...' out of the stores and into their homes, Peter Grant and Jimmy Page had absolutely no intention of releasing it as a single. "It was never, ever going to be released as a single[127]," Page again confirmed to Mick Wall. "The whole thing was we wanted people to hear it in the context of the album. Also, I said 'It'll help the album sell because it's *not* a single'." Page's understanding of supply and demand proved correct. With no alternative but to purchase the LP, *Led Zeppelin IV* just kept selling, resulting in a 90-week stay in the US charts and almost the same again in the UK. "I always knew 'Stairway...' was good," Jimmy said, "[But] I didn't know it was going to be an anthem."

An anthem, and indeed, so much more. With its lilting vocal, steadily building momentum and explosive finale, 'Stairway To Heaven' was destined to become an ageless poster boy for both *Led Zeppelin IV* and the band. By the end of 2014, 23 million copies of the album had been sold in the USA with nearly another two million purchased in Great Britain. When one factored in a further five million units shifted in territories as diverse as Canada, Australia, Germany, Spain and Holland, and over four million radio plays (and counting) in North America

---

127 While Page kept his word, a number of promotional copies featuring 'Stairway To Heaven' were pressed for radio purposes. They have subsequently become one of the most sought-after items of Led Zeppelin-related ephemera.

alone, the sheer weight of numbers was staggering to behold. But Jimmy Page has never been interested in topping it. "No, that was never the intention," he told *Classic Rock*. "That's not the thing to do if you want to keep creating great stuff. To try and top 'Stairway To Heaven' would have been like chasing your own tail."

Perhaps. Yet, what 'Stairway To Heaven' as a song and *Led Zeppelin IV* as an album did do was seal the band's legend in perpetuity, those seven fine tunes and one unimpeachable anthem granting them an almost untouchable status within the rock community. Indeed, if Jimmy Page chose never to pick up a guitar again after the winter of 1971, so be it. His contribution was made. "I thought 'Stairway...' would hold up as a piece of music... and make a bit of a splash," he said. "Of course, one can never hope in your secret dreams that things could last the way they did, [so] I never really expected that. But, you know, I was always aware of how good our music was. That was the difference," he concluded. "The four individual parts making this fifth monster..."

CHAPTER 18

At around the same time Led Zeppelin released their fourth album, Jimmy Page bought a small, but striking house in the Scottish Highlands. Sitting pretty on the south side of Loch Ness, the location was certainly picturesque, surrounded by copious woodland with the high, green hills and crystal clear waters of Foyers Bay nearby. Unlike some of the grander, more ornate piles in the surrounding area, however, the house's distressed condition meant it was of little interest to prospective buyers or investors. "It was in such a state of decay," Page later told Howard Mylett, "nobody wanted it." He went ahead and bought it anyway. For a man with a reputation for being careful with his money and investments, such a purchase seemed out of character. "All I'm saying," Jimmy continued, "is that it's an interesting house and a perfect place to go when one starts getting wound up by the clock." Indeed. Yet, the main thrust of his curiosity was surely that Boleskine House had been the former residence of Aleister Crowley, a man of great and abiding interest to Jimmy Page.

At the very least a divisive figure – a description he might have appreciated or even revelled in – Edward Alexander Crowley[128] was

---

128 Crowley would adopt the name Aleister in his teenage years.

born on October 12, 1875 in the town of Royal Leamington Spa, Warwickshire. The fact that Crowley shared the county of his birth with England's finest playwright was not lost upon him. "It has been remarked a strange coincidence," he once said, "that one small county should have given England its two greatest poets. For one must not forget William Shakespeare." The progeny of devout Christian Fundamentalists[129], Crowley was also a child of wealth, his father's share of the family brewing business meaning his young son would never have to work for a living. As a result, Crowley confessed to notions of superiority, or as he put more accurately put it, "[My] aristocratic feelings were very strong." He is reported to have practised them often and without much in the way of impunity until a reported attempt to bash an errand boy with an iron-tipped stick led to him being chased home in fear for his life.

When Crowley was 11, his father died. Having seen the older man as something of "a hero and friend" for both the passion and depth of his faith, Crowley lost one of his principal anchors. The situation worsened when his mother Emily moved their shrinking family[130] to London to be nearer her own brother, Thomas Bond Bishop. Now ensconced in a strange new environment with a woman he later called "a brainless bigot"[131] and a "perfidious and hypocritical" uncle whose rigorous self-belief and skewed notions of piety appalled him, Crowley did the only logical thing he felt at his disposal: he rebelled. And a very good job he did of it too, with the next 60-odd years of his life given to the wilful pursuit of knowledge in all its forms: intellectual and forbidden, sacred and profane.

---

129 Crowley's father, Edward, was a former Quaker who had converted to the 'Exclusive Brethren' – a faction of the Plymouth Brethren – in adult life. Unshakable in the strength of their religious convictions, the Plymouth Brethren believed that each word of The Bible was divinely inspired.

130 A baby daughter died some seven years before Edward Crowley passed away in 1887, leaving Aleister an only child.

131 Emily Crowley had her own name for her son: 'The Beast'. Reportedly, Crowley loved her description so much, he commandeered it for his own purposes, adding an honorific to create the nickname 'The Great Beast'.

In reality, it would take a separate and lengthy biography to adequately explore the life and ideas of Aleister Crowley. But a little information about the man would surely not hurt. His love of mountaineering, for instance, was just one small yet typically controversial facet of his nature. Originally feted for his early climbs in the Bernese Alps and a spirited, if unsuccessful attempt to conquer K2, another vainglorious attempt on Kanchenjunga[132] in 1905 resulted in a black mark against Crowley's name, with colleagues pointing accusatory fingers about his role in the loss of five lives on the expedition. Crowley's education, too, threw up its fair share of tall stories, his days at Malvern College and Cambridge University littered with tales of prostitutes, sexually transmitted diseases and heated debates with teachers about the value of Christianity, a religion he would soon reject in favour of his own form of esotericism.

As Crowley's progressed, his obvious fondness for riotous living, authorship of several works of erotic fiction and countless sexual dalliances with both men and women led him to being pilloried by the press and shunned by certain sections of society. He didn't seem to much care. In fact, at times, Crowley appeared to revel in his otherness. "Ordinary morality," he once opined, "is for ordinary people." That said, there were real tragedies along the way that might have left deeper cuts. Wives fell by the wayside. Mistresses committed suicide or lost their minds. His son died in childhood. Having squandered much of his inheritance as a young man, Crowley was also increasingly forced to seek donations from friends and devotees, or handouts from the various organisations with which he aligned himself over the years to keep from penury.

Then, there was the addiction to hard drugs. Always an enthusiastic imbiber – cocaine, hashish and opium were all tested for their efficacy – Crowley's real love was opiates or, more specifically, heroin. In fact, when many had either deserted, forgotten or simply been alienated by him, and Crowley faced the end of his days as a guest in a Hastings boarding house in 1947, heroin was still omni-present. "Having to

---

132 At 28,169 feet, Kanchenjunga is the third-highest mountain in the world and was not conquered until 1955.

talk," he wrote of his experiences with narcotics in 1922's *Diary Of A Drug Fiend*, "destroys the symphony of silence."

Variously described as "an egotist, polemicist and pornographer", who was also capable of inflicting "immense physical and emotional cruelty" on those around him, Aleister Crowley was obviously not without his faults or several hundred detractors to point them out. Yet, away from the myriad examples of his unpleasantness and cock-crowing was a man of questing intellect and many accomplishments. In addition to being a fine poet, able sportsman (at least until the drink and drugs had their way) and tournament-level chess player, Crowley was also one of few souls who assumed the role of both propagator and prophet for a religion: 'Thelema'.

Again, it would be madness to try and cover every aspect of Crowley's law of Thelema within the pages of a book devoted to another subject.[133] After all, it was a huge part of his life's work, Crowley dedicated myriad volumes to it and many a student, scholar or writer (this one included) might come unstuck on even the simplest of his theories. Suffice to say, Crowley's journey to Thelema reportedly involved an extensive period of previous learning, with his philosophical and mystical travels bringing him into the ranks of the Hermetic Order Of The Golden Dawn during the late 1880s. Another prolonged study of French occultist Eliphas Levi – whom Crowley later claimed to be the reincarnation of – and the writings of humanist and physician François Rabelais followed. Similarly, a possible initiation into the Freemasons in 1900 and further time spent familiarising himself with Elizabethan magus John Dee and his Enochian invocations (Crowley was also said to feel a strong spiritual connection with Dee's mercurial assistant, Edmund Kelly) provided more grist for the spiritual mill.

---

133 For those seeking more detailed information on the life of Aleister Crowley and Thelema, one simply has to turn to 'The Great Beast' himself. Over the course of his Life, Crowley compiled a comprehensive 'Libri' of methodologies, occult practices and various scriptures around his Thelemic teachings. Further, during the twenties, he wrote his own autobiography – or in his words 'Autohagiography' – *The Confessions Of Aleister Crowley.* There are also many biographies about Crowley to be found, ranging from Richard Cammell's 1962 study *The Man, The Mage, The Poet* to Colin Wilson's 1987 book *The Nature Of The Beast,* and beyond.

But after copious study and no doubt enlightening expeditions through India, Mexico and France, it was actually on a trip to Egypt with his wife, Edith Rose, during April 1904 that Crowley's search for hidden knowledge via ceremonial, sexual and sometimes drug-assisted means came to a sudden end and vivid new beginning. In his version of events, on hearing a disembodied voice calling itself Aiwass – who in turn claimed to be a messenger of Egypt's patron god Horus – Crowley began writing down everything the non-corporeal entity said. Three days later, he had *The Book Of The Law* (or *Liber AL vel Legis*). Proclaiming that man had entered a new age (or 'Aeon of Horus') with Crowley as its prophet, the Book had one supreme command at its moral centre: "Do what thou wilt shall be the whole of the law. Love is the law, love under will."

The "will" part of this edict was of critical importance to Crowley's vision of 'Thelema'[134]. A key enabler to achieving one's overall destiny in life, but also a more immediate path to be followed when seeking harmony with one's natural surroundings, Crowley's notion of 'true will' was not driven by ego or desire per se. Instead, it was more about directly connecting or aligning one's real self with the divine nature of the universe. And in so doing, that real self would be liberated from inner conflict and false desire, allowing instead the opportunity to get on with the business of achieving or actualising true potential. No resistance, no impediments to progress. Just one 'magickal' path. "All you have to do," said Crowley, "is to be yourself, do your will and rejoice." In his mind, this was willpower as it should be: vibrant, purposeful and powerful.

As evidenced, at the end of Aleister Crowley's life, it was difficult to ascertain exactly how his beloved religion and philosophy of Thelema,

---

134 There are many historical precedents for the word 'Thelema'. It is present in early Greek and Latin translations of the Hebrew Bible, and later appeared in the Renaissance as the name of a representational character in the fictional work of Dominican monk Francesco Colonna, who in turn influenced the writings of the aforementioned François Rabelais. Each time and in each iteration, Thelema is connected to notions of the will.

and the potentialities of accessing one's true will had benefited him. Addicted to heroin, largely reliant on the kindness of his few remaining friends for money and living in a humble guest house, Crowley's reduced circumstances were a far cry from the spirited intellectual battles fought in the classrooms of Cambridge University and the globe-trotting adventures of his prime. In fact, when he died aged 72 on December 1, 1947, only a dozen or so people reportedly attended his funeral, with the excerpts read from *The Book Of The Law* over his coffin erroneously picked up by the local press as a 'Black Mass'.

Yet, by the mid-sixties, Aleister Crowley was again in the ascendant. Already the subject of a sympathetic biography by his friend Charles Richard Cammell[135] that portrayed him less as a 'mystical ogre' and more a 'wise and witty old mage', Crowley was also the beneficiary of a more general upsurge of interest in all matters pertaining to the occult. "[It is] a curious historical phenomenon that in the last decades of every century, there is a sudden revival of interest in the paranormal," said original 'Angry Young Man' (and writer of *The Occult*) Colin Wilson. "In the last years of the 16th century, it was John Dee. A century later [incredibly] Sir Isaac Newton, who was a dedicated alchemist. A century [after that] came Cagliostro, and then a century later still, a whole 19th-century movement that included Lord Lytton, Eliphas Levi, Madame Blavatsky, Aleister Crowley and the Golden Dawn. In the 20th century, it all started again with a book called *The Morning Of The Magicians* by Louis Pauwels and Jacques Bergier, which became a best seller in the 1960s."

In Aleister Crowley's case, it was perhaps easy to see why his star had begun to shine again. In a new age of sexual freedom, mind-altering drugs and greater philosophical challenge, Crowley's gospel of true will, personal liberation and experimental 'sex magick' was enormously appealing to a generation keen to remove the final shackles of post-war

---

135 As mentioned earlier in these pages, CR Cammell's biography about Aleister Crowley was one of the first serious studies of his work. Interestingly, Cammell's son Donald (another member of the 'Chelsea set') would go on to become a cult film-maker, writing and co-directing 1968's *Performance*, a marvellous study of identity, murder, madness (and possibly, magic) that starred Mick Jagger and James Fox.

austerity and get on with their collective and individual destinies. As if to make the point, the Beatles even placed Crowley on the cover of their own firmament-exploding *Sgt. Pepper's Lonely Hearts Club Band*, his hollow, mesmeric eyes staring out at record buyers alongside the likes of actress Marilyn Monroe, comedian Stan Laurel, politician Karl Marx and many other famous faces. "We just thought we'd like to put together a lot of people we like and admire," said Ringo Starr at the *Sgt. Pepper...* launch party in May 1967. Evidently, Aleister Crowley was no longer "The wickedest man in the world," but more "a naughty uncle who could teach the kids a thing or two about living."

Jimmy Page had a clearer understanding than most about these changes in cultural and philosophical perspective. A former art student who had spent an inordinate amount of time in the company of musicians and 'creatives', he had also no doubt been exposed to the free-thinkers of London's Chelsea set and their infatuation with both Eastern and Arabic philosophies. More, Page's arrival in America with the Yardbirds had perfectly coincided with the rise of San Francisco's hippie movement, these former beatniks transforming into something much more bizarre and exotic, with complimentary ideas to match.

And, of course, Jimmy had watched with some interest as Robert Plant's early explorations into the writings of Tolkien had led him in turn towards Celtic and Nordic mythology, the subsequent influence of writers such as Lewis Spence and Edmund Spencer very possibly contributing to the lyrical themes present in 'Stairway To Heaven'. "There has been a major revival, a spiritual revival throughout the world," Page later said. "There's a great interest in the Celtic mysteries and the Dark Ages, and the areas where a lot of these truths were erased for the sake of the church. But I'm quite fascinated by these things."

In point of fact, Jimmy Page's fascination with such things could be squarely traced back to late childhood, when he first encountered the work of Aleister Crowley. "I read *Magick In Theory And Practice* when I was about 11 years old," he said. "But it wasn't for some years that I understood what it was all about." By his late teens, Page was beginning to develop a much clearer understanding of some of Crowley's fundamental tenets, his knowledge enhanced by further reading around the subject and, no doubt, similar esoterically themed tracts. He later expanded on this theme in an interview with writer Nick Kent. "The first book I read about Aleister Crowley was *The Great Beast* and it created an intense curiosity," Jimmy confirmed in 2003. "The more I read about him, the more fascinated I became about him, because he'd tied up so many traditions in Western magic – he'd introduced Yoga to the west as well – and because I found his system worked. Plus, all the aspects of ritual magic, talismanic magic, I could see they worked."

As evidenced, to properly embrace Crowley's ideas meant the abnegation of one's conscious desire and unshackling of erroneous distraction in favour of the pursuit of true will. Again, Page had no issue with such a concept. In fact, he readily embraced it. "What I can relate to is Crowley's system of self-liberation in which repression is the greatest work of sin," he later told Chris Salewicz. "It's like being in a job when you want to be doing something else. That's the area where the true will should come forward. And when you've discovered your true will, you will forge ahead like a steam train. If you put all your energies into it, there's no doubt you'll succeed."

These remarks were made in 1977, but they could have easily described Jimmy Page's actions and beliefs 10 years before when, as leader of Led Zeppelin, he pushed both himself and the band forward like a relentless locomotive towards superstardom. Whether one shared his beliefs or not, whatever Page had found in Crowley seemed to work for him and his group. "The four musical elements of Led Zeppelin making a fifth is magick into itself," he once said. "That's the alchemical process."

Though Jimmy Page had obviously been taken with the work of Aleister Crowley, he had been more or less content for such matters to remain under the radar and out of the public domain. But that began to change in 1970 when the phrases 'So mote be it' and 'Do what though wilt' appeared on the run out groove (or lacquer) of early pressings of *Led Zeppelin III*. Inscribed during the final mastering of the LP by engineer Terry Manning under Page's instructions, the link to Crowley's religion and philosophy of Thelema could not be clearer. Given that rock music's still relatively new, but incredibly engaged audience keenly devoured every lyric, word and image upon the record sleeves of their favourite bands for hidden meanings, it was also inevitable these inscriptions would generate excitement, rumour and intrigue.[136]

However, Page's decision to actually purchase Boleskine House was a much larger gesture in confirming his fascination with Aleister Crowley. By all accounts, until Jimmy bought the Scottish home, his collection of Crowley-related ephemera had been limited to the acquisition of private manuscripts, first editions of books, artwork, items of clothing and other ceremonial vessels. But proper brickwork sitting atop a loch already legendary for its monsters (or at least cryptids) was simply too tasty a morsel for the press to ignore.

Even some cursory digging around the history of Boleskine House was enough to set the hares running and typewriters pinging. Allegedly built on the site of a 10th-century kirk (Scottish church), which according to Page "had been burnt down with its congregation", locals had long given the manor house and its nearby graveyard a wide berth. But what they deemed a suspicious plot of land with a possibly terrible past was of little concern to Aleister Crowley when he bought the 'Manor of Boleskine and Abertarff' from the Fraser family in 1899. In fact, Crowley believed it the ideal, secluded location in which to better isolate himself while performing a series of magical rituals known as the 'Sacred Magic of Abramelin the Mage'[137]. A complex task that required months of preparation, chastity and abstinence from alcohol, Crowley had been attempting to invoke his 'Guardian Angel' or 'Higher Self' in the grounds above Loch Ness. Though he never completed the invocation, he did write of it in his autobiography. "There should be a door opening to the north from the room of which you make your oratory," Crowley instructed. "Outside this door, you construct a terrace covered with fine river sand. This ends in a 'lodge' where the spirits may congregate..."

---

136 There has been some dispute about exactly what inscriptions were featured on the very earliest pressings of *Led Zeppelin III*, with some claiming the run out groove actually bore both phrases. Whatever the case, because later copies of the LP only ran part inscriptions (or none at all), these early examples have become collectible items.

137 Said ritual was taken from a magical text (or 'Grimoire') named *The Book Of Abramelin*, which in turn told the story of an Egyptian mage passing on various magical secrets to his own son.

With stories of summoning the '12 Kings and Dukes of Hell' as a part of the Abramelin ritual and burning kirks a part of local legend, Boleskine House's grim history and supercharged atmosphere was bread and butter to journalists eager to learn more about Page's exact reasons for buying the property. For the most part Jimmy played coy, though he was willing to concede the Scottish manor had its own singular qualities. "I hadn't originally intended to buy it," he later told Led Zeppelin archivist Howard Mylett, "but it was just so fascinating. It's not an unfriendly place when you walk into it. It just seems to have this thing." To further enhance its essential character, Page invited his friend Charles Pierce to paint some murals upon the interior walls of Boleskine. An interior designer and fellow student of the esoteric, Pierce's resultant images were reportedly just as one might have imagined them.

However, it was neither the presence of arcane inscriptions on LPs nor the purchase of Boleskine House that was mainly responsible for alerting both the press and fans of Jimmy Page's enchantment with 'the hidden world'. Instead, it was the symbol he had chosen to represent himself with upon the release of *Led Zeppelin IV* in 1971. Emblazoned on his sweaters and speaker cabinets and soon to be embroidered on his stage suits, 'ZoSo' was and, indeed, would remain the guitarist's biggest mystery. Further, unlike Robert Plant, John Paul Jones and John Bonham, who appeared happy to explain their personal sigils when asked, Jimmy's choice to withhold the meaning of 'ZoSo' only resulted in further enhancing its almost monastic charisma.

Of course, soon after its declaration to the world, theories began to rapidly surface as to what 'ZoSo' actually meant or represented. For some, the answer could be found in an alchemical textbook dating back to 1557 entitled *Ars Magica Arteficii*[138]. Produced by the Italian polymath Gerolamo Cardano, a sigil (or glyph) illustrated among the pages of this

---

138 The sigil in question was reproduced by the English artist and historian Fred Gettings in his *Dictionary of Occult, Hermetic And Alchemical Sigils*. According to author Barney Hoskyns, another 19th-century dictionary of symbols titled *Le Triple Vocabulaire Infernal Manuel du Demonamane* by Frinellan (aka Simon Blocquel) also reprinted this sigil. The dictionary was published by Lille, Blocquel-Castiaux in 1844.

ancient grimoire bore more than a passing resemblance to Page's own symbol, with the heavily stylized 'Z' referencing the astrological signifier for Capricorn – to wit, Jimmy's sun-sign. The remaining 'oSo' was also pregnant with potential meaning, but no less easy to decipher. Once again open to interpretation, certain sources have it that this part of 'the equation' might be directly linked to Page's admiration of Crowley by process of its design, though others point at another alchemical symbol, this time for Mercury (or even Mars) as a plausible explanation for 'oSo'.

In truth, no one really knew and Page wasn't telling. Though journalists have repeatedly questioned him about 'ZoSo' since the symbol first emerged, Jimmy in return has consistently kept his counsel on the matter. Occasionally, he has laughed off such enquiries, while at other times opening the mystical curtain for the briefest of seconds only to draw it closed again at speed. "Let's say we were breaking a lot of rules and that was our intention," he told writer Mick Wall in 2003. "My symbol was about invoking and being invocative. And that's all I'm going to say about it." But in the main, Page's response to all enquiries concerning 'ZoSo' has been constant, increasingly empathic and distressingly familiar. "Next question," he tersely instructed *The Guardian* when quizzed on the subject in October 2014. Forty-odd years gone and we're still none the wiser. Of course, in occult terms, the less Jimmy Page said about 'ZoSo', the more the talismanic symbol retains its inherent strength, that old saying 'The root of all power is in naming' not lost on him then or now.

While the symbolism of 'ZoSo' and the pursuit of his true will might have paid enormous spiritual (and financial) dividends – "As far as I was concerned, it was working so I used it," he later said – Page had increasing trouble representing his broader views on the occult in the press. At first, he appeared content enough to discuss the likes of Aleister Crowley and more general esoteric matters with journalists. But as time went on and enquiries and stories became more invasive or sensationalistic, Jimmy began to couch his answers more carefully, or simply not answer at all. "Well, Jimmy always did have an aura about him," said writer Chris Welch. "[And] in the early days, he was quite happy to talk about his interest in Aleister Crowley and to share his views [on the subject].

As time went on, however, if the subject of magic or drugs came up, well, he was less happy to [engage]. He stopped talking about it when he felt it had got out of hand. [But] by then, he'd also mastered the art of deflecting questions, which just added to the overall mystery…"

One felt a degree of sympathy for Jimmy Page in this respect. Had he, for instance, waxed lyrical to the media about the work of Scottish author and political reformer Samuel Smiles, things might have been very different. After all, like Aleister Crowley, Smiles was an educated man whose thinking was attuned to the grander ambitions of the Victorian age. And like Crowley, he too believed that the pursuit of knowledge brought both liberation and potential greatness to the individual. "Knowledge is of itself one of the highest enjoyments," he said in 1845. "The ignorant man passes through the world dead to all pleasures, save those of the senses. Every human being," he concluded, "has a great mission to perform, noble faculties to cultivate [and] a vast destiny to accomplish." That said, Smiles' philosophy of 'Self-Help' came for a Chartist perspective and involved neither invocations to raise dormant spirits or spells to capture them in achieving his aim. By speaking so positively of Aleister Crowley, Page had aligned himself in the public mind to 'Magick' and all the connotations therein. More, he knew it. "There's no point saying more about [talismanic magick]," he told Brad Tolinski in 2012, "because the more you discuss it, the more eccentric you appear to be…"

However, despite concerns about misrepresentation, being deemed an eccentric, intellectual theorist or even "evangelist" for the philosophy and religion of Thelema, Jimmy Page's sincere fascination with the occult and pursuit of true will did confer another potential benefit on both him and Led Zeppelin: the power of 'mystique'. While the very mention of 'magick' may have given some the willies, for others it had an allure all its own, and one that could be commercially linked. Even since Lucifer was cast from heaven, rebellion equalled sales and Page's extracurricular explorations and increasingly enigmatic image tied right into this nefarious, but profitable business model – whether he wanted it or not. In fact, the more elusive Jimmy was in discussing the likes of Aleister Crowley, Rosicrucians and Wicca with the press, the more his mysterious stock rose. Again, though it might have irritated him, he was not unaware of the effect. "I'm no fool," he once said. "I know how much the mystique matters, so why should I blow it now?" There was a flipside. While "the cult of 'ZoSo'" and the overall sense of mystery surrounding Page and Zep continued to beguile their audience, it was only a matter of time before it brought other, less pleasant headlines with several future tragedies being callously linked to their dalliance with "the dark side".

Back in 1972, however, Isaac Newton's third law – "For every action, there is an equal and opposite reaction" – had yet to be distorted by strange accusations or high-jacked by lazy journalism. In fact, following the release of *Led Zeppelin IV* and the embracing of 'Stairway To Heaven' as an anthem for the masses, both Page and his band seemed untouchable, their musical airship floating sky-high over the continents. Even the usually taciturn John Bonham seemed ecstatic with the band's progress. "My personal view is [the album is] the best thing we've ever done," he said at the time. "It's the next stage of where we were at and the playing's some of the best we've ever done. Jimmy's like... mint!"

There was one more curiosity to be had for the 'mint'-like Jimmy Page. When Led Zeppelin returned to the echoing concert halls, vast arenas and grassy sports grounds for yet another round of touring in the spring and summer of 1972, a new flag could be seen waving back at the guitarist from the audience at several shows. Obviously homemade but still striking to behold, it was not unlike the 'Jolly Roger' in its overall construction, the banderol's anti-colours cast in simple black and white. But instead of a smiling skull and crossbones festooned at the centre, these cloths bore another, very different symbol: 'ZoSo'. For Page, its meaning was obvious. For the rest of us, then as now, it remains an impenetrable mystery.

CHAPTER 19

Over The Hills And Far Away

Having recorded what many feel was the best album of their career thus far and seen it gallop up the charts in several continents, it would have been almost rude of Led Zeppelin not to bring their wares back to the stage in 1972. "Ha!" Chris Welch laughed, "well, they'd have been mad not to tour after the success of the fourth LP and 'Stairway To Heaven', wouldn't they? Zep were many things, but mad they were not." They were, however, exceedingly keen to use the success of *Led Zeppelin IV* to extend their reach beyond their normal, happy hunting grounds of Europe and the USA. "The world was beckoning," said Jimmy Page. More than happy to follow, Led Zeppelin chose to begin 1972 with their very first 'Australasian' tour.

With the logistics of transporting equipment, stage lights and personnel over 10,000 miles proving cost prohibitive for even the biggest bands, the likes of Australia, New Zealand and South-East Asia were still virgin territory for most rock acts at the time. But if ever there was a manager to buck the trend and establish new and profitable ways of including them on his group's touring itinerary, it was Peter Grant. Unfortunately, it began rather badly for all concerned. When the group landed in Singapore for a scheduled concert at the National Theatre on February 14, their long hair contravened a local edict and they were not allowed to disembark from the plane. Ostensibly a law to curb 'Gangsterism' among the Singaporean young, it was explained to Grant by officials that if Jimmy et al. simply cut their locks, entry would be granted. Led Zeppelin departed the country soon after. A similar fate awaited the Bee Gees only a month later, though this time the resolutely hirsute pop trio were allowed to perform one concert with hair intact before being escorted back to the airport and onto a plane.

Though Jimmy Page had previously toured Australia once with the Yardbirds, he must still have been surprised by the extent to which his new band was embraced by fans when they arrived in the country during mid-February 1972. Booked for five dates in five cities – with one further concert to be held at the Western Springs Stadium in Auckland, New Zealand – tickets to see Led Zeppelin had been snatched up in droves, an estimated audience of over 80,000 turning out for their first gig at Perth's Subiaco Oval on February 16. With Robert offering the assembled throng a hearty greeting at the start of festivities – "We took 36 hours to get here, so we're going to have a good time!" – and the group performing for over two and a half hours, "Perth," according to *The West Australian*, "had probably never seen a concert quite like it. [In fact]," the paper continued, "some were so keen to see the most popular English heavy rock group to ever appear live in Perth that they did not mind climbing fences to get in."

The police, on the other hand, minded quite a bit. When some 500 fans tried to get into the concert without paying, local officers met their efforts with equal force, the resulting clashes leading to a near riot outside the concert's perimeter fence.[139] It didn't quite end there. A few hours later Led Zeppelin themselves were the subject of the Perth police force's attentions, when the band's rooms at the Scarborough hotel were raided in search of drugs. Though nothing was found, Jimmy smelt a

139 According to Australian media reports, fans' efforts to get into the Subiaco Oval without paying were extremely well-organised, with several enterprising individuals arriving at the gig with bolt- and wire-cutters, and even ladders. "They armed like they were ready to storm a Norman castle in the dark ages," said a spokesman for Channel Seven at the time.

rat, or at least the scent of lawful retribution. "I'd like to know if today's raid was some sort of a rebuff for last night," he told *The Daily News* at the time. "We had nothing to do with any of what happened and then this morning, at some unearthly hour, we were pulled out of bed and treated in a totally derogatory manner. I thought we could get away from this sort of thing out here [and] I'm just dumbfounded by it all. We just didn't expect anything like this to happen in Australia."

The rest of the tour proved less fraught, though problems continued to dog both the band and their entourage. Water damage to the stage caused by freak rainstorms delayed their scheduled appearance at Adelaide's Memorial Drive Arena on February 18 by 24 hours. That said, when it did go ahead, both audience and press were left bruised but delirious by the group's assault, with Jimmy seemingly responsible for inflicting most of the damage. "The controlled violence with which the UK group produced many of its sounds, hurled out of two giant banks of speakers at the 8,000-strong crowd, has never been seen here," said *The Advertiser*'s Richard Mitchell. "From the start, all eyes were on brilliant lead guitarist Jimmy Page. He used six and twelve-string acoustic guitars with the ease that many had flocked to see. His electric guitar work was extraordinary. At one stage, using a bow, he smashed out a string of piercing notes only to end with a run of delicate sitar-sounding music. Thunderous applause followed all his work."

Rain again threatened to put the kibosh on Zep's gig at Melbourne's Kooyang Stadium a day later, with the group forced to temporarily leave the stage before being cajoled back on by the baying crowd. "It was raining so heavily, we were in danger of being electrocuted," Robert Plant later told *On The Air*, "so we had to say, well, we can't do any more. Then, of course, the crowd were like 'Noooo!'" In Auckland, there was no inclement weather to spoil the show though, on this occasion, tour manager Richard Cole was left somewhat confused when the band arrived at their hotel. "There was a room booked in advance for 'Mr. Led Zeppelin'," Plant laughed. "Wow. 'Led' finally got his own room..."

By the time Led Zeppelin arrived in Australia's capital Sydney for a sold-out concert at the voluminous Showground on February 27, the media were out in full force to greet them, each band member being vigorously pursued around their pre-gig press party by a cast of journalists, TV pundits and even the odd celebrity, with author/noted feminist Germaine Greer happily chatting to a bemused-looking Robert Plant as the cameras rolled around them. While Australia appeared to be head over heels in love with Led Zeppelin, just two days after a last concert at Brisbane's Festival Hall, the band were gone, curiously never to return. "Maybe they didn't like the rain," quipped one wry Aussie reporter.

Over the course of the next 10 months, Led Zeppelin would perform similar smash and grab raids on the hearts and pockets of eight more countries, with Holland, Belgium, Switzerland and Japan all meriting brief visits before the group were bundled off to their next rendezvous.

As ever, America was where Zep chose to spend the majority of their touring time, with 16 dates (and a further one in Montreal, Canada) bringing them from Detroit and Houston to New York and Seattle throughout June 1972. For Jimmy Page, the nightly mission was always the same. "The music," he said at the time. "Every night I want [the music] to change, to develop. I can't even envisage what that must be like, playing the same thing over and over. I just... can't."

For Peter Grant, however, so strong was Led Zeppelin's pulling power in the States that a further change to their financial operating model was required. In an unprecedented move, the wily manager now demanded 90% of the band's gate receipts from US concert promoters. Astoundingly, he got it. "I'm not sure you could give Peter 100% credit for ushering in a new era in how bands operated on the road," said Chris Charlesworth by way of explanation. "The original model of armies of roadies and huge trucks going from gig to gig probably started with Cream and then the Who after that. And of course, the man who really started it all was Frank Barsalona, who ran Premier Talent from New York in the sixties. He was responsible for putting together the original syndicate of promoters across the USA – Barry Fey, Bill Graham and maybe 12 others. But Peter Grant, well, Peter turned it into a fine art. He finessed it into something else entirely with the Zep tour machine and then the group getting 90% of the gate. But both Page and Peter knew it was America where the audience was the biggest and the financial rewards were greatest. They pursued it, and through Jimmy's management of the music and Peter's management of the business, they got it."

Nevertheless, one or two flies in the ointment remained. While Grant was no doubt revelling in his latest financial wheeze and *Rolling Stone* again sharpening their critical pencils as a result, Led Zeppelin were still being upstaged in the press by another band on the road in America at the same time. "The bloody Stones were getting all the headlines," growled John Bonham, "and that really pissed us off." Though Zep were outselling Mick Jagger's motley crew by a margin of at least four to one in the LP charts, the Rolling Stones were still "original 100% rock'n'royalty" and the music papers wouldn't let Page and co. forget it.

With Mick and his new bride Bianca 'white hot' in media terms and guitarist Keith Richards' latest adventures and ever-calcifying image a source of ceaseless wonder to journalists, not a day went by when one or either of them were caught peering out from the pages of the magazines or tabloids. Having seen off all comers to finally take the rock crown with their last album, this championing of old school British blues boys was a slap in the face not only to Led Zeppelin, but also their erstwhile manager. To remedy the situation, Peter Grant took strong measures. For all future touring commitments, he would employ PR consultant Danny Goldberg to promote Zep's efforts. His task would not be easy.

Another causal irritant not only for Grant but potentially for Jimmy Page was that when Led Zeppelin did receive coverage from the American press, it was often focused on Robert Plant. Now more resembling some sculpted bronze deity than "hairy hippie newbie", Plant's combination of leonine good looks and easy charm not only endeared him to Zep devotees, but when one threw in his almost encyclopaedic knowledge of old blues and rock'n'roll records, music writers, too. Basking in the nightly adulation of thousands of screaming fans and growing increasingly confident as a result, "the new boy from West Bromwich" was in serious danger of becoming the public face of Led Zeppelin. "By 1971, 1972, Robert was no longer the neophyte," said Dave Lewis. "He'd grown in confidence, begun to recognise the depth of his abilities and had the audience eating out of his hand. Great for Zeppelin, of course, but it also created a subtle shift in the balance of power. It wasn't just 'Jimmy's band' anymore..."

Obviously, there were clear reasons as to why Robert Plant was beginning to feature more strongly in the press. But in his own way, Jimmy Page was as much responsible for this change of emphasis as anyone else. While Page had been the visionary architect of Led Zeppelin at the start of their inexorable rise, he was also eager for the public to see the band for their individual as well as collective talents rather than just an enabler for his own ambitions. Indeed, it was Page that pushed Plant hard into taking over as sole lyricist by the time of their second album, as well as encouraging John Paul Jones – and to a lesser extent drummer John Bonham – to provide song ideas and arrangements.

However, whether Jimmy Page had anticipated exactly how much the press and public would latch onto Robert Plant as the face of Led Zeppelin was another thing altogether. "I think Jimmy began to realise that he'd created a bit of a monster with Robert," confirmed Chris Charlesworth. "At the beginning of Zep, Robert was this relative unknown, but as time went on, he started to become the 'golden god' and that had an impact on how the band – and as importantly, Jimmy's leadership of the band – was publicly perceived. Robert was also much more affable and friendly with the press, and as a result, that made for a better interview and more coverage for him. That must have been hard for Jimmy. Up to then, he'd been at the wheel of the car."

Whatever issues Page and Plant faced due to increasingly uneven press coverage behind the scenes, there was no public signs of discord when the two flew into Bombay (now Mumbai) in October 1972 following a recent spate of Japanese dates with Led Zeppelin. "Man," it's great to be in India for [another] visit," Plant told Bombay's *Junior Statesman* on arriving at Bombay's five-star Taj Mahal hotel[140]. "Do you know why

---

140 While staying at the Taj Mahal, Page and Page befriended local rock singer Nandu Bhende and his band, Velvette Fogg, with Robert even sitting in on drums for a number or two during their rehearsals. A few nights later, Jimmy and Robert were at it again, this time playing an impromptu set with bassist Xerxes Gobhai and drummer Jameel Shaikh at Bombay club The Slip Disc. If reports are correct, the newly formed quartet bashed out a fine version of 'Whole Lotta Love' before Page and Plant were paid for their efforts with a bottle of Scotch.

we're here? To see if we could set up a recording studio..." Though said studio would remain a pipe-dream, there was little doubting the sincerity of affection both Jimmy and Robert had for India. Their third visit to the country in just over a year, the duo had actually made a direct beeline for Bombay when Zep were denied entry to Singapore some eight months before. Accompanied on that particular jaunt by ever-present tour manager Richard Cole, Page and Plant spent much of their time filming fakirs, market stalls and more general scenes of street life with an 8mm camera, capturing "the sweep and vibe" of the city as they went. But this latest visit (doomed studio construction aside) had another, more specific purpose. "I was keen to work with Indian musicians," Jimmy later told the BBC, "and to see how it would work as a fusion with music that they'd never heard before."

Since he'd bought his first sitar in 1965 and began studying the music of Ravi Shankar, Jimmy Page had been fascinated with Indian music, a preoccupation that had only grown deeper when exposed to pioneering "world-folk stylists" such as Bert Jansch and Davey Graham. As outlined in preceding chapters, the likes of 'White Summer' and 'Black Mountainside' – though played on guitar – had both emanated from the same distinct "Celtic-Indian" D-A-D-G-A-D tuning, with Page's string work on each track highly evocative of the drones and bends redolent in Jansch and Shankar's own instrumental/sitar musings. Additionally, Jimmy's use of the violin bow on the Yardbirds' 'Little Games' and more comprehensively onstage with Zep during 'Dazed And Confused' again carried distinctly South Asian-sounding hues, those queasy quarter and micro tones deliciously unsettling to the Western ear. Now, he was after the chance to extend his experiments still further by blending the songs of Led Zeppelin with some of the best classical musicians in India.

Armed with a brand-new Stellavox quadraphonic tape recorder, Page and Plant entered a small studio in downtown Bombay (probably in the last week of October 1972), booked especially for the occasion by revered composer, flautist (and close friend of Ravi Shankar) Vijaya Raghava Rao. Greeting them inside were the Bombay Symphony Orchestra, best known locally for their work on the soundtracks of Bollywood movies. "These musicians were classically trained within their own idiom and they had this very strong character of their indigenous music," Jimmy later said. However, with no defined arranger on hand to act as conduit between the two separate teams, it took a little while to get into the swing of things. "Well, it was tricky, tricky to work with musicians you've never met, with no Indian arranger there to convey what you want," Page continued. "But I just knew it would work, and it did work."

The two tunes Jimmy chose for the session were 'Four Sticks' and 'Friends'. With elements that would lend themselves beautifully to this type of experimentation, Page was nonetheless amazed at how those gathered breathed new life into his and Plant's compositions. "'Four Sticks' for instance, is pretty complex, even for the incredible technical abilities these musicians had," he said. "But they were able to play it by [applying] their own technique to it. They were incredible players who certainly kept me on my toes." While 'Four Sticks' was performed by the ensemble "as an instrumental... an exercise," Robert got his chance to contribute on 'Friends', stepping up to the microphone as Jimmy's oddly tuned guitar led a crack team of swooping sitars, sarangi and tablas behind him. "I already knew these sounds and instruments," said Page, "I was familiar with northern and southern India. I knew what they could do in [enhancing] our songs."

A nascent experiment in temporarily stepping outside the Led Zeppelin bubble while also involving themselves in one of the first proper crossovers between rock and Indian classical music, one might have thought Page and Plant would have been in a rush to release 'Four Sticks' and 'Friends', perhaps as part of an EP or – say it quietly – even a limited edition single. Yet, while Jimmy was satisfied with the overall execution of the tracks, he had reservations about the quality of the actual recording. As a result, the 'Bombay Sessions' were placed in storage where they would remain – bootlegs not withstanding – for over 40 years, until Page finally allowed them to see light of day.

While these orchestral variations on 'Four Sticks' and 'Friends' were temporarily destined for the vault, there was plenty of other new material for Led Zeppelin to concern themselves with by the end of 1972. In fact, tours allowing, the band had been hard at work in the preceding months on following up their monstrously successful fourth album. Again, Page was at the heart of the storm, his oft used phrase 'Onwards and upwards' now almost a mantra for each new Zep release. "By that time," Robert Plant later told *Guitar World*'s Steve Rosen, "all the way down there was a conscientious air about Jimmy's work. And Jimmy's catalystic efforts to get everybody moving one way or another. It's remarkable we kept it going... really, there wasn't one record that had anything to do with the one before it."

Having enjoyed such a productive time at the sprawling, if somewhat chilly setting of Headley Grange, the band were obviously eager to return to Hampshire to try their luck again. But when the house proved unavailable, a new venue had to be found. With the Stones still in semi-permanent exile (both geographically and by album title), Mick Jagger's rather more opulent Stargroves and its surrounding grounds was once more presented as a possible option. Presumably negotiating better day rates than before from the wily singer, Led Zeppelin moved lock, stock and mobile studio to East Roundhay in mid-April 1972 to begin recording. Returning to join them on this occasion was engineer Eddie Kramer. "We'd had a falling out[141]," he recalled to *Uncut* in 2009, "and I didn't hear from them for a year. Then I got a call to come to England as if nothing had happened." Indeed, the band Kramer found at Stargroves was in an extremely relaxed mood. "I remember they were all walking like Groucho Marx in sync," he later said. "With back steps and forward steps in time to the music, just like kids." However, there was no mistaking the man in charge. "Yes, Jimmy was still the boss, very, very clearly..."

Led Zeppelin's tenure at Stargroves was brief, but nonetheless yielded positive results. With both Page and John Paul Jones having installed studios in their respective homes, demo tapes could be presented to

---

141 Billed as 'Director of Engineering' on *Led Zeppelin II*, Kramer had been invited back to oversee a recording session at New York's Electric Ladyland studios for the band's fourth album. But when a curry was spilled on the studio floor and Eddie asked Zep's roadies to clean it up, an argument between he and the band ensued. "Don't talk to our roadies like that," (they said). "We're leaving." Twelve months later and they were all friends again.

their fellow band members in near complete form, cutting down on arrangement time or needless prevarication. Of course, Zeppelin being Zeppelin, there was always room for tweaks and random experimentation, but there was also now a template to refer to should they need it. This was especially true of Jones' intricate keyboard parts. "More than ever before, keyboard-type instruments were prominently displayed in the band's sound," Eddie Kramer later told *Guitar World* in 1986. "This was of course due to John Paul, [whose] contributions to Led Zeppelin were enormous yet relatively unsung. In [the group], his keyboards provided a necessary diversion. I'm sure he would have loved to have played more keyboards, but Page probably directed it, because he was the band's master of ceremonies. Still, the amount... John contributed was well in proportion."

By the sounds of it, Led Zeppelin used every available inch of Stargroves to capture every inch of their sound. In John Bonham's case, with no minstrel's gallery to call his own a la Headley Grange, the drummer's kit was set up in a conservatory-like area on the mansion's ground floor. Robert Plant was consigned a similar space in which to record his vocals towards the back of the house, though he and Jimmy took to recording in the gardens surrounding Stargroves when the sun was shining. "The lads were really happy there," Eddie Kramer later told author Stephen Davis, "recording with the amazing acoustics of the old mansion and frolicking around in its park-like setting." When Page wasn't recording acoustic guitars among the flora and fauna of Stargroves, he was busy exploring inside its walls to find a sweet spot for his amplifiers. Again, the solution came by appointing the equipment its own room, or alternatively pointing the speaker cabinets up towards the chimney. "I believe he was using a Vox AC-30," said Eddie Kramer, "and/or a Hiwatt cabinet with a Marshall amp." Page was also using Stargroves' main bedroom as his own personal sweet spot, having claimed ownership of Mick Jagger's private boudoir shortly after arriving. "Well, Jimmy was in charge," Kramer continued. "It was his playground..."

With further recording completed between tour commitments at London's Olympic Studios and New York's Electric Ladyland during the early summer of 1972, Led Zeppelin actually had their new LP in the can long before Jimmy and Robert set off for Bombay to record 'Friends' and 'Four Sticks' in the autumn of the year. But as ever, a problem with album sleeves saw the release date of their latest opus pushed back by several months. On this occasion, the issue began not with a disagreement between band and record company, but rather a cheeky example of artistic differences with those chosen to design the LP's lavish cover.

By the time Led Zeppelin were looking for prospective designers for the gatefold sleeve of their fifth disc, Hipgnosis were well on their way to achieving international notoriety. Founded by film/art school students Storm Thorgerson and Aubrey 'Po' Powell in the late sixties, the graphic design team prided themselves on cutting-edge visuals, using manipulated photographic techniques to create striking, often surreal album art. Friends of wayward genius Syd Barrett since meeting in Cambridge, Thorgerson and Powell had got their first break providing Pink Floyd with the cover of their second LP, 1968's *Saucerful Of Secrets*. But subsequent commissions from the likes of the Pretty Things and Free and a growing reputation for taking things to extremes had brought their work to the attention of Jimmy Page and Led Zeppelin. Unfortunately, Hipgnosis' equally well-established habit for trading on comedic puns almost undid the collaboration before it blossomed.

If reports are correct, when Storm Thorgerson first met with Jimmy, Robert and Peter Grant, he was probably informed that Zep's new album was likely to be called 'Houses Of The Holy'. An intriguing title whose meaning Page later confirmed was inspired by the notion that humankind are "houses of the Holy Spirit, in a sense", the possibilities for suitable cover art were only constrained by Thorgerson's imagination. But Storm was as mischievous as he was talented. When he returned to meet with Jimmy a few days later, he presented the guitarist with a doctored photograph of a fluorescent tennis court, in the middle of which was placed a racquet. Page – not unreasonably – asked what it all meant. Storm replied, "Racquet. Racket. Geddit?" Having just implied that the music of Led Zeppelin was a bit on the noisy side, Jimmy asked Thorgerson to leave.

Insulted, but no doubt seeing the funny side behind Hipgnosis' design – "Some balls," quipped Page – Zep chose to press on with the company, though this time it was with Storm Thorgerson's business partner Po Powell instead. "Well, we obviously got on better with Po than with Storm," Jimmy later told *Classic Rock*'s Paul Elliot, "[and] if people didn't like one person, then they'd work with the other one." It turned out to be a wise choice. Basing his idea on the conclusion of the novel *Childhood's End* by science fiction writer/inventor Arthur C. Clarke, Powell created a collage print of a group of mysterious children ascending a rocky, almost alien hill against an eerie orange sky. Actually photographed in the worst of weather over a 10-day period at the Giant's Causeway in Northern Ireland, the Hipgnosis designer had only used two kids for the shoot[142], but later multi-printed their images in various poses to give the appearance that the rocks were being swarmed by nubiles. When asked to make each child gold or silver, Po duly complied, only to see an error in post-production turn them all purple. Not the effect requested by any means, but when Powell viewed it again, the unusual colouring seemed to work even better and he decided to submit it to the band anyway.

Suffice to say, Jimmy Page and Led Zep loved it. Seeing the children's tentative, yet determined climb towards an unseen summit was not only a metaphor for approaching "the expectancy of the music contained within", but also wholly representative of "Innocence... the idea of us all being vessels of houses of the holy", Page was enrapt by Po Powell's work. Just as well, because the technique involved in printing the LP's sleeve proved so elaborate it took another two months to complete, pushing the release date further back, to the spring of 1973. Thankfully, that gave Peter Grant and Jimmy just enough time to inform Atlantic Records that – as with *Led Zeppelin IV* – the band's name and the album's title would not appear on the cover. However, to slightly appease the label's marketing department – and no doubt save Ahmet Ertegun a few sleepless nights – they did agree to clothe the disc with a wrap-around

---

142 The children in question were Stefan Gates (now a TV presenter) and his sister, Samantha. They can also be seen on the inner gatefold sleeve of the LP, which was photographed at Dunluce Castle, again near the Giant's Causeway.

paper band spelling out the missing details for UK buyers. In the end, it was the least they could do...

Armed with another suitably arcane cover whose meaning fans could ponder to their heart's content over months to come, Led Zeppelin finally released their new album *Houses Of The Holy* on March 28, 1973. When asked at the time how he would describe the contents, Jimmy was keen to promote Led Zeppelin as once again challenging itself to create something truly novel. "People still have this preconceived notion of what to expect," he said. "But this will be something really new. If you carry on on just one plane, you just repeat yourselves." He was, of course, right. But it was the very diversity of material on *Houses Of The Holy* that had some scratching their heads in confusion rather than clapping their hands in joy.

As one had perhaps greedily come to expect from Zep, the album began strongly with the braying gallop of 'The Song Remains The Same'. Originally an instrumental that Page had jokily entitled 'The Plumpton And Worcester Races' in honour of his and Plant's respective country houses, the tune was soon renamed 'The Overture' when Jimmy thought it might work best as a segue into another track. However, after Robert took a shine to the melody and decided it needed lyrics, the title was changed again, first to 'The Campaign' before eventually settling on 'The Song Remains The Same'. "It was originally going to be an instrumental, but I guess Robert had different ideas," Page later told *Guitar World*. "You know, 'This is pretty good, better get some lyrics quick!'"

Full of glistening 12-string Rickenbackers, countrified lead lines, courtesy of Page's Fender Telecaster, and a coy but clever half-time rhythmic shift in the middle of the track, 'The Song...' also featured a slightly sped-up vocal, taking Plant's planet-spanning wordplay into the clouds. "California sunlight, sweet Calcutta rain," chirped the helium-voiced singer, "Honolulu starbright, the song remains the same." For Eddie Kramer, Jimmy's decision to enhance Plant's already impressive vocal range with a little studio trickery was all about creating yet another texture to brighten his existing army of six- and 12-string guitars. "I believe Jimmy later had Robert's vocals speeded up a bit so they became another layer to all those gorgeous guitars."

Next up came a complete volte-face in both tempo and mood with 'The Rain Song'. Conceived and demoed by Page at Plumpton Place in his brand new home studio[143], the tune began with a witty riposte to a former Beatle. Having heard on the grapevine that George Harrison had criticised Led Zeppelin for never writing ballads, Jimmy stuck the two opening notes of Harrison's own 'Something' at the beginning of the track. After that, however, it was all Page's own work. Written on his beloved Danelectro in yet another alternate tuning (this time D-G-C-G-C-D), 'The Rain Song' was a gorgeous amalgam of lush chords, melancholy instrumental passages and, with its strangely uplifting conclusion, an ideal opportunity for John Bonham to showcase the more delicate side of his percussive nature.

There was one more part to be negotiated. On his original demo, Jimmy had outlined a Mellotron line for 'The Rain Song'. An early attempt at a sampling keyboard where each key triggered the playback of a single, pre-recorded note, the Mellotron was a hellish contraption to master, which may have been why Page was eager to get John Paul Jones involved as quickly as possible. "Well, I didn't do [the Mellotron part] very well on the demo," he laughed, "but it gave [the track] a guideline [for] John Paul Jones." For his part, Jones was over the moon at the prospect of tackling one of the most unsympathetic instruments ever invented. "To walk up to the Mellotron, not knowing if it was going to be in tune or what it was even going to do, was a terrifying experience..."

At first, transferring the melodic core of Page's demo track into the bones of Led Zeppelin was not easy. "It was hard until we got the feel of it," Jimmy later admitted to Stuart Grundy. "It was one of those cases where you keep going at it, initially because we'd played all the instruments ourselves, and it was a matter of sorting out which overdubs were the least important or maybe inserting a new phrase." Also helping things along was Robert Plant, whose mind had again wandered into the ever-fertile territory of doomed relationships to inform his bittersweet

---

143 Page's home studio featured a Vista console enhanced by parts from the same Pye mobile used to record one of rock's finest ever live LPs: the Who's 1970 in-concert set, *Live At Leeds*.

lyric. "[The idea] was just a little infatuation I had," he later told Q. "If I had done it the day after, it would have been no good."

When finally mastered by the band and committed to tape by Eddie Kramer, 'The Rain Song' proved one of the highlights of *House Of The Holy*. Blessed with Page's chiming guitars, John Paul Jones' swooping, Mellotron-assisted orchestrations and some wonderfully restrained brushwork courtesy of John Bonham, Robert's capricious tale of love won and lost over four seasons was in Jimmy's words destined "to become a bit of a classic in the end".

If 'The Rain Song' introduced a melancholic aspect to *Houses Of The Holy*, then 'Over The Hills And Far Away', 'Dancing Days' and 'The Ocean' all served as joyous antidotes, with each tune full of bouncy charm and witty, whistling melodies. Taking the former first, 'Over The Hills...' had actually begun life as 'Many, Many Times' before someone presumably spotted that the title was a tad too close to the band's own 'How Many More Times' for comfort. The solution was easy enough. With two kids to now call his own, Robert Plant simply stole a line from a children's book by Beatrix Potter (*The Tale Of Pigling Bland*), and the track had its name, and indeed, much of its lively atmosphere. Driven along by Page's persistent acoustic guitars (a six-string at the introduction, then a 12-string coupled with an electric to add a little more drama), 'Over The Hills...' really did belong, however, to Led Zeppelin's mighty rhythm section. Now closer than twins, Bonham and Jones' intricate bass/drum interplay and energetic dancing around Robert's vocal were as clever as they were technically daring. "The rhythm section on 'Over The Hills...' is exceptional," JPJ later told Q. "There are a lot of very, very tight, exciting moments in it."

'Dancing Days' was in its own way just as satisfying, if a little on the eccentric side. Reportedly inspired by a stray melody Jimmy and Robert had heard while holidaying in Bombay, the track's backwards-sounding sitar-like riff, irregular slide guitar intrusions and jerky chord structure all seemed individually designed to disorientate the listener. Yet, in combination, they conspired to rescue 'Dancing Days', turning it instead into a very fine, albeit very weird pop song. Curiously chosen as the first tune to be offered up to radio in advance of *Houses Of The Holy*'s release (it was played by BBC DJ Emperor Rosko five days before the album hit stores), 'Dancing Days' also served as the B-side to the US single release of 'Over The Hills And Far Away', the odd pairing reaching a somewhat disappointing number 51 on the *Billboard* Hot 100 in April 1973.

'The Ocean', on the other hand, could neither be described as particularly easy to whistle nor wilfully eccentric, though for some, it was probably superior to both 'Over The Hills...' and 'Dancing Days'. Opening with a riff that sounded as if it had been written in a tumble dryer, each note flying this way and that like a bunch of rabid socks, 'The Ocean' – as with 'Black Dog' before it – was yet another Zep track that struck fear into the heart of drummers everywhere, its 15/8 time signature only to be attempted after a stiff drink or two. But once Bonham, Jones, Plant and Page settled down into verse and chorus, the song took on a new dimension, 'The Ocean''s lyric becoming both metaphor and tribute to "the enormous army of denim" that Zeppelin found staring back at them each night in the arenas, concert halls and stadiums of the USA and beyond. Introduced at many a future gig with the words "This is about all of you", its madcap riffing, doo-wop outro and winking tribute from Robert to his daughter Carmen ("I'm singing all my songs to the girl who won my heart") made 'The Ocean' a technical marvel, a gem of a tune and something of an insider anthem, too.[144]

Thus far in their recorded career, Led Zeppelin had seldom put a foot wrong, the band's ability to turn their hand to most any musical style and make it work for them as enviable as it was ingenious. However, in the case of 'The Crunge' and 'D'yer Mak'er', some felt they had stumbled over their shoelaces by taking on funk and reggae. Born out of an impromptu jam at Stargroves, when John Bonham's insertion of an extra half-beat against a stray bass riff from John Paul Jones triggered

---

144 In addition to those strange time signatures and insider references, 'The Ocean' also appears to feature a ringing phone at one minute 37 seconds into the track. After ringing again four seconds later, the sound then disappears for good. A cult tune that obviously bears repeated listening, rap trio the Beastie Boys were so fond of 'The Ocean' they sampled its opening riff for 'She's Crafty', the third track from their own 1986 debut album, *Licensed To Ill*.

"one of those moments", 'The Crunge' was soon off its marks and running. "Bonzo would dictate an unusual time signature when we'd be writing, or in a jam he would come up with something," Jones later told *Musician*'s Matt Resnicoff. "Or again, he would start a riff that was strange, unusual or just interesting. 'The Crunge' was like that." Keen to put his own mark among all that drum and bass, Page in turn added a short, but memorable chord sequence that had been stored in the back of his head for at least a year or two, and Led Zeppelin almost had a song, if not quite a tune. Sadly, so it would remain.

Obviously in a playful mood when it came to writing lyrics, Robert and John Bonham at first wanted to mumble over 'The Crunge' in Black Country accents. "Bonzo and I were going to go in the studio and talk 'Black Country' through the whole thing," Plant laughed. "'You know', like 'Aah bloody hell, how you doin'? You all right mate?'" Nonetheless, sanity prevailed. "Well, it [sort of] evolved... and at the end of my tether, it came out." The 'it' in question was a more than passable James Brown impersonation from Robert, with the West Bromwich-born singer squealing and scatting like the Godfather of Soul while desperately trying to find "that confounded bridge"[145]. Either a skewed, if novel, experiment into the intricacies of dance music, or a "lame James Brown take-off that was impossible to dance to," 'The Crunge' still remains one of John Paul Jones' favourite Zep tracks. "It's got that extra half beat, which was a brilliant, brilliant thing."

'D'yer Mak'er' divided opinion even more than 'The Crunge'. Starting life as a fifties doo-wop pastiche (hence the nod to Rosie & the Originals on the sleeve inset), a flick of the wrist from Bonzo on the off-beat had sent the tune off in a completely different direction,

---

145 Many of James Brown's early recordings were done live with little in the way of rehearsal. Hence, Brown would shout out directions to his band as he went, with the phrase "Take it to the bridge" yelled coming out of either a chorus or instrumental passage. By the time he was successful, James would simply add it to the likes of 'Sex Machine' for extra flavour. Plant's use of the phrase was both tribute to Brown ("Love him," the singer said, laughing) as well as another in-joke: 'The Crunge' doesn't actually have a bridge.

with the drummer, Page and Jones soon following each other down an uncertain path towards reggae music. While some of the trio remained a tad unsure about the development, Plant was on it like a rash, yet again concocting a sad-eyed story about a man – this time informed by letter – that his lover was departing was for pastures new. "When I read the letter you wrote me, it made me mad, mad, mad," he sang, "When I read the news it brought me, it made me sad, sad, sad..."

Had Zep named the track 'Dear John', maybe things might have been different. But basing the song's title on an old English vaudeville joke about the phonetic pronunciation of 'Jamaica' made it feel at best a bit cheesy, at worst plain daft. Even John Paul Jones agreed. "Not my favourite song, personally," he told writer Alan di Perna in 1991. "It makes me cringe a bit. It started off as a joke, really... just us sitting around playing some stuff. It got into that reggae rhythm and we put it down... but I wasn't happy with the way it turned out. Robert really liked it, [but] even in a band, people have different opinions about the songs." In the end, Plant had his victory of sorts. When released as a single in the USA in September 1973, 'D'yer Mak'er' reached number 20 in the charts.

Still, both 'The Crunge' and 'D'yer Mak'er' were inessential throwaways next to the chilly centrepiece of *Houses Of The Holy*: 'No Quarter'. Hatched at the keyboard of his home studio in East Sussex, John Paul Jones had originally presented both the chords and a partial arrangement of 'No Quarter' to the rest of Led Zeppelin at Headley Grange during recording sessions for the band's fourth album. Attempted at that time with a slightly more up-tempo feel, all agreed there was something special about the song, but it was placed temporarily on hold in favour of other material. But when Zep were ready to record *Houses Of The Holy*, Jones had finessed it sufficiently for 'No Quarter' to be given another run-through, with Page and Plant's own ideas now incorporated into the pot.

Cut at Olympic Studios with Andy Johns making an all too brief return as engineer, 'No Quarter' was first and foremost another shy monolith to John Paul Jones' skills as both a songwriter and keyboardist. "He's just a hugely underrated musician and arranger," reiterated Eddie Kramer. Full of unconventional electric piano, synth and bass pedal lines, Jones' core composition was awash with unexpected shifts in melody and mood, giving an uneasy, almost melting aspect to the tune. But as with all of Led Zeppelin's finest, it was the work of JPJ's fellow band members that took something already very good and made it truly remarkable. In the case of John Bonham, this translated as providing a wondrously sympathetic drum track that teased out every nuance and twist at hand. Robert Plant's contribution was equally noteworthy, his careworn lyric bringing to life a nameless band of messengers tasked with delivering news "that must get through" no matter the sacrifice or casualties involved. "They hold no quarter, they ask no quarter..."

As producer, Jimmy Page had concentrated on enhancing the already cauldron-like atmosphere of 'No Quarter' to a new level of psychic disturbance. To begin, he utilised a pitch-control to lower the song by a semi-tone, which in conjunction with its now snail-like tempo, made each change of chord or melodic variance sound even more intense and claustrophobic. Page also busied himself treating Robert's voice with various sound effects, the singer's sighs and whispers taking on a watery quality that sat superbly well on Jones' already oscillating keyboard line.

Finally, Jimmy dispensed with his usual amplification and ran his guitar directly into the studio desk. By further pumping the signal with generous amounts of compression and limiter (and sprinkling in a little Theremin here and there for good measure), it gave his Les Paul a glacial distortion that again only added to the song's wintry timbre. All in all, this was the work of a producer at the very top of his game "Jimmy's best quality as a producer was his ability to work with the elements he had on hand," Eddie Kramer later told writer Joe Lalaina. "He knew how to pull the best performances out of Led Zeppelin, including himself. He was able to mentally mix all the elements together, be a continual inspiration and very single-mindedly pursue the best in every track."

From the alien landscapes and shifting seasons of 'No Quarter' and 'The Rain Song' to the cramp-inducing funk and instrumental gymnastics of 'The Crunge' and 'The Ocean', *Houses of The Holy* was a veritable smorgasbord of an album, its sense of ambition and musical reach almost bordering on arrogance. But again, that was at least half the point of the exercise for Jimmy Page. "You can either stay in a complete rut," he had said of extending Led Zeppelin's perimeters in

1971, "or after three years, you can start moving and flowing a bit more." Indeed, this sense of flux and mutability wasn't just confined to the music of *Houses Of The Holy*. With the possible exception of 'No Quarter', the rumbling mystical undercurrents that had informed so much of Robert Plant's lyricism on previous Zep albums was now all but gone, seldom to return again. In fact, despite its somewhat pompous title, *Houses...* was actually quite a jolly-sounding album, with images of "suppin' booze", "hitting on the moonshine" and fleeing from the "Keepers of the gloom" helping create an upbeat, free and easy tone throughout. "*Houses Of The Holy* was a very inspired, fun time," Plant later said, "and there was a lot of imagination on that record."

Yet, despite its lighter feel, bolder emphasis on orchestration and overdubs, and Page again straining at the leash to push Led Zeppelin's boundaries as far as he could, the critics remained unconvinced. Instead of giving kudos to the band for refusing to revel in the familiar, they actually seemed aggravated by Zep's need to explore their own musical corners for inspiration. "Plant and Page are strangely sluggish and vacant, exploding only occasionally on 'Dancing Days' and 'The Rain Song'," said *Disc & Music Echo*. "On two or three listens, *Houses Of The Holy* comes over as an inconsistent work." After extending a partial olive branch for their noble works on *Led Zeppelin IV*, *Rolling Stone* was also back to prodding at the group with the soiled end of a pointy stick. "*Houses...*'" they concluded "[is] a dose of pabulum." Still, at least *Sounds* was partly on the band's side. "If you're looking for the heaviest of rock with which Zep first blasted your ears, you'd be disappointed... [but] from an advancement point of view, this is a fine LP."

Though previous drubbings were sometimes harsh, or – in the case of *Led Zeppelin II* – almost incomprehensible to understand, on this occasion it was not so difficult to see why the group's new release might have confused or irritated the critics. Unlike its illustrious predecessor, *Houses Of The Holy* seemed to lack a cohesive centre, with Zep pulling its contents every which way in an effort to placate their own restless musical spirit. At times, this made for a bumpy ride, with Indian scales clattering into reggae beats and icy keyboard blasts shunted aside by trampolining rhythms and bendy guitars.

Further, while 'The Crunge' and 'D'yer Mak'er' had allowed Zep to amuse themselves as well as again tug at the boundaries of their sound, neither tune was essential listening, their presence on the LP questionable at best. As usual, Jimmy leapt to the band's defence. "Maybe you could attack 'The Crunge' or 'D'yer Mak'er' for being a bit self-indulgent," he told *NME* at the time, "but they're just a giggle, just two send-ups. If people can't even suss that out, on that superficial a level, then you can't expect them to understand anything else on the album." Page probably had a point. But truth be told, neither 'The Crunge' or 'D'yer Mak'er' were particularly funny.

All in all, however, these were but minor quibbles. *Houses Of The Holy* remained a fine LP and provided yet more proof that Led Zeppelin were never going to rest on their laurels or simply milk the hard rock template of their earliest incarnation for the sake of sales. "The key to Led Zeppelin's longevity has always been change," Jimmy later said. Such a resolute stance did them no harm either. Despite their ever-broadening eclecticism, the band were duly rewarded with yet another huge seller, the album bouncing to the number one spot on both sides of the Atlantic soon after its release in late March 1973, and staying on the charts for a further 21 and 39 weeks in the UK and USA respectively. Once again, fan power had triumphed over journalistic sniping and Jimmy Page was more than happy to acknowledge it. "We didn't let [anything] get in the way," he said at the time. "My main goal was just to keep rolling."

In reality, Page was hideously understating Led Zeppelin's position and the exact space the band now occupied within the larger rock pantheon. Seemingly impervious to criticism and thus able to explore whichever musical style amused them at any given moment before watching it sell in the millions some months later, Zep were entering a new and matchless phase in their career by mid-1973. It would be a time marked by financial records being broken, then broken yet again. A period where vanity projects, new business enterprises and celluloid adventures would go hand in hand with images of golden gods, ageless hermits and shooting laser beams. Led Zeppelin were about to 'Go imperial', and for the next two years at least, the world could only watch agog at the sheer scale of their empire building.

CHAPTER 20

Going To California

A s Led Zeppelin readied themselves for their ninth US tour in early
May 1973, Jimmy Page was still only 29 years old. By industry
standards he already ranked as a battle-scarred veteran of the music wars.
Within the space of little over a decade, Page had been a rock'n'roll
latecomer with Neil Christian & the Crusaders, an in-demand session
guitarist to the stars, a fledgling psychedelic pop hero with the Yardbirds
and all this before forming what had now become the biggest rock band
on the planet. As victories went, each campaign deserved its own medal.
"Onwards and upwards," he often said. Given how far Jimmy had come,
it was probably time for Peter Grant to build him a new ladder.

Of course, an additional benefit that such a life had conferred on
Page was being able to watch the development of the music business
from all sides of the equation. For a man always given to observation,
it must have been quite the study. When Jimmy got his original break
in sessions with Tony Meehan all those years before, for instance, the
Beatles had not even had their first number one, let alone become
the "group that would change everything." "They weren't really any
better than any of the London bands," Jimmy later said of witnessing
the Liverpudlian quartet's first gig in the capital at Leyton Baths in
early 1963. "[But], then it was their song-writing that came through."

Yet, roll on a decade and the Mop Tops were no more, the new form of pop they invented from inside the walls of Abbey Road to be enjoyed in perpetuity, but never added to. The next wave of performers seeking to create something genuinely new had also faltered in the wake of the Beatles, and Page was again a witness. As Led Zeppelin began their ascent to superstardom in late 1968, Cream were just coming to the end of their road, the trio's four-album run having laid down some of the foundations for what would become known as progressive rock. Five years on, however, and both Jack Bruce and Ginger Baker were 'cult artists' rather than the all-conquering heroes who ravished the Royal Albert Hall in November 1968, their commercial appeal now selective rather than universal. Even Eric Clapton appeared lost at sea, his early, promising, post-Cream experiments with Blind Faith, Delaney & Bonnie and Derek & the Dominos having floundered in the face of personal battles with alcohol and drugs. With Jimi Hendrix tragically dead at the age of 27, Jeff Beck continuing to fight his own shadow in a succession of under-performing outfits and the man they once called 'God' holed up in a Surrey mansion seemingly addicted to heroin, only the Stones, the Who and Jimmy's own band had made it out of the sixties thus far intact. In comparison to some, Page must have felt blessed. "Whatever Cream had, it destroyed them," he tellingly told *Melody Maker*. "But it hasn't destroyed us..."

Of course, nature abhors a vacuum and for each withdrawing guitar hero or imploding group, legions more had risen up to take their place, and some of them undoubtedly influenced not only by Cream but Led Zeppelin too. Of these 'third wavers', Black Sabbath and Deep Purple were surely the most promising of the bunch, with both modifying Page's original template for "a marriage of blues, hard rock and acoustic music" to suit their own distinctive needs. In Purple's case, this meant taking complex blues and jazz figures and hard rock rhythms to almost symphonic heights, with singer Ian Gillan's Little Richard-like falsetto providing the cherry atop all that instrumental virtuosity. "I could tell the fashion was going to be for screamers with depth and an overall blues feel, which is why I got Ian in," said Deep Purple guitarist and original 'Man in Black' Ritchie Blackmore somewhat sardonically.

Sabbath, on the other hand, concentrated the thrust of their attack on the more primal aspects of the Led Zeppelin formula, abandoning any notion of acoustic softness in favour of almighty power chords and killer riffs. "Zeppelin paved the way for us," Black Sabbath bassist Geezer Butler later told *Classic Rock*. "They were our favourite band by that time, [and] it was all that we listened to... lying down on the floor, smoking our dope and listening to Zeppelin." Such was the blunt force and sheer trauma of Black Sabbath's music, it had critics tripping over themselves to give it a suitable name. The one that stuck was 'heavy metal', a phrase first coined by the Canadian-American group Steppenwolf in their song 'Born To Be Wild', composed by their guitarist Mars Bonfire, aka Dennis Edmonton. "Zeppelin were the hardest thing until we came along," continued Butler. "They very much started the genre and we cashed in on it." Even Cream's Jack Bruce was pointing an accusatory finger in the direction of Zep here. "I don't take the blame for inventing heavy metal," he laughed. "Hang that one on Led Zeppelin."

Not according to Jimmy Page. As the number of bands playing 'hard rock', 'cock rock' or plain old 'heavy metal' began to multiply both in the UK and the States, Page felt continually compelled to defend his band's corner, with the guitarist keen to put critical distance between Zep and the more 'unsubtle' groups that followed in their wake. "Yes, I heard [the term] 'heavy'," he later reiterated to *Melody Maker*'s Michael Watts, "[and] I remember... when we were equated with Black Sabbath, Deep Purple and Grand Funk Railroad, but we were nowhere near any of those. I mean, 'Stairway To Heaven' isn't a number that Grand Funk Railroad would come up with. Still," Jimmy conceded, "I've only ever heard one Grand Funk number on the radio, so I dunno, I dunno..." As well-intentioned as it was, the caveat wasn't really necessary.

Page was also somewhat defensive on the subject of riffs. Having birthed the mother of them all with 'Whole Lotta Love', one felt Jimmy might have smiled benignly when the likes of Black Sabbath's 'Paranoid', Deep Purple's 'Smoke On The Water' or latterly Grand Funk's '(We're An) American Band' all seemed to draw from the same simple well. However, as he was at pains to point out, not all riffs were the same. Not by a long shot. "Yeah, we play on riffs, but they're not all as straightforward as they appear," he said. "For instance, 'Black Dog'. I'd like to see another band play the riff to that accurately. There are riffs," Page concluded, "and there are *riffs*."[146]

As *Houses Of The Holy* so clearly illustrated, while Jimmy Page and Led Zeppelin had banked on riffs to provide emotional punch and visceral power at the beginning of their career, the desire not to be defined by them was growing ever stronger with each album. In fact, Zep now seemed to have more in common with the new wave of prog-rock acts than anyone else. 'The Song Remains The Same', for instance, bore several passing similarities to the work of Yes, its dextrous rhythms and balance of mood and texture closer to Chris Squire's quixotic art-rockers than either Purple or Sabbath.

'No Quarter' recalled elements of Pink Floyd, its slow swirls, dragging chords and sense of unease exploring similar territory to 1971's *Meddle* and the soon-to-be gigantic *Dark Side Of The Moon*. But again, this was no band-wagon jumping on Jimmy or Zep's part, more just a consolidation of the original idea behind the band. "Light and shade," Page had said. Now, he had simply expanded the model to include all points in between. "I hated Zep being referred to as just a 'heavy metal' band," said Chris Welch. "They were powerful, but they had nothing to do with heavy metal. They could rock with the best of them, often better than all of them. But they could also be incredibly light with their sound, clever with their arrangements and great at the recording stage. That whole 'light and shade' thing was very apt. Just look at 'Stairway...' or 'No Quarter'. They were operating in a different space..."

In keeping with his style, Jimmy Page was as eager to put clear daylight between Led Zeppelin and the growing prog-rock movement as he had been with any notion that his band were heavy metal. He was also blunt

---

146 Indeed, rumour has it that one of the reasons Jimmy loved playing 'Black Dog' so much was precisely for its complexity, seeing Jones' hellish riff as a warning sign to other bands who thought they could encroach on Zep's territory. No doubt, the bendy time signature and stop/start wobbles of 'The Ocean' was yet more proof of Page's desire to see off all comers in the battle to create the ultimate riff.

when doing so. "Yes? Well, I don't particularly hate them," he told *Melody Maker*. "I think they must get excited during their rehearsals, but once the thing's recorded it must be really painful because they've got to play it note for note. Yes have relevance because they're bridging a particular gap, but it's not one I especially like, although I know I can do it. I had to when I was playing session work, to live within the confines of something. But I couldn't do the same thing every night." Neither heavy metal nor prog, hard rock or soft, in his mind, Led Zeppelin remained precisely what Page had always envisioned them to be. Hard as a diamond, gentle as a lamb and utterly beyond classification.

Whether one shared Jimmy Page's sentiments about the merits (or indeed, demerits) of Yes, Deep Purple or anyone else for that matter, it was difficult to argue with him when faced with Led Zeppelin's sustained level of success. Unlike many of their peers, there had been no drama in the band's ranks on their way to stardom or bitter fall-outs when they had achieved it. Instead, Zep continued to present itself as a bold, impenetrable and mysterious unit trading on both individual and collective excellence, with each album they released pushing them further into a space all their own. As chairman of the board then, Page was surely allowed to voice his opinions or even howl them from the rooftops of each country he and Zep visited. But in the main, his concerns appeared to centre less around other acts and more about focusing on the needs of his own merry band. "I'll always be committed to this group, I should think, always..." Just as well, really, because he and Led Zeppelin were about to take on one of the biggest, showiest and most profitable tours of their young lives.

Led Zeppelin were already on the road in Europe when *Houses Of The Holy* was released in March 1973, this latest batch of dates in France, Scandinavia and Germany coming off the back of an already comprehensive UK tour that bookended the previous year. Following standard protocol, they had previewed many of the songs that ended up on *Houses...* along the way, with some tunes ('Dancing Days', 'The Ocean' and 'Over The Hills...') getting in-concert run-throughs as far back as mid-1972. "You couldn't do that now, though," Page said in 2014, "everybody's got smart phones so the surprise would be ruined..."

304

Still, Peter Grant would find a way to capture Led Zeppelin's live show for posterity – if not as majestically as he might have wanted – in the coming months.

Back on May 4, 1973, however, it all began again for Zep in America with the opening show of 33-date tour that was to take them through 30 cities over three-odd months, this time with a vacation in the middle, though not necessarily as a reward for any good behaviour on the band's part. Kicking off before a crowd of 49,236 at Atlanta's Fulton County Stadium for a reported sum of $246,180, the numbers now involved for Led Zeppelin's live appearances were staggering, but they were only warming up. One night later, the quartet trampled the US concert attendance record underfoot when they played to 56,800 people in Tampa, Florida, exceeding the Beatles' previous tally of 55,600 for their gig at New York's Shea Stadium by 1,200 ticket stubs. What was even more remarkable was the fact that there was no support act on the bill. Just two and a half hours of undiluted Zep. "I will never, ever forget the reaction when they came onstage," Atlantic president Phil Carson later told *Classic Rock*. "Just mindblowing!"

Obviously, this was rock music being consistently played out on a scale never attempted before. While Woodstock and Altamont had seen larger numbers through their gates, those festivals had featured many different acts and, equally importantly, were free to enter. Led Zeppelin, on the other hand, were pulling punters in the tens of thousands on their name and reputation alone for $6.00 a pop. For some, all that power might have boggled the mind. For frontman Robert Plant, it was more a case of finding a coping strategy and hiding behind it as best he could. "I think it was the biggest thrill I've had," he said after the Tampa Stadium show. "I pretend... I kid myself... I'm not very nervous in a situation like that. I try to bounce around just like normal. One would think it would be very hard to communicate with 60,000 people some have got to be quite a distance off [and] there were no movie screens showing us, like in Atlanta [the night before]. The only thing they could pick on was the complete vibe of what music was being done."

There really were no worries over vibe or music at Tampa. Their set honed to perfection from several previous months on the road, the quartet kicked off its record-breaking performance with now sturdy set-opener 'Rock And Roll' and just kept on going. From vintage jewels ('Dazed And Confused', 'Whole Lotta Love' and 'Moby Dick') to modern gems ('Over The Hills...', 'The Song Remains The Same' and 'The Ocean'), the Zep machine was a study in ruthless efficiency and relentless improvisation. In short, everything was despatched brilliantly and nothing ever sounded quite the same as it had before. Even when they calmed the crowd's nerves by introducing the soothing strains of 'The Rain Song', the level of energy coming off the stage was palpable. "But that was it," Plant later said. "It was all about extreme energy."

Mirroring the bold fashion choice he had made at Led Zeppelin's debut gig in Gladsaxe, Denmark on September 7, 1968, Jimmy Page marked his band's appearance at Tampa Stadium by donning a striking white suit over a jet black shirt, his leather shoes combining both monochrome colours for maximum rock star effect. As the tour progressed, Page would become even more dapper, though the latest addition to his arsenal of guitars arguably outshone just about anything he chose to wear. Weighing in at a hefty 34lb, with its cherry red mahogany body as curvaceous as anything painted by Picasso, Jimmy's Gibson EDS 1275 double-necked axe was as stunning as it was pragmatic.

The guitar had actually made its 'catwalk debut' some two years before at Belfast's Ulster Hall on March 5, 1971, its acquisition by Page empathically solving the problem of how to bring 'Stairway To Heaven' out of the studio and onto the concert stage. "I'd recorded the thing and then wondered how I was going to do it," he later confirmed to *Guitarist*, "so I got the double-neck specifically for doing 'Stairway To Heaven' live." Finding the right guitar to do so turned out to be something of an involved process. Having recorded certain passages of the song on separate six- and 12-string guitars, Page now needed an instrument that combined both in one body. A long-time fan of Earl Hooker, Jimmy had reportedly seen the Chicago bluesman wielding a double-necked, six-/12-string Gibson on the cover of his superb 1969 LP *Two Bugs & A Roach* and approached the company to purchase the same model. Unfortunately, by then it was out of production, but Gibson set about custom-building a new version specifically for Page.

Though a cumbersome proposition, the EDS 1275's particular qualities were ideal for performing Zep's anthem for the ages each night onstage. "I used to have the switch in the middle so that both necks were on at once," said Jimmy, "so you'd get all that sympathetic resonance coming through from the other neck. I used to end 'Stairway To Heaven' like that." By the release of *Houses Of The Holy*, Page found he could also use the guitar to enliven some of that album's material too, with the double-neck now being called into live action for 'The Song Remains The Same' and its segue partner 'The Rain Song'. Over subsequent years, the image of Jimmy Page holding his Gibson EDS 1275 aloft before the crowd at the end of 'Stairway...', 'The Rain Song' and several other Zep classics[147] would become an iconic one, both guitarist and guitar finding themselves the subject of a famous poster adorning the bedroom walls of many a teenager throughout the seventies. "That Gibson was as instantly recognisable as Paul McCartney's violin bass, Pete Townshend's black and white Rickenbacker or Hendrix's white Woodstock Strat," said Chris Charlesworth. "Everyone knew when it appeared on stage, 'Stairway To Heaven' was on the way."

As large and unwieldy as Page's double-neck Gibson was, it paled into insignificance when compared with another piece of kit Led Zeppelin acquired for their 1973 US tour. With the band committed to a multitude of dates in a spray of American cities often hundreds of miles apart, it made sense to travel between gigs in the most expedient way possible. To this end, Zep had long utilised a snug executive aircraft to fly them around, a practice long established within the entertainment industry for those wealthy enough to afford it. Since the late sixties, performers such as Frank Sinatra and James Brown had hired or purchased their own

---

147 Page's EDS 1275 was also used to perform 'Celebration Day' and 'Tangerine' on later Zep tours, with Jimmy mothballing his distinctively shaped 12-string Giannini GWSCRA12-P Craviola acoustic in favour of the double-neck on the latter tune. Another guitar – a 1969/70 Les Paul Custom repainted red and christened 'Number Three' – also saw considerable use by Page on the 1973 US tour. It was later put aside for almost a decade before resurfacing with a Parsons B-Bender newly attached to its body.

planes to make the business of touring as stress-free and comfortable as they could. But with the advent of 'The Starship', Peter Grant and Led Zeppelin had stepped up the luxury factor to a whole new level.

A souped-up Boeing 720B airliner replete with thick wall-to-wall carpets, a shower, double bed (including a safety belt "for horizontal take-offs and landings"), TV lounge, fake fireplace and its very own bar, The Starship didn't come cheap at $2,500 per hour. But for all the expense, it did afford the band and their entourage their own private members club high above the clouds of the USA. "Having a plane like that at their disposal they could pretty much base themselves anywhere and just fly out to gigs," said Atlantic's Phil Carson. "In those days, there was no real airport security [so] the plane would taxi up to the predestined point nowhere near the terminal... then this line of limousines would come." With the champagne, Jack Daniels – and in John Bonham's case, a case or two of Ballantine's beer – in free supply and two specially hired stewardesses named Bianca and Suzee to serve it, Zep's very own "rock'n'roll airship" would again become another facet of their ever-growing legend, with endless stories of on-board bad behaviour spilling out in the press over subsequent years. "We weren't the only band that had its own plane," Jimmy later said, "but we were the only ones that had had a grown-up plane." As time would tell, XXX-rated, too.

As many a journalist was all too aware, Led Zeppelin's gift for partying wasn't just confined to the air, with the band and their entourage's penchant for 'having a good time all the time' already written in stone well before the US tour of 1973. In fact, since Zep had first touched down on American soil four-odd years before, tales of wine, women, groupies and mudsharks had been following them around like a stray dog in search of an owner. Many of the legends seemed concentrated around Los Angeles, the band's tendency to hold court at Sunset Strip's famous (or infamous) Rainbow Bar & Grill or Rodney Bingenheimer's English Disco marking them out as visiting "British rock gods" to a local populace of otherworldly beings and various other hangers on. "This was a city," one journalist said, "that attracted the weird and wonderful. There were even people there who would communicate solely by making whistle and clicking noises. All human life, and then some..." Zep, however, loved such magnificent distractions. "Unlike some artists who valued their seclusion," wrote journalist Dave DiMartino, then a 15-year-old simply witnessing the festivities, "Led Zeppelin would be highly visible during their visits [to LA]." And, no doubt, contributing to a growing powder keg of rumour and intrigue while they were at it.

When Zeppelin weren't visiting the Rainbow, they could be found at the nearby Continental Hyatt House hotel, or to give it its more familiar nom de plume, "The Riot House". Hiring an entire floor all for themselves – usually the ninth; it had a swimming pool – it was here that Zep relaxed, indulged their excesses or created "sheer bloody havoc", depending on mood or whim. Often at the heart of the storm was John Bonham, whose titanic beer consumption, in combination with homesickness and crushing between-gig boredom saw him pass the hours by terrorising fellow band members, road crew and hotel staff alike. "For Bonzo's birthday party, the group gave him a motorbike," Phil Carson recalled to *Classic Rock* in 2013. "I recall him riding it down the hotel corridor. That's when things started to get a little scary." Yet, when Bonham's or anyone else's enthusiasms threatened to get the better of them or, worse still, invoke the interest of local law enforcement agencies, Peter Grant was on hand to clean up the mess. "Peter was always so calm when faced with any sort of threat [to the band]," Atlantic's A&R director Alan Callan later told Q. "He saw overcoming it as simply lancing a boil."

Now officially in charge of championing Led Zeppelin's American successes was Danny Goldberg. A publicity man par excellence, who as previously seen was employed by Grant and Page to ensure the band were given their rightful due in the press, Goldberg was also responsible for derailing any potentially damaging news stories that might harm his new charges. But for him, Zep's sometimes boorish displays of bad behaviour were more about bored, unruly and extremely privileged children at play as much as any deliberate attempt on their part to undo the fabric of American society. "It was that feeling of 'We can do absolutely anything', [or] 'There were no rules'," he later told *Guitar*

World's Steve Rosen. "And that whole phenomenon of having a whole floor, it was just like one big playground. So what if [Bonzo] or Richard Cole drove a motorcycle through the hallway? What was notable... was it just epitomised their whole [anarchic] attitude."

One person unlikely to be found exploring the nooks and crannies of "The Riot House" on the back of a motorbike at some ungodly hour was Jimmy Page. According to Goldberg, it simply wasn't his style. "Jimmy never rode through the hallways or threw TVs out of windows, but he loved it when other people did. Jimmy was more the kind of person who would manipulate someone into doing those kinds of things... then laugh to himself watching everyone make fools of themselves." Undisputed leader of the band and a veteran of the road to boot, Page was no doubt mindful of maintaining his status in the pecking order. But as ever with the guitarist, his essential nature found him content to mostly perch on the periphery, carefully observing the action, than place himself at its epicentre. From business meetings to high jinks, Jimmy was a man apart. "He tended with a large group of people to lay back and see what everyone else was saying," Goldberg again told Steve Rosen in 1986. "A lot of the power over the group came from those moody silences. He had a very specific sense of himself." Yet, by his own admission, Jimmy Page wasn't always on the outside looking in. "Let's put it this way," he later told *Mojo*, "I certainly wasn't going to bed with a cup of cocoa..."

In fact, when Los Angeles first took Led Zeppelin to its collective bosom, Page had very much been at the forefront of the action, the guitarist beginning an affair with one of Sunset Strip's more famous faces while on the group's endless American tour of 1969. Now celebrated as 'the world's most famous groupie', Pamela Ann Miller was then simply a precocious high school student from Reseda, California who had become deeply fascinated with pop and rock stars as a teenager. Deciding to pursue her interests in the flesh, she moved to downtown LA during the mid-sixties, ingratiating herself among the city's then flourishing musical community.

Soon enough, Miller found herself working as a nanny for composer/ humorist/artistic polymath Frank Zappa, their friendship eventually leading to her joining the GTOs[148], a troupe of like-minded young women who mixed theatre, performance art and spoken-word skits while Zappa's backing band doodled along behind them. "The GTOs were one of the first girl groups," Pamela later said. "We were a really outrageous, loud group of girls who just wanted to turn heads and have fun." After releasing their only album *Permanent Damage* and performing one concert (albeit for six hours) in the summer of 1969, the GTOs broke up, with various members of the troupe being either detained or arrested for drug possession.

However, it was her ability to act as a 'muse' to rock musicians rather than her talent as a singer or dancer that brought 'Miss Pamela' (as she became known) to notoriety. "There were very few girl groups, so for most girls, all they could do to be around the music was to be with the guys in the bands," she told *The Guardian*'s Kathryn Bromwich in 2015. "In those days it was much easier to meet bands, and there weren't as many girls trying to do it. So it wasn't difficult if you were a pretty girl to meet [the likes of] Mick Jagger[149]. They were hanging out in clubs in Los Angeles and you could just say hello. There was a different feel in the air. You could just hang out and there was not a lot of judgement going on. As 'groupies', 'muses', whatever, we were friendly with a lot of these people. Some of the girls didn't sleep with the guys, they just wanted to be backstage and be part of the scene." For Miss Pamela, however, there was always one over-riding factor. "The music. As any good groupie will tell you, it was always about the music. That was in the blood stream. We were into sex, drugs and rock'n'roll."

Miss Pamela first caught Jimmy Page's eye at a hip LA club called Thee Experience. According to her, "He was such a beautiful guy, such a perfect specimen... the epitome of the perfect rock god." Nonetheless, when Page reportedly sent Richard Cole over with his room number

---

148 Formed by Zappa, Girls Together Outrageously – or Only, Occasionally or Orally, depending on the day or mood – comprised seven members, including Miss Pamela, Miss Sandra, Miss Mercy, Miss Sparky, Miss Cynderella and Miss Christine.
149 Miss Pamela reportedly had a brief affair with Jagger.

at the Hyatt written on a piece of paper, she dodged the advance. "I guess he thought I'd show up there, which I didn't," she told *Q*'s Dave DiMartino. "That always made you seem more intriguing to whoever it was." Inevitably, it didn't stay that way. When Jimmy called Pamela directly and invited her to a gig in San Diego, romance subsequently blossomed. "I met him there and that was it. From that moment on, we were sort of enmeshed. We rode home in the back of a limo, and whatever I did was perfect. 'Oh Miss P... I've been looking for you all my life'. Of course, years later, we found out he said the exact same thing to all the girls, but you know, it seemed very sweet at the time." Sweet, but not entirely innocent. "He did keep whips coiled up in his suitcase on the road, but he never attempted to use them on me," Miss Pamela told *Uncut* in 2009. "But then Jimmy had a wicked sexual side which made him a transcendent lover."

By 1973 or thereabouts, things had evidently moved on, though Page was again subject to rumours of on-the-road affairs. Having previously been linked to Miss Pamela, the gossip mill now had his name entwined with a raven-haired teenage model named Lori Mattix, then gracing the covers of celebrity lifestyle magazines like *Star*. According to several tales – mostly told by Lori and Pamela themselves – Jimmy unceremoniously dumped his former flame at Rodney's English Disco in LA and took up with Mattix the very same night. "Jimmy said 'Wait outside and I'll get the limo'," Pamela confirmed to *VH1*. "So, I'm standing out there very innocently, and he walked out with Lori! Groupie egg on face. That mother fucker..."

In Mattix's account, she was later 'mock-kidnapped' (possibly by Richard Cole) and brought to Page's room at the Hyatt where he met her wearing a hat, cane and a Cheshire cat grin. Again, Jimmy's latent charm seems to have won out. "He had this wonderful calm demeanour about him," she later said. "Something very mysterious, [but] always really kind and sweet. When you do meet him, when you do get to know him, you just fall in love with him because he's so sweet." In due course, Page's name would be linked to several more women, each with few, if any bad words to say about him. "I mean God, I was a baby really, [but] we fell madly in love," said Lori. "There was a magical innocence to him, and it really was one of the most beautiful times in my life..."

Another word that had begun to feature heavily in the general scuttlebutt and gossip surrounding Led Zeppelin, and indeed, the broader rock community by 1973 was 'drugs' – or more specifically cocaine. Unlike marijuana or acid, whose casual use (or otherwise) had contributed heavily to the music and cultural make-up of the sixties, cocaine was neither used as a mild relaxant or wildly variable "door to other worlds". Instead, its effect was all about 'the boost' – from the amplification of physical and creative energy to the heightening of social and artistic confidence.

More importantly, cocaine seemed to have few of the more obvious drawbacks associated with either alcohol, pot, LSD or other Class A drugs such as heroin. With no obvious smell or smoke surrounding it, it was discreet and quick to administer, while also difficult for police to immediately detect. In sensible doses, it did not traditionally render its user drunk, incapable or prone to nodding off for hours on end. On the contrary, cocaine's qualities as a stimulant seemed specifically designed to plug into the demands of a new decade where the image and delivery of rock music was becoming ruthlessly efficient and increasingly imperious. As one critic put it, "rock had entered the business age", and cocaine matched its requirements pound for pound and kilo for kilo. The long-term physical problems, crushing psychological comedowns and occasional episodes of psychosis would all come later, of course. But for the time being – and several years to come – cocaine was the drug of choice for jobbing rock gods and their court of helpers, handlers and hangers on.

Singling out Jimmy Page, Led Zeppelin or their entourage for the possible use of cocaine in such a time would be utterly ridiculous. As all-pervasive in the music industry during the seventies as long hair, flared trousers and broken promises, the drug was everywhere and on hand to everyone who could afford it. However, for Jimmy Page, there were no stern denials issued regarding cocaine use or any other narcotic for that matter. No judgements for or against and absolutely no moralising or distancing himself from any of it. On the contrary, Page seemed to infer a practical acceptance that drugs (hard and soft) had – and would – play a role in the delivery system of the music. "I don't regret it at all because when I needed to be really focused, I was really focused. That's it," he told writer Nick Kent of his experiences with cocaine and other drugs during a particularly candid exchange in 2003. "...You've got to be really on top of it."

No one could deny that either Jimmy or Zep were anything other than on top of things during their sojourn across the States in the early summer of 1973. Building on the records broken in Atlanta and Tampa, the group now pushed on through St. Louis and Dallas, Denver and San Diego, their shows growing longer (three hours wasn't unusual), the sets more theatrical and the performances ever more extravagant. "By 1973," Phil Carson later told *Classic Rock*, "they had built their empire and they were now surfing the wave." With *Houses Of The Holy* still riding high in the charts and the group's sprinkling of several of its songs each night onstage only drumming up more interest in the album, Led Zeppelin were literally printing money as they went from state to state. In fact, as one US promoter went to the press confirming Zep had raked in $1,000 a minute at San Francisco's Kezar Stadium on June 2, Peter Grant was regaling Britain's media with much the same message, Zep's wily manager telling the *Financial Times* that the band were now due to earn $30 million in America over the course of the coming year.

Faced with such staggering numbers and no apparent end in sight to the group's popularity, Led Zeppelin's success was verging on the preposterous. "It was just a culmination of all the touring they'd done before," said Carson, "and the sheer quality of their records." Yet, with each new attendance record smashed and another million dollars earned, Page and Zep were slowly running out of ornate castles and suitably high towers from which to shout their victories and raise their flags. Happily, they did not lack for imagination. Having conquered the charts, eaten up continents with their touring and sold more tickets than PT Barnum while doing so, the band now chose to focus their attentions on a brand-new enterprise: making a concert film. Nonetheless, for those relishing the spectacle of bread, circuses and huge coliseums with Jimmy Page cast in the role as Led Zeppelin's 'Electric Caesar', they were in for a surprise. While Zep would certainly provide the former, Page would cast aside his purple robes in favour of the rough serge wool and pointed hood of a hermit's garb.

CHAPTER 21

The Song Remains The Same

With only a smattering of TV appearances and a single song contribution to 1969's *Supershow*[150] music documentary to their name, Led Zeppelin had run shy of cameras, a conscious decision taken because Jimmy Page lacked confidence in the medium's ability to project their music in the way he wanted it to sound. This absence from film and TV also tied in beautifully with the air of mystery both Jimmy Page and his band were ever keen to cultivate. Nonetheless, the truth was that Zep had been trying hard to find the right cinematic vehicle for their talents since January 1970 when Stanley Dorfman and Peter Whitehead were commissioned by Page and Peter Grant to film the group at London's Royal Albert Hall. On that occasion, progress was supposedly stymied by the quality of footage shot, but that had not stopped Jimmy and Grant from searching other potential avenues. In the end, Page didn't have to travel far for an answer.

150 Directed by John Crome, *Supershow* (or *The Last Great Jam Of The 60s!*) was designed to bring together artists from blues, rock and jazz for a 'giant supersession'. Loosely based on the Stones' *Rock 'N' Roll Circus*, *Supershow* featured performances by Eric Clapton, Buddy Guy, Jack Bruce and Jon Hiseman's Colosseum among others. Led Zeppelin's contribution to the film was 'Dazed And Confused'. *Supershow* received a limited theatrical run at London's Lyceum in November 1969, with Zep later redeeming the footage of 'Dazed And Confused' for their own commercial purposes.

A New Yorker by birth, filmmaker Joe Massot had arrived in London at precisely the time it began to truly swing. Having previously met the Beatles on the set of their 1965 comedy adventure *Help!*, he approached them to appear in his own documentary short *Reflections On Love* a year later. Striking up a friendship with George Harrison, Massot subsequently asked 'the Quiet One' to write the music for his directorial debut, the psychedelic farce *Wonderwall*. A cult item even in 1968, *Wonderwall's* mix and match soundtrack of Indian ragas and more straightforward rock tunes might have befuddled the ear, but Harrison's involvement in the movie nonetheless marked the first solo musical outing by a member of the Fab Four outside the band, as well as the first release by their newly founded Apple Records.

Fast-forward to 1972 and Joe Massot was still in London, but now pitching the idea of a movie featuring Led Zeppelin to Jimmy Page at Plumpton Place.[151] Enthused by their discussion but almost always busy, Jimmy batted Massot's idea over to Richard Cole who duly passed it on to Peter Grant for his consideration. At first, Grant felt that the director was not well-known enough to merit such a potentially high-profile gig. But a year later, and with Zep smashing attendance records right, left and centre in the USA, Peter decided the time was right to finally capture the quartet in all their cinematic glory, and Joe Massot was to be his man. Soon enough, Massot would wish he wasn't.

It began well enough, however, with both sides harbouring only the loftiest of ambitions and the highest of expectations for the project. "We didn't want the film to be an in-concert type of thing," Page later told writer Peter Doggett. "It had to have bigger dimensions [than that]." Massot was equally wary of his movie being just a simple record of Zep performing before a live audience. "I told Jimmy that there was no point in making another *Woodstock* or *Concert For Bangladesh*," he

---

151 In 1970, Joe Massot temporarily moved to Wallingford in Berkshire, his rented cottage close to Jimmy Page's then home at Pangbourne. When Massot became acquainted with Jimmy's partner Charlotte Martin, she in turn introduced him to the Zep guitarist. Bonding over a shared love of antiques, the friendship was duly sealed when Page invited Massot to see his band perform at the Bath Festival.

said. Instead, the director wanted to bring the band's personalities and individual interests into play, presenting them as fully rounded people rather than unknowable figures on a stage. "[I wanted] to represent them as individuals and then incorporate those four sections into a film structure. All the individual sequences were to be integrated into the group's music and concerts." It didn't quite stop there. As well as filming four 'character portraits' or 'fantasy sequences' for each member of the band, Massot also planned to turn the camera on Zep's manager. Given the fact that Peter had always wanted to be a film star, this was probably music to his ears. However, Grant's presence in the film would be far from jovial, his screen time taken up with gangster skits and an uncomfortably real demonstration in the politics of power.

Realistically, Joe Massot's dream of crafting the perfect Led Zeppelin flick was probably doomed from the start, with the director given just 48 hours notice to get himself and his crew to the States to begin filming the band in all their pomp. In fact, his first overall impressions of the Zep machine proved ominous and unsettling. Arriving at Baltimore's cavernous Civic Center on July 23, 1973, Massot's camera was immediately called into action backstage as Peter Grant began the process of slowly dressing down, then quickly terrifying a concert promoter for the alleged crime of allowing unlicensed Zep merchandise to be sold on the premises.

A grim five minute's worth of footage made worse by Peter's escalating temper and Massot's "close quarters access", Chris Welch captured the scene with pinpoint accuracy in his own fine book, *Peter Grant: The Man Who Led Zeppelin*. "As he builds to a crescendo, Grant's anger is targeted not just at his present victim but at all American rock promoters, and finally at America in general, as if the whole country is out to make a buck at his expense. It's a genuinely chilling scene," Welch concludes, "and it remains the only footage of Peter Grant in action, browbeating in the manner only he could." Perhaps wisely, Massot chose not to raise the fact he was still waiting for a proper contract for his filmmaking services at this juncture.

The real jewel to be caught on film by Joe Massot and his crew was not Grant's terrifying presence, however, but Led Zeppelin in their natural environment – on the concert stage. In agreement with the band and their manager, this would take place over three nights at New York's Madison Square Garden, from July 27–29, giving Massot a further three days post-Baltimore to gather his thoughts before the cameras rolled in earnest. On the way to NYC, he did just that, reportedly filming snippets of Zep both onstage and backstage at Three Rivers Stadium in Pittsburgh, while also picking up incidental footage of the highways and byways of America as the group and their entourage travelled towards the Big Apple and into the belly of the beast. With esteemed camera operator Ernie Day and assistant Robert Freeman in tow, Massot continued to seek assurances around payment and filming access for his crew, but prising open Led Zeppelin's legal and financial armour was not an easy task. "Getting Led Zeppelin to sign anything or grant me any real power was very difficult. But I trusted them. What I wanted was to make a great movie…"

Before filming commenced at the Garden, Led Zeppelin and Joe Massot discussed the cinematic rules of engagement. For continuity purposes, the director asked that the band wear the same outfits for all three shows. While Page, Plant and Bonham acquiesced, John Paul Jones refused Massot's request, presumably on the grounds of personal hygiene. For his part, Jimmy seemed less concerned about the state of his stage clothes and more worried about potentially intrusive cameramen, the guitarist seeking an assurance from the director that his band were given all the space they needed to entertain 60,000 screaming New Yorkers over their three-night run. "I didn't want to be distracted while I was trying to perform," Page told *Guitar World*'s Brad Tolinski in 2008, "[so] I warned all the cameramen to stay away from me, within reason."

Ultimately, the resulting marriage of Led Zeppelin's in-concert firepower at MSG and Joe Massot's film cameras proved neither utterly brilliant nor woefully bad, with the band's overall performance best described as strong and stout rather than truly transcendent. Even the usually defensive Jimmy Page was willing to concede something had been generally amiss. "It wasn't a terribly good night, and it certainly wasn't a magic one," he later said of the group's final gig in New York, from which much of the final footage was extracted. That said, when Zep were on form during their set, the results were truly thrilling, with the slow-burning of 'The Rain Song', chilly atmospherics of 'No Quarter' and blunt-edge trauma of show opener 'Rock And Roll' all barely contained by the 35mm film stock Massot used to record them.

Indeed, Page himself went above and beyond the call of duty several times, the spraying barrage of notes issuing forth from his double-necked Gibson EDS 1275 during 'The Song Remains The Same' and heartfelt solo flights throughout 'Since I've Been Loving You' just two of the stand-out moments captured on celluloid. And for those seeking continued proof of his gifts as a showman, one only had to look to 'Dazed And Confused'. Dressed all in black with astrological and alchemical symbols of moons, stars and dragons sewn into his clothing, Jimmy's summoning of the four winds with his violin bow before the assembled throngs was pure theatre, these larger than life gestures a winking precursor to the atonal maelstrom of screaming cats, injured planes and trapped demons he let loose only moments later. All in all, it was an electric display from a man who had last seen sleep some 120 hours before in Baltimore. "The only way I prepared for the filming was by staying up for five nights!" he said, laughing, to *Guitar World*. "I mean, we were in New York, we were making a movie... and it was difficult to shut down that kind of electricity. You'd try to go to bed... but it was just more fun to go out and enjoy yourself."

Yet, however one viewed the frames, Joe Massot's filmic record of Led Zeppelin at Madison Square Garden didn't quite confirm the group's long-established reputation as visiting deities temporarily on leave from Mount Olympus, with one or two songs, among them 'Stairway To Heaven', strangely lacking their usual spark and spirit. Worse, it also soon came to light that there were several technical errors in the footage that would be difficult to resolve at the editing stage. "We did three nights of filming," said a non-plussed Page, "but there were intros missing, endings chopped, that type of thing. The film crew were really out of it, I think. Well, I know they were because I was there watching them!"

One of the more glaring omissions was on 'Whole Lotta Love', the last few seconds of which seemed to be entirely absent. With little time to prepare angles or familiarise himself with the group's live set, Joe Massot might be forgiven the odd mistake. But this was Led Zeppelin, and Peter Grant was in no mood for fun and games, let alone accidentally cutting off the climax of one of their finest tunes. "They filmed three bloody nights at the Garden," he growled, " and never got one complete take of 'Whole Lotta Love'..."[152]

Luckily for Massot, there was an opportunity to paper the cracks. As previously agreed with Page and Grant, they still needed to film four individual framing devices with the director. If correctly edited, these could now be used to plug holes in the concert footage, as well as provide additional context, broader characterisation and an element of fantasy and mystique. But again, there were difficulties to overcome, with Led Zeppelin's life off the road a million miles away from the protean antics displayed in New York. "Jimmy is 'Led Wallet' because he's always got a heavy wallet [which] stays in his pocket and Robert lives on a farm... with his goats," said Peter Grant of the band's interests while not on tour. "John's happy as long as he's got a pint of bitter and John Paul Jones is the antithesis of the pop star... he only comes out when there's a concert to play or an album to make." With back stories like these to work from, turning Led Zeppelin into the superheroes filmgoers wanted to see was never going to be easy.

And so it proved. Commencing work after the American tour had long concluded, Joe Massot was given but days to film his now infamous 'fantasy sequences' with Led Zeppelin during October of 1973. Again working to the strictest of time schedules, the director's

---

152 Grant's overall disposition was probably not improved by the fact that on the second night of Led Zeppelin's stay at Madison Square Garden, $186,700 of the band's money was stolen from a safety deposit box at the Drake Hotel. Put aside to pay expenses and wages at the end of the tour, the loss was substantial enough for a press conference to be called, at which Peter got into an altercation with a photographer who soon pressed assault charges. Thought to be an inside job – Richard Cole, who had the keys to said security box, even took a lie detector test to prove his innocence – the stolen money has never been recovered.

brief was to essentially turn up at the house of each band member, discuss how they might wish to be portrayed and then roll the cameras. "I became a psychiatrist," he later told Peter Doggett. "It was weird. I'd go to each one's home, he'd show me around, we'd talk about the film and two days later we'd be making it." Unfortunately, this lack of vital preparation was to become glaringly apparent in the final footage, which was at best undistinguished, at worst truly laughable.

The runt of the litter was surely John Paul Jones' segment. Temporarily transformed into the wayward leader of a band of lusty thugs, Jones found himself terrorising the inhabitants of an unidentified village from the back of a horse before returning home to read passages from *Bedknobs And Broomsticks* to his devoted wife and children. Allegedly an "allegorical, symbolic tale", contrasting images of violence and brutality with the seasoned calm of domestic life, JPJ had reportedly got part of the idea for the sequence after watching the Disney TV feature *The Scarecrow Of Romney Marsh,* featuring smuggling anti-hero Doctor Syn. But when he was reportedly refused a licence to use the character[153], John Paul and Massot were forced to improvise. "The whole thing turned out to be like the *Horse Of The Year Show,*" Jones quite rightly said. Of equal embarrassment was the state of the bassist's hair. Having shorn his locks soon after the end of Zep's last US tour, John Paul was forced to don a wig for continuity purposes when filming the snippet. Looking more like a deranged pageboy than one quarter of the world's most successful rock group, JPJ's "mad syrup" was arguably more terrifying than his turn as a horse-riding sadist. "They wouldn't even let me cut it," he later moaned.

While Jones had long traded on his visual anonymity and could therefore argue no one was expecting an Oscar-winning performance from him in Zep's "little film", the same could not be said of Robert Plant. Lead vocalist and, for many, the visual entry point of the Led Zeppelin universe, Plant's framing sequence had to be at least as dashing

153 Created by novelist Richard Thorndike in 1915, the Reverend Doctor Christopher Syn has featured in seven novels, at least three films/TV series as well as numerous theatre, radio and comic adaptations.

and ostentatious as his onstage persona. Sadly, like JPJ's effort, it turned out to be a huge disappointment. Filmed in and around Raglan Castle and Cardigan Bay in Wales, Robert was cast in the role of a steely Arthurian knight on a quest to rescue a beautiful princess, played by winsome blonde model Virginia Parker. So far, so very Plant. But truth be told, his excessively manly poses and comedic wielding of a steely broadsword were a hoot from start to finish. At times, even he couldn't keep a straight face.

Peter Grant's efforts really weren't much better. Presumably apportioned his own snippet at the behest of the band, Grant's brief turn as a thirties gang boss dispensing mob justice by machine gun with lackey Richard Cole in tow looked incredibly stagey and nowhere near as menacing as he had appeared when dealing with his delinquent promoter in Baltimore. However, the film shot of Zep's manager driving a vintage car around the countryside with his beloved wife, Gloria, by his side was much more enjoyable, with Grant's glee obvious to all.

By setting aside any and all pretensions to fantasy or horror, sword or sorcery, and guns and crime, John Bonham's individual segment was by far the most entertaining to watch. Caught in his natural habitat – in the pub, at the snooker table, herding his bulls, driving a tractor, and still finding time to cheekily goose his wife, Pat – Bonham looked every inch the happy farmer. Even when tearing around on custom motorcycles or drag racing on a track in Northamptonshire, Zep's drummer seemed either genuinely unaware or, more likely, completely unconcerned by the presence of Joe Massot's trailing cameras. In short, this was not your average rock star. "The [crew] came down to my place for a week, and if I was going out somewhere, they'd sometimes get to know about it and just be there," he later said. "They were pretty tactful. Other times, they'd just follow me about." One of the more touching sequences shot focused on Bonham's relationship with his young son, Jason. By then eight or nine years old, Bonzo had got the boy a mini-replica of his own Ludwig drum kit, at which Jason could be seen bashing away in the same distinctive style as his dad.

For Fairport Convention drummer Dave Mattacks, who had now got to know the members of Led Zeppelin well via their shared travels on the road, Bonham's keen interest in teaching his son the drums was completely in keeping with the strong family side of his nature. "Fairport's bassist, Dave Pegg, and I were invited to Bonzo's place for dinner one evening," Mattacks confirmed in 2015, "and we had such a great time. And I just remember this huge jukebox Bonzo had in one of the rooms with a tiny, wee drum kit in front of it. John said 'I've got Fairport's 'Walkawhile' on the jukebox and I've taught Jason to play along. Want to hear him?' Well, we did. So, he calls Jason, puts on 'Walkawhile' and lo and behold, Jason plays along. And he was good. I mean, he couldn't have been more than 9, 10 years old, but he was good..."

Obviously in the mood to play, Bonzo then performed a little miracle of his own. "Afterwards, we're talking in the same room," continued Mattacks, "and I said to John, 'Hey, what's the deal with 'The Crunge'? I can't find where 'the one' is, it sounds like 9/8, but I'm not sure that it is. So John says, 'Let me show you', and he sits himself down behind Jason's tiny, tiny drum kit and just started playing. I kid you not, it sounded exactly like [the record] – that huge Bonham sound. John proved in one bizarre moment, it's little or nothing to do with the equipment, it's all about the player. You can buy the same kit, you can set up the same way, but nobody sounded like John. Funnily enough, his son Jason probably ended up coming the closest..." But not just yet.

Inevitably, Jimmy Page's segments were shot well after his band mates. First up was a short, somewhat bizarre interlude filmed at Plumpton Place, with Jimmy sitting with his back to camera playing a hurdy-gurdy alongside a moat as a pair of black Australian swans swam by. As Massot's lens crept ever closer, Page finally turned around, his eyes now a blazing red instead of their normal hazel green. An obvious special effect shoehorned into frame to reinforce his ever darkening image, Jimmy's demonic visage was probably meant to scare the bejeesus out of the audience. But in reality, it just looked a bit cheap. For BP Fallon, who had then recently joined the Zep organisation as their British publicist (or 'Master of Entertainments'), though Page might have been more than eager to play up the mystery, he was still no eater of souls. "Satanism?" he laughed. "Jimmy and I were more interested in sitting around listening to old Sun 45s that we'd got hold of from [the]

Rock On record stall in Soho! Just because you've got black swans swimming around in your moat doesn't mean you're in communion with Beelzebub..."

Nonetheless, Page's continuing interests in the occult were again underlined when he invited Joe Massot and his crew to join him at Boleskine five days before Christmas in December 1973. While Page had little time to visit his eerie Scottish mansion due to various touring/recording commitments[154], it was obviously still vital to him that his main segment for the movie project was filmed there. More, there were other very specific requirements that had to be adhered to. "Jimmy insisted that his segment was shot on the night of the full moon," Massot later confirmed.

The actual shoot itself proved arduous to accomplish and hellishly cold to boot. With chill winds bouncing off Loch Ness and ice on the ground making conditions treacherous on foot, Page's decision to be filmed traversing up a steep mountainside near the midnight hour did not immediately sit well with Joe Massot. "Well," he later said, "it was quite difficult lighting the mountain at night." But as Jimmy soon found out, not quite as difficult as actually climbing it. "It hadn't occurred to me when I was scrambling up that mountain that I'd have to do half a dozen takes," he later told Q. "Suddenly, it hit me that I'd bitten off more than I could chew. In the [final] film, it didn't look anywhere near the distance I covered. It just looked like I was having a promenade."

The action began in earnest when Page reached the top of the summit. "Jimmy wanted to say something about time and the passage thereof," continued Massot. "[His] was a symbolic tale about a young man fighting his way to the top to meet with the old man of the mountain... Father

---

154 At least one source has it that due to his work commitments with Zep, Page only managed to spend a matter of weeks at Boleskine since its purchase in 1970. He would eventually ask his childhood friend Malcolm Dent to look after the property in his absence. Though something of a sceptic about Boleskine's colourful history, Dent did concede odd things happened there. "Doors would be slamming all night," he later told *The Scotsman*, "[and] you'd go into a room and carpets and rugs would be piled up. We used to say that was Aleister doing his thing."

Time, in symbolism. Jimmy played both parts." In the final scene, Page is helped to the summit by an old man holding a lantern, only to find that the hermetic figure is actually just an older version of himself. With effects achieved in post-production, Jimmy's face ages backwards and forwards in the half-light, his features moving between child to wizened hermit as the footage progresses. "The transformation was done with a life mask, which I still have," he told *Guitar World* in 2008. "Using that as a foundation, they created different faces that showed me as I might look after various ages of life... then they joined the faces together."

Though Massot's explanation of Page's fantasy sequence fitted well with the film he shot at Boleskine, there were other philosophies at play in the scene that Jimmy was keen to clarify. "I was hermetic," he again told *Guitar World*'s Brad Tolinski, "I was involved in the hermetic arts. But I wasn't a recluse... or maybe I was. My segment," he continued, "was supposed to be the aspirant going to the beacon of truth, which is represented by the hermit and his journey towards it. What I was trying to say through the transformation was that enlightenment can be achieved at any point in time. It just depends on when you want to access it. In other words, you can always see the truth but do you recognise it when you see it or do you have to reflect back on it later."

Of course, by making public his private fascinations on film, Jimmy Page was again tempting speculation about dabbling in the dark arts. But like BP Fallon, his former lover Pamela Miller felt any such links were unfounded. "I just think it was a sincere fascination," she later said. "I think Jimmy took a lot out of it, and it came through in the music... that amazing depth and mystery. He was simply interested in otherworldy things. All that selling your soul to the devil, that's all bullshit, none of that ever took place."

With additional footage in the can, Joe Massot set about pulling together a cut of the movie he could show to the band. A $25,000 KEM console was purchased at his own expense to begin the editing process, with the director working furiously from thousands of feet of the 16 and 35mm film stock he had gathered in New York and England. After several weeks on the job, Peter Grant – not unreasonably – asked to see some of the results. Massot provided him and Zep with a few sample cuts, one of which featured them performing 'Stairway To Heaven'. Neither group nor manager were impressed and Grant stopped taking Massot's phone calls soon after. Jimmy Page also proved "unavailable". Still without a proper contract and having to meet the majority of his own costs, Joe was becoming frantic. Yet, somewhat surprisingly, it was at this point that an olive branch was thrown to him from the unlikely direction of Robert Plant, who asked Massot to set up a screening of all his efforts thus far.

So it was in late spring of 1974 that Zep, Peter Grant, the director and some of the group's entourage gathered together to view the results at a preview theatre in central London. Again, it did not go well. When confronted with the sight of Page dressed as an aged hermit – free-flowing false grey beard and all – John Bonham reportedly began guffawing with laughter, dropping most of the chips he had brought with him to snack on. Suffice to say, Jimmy was not pleased with his drummer's impertinence, the guitarist's dissatisfaction perhaps amplified by a sinking feeling that of the film shot, Bonzo seemed to steal the show both on and offstage. Matters worsened when additional footage seemed only to confirm the enviable size of Robert Plant's member, itself barely constrained behind a wall of tight denim. "They thought it was my fault Robert had such a big cock," Massot later said, laughing. But more regrettable than amateurishly shot fantasy sequences or barely controlled crawling king snakes was the unmistakable fact that portions of the music still seemed out of synch with the band performing it, with several intros and endings simply either missing or not tallying with the soundtrack itself.

Inevitably, there would be no happy ending between Joe Massot and Led Zeppelin. After Peter Grant visited the director at his London home to view more segments and again found them wanting, Massot was informed that the group would now proceed without him. At this point or soon afterwards, he was offered a perfunctory sum for his work in exchange for the film stock. Already aware that both band and manager were tiring of him and the project, but still lacking that all important piece of paper outlining exact business terms, Massot had already taken the precaution of hiding the footage at a friend's garage. Thus, when a "representative" of the group came calling to pick up what Led Zeppelin considered rightfully theirs, he left empty-handed but for the KEM editing machine. With the two parties now completely estranged, the whole matter was subsequently handed over to the lawyers to sort out, with Joe Massot eventually receiving some recompense for his efforts and Zep their film.

At this juncture, it appeared that Led Zeppelin might abandon the project for good. Given later shenanigans, it would have been both much easier and cost-efficient to do so. But having already gone to some expense to get this far, Page and Grant were reluctant to drop the idea. Hence, they sought out another filmmaker capable of completing what Joe Massot had started. The man brought in to replace him was director Peter Clifton, a 29-year-old Australian who had previously worked with Jimi Hendrix during his glory years as well as recently overseeing production on *The London Rock 'N' Roll Show*, a faithful visual document of Jerry Lee Lewis, Little Richard and Chuck Berry's storming of Wembley Stadium in front of an ocean of Teddy Boys in August 1972.

Clifton had his work cut out from the off. "I only met Joe Massot once, and he was a nice guy," Clifton later told Chris Welch. "Peter Grant arranged for me to visit his home... and view his attempt at making a Led Zeppelin film. It was complete mess. There was no doubting Joe's talent, but he was in deep waters with his filming attempt." Though Massot had the bones of a great movie in his hands, a "lack of filmic continuity" and those "glaring holes" in the key footage stymied any sense of real coherence. In Clifton's opinion, extensive re-shoots were called for, and quick.

With few if any alternatives to hand, Grant signed off Peter Clifton's recommendation. Like Joe Massot before him, Clifton seems to have gleaned no real joy from working with Led Zeppelin. Desperate to narrow the various gaps in Massot's stock, he persuaded the group to reconvene at Shepperton Studios for five days of additional shooting. Here, Zep tried to recreate the majesty of their Madison Square gigs while the director in turn set about capturing a number of close-ups and long and wide shots he could then insert into already existing footage. While Clifton was originally entranced to have a band of Zep's stature performing for him at such close quarters – "They started playing 'Black Dog' for me [and the crew] and we all got such a shock" – things began to quickly sour. When the director's efforts to patch together new and old film proved more costly and time-consuming than anyone had anticipated, Peter Grant came calling, and often, allegedly abusing Clifton's camera operator/editor Ernie Day when the Hollywood veteran offered an opinion on where improvements might be made. Given that Day had previously worked on David Lean's 1962's masterpiece *Lawrence Of Arabia*, his views might have been worth hearing.

Though Peter Clifton's dealings with the band were predominantly run through the immovable force that was Peter Grant, he retained the distinct impression that behind the scenes, it was Jimmy Page who was really pulling on his strings. "Jimmy needed Peter and Peter loved Jimmy. So having Peter on his side made Jimmy realise that he could make anything happen. Yet, the pair of them turned breaking appointments into an art form." Indeed, when Clifton did eventually get some one-to-one time with Zep's leader, he found their meeting largely unhelpful, with Page supposedly more interested in showing him rushes from another film project he was working on (and to which we will return in due course) rather than concentrating on matters at hand. "Jimmy was the most difficult [member of Zep] to deal with," Peter later told Chris Welch, "because he was the most inarticulate and introverted."[155]

155 Though Peter Clifton saw the film out to the bitter end, his relationship with Led Zeppelin continued to falter. After post-production was completed, Clifton alleged that Peter Grant had his house searched for stolen negatives. Both the director and his family were on holiday at the time. While some stock was discovered, Clifton contested this was simply a collection of the best "home movie" footage shot of Zep and that he had fully intended to give it to band and manager as a gift. The director also reportedly became incensed with the decision to remove the names of those who had worked on make-up, special effects and editing from the film's final credits sequence. In short, Clifton's assessment of his time with Led Zeppelin does not make for pleasant reading. "(They were) the rudest, most arrogant and inhumane people I ever encountered in my 25 years of filming music." That said, there appeared no harsh words for John Paul Jones – "Jones was very sweet, actually, and sparkled as a musician." In later life, Clifton and Grant appeared to reconcile most, if not all their differences. "Peter had changed," the director told Chris Welch in 2001, "and became quite humble."

In the end, Led Zeppelin got their film, but it took them three years from inception to execution to "push the bloody thing" into movie theatres. For a plethora of reasons that will soon become apparent, both Page and the band were repeatedly side-tracked by personal difficulties, horrid accidents or other acts of God (or nature) throughout 1975 and early 1976, with each new occurrence or enterprise taking them away from what at a total cost of $350,000, Peter Grant later dubbed "the most expensive home movie ever made". Even more comically, when the film was finally ready to be shown to Ahmet Ertegun for his seal of approval in the summer of 1976, the Atlantic boss fell asleep, having travelled to a midnight screening at Grant's invitation directly after his wife's birthday party. So upset was Peter at his friend's reaction that he left the theatre in a huff, with Ertegun quickly following him to minimise any perceived slight.

Subsequently sold to Warner Bros. for theatrical distribution (a deal that saw Zep more than recoup their original investment), the film Led Zeppelin christened *The Song Remains The Same* finally received its world premiere at New York's Cinema 1 on October 20, 1976. A starry event, with all members of the band, the Stones' Mick Jagger and country-rock chanteuse Linda Ronstadt also in attendance, the movie house was specially equipped with quadraphonic speakers so as to better enhance the overall sound quality of the concert footage. Unfortunately, when *The Song Remains...* opened in San Francisco and Los Angeles a week or so later, there were no such speakers on hand, resulting in a vastly inferior aural experience for the audience and the severe embarrassment of Jimmy Page.

The sound problem – with a little help from director Peter Clifton – had been rectified by the time the movie arrived in London, but superior technology could not save it from those critics who had already happily proffered their opinion in the US press. According to *Circus'* Robert Duncan, *The Song...* appeared to have been crafted by "junior college students who had just discovered LSD", while *Rolling Stone* took a blowtorch to both the film and the band. "While Led Zeppelin's music remains worthy of respect – even if their best songs are behind them – their sense of themselves [in *The Song Remains The Same*] only merits contempt." Still, it was on British shores that the most brutal and incisive critical shot was fired. "This is one dumb movie," pronounced *NME*'s Nick Kent. "It's dumb because it's excessive, pretentious and grossly narcissistic in turn."

With charges of pomposity, pretension and self-indulgence now squarely levelled at Led Zeppelin, it appeared that *The Song Remains The Same* might well die a commercial death. But the sheer number of people who wanted to see "the magic and mystery" up close and personal ensured its moderate success. By early 1977, the movie had taken a respectable $10 million at the box office, with its profit margins further enhanced by million-plus sales of the soundtrack LP, which reached number one and number two in the UK and US respectively. As ever produced by Jimmy Page with Eddie Kramer again back as engineer to assist him, the double album was in many ways far better value for money than a ticket to see its parent film and – given its hi-fidelity mix – a real step-up from most Zep concert bootlegs doing the rounds at the time. But even Page sounded hesitant as to its value, with an air of penitence sitting heavily over his remarks. "First and foremost, it's a soundtrack album and as such, simply has to be available. There was no editing, really," he continued. "[And] there are loads of howling guitar mistakes on it. Normally, one would be inclined to cut them out but you can't when it's a soundtrack. In its own way... it's an honest album."

Despite all its flaws, and there were many, *The Song Remains The Same* had a number of redeeming features. Certain songs – 'The Rain Song', 'Dazed And Confused' and an extended 'Whole Lotta Love' with its 'Let That Boy Boogie' jam, for instance – still contained the power to transport an audience, and not just those watching the original shows at the Garden back in July 1973 either. For the time being at least, the film also stood as the only decent visual documentation of Led Zeppelin in concert during a period that many would argue was when they were nearing or even at the peak of their powers. As such, it offered a unique insight into what the fuss around Led Zeppelin was all about, as well as allowing us to witness Jimmy Page's uniquely persuasive guitar style.

Whether an off night for him or not, Page's ownership of the stage when soloing furiously throughout 'Heartbreaker' and 'Dazed...' or playing simple bedding chords on the likes of 'Whole Lotta Love' while duck-walking like Chuck Berry was – and still is – a joy to behold. Even *NME*'s Nick Kent thought so. "The camera takes fairly kindly to Page throughout," said the journalist. "His 27-minute 'Dazed And Confused' shows [him]... as a man possessed. Hurtling out the power chords using virtually every limb available to his slight form to bring the point home, often adopting a drop kick move which traverses him around the stage handsomely." But however agile and lithe Jimmy was, he was always going to face the stiffest of competition from Robert Plant. A mesmerising presence, given to teasing his audience, Plant was clearly a hit with female fans. In fact, at one point during 'Since I've Been Loving You' a girl in the audience appears utterly transfixed, sexually overwhelmed by Robert's seductive smile and whatever else caught her eye.

Yet, however magnificent the drumming of John Bonham, the "keyboard mojo" of John Paul Jones or the unearthly howls emanating from Page and Plant, *The Song Remains The Same* still felt like an error in judgement: its frankly daft fantasy segments excessive, imperious and easy to lampoon and, as one critic put it, "the group's live performance not quite 'God-like' enough to merit the fuss or running time." Further, because of its tortuous, three-year route to the screen, the film's final arrival in late 1976 appeared almost anticlimatic, representing a memento of times past (albeit good ones) rather than compelling new evidence of Zep's latest incarnation. Then, of course, were the questions raised around the actual making of the movie. Given Joe Massot and Peter Clifton's claims of financial ill treatment and worse, Peter Grant's surreal gangster scenes and his verbal crushing of a Baltimore promoter now took on both an uncomfortable air of veracity and a real sense of menace, this ugly side of the Led Zeppelin machine a pre-sentiment of even more unfortunate incidents in the future.

Back in mid-1974, however, *The Song Remains The Same* remained little more than an irritating oversight to be solved for Jimmy Page and the band by the ever-dependable efforts of their manager. Besides, Led

Zeppelin now had bigger fish to fry, with Page's dream of complete artistic and financial control for the group he had started six years before taking a new and decisive turn for the better.

CHAPTER 22

Kashmir

While *The Song Remains The Same* occupied the days and haunted the nights of film directors Joe Massot and Peter Clifton with both men struggling to keep Led Zeppelin's glorious vision from collapsing into grand folly, the group's actual attentions had long since moved on to other things. With the best part of five years spent either in the studio or on the road, 1974 was deliberately set aside as a year of relative inactivity, a period when each band member could relax from their responsibilities as rock gods and reflect on "all the good times and money earned".

For all concerned, this meant spending quality time with their families at their respective estates, farms and houses, their individual lives away from Zep as diametrically opposed as they could possibly be from the madness encountered in America and elsewhere. Indeed, John Paul Jones' absence from the collective fold may well have triggered something of a long night of the soul, with the bassist approaching Peter Grant in mid-1974 to inform him of his intention to leave Led Zeppelin for good. "He turned up at my house and told me he'd had enough," Grant later confirmed. "He said he was going to be the choirmaster at Winchester Cathedral." A huge, and it has to be said, unlikely leap in career that would have profound ramifications not only for Jones but also his colleagues, Peter asked the bassist to think carefully about his decision. "I said 'If you want to leave, well, you've got to do what you've got to do'. But I told to him to think about it. I told Jimmy, of course, who couldn't believe it, but it really was about the pressure. He was a family man, was Jonesy..." After due consideration, Jones elected to stay put.

John Bonham, too, had succumbed to severe misgivings as to the amount of time Led Zeppelin took him away from his family, with the drummer's drunken spells while on the road often triggered by feelings of homesickness as much as boredom. Indeed, there was the distinct feeling with Bonham that just one day away from his farm might well be one day too much. "The band were flying somewhere from England and we're all up there in first class, and Bill Wyman of the Stones was there with his girlfriend at the time, Astrid," tour manager Richard Cole remembered in 2009. "Anyway, she was talking to Bonzo and when we were getting off the plane, Astrid pulled me to one side and said, 'Richard, why do they bring a farmer on the road with them?' I said, 'What are you fucking talking about? He's the fucking drummer.' 'Oh,' she said. 'All he was talking about was all the cows, sheep and goats that he owns...'"

Like JPJ, Bonzo and Robert Plant (another country squire-type when time allowed), Jimmy Page found the transition from road warrior to homebody not without its difficulties. In fact, the contrast and come down between the high-energy antics of his life on tour and the clear skies over Plumpton Place could not have been starker. But for Page, returning home after months spent in hotels, studios and planes (no matter how luxurious) offered many a potential benefit, not least of which was a break from his three travelling companions. "We only really socialised when we were on the road," Jimmy later said, "[and] we really came to value our [individual] family lives. Our families helped to keep us sane."

There were other interests in which Page could indulge while back on British soil. In addition to Plumpton Place and Boleskine, he had recently bought another equally striking property, this time in central London's affluent Holland Park. Designed and built to the exact specifications of renowned architect William Burges between 1875 and 1881, 'The Tower House' was a testament to the French Gothic Revival style that had enjoyed a brief upsurge in popularity throughout Victorian Britain at the time. With its red brick façade, Cumbrian green slate roof and jutting cylindrical tower easily marking it out from the surrounding houses, The Tower House had enjoyed a rich history of ownership before Page came calling. From esteemed archaeologist Richard Popplewell-Pullan and two army colonels (Messrs. Minshall and Graham respectively) to Poet Laureate Sir John Betjeman. "I don't see how anyone can fail to be impressed by its weird beauty," said Betjeman "[or] awed into silence from the force of this Victorian dream of the Middle Ages."

After a brief period of neglect, The Tower House was given a facelift in the mid-sixties by Lady Jane Turnbull before being sold on for £75,000 in 1969 to Irish actor and all round force of nature Richard Harris. "I loved the eccentricity of it," he said at the time. "It was built by Burges who also built Cork Cathedral and it was the focal point of Kensington for me when I arrived in London." An astute soul given to purchasing, renovating and then quickly selling on properties, Harris nonetheless tarried awhile in Holland Park, despite the fact he thought that ghosts of children who previously lived at the house still inhabited certain rooms. To placate any restless spirits, he actually bought toys for them. "I love ghosts," he said of his nightly visitors, "I depend on them to guide me through."[156] By 1972, however, The Tower House was finally in Jimmy Page's hands, the guitarist paying £350,000 after Richard Harris brought in Burges' original decorators Campbell Smith and co. to carry out a complete restoration of its stone and plasterwork. "I wanted Burges to be proud of us," said the actor.

---

156 Though Richard Harris claimed to have initially enjoyed the ghosts of The Tower House, there is also reason to believe he may have tired of them. In later interviews, the actor confessed he had been "pestered" by one particular spirit (a boy), which in turn might have been a factor in his decision to sell on the property to Jimmy Page. However, given Harris' proven track record in property investment (it made him tens of millions), this seems highly unlikely...

Outbidding fellow superstar David Bowie (to whom we shall return soon) for the big first prize, Page and his new acquisition were actually a perfect fit, the house's extraordinary inner decorations mirroring his own particular interests in arcane, Gothic and Pre-Raphaelite forms. With painted ceilings full of astrological signs, a library with a sculpted mantelpiece depicting the Tower of Babel at its centre and a further explosion of murals, detailed woodwork and other objects of art (pagan and otherwise), Jimmy could spend forever exploring The Tower House's various nooks and crannies. "I was still finding things 20 years after being there," he told the *BBC News Online* in 2012, "a little beetle on the wall or something like that. It's Burges' attention to detail that I find so fascinating."

Of course, with each townhouse or country pile purchased by Jimmy Page came a further drain on his finances. He probably wasn't losing any sleep. Already a multi-millionaire with an extraordinary source of potential income to be tapped each time Led Zeppelin released a new album or again took to the road, any real concerns around money – then or in the future – were now well behind him. Nevertheless, Jimmy and manager Peter Grant had long planned a bold new move to further enhance the 'bank of Led Zeppelin'. Their latest wheeze, and one fully supported by Robert Plant, John Paul Jones and John Bonham, was to launch their very own record company.

Led Zeppelin were certainly not the first band to harbour such lofty ambitions in this area. In 1968 the Beatles formed Apple Corps Ltd., a sizeable undertaking that found the Fab Four dabbling in film, electronics, retail and even clothes. While most all of these enterprises haemorrhaged money, Apple Records proved far more durable, their long-term ability to sell 45s and LPs by the truckload making it a success when all else failed. Learning from the Beatles' mistakes, the Stones kept their operating model much simpler when launching Rolling Stones Records two years later. Having freed themselves from Decca and Andrew Loog Oldham's managerial successor, the shrewd, but extremely short-term Allen Klein, Jagger, Richards et al. were able to control their own destinies in a distribution deal with Atlantic Records. As such, profits were maximised and overheads kept low.

To old showbiz stagers like Jimmy Page and Peter Grant, taking Led Zeppelin in a similar direction really was a no-brainer. So when their five-year contract with Atlantic came to end on October 28, 1973, they sat down with Ahmet Ertegun to hammer out an agreement similar to the Stones. With Zep now responsible for nearly 25% of Atlantic's overall sales, Ertegun was reluctant to lose primary control of what had become the record company's leading cash cow. But he was also perspicacious enough to understand that by acting as distributors for a new, multi-million selling company, Atlantic would still make a pretty penny. In short, a deal was there to be done. By January 1974, the mechanics of it were in place and Zep had the makings of their own label.

The first question was what to call it. At first, the suggestions were either tragic, uninspired or simply unusable, with the likes of 'Slag', 'Slut', 'Eclipse', 'Stairway' and even 'Led Zeppelin Records' all considered for a millisecond or so before being rightly discarded. But then Jimmy Page curiously suggested 'Swan Song'. In common parlance 'a final gesture' or 'last performance', Page was actually more interested in connecting with the origin of the phrase, which lay in the belief that though largely quiet throughout their lives, swans emitted a beautiful song or lament in the moments before their death. "[It is]," he said, "one of the most beautiful sounds in the world." Initially used by Jimmy as the title of an instrumental he had been working on, 'Swan Song' was now given the considerably bigger responsibility of being the name of Zep's new record company.

With companies came logos and labels. Again Jimmy Page was found to be on point, the guitarist suggesting two swans not unlike the West Australian kind that paddled around his moat at Plumpton Place to serve as inspiration for the former, while also picking out a distinguished, if ambiguous, image by the obscure American symbolist painter William Rimmer (1816–1879) as the basis for the latter. Entitled *Evening (Fall Of Day)*, Jimmy had found the painting in question in a 1971 art book called *Dreamers Of Decadence* and it was said to depict the winged sun god Apollo ascending from Earth at the close of day.

Given that in Greek mythology – a theme well-represented in the various murals dotted around The Tower House – the swan was said to have been consecrated to Apollo and therefore held as a symbol of beauty and harmony by the god and those who worshipped him, there was surely some connective tissue here with the label's name. But others saw different connotations in Led Zeppelin's slightly altered version of Rimmer's original painting, with the Swan Song label supposedly depicting Icarus falling earthwards after flying too close to the sun. "Well, there's the story of Icarus and Daedelus, isn't there?" Jimmy later confirmed to *Mojo* in 2015. "If you think about it in relation to the original Led Zeppelin idea of a lead balloon, [it's] carrying on the original idea of that, isn't it? The idea of the swan song is the dying song of the swan, OK? So there's a parallel."

Another less credible theory was that Swan Song's subtle modification of William Rimmer's *Evening (Fall Of Day)* was in fact a clever artistic cipher for the most notorious of all the fallen angels; to wit, 'The Morningstar', 'The Lightbringer' or, to give his more familiar name, 'Lucifer'. Though Page denied any such association, the rumour mill would run and run on the subject of Swan Song's 'ascending/descending/god/angel/devil' for a while yet, the real truth of the image's meaning further obscured by yet another arcane project Zep's ever-more mysterious guitarist would soon involve himself in.

Away from the myriad possibilities of Swan Song's Delphic symbolism, the practicalities of the label proceeded apace, with a suitable premises found for its offices at 484 Kings Road in London's Chelsea district by the spring of 1974. Strongly associated with fashion and art since the 1960s, when cutting-edge boutiques such as *Granny Takes A Trip* and *Alkasura* drew the great, good, young and trendy through their doors each weekend, the Kings Road had taken a bit of beating by the mid-seventies, its shop fronts now perhaps more shabby than 'shabby chic'. But this didn't seem to bother Peter Grant or the group in the slightest, who were happy to set up shop in a badly lit office block overlooking local traffic and directly above a Royal British Legion club.

For a band and organisation used to shamelessly parading its wealth in the press and travelling on Starships or in the back of limos, the Swan Song base looked like something of a comedown. Yet, with Peter Grant, Page and the band all more likely to make decisions by telephone in the comfort of their country homes rather than travel daily into the smoke for pointless meetings and needless prevarication, practicality won out over opulence every time. "For all their millions, Zep didn't spend a penny doing the place up," Swan Song's long-serving secretary Cynthia Sach later said.

On the occasions that the band did venture into Swan Song's offices, however, they usually brought good manners and levity with them. John Bonham, for instance, was extremely well-liked by staff, his lack of pretence and general air of affability doing much to diffuse nerves among any new recruits. Robert Plant and John Paul Jones, too, had little in the way of airs and graces, one of them content to wax lyrical about his beloved Wolverhampton Wanderers while telling the odd joke, the other more than happy to blend into the wallpaper as he went about his business. "Jones was so quiet," said one employee, "you sometimes forgot he was there."

In fact, it was only when Grant and Page appeared at Kings Road that there was a collective straightening of backs, with Peter's frequent bad moods to be avoided at all costs and Jimmy's quiet, but attentive gaze and will-o-the-wisp personality marking him out as a man apart. "Jimmy was an inquisitive man in awe of his own talent and prescience," Swan Song's office manager/head of promotion Unity MacLean later told *Uncut*. "He was a little bit like quicksilver. Hard to get hold of." Daniel Tracey, a teenager then gaining work experience at the label's office, went a little further. "Unity told me not to look at [Jimmy] or speak to him," he said. "He came in, looking very smart with a black frock coat and scarf. But I'm not joking. It was like an icy cold blast blowing into the room on one of the hottest days of the summer." As ever, Page's legend prevailed.

While the primary role of Swan Song was to provide Led Zeppelin with even more artistic and financial independence, both Jimmy Page and the band were also eager that the label find strong new acts and, wherever possible, sign them. However, based on their own experience of the business, Zep were more predisposed to helping those who could help themselves than act as artistic nannies or wet nurses. "We'd been thinking about [the idea of Swan Song] for a while and we knew if we formed a label there wouldn't be the kind of fuss and bother we'd been going through over album covers and things like that," Page later said. "Having gone through, ourselves, what appeared to be an interference, or at least an aggravation, on the artistic side by record companies, we wanted to form a label where the artists would be able to fulfil themselves without all of that hassle. Consequently, the people we were looking for for the label would be people who knew where they were going themselves. We didn't really want to get bogged down in having to develop artists, we wanted people who were together enough to handle that type of thing themselves."

In the main, the first raft of Swan Song's signings fulfilled at least some of Page's stated criteria with each act bringing something old, new, borrowed and, indeed, blue to the table. From Glasgow, Scotland came Maggie Bell, a razor-gargling, ultra-passionate singer in the mould of Janis Joplin. Managed by Peter Grant since her days fronting R&B stalwarts Stone The Crows in the late sixties, Jimmy would eventually lend a hand on Bell's first solo album for Swan Song – 1975's patchy, but eminently listenable *Suicide Sal* – contributing some tasty bursts of blues guitar to 'If You Don't Know' and a genteel, countrified solo on 'Comin' On Strong'. "I liked Maggie, I was asked to do it and I thought 'Why not?'" Page later told *Mojo*. "My [parts were done] at Tittenhurst Park, the John Lennon studio... I went down there, stayed a couple of hours and just laid down a couple of overdubs."

Another group happy to tuck themselves under the wings of Swan Song were the Pretty Things. Veteran shape-shifters who could list pop, blues, R&B, psychedelica and groundbreaking rock operas (1967's marvellous *SF Sorrow*) on their CV since forming back in the early sixties, the Pretties often came close to breaking into the big time. But with a long-established reputation for being difficult to work with, endless line-up changes destabilising their core and a bad luck streak that would shame Albert King, they were best known as a cult act with a lively past rather than hungry contenders eager to break into the charts. Jimmy Page was eager to change all that. "The Pretty Things were a band that were really changing their music and had done because they probably did one of the best singles way back in the day with

'Rosalyn'," he later told writer Michael Bonner. "That's wild! That's serious! When someone said, 'Oh, some tapes have come in,' I was keen to hear what they'd done because it was always so good! Good writing, good performance from everybody. A fine band."

The canniest of Swan Song's signings was Bad Company, though Zep's new label would have to share the group with Island Records, to whom they were contracted in the UK. A small inconvenience perhaps, but of no great import to new manager Peter Grant, who made certain the lion's share of their earnings would be generated in the States. Formed from the ashes of Free by vocalist Paul Rodgers and drummer Simon Kirke, and aided and abetted by former King Crimson bassist Boz Burrell and Mott The Hoople escapee/lead guitarist Mick Ralphs, Bad Company had the makings of a true rock supergroup from the off. As such, Grant and Swan Song were on them like a rash. "Well, Peter had the original idea of putting a record label together and then he also had designs to sign Paul Rodgers and Bad Company," Jimmy later said. "Theirs was [always] going to be one of the first releases out there."

As part of Free, Paul Rodgers had flown high. Lead singer of one of the few acts talented enough to mount a serious challenge for Zep's early blues rock crown, they had sold records in the millions with their signature tune 'All Right Now' destined to become a dependable part of many a radio DJ's kit bag. But egos, in-fighting and the persistent drug problems of their brilliant but troubled guitarist Paul Kossoff meant Rodgers was starting all over again with a new group on a new label. More than that, he was also taking career advice from the most unlikely of sources. "I remember getting a pep talk from John Bonham," Rodgers later told *Guitar World*'s Alan di Perna. "He summoned us to a board meeting [for Swan Song] in a hotel... when we were in New York and said, 'Now listen guys, we've got a lot of money invested in this label. Don't you go fuck it up. You behave yourself.' Now, this is from John Bonham..." It might be worth noting that at this juncture Bonham had recently taken to wearing a top hat, white boiler suit and Doc Marten boots onstage and off, his new clothes directly aping the attire of 'The Droogs', an ultraviolent gang of rapists and killers featured in Stanley Kubrick's controversial 1971 movie, *Clockwork Orange*.

Still, Led Zeppelin's resident wild man needn't have worried. Bad Company were to be Swan Song's first real success. The band's self-titled debut album – and indeed the label's inaugural American release – was an instant hit on both sides of the Atlantic when it hit the shops in June 1974. Reaching number one and number three in the US and UK, the LP also spawned two huge hit singles with the slow-burning 'Can't Get Enough' and 'Movin' On', both tracks helping *Bad Company* to stay on the British charts for 25 consecutive weeks and sell five million copies Stateside. Help came from board level when, to the delight of a 5,000-strong crowd, Jimmy got up to jam with Bad Co. on September 4, 1974, in New York's Central Park, much to the chagrin of bill toppers Foghat, who were obliged to follow this spectacular unexpected guest appearance.

All of this surely worth a party or two. "Well, there were actually three separate launch parties (for Swan Song) in New York, Los Angeles and London," Rodgers later confirmed. "The English one was actually pretty incredible. It was held in this string of caves down in the south of England [and] I've never really got over it..."

Rodgers was not understating the lunacy of Swan Song's three launch parties, which have subsequently gone down in rock folklore as among the more lavish and debauched soirées of their time. Obviously eager to play right into their own growing legend, Zep and Grant had pulled out all the stops when introducing the label on both American coasts, hiring a goodly portion of New York's Four Seasons Hotel on May 7, 1974 and LA's luxurious Bel Air three days later. At both venues, the great and the good could happily mingle alongside Zep and their new signings with legendary comedian and guest Groucho Marx proving that at 84 years old, he had lost neither his gift for ribald humour or downright rudeness. "Show us your tits!" he was said to have remarked when meeting singer Maggie Bell in Los Angeles.

However, it was at Chislehurst Caves in October 1974 that Led Zeppelin truly excelled themselves, turning part of a 22-mile stretch of subterranean man-made tunnels into something the Roman Emperor Caligula might well have been proud of. "There'd been gigs at Chislehurst back in the time of cavemen, I think," Jimmy later told Phil

Alexander, "and it was flagged up as a place that would be cool to have a launch, so that's where we did it."

Employing a cast of professional fire-eaters, stage magicians (and possibly a few real ones, too), various other lunatics and a near-endless supply of booze, the 'Chislehurst games' have become the stuff of legend. "There were strippers dressed as nuns doing things with candles and crucifixes," said Bad Company's Paul Rodgers some 30 years later. "There was all sorts of drinks and other goodies. I don't think anyone slept properly for three months afterwards. I think that one was [soon] after that that we shakily signed a contract [with Swan Song]. Now I understand what it was all about. It was to lull us into a false sense of security, and it certainly worked, because we had a great time for many years after." The Pretty Things' drummer Skip Allan also confirmed that when it came to throwing a party to be proud of, Zep were simply unrivalled. "Everything you've heard about Led Zeppelin, quadruple it. That's what it was like. Total lunacy."

With the multiple-venue theatrics of its launch and the multi-platinum sales of *Bad Company*, Swan Song had proved itself capable of generating the same levels of publicity and chart-topping success as any established record label.[157] But now it was time to bring in the big guns. Having seen nearly 18 months pass since they had released any new product, and with footage of the band's last live performance at New York's Madison Square Garden in July 1973 still being mulled over by various film directors and editors, a return to action from Led Zeppelin was long overdue. But truth be told, despite their obvious lack of profile, the group – or at least parts of it – had never stopped working. In fact, since Zep withdrew from public view all those months before, Jimmy Page had been furiously stockpiling new material on his eight-

---

157 While true to say that Bad Company would continue to do great business for Swan Song, of the label's early signings, they really were the only act to do so. For a variety of reasons (including a proper lack of promotion), Maggie Bell and the Pretty Things struggled to penetrate the charts, with Bell's *Suicide Sal* and the Pretties' first album for Swan Song – the underrated *Silk Torpedo* – both proving to be commercial disappointments.

track home studio at Plumpton Place. "For me," he later said, "being at home meant I could continue to work on what we were doing."

Away from the prying eyes of the media, Led Zeppelin had actually planned a return to the fray as early as November 1973 to begin work on their sixth album. Dispensing with the previous setting of Mick Jagger's palatial Stargroves in favour of a return to Headley Grange – "I wanted... that wonderful hall ambience," said Page – a mobile studio belonging to Faces bassist Ronnie Lane was specifically hired for the sessions. Coming with it was engineer Ron Nevison, then a brand-new recruit to Zeppelin's cause. "I'd built [the] mobile studio... for Ronnie and successfully used it to engineer much of the Who's *Quadrophenia* album," he later told writer Brad Tolinski. "Since I was the 'hot guy at the time', Zep called up to see if I'd engineer the sessions." However, when there was no sign of John Paul Jones at the appointed time, the keys to the Hampshire mansion and Lane's roving recorder were handed over to Bad Company for use on their debut LP.

Though the band made little of JPJ'S absence, rumours have grown in subsequent years that it was at this juncture – and not, as previously stated, in mid-1974 – that Jones put in his request to leave Zep for the choirmaster's position at Winchester Cathedral. According to Jimmy, the whole story was nonsense from top to tail, with the bassist's late return from a family holiday – and not some mild existential crisis – to blame for his failure to arrive at Headley Grange. "Tell me who your source is on that one?" Page snorted when the 'Choirmaster conspiracy' was put to him by *Record Collector* in 2014. He also poured cold water on the same question when it was asked by *Mojo* a year or so later. "I heard he was late back from holiday. The rest sounds like *Wikipedia* nonsense."[158]

---

158 Actually, when one turns to *Wikipedia*, Page has been quoted as saying that it was illness rather than a late return from holiday that was to blame for John Paul Jones' non-appearance at Headley Grange. "It took a long time for this album mainly because when we originally went in to record it, John Paul Jones wasn't well and we had to cancel the time," he told *Rolling Stone* in 1975. The plot thickens.

Whatever the bones of it, John Paul Jones was very much present and correct when Led Zeppelin reconvened at Headley Grange in January 1974 to again start work on the album. This time around progress was assuredly swift, with the songs Page had brought with him from Plumpton Place now banged into shape while several other fresh compositions quickly joined them. By close of recording several weeks later, Zep had eight tracks to hand, or as Robert Plant more accurately called them "some hot ones... real belters... real off the wall stuff."

Nonetheless, the band's burst of creative energy brought with it another set of challenges. Having caught over 40 minutes of tunes on tape, they now had enough material for "one and a half" LPs. Reticent to throw out any of their new babies with the bathwater, the group made the decision to revisit some previously unheard gems and add them to the list, thus creating a double album. "We figured let's put out a double and use some of the material we had done previously but never released," Page later told *Trouser Press*. "It seemed like a good time to do that sort of thing."

Unearthing a further seven songs dating back as far as July 1970 to join the batch recently cut with engineer Ron Nevison at the Grange, Zep soon had enough for four sides. With additional overdubs recorded at London's Olympic Studios and the whole package mixed by engineer Keith Harwood – "I had a great relationship with [Keith] and he was really sympathetic to the band," Jimmy later reasoned – everything was in the can by the autumn of 1974. In line with the group's return to the road in America, a release date of January 1975 was now actively targeted.

As usual there were delays and, again, most of them focused around the cover of the LP. Since finishing work at Headley Grange, Page had been keen on the album's eventual title adequately capturing the effort and energy that went into its recording. He settled on the rather marvellous phrase 'Physical Graffiti' and now wanted a sleeve design worthy of it. "I actually remember meeting with Hipgnosis and telling them what I wanted," he later said. "When I uttered the album's title, there was a hush. Nobody said anything..."

With Hipgnosis seemingly stumped, the man finally trusted to deliver Jimmy's specific vision "of looking into these different rooms and seeing all these different situations going on in each of them" was US graphic designer Peter Corriston. Scouting New York for weeks before finding a building that offered the precise specifications, Corriston eventually settled on a tenement block in Manhattan's Lower East Side (96 and 98 East 8th St, St. Mark's Place, to be precise). "I had come up [with] a concept for the band based on the tenement, people living there and moving in and out," he later told *The New York Times*. "The original album featured the building with the windows cut out on the cover and various sleeves that could be placed under the cover, filling the windows with the album title, track information or liner notes."

Along with these vital snippets were also several photos, including shots of the Queen, Laurel & Hardy, King Kong and, rather intriguingly, Led Zeppelin in drag; photos reportedly taken at a party thrown by Ahmet Ertegun at LA's infamous Riot House. Page was in no doubt as to which member of the band looked the most – and least – fetching when dressed in woman's clothing. "Who made the best and worst woman?" he said to *Guitar World* in 2005. "Oh, I think Robert Plant takes it for both, doesn't he?"

Inevitably, the intricate tracings of the LP's sleeve design took more time to achieve than first thought. With the cover having to be especially die-cut so as to allow for the windows' "peek-a-boo holes", and the band as ever allowing nothing into the public domain until they were completely satisfied with the results, *Physical Graffiti* arrived in stores a month or so behind schedule on February 24, 1975. Worse still, Zep were already well into the first leg of their latest US tour, meaning those inspired to seek new product by the group after witnessing them live were to be temporarily disappointed. That said, when they did get hold of the LP, its contents were surely worth the wait. Running a gamut of styles, from country stomps, acoustic whimsy and tender ballads to orchestral blues, scorching hard rock and middle-eastern wig-outs, *Physical Graffiti* was easily the most diverse album of Led Zeppelin's career and arguably the best thing they would ever put their name to. "It was," Page said with no particular ceremony or great exaggeration, "a high water mark for us. Even Led Zeppelin's mediocre was always better than anybody's best..."

Physical Graffiti commenced with the cut, thrust, cacophony and clatter of 'Custard Pie' and 'The Rover', two tracks recorded nearly two years apart, but now seamlessly conjoined to provide the album with its adrenalised start. In the case of 'Custard Pie' – hot off the press from Headley Grange – it really was all about Page, his shin-kicking, Chuck Berry-like riff driving the song along in a series of bold stops and starts. Part-referencing the style and swing of Sonny Terry & Brownie McGee's own 'Custard Pie Blues' and with Plant certainly appropriating the phrase "Shake 'em on down" from Bukka White's tune of the same name, those glaring signposts to the work of old blues men were again there for all to hear. But with Jimmy letting rip with a tinny, scalding solo (his guitar filtered through an ARP synthesiser to produce its waspish tone), JPJ bouncing a funky clavinet off Bonham's tank-solid bass drum and Robert wailing away on harmonica like a man possessed, one really didn't much care who had provided the influences.

'The Rover', too, was all bruising guitars and "none-shall-pass" drum patterns, though this time, Led Zeppelin put as much emphasis on melody as they did on energy. Born out of an acoustic blues jam at Stargroves while recording *Houses Of The Holy*, 'The Rover' found Plant singing for peace, love and solidarity while Jimmy, John Paul and John negotiated clever leaps between vamping verses and mellifluous choruses. In this febrile stew of clumping riffs and subtler chord changes Jimmy was particularly effective, his beautifully constructed lead lines recalling the discipline and inventiveness of endless days and nights spent working as a session musician.[159]

---

159 While Page's guitar work on 'The Rover' is among the best of his career, there were also some fraught moments along the way, with engineer Ron Nevison accidentally erasing one of Jimmy's Les Paul overdubs on the track. Though Keith Harwood – who had "safety copies" of the original recording – was able to salvage much of the mistake during the mixing process, Page remained unimpressed with Nevison's error, even going as far as to put "Guitar lost courtesy Nevison" among the LP's sleeve notes. "I remember Ron Nevison saying 'Oh, nevermind...' when I'd ask him something," he told writer Mark Blake in 2005. "I thought he should have changed his name to 'Ron Nevermind', because after *Physical Graffiti*, that's what I thought of him. No, he didn't work with us again..." Thankfully, Nevison continued to work with many other acts as both engineer and producer over subsequent years, including Bad Company, Meat Loaf, Heart, Joe Cocker, Chicago and UFO, among others.

In fact, much of *Physical Graffiti* would reflect Page's continuing mastery of six and 12 strings, his bold use of acoustic and electric guitars, amps and various sound effects brilliantly employed to create mood, texture and occasionally menace. "I'm actually really sloppy," he told *Melody Maker* of his instrumental prowess at the time. "[And] I don't read, except for the musical equivalent of a seven-year-old. But that's how it was on the sessions. If there was any bit I wasn't quite sure about, by the time they were ready to count in, I'd got it off." Still, for all of Jimmy's self-deprecation, he also understood his rare ability to transmute base metal into something a bit more sparkly. "I'm just totally uneducated. But it doesn't really make any difference because every now and then something good will come through..."

There was more proof of this instrumental alchemy on 'Ten Years Gone', a truly impressive deep cut at the heart of *Physical Graffiti* that Page had worked up to speed with Zep at Headley Grange in early 1974. Featuring a winsome lyric from Plant that told of the heartbreaking ultimatum he received from his partner 10 years before, the singer's decision to choose music over love was now supported not only by the bag of hefty royalty cheques every quarter, but also a guitar master class from Jimmy.

Whether displaying an encyclopaedic knowledge of folk, jazz and blues chords or creating a swell of Oriental-themed harmonies to help push the tune along in its more contemplative moments, Page's performance on 'Ten Years Gone' was up there with his very best. "I demoed it at home, the guitars... everything," he later said of the track. "I really was quite passionate about getting that one together." Impeccably arranged and immaculately performed, the venerable producer and career resurrectionist Rick Rubin called 'Ten Years Gone' "The sound of nature coming through the speakers" and he probably wasn't wrong.

Elsewhere, Page was equally in his element when balancing arrangement and performance with innovation and execution. On the vexatious 'Sick Again', he seemed intent in piling on as many overdubs as possible to create an unctuous enough soundtrack to match Plant's bawdy tale of on-the-road excess. The trick was repeated again on 'The Wanton Song'. Like 'Sick Again', another new tune full of propulsive rhythms, combustible Les Pauls and sexual braggadocio, Jimmy this time concentrated on effects wizardry to provide extra spark from six strings, his use of Leslie rotary speakers and backwards echo conjuring up the noise of both injured church organs and out-of-control trains.

The Leslie speakers were back again on 'Night Flight', a chipper little number rescued from sessions for Zep's iconic fourth album and now given a new lease of life on *Physical Graffiti*. With Page's axe swirling against a massed wall of keyboards courtesy of John Paul Jones, Robert was free to wail away to his heart's content, the singer's hearty cries of "Oh mama, well I think it's time I'm leavin', there's nothin' here to make me stay," making the hairs on one's neck stand up like well-trained circus lions.

While the individual members of Led Zeppelin were well-represented in concert, with solo spots from Jimmy, JPJ and Bonzo long a part of the band's set, such occasions on record had been few and far between. Perhaps that was the point. Still, it was a genuine pleasure to once again hear Page strike out on his own with 'Bron-Yr-Aur'. Written at the titular Welsh cottage back in 1970 during the same period that produced the likes of 'Friends' and 'That's The Way', at just two minutes, six seconds long, 'Bron-Yr-Aur' was (and always would be) the shortest composition ever to make it onto a Zep LP. But its inclusion on *Physical Graffiti* proved wise and measured, with Jimmy's jaunty folk instrumental – cut on his favoured 1971 Martin D-28 acoustic and using the same C6 tuning as 'Friends' – lending side three of the album a certain lightness of touch among all the rock, roll and other progressive interludes.

This more stripped-down approach was also present on 'Boogie With Stu', a track once again exhumed from sessions for *Led Zeppelin IV*, this time featuring Jimmy's old friend, Rolling Stones tour manager and barrel house piano expert Ian Stewart. When dropping off the Stones' mobile studio at Headley Grange in late 1970, Stewart had idly perched himself at a stray baby grand that happened to be in the hall of the cavernous mansion and started playing. The result found Page grabbing a mandolin and his fellow band members and then punching the record button. "Stu was playing a piano that was unplayable [and] that was incredible," he told *Mojo* in 2010. A shy man by nature, Stewart was nonetheless a master of all things boogie-woogie, having eaten up the piano styles of Johnny Johnson, Otis Spann and Lafayette Leake while still a teenager. Therefore, for Jimmy to catch him banging away on tape with Zep was quite the coup. "It was too good to miss because Stu wouldn't record," Page confirmed. "He just wouldn't do solo stuff. [But], it did for us..." Initially titled 'Sloppy Drunk' to reflect its loose-limbed feel, the jam between Stewart and Led Zeppelin was nonetheless given a proper spit and polish for its appearance on *Physical Graffiti*, with Page again adding an ARP synth to create a suitably slapping guitar sound and Bonham providing an enhanced, skiffle-like backbeat to further enliven proceedings. Additionally, given that the finished tune was inspired by Chicano teen idol Ritchie Valens' 'Ooh My Head' – and there were growing rumblings around the group's previous appropriation of riffs from old blues songs – Zep were keen to give credit where it was due. Unfortunately, as evidenced in a previous chapter, Valens had perished in a plane crash some 25 years before. They thought the problem could be solved by naming his mother among the writing credits, but Valens' publishers still filed suit for copyright infringement, leading to the first of several out-of-court settlements that would eventually dog the group. "It went quite wrong, really," Page later said of the incident.

Zep were on much safer ground with 'Houses Of The Holy', a track that sounded like no one other than themselves. Though bearing the name of their fifth album, the band had deliberately held off using it on the previous LP largely for reasons of comedy. "We had a perverse sense of humour," Jimmy later told *Mojo*'s Phil Alexander, "so we made the decision to leave it off [the LP] and include it on the next one." There may have been another factor at play. Given its sprightly feel, sticky off-kilter guitar riff and happy-go-lucky disposition (Robert bounded along like he was on laughing gas throughout), the tune might have been a tad too similar in construction to the arguably superior 'Dancing Days' to merit inclusion on *Houses Of The Holy* – proposed title or not.

One song that could simply not be excluded from *Physical Graffiti*, or any other Led Zeppelin album for that matter, was 'Trampled Under

Foot'. Powered by John Paul Jones' restless, shifting clavinet pattern, Bonzo's thumping snare and Jimmy's 'Now you hear me, now you don't' wah pedal intrusions, Zep had rehearsed 'Trampled...' within an inch of its life at Headley Grange during January 1974 to master JPJ's funky central riff. Their efforts were duly rewarded with the track rattling along like some lost Stevie Wonder classic while Robert cleared his pipes over the top. "Greasy slicked down body, groovy leather trim, I like the way you hold the road, mama, it ain't no sin." Full of lascivious wordplay (it's a fair bet Plant wasn't just talking about a man's love affair with his car here[160]) a rack of meaty hooks and some extremely deft clever rhythmic accents, 'Trampled Under Foot' was destined to become both a concert hall favourite as well as a minor US hit, the song reaching number 38 in the charts when released as a single in February, 1975.

It wasn't all cartwheels and lollipops, though. While 'Down By The Seaside' and 'Black Country Woman' were both likable enough, it is debatable whether either track would have been called into action but for the fact that Zep had four sides of vinyl to fill. A curious concoction written at Bron-Yr-Aur in 1970, '... Seaside' was perhaps the better of the two tunes, with JPJ's electric piano floating airily alongside Page's rambling guitar and Robert's lilting vocal before Bonzo broke into his stride, leading an lively, up-tempo middle-section that calmed down again only moments later. As an exercise in Jimmy's much stated desire for light and shade, it all worked admirably well. Yet, at times, one couldn't help but feel that 'Down By The Seaside' was not unlike Crosby, Stills, Nash & Young jamming along with Yes.

Again, 'Black Country Woman' also had its merits. Another refugee from the Stargroves sessions of 1972, '... Woman' has subsequently become best known for the fact that it was actually recorded on the lawns of the mansion as a plane flew overhead, with Plant's laughing

---

160 The lyrics to 'Trampled Under Foot' – originally called 'Brandy & Coke' – were actually inspired by Robert Johnson's 1936 tune 'Terraplane Blues', which found the legendary bluesman extolling the virtues of a classic car (Hudson Motors' six cylinder 'Terraplane') as a sly metaphor for sexual infidelity.

instruction to keep the tapes rolling – "Nah, leave it, yeah" – captured for all time. And indeed, 'Black Country Woman''s relaxed gait was a large part of its charm, the group sounding baggy and breezy as they danced their way around a traditional country blues Robert had originally called 'Never Ending Doubting Woman Blues' (quite the title there). However, for all its genial manners and air of informality, the tune was at best inessential, at worst simply there to fill a gap.

The same could not be said for *Physical Graffiti*'s three remaining songs, two of which were worthy of the highest honours, the other meriting a new category of medal entirely. With 'In The Light', Led Zeppelin again excelled themselves in the potentially tricky domain of progressive rock, the tune's endless drones and high-pitched block vocals then falling away to doom-laden guitar riffage before finally fading out in a Beatles-like blaze of melodic, multi-tracked glory. A particular favourite of Jimmy's, 'In The Light' was one of the album's undoubted highlights, with his tumultuous guitar overdubs at the tune's finale really deserving a paragraph of their own. But for Page, it was actually John Paul Jones' eerie ability to make his keyboard sound like a shehnai (an Indian/Pakistani 'oboe') that should be mentioned in dispatches. "I must say," he told *Musician* in 1990, "John Paul came up with some fantastic things, you know. The synthesiser introduction on 'In The Light' was just fantastic."

'In My Time Of Dying' might have been even better. A magnificent return to their blues rock roots recently cut – like 'In The Light' – with Ronnie Lane's mobile studio at Headley Grange, the song actually had several antecedents. Originally coming to life at the turn of the century as a gospel refrain, it was subsequently updated by both Charley Patton and Blind Willie Johnson in the twenties as 'Jesus Is A Dying Bed Maker' and 'Jesus Make Up My Dying Bed', before eventually being covered by Bob Dylan on his 1962 debut album, with American folk's master poet finally naming it 'In My Time Of Dying'. In somewhat cavalier fashion (and unlike 'Boogie With Stu'), Zep chose to ignore the song's previous lineage and credit themselves as sole writers, though in truth the song that appeared on *Physical Graffiti* bore little or no resemblance to anything that had gone before.

Moving along like some mad blues symphony, Led Zeppelin's 'In My Time Of Dying' might have begun slowly with just the sound of Plant's lonesome voice and Page's cavern-dwelling slide guitar, but it revved up soon enough. Borne along by John Bonham's trademark "Headley Grange drums" and Jones' loopy fretless bass, the track ultimately became "a bible-sized shit-storm" of bottleneck six-strings, wailing vocals and caveman rhythms, with Jimmy, Robert, JPJ and Bonzo collectively railing against the dying of the light over 11 glorious minutes[161]. So galling was the pace, in fact, that Bonham came perilously close to collapse by the end of the take, his coughing enquiry – "That's got to be the one, hasn't it?" – as much a plea for mercy as anything else. "Oh my Jesus" indeed...[162]

Topping all of them, of course, was 'Kashmir'.

Arguably the zenith of Led Zeppelin's achievements, 'Kashmir' had long been floating in Jimmy Page's consciousness, albeit under another name: the ubiquitous 'Swan Song'. Desperately eager to try and get the band involved with the tune, he brought it to rehearsals, but its multitudinous structure drew no great enthusiasm from his colleagues. "It was [attempted]," Jimmy later said, "[but] not with any real conviction because it was a really complex thing to do." A maze of acoustic/electric/acoustic passages, 'Swan Song' evidently didn't do a great job of selling itself to Plant, JPJ and Bonzo. However, Page knew there was something there. After several further passes at his home studio in Plumpton Place, he gradually began to fixate on the track's fanfare-like ending. Here, the breakthrough was made.

---

161 With 'Bron-Yr-Aur' clocking in at just over two minutes and 'In My Time...' an exhausting 11 minutes or so, *Physical Graffiti* features both Zep's shortest and longest recordings.

162 At 'In My Time Of Dying's mighty climax, Robert Plant repeatedly roars the phrase "Oh my Jesus". But some eagle-eared fans have deduced that at times, Zep's vocalist might also be shouting 'Oh Georgina'. When Page was asked by *Mojo* in 2015 as to whether Plant was in fact name-checking a then recent female conquest instead of the Lord, the guitarist collapsed into a fit of giggles. "I'm not getting into that," he laughed. "I just can't!"

"I had a long piece of music I'd been working on, and just on the tail end of it, I... had that riff, that cascade with the brass parts," he confirmed to the BBC's Gavin Esla in 2015. "Then, that [riff went] into the [main] riff and I thought 'Oh, oh... this is something I really want to try.' So I started working on that at home. It [the main riff] was going round, just going round and catching up with itself. I just couldn't wait to get into Headley Grange with John and do this. He loved it, and we just played it over and over again."

As the duo worked hard on finessing Page's lumbering riff and the cascading flurry of notes that followed it, other ideas started to spark in Jimmy's head. "While I was working with John at Headley Grange," he later told *Record Collector*. "I had the idea of using an orchestra. Of course, John took to it immediately. Well, the whole band did. [So] the staccato parts became the brass and string parts." Continuing to mine various sources for inspiration, Page looked to classical composer Benjamin Britten's 'Variations On a Theme Of Frank Bridge' and 'The Young Person's Guide To The Orchestra' as the basis of how those orchestral parts might fit into the overall composition. From there, it wasn't much of a leap towards another torturous instrument Zep had nonetheless exploited to fine effect on previous recordings. "Well," John Paul Jones laughed, "the Mellotron was a bit of an afterthought, but things were heading that way already..."

The last component came from Robert Plant. While holidaying in and around South Morocco shortly after the excursions of Led Zeppelin's 1973 US tour, the singer found himself driving on a roughly cut desert road between Tan-Tan and Guelmim. Struck by the fact that there seemed no end to the long, narrow stretch he was navigating – "It was like a channel" – Plant began conjuring up a lyric full of endless sandscapes, searing sun, Berber tribesman and a quest for the mythical land of Shangri-La. After pulling his words into coherent shape, he came up with the title 'Driving To Kashmir', later truncating down to one single, but eminently memorable word.

The rest really was an exercise in mechanics and hard graft. Confident that he had something potentially monstrous on his hands – "It just felt so intense" – Page stuck with his idea, broke with tradition and employed outside help to get the song over its final hurdle. Hiring Olympic Studios as the setting, Jimmy also hired a small group of brass and string players to bolster its already orchestral sweep, with trumpets and trombones fleshing out the melody and a low-slung cello specifically used to double the main guitar riff. When JPJ's strangely alluring, distinctly Eastern-sounding Mellotron part was added to the recording, Led Zeppelin had finally erected the monolith at the centre of *Physical Graffiti*. "We were all trying to push each other," Jimmy later said, "to create something new, something that hadn't been heard before..."

That they certainly did. With 'Stairway To Heaven', Led Zeppelin had crafted a song specifically designed to pull the listener along to it, each new passage and chord struck building inexorably towards an emotional, heady climax. 'Kashmir', however, offered no such easy denouement. Instead, it provided a journey to far more distant and unsettling lands, with one having to closely follow the path of Jimmy Page's ever-circling, talismanic riff to stay safe from surrounding danger. Brilliantly structured, gorgeously orchestrated and – by eschewing the traditional Western scale – wilfully exotic, 'Kashmir''s wondrous world of Mellotrons, cascading fanfares and narcotic drum patterns[163] found Page and Led Zeppelin operating on a whole new level of musical complexity. *Tight But Loose*'s Dave Lewis was quick to agree. "It was just six years from 'Good Times Bad Times' to 'Kashmir'. Six years. Who'd have thought that could happen? Jimmy did. Just like the Beatles went from 'Love Me Do' to *Sgt. Pepper...*, Zep made those leaps in musicality and composition. Each member was hugely important in

---

163 One tall tale has it that John Bonham might have had some pharmaceutical help when creating 'Kashmir''s unique "soporific" drum pattern, the sticksman reportedly turning up to rehearsals for the song armed with a bag of 100 Mandrax tablets (or 'Quaaludes', as they are better known in the USA). Legendary for their sedative effects, the story goes that Bonzo's resultant, crab-marching beat was more to do with his being heavily 'under the influence' than any great desire to play particularly slowly. As one source said, "File under 'Unlikely'..."

achieving that, but it was Jimmy at the start who knew he could do it, that they could do it."

Though Page was undoubtedly sure that Led Zeppelin had hit the mother lode with 'Kashmir', he was still reticent to boast about it too much at the time. "'Kashmir' really was groundbreaking, with the orchestra and stuff. [It was] brilliant," he later said. "But you know, when I was doing the promotional stuff [for the LP], I didn't really bang on about it that much because of the fact that we'd used an orchestra. So I was actually talking more about 'Trampled Under Foot' or 'In The Light'. But, you know, I knew what 'Kashmir' was. I knew what 'Kashmir' was before we'd even recorded it."

With the likes of 'In My Time Of Dying', 'In The Light' and 'Trampled Under Foot' as good as anything they had ever cut and 'Kashmir' gathering together Led Zeppelin's individual talents into one exquisite, collective whole, *Physical Graffiti* was arguably the band's most complete album yet. And for once, some of the critics weren't holding back on the superlatives in praise of the group, with *Melody Maker*'s Michael Oldfield leading the charge. "[*Physical Graffiti* is] a work of genius, a superbly performed mixture of style and influences that encompasses not only Led Zep's recording career so far, but also much of rock as a whole. They can take as long as they like with the next album. *Physical Graffiti* will last 18 months or 18 years. And then some."

Now bucking the trend set in their previous encounters with Zep, *Rolling Stone* also seemed to warm to the LP, even if writer Jim Miller singled out Jimmy for the majority of praise. "The album's, and the band's, mainspring is Jimmy Page, guitarist extraordinaire. It was Page who formed Led Zeppelin in 1968, after the model of such guitar-oriented blues-rock units as Cream, the Jeff Beck Group and the Yardbirds, where Page, a former session man, had first come to prominence. And it is Page who continues to chart Zeppelin's contemporary course, not only as the group's lead guitarist, but also as the band's producer. *Physical Graffiti*," he continued, "testifies to Page's taste and Led Zeppelin's versatility. Taken as a whole, it offers an astonishing variety of music, again produced impeccably by Page."

Still, there remained trace elements of the magazine's previous, sour dissatisfactions concerning the worth of Jimmy's colleagues. "Not that this album will convince the doubters," Miller concluded. "Anyone with an antipathy to the posturing of Robert Plant or the wooden beat of John Bonham, be forewarned: A Led Zeppelin is a Led Zeppelin is a Led Zeppelin."

In his review of *Physical Graffiti*, *Sounds'* Steve Peacock chose to concentrate on a perhaps more plausible chink in the double-LP's armour, with his dissatisfactions centred around its overall length and use of filler material. "...*Graffiti* is the first Zep album since the first Zep album that I can imagine myself wanting to explore beyond the call of duty," he said at the time. "It is by turns brain-numbingly intrusive, exhilarating, over-stretched and effectively concise... [but] if the albums were sold separately, I'd buy sides three and four." It was a view that writer Chris Welch was happy to expand upon in 2015. "*Physical Graffiti* was a good album with some obvious stand out tracks," he confirmed. "'Trampled Under Foot', 'Houses Of The Holy' and 'Kashmir', of course. But I also thought there were quite a few filler tracks on there, too. Heresy, but might it have been better as a single album?" In fact, for Welch, try as they might, Zep would never quite deliver the ultimate testimony to their talent. "I'm being a bit controversial here I know, but I actually don't think they made the ultimate 'Zeppelin' album. The first two were pretty solid, but I just don't think they achieved making the ultimate statement. The Beatles did it with *Sgt. Pepper's...*, but no, I don't think Zeppelin did. I know they wanted to..."

One thing that most all could agree on was how much thought and effort Page and Led Zeppelin had put into the running order of *Physical Graffiti*, with its songs deliberately sequenced to create a real sense of ebb and flow over 83-odd minutes of music. "The real genius of *Physical Graffiti* is in its sequencing," said Dave Lewis. "Like the White Album or *Exile On Main Street*, it all flows perfectly. The tracks bleed into each other so well, from straight ahead rock to wild exploration. Melancholy, darkness, light and with 'Sick Again' ending it all so wonderfully." Unsurprisingly, Jimmy was wont to agree. "The running order of the songs on *Physical Graffiti* was very important," he told writer Mark Blake. "It wasn't just thrown together haphazardly."

A peach of an album no matter how you chose to play it, *Physical Graffiti* once again reaffirmed Led Zeppelin's unrivalled commercial dominance both in Europe and the States. Going Top Five in France, Austria, Spain and Norway soon after its release in late February 1975, the double set also predictably went to number one in both the UK and USA, spending 27 and 41 weeks respectively in and around the Top 30 of both countries. However, on this occasion *Physical Graffiti* was also joined by all five of Zep's five previous LPs in the charts, marking another record for a band that now specialised in breaking them. "The audience was ahead of the record company," a representative of Atlantic later said. "I never saw an album sell as much as *Physical Graffiti*. You'd go to stores and there were lines [with] everybody waiting to buy the same record."[164] As Swan Song's first official release by the band, Peter Grant – as improbable as it might seem – was probably turning cartwheels with such news. "*Physical Graffiti?*" said Dave Lewis. "Yep, it put Swan Song on the map, didn't it? It really takes some beating, that album..."

With over one million copies of the LP sold before it even it even arrived in shops, their latest US tour already breaking as many records as their album sales and a cavalcade of equally in-demand concert dates booked well into the summer of 1975, Led Zeppelin continued to exude invulnerability from every pore of their being. "I genuinely don't think people understand how big Zep were by 1975," Dave Lewis confirmed. "They were really bigger than life. In a pre-internet world, they were like... gods or something, though, of course, getting to that point hadn't been easy. But, then... well, the wheels started to come off. In fact, the whole story of Zep post-1975 became a bit of a tragedy."

---

164 In 1975, *Physical Graffiti* was the first album to ever reach platinum status (one million units in the USA) on advance orders alone. By mid-2015, worldwide sales of the LP were closing in on 16 million units.

Indeed it did. But there would be at least one last blaze of glory before the airship began its final descent to Earth.

CHAPTER 23

In The Light

Some argue it was 1973 that was the golden year to see and hear "the miracle in action". Yet others have it that 1972 was actually the one. Based on later recorded evidence, they might well have a point. For a nostalgic few, 1970 was another strong contender, with the band's lusty show at London's Royal Albert Hall just one outstanding highlight among an ocean of memorable gigs. But for many, Led Zeppelin reached the very peak of their powers in 1975. "Majestic", "Brilliant", "Simply untouchable" ran some of the headlines, and from the outside looking in, there was little doubt as to their supremacy. "1975," said an admiring Dave Lewis, "was when Led Zeppelin really ruled the roost. At that point, I really don't think there was a bigger or better live band on the planet."

Having been absent from view for the best part of 18 months, Zep's return to the road in early 1975 marked one of the most highly anticipated tours of the year, if not the decade. In the event that any proof was needed, when the group announced they were to play 34 US dates from mid–January to the end of March, all 700,000 tickets sold out in a matter of days, with 60,000 of them snapped up in just four hours for their three shows at Madison Square Garden. "By that point," Chris Welch laughed, "it had all gone thoroughly bonkers."

But for all the attendant hoopla, it didn't start particularly well. Following two warm-up dates in Rotterdam and Brussels, and only days before the beginning of their American onslaught, Jimmy Page put the fear of God not only into the band but also manager Peter Grant when he injured one of his most prized assets. Catching the ring finger of his left hand in a metal door when exiting a train at London's Victoria Station after travelling up from Plumpton Place, a collective gasp of breath shot across the entire organisation as news of the accident hit. "I just went numb with shock," Page later said of the moment his digit cracked.

With a lighting rig the size of a large rocket, a 70,000-watt PA system, a 45-man road crew and a fleet of large trucks already booked and ready to go, any cancellation or deferment of the American gigs would cost time, effort, wages and, much worse, huge loss in revenue. Faced with such a potentially grim scenario, Jimmy was left with little alternative but to grin and bear it, the guitarist using painkillers, Jack Daniels and several ice packs to get him through Zep's first tranche of US dates, while also dropping his own lengthy showpiece – 'Dazed And Confused' – until his fingers felt up to the task. "It [was] so damn futile," he later growled, "I couldn't play the fucking way I know I should."

There were other, early wobbles to contend with before Led Zeppelin reached their stride. As evidenced, niggling design issues with the sleeve of *Physical Graffiti* meant that the double-LP landed in US record stores several weeks after the band had commenced their tour. In the end, the delay proved of little consequence to sales (indeed, steadily growing anticipation for the latest album may well have worked in their favour), but its lateness in arriving nonetheless irritated Page and Peter Grant. Further, the American winter had a particularly deleterious effect on Robert Plant's health, with the singer succumbing to influenza after only three gigs. Dragging himself through the opening dates, Plant was finally forced to raise the white flag in Chicago, with the group uncharacteristically having to cancel a show in St. Louis while Plant recovered. Normally a beacon of health both on and off the road, Robert had also been in the wars a year before, when a "hush-hush" operation on his throat temporarily halted progress during the recording of *Physical Graffiti*. Indeed, there is some evidence to suggest that even after he returned to active service at Headley Grange, Plant's voice was still not fully recovered, his usually limitless range sounding somewhat fragile and out of step on the outro of 'The Rover'.

On this occasion, Robert's brush with ill-health allowed his three colleagues the opportunity to veer off schedule for a precious day or two, with each member having very specific ideas as to where the group's private plane – the omnipresent Starship – might take them, Jones favouring the Bahamas, while Bonham argued for Jamaica. When the Starship's pilot threw cold water on it all by pointing out that the plane was not licensed to leave American airspace, Page got his way, with everyone heading to Los Angeles where he could cuddle up with Lori Mattix. On the plane Bonham was sparko, a casualty of Smirnoff blue label, while Jones belted out 'My Old Man Said Follow The Van' on organ as Peter Grant sang along. Watching all this from close quarters was *Melody Maker*'s Chris Charlesworth, who'd drawn the plum assignment of reporting on Zep's triumphant return to the US from both the ground and air. What he saw impressed him enormously, but troubled him, too. John Bonham now seemed to positively hate the prospect of leaving his family for even the shortest time, which maybe explains why his drinking was accelerating to new levels while on tour, with rumours of heavy drug use to match. "Bonzo had been drinking vodka on the way to the airport and passed out soon after getting the plane, so the roadies put him to bed," said Charlesworth. "After about three hours he woke up and, well, he lurched down the aisle, saw one of the stewardesses and tried to mount her. Very upset she was, almost inconsolable, and for all the right reasons..."

Though Grant tried to manage the situation by repeatedly apologising to the girl while packing a clearly still very drunk Bonzo back from whence he came, in the end it was actually Jimmy Page who took control of the situation. "Yeah, it was Jimmy who managed to calm the stewardess down and a very good job he did of it too," recalled Charlesworth. "He put his arm around the girl, spoke very softly to her and apologised profusely. Charm personified, Jimmy. A leader doing his work, you might say..."

A deeply unsavoury episode that only served to strengthen Bonham's reputation as a 'house angel/street devil', the Starship incident also confirmed that beneath their apparently indestructible image, Led Zeppelin were beginning to genuinely feel the burn of fame. Aside from Bonzo's acting out and JPJ's recent doubts about his place in the band, there were other cracks that needed rapid papering. Peter Grant's constitution, for instance, was showing signs of siege, those occasional visits to health farms halting his weight gain only for a time before a quick return to bad habits undid all the good work. Grant's emotional state, too, had taken a recent pounding with Zep's manager undergoing a painful and protracted divorce from his wife, Gloria. Even Richard Cole, a man seemingly made of titanium and concrete, was showing signs of wear and tear, his disappointment at not having been given a senior role at Swan Song leading to bad moods and an ever-escalating use of drink and drugs.

Suffice to say, when Zep fully reconvened their musical activities at North Carolina's Greensboro Coliseum on January 29, their performance was a tad muted. Nevertheless, Charlesworth had a taste of rock dynamics at their very highest level that he remembers to this day. "You felt as if you were actually travelling with the President on Air Force One when you were on the Starship," he said. "At that point, Zep were in their own bubble, a luxurious, huge bubble. They had their own plane, police escorts to and from the airport and were travelling in the best limos to the best hotels or biggest gigs. Even the hangers on got nice hotel rooms, including me. You really were in the presence of rock royalty, and let's remember, this was all being road managed by Richard Cole on Peter Grant's instructions. A lawyer accompanying them, doctors on hand, security men keeping unwanted people away – it was an incredible operation."

While John Paul Jones' recent brush with the choirmaster's position at Winchester Cathedral hinted at his own dissatisfactions with the rigours of the road[165], Jimmy Page was also not immune to the price fame was

---

165 One story suggests that as his children grew older, JPJ became increasingly reticent to tour during school holidays, preferring the company of his family to the howls and whoops of Zep's audience.

exacting from Led Zeppelin. Though now more than a decade on from the various maladies that had ended his tenure with Neil Christian & the Crusaders, Page was still not the healthiest of souls. As engineer Eddie Kramer confirmed, Jimmy often suffered from stomach problems, with the additional burdens he placed on himself as producer, primary songwriter, lead guitarist and leader of the band surely not helping his condition. By 1975, Page also began to show visible signs of wear and tear: spectrally thin, his arms and torso were more akin to a gangly, underfed teenager than a man entering his thirties. As time came to show, some of this might have been for purposes of image, but as the joke went, "When Jimmy turned sideways, he actually disappeared." There were other rumours, too. Like many in the Led Zeppelin camp, there were now concerns that Page was occasionally dallying with the hard end of Class A substances, with hints that heroin as well as cocaine were on the guitarist's pharmaceutical menu.

Still, if Page and his colleagues were ever in danger of falling prey to their excesses or becoming corrupted by the power they could wield, Peter Grant was always on hand to smooth every surface, and nullify every threat. No matter his own personal circumstances, "Big Gee" ensured the train – or in this case, the Starship – kept 'a rolling: "Grant had the Zep operation working like clockwork," reasoned Charlesworth. "They were the first band to locate themselves in one city within two hours' flying distance and then travel from there to 10 or so gigs via plane. They didn't even have to unpack their cases. On Peter's instruction, Richard Cole would be there after every gig, with these big red bathrobes ready to wear as they came offstage. He'd scoop 'em up after the encore and whisk them away to the airport while the crowd were still in the stadium cheering for more. Come 1975, Zep were like a small army with Jimmy and Peter Grant calling the shots and wearing the epaulettes..."

Following a distinctly rocky start, then, Zep were soon back to their peripatetic best, with the group roving across the States and Canada like a flock of frisky cockerels throughout February and March of 1975. As ever, the quartet peppered their concert set with several new tunes: the rollicking 'Sick Again' took up a regular and well-deserved spot as the second number of the show, while 'Trampled Under Foot' became a mid-gig highlight as well as something of an updated showcase for the keyboard skills of JPJ. Unfortunately, however, neither 'In The Light' (which again was perfect for displaying Jones' synth talents) or 'The Rover' made the transition from record to stage, though in the case of 'Custard Pie', the song was rehearsed for inclusion on the tour before being mysteriously discarded again.[166]

Of *Physical Graffiti*'s other tracks, predictably both 'In My Time Of Dying' and 'Kashmir' took pride of place in the band's readjusted set list, though in the latter's case, the results could be uneven, especially at earlier gigs. While Zep made a magnificent fist of raising the bones and spirit of an old blues song to a brand new generation with 'In My Time...', the inherently hypnotic quality of 'Kashmir' caused them all sorts of stumbles, with various members of the band losing track of where they were and what was coming next, especially in the song's convoluted middle-section. Through sheer effort of will – and no doubt, a few choice comments from Page – the in-concert teething problems 'Kashmir' had succumbed to were soon rectified.

Offstage, there continued to be other niggles, irritations and, in one case, genuine cause for concern. Before, during and after several shows audiences turned surly, with pockets of violence erupting at certain venues as emotions ran high. "At Greensboro Coliseum," Chris Charlesworth later confirmed, "about 500 fans tried to storm the rear of the arena, with bottles and debris flying here, there and everywhere. In fact, three of the band's five limos took a hit." Another date in Boston was also cancelled (though also later rescheduled) when a similar riot broke out over ticket sales, while in Philadelphia on February 8 a security guard set upon a fan so badly that Jimmy was forced to intervene from the stage. "There is a responsibility to the audience," he later reasoned, "[because] we don't want anything bad to happen to these kids." For those seeking a touch of irony, Robert Plant was now regularly announcing John Bonham

---

166 As was nearly always the case with Zep, certain songs from *Physical Graffiti* had received a public airing well in advance of the LP's release, with 'Black Country Woman' and snippets of the riff from 'The Rover' played onstage as early as 1972.

as 'Mr. Ultraviolence' before his solo spot on 'Moby Dick', the singer obviously poking fun at his old friend's *Clockwork Orange*-inspired attire.

Perhaps in their own way as distressing as the occasional outbreaks of civil disobedience and over-zealous security staff were reports of death threats to the band. While Page had personally received some very odd letters in the past – his well-publicised interests in the occult acting as something of a lightning rod for certain factions of society – the 1975 US jaunt saw an upsurge in such correspondence. "We had some vague death threats earlier in the tour," Jimmy explained to *Rolling Stone* at the time. "I imagine that makes the armed guards a necessity, but... *Christ*. This is one thing that really bothers me. I don't think we're a band that's hated by any means. I get good, warm feelings from our fans [and] we're not the sort of band people really want to be nasty to."

There was one more unnerving occurrence that surely gave both Page and those charged with protecting him serious pause for thought. During Zep's now well-established three-night stand at LA's Forum (March 24, 25 & 26), which also incidentally marked the end of the band's US tour, a woman reportedly asked to meet with Jimmy backstage. When her request was denied by Danny Goldberg, she elected to leave a note. It warned of a "bad energy" surrounding Page. The person in question reportedly turned out to be Lynette 'Squeaky' Fromme, a former member of Charles Manson's notorious killer cult The Family, and soon to be convicted of the attempted assassination of US President Gerald Ford. "I don't know about that," Jimmy later told *Mojo*'s Phil Alexander. "That's not to say it didn't happen, but it could well have been kept out of my sight. There were a lot of weird things that went on around that time, some of which you heard about, some of which you didn't. In some cases, it's just as well that you didn't hear about them to be honest..."

With Zep's 1975 'winter to spring' jaunt across the USA and Canada, the band not only regained its touring muscles after nearly a year and a half of inactivity but also re-established their brand and presence in what had always been the group's biggest financial market. Equally, away from the vast profits generated by such a lengthy spell in the stadiums and arenas of the States, Led Zeppelin also received some of the better notices of their career. For one, the previously nemesis-like

Rolling Stone now seemed intent on building bridges with Page and co. After the pleasant(-ish) review accorded *Physical Graffiti*, the magazine now sent a sympathetic voice in the form of rookie reporter Cameron Crowe on the road with them.

Still a teenager at the time, Crowe came with few if any of the pre-conceptions that had marred *Rolling Stone*'s previous dealings with Zep. Instead, he seemed content to simply enjoy the music and watching the games unfold than reopening any old wounds concerning the band's crowing about dollar signs. "At a party hosted by Zeppelin in honor of the Pretty Things [in LA]," wrote Crowe in the spring of 1975, "Bonham threw several stomach punches at *Sounds* correspondent Andy McConnell. McConnell, who'd had an amicable meeting with the drummer earlier that afternoon, shined a flashlight in Bonham's face and cracked, 'You're an ugly fucker aren't you?' Bonzo responded by knocking McConnell across the room."[167] Business as usual, then.

The general mood of reconciliation concerning Led Zeppelin was also apparent in *Billboard*'s assessment of the band, with the publication happily flying the groups' colours from their own mast. "The band has long been the target of critical barbs for their crashing volume and seeming sameness of their material," reasoned the publication, following Zep's last date at the LA Forum. "Yet, in an age when headline acts are often boring, sloppy and create no excitement at all, this British quartet stands out as a masterful example of what rock'n'roll was meant to be." Whether it was master US publicist Danny Goldberg's good work finally coming to pass or simply a new breed of writer ready to assess the group without the weight of the past on their shoulders it appeared Zep were finally getting their critical dues from Uncle Sam.

---

167 It wasn't all punch-ups. At the same party, Jimmy finally got a chance to meet one of his all-time folk heroes, the wonderful Joni Mitchell, whose tune 'Woodstock' Zep had recently taken to incorporating into passages of 'Dazed And Confused'. However, as he confessed on the night, Page was unsure at first as to how to approach her. "If she's been hit on half as many times as I've been hit on tonight," he told Cameron Crowe, "she (won't) want to know." In the end, the two struck up an easy conversation.

In the same way that Led Zeppelin were receiving just kudos for their work in the States, UK audiences were about to be granted the full spectacle of what their US cousins had grown used to in previous years. At the beginning of 1975, Robert Plant strongly hinted that Zep wanted to create something truly special when they returned to the British stage. "We want to find somewhere," said the singer, "where we can make it into a bit of an event." The band were now ready to deliver on their promise. In a bold and at the time innovative move, Zep announced three shows at London's Earls Court, a massive exhibition centre capable of holding at least 17,000 people per night. Presumably giddy at the prospect of seeing their heroes on such new and exciting terrain, tickets for each concert sold out in a matter of hours, forcing Peter Grant to schedule two further gigs on May 17 & 18. When the numbers were finally in, over 85,000 had paid up to £2 each for the band's homecoming. This was a long way from entertaining the locals at The Fishmonger's Arms in Wood Green.

Of course, there were a few downsides to the package. With Earls Court being the only location at which Zep would appear, fans faced the prospect of travelling from all over Great Britain to watch them perform in London[168]. Conversely, the quartet's "full American show" was being flown over for the gigs, meaning that laser displays, flashing backdrops, dry ice machines and the odd explosion or two were also coming to town. To cap it all, a huge TV screen was to be installed way above the band's heads, providing a live feed from cameramen filming below so that everyone – even those at the very back – would not miss a second of the action taking place onstage. Unsurprisingly, promoter Mel Bush sounded positively evangelical when addressing the press. "[There is a] demand for these shows," he said, "unprecedented in the history of rock music." Now, all Led Zeppelin had to do was be utterly brilliant.

---

168 To counter worries over travel and general access to the venue, Peter Grant and promoter Mel Bush struck a deal with British Rail, which agreed to publicise the ease with which fans could get to Earls Court. The wheeze became known as the 'Zeppelin Express Physical Rocket' train service. One really couldn't make this stuff up.

Sticking rigidly to script, that they were. A "monument in mind-blowing excess", the band's five-night stand at Earls Court probably deserved all the superlatives that were thrown at it at the time and, indeed, in decades since. With Zep serving up their audience treasure upon treasure over the course of a set lasting on average an astounding 240 minutes, there was little doubting their sincerity to provide value for money or a spectacle worthy of a Roman circus. Delivering over 60,000 watts of audio firepower (the sound level was crushing at times), vast amounts of dry ice billowing from the stage at regular intervals and an enormous sign screaming their name, just in case one had forgotten who was onstage, Led Zeppelin were unafraid of making the grand gesture. But as the bootlegs also confirm, the songs were pretty epic in scope, too.

Whether delivering barn-storming rockers ('Sick Again', 'Rock And Roll'), progressive head music ('No Quarter', 'The Song Remains The Same'), a 20-minute acoustic interval (now incorporating 'Bron-Y-Aur Stomp') or the cream of their crop ('Stairway To Heaven', 'The Rain Song' and 'Kashmir'), the band were simply peerless. "This," one wag at *Melody Maker* quipped, "was the best exhibition Earls Court have ever put on." In fact, when the Zep came to a halt after the stutter and flow of 'Black Dog', 'Heartbreaker' and 'Communication Breakdown' at the end of their final night at Earls Court, there appeared to be genuine puzzlement in the crowd. After nearly three and a half hours of fine tunes, riveting musicianship and the highest of musical drama, no one, it seemed, factored in it actually had to end. "Well," said Charlesworth, "At that point, they were in a class of one, weren't they?"

Having the time of his life at the centre of it all was Jimmy Page. At heart the same music-obsessed youth John Hawken had witnessed throwing shapes and poses on the stage alongside Neil Christian in 1962, the only difference now was that Jimmy had better toys to play with and longer songs in which to show them off. And what a consummate showman he had become. Gibson Les Paul dangling almost at his knees, cigarette jammed insouciantly into the side of his mouth and pale and thin[169] as a sheet of paper, Jimmy was the archetypal British rock guitar god. Clapton might have held the title for a while, Beck was surely the best at getting round the neck, Keef had the renegade outlaw angle all sewn up and windmill maestro Townshend would always be the most athletic. Yet, when it came down to it, Page was now really the one calling the shots. "Sure, Jeff Beck was probably a better player and Eric was a real purist of the blues, and you know, no disrespect to either of them," said Dave Lewis. "But Jimmy had that persona, that aura and air of mystery that separated him from the others..."

By 'Earls Court 1975', Jimmy Page was also the proud possessor of one of the very best suits in rock'n'roll. Like the legendary Johnny Cash, Page had always been a man who knew the power of wearing black, though in his case he added a few more colours to the palette to enhance the effect. Sewn on to a short jacket and semi-flared trousers was an array of elaborately rendered dragons, the fiery, mythical creatures ablaze with the rich oranges, reds and whites sometimes found in Chinese and Japanese art. Twisted around the fabric of Jimmy's suit in bold, flowing patterns, these oriental fire-breathers[170] (if that's indeed what they were) appeared to almost come alive under the stage lights, giving the guitarist's onstage movements a new, other-worldly dimension. When one added the various other glyphs and talismanic sigils also emblazoned on the fabric – astrological signs for Capricorn, Scorpio and Cancer as well as the ever-present 'ZoSo' – Page's 'Dragon suit' was as much a mage's ceremonial robes as any radical fashion statement.

169 By the sounds of it, Page was quite regimented about keeping his weight in check. Though only 130 pounds at the time of Zep's 1975 US tour, he appeared genuinely keen to lose a bit more while on the road. "[Jimmy] often wouldn't eat for days on tour – he weighed 130 pounds and wanted to get down to 125," wrote Lisa Robinson for *Vanity Fair*, "... he'd been making vitamin-enriched banana daiquiris in his room – for sustenance..."

170 In Western tradition, dragons were often seen as arbiters of chaos and wrongdoing, the creatures perceived as evil. However, in East Asian mysticism they are a far more benevolent entity, representing fertility with additional links to heaven and the purity of water. As touched on before, the dragon is also linked with alchemical symbolism in China, denoting spiritual power and notions of immortality.

Of course, Page had become increasingly adept at managing and manipulating his own image over preceding years. From his earliest days in the Yardbirds, he had juxtaposed Nazi and Confederate symbols to create intrigue and more than a little controversy too, with one Scottish crowd actually spitting at him in 1966 for wearing the then notorious 'Iron Cross' as part of his stage outfit. In fact, the 'Birds had often run into problems for their outlandish garb, with the band regularly confronted on the streets of the USA. "Indeed," Chris Dreja later said, "it was 90% straight Americans [at that time] and they found Jimmy very weird. The Confederate hat and Nazi regalia pinned on the same costume didn't go down too well." Further, the theme of dragons wasn't exactly new for Jimmy either, with his Yardbirds-era, Jeff Beck-gifted Telecaster brandishing a vivid painting of the creature on the front of the guitar. Still, the 'Dragon Suit' was entering bold new territory even for Jimmy, its eerie colours and mystical connotations making him look to all intents and purposes like a modern-day Paganini.

That said, it was more likely that Page was simply playing with his own archetype and the fashion demands of a post-glam rock god than summoning up any demons on the stage of Earls Court. After all, "Well, much has been made of the whole Dragon suit thing, of Jimmy 'the showman'," said Dave Lewis. "But if you look back at the earliest part of the band's career, it was all jeans, beards and plimsolls. It was only when the industry changed that Jimmy really went with that. Of course, he always had a flamboyant streak – you only have to look at what he wore in the Yardbirds to find it. And there's the art school connection to be taken into consideration too. But I think Jimmy's visual development as a showman – the dragons, the shooting lasers – grew with the success of Zep. That's not to say he didn't revel in it at times, but so did the fans. Say what you will, Jimmy Page was the coolest man in rock 'n' roll'. Probably still is."

For John Paul Jones, who once boasted that by simply putting on a baseball hat, he could walk off the stage at any Zep gig in any city and disappear unnoticed into the crowd[171], Page was just doing what

---

171 Keen to blend into the wallpaper whenever he could, Jones frequently changed the length and style of his hair to further enable his anonymity.

he did best: providing American and British crowds with a 'guitar superhero' they could watch in awe, play on their stereo or pin to their walls in the form of a poster. "[Showmanship's] very important," JPJ told *Guitar World* in 1991. "It's just that I was never very good at it, mainly because I'd always forget! I'd say, 'I really must do this move or that move', but then the music would start and I'd forget about everything else and just end up concentrating on playing. But Jimmy, well, he was a born showman and a great musician. It was all very easy for him."

Though they would later play to larger crowds and sell even more records, it would not get any bigger for Led Zeppelin. By performing over five nights at Great Britain's largest exhibition centre, a line in the sand had been drawn for the group with even Peter Grant now unsure as to where they could meaningfully go next. "[Peter] said, 'Look, there's nothing else I can do for you guys,'" Robert Plant later said. "'We've had performing pigs and high-wire acts, [but] there's no more I can do because you guys now really can go to Saturn.'" Yet, for all the thousands of people in attendance and the waves of adulation subsequently generated, the Earls Court gigs were not a financial success. Strangely, for the always cost-efficient Jimmy Page, on this occasion at least the numbers didn't seem to matter. "We were so determined to do the same sort of show and more [than] we'd being doing in America that we came out of it with only a few hundred pounds over the five days," he later told *NME*. "But it didn't matter because the vibe was so electrifying."

Faced with confirming their own godhead or flying a rocket ship into space to try and find a venue big enough to house them, Led Zeppelin decided instead to scatter to the four winds Page had called to each night onstage. With a lengthy break before they were next due back on the American road in the late summer of 1975, there was time enough for each band member to take a holiday or simply stay at home contemplating recent victories. In Jimmy and Robert's case, they brought their respective families together for a holiday on the Greek island of Rhodes, though Page left early for a another appointment in Italy. The rest, however, decided to stay on.

It proved a fateful decision. On August 4, 1975, the Austin Mini Plant had hired to get everyone around spun off track and hit a tree. The resulting crash brought injuries to almost all passengers[172], with his daughter Carmen suffering a broken wrist and son Karac a fractured leg. Plant's wife, Maureen – who had been driving – was the most severely injured, sustaining both a fractured skull and broken pelvis that would lead to a period in intensive care. Plant, too, took a real pounding, with the singer's elbow, ankle and several other bones all fractured in the accident. "I was lying there [in hospital]," he later said, "in some pain trying to get cockroaches off the bed and the guy next to me, this drunken soldier, started singing 'The Ocean'..." Though in the south of France at the time of the crash, Peter Grant responded almost immediately, despatching Richard Cole to arrange for the party to be airlifted back to London for treatment.

Horrible for all concerned, the incident in Rhodes unsurprisingly also had profound ramifications for Led Zeppelin. When it became clear that it would take quite some time for Plant, his wife and their children to recover from their injuries, plans for the upcoming US tour were promptly scrapped. With over 100,000 tickets for their opening shows in Oakland already sold and a further tranche of dates scheduled for Pasadena, New Orleans, Florida and elsewhere also on sale[173], the loss to Zep's coffers was to be substantial. "It was just strange that it happened within a week of [US tour] rehearsals," Jimmy later said. "It was just like someone saying 'No, you're not going to do it.'"

More, despite the fact that Plant was in extremely poor health, the decision to bring him back to England had jeopardised his tax exile status, meaning that he and the rest of the band could potentially lose a small fortune unless he departed from Blighty soon. "We had the second tour of the US all lined up," Grant later confirmed to Chris Welch, "as we

---

172 Reportedly, Jimmy's daughter, Scarlet – who was holidaying with the Plant family – was also in the car at the time of the crash, though it appears she was uninjured.

173 In addition to Zep's US dates, the band had been scheduled to play warm-up gigs in Scandinavia, as well as a brace of concerts in South America following their latest Stateside jaunt. All were suspended in lieu of Robert's injury.

were going to be away from England all year." Faced with such stacked odds, Robert was promptly decamped to the safe financial haven of Jersey where he could convalesce and the group might also join him.

An unfortunate contrast to the triumph of Earls Court, Plant's accident put a halt in Zep's gallop just as the group were reaching the finishing line. However, all was not lost. Far from it, in fact. Never one for letting anything get in the way of his true will, Jimmy Page was soon pushing Led Zeppelin onwards and upwards again, taking his band's dilemma by the scruff of the neck in a way even he described as "urgent and attacking".

"Yep," Robert laughed, "we made 'The Wheelchair Album'..."

CHAPTER 24

Achilles Last Stand

Thus far, 1975 had been quite the year for Jimmy Page. With *Physical Graffiti*, he and Led Zeppelin had crafted, then released what many would come to believe their finest album. Though suffering a somewhat rocky start, the band's latest brace of American dates had also been a triumph. Breaking box-office records as they went, the tour acted as a commercial springboard for Zep's recorded output, with not only *Physical Graffiti* but all five of their previous LPs re-entering the US charts. The group's success was not only confined to the States. Overwhelming popularity at home saw Led Zeppelin perform an unprecedented five nights at London's Earls Court, with 17,000 fans attending each gig in a state best described as wonderment and awe. "How can anyone," wrote Jack Haynes to *Melody Maker* after witnessing the concerts, "even try and put the experience into words?" Number one albums on both sides of the Atlantic. Multi-platinum sales. Ticket demand at an all time high. In short, Page had good reason to be turning cartwheels.

Nonetheless, away from the stage and recording studio, there were problems. By all accounts, Jimmy's romantic life had recently seen its fair share of ups and downs, after the guitarist appeared to encounter temporary difficulties with long-term girlfriend Charlotte Martin. An affair with Krissy Wood had seen the British model leave her husband –

former Face and then brand new Rolling Stone guitarist Ronnie – for Page, only for things to stumble soon after, with the pair both returning to their respective partners over subsequent months. Elsewhere, Jimmy was also rumoured to be involved with Bebe Buell, a stunning brunette actress/model/singer who had been named *Playboy* magazine's 'Playmate of the Month' in November 1974.

It didn't end there. In addition to Wood and Buell, Page was still nominally attached to Lori Mattix, his not-so-old flame whenever he visited Los Angeles. Only former paramour Pamela Miller now seemed to be out of the picture, though as time would tell, not quite out of the story just yet. "In early 1975... Jimmy had Lori... waiting for him to get tired of Krissy and Bebe," author Stephen Davis later told *Uncut*. "His life was intense." And very probably, physically exhausting too.

Of course, Page had a proven track record in handling difficulties – professional, romantic or otherwise. Known for his "iron discipline", the only time Jimmy ever seemed to publicly lose the run of himself was when critics refused to accept or acknowledge the quality of Led Zeppelin's music. In this regard, one had some genuine sympathy for him. A session musician for many a year, Page had played alongside the very best bands and performers, thus knowing full well the true worth of his own group. Therefore, when Zep were criticised for their "lack of artistic flair", "crass obviousness" or plain old "thud and blunder" without any great justification, his blood pressure must have rapidly approached boiling point.

Yet, Robert Plant's accident on August 4, 1975 presented Page and the band with a whole new set of issues to contend with. Up to this point, he, manager Peter Grant and Zep as a whole had exercised a steely determination over their collective fate, utilising hard graft, business nous and occasional musical genius to always keep them on track. Due to a simple but unexpected bend in the road, that control was now potentially compromised. A tour had been cancelled, and worse still, due to the extent of Robert's injuries, there were no guarantees as to when – or even if – Led Zeppelin might return to the fray.

"Robert's leg was in plaster and apparently it wasn't 100% that it was going to heal properly," Jimmy told *Musician*'s Matt Resnicoff in 1990. "That's what I was told at the time anyway. So, as you can imagine, it was all a bit hairy... there was a lot of tension there." Despite this potentially grim prognosis, the guitarist was in no mood to let the band slip away. Calling on 'Thelema', 'true will' or whatever else you might choose to name it, Page personally set about removing as many obstacles as he could. Determined to get Zep working again as quickly as possible – and very possibly gain critical distance from all those romantic entanglements too – he became the prime mover in persuading Plant and the others to record a new album as soon as the singer's health allowed. "It was like two fingers to [the] things that destroy other bands," he later told author Chris Salewicz. "We just required the challenge of working fast and simply, [so] we all went back to square one... a basic structure and a minimum of rehearsal."

Briefly meeting up on Jersey where Robert was facing the dual challenge of managing his convalescence while also avoiding the UK taxman, Zep discussed their new project in rough terms. After this collective spell together, Plant then moved onto Malibu in pursuit of the late summer sun and further recuperation. However, he was soon joined by fellow tax exile Page, leading to a fertile spell of song-writing, with Robert's understandably more reflective lyrics being fused to Jimmy's rather more spirited riffs and chord progressions.

Come October 1975, the duo were ready to present the results to Bonzo and JPJ at SIR Studios in Hollywood, with the whole band now banging the compositions into some sort of shape. Yet, Jimmy was still keen not to overcook the pot. "A bit of analysis and structure," he said, "but not too much. It was all about retaining that sense of spontaneity." After three or so weeks of rehearsal, they were ready to record. The destination this time was Musicland Studios in Munich, Germany, where Zep arrived in early November. Though long a favourite city of Page's – he reportedly first became acquainted with its charms while in the Yardbirds – the onus from day one was squarely on work. "Apart from one night out in Munich," he later said "the rest of the time was spent in [Musicland]."

By now, Led Zeppelin were well-used to marshalling their energies in the stale environment of the studio. Indeed, they could set their clock as to what worked for them. "The approach to recording was always very similar," Jimmy told *Metal XS* in 2015. "First capturing the ambiance of the room, in this case, Musicland. The reflective surface, the drums... and getting the energy that you're trying to encapsulate in the recording." Then, it was simply a case of seducing whichever muse wished to come out and play. "If [one song] wasn't quite happening, we'd stop and go on to something else," he continued. "The essence was always in capturing the atmosphere, the feeling."

That said, on this occasion, there were differences to negotiate, not least of which was Robert's fragile condition. With his leg still heavily in plaster, Zep's singer was forced to record his vocals by either propping himself up to the microphone on crutches or from the seat of his wheelchair. He was not a happy camper. "Physically, I was really frustrated, [and] I think my vocal performance on it is pretty poor. It sounded tired and strained," he later said. Feeling under the weather, under strain and a tad claustrophobic to boot, Plant was obviously not himself. "I was just furious that I couldn't get back to the woman and the children that I loved[174]," he continued. "And I was thinking, 'Is all this rock'n'roll worth anything at all?'"

Thankfully for Robert – though perhaps not for the rest of the band – Led Zeppelin were on "a hell of a schedule" in Munich, with only 18 days of studio time booked before the Rolling Stones came knocking at Musicland's doors to take over the complex for the recording of their own album, *Black And Blue*. For many a group, this timeline might have caused a collective breakdown. But Page was in his element, the former sessioneer determined to capture everything he could before Jagger and co. ended the party. "[I] just had to lay it down, more or less," he later remembered to A-Zeppelin. "First track... second track, you know, really fast working on that."

There was no hint of exaggeration here from Jimmy. Working up to 20 hours a day alongside engineer Keith Harwood, their furious pattern

---

174 Plant's wife Maureen did make several weekend trips to Munich to cheer up the singer, though according to Peter Grant, "Robert was pretty depressed when she went away."

of industry even included waking each other up at the recording/mixing desk every time sleep threatened to undermine their efforts. The whole thing came to a surreal head when Page was left with only a matter of hours to complete all his guitar overdubs for the LP. Nonetheless, the deed was somehow achieved.[175] "All the guitar overdubs on *Presence* were done in one night," he later recalled. "I didn't really think I'd be able to do that... but everything sort of crystallised and was just pouring out. But I was very happy with the playing on that whole album. There was a certain maturity to it, I think..."

A whirlwind in the making, Led Zeppelin's sixth album was completed on November 27, 1975, precisely a day before the American holiday of Thanksgiving. Feeling that the word perfectly encapsulated the heady mood of optimism he felt on finishing the project, Plant duly suggested 'Thanksgiving' as the LP's title. Unfortunately, Robert's [rather good] idea didn't tally well with what the designers at Hipgnosis had in mind. "There was no working title for the album," Jimmy later explained. "The record-jacket designer said, 'When I think of the group, I always think of power and force. There's a definite presence there'." Under orders from Jimmy to provide something that encapsulated this concept, Hipgnosis' George Hardie went all out to create the most eye-catching – and some might say downright peculiar – sleeve he could.

Using fifties-style *Life* magazine-like photographs of ordinary Americans at home, work or at play as the foundation of the design, Hipgnosis inserted a small black obelisk in the midst of each image, its presence in the family living room, the office or even on the golf courses deliberately creating an inexplicable, slightly eerie element to the scenes of thorough nondescript ordinariness surrounding it. Cheeky as ever,

---

175 Some reports have it that Page actually asked for two further days grace from the Rolling Stones camp so the whole project – including his guitar overdubs – could be completed in Munich. However, when the Stones finally arrived to pick up the keys, Mick was "reportedly amazed" that Jimmy and Zep had met their self-imposed deadline. Given that the making of certain Stones albums have run to months (if not years), Jagger's reaction should come as no great surprise.

Hipgnosis had clearly drawn their inspiration from Stanley Kubrick, with 'The Object[176]' bearing more than a passing resemblance to the unfathomable monolith at the centre of Kubrick's 1968 sci-fi movie *2001: A Space Odyssey.* "The cover was very tongue-in-cheek, to be quite honest," Page later laughed. "Sort of a joke on *2001.* I think it's really quite amusing."

That said, at the time Jimmy was intent on keeping a very straight face when it came to enquiries about the cover to Zep's new LP. "There is a link between the artwork and the music, [but] the artwork is such that you could look at it and put your own interpretation on it," he told *Melody Maker's* Harry Doherty. "I'm sorry to be elusive, but I don't think I should say that it's this, that or the other because it's an ambiguous thing. It's not right for me to lay down my own impression because somebody else might have a more illuminating one." One thing he was willing to emphatically clarify, however, was the record's name. Batting aside Robert's suggestion of 'Thanksgiving', Page also ignored Hipgnosis's preferred title of 'Obelisk'. "[They] wanted to call it 'Obelisk'," he said. "To me, it was more important what was behind the obelisk." But Page did like George Hardie's original term 'Presence' when describing the band. Again exercising that famous iron will, the guitarist held out until there were no more objections. Jimmy favoured 'Presence'. *Presence* it was.

As Hipgnosis began pulling together the final design specifications for the LP's sleeve – inevitably, the intricacies of the cover were again to cause minor delays[177] – the band were free to kick their heels until

---

176 According to John Bonham, Hipgnosis' specially designed 'Object' did indeed have mysteries properties. "While I was away my wife (was sent) one of these objects (at home)", he said in 1975. "They had a tape machine running and the children were singing. Anyway, and this is the gospel truth, when they played it back, there was another 'sound' on the tape. That's something to think about, eh? She put it outside. She wouldn't have it in the house." Others, however, have likened the obelisk-like shape to "a piece of liquorice twist stuck on top of a bible."

177 Though there were minor delays in its production, *Presence's* final sleeve design was impressive enough to see both George Hardie and Hipgnosis nominated in the category of 'Best Album Package' at 1977's Grammy Awards.

its release. Still in tax-exile mode, all four returned to Jersey during December 1975 where a hastily scheduled appearance at a local bar threatened to descend into farce before it had even begun. Determined to exercise their gigging muscles after such a long period off the road, Peter Grant organised a brief set for Zep at Behan's West Park nightclub.

Unfortunately, when the owner announced to those assembled (and there weren't many) "Tonight, we present Led Zeppelin!" no one batted an eyelid, thinking it was all a joke. It was only when the group sheepishly emerged from the wings that the penny actually dropped. Handing in a short but sharp set to the now delighted punters, a frail Robert was still forced to perform sitting on a chair. Nonetheless, on New Year's Day, 1976, he took his first unaided steps since the accident. "One small step for man," he quipped, "and one giant step for six nights at Madison Square Garden..."

One year and five weeks on from the release of *Physical Graffiti* – an impressive feat, given Plant's precarious state of health during at least some of that period – *Presence* landed in record stores on March 31, 1976. To say it was Jimmy Page's baby would be understating the case and then some. Though Robert, Bonzo and JPJ all made their undoubted mark, *Presence* was an album dominated by Page, its production and arrangements, influences and compositions representing an almost musical totality on the guitarist's part. In simple terms, by refusing to let the group capitulate in the face of Plant's injuries or wallow in any notions of self-doubt, Page had mounted something of a one-man rescue mission on *Presence*. Given the results (and some of Robert's barbed lyrical swipes on the disc), whether assembling Zep so soon after the events in Rhodes was the wisest of decisions remained debatable. But it is, nonetheless, what he did. "*Presence* is as dark, light or joyful as you want to see it," Jimmy later said. "There's a real collection of energies there..."

Leading from the front was album opener and Page's opening statement, the all puns intended but still quite breathtaking 'Achilles Last Stand'. A cantering rocker full of melodic twists and turns, '... Last Stand' was a travel brochure of a song, with Plant's lyrics detailing the band's recent globe-trotting adventures in avoidance of the tax man, particularly he and Jimmy's road trip across Morocco and Spain just before the pair fatefully ventured onto Rhodes. "Into the sun, the south, the north," sang Robert, "at last the birds have flown..." Full of references to the Atlas mountains, "sandy lands" and "eternal summer's glow", Robert reportedly became so excited after hearing the track during a playback in Munich he actually fell over, threatening to undo all the good work on his recovery thus far.

However, 'Achilles Last Stand' really did belong to Jimmy. Flirting with Arabic scales and Flamenco flourishes, Page's guitar sounded as well travelled as Robert's lyrics, his Gibson Les Paul creating a soundtrack that helped conjure up all that blistering sun, sand and dust in the comfort of one's own living room. Intent on building up '... Last Stand' "like the façade of a Gothic building, with layers of tracery and statues," Jimmy had poured overdub upon overdub at Musicland until reaching his stated goal. "'Achilles Last Stand' has the most overdubs," he later told writer Lisa Robinson. "There must be half a dozen going at once. I knew that every guitar overdub had to be very important, very strong within itself to identify each section." A frantic companion piece to the equally cosmopolitan 'Kashmir', 'Achilles Last Stand' was destined to become another of those Page/Plant compositions that found a new and much more complicated life when later introduced on the concert stage.

'For Your Life' was a far more straightforward tune, though with a little digging it did offer real clues as to Robert's state of mind after the fateful events of Rhodes. Based around a typically dirty-sweet riff from Page, the track had been born "on the spot" during a studio jam in Munich, with Robert adding some tart lyrics he brought with him from Malibu. Obviously reflecting on all those wild nights in LA only to now find them seriously wanting, Plant sounded tired both of his injuries and the whole rock star existence. "In the city of the damned... you go no lower, the next stop's underground."

While Zep's singer wrestled over memories of groupies, cocaine, squeezed lemons and the vacuous nature of LA nightlife, Jimmy was working in a brand-new guitar, with 'For Your Life' marking the introduction of a 1964 Lake Placid Blue Fender Stratocaster to his instrumental palette. Reportedly purchased in 1975, the Strat not only allowed Page to add rumbling, tremolo-bar assisted chord crashes to 'For Your Life', but also a deliciously trebly solo, its splenetic tone a striking contrast to the usual thickness of his Les Paul.

Another song that caused severe tapping of the foot was 'Royal Orleans'. Birthed this time in Hollywood during Zep's frantic rehearsal period of October 1975 – "We started screaming in rehearsals," Jimmy later confirmed, "and never really stopped" – 'Royal Orleans' found the band at their very funkiest. All stops, starts and bumps on the musical road, the track's various meanderings sounded like a hard rock version of Sly Stone, James Brown and the Meters, with JPJ and a bongos-wielding Bonzo having the time of their rhythmic lives (indeed, their peerless work on the song earned the duo their only song-writing credit on the album). Not that Page was outdone, though. Beefing up the song's various strands via the use of copious overdubbing, Jimmy was again a dominant force on 'Royal Orleans', his inventive, wobbling solo almost lost among all those other sliding riffs and chopping chords.[178]

This manipulation of time, tone and melody was also present on both 'Candy Store Rock' and 'Hots On For Nowhere', two tunes that in some ways exemplified the general sense of quirkiness at the heart of *Presence*. With 'Candy Store Rock', Jimmy had initially "leant" on Scotty Moore for inspiration, borrowing one or two of the guitar-slinger's old riffs from those fifties Sun sessions with Elvis Presley for his own specific purposes. Nevertheless, as with so much of Zep's work, what Page had originally borrowed became something else entirely when the band were finished with it: in this case, "a rollicking, timpani-infested, psycho-shuffle", with Jimmy's rockabilly guitar lunges, Plant's cod-Elvis impersonations and JPJ and Bonzo's jumping beat creating an uncategorisable stew that even they found hard to describe. "['Candy Store Rock']," Robert later told Dave Lewis, "is far beyond the realms of pop, jazz... well, anything."

---

178 The title of the song actually alludes to the 'Royal Orleans' hotel in the city of New Orleans. Located at 621 St. Louis St., it was a favourite haunt of the band while touring the South.

In its own way, 'Hots On For Nowhere' was even more out there, but for very different reasons. Pinging around several odd guitar figures – again being applied with maximum wang-bar abuse by Jimmy on his new LPB Fender Strat – Plant's 'sing-songing' vocal actually disguised a rather blunt lyrical attack on two of his closest allies. "Now, I've got friends who would give me the shoulder," he sweetly intoned, "I've got friends who would give me fuck all..." Very possibly annoyed at having been dragged back to the microphone before he was ready, Robert's not-so-veiled shot across the bows at Page and Peter Grant would not have gone unnoticed at the time by either. The first instance of open rebellion – or at least pithy insurrection – from the normally placid vocalist, it would not be the last, with Plant's tendency to dig in his heels when Page tried pushing him forward becoming a real bone of contention between the two over subsequent years.

Back in 1976, however, the duo appeared wholly reconciled in time for 'Tea For One', as Robert's words mourned the protracted absences from wife Maureen while recording *Presence* in Munich. "'Tea For One' sums up that period for me, really," Peter Grant later told Chris Welch. "That was Maureen's song." Written by Plant under the lyrical guise of a lonely man counting down the hours until he next sees his lover – "It's about ultimate loneliness in a hotel room," Page later said – 'Tea For One' had all the forlorn qualities of the very best midnight blues songs, even if its similarity to Zep's own 'Since I've Been Loving You' was a little too close for comfort around the song's bridge.

That said, like 'Since I've Been Loving You', 'Tea For One' also acted as a platform for one of Jimmy's finest and most emotionally satisfying solos, even if the prospect of actually committing it to tape had filled him with dread beforehand. "It suddenly hit me... that everybody had played a blues number and there were so many musicians whose forte it was, like Eric," he confirmed to *Guitar Greats*. "[So], it was one of the last solos to go on, because I feared it a bit and it had this atmosphere to it. [But] when I heard it back, I was really pleased with it."

Finally, tucked away at the centre of *Presence*, and acting as gatekeeper between sides one and two, was 'Nobody Fault's But Mine'. Built upon a slow, mesmerising central riff from Page and a hide-and-seek backbeat from John Bonham and JPJ, 'Nobody's Fault...' might have had more rhythmic stops and starts than a faulty traffic light, but in its own way the tune shone as brightly as 'Achilles Last Stand'. A triumphal return to the type of hard blues rock that had established the band's reputation and featuring madcap, almost atonal harmonica blasts from Robert, there was yet another flavour to be had from the track which did not immediately recall the Mississippi Delta.

With its three distinct guitar parts – "Two in unison, one in octave" – and wavering Arabian melody line, 'Nobody''s Fault...' again carried a sense of Plant and Page's recent travels to Africa and beyond. "I couldn't say there was a number [completely] built around a Moroccan rhythm on the new LP," Jimmy told *Melody Maker* at the time, "but I definitely learned a lot from Morocco which I can relate to on songs. The whole thing that goes on in Morocco is incredible. It's trance music basically, and when you see the sorts of things that are done by the power of music as such, one couldn't help but sort of reassess what one thought one knew already." According to Page, all such expeditions to foreign climes fed into the music he was writing for Led Zeppelin. "There have been sort of phrases and melodies, rhythms that have been picked up on [with] the travels though Morocco and places like that, which all get consumed. You take it all in and it comes out in the music...[179]"

Playful, wilfully eccentric and even occasionally joyous, *Presence* found Jimmy Page knee deep in the rock'n'roll and blues that originally inspired him as a teenager. More, with 'Achilles Last Stand' and 'Nobody's Fault But Mine', he and Led Zeppelin had again successfully negotiated the tonal complexities introduced on the likes of 'Friends' and 'Kashmir', the music of North Africa and south-western Spain now as deep in the band's veins as that of Chuck Berry, Elvis Presley

---

179 While the music of 'Nobody's Fault But Mine' might have contained vague hints of Jimmy and Robert's travels in Africa, the actual lyric of the song bore remarkable similarities to Blind Willie Johnson's own 1928 classic of the same name. Unfortunately, Johnson's name was omitted from the writing credits of the version that appears on *Presence*. Plant would later rectify said omission by giving full credit to Johnson when introducing the song live in concert.

or Howlin' Wolf. Of course, like every Zep LP before (and after) it, *Presence* wasn't quite perfect. All those fifties-style riffs and stop-go rhythms had a tendency to bleed into one other, and by his own admission, Robert Plant wasn't quite 'on point' at times. But given the circumstances around its recording, getting anything at all on tape was surely cause for celebration. "*Presence* was a forced album, one made on the haunches so to speak," said Dave Lewis. "Three weeks from start to finish, no messing around."

Lewis also cut to the quick as to who the real driving force behind *Presence* was. "*Presence* is really Jimmy Page's album," he continued. "Every song, every riff, every note, Jimmy's driving it. And as for 'Achilles Last Stand'... well, it's astounding and captures the essence of him. Pure grace under pressure. From coming off stage at Earls Court in 1975 when he and the band were at the top of their game, then for it all to fall away and then to try and get that sense of perfection back. I think '... Last Stand' personifies that. 10.26 minutes of pure guitar genius and surely his best work. The Stones were coming into the studio, he had a day to do the overdubs, but somehow he managed it. Yes, 'Achilles Last Stand' for me is Jimmy's finest achievement with Zep, no question."

In March 1976, however, the critics seemed less sure about *Presence*, with opinion somewhat divided as its overall worth. For *Melody Maker*'s Chris Welch, there was absolutely no question as to the record's qualities. "Led Zeppelin have come among us again," he said, "[with] an album that has pace, direction and tremendous style." *Rolling Stone*'s Stephen Davis was also giving, though with certain caveats attached. "*Presence* confirms this quartet's status as heavy metal champions of the known universe, although Page and Plant are masters of the form, emotions often conflict and results are mixed. But make no mistake, *Presence* is another monster in what by now is a continuing tradition of battles won by this group of survivors." Yet, *NME*'s Charles Shaar Murray, was less seduced by the LP and not afraid to say so. "No Mellotrons, no acoustic guitars, no hats-off-to-Harper or reggae piss-takes," he wrote in his review. "Now the bad news. There ain't one single candidate for 'The Led Zep All Time Killer Hall Of Fame' in the whole caboodle..."

There was some truth in Shaar Murray's remarks. With the exception of 'Achilles...' and 'Nobody's Fault...', *Presence* did lack some of the classicism and finesse of Zep's best work, the frantic circumstances of its recording lending the album a real immediacy and freshness, but also a feeling of hurriedness about certain tracks. No great surprises there. For Jimmy Page, this was actually to the disc's benefit. "There's a lot of urgency about it," he said. "There's a lot of attack to the music. I think that's reflecting a state of mind of being constantly on the move. You know, no base because of the [tax] situation. That is definitely reflected."

Also reflected in the lyrics and on the album's cover sheet were other aspects of the making of *Presence* that were perhaps more problematic. As evidenced on 'Hots On For Nowhere', Robert Plant's anger at his circumstances (within the group as well as without) seemed palpable, with no prizes given for guessing the object of his apparent ire. John Paul Jones and John Bonham might also have had reason to feel somewhat dissatisfied. Steadily ramping up their share of song-writing credits since the release of 1969's *Led Zeppelin II*, Page's decision to join Plant in Malibu to work on new material had deprived them of the opportunity to contribute more strongly to the LP during its initial stages, as just one tune ('Royal Orleans') in the credits bore out.[180]

Given that Led Zeppelin always showed a united front in public and Jimmy had built the band on the dual foundations of steely discipline and innate professionalism as well as "bloody good music", it is impossible to know exactly how irritated Plant actually was or whether JPJ or Bonzo actually felt excluded from the writing process. (God knows, they might have been happy enough for the break.) However, manager Peter Grant later gave a clear indication of how difficult the record had been to complete. "An uphill struggle," he told Chris Welch. "It was difficult in the writing and rehearsal stage and then we were pressured into recording it quickly. It's not," he concluded, "one of my favourite albums..."

---

180 Indeed, unlike any other Led Zeppelin LP, *Presence* features absolutely no keyboards, with John Paul Jones just contributing bass.

Despite a tortuous birthing process, like *Physical Graffiti*, *Houses Of The Holy* and most every Zep album before it, *Presence* had no trouble scaling the heights of either the US and UK charts. Landing at number 24 in the *Billboard* Hot 100 at the end of March 1976, the LP reached the top spot within two weeks, securing platinum status and then some. The story was much the same in Great Britain, where *Presence* shipped gold on the day of its release, the LP's arrival at number one six days later confirming Zep's fifth consecutive chart-topper at home. As ever, the mathematics was impressive. Unfortunately, unlike its distinguished predecessors, who both enjoyed a robust shelf-life after their initial launch, *Presence* did not prove itself a sustained best seller, with the disc making a graceful exit from public view in a matter of weeks rather than months.

Jimmy Page couldn't have cared less. Having sweated blood to write, record and produce it over 18 hellishly busy days, *Presence* represented something far more than just sales to the guitarist. An electrified homage[181] to the sounds of his youth and the myriad musical discoveries made since then, the album was also Page's declaration that despite whatever got in the way of his band, he would drive right through it, even dragging his colleagues along if necessary. "It was a gamble to see if we could meet the deadline or not," he later told *Melody Maker*. "Fortunately, we did. We worked every minute of the day, and it was great to do it like that." For Chris Charlesworth, Page's dogged dedication to the cause while making *Presence* was unsurprising. In fact, it was just part of his job spec. "I think Jimmy and Zep were all about hard work," he confirmed. "Page was this incredible musical leader who personified focus, work ethic and personal discipline. If Robert had turned up in Munich in an iron lung, Jimmy would have got that album made!"

Variously described by Jimmy Page as the band's "most important" record and a "personal favourite" of his, *Presence* also served to keep

---

181 With the exception of an acoustic bedding track on 'Candy Store Rock' – incidentally released as a US single in June 1976 (it did not chart) – *Presence* features only electric guitars.

Led Zeppelin's flag flying at a time when their singer would have had trouble even hoisting it. But even as Robert Plant began to more fully recover from his injuries, Page was already contemplating the group's next move, his ambitions for Zep and interest in music as a whole as keen as ever. "We're only scratching the surface," he said in March 1976. "...There are no horizons as to what can be done. It just takes a lot of work, writing and recording. You can bet your life that in the next five or 10 years, they'll be some amazing things coming up."

And some quite awful things, too.

CHAPTER 25

Unharmonics

With *Presence*, Led Zeppelin reasserted their commercial position once more, the album's number one placing in the UK and US charts confirming them as rock music's premium selling act. That they did so with Robert Plant not swinging from the chandeliers but seated quietly on a chair while recovering from a car crash surely made the achievement all the more remarkable. "After the 1975 tour," said Chris Charlesworth, "I'm not sure Zep hadn't anything left to prove, even to themselves. But Jimmy obviously wasn't ready to stop." On the contrary. Pulling the band up by their bootstraps, Page had worked ceaselessly until *Presence* was in the shops and Led Zeppelin were back in their rightful place: on top of the tree looking down at everyone else. "[*Presence*] was a sort of test, really," he later said. "We could have come unstuck. But..."

Nonetheless, there would be no live dates in support of the record. Though Zep had finished their year-long tenure as tax exiles and were now able to return to Great Britain without threat of financially punitive measures, rumours of another 'Back to the Clubs tour' remained precisely that. "We weren't ready to do it," Peter Grant later reasoned. "It was a bit of a worrying time." With Plant still a tad on the rickety side and Jimmy having to deal with his own share of triumphs and troubles – to which we shall return in a moment – a small-scale run of UK dates was the last thing on anyone's mind. Even America would have to wait its turn, as the group and its leader sorted out all those matters that had gone unattended while they were on the run throughout 1975 and early 1976.

For Page, this period of relative downtime was marked by a series of highs, lows and, in the words of Peter Grant, the odd "unwanted squatter... to get rid of". It began badly. On May 14, 1976, Jimmy received the worst type of news when he learned that his former band mate Keith Relf had died. Only 33 years old, the singer had been writing songs in the basement of his home in Surrey when a faultily grounded guitar electrocuted him. At the time, Relf was busy pulling together his post-Yardbirds group Renaissance for a new album and possible tour.

"Keith wasn't particularly well then," said Renaissance's keyboardist John Hawken. "[But] he was still putting himself out there, writing these songs, trying to get the band going again [while] also caring for his young son, Danny. That he actually died while working on one of our songs... well, it was such a tragedy to befall such a soft and gentle man. A good soul was Keith." For Jim McCarty, who subsequently took up the reins of the reformed Renaissance[182], the loss of his teenage friend and song-writing partner for over a decade was equally hard to take, with Relf's passing also bringing his days as a Yardbird back and everything that had happened since into sharp focus. "Keith was a nice guy, a sensitive soul and I still miss him," said the drummer in 2015. "But what he did, he did well, and you know, Keith really had something as a frontman. He had a really special atmosphere about him. We were both quite sensitive in our own ways, and Jeff [Beck] too. But Jimmy, make

---

182 When Keith Relf died, Jim McCarty took on much of the responsibility of pulling Renaissance back together, though the resultant project was renamed Illusion (in honour of Renaissance's second album). "Jim picked up the reins and did double duty on [writing] the songs," said John Hawken. "And I have to say, that first Illusion album in 1977 was my favourite record of all the ones I've worked on. Just fabulous song-writing."

no mistake, Jimmy was a tough guy. Jimmy could work hard, play hard and that's how he managed to cope with it. I think my only real regret was that I wasn't quite tough enough for it. I didn't have that hardness. Keith didn't. Jeff didn't. But Jimmy did..."

While Page was no doubt upset by the sad news of Keith Relf's death, he had much else to contend with at the time, as his much-written about interest in the occult was again about to put him back in the media spotlight. In truth, after the brouhaha of his purchase of Boleskine in 1970, press curiousity concerning Jimmy's fascination with the life and work of Aleister Crowley had to some extent settled, with only the odd spurious enquiry or printed reference here and there for the guitarist to contend with.

In part down to the good work of publicists Danny Goldberg and BP Fallon, Jimmy had also done his bit to manage the situation, either patiently – albeit firmly – explaining his views when such topics were raised, or by casting a withering glance (rather than a spell) at any journalist whom he felt took the subject too far. "I'm not saying anything more about [Crowley]," he told *Melody Maker*'s Michael Watts in 1974. "You know, Pete Townshend always mentions Meher Baba[183], but I just don't want to know about telling everybody anything about Aleister Crowley. From what I've read... and as far as the papers' sensationalism goes, [the coverage] doesn't bear any relevance to the man whatsoever. No, [I] don't do any spouting." Of course, it wasn't all controllable. Certain writers, for instance, had a field day with the long black candles Page reportedly lit in his hotel rooms while on tour – but in the main, progress was being made.

To illustrate that fact, a notable effort to bring some intellectual rigour to Page's fascinations was made by *Crawdaddy* in February 1975, when the cult American rock magazine sent esteemed novelist William S. Burroughs to interview Zep's guitarist backstage at New York's Madison

---

183 Meher Baba was an Indian spiritual leader who claimed to be God in human form (an 'Avatar'). Drawn to his teachings about reincarnation, the nature of life and the link between the universe and imagination, the Who's Peter Townshend became an avid follower of Baba in the early 1970s.

Square Garden. A controversial figure in his own right[184], perhaps best known for his non-linear writing style (1959's *Naked Lunch*) and early use of literary cut-up techniques (the 'Nova Trilogy' of 1961, 1962 and 1964), Burroughs had also spent much time in Tangiers during the early 1950s. More, his own studies brought him into close proximity with the works of Hassan-i-Sabbah, a 12th-century Persian mystic and Islamic theologian well versed in alchemy, astronomy, mathematics and their correlation to music. As such, the author had a more than passing familiarity with the trance-like rhythms and Arabic scales Jimmy would later employ on the likes of 'Achilles Last Stand' and 'Nobody's Fault But Mine'.[185]

In a conversation that encompassed Aleister Crowley, Gnosticism, Orgone accumulators (a device constructed to contain 'universal life energy') and psychic healing, Page more than held his own, making several intelligent points on the responsibilities of crowd control and the possible dangers of infrasound. Even if on occasion it all threatened to descend into the realms of impenetrable pseudo-science – Burroughs often seemed to be writing more about his own views than those of his subject – it still made for interesting reading. "Cor! Yeah!" Jimmy later said, laughing, to *Mojo*'s Phil Alexander. "I really was thrilled [he] was going to do an interview with me. He was an all-time hero. Burroughs wanted to talk about trance music. He could see parallels between [it] and the sort of riff music coming out of say, Chicago. He knew about both. There's a long tradition in trance music invoking spiritual healing and I totally understood what he was talking about: the transcendence."

184 Rightly lauded by the Beat Generation for the quality of his writing, Burroughs' life was nonetheless marred by various controversies. When living in Mexico in the 1950s, he accidentally shot and killed his partner, Joan Vollmer, during a drunken performance of "our William Tell act". His copious use of drugs – from hallucinogenics and speed to alcohol and morphine – was also the stuff of legend.

185 At the time of his meeting with William Burroughs, Page had not actually been to Morocco. It seems a fair bet that Burrough's championing of the country and its music – "I think [Zep's music] has quite a lot in common with Moroccan trance music," the writer told Page at the Garden – might well have been a major factor in Jimmy and Robert's subsequent visit there in the summer of 1975.

There were several ways of looking at Page's meeting with William Burroughs in 1975. For some, it was "A true exchange of 'heads'." For others, the pair were just two like-minded philosophers – "Do what thou wilt..." and "Nothing is true, everything is permitted" – casually chatting over a beer and a cigarette. And of course, for the more cynical among us, it could all have been a clever wheeze designed by Zep's US publicity arm to emulate – or even trump – novelist Truman Capote's on-the-road report on the Rolling Stones for *Vanity Fair* in 1972. Call it what you will. But the New York summit held between the bespectacled academic and long-haired rock god surely helped illuminate Jimmy Page's continuing fascination with matters pertaining to the occult and the seriousness with which he took it. "I was also bloody moved," Jimmy concluded, "that he'd been to see us and [by] how much he'd got out of it."

For those seeking further proof of the sincerity of Page's interests, they had to look no further than his then recently opened bookshop, Equinox. A modest space located at 4 Holland Road, Kensington[186], Equinox joined the exclusive likes of Atlantis in Bloomsbury and Watkins' Books near Leicester Square as one of the few London stores trading solely in esoteric-themed literature. Something of a personal crusade for Jimmy, Equinox – or to give its proper name, The Equinox Booksellers and Publishers – provided two distinct services. One, the sale of books dedicated to subjects such as "yoga, diet and mysticism", the other, the publication of books Page felt were worthy of greater interest. "There was not one bookshop in London with a good collection of occult books," he later said, "and I was so pissed off not being able to get the books I wanted."

True to his word, Jimmy reportedly published two specific books via Equinox by 1976. In the case of *Astrology, A Cosmic Science*, the onus was

---

186 According to some reports, Equinox was tastefully decorated with images of Egyptian deities (Thoth, Horus) and other Art Deco imagery. Paintings by the likes of English occultist/writer/artist Austin Osman Spare and Aleister Crowley were also hung upon the walls. Jimmy was a particular fan of Spare's work, purchasing his 1907 self-portrait *Portrait Of The Artist*.

on an almost humanistic approach to the subject at hand, with American author Isabel Hickey providing a "spiritual textbook" on the study of divining information about human affairs and world events from the movements of planets and stars. *The Book Of The Goetia (Of Solomon The King)* – as edited by Aleister Crowley in 1904 – had a somewhat different thrust, its concerns in part pertaining to the invocation of spirits in the practice of ceremonial magic. Page was well aware that such diverse and specific tracts would never be best sellers. That was not the point. "I basically wanted the shop to be a nucleus," he later said, "that's all."

An affair of the heart, Equinox inevitably brought its fair share of curiosity seekers through the door in Kensington, with many a fan visiting the shop at least once in the hope of catching a glimpse of Jimmy. There were even rumours that the odd fellow musician made an appearance here and there to see what all the fuss was about, though they may well have left disappointed. "Well, it was the time, [and the occult] was still quite fashionable," reasoned Chris Welch. "Bands and musicians were very interested in such things, though with some of them, I don't think it really went much deeper than reading Dennis Wheatley books or watching Hammer Horror films!"

In the end, it was neither his conversations with William Burroughs nor the opening of an antiquarian bookshop in an affluent London suburb that again roused the media's interest in Page's connections to the occult. Instead, it was the Zeppelin man's long-gestating association with Kenneth Anger that really set off the fireworks, their sour-faced falling out over the soundtrack to Anger's movie *Lucifer Rising* spilling out of Jimmy's house in Holland Park and straight into the pages of the press.

Author, actor but mostly director/filmmaker, Kenneth Anger had been a figure of some controversy in both American and European cinema long before he met Jimmy Page. Born in Santa Monica, California at the end of the twenties, Anger first came to attention in 1947 with the hugely experimental *Fireworks*, his short but striking film full of erotic and Sado-masochistic overtones that reflected aspects of the director's own homosexuality. "*Fireworks*," he later told the *Austin Chronicle*, "is all I have to say about being 17, the United States

Navy, American Christmas and the Fourth of July." Following a brief, financially forced detour into book writing, which produced the still mildly notorious *Hollywood Babylon*[187], Anger got back on track with a new series of underground shorts, his quasi-mystical biker homage *Scorpio Rising* (1961) and arcane *Invocation Of My Demon Brother* (1969) drawing both critical kudos and cult interest. Yet, it was his own obsessions with Aleister Crowley and the religion of Thelema that led to Anger's dalliance with Page.

Like Jimmy, Kenneth Anger had become interested in alternative philosophies and religions as a teenager, his early reading of L. Frank Baum's *Oz* books opening a door into Rosicrucian studies, before further, tentative explorations led him first to *The Golden Bough*, Sir James Fraser, William Butler Yates and then the ceremonial magic of Eliphas Levi. From there, it was but a short intellectual walk to Aleister Crowley. By 1955, he and friend Alfred Kinsey[188] had travelled to Cefalu in Sicily to locate the infamous 'Abbey of Thelema', the very site where Crowley had set up a commune in the early 1920s before Italian Fascist leader Benito Mussolini ran he and his followers out of the country after several wild (and probably very inaccurate) stories concerning animal sacrifice and depraved sex rituals at the property were printed in the British press. Once found, Anger set about trying to restore some of the erotic murals and frescos left behind on the walls of the Abbey, as well as re-enacting a few Thelemic rituals in honour of absent friends.

---

187 Essentially a collection of celebrity tittle-tattle, lurid gossip and tall stories (without source or attribution), Anger's *Hollywood Babylon* made various claims regarding the private lives of Fatty Arbuckle, Mae West, Rudolf Valentino and Walt Disney, among many others. First published in France in 1959, *Hollywood Babylon* was not released onto the American market for another 16 years.

188 A zoologist, psychologist, biologist and, indeed, etymologist, Alfred Kinsey was perhaps best known for his work into human sexuality, with his reports – *Sexual Behavior In The Human Male* (1948) and *Sexual Behavior In The Human Female* (1953) and the later 'Kinsey Scale' – seen as ground-breaking studies in the field of 'Sexology'.

Page and Anger appear to have got off to a fine start, with Jimmy already well aware of Kenneth's work both as an avant-garde filmmaker and devotee of Crowley. In fact, Page had seen *Scorpio Rising* and *Invocation Of My Demon Brother* at a film festival in Kent in the late sixties. He also knew of Anger's previous efforts to restore the Abbey of Thelema, having been privy to the letters the American wrote to Crowley's old friend Gerald Yorke asking for funds. "I could see Anger was passionate about this stuff," Jimmy later explained to *Classic Rock's* Pete Makowski, "so that, along with his creative output, made him someone I [wanted] to meet."

In Kenneth Anger's mind, that first meeting took place sometime during 1971, when he and Page supposedly attended Sotheby's auction house in London to bid for a rare Aleister Crowley manuscript. Anger states that Jimmy successfully outbid him for the book. Page, on the other hand, has little or no recollection of the event. "I don't exactly remember where I met him," he later said, "I don't think it would have been in an auction room... I would have someone else doing [the bidding] on my behalf." However it went down, the two soon found a way into the other's orbit, with invitations extended to their respective homes in Sussex and London. According to Page, the idea of a possible film collaboration was raised quickly by Anger. "It was at his [London] apartment that he outlined this idea for a film that became *Lucifer Rising*. It was there he asked me to take the commission to do the music, and I agreed that." By February 1972, the director had announced Jimmy's participation in the project to Hollywood movie magazine *Variety*.

This was not the first time Kenneth Anger had attempted to get *Lucifer Rising* off the ground or seek the assistance of a rock star in the creation of a soundtrack. In fact, he had already shot footage for the film in the mid-sixties, large parts of which ended up being used for his own *Invocation Of My Demon Brother*. Interestingly enough, that particular short also featured a brief cameo from Rolling Stone Mick Jagger, whom Anger had befriended – alongside band mate Keith Richards and their respective partners, Marianne Faithfull and Swedish model/actress Anita Pallenberg – following his arrival in London in 1968. On that occasion,

Jagger had provided the director with *Invocation...*'s accompanying score, writing a suitably spooky piece on drums, a then new-fangled Moog synthesiser and, rather more improbably, a rasping piano accordion. It was now Jimmy Page's turn to get involved. It would not be a smooth journey.

The 'plotline' to Anger's *Lucifer Rising* was always ambitious, and not easily deciphered unless familiar with the work of Aleister Crowley and the religion of Thelema. In essence, the film was to follow a ritualistic or symbolic recreation of the coming of the 'third aeon' – or 'Aeon of Horus' – as told to Crowley in the Thelemic sacred text, *The Book Of The Law* during his travels in Egypt during 1904. "Aleister Crowley identified Horus as the god of the New Aeon," Anger later told journalist Christopher Knowles, "which is supplanting Christianity in his concept. In my own mind, all these things tied together."

Page would later offer his own interpretation of the ideas behind *Lucifer Rising*. "Within the framework of it, Anger was saying there's a dawning," he told *Classic Rock*. "You have Isis, who would correlate to the early religions. Isis is the equivalent of man worshipping man, which is now where we have Buddha and Christ and all the rest of it, like the three ages. And then the child is Horus, which is the 'age of the child'. Which is pretty much the new age, as it was seen."[189] It was in this prophesied third aeon that Thelemites believed that humanity would enter a time of true understanding and self-actualisation.

The role of Lucifer in Anger's film was also radically different to common tropes or popular misunderstandings of the character. Completely unconnected to the traditional 'Satan' of the Bible, this Lucifer was less evil personified and more the fallen angel of Milton's *Paradise Lost*, his responsibility before rebelling against God having been that of 'Lightbringer', 'Morning Star' or 'Dawn-bearer'. Illumination, in all its symbolic glory, it seemed, was the key here. "Lucifer," Anger

---

189 Page was probably referring to the connection between the 'Aeon of Horus' and the astrological 'Age of Aquarius', which in turn was linked to the rise of the 'New Age' movement of the late sixties and early seventies, with its greater emphasis on alternative philosophies, religions and medicine.

once said, "is the teenage rebel. [He] must be played by a teenage boy. It's typecasting..."

Indeed, when the director originally tried to get the film off the ground in the mid-sixties, he had cast Robert 'Bobby' Beausoleil in the titular role, the Santa Barbara-born music loving teen[190] being age appropriate and 'James Dean-handsome' enough for Kenneth's singular vision. "The concept was that I would be representing the coming of the new age," Beausoleil later told writer Bill Landis. "In a mythological sense, we have come through matriarchy, we have come through the mother goddess. We have come to patriarchy where the goddess is male. And the Aquarian Age is supposed to represent the age of the child. This was the character I was supposed to play."

Unfortunately, the two soon fell out, with Anger making his way to London and Beausoleil later becoming involved with Charles Manson, on whose bidding he murdered musician (and fellow 'Family' member) Gary Hinman in 1969. As the records would come to show, however, though sentenced to death for the crime (it would later be commuted to life), Bobby Beausoleil was by no means out of the picture just yet.

By the time Jimmy Page properly came on board for *Lucifer Rising* in 1972/3, Kenneth Anger had been pulling together the threads of his new version of the film in various locations and with various people for almost four years. Requested by the director to play the role of Lucifer, Mick Jagger had turned it down[191], instead recommending his own brother Chris for the part, a courtesy Anger gratefully accepted. The Stones singer's now former girlfriend Marianne Faithfull was also signed up to the project (in the role of mythological goddess 'Lilith'),

---

190 A face on the LA and San Francisco music scene of the mid- to late sixties, Beausoleil was an early member of Arthur Lee's the Grass Roots, who later changed their name to Love and found fame with the seminal 1967 LP *Forever Changes*.

191 Some contend that Mick Jagger's association with Anger was an influence on his lyrics to the Stones' 1968 track 'Sympathy For The Devil'. However, after the events of the Altamont Festival a year later and more general accusations of the band being in thrall to demonic forces, Jagger distanced himself considerably from the American filmmaker.

joining the band's personal photographer Michael Cooper, who in turn agreed to help with photography on the movie. Completing the Rolling Stones connection was Donald Cammell. A fine filmmaker in his own right, Cammell had not only put Jagger through his acting paces as co-director alongside Nicholas Roeg on 1968's controversial, mind-warping *Performance*, but was also the son of Aleister Crowley's close friend, Charles. Now Anger chose him to portray 'Osiris', the Egyptian god of the afterlife and resurrection. Gleaning a much-needed £15,000 from the UK's National Film Finance Corporation to help finance further shoots[192], Anger and his merry band decamped first to Germany, then Egypt. Regrettably, it was precisely here where Crowley received his original vision of Thelema that the director and his own 'Lucifer' clashed, resulting in Chris Jagger being fired from the movie. Anger was yet again without a leading man.

He did, however, now have reams of film footage and, thanks to Jimmy Page, a new editing machine on which to cut it. Having "acquired a three-screen editor" following the completion of *The Song Remains The Same* (possibly the same one liberated from Joe Massot), Jimmy now handed the device over to Kenneth Anger for his use on *Lucifer Rising*. Further, Page had seen 30-odd minutes of Anger's work and was keen for him to expand it from a proposed short into a full-length feature. "He had this vision of a 93-minute film," the guitarist later said. "So the next logical step was to give him the facilities to continue, which is what I did."

Pivotal to this decision was the fact that Page had already heard his music in conjunction with Kenneth Anger's images. "What you have to understand about the music to *Lucifer Rising*," he told *Mojo* in 2015, "is that I had the music *before* the film. Anger came to me and I thought I had something that would fit that film." That "something" was a pre-existing piece that Jimmy had composed on a 5ft long bass tanpura

---

192 Anger had shown several minutes of footage from *Lucifer Rising* to the NFFC in 1971 to help gain its financial help. However, the subsequent grant did not go well in the British press, with the *Sunday Telegraph* running the headline 'Devil Film to Get State Aid'.

purchased in India some years before. A "deep, resonant beast" that created a "majestic drone," he supplemented it with various instruments, including a synthesiser, Mellotron and tabla drums. To complete the trance-like package, Page added a phased Buddhist chant and further horn effects. "It sounded like the horns of Gabriel," he confirmed to Pete Makowski in 2006. "It was a good piece." And even better when played alongside Anger's footage. "He came down to my place in Sussex and brought a projector with him," said Jimmy. "He put it on and played the film. The music was perfectly in sync with everything that was going on. It was astonishing..."

Confident that their partnership would produce a work of real and enduring distinction, Page allowed Kenneth Anger to move into the basement of The Tower House in Kensington. Here, the director would have the space and silence he required, while also keeping his costs (ever an ongoing issue) to a minimum. In many ways, it sounded like the perfect set-up; Anger with a firm base of operations and reasonable access to Page, Jimmy on hand whenever his commitments to Led Zeppelin allowed. Surely, in such a fertile environment, ambition was at last on its way to becoming actuality.

And so it seemed, at least at the start. In April 1973, Kenneth Anger allowed several minutes of footage from *Lucifer Rising* to be screened at a personal appearance he made at the State University of New York. But then came radio silence. 1974 passed. As did 1975. Come the autumn of 1976, however, and things suddenly turned nasty. In Page's reckoning of events, his housekeeper discovered that Anger was giving a guided tour of The Tower House to several people. When Jimmy's partner Charlotte Martin was informed of the incident, she took the director to task. Loudly. "Kenneth took umbrage," Page later confirmed, "that he couldn't show people around."

Obviously furious with what had happened, Jimmy and Charlotte asked Anger to leave. The director vacated – or was evicted from – the premises, with the fireworks going off soon after. "I started getting all this hate mail directed at my partner and myself," Page told writer Christopher Knowles. Arriving in the form of newspaper cuttings and articles "underlined in red ink", Jimmy took them to be an attempt at "some kind of curse, [but] it fell flat."[193] Nonetheless, when the film director accused Jimmy of holding onto or man-handling his possessions after he had left The Tower House, the guitarist came out fighting. "What a snide bastard," he growled. "His stuff was all over the place, so I just got some roadies to get it all together for him. Christ! He even turned that one against me. I just wanted to see the bloke finish the bloody film." In retaliation, Jimmy had even considered delivering Anger's remaining belongings to his new address via hearse. "But I thought that might be a tad dramatic."

Ultimately, all of this might have remained a private matter. But the pair's rapidly deteriorating personal and professional relationship was soon dragged kicking and screaming into the public domain when Kenneth Anger chose to air his grievances against Jimmy (and, to a lesser extent, Charlotte Martin) at a press conference. Though Anger's principal beef with Page seemed to centre on his failure to deliver a long enough soundtrack for *Lucifer Rising* ("He gave me 20 minutes, I needed 40," Kenneth later said), it didn't quite end there.

Evidently not one to hold back any dissatisfactions, the director's scattergun approach also found him firing away at Page's betrayal both of his own beliefs and commitment to *Lucifer Rising* – "...his behaviour is totally contradictory to the teachings of Aleister Crowley and... the ethos of the film" – as well as pouring scorn on the Zep guitarist's gifts as a musician. "I'm beginning to think he's dried up," scowled Anger. "He's got no themes, no inspiration and no melodies to offer. *Presence*," he sourly concluded, was "very much a downer album."

Insulting a man's religion and musicianship was bad enough. Yet, Anger wasn't quite finished. In a none too subtle reference to "a problem dragging him down", and making him act like "Jekyll and Hyde", the filmmaker also seemed to be implying that Jimmy had a serious drug habit. Though he fell short of naming the exact nature of Page's addiction at the time, he was more candid 30 years later in an

---

193 According to author Mick Wall, Anger placed "The Curse of King Midas" on Page: "Turning Jimmy into a statue of gold – a metaphor for illness despite wealth."

interview with *Classic Rock*. "Dealing with anyone that's on heroin... [is] like knocking on thick glass between you and that person."

There were, of course, mitigating circumstances around Jimmy Page's ability to commit his full attention to *Lucifer Rising*, the main one being his continuing leadership of the world's largest rock band. But curiously, it was Anger's attack on Page's professionalism rather than charges of artistic drought or inferences of drug addiction that seemed to rile him most. Evidently, Jimmy was still very much a session musician at heart. "He's implying he's received nothing from me, which is totally untrue," he said. "You know I did the film's music. I gave him everything in plenty of time, OK?"

Page was also unafraid to highlight the fact that Anger's own progress on the movie was hardly the stuff of Olympic-level sprinting. "I think you hit the nail on the head when you pointed out how long he [Anger] had been working on the film," he confirmed to writer David Hancock in November 1976. "I not only delivered the music but I lent him the machinery we'd had for work on our movie *The Song Remains The Same*. He hadn't got the money to hire the stuff so I let him have all our editing machinery and everything so he could finish his film." Page also had another theory as to what might have caused Anger's various outbursts. "In fact, if you read between the lines it'll be apparent that maybe the creditors were on his back for him to deliver the finished film and because he hadn't got it, he used me as a scapegoat and an excuse."[194]

An ugly end to a potentially enthralling collaboration, Kenneth Anger and Jimmy Page eventually retreated to their respective corners, both grumbling as they went. In the case of *Lucifer Rising*, its tortuous, bedraggled route to the big screen would continue for several years yet, with Anger finally distributing the finished film in 1980. Bizarrely, the

---

194 This was not the first time such an accusation had been levelled at Kenneth Anger. Back in late 1967, the director had accused Bobby Beausoleil of stealing some of the original footage shot for *Lucifer Rising*. Strenuously denying the allegation, Beausoleil instead pointed the finger at Anger himself, implying that the director had already spent all the funds invested in the movie and was claiming the film stock had been stolen to simply avoid his creditors.

man who replaced Jimmy on soundtrack duties was none other than Bobby Beausoleil. Having read about Page and the director's fall-out from his cell in California's Tracy prison, Beausoleil wrote to Anger offering his services. With both men obviously in a forgiving mood, a deal was done. Utilising the help of a prison schoolteacher (Minerva Bertholt), Bobby was given access to various instruments and recording equipment, and even formed a band – The Freedom Orchestra – to help him complete the project.

For those hoping to hear Jimmy Page's own contributions to *Lucifer Rising*, they would be in for a long, long wait. Nearly 35 years, to be precise. Obviously glad to be shot of both the film and Kenneth Anger – "Pure bitchiness," Page said acidly at the time. "The only damage [Anger] can do is with his tongue" – he quickly distanced himself from any mention of *Lucifer Rising* and refocused his energies on Led Zeppelin and other associated matters.

Nonetheless, "this everyday story of musicians, magicians, murderers and myths" had again tugged Jimmy back into potentially choppy waters with the press. While he might have entered the project with only the best of intentions, now all anybody was hearing were words and phrases such as "addiction", "magical spells" and the "Manson Family". All well and good when it came to keeping up that mysterious rock star image or even adding a fresh air of danger to a band now entering its ninth year in the business. But soon enough, all the talk of curses and dabbling in the 'dark arts' would be turned against him and Led Zeppelin for the most erroneous, stupid and tragic of reasons.

Back in October 1976, however, and Page was on more familiar terrain, even if his interests were still in part connected to the motion picture industry. Three years in the making, and already covered elsewhere in these pages, *The Song Remains The Same* finally made it to movie theatres in both the US and UK. Grand, time-consuming and now out-of-date folly or legitimate, timeless in-concert testimonial to one of the great rock groups, *Time Out*'s sweet and sour review of the film was fairly emblematic of the critical reaction the film received.

"Essentially a chord-by-chord documentation of their 1973 Madison Square Garden concert, the heavy metal onslaught is intercut with lavish psychedelic effects, New York by night, seedy backstage wrangles and five fantasy sequences. It's gruellingly long, four-track stereo relentless and the music a mechanical recreation of Zeppelin standards." Yet, for all the movie's faults – and there were more than a few – *The Song Remains...* soundtrack confirmed demand for all things Led Zeppelin remained undiminished. Released on October 22, 1976, the double LP reached number one and number two in the UK and USA respectively, with two-odd million people more than content to usher Zep back into their homes.

The band's record label Swan Song could not quite boast such impressive numbers. While Bad Company's rootsy, if workman-like, blues rock continued to beguile – particularly in America where the band scored two US Top Five placings with 1975's *Straight Shooter* and 1976's *Running With The Pack* – elsewhere things were less rosy. As evidenced, Maggie Bell's *Suicide Sal* had not found the audience it probably deserved, and despite Jimmy Page's emphatic backing, neither had the Pretty Things. Having already missed the commercial target with the amusingly named but blank-firing *Silk Torpedo*, the group's follow-up *Savage Eye*[195] also failed to entice audiences. For singer Phil May, who had experienced his fair share of chart disappointments, the writing was already on the wall. "[We] were staggering around like an elephant that's been shot."

Gambling that an injection of new blood around the place might lead to richer dividends (and perhaps end the over reliance on Bad Company's success), Peter Grant, Jimmy and the rest of Zep went looking for fresh acts. First to be signed was long underrated Welsh singer-guitar player Dave Edmunds, who had scored a Christmas number one in 1970 with the good-natured twang of 'I Hear You Knocking'. Brought in on Robert Plant's express recommendation, Edmunds would cut several impressive LPs, but he was unable to become a truly effective pop star until he actually left the label to record with his new band Rockpile in 1980.

---

195 While *Savage Eye* was another reasonable effort from the band, the LP would be their last with Swan Song.

Detective's appeal was even more selective. A wired amalgam of funk, hard rock and R&B, the group's debut LP reportedly cost "a bloody fortune" to record yet still sold poorly, its release in early 1977 imprecisely timed to coincide with a musical revolution then sweeping Great Britain that would have profound implications for even a band as mighty and powerful as Led Zeppelin. But more of that later. Ironically enough, Detective's feverish stew of lusty howls, hard guitars and funky beats had more than a little in common with Zep's own mid-seventies output, leading Jimmy Page to ask the group's producer, Jimmy Robinson, the following question. "Uh, don't you think it sounds a little bit like... us?"

It was not the only thing Page had in common with Swan Song's latest signing. In fact, Detective's hard-living, royally connected[196] lead singer Michael Des Barres had been dating Jimmy's old flame Pamela Miller since 1974. By the time of the band's second release, the equally chart shy *It Takes One To Know One* (1978), the two would be married. Ever discreet, Page made no comment on the union, though Michael's explanation of the Detective sound might well have described the guitarist's own brief affair with the delightful 'Miss Pamela'. "We were precisely what rock'n'roll should be," Des Barres later told *Uncut*'s David Cavanagh. "Magic and chaos mingled..."

Between Robert Plant's near fatal accident, the "pure anxiety" of recording *Presence*, "the up, downs and all around" that constituted *Lucifer Rising* and Swan Song's equally topsy-turvy fortunes, the months between August 1975 and November 1976 had been an unparalleled period of emotional turbulence for both Jimmy Page and Led Zeppelin. Once rock solid in their dealings with the world, recent events had tested them as never before. "All this while they were meant to be on a break, too," Chris Charlesworth laughed. "They probably needed another one just to get over it." There would be no break, however. Having been off the road since those five magical nights at Earls Court

---

196 The only child of Marquis Philip and Marchioness Irene Des Barres, the Detective vocalist's full title was in fact 'Lord Marquis Michael Philip Des Barres'.

(and their hastily scheduled appearance at a Jersey nightclub[197]), Led Zeppelin were finally ready to again meet their public with a world tour scheduled for much of 1977. "New roads to travel, new songs to sing," as the saying went. Unfortunately, the journey Zep now set out on was a long, slow march towards their own demise.

197 While Led Zeppelin had indeed been off the road for the best part of a year and a half by November 1976, various band members had already been treading the boards, albeit with other bands. Jimmy and Robert joined Bad Company at the LA Forum on May 23 for a rowdy take on 'I Just Want To Make Love To You', while John Paul Jones sat in on piano with the Pretty Things at the Marquee four days later.

CHAPTER 26

Nobody's Fault But Mine

Rehearsals for Led Zeppelin's return to the stage first began at north London's Ezyhire Studios in November 1976 before moving west to Fulham's slightly larger Manticore complex two months later. As ever, Jimmy Page was leading from the front. Instead of easing the band in gently with one or two of their simpler, older tunes, he suggested they tackle *Presence*'s hideously complex 'Achilles Last Stand' first. "We could have eased into the familiar stuff," Jimmy told *Melody Maker* at the time, "but we went straight into the deep end by trying out 'Achilles...'. I thought I'd have to use the twin-neck [guitar], but it actually sounded better with the six-string using different effects. When we did that first rehearsal, it just clicked all over again. Something epic is going to happen musically. That's the way I feel with this next tour." Obviously, Zep's leader was brimful of confidence and raring to go. But the world he and the group were re-entering had radically changed since they last visited nearly two years before.

With Led Zeppelin off the road since mid-1975, a plethora of groups had tried to ease themselves into the space they left behind, some with much more success than others. Though there were no serious takers for picking up the folk side of their back catalogue, or indeed, Page and the band's heady experiments with Eastern and Asian music, plenty had drawn inspiration from the seam of bluesy hard rock that ran deep at Zep's core. Aerosmith, for instance, were clearly indebted to the bump and grind of 'Whole Lotta Love', 'Celebration Day' and 'Black Dog', with the Boston quintet's ability to capture "the Zeppelin essence" while also adding elements of R&B and pure pop sheen leading them to multi-platinum status in the US while Page and co. were in absentia. It surely helped that Aerosmith's singer Steve Tyler and guitarist Joe Perry were also long-time, fully paid members of the Yardbirds and Zep appreciation society. "I'd sit in front of the record player for countless hours," Perry later said, "trying to absorb Page's electric mojo."

"Cartoon rockers" Kiss, too, had managed to compress Zep's wide-open musical bandwidth into something much smaller, but still distinctly commercial. Dismissed by critics as "big dumb rock," the face-painted New Yorkers were actually far smarter than they first appeared, with simple, but effective fare such as 'Deuce', 'Parasite' and most especially 'Makin' Love' as beholden to Jimmy's early library of riffs as their own obvious affection for the Beatles and Brit glam-rockers like Slade and Sweet. Again, the conceit had worked, with Kiss packing out the very arenas and aircraft hangers Led Zeppelin had left empty in 1975. If there was one group, however, who came closest to embodying the experimental spirit of Zep, it was surely Rush. Though nowhere near as successful as Aerosmith or Kiss (at least not yet), Rush's ability to mine the same progressive-rock soil that parts of *Houses Of The Holy* and *Physical Graffiti* were built upon boded well for their future, the Canadian trio well-placed to provide succour for those seeking Led Zeppelin's more eclectic side should the airship ever leave planet Earth behind.

While these "Sons of Zeppelin" had been busy in the States following their heroes' musical and commercial blueprint, Great Britain's newest batch of groups seemed intent on tearing down anything to do with Page, Plant, Jones and Bonham. Born in a clothes shop only 54 doors up from Swan Song's offices on London's Kings Road[198], the Sex Pistols'

198 Before forming the Sex Pistols, core members Johnny Rotten, Steve Jones, Glenn Matlock and Paul Cook all either worked, congregated in or stole from Sex, a fetish fashion store located at 430 Kings Road and run by designer Vivienne Westwood and businessman/entrepreneur/art terrorist Malcolm McLaren. McLaren would later manage the band, overseeing them from promising punk terrorists to the "fabulous disaster" they later became.

meaty stew of monarchy-baiting lyricism, arch social complaint and "killer fucking tunes" was unsubtly leading the charge for 'punk rock' at home, and the movement was gaining serious traction.

Powerful, bilious and raw, punk's complete lack of respect for technically brilliant guitar solos, 20-minute drum workouts or lyrics about elves, goblins and hobbits was a sharp slap in the face for all those acts who had long traded on the very same. Dismissing the likes of Zep, Yes, Emerson, Lake & Palmer and "the other wizard-hatted proggers" as no more than bloated, irrelevant dinosaurs, the Pistols, the Clash and those about to come in their wake were ironically trading on the same short, sharp riffs and killer hooks that had made the likes of 'Communication Breakdown'[199] so exciting and fresh almost a decade before.

If Jimmy Page felt frightened of this new surge of rebellious blood rising up from the squats and clubs of West and Central London, he certainly didn't show it. In fact, instead of pulling up the drawbridge of Plumpton Place or placing archers at the lead-lined windows of The Tower House, he actually ventured out to see what all the fuss was about, albeit with a few burly members of the Zep entourage in tow. Grabbing hold of Robert Plant for 'moral support', Page and his cohorts hot-footed it to punk stronghold The Roxy in January 1977 to witness one of the finer exponents of what was then being termed "Year Zero".

Anarchic, comedic but surprisingly tuneful, the Damned were then readying themselves for stardom (or infamy), having recently released punk's first legitimate single, the wonderful 'New Rose', some four months earlier on the perfectly named Stiff Records. Though his own band had absolutely nothing in common with these young upstarts, Jimmy was rightly entranced. "It was phenomenal," he later told *Mojo*.

---

199 Johnny Ramone – who with his band the Ramones was one of the leading lights of New York's seventies punk scene and therefore partly responsible for inspiring Great Britain's own version of the movement – once credited Jimmy Page's attacking, percussive down-strokes on 'Communication Breakdown' as a major influence on his own guitar style.

"The Damned came out in these little outfits... Captain Sensible might even have been dressed up like a nurse... and I was thinking 'Oh, what's this going to be like?' But the energy coming off them nailed you to the wall."

Nonetheless, when Page, Plant and new recruit to the cause John Bonham returned to the club a week later, the reception they received was far less friendly. Now clearly identified as 'the enemy', matters did not improve when Bonzo reportedly challenged Damned sticksman Rat Scabies to a 'drum-off'. In Bonham's perhaps beer-addled mind, this was probably more good-natured badinage than any serious attempt to assert he and Zep's musical supremacy.

Yet, while Scabies thought the challenge hilarious and was well up for any battle – despite the mad name, Rat was actually a fine player – it did not fly well with those gathered. After calling him "an old fart", the punk contingent continued to barrack Bonzo and the rest with visiting Sex Pistol and soon-to-be 'Public Enemy Number One' Johnny Rotten even laying his head at Robert Plant's feet in a gesture of mock worship. When 'Percy' began giving serious consideration to kicking Rotten with a well-aimed cowboy boot, one of the Zep crew intervened. "'That's a very bad idea,' he said to me," remembered Plant, "'because if you do that, it'll be the last thing you ever do...'"

Given that Rotten and the rest had just trampled all over Led Zeppelin's ham-fisted olive branch, one might feel Jimmy Page had reasonable cause to rubbish both punk and its leading players. But he remained oddly supportive of the music at the time, and for decades to come. "Punk was actually quite refreshing," he later told *Guitar World* in 1991. "Maybe bands like ourselves were getting a bit stodgy by then." As for the insults and accusations that Zep were nothing more than 'old farts' and 'dinosaurs', again Page remained stoic and sure of he and his band's own gifts. "Did it bother me? No, it really didn't," he said. "I was more interested to hear what these bands were doing. I already knew what *I* was doing."

Away from the pantomime theatrics of The Roxy, Zep continued to prepare themselves for their latest tour, which was scheduled to kick off at Fort Worth, Texas on February 27. In anticipation of the 49 US dates ahead of them, the group focused on refreshing the bones of their set, turning to old album favourites (but still "stage virgins") such as 'The Battle Of Evermore' and 'Ten Years Gone'[200] to provide new in-concert thrills for their audience. Oddly enough, little material from *Presence* was tried out by Zep at this juncture[201], with only 'Nobody's Fault But Mine' and the aforementioned 'Achilles Last Stand' added to the show's running order. Given that the recording of the LP constituted a "dark and dense period" in the band's life, parking its contents was probably quite deliberate.

However, just as the engines were revving up for Zep's departure to the States, a spanner was thrown in the works when Robert Plant was diagnosed with laryngitis. The kiss of death to any singer, Zep and their manager Peter Grant had no alternative but to give Plant a month to recover and heavily reschedule the tour, eventually breaking it up into three distinct stages that would run between spring and late summer. "Less than ideal," said Big Gee at the time, "but absolutely necessary."

False dawns and false starts now behind them, Led Zeppelin finally made it to America on April 1, 1977 for their opening date at the Memorial Auditorium in Dallas, Texas. Right up until showtime, however, it was not Plant's voice that was of concern, but his foot. Though now nearly two years on since the accident in Rhodes, concerns still lingered as to whether Robert's injury would compromise his abilities onstage. In common parlance this was squeaky-bum time both for him and for Led Zeppelin. "The only thing I didn't know," Plant later told writer Ray Coleman, "...was whether I was going to be able to pace myself

---

200 By bringing 'Ten Years Gone' into Zep's set, Jimmy also brought a new guitar. A 1953 Fender Telecaster, the 'Botswana Brown' featured a built-in 'B-Bender system' allowing Page to bend said B-string up a whole tone (two frets) to C-sharp. The instrument would become a particular favourite of Page's in coming years, its original maple neck reportedly replaced by the rosewood one taken from his famed Yardbirds 'Dragon' Telecaster.

201 While 'Candy Store Rock' was rehearsed for possible inclusion in the band's set at Manticore, it was never played live. *Physical Graffiti*'s 'Custard Pie' suffered the same fate.

out with my foot problem... and at that first gig at Forth Worth, I was petrified. Since Earls Court [in 1975], all this horrendous physical hoo-ha had taken place, and for 10 minutes before I walked up those steps in Dallas, I was cold with fright."

Suffice to say, Robert Plant stood his ground and so did Zep. Kicking off with the Gibson 1275-led glory of 'The Song Remains The Same' and rabbit-punching 'Sick Again', the quartet handed in a joyous, near three-hour set specifically designed to re-acquaint the States with what it had been missing. Whether dipping backwards into the late sixties ('White Summer'/'Black Mountainside'), stealing gold from their illustrious fourth disc ('Stairway To Heaven', 'Rock And Roll') or acknowledging their most recent, if troubled history ('Nobody's Fault...' and 'Achilles...'), Led Zeppelin proved they had lost none of their lustre or enthusiasm for the game. So confident were the group, they even dropped 'Whole Lotta Love' from the set. "Sure it was emotional," gushed Plant to the *LA Times*' Robert Hilburn after the lights had faded. "[But] we just cleared the biggest hurdle of our career."

As ever with Zep, their first few US shows found the group either wobbling over new stage material or fighting nightly wars with their PA system. But as Robert Plant correctly deduced, by putting Fort Worth behind them, a giant leap forward had been made. Or at least until Jimmy Page succumbed to food poisoning during the band's third successive show at Chicago Stadium nine days later. Grinding his way through five numbers, Page was finally forced to throw in the towel after a particularly gruesome rendition of 'Ten Years Gone'. Obviously in pain, the guitarist stumbled offstage, causing Plant to call a five-minute timeout on behalf of the band.

When it became plain that Jimmy was in no state to continue, tour manager Richard Cole came to the rescue. Stepping into the spotlight to address the audience, Zep's oft-put upon tour manager faced down the audience and cancelled the show. "It was the first time we ever stopped a gig like that," Page later told *Circus*. "We always have a go... but the pain was unbearable. If I hadn't sat down, I'd have fallen over." Though sympathetic to his chum, Robert was obviously not taking

Jimmy's malady too seriously. "Jimmy was feeling ill... but it was only a false pregnancy, so that's all right."

By the following night, Page had recovered sufficiently to resume the concert stage in Chicago. And what a sight he was. Dressed like a deranged Nazi storm trooper replete with sunglasses, SS leather jack boots and military visor cap, Page brought new meaning to the words 'Guitar Hero'. Thin as a rail, covered from head to toe in black and wielding his trusty Gibson double-neck like a two-headed battleaxe, Jimmy's sense of style was now as flamboyant as his playing. Page must have thought so too. Re-emerging from the wings before 'Achilles Last Stand' in a pristine white satin suit especially embroidered with red poppies and now familiar dragon motifs, this was as much a Paris cat walk as a rock extravaganza. "The coolest man in rock'n'roll," Dave Lewis once said. Nobody was arguing against him in Chicago on April 10, 1977.

With all the kinks now more or less ironed out, Zep continued on their merry way, playing to packed houses throughout April in Minnesota, Ohio and Kentucky, among other destinations. Yet it was at Michigan's Pontiac Silverdome on the last day of the month that the band truly reaffirmed their own unique standing by setting a new world record for audience attendance by a single artist or group at an indoor venue. When fellow old-stagers the Who appeared at the Silverdome in December 1975, they had managed to pull a mind-boggling 75,962 punters through the turnstiles. Now, Zep took that total up a notch to 76,229 with the group earning some $792,361 for their efforts.

Breaking for two-odd weeks after the gargantuan events of Michigan, Led Zeppelin were still receiving various garlands even when off the road. After strolling nonchalantly up the steps of the Grosvenor House hotel in London's swanky Mayfair on May 12, 1977 to attend the 23rd Ivor Novello Awards, the group (minus an absent John Bonham) were presented with a trophy for their 'Outstanding Contribution to British Music'. Having taken the best part of a million dollars for one night's work only 12 days before and with an anticipated profit of another $30 million being talked up by the end of the US tour, the gong was perhaps as much about the group's overwhelming financial successes as their ability to write great songs.

Again looking dapper in another pristine white suit – albeit without poppies or dragons for this more formal occasion – and cracking the same Cheshire cat grin that had served him so well for the last nine years, Jimmy Page appeared positively chuffed when posing for photographs at the Ivor Novello Awards. And for good reason, too. Standing next to Robert Plant, John Paul Jones and his real partner-in-crime Peter Grant, Page's dreams of forming the perfect band had now come to almost perfect fruition, his intransigent will rewarded with untold riches, golden trophies and the adulation of millions. In short, the plan had come off.

"I remember him well back in the summer of 1968 when he came in for that first interview at *Melody Maker*," Chris Welch said in 2015. "Very, very charming was Jimmy. Good looking too, very young looking actually, and with a good sense of humour. Not sly, but maybe... impish. Anyway, I recall him telling me about his new group, which he was calling Led Zeppelin. I started writing the name down in my notebook as 'Lead'. But he stopped me immediately and said, 'No, that's not how you spell it. It's L-E-D'. Very Jimmy, that. He could give the impression of being almost diffident but he's always on the case. Always. Jimmy always knew where he was going. But then," Welch concluded, "came 1977 and the American Incident. And God, poor Robert. From there on in it really became the 'Annus Horribilis' for Led Zeppelin."

The first real blow to the empire Page had built with Led Zeppelin was dealt some three months after the band's resounding triumph at the Ivor Novello Awards. Back on the road for the third and final leg of their city-hopping US tour after having re-conquered LA with six straight nights at The Forum – "The only rock group in history to sell out six shows!" screamed the posters – Zep rolled through Seattle and Florida before arriving on July 23, 1977 at the cavernous Alameda County Coliseum in Oakland, California. On paper, it was just another gathering of the tribes, really, albeit one taking place on a sweltering hot West Coast Saturday.

But then things went seriously wrong.

As evidenced, Peter Grant's brusque, no-nonsense managerial style and gift for both mental and sometimes physical intimidation had always lent an air of menace to Led Zeppelin's business dealings. Grant's "right hand man" Richard Cole was also no slouch when it came to strong-arm tactics, being perfectly capable of giving a verbal dressing down to those who deserved it (and some who probably didn't) while also rendering anyone unconsciousness with one, well-aimed punch. And lest we forget, on occasion there was a definite need for such behaviour. From disreputable promoters, T-shirt hawkers and bootleggers to crazed fans, "wannabes" and gatecrashers, Led Zeppelin were at risk either financially or physically every hour of every day. Grant had even gone as far as to hire decoy limousines after fans had repeatedly thrown themselves at the cars when the group tried to leave venues after concerts. "They really needed heavy security," the Pretty Things' Phil May later told *Uncut*. "They'd go to a club in LA and if they didn't have 18 gorillas around, they wouldn't get a moment's peace."

Perhaps more than anyone in the group, Jimmy Page knew of the dangers surrounding Led Zeppelin. Having already received a reported visit backstage from Lynette 'Squeaky' Fromme of Manson Family fame in 1975, he had also been privy to the attentions of another worrying fan around the same time. "Actually, it was a lot more serious than I thought," he later told writer David Hancock. "The guy was a real crazy and had all these photographs on the wall with circles around them. It was a real Manson situation and he was sending out waves of absurd paranoia. I got to hear of it and hired a security guard along for the tour. It was actually a lot worse than everyone at first believed. Eventually this guy was tracked down and got carried away to hospital. He would have had a go, though. But I don't think too much should be drawn from all those experiences. It was certainly nothing to do with the [Manson] Family or anything like that, because I met some of them later. In America, there's just a lot of lunatics living on the edge and it was one of those things."

With such threats to life, limb, mind and pocket, building an impenetrable wall around Led Zeppelin seemed to make real sense.

Yet, as time went by, rumours began to spread that the band's own security staff were now taking things too far, their heavy-handed tactics of even more concern than those they were employed to stop. At the London premiere of *The Song Remains The Same*, for instance, a story spread that Zep's minders had thrown a photographer from a first-floor roof onto a parked car below when he became a little too intrusive with his camera lens. Another tale had an over-zealous fan hit across his fingers with a hammer after getting a little too close for comfort to the band onstage.

By the 1977 US tour, these anecdotes were gathering pace and intensity. Drugstore staff had reportedly been intimidated by Zep employees, who demanded their prescriptions be filled immediately 'or else'. A further report told of a restaurant in Philadelphia being levelled by the group's staff, resulting in $20,000 of damages. Boorish behaviour to visiting female fans – always a concern at the best of times – was also becoming rife. "No head," went the slogan, "no backstage pass." There were even outlandish stories of guns, knives and knuckledusters being pulled on anybody who said or did the wrong thing. And so it went.

Of course, there was no evidence to suggest that the band themselves were involved in any of these reported incidents. In fact, Robert Plant seemed completely unaware of where things might be heading when interviewed in April 1977. "All this stuff about us being barbarians is perpetuated by the road crew," he joked with writer Lisa Robinson. "They check into hotels under our names. They run up disgusting room-service bills and then they take the women of the town by storm by applying masks of the four members of the group. It gets us a bad name. And sells a lot of records."

Page, too, was keen to reiterate that when it came to matters of violence – implied or actual – Led Zeppelin were essentially clueless. "I know now that a lot of violence that went on was kept from the group, so we rarely knew anything about it," he later told Nick Kent in 2003. "It was only near the end that I saw it truly manifesting itself. It had got very heavy by then and was so far removed from what the true spirit of the band was about. The bad elements in the organisation grew out of control and it became a terrible misuse of the power of the band... people around us abusing our power."

On July 23, 1977 in Oakland, it all reached an ugly crescendo, though conflicting accounts of precisely what occurred still blur the issue. It seems fairly certain, however, that tempers had been steadily rising backstage at Alameda County Coliseum all day, with concert promoter Bill Graham's own road crew and Zep's security team butting heads at least once before "it all went to rat shit". Having watched Led Zeppelin's meteoric rise to stardom from the wings of San Francisco's Fillmore West and Winterland in the late sixties, Graham was now a distinguished veteran of the industry and something of a West Coast legend in his own right. "Bill," said one industry insider "was probably the most powerful concert promoter on the western seaboard, if not all of the States." As such, he, Peter Grant and Zep had always enjoyed a financially beneficial, trouble-free relationship. But that was about to change. "I'd [already] heard about the ugliness of their security, how they were just waiting to kill," he later wrote in his own autobiography, *My Life Inside Rock And Out*. "They had these bodyguards that were immense. A couple had police records in England. They were just thugs."

Reportedly, the first altercation at Oakland was sparked by an off-the-cuff comment from Jim Downey, a member of Bill Graham's road crew, to Peter Grant as he was walking from the stage. "Jim said to Grant, who looked very tired, something like 'Do you need help?'" Graham later told the press. "From what I can tell, offence was taken to that statement." The offence in question seemed to manifest itself with Grant's new 'Security Co-ordinator' John Bindon – a West London hard man, bodyguard, occasional actor[202] and according to the Pretty Things' Skip Allan "an absolute nutter" – allegedly striking Downey's head against a concrete wall. It then got worse.

Accompanying his father and Led Zeppelin on the final leg of their 1977 US tour was Peter Grant's then 11-year-old son, Warren. He appeared to be having a whale of a time, too. "I was on the 1977 tour for quite a few weeks and I travelled on the Starship,"

---

202 John Bindon actually appeared as a London mobster alongside Mick Jagger in *Performance*. He was also cast as a crime boss in the seminal 1971 Brit-flick *Get Carter*.

he later told Chris Welch. "It had 'Led Zeppelin' painted on the side and I remember sitting in huge seats and seeing the bar, of course. At the back, there were circular beds with curtains around them, where they could kip, or whatever. I'm sure they weren't just there for kipping!"

As the story goes, Warren Grant was happily roving backstage in Oakland when his attention focused upon a wooden Led Zeppelin sign being removed from the band's trailer by another of Bill Graham's team, security guard Jim Matzorkis. By all accounts, Matzorkis was taking down the sign to put it in storage. The child asked him for it and was refused. According to Warren, things might have then become a little physical. "I was a young kid, I complained and the guard pushed me," he later said. "All I saw was this guy running." But not fast enough.

On a break during Zep's show – the incident might well have occurred while the group were in the midst of their acoustic set – drummer John Bonham had seen what took place and came charging to the youngster's aid. In some accounts, Peter Grant, Richard Cole and John Bindon accompanied him. No shrinking violet himself, Bonzo allegedly placed a well-aimed foot in the security guard's genitals and then walked back to the side of the stage. Understandably, Jim Matzorkis fled from sight as quickly as he could. It wasn't over quite yet.

At some point in the proceedings – probably after the show had finished – Bill Graham approached Peter Grant about the incident. Given that Graham had a temper possibly equalling Led Zeppelin's own cantankerous manager, this was unusual behaviour, but he genuinely hoped to clear the air. At first, it appeared to work. Grant demanded to meet with Jim Matzorkis. Graham demanded that if he did, there would be no blood spilt. "I said 'Peter, you're a very big person, give me your word, nothing physical'. He said 'Bill, I give you my word'." When Bill Graham went to find Matzorkis hiding in a nearby trailer, Grant, Cole and Bindon followed. Introductions were made and then, according to Graham, he was ejected from the vehicle while John Bindon (and possibly Peter) allegedly went to work on the security guard. Richard Cole, in the meantime, held the door shut as they did so, fending off attempts on the part of Graham and his team to get past him with an aluminium pipe[203]. After a minute or two, Jim Matzorkis finally managed to break free. He was later treated at a nearby hospital for cuts, bruises and a broken tooth.

Suffice to say, the atmosphere backstage at Oakland turned murderous. Enraged by an assault on one of their own – and on their own turf, to boot – Bill Graham's security staff and road crew were all for seeking immediate retribution on Grant and co. Graham, on the other hand, wanted no more violence, promising his team he would deal with the matter legally as soon as possible. After all, Led Zeppelin were scheduled to play a second show at the same venue the following afternoon. For the already beleaguered promoter, having 60,000 rioting fans on his hands should a cancellation occur was potentially even more calamitous than what had just happened.

Overnight, Led Zeppelin's lawyers went to work drafting a "Letter of Indemnification" to ensure that Bill Graham would take no legal action against those involved. With the missive finally arriving only an hour before Zep were scheduled to walk onstage in Oakland for a second time, though nothing was officially said, the underlying point being made was crystal clear. Without an appropriate signature, the group might not appear. Nonetheless, there were holes in the document one could drive a bus through. First, Graham had no right to sign anything on behalf of his injured security guard. Further, given the circumstances, any signature obtained from him would now be "under duress". In short, the letter carried little or no legal weight. Graham therefore scribbled his name, Led Zeppelin played their set and the following morning – on Bill's tip-off to the local Sherriff's Department – Peter Grant, John Bindon, Richard Cole and John Bonham were arrested at their hotel on a charge of assault and battery.

The fallout following the Oakland Incident made uneasy reading for both Peter Grant and Led Zeppelin, with a justifiably angry Bill Graham having a field day with the media. "I could never in good

---

203 Reports have it that Richard Cole – or possibly another member of Zep's team – did indeed hit Bill Graham's production manager, Bob Barsotti, with an aluminium pipe, though whether this was before, during or after the trailer incident remains unclear.

conscience book them again," he said at the time, "[and] I cannot help but wonder how much of this in fact went on in the past with these people." *Rolling Stone* was also quick to pick up the story, with journalist Merrill Shindler's icy narrative of events leaving absolutely no doubt as to whose side the magazine was on. To add financial injury to Zep's ever-escalating woes, Graham duly filed a $2 million lawsuit against those deemed responsible, thereby potentially stinging everyone in the pocket as well as in the press. "It could have got a lot worse," Peter Grant later said of the affair. "It was just a very regrettable incident. But we were up against Bill Graham's security guys with their gloves filled with sand. We didn't want to get into that. There were wives and children with us."

At the time, Jimmy Page appeared shaken by the negative coverage around the event, although his remarks still remained measured and understandably supportive of his own team and their part in any alleged assault. "I wasn't there," he said, "but I do know it was nothing really heavy. Certainly nothing heavier than I'd witnessed out front during the concert." Time did not greatly change his mind either. Two years on and Page again appeared reluctant to fully accept Graham's version of events. "I didn't see it, you know, so I can't say exactly what happened, [and] there were no million dollar law suits put out on me," he told *NME*'s Chris Salewicz in November 1979. "You must remember Bill Graham has a very heavy reputation, that all his security people have a reputation for heaviness. [And] as for Peter, well, he's a very big guy and if people are coming up to him all the time and calling him a bastard and telling him to piss off to his face, then he's probably going to react accordingly."

Back in February 1978, the legal issues around Oakland were finally resolved, though certainly not to the satisfaction of Bill Graham. Pleading 'Nolo contendere'[204], Peter Grant, Richard Cole, John Bindon

---

204 A Latin phrase, 'Nolo Contendere' literally means 'I do not wish to contend' (it is also referred to on a plea of 'No contest'). In legal terms, by entering 'Nolo contendere', one does not accept or deny responsibility for the charges but agrees to accept punishment. It also differs from a straightforward plea of 'Guilty' because it cannot be used against the defendant in another cause of action.

and John Bonham were all found guilty of assault, given suspended prison sentences and fined between $500 and $750. Because there was no requirement for the four to actually appear in court due to the terms of their plea, the civil suit filed against them would also not be heard. In Graham's mind – given the severity of the crime – Grant and his cohorts appeared to be getting off rather lightly. "I can't believe that anyone can go into a trailer, kick the shit out of someone and then the Judge says 'Tut, tut, just be good boys from now on'," he growled. "They'll never learn."

While the leniency of the sentences meant that everyone escaped jail, the aftermath of what occurred in Oakland did not recede any time soon. Not only did Peter Grant come to bitterly regret his actions[205], but Page was still answering questions about the incident some 11 years later. "There are all these horrific stories about what's supposed to have happened there, [but] I don't think it was as bad as it was built up to be, to be truthful with you," he told *Musician*'s Charles M. Young in 1988. "I'm not saying it didn't happen, but you know what it's like over there. If you sneeze on someone, they'll sue you. I'm not denying somebody got hit, because they did. It just wasn't anywhere near... it just got blown out of all proportion."

Ultimately a sorry affair that tainted Led Zeppelin's image, reputation and standing at home as well as in the States, the events at Oakland should have been the only lowlight of what had been an otherwise triumphant comeback for the band. But there was far worse news to come. Only days after Peter Grant and Bill Graham severed their once amicable relationship, Robert Plant took a phone call from his wife in England informing him that their five-year-old son, Karac, had died suddenly

---

205 Dire Straits manager Ed Bicknell became a close friend of Peter Grant during the last decade of Grant's life. According to him, the Zep man read Bill Graham's autobiography when it was published and was moved to tears by the promoter's description of what happened at Oakland. "He was in tears on the telephone," Bicknell later told Chris Welch for his book *The Man Who Led Zeppelin*. "He said 'This book has come out and it tells the full story... I don't want to be thought of as a bad person.' Towards the end of his life, Peter had his regrets. "Oakland," Bicknell concluded, "was a source of great regret to him."

from a viral infection. Obviously devastated, Robert – accompanied by John Bonham, Richard Cole and assistant Dennis Sheehan – left for home immediately, causing Zep's remaining US dates to be cancelled.

After their son's funeral – which was attended by Bonham and Cole, but not by Page, John Paul Jones or Grant[206] – Plant and his wife Maureen went into seclusion, cutting themselves off from the world to deal with their grief. Given some of the press coverage that followed, it was the best thing they could have done. Obviously in pursuit of easy sales (when they might have been better served pursuing a sensitivity chip), a publication or two tried to draw links between the recent tragedy and Jimmy's interest in the occult. With various stories and theories already running about "The Zeppelin curse", "Bad karma" and Page's personal deal with the devil bringing bad luck upon the group, this was opportunistic journalism at its worst. "All that rubbish about a curse on the band," said a rightly aggrieved Chris Welch, "or it being God's punishment on them and Jimmy. Oh, really? Come on..."

Swan Song office manager Unity MacLean was just as eager to rubbish any such claims or bug-eyed theories. "You've got to weigh up the balance here," she later told *Uncut*. "It was a freak accident that Robert's little boy died. The poor child became dehydrated. It means they can't bounce back. People don't realise how quickly a child can go downhill. It wasn't anything to do with 'a curse'." No doubt disgusted by coverage attempting to draw parallels between his interest in Aleister Crowley and involvement with *Lucifer Rising* and Zep's travails, Page chose silence as his weapon. Let them write what they liked. He would not even dignify it with a response.

The death of Karac Plant coupled with the events of Oakland rightly brought Led Zeppelin to a stuttering halt in the summer of 1977. Diaries were wiped, engagements suspended and plans put on hold. For the first time since Jimmy Page formed the group in 1968, they were on an

---

206 Due to various circumstances, on the day of the funeral Jimmy was in Egypt, Peter in Long Island, New York and John Paul on holiday with his family (unfortunately, not contactable by phone at the time). According to Richard Cole, Robert was "very hurt" by their absence.

indefinite hiatus, their future uncertain, perhaps even hanging in the balance. "No one pushed Robert to do anything," Richard Cole later said. "Jimmy, Peter and the band sat back and said, 'When you're ready, let us know what you want to do...'"

For the best part of a year, the answer was nothing.

CHAPTER 27

Wearing And Tearing

Led Zeppelin finally returned to active recording duty at Abba's newly opened Polar Studios in Stockholm, Sweden on November 6, 1978. On the face of it, it was an odd choice of venue at which to reconvene: "The world's biggest pop group," ran one joke at the time, "playing host to the world's biggest rock group". Yet Solar was as good a place as any for the quartet to make their musical comeback. Clean. Clear. Pristine. Modern. All the things, in fact, that might help Zep put their recent past behind them and enable them to find a new way forward. If they still could, that is.

Indeed, just a year before, some genuinely believed the world had seen the last of Led Zeppelin. The bloody mess in southern California. The tragic death of Karac Plant. Then the quiet retreat, followed by an eerie silence. From the outside looking in, the signs pointed to a group capsizing under the weight of its own despair, its time perhaps finally done. Worse still, there was even some credence to support this bleak view, with both Zep and their troubled manager having to navigate several dark passages before finding the way back towards the light.

In Peter Grant's case, his personal woes had continued to intensify long after that mad afternoon in southern California. Following his recent divorce, he found himself almost immediately in the midst of a new battle, this time for the custody of his children. Dangerously overweight, drinking and drugging too much and stressed way beyond his own natural limits, there was now little or no calming Peter down, with the walls of his Swan Song office often shaking as a result. "There had always been an underlying current of anger [at Swan Song]," Unity MacLean told *Uncut* in 2011, "and there was a lot of anger in Peter Grant."

By early 1978, this unstable mix of internal pressure, dangerous chemicals, latent gall and impending court cases simply proved too much for him, with Grant suffering a mild heart attack. Already diabetic, he was immediately ordered by doctors to cut out sugar, spirits and fatty foods in order to better manage his condition and lose weight. A mighty task for a mighty man, then, and one that would take him time to right.

Elsewhere, it was marginally better, though there were still hurdles here and there to be overcome. With the band pretty much scattering to the four winds after the events of late July 1977, each member of Led Zeppelin had been left to contemplate the future in their own way. For renowned family man John Paul Jones, this was a simple task. Zep's enforced hiatus simply allowed him to spend more time with his wife and children. Rumoured not to have greatly enjoyed the last US tour pre or post-Oakland – "The bigger places weren't as much fun... presumably the crowd were having fun, but we couldn't really see them..." – the bassist seemed wholly content to now shut the door behind him and play house for a while. Thankfully, he continued to write songs – "the odd tune," JPJ later laughed – on his brand new toy: a gleaming polyphonic analogue synthesiser Yamaha had christened 'The GX1'. Both the songs and the synth would make their impact felt soon enough.

John Bonham also seemed glad of the chance to let the dust settle, his role in the assault of Jim Matzorkis perhaps not as pronounced as that of Peter Grant, Richard Cole and John Bindon, but surely serious enough to give him pause if he let it. "Bonzo was a huge adult with the emotions of a six-year-old child," Zep's US publicist Danny Goldberg later told *Q*. "[He] had artistic licence to indulge in any sort of infantile or destructive behaviour that amused him." In reality, making excuses for Bonham's boorish on-the-road behaviour was becoming progressively harder, with Oakland only the latest in a series of other similarly regrettable incidents: allegedly punching the face of a promotional assistant in 1973, putting the fear of God into a female stewardess on board the Starship in 1975, and even waving a gas gun above his head in a Monte Carlo restaurant in plain sight of several visiting mobsters before Richard Cole had the good sense to knock him out cold.

Yet with Bonham, all such behaviour seemed to stem from one inevitable source. "I think when he was on tour, he missed Pat and his family so much, it was drink, drink, drink and then his temper would come out," said his sister, Debbie, in 2003. "But to paint him solely as an illiterate thug was wrong." For the time being at least, Bonzo would face no such temptations. With Zep off the road, it was now a tractor seat rather than the drum stool that occupied his days. "Bonzo was a thoroughly nice bloke when he was sober, though as everyone knows, he could also be one mean drunk," said Chris Charlesworth. "Really, he was just a home-loving farmer at heart. It was only when you took him away from the cows and sheep and put him on the road with Zep that the problems seemed to start."

When it came to Led Zeppelin's two front men, again, all appeared quiet. Following the premature end of the band's US tour, Jimmy Page was quick to assume his role as leader, stepping out in front of the press to clarify Zep's position. Though he would not be drawn on daft questions pertaining to "curses" or "bad karma", Page was nonetheless eager to rubbish any rumours that the final chord had been struck. Using Capital Radio DJ Nicky Horne's show *Your Mother Wouldn't Like It* as his main media platform, on October 3, 1978, Page reiterated that Led Zeppelin would be back, but only when they were ready.

In the past, that 'ready' had traditionally been in the hands of Jimmy Page. But things had changed. Zep's future now seemed dependent wholly on Robert Plant. Knocked sideways by the death of his son, no one could blame Plant for taking his time in returning to the group or ruminating over his last two years within it. After all, since the accident in Rhodes, Robert's life had been a rollercoaster of hospitals, recording studios, stadiums and silence. Determined to clear his head (or, as likely, numb it completely), the singer reportedly spent his nights drinking beer in the gardens of his West Midlands home, that previously svelte waistline expanding an inch or two as a result.

Nonetheless, by January 1978, there were definite signs Plant was starting to overcome his malaise. Obviously itching to do something, he and long-time Zep sound engineer Benji Lefevre threw in their lot with Birmingham punk band Dansette Damage. Traipsing over to Old Smithy Studios in Kempsey, Plant ending up producing the group's first single, 'NME/The Only Sound', even adding some yelping backing vocals to the tune for good measure. A novel way to idle away a few stray hours, Zep's mighty but now veteran singer must still have had trouble stifling the giggles when the Dansette's own vocalist launched into the line "Being an old fart just ain't my rave...."[207] Again, the times, as they say, were changing.

Yet, despite Robert Plant's return to the musical fray via a good-natured dalliance with punk, it was obviously not enough to make him consider engaging with "the great machine". Indeed, as winter rolled into spring, Plant still appeared unsure, with a now recovering Peter Grant becoming increasingly concerned with the singer's state of mind. "I knew it would take a while for [Robert] to recover from the tragedy," he later told Chris Welch, "but I also knew he would eventually return to the fold. Even so, it was a long uphill struggle to get Robert to work again."

In the end, it might well have been Jimmy Page – albeit by indirect route and probably by accident (though possibly not) – who finally

---

207 Wisely deciding to keep his involvement with Dansette Damage under the radar – he risked looking like a bandwagon jumper, the Dansettes risked ridicule from their fellow punks – Robert Plant kept his name off the single's cover sleeve. Instead, he was credited as 'The Wolverhampton Wanderer' in honour of his beloved football team. However, the group also gave their thanks to a mysterious 'Uncle Bob' elsewhere on the sleeve. A love letter of sorts to Britain's then pre-eminent punk newspaper, the Dansettes' 'NME' received a positive review from the titular publication. One wonders if that might have changed should Percy's involvement have become clear at the time...

managed to reel Plant back to Led Zeppelin. "Well," said Chris Charlesworth, "there's an old story that Jimmy had been jamming with his old mate Roy Harper while Zep were inactive and the two of them discussed Harper doing something with the band if Robert didn't want to return. Anyway, Roy happened to mention his involvement with Page to a journalist in an interview with a farming magazine. Like half the musical community at the time, Harper had obviously bought some sheep. But because of the type of publication it was, Roy's comments completely bypassed the rock press. It didn't bypass Robert Plant, however. Being a farming type himself, Percy actually subscribed to this magazine and was astounded to read he might be replaced by Roy bloody Harper! So, after eight, nine-odd months away, Plant calls Page and it's all on again. A tall tale, perhaps. But some think it happened that way…"

Whatever the truth behind Robert's return, he, Page, Jones and Bonham took their first steps back into collective music-making by regrouping at Clearwell Castle near Gloucestershire's verdant Forest of Dean in May 1978. Here, amidst all the gothic towers and oddly twisting trees, the band indulged themselves with rock'n'roll standards, old blues covers, established favourites from their own stage set and even a smattering of new ideas to ease themselves back into the job of being 'Led Zeppelin'. For Jimmy, the experience sounded not unlike that of hooking up with an old flame after years spent apart. "[It] was basically a period of saying 'Hello' to each other musically once again," he told writer Simon Pallett. "We hadn't played together for so long, [so] Clearwell was the first actual playing we'd done for what seemed like an eternity… [but] it really was just limbering up."

With re-introductions now out of the way and the bit back firmly between their teeth, Zep started limbering up in earnest for the trip to Sweden. Obviously reinvigorated by his time off in Gloucestershire, Robert Plant led from the front, his shaggy head seemingly everywhere all at once. During the summer of 1978, Zep's vocalist not only popped up for a guest spot on anarchic kids TV show *Tiswas* alongside old pal/ presenter Chris Tarrant, but also joined local Brummie heroes Melvin's Marauders onstage at Wolverly Memorial Hall for a spirited attack on

Elvis' 'Blue Suede Shoes', among others. From there it was off to Ibiza, where in the midst of a quick holiday he still found time for a beery jam with visiting pub rock legends Dr. Feelgood at the aptly named Club Amnesia. Come September and Robert was at it again, emerging from the wings at Birmingham Town Hall for a feisty take on Arthur Crudup's 'My Baby Left Me' alongside fellow Swan Song signing Dave Edmunds.

While Plant now appeared match-fit and raring to go, Jimmy Page had kept his head down while Robert was shaking his onstage. Aside from putting in an appearance at Richard Cole and Bad Company drummer Simon Kirke's joint wedding at Chelsea Registry Office (and the party afterwards at Fulham's Golden Lion) on September 16, Jimmy's profile remained spectrally quiet throughout much of 1978. Even the prospect of joining Plant, John Paul Jones and John Bonham – and the Who's Pete Townshend and Pink Floyd's David Gilmour – for an all-star sing-along with Paul McCartney and Wings at Abbey Road's legendary Studio Two[208] failed to tempt him back to his old session stomping ground.

Jimmy was, however, present and correct when Led Zeppelin finally began their run-in towards Stockholm at Ezyhire Studios in early October 1978. Undertaking a furious period of rehearsals, the group now concentrated solely on new material, stirring up some 10 songs in all, seven of which would make up the final cut for their latest album, with the remaining three having to wait their turn before release. That said, there would be no lazy repetition or ploughing the same furrow when it came to the new brood of tunes. As ever with Zep, the onus was still very much on "terra incognito", their determination to find

---

208 Nicknamed 'The Rockestra' by Paul McCartney, the Abbey Road gathering on October 3, 1978 also featured contributions from the Shadows' Hank Marvin, the Faces' Ronnie Lane and Kenney Jones, as well as Gary Brooker and Tony Ashton. Of the tracks recorded with Plant, JPJ and Bonzo, two – 'So Glad To See You Here' and 'Rockestra Theme' – later surfaced on Wings' 1979 LP, *Back To The Egg*. Robert, John Paul and Bonzo were also guests at Wings' 'Concerts For Kampuchea' at Hammersmith Odeon in December of 1979. Again, Jimmy did not attend.

undiscovered terrain as strong as it had been in 1968. "We didn't get caught in a formula," Page later told American radio DJ Redbeard, "and we didn't do singles. We never repeated ourselves. We always avoided that trap."

By November, the quartet and their omnipresent (and now fully recovered) manager Peter Grant had landed in Sweden and were on their way to Polar Studios. While the new venue might have represented a mild risk for a group more used to recording in already established venues throughout the USA and UK, Polar nonetheless had much to commend it. A former cinema now transformed into a state-of-the-art 32-track recording complex[209], its location also afforded Page and co. the perfect opportunity to avoid any messy financial run-ins at home with the Inland Revenue by cutting the LP abroad.

In essence, Led Zeppelin's Polar experience was akin to a weekly commute, with the band flying into Stockholm to begin work on Monday afternoon and then flying out again the following Friday evening. Yet, unlike previous gatherings where everyone more or less turned up at the studio en masse for recording, this time around Zep was divided into day-jobbers and night-dwellers, with Plant and Jones taking the early shift while Page and Bonham were more content to burn the midnight oil. "Well, there were two distinct camps by then," JPJ later told *Rolling Stone*, "and we [Robert and I] were in the relatively clean one."

Though not completely explicit in his remarks, it was still clear that Jones was referring to the fact that by late 1977, both John Bonham and Jimmy Page were struggling with various addictions. Bonzo's alcohol problems had now escalated far beyond a few beers in his local pub, the drummer's increasing fondness for vodka a cause of growing concern for those around him. More, one could see it clearly in his appearance. Though still only just 30 years old, Bonham had recently begun to more resemble a man at least a decade older, the T-shirts and sunglasses

---

209 As well as a then cutting-edge 32-track Studer board, Polar's main space – Studio A – also featured four separate/isolated rooms, each one with distinct acoustics and baffle boards.

unable to disguise his sagging paunch or baggy eyes.[210] On the other hand, the rumours surrounding Page were more narcotics-based, with the guitarist's name continuing to be linked in whispered allegations to both cocaine and heroin. By 2003, he seemed to admit that at least some of these rumours might have been true. "I don't regret it," Jimmy said in response to writer Nick Kent's enquiries about his use of drugs, "because when I needed to be focused I was really focused. That's it."

Such odd patterns in time management and the distribution of labour were bound to have an effect on the recording of Zep's new LP, and so it proved. With JPJ and Plant left to their own devices during the daylight hours, they began to work together much more than before, a fact soon to be reflected in the prominence of Jones' song-writing credits on the album. "John Paul had just bought his Yamaha dream machine, the same one that Stevie Wonder had," Jimmy later told *In The Studio*, "and it enabled him to write complete songs to which Robert then wrote lyrics. I was cool with that stuff. It was really good."

That said, neither Page nor Bonham could be accused of coasting. Though often arriving at Polar just as Robert and JPJ were doing up their coats to leave, Zep's drummer and guitarist were both on reasonable form at Polar, their contributions both precise and still inventive. Indeed, once the week in Stockholm was over, it was Jimmy that gathered up the master tapes, bringing them home to Plumpton Place where he would work on overdubs and general production at his own studio before setting off for Sweden again the following Monday. "We recorded [the LP] in just three weeks," he said. "That's really going some. You've got to be on top of it."

As Page said – and just like *Presence* before it – Zeppelin's decision to work at a clip in Stockholm paid off in spades. By mid-December 1978, all four were back home with a tape of their new LP in their back pockets, and even a provisional title and release date. According to some

---

210 Though John Bonham's principal vice was alcohol, like Page, there were allegations he was also a heroin user at the time. "I know the heroin thing was reported about John," Debbie Bonham later told Q. "But it was never brought home to the family. How true it all was, I just don't know."

press reports before Christmas, the band's eighth studio album was to be called 'Look' and in the shops by February 12, 1979. Zep being Zep, said disc did not arrive in February. Or March, April, May, June or July, for that matter. But subsequent stories of a return to the stage "in the grandest possible fashion" carried considerably more weight.

After all that came before, early indications pointed towards Led Zeppelin gently easing their way back into the limelight, with the band perhaps undertaking a short European tour or even a pilgrimage of the UK's smaller halls and clubs in the spring of 1979. Such a low-key approach, however, was never really on the cards. Dead set on making a grand gesture, manager Peter Grant genuinely believed that Zep's return should be an epic event and one truly worthy of their status. "It seemed logical to me that if we were to regain our position as the world's biggest group," he said, "we'd better play the biggest place possible." On May 22, that location was finally revealed as the Knebworth Festival. Set on the grounds of one Hertfordshire's most lavish stately homes, with fields and trees as far as the eye could see, this was to be no sneaky walk on from the wings. "No," laughed Dave Lewis, "this was eyes of the world stuff..."

The date set for the group's comeback was Saturday, August 4, but due to immense demand for tickets, a second show was promptly scheduled for a week later. In keeping with the festival theme, Led Zeppelin were not to be the only performers on either night, with several support acts employed to whet the crowds' appetite in advance of the main event. As always with such things, wild rumours circulated as to who might be propping up Zep, with names like Van Morrison, Dire Straits and even scruffy pop punks the Boomtown Rats all reported to be in the frame. In actuality, it was old folkies & old friends Fairport Convention, American country rockers Commander Cody, musical polymath Todd Rundgren and, somewhat improbably, Cockney pub duo Chas & Dave who were charged with the task. As a bonus ball (and possibly to help ticket sales along for night number two), Keith Richards and Ronnie Wood were to step away from their day job with the Stones and perform as 'The New Barbarians' alongside jazz bass supremo Stanley Clarke and former Faces pianist Ian McLagan. For those seeking a Bruce

Springsteen substitute, Southside Johnny & the Asbury Dukes were also along for the ride on both dates.

With Jimmy, Robert and Bonzo had already joined Bad Company at encore time for an animated rendition of Don Nix's hoary R&B classic 'Going Down' at Birmingham Odeon in early April, all that was left to do was to gather up John Paul Jones and head into rehearsals for Knebworth. Arriving at Bray Studios in Berkshire in late June, Zep went about the business of pulling together their song list in deadly serious fashion, the band stripping down to shorts and T-shirts in an effort to combat the effects of an atypically dry British summer. As the group battled the heat, the technicians and designers battled with the mechanics of their stage set, as a huge new lighting rig, laser effects and video cameras were all put to the test. Curiously for the normally stoic Zeppelin, nerves were starting to show, with Plant even daring to suggest that for those eyeing a 'heroes' return', they best look elsewhere. "It's not a question of are we heroes anymore," he said. "Heroes are in books. Old books." Ever the leader, Jimmy Page kept quiet. No interviews, but for a quick comment that he was "vibing up for the shows". If something was going to go wrong, it would not be Page that blinked first.

With the clock now running down, Led Zeppelin made their final preparations for Knebworth by playing two warm-up dates in Denmark at the intimate setting of Copenhagen's 2,000-seat Falkoner Theatre on July 23 & 24. Some 11 years before, they had torn the doors off Scandinavia, using the region as a frisky warm-up before their onslaught on the USA and UK. Unfortunately, it was a different group that took to the stage this time around, one that sounded creaky and frankly under rehearsed, the energy that had always defined and sometimes rescued them now replaced by long spells of instrumental awkwardness and lax rhythmic interplay. Worryingly, Page often seemed the worst offender, his fingers meandering around the fretboard rather than creating sparks. By the second gig, there were signs that these kinks were being ironed out, but unless Jimmy really had a magic wand to hand, it looked like Zep might be heading towards an embarrassing collapse on August 4.

The calm before the storm came at the band's first soundcheck on the grounds at Knebworth, with an unexpected guest adding a much-needed burst of humour among the ranks. "We were doing 'Trampled Under Foot' at the soundcheck," Page recalled to *Mojo* in 1999, "[and] I was playing along, concentrating on the guitar. I looked around and there was [Bonzo's son] Jason on the drums! It was so John could go out front and listen to the sound balance. I remember John just standing there, laughing."

Now 13 years old, Jason Bonham had been raised by his father on a staple diet of only the very best drummers, with the teenager gorging himself on the work of percussive greats such as Buddy Rich, Elvin Jones and Motown legend Bernard Purdie. Having long graduated from his mini-Ludwig kit, Jason was now in training on the real thing. He was also extremely loud. "When we did the first soundtrack for Knebworth, the police told us we could be heard 13 miles away," Robert Plant later told *Talks Music*. "That was basically Jason running around the kit. And he was the son of the real one!" The 'real one' was justly proud. After watching Bonham Junior go through his paces from the field below, Bonzo quipped, "It's the first time I've ever seen Led Zeppelin!" It turned out to be a curiously prophetic comment.

So it was that after 24 months' absence from the stage and over four years since they last played Great Britain, Jimmy Page and Led Zeppelin were finally ready to take on their largest ever British gig. Yet, they must have wondered what exactly it was they were taking on. After all, it was only two years before that Clash bassist and punk pin-up Paul Simonon had declared them an irrelevancy. "Led Zeppelin? I don't need to hear the music," he growled to *NME*. "All I have to do is look at one of their album covers and I feel like throwing up." By now, however, punk itself had fallen, with the Sex Pistols turned into a farce by the exit of their combustible singer Johnny Rotten and the continuing antics of manager Malcolm McLaren. Even the Clash had given it all up as a bad job, chucking away their stencilled shirts and Situationist slogans in favour of sharp suits and a spirited attack on the pockets of America.

In fact, everywhere Page and Zep looked there were signs of change, uncertainty and loss. In the States, Aerosmith and Kiss were teetering on towards the abyss, as drugs and drink threatened to undo both bands, leaving only Rush seemingly ready to embrace the challenge of an impending new decade. At home, long established hard rock groups such as Thin Lizzy, UFO and Judas Priest faced 'The New Wave of British Heavy Metal' head on, the youthful likes of Def Leppard and Iron Maiden readying themselves to do battle with the old guard. Elsewhere, Black Sabbath were without a singer, Deep Purple had long broken up and Pink Floyd were in the process of building an enormous, insurmountable wall around themselves. The Who, compromised by the death in September 1978 of drummer Keith Moon, were at a crossroads, leaving only the Rolling Stones, seemingly impervious to changing times, to march blindly on. Where Led Zeppelin sat in the overall scheme of things was anyone's guess. Only Jimmy Page seemed certain. "Everyone was saying we didn't have the following anymore," he later said. "But I knew we did. There was no doubt..."

Page was right. What the 1979 Knebworth Festival confirmed beyond all else was that despite the protests of punk and new wave, the chilly advance of 'synthpop' and the "ups, downs and all arounds" of their peers and progeny, Led Zeppelin were still the world's biggest rock band and had an audience to prove it. Flying in by helicopter just half an hour before they were due onstage, the band was greeted by the sight of over 100,000 people below, Knebworth having transformed itself into a giant village in which the faithful hordes were gathered in anticipation of Zep's return. "I remember arriving by helicopter over the crowd," said John Paul Jones. "That was a sight and a half, you know... an emotional homecoming."

While the competing smells of beer, dope and patchouli oil hung in the air, making it appear as if punk had never happened, Zep's own especially assembled army were busy making doubly sure that not one ounce of anarchy was loosed upon Knebworth. With 500 police, 400 roving stewards, 40 on-site counsellors and 350 Red Cross/St. Johns' Ambulance staff working front of house, and a further 150 crew taking care of business backstage, this was a huge, almost imposing operation, and one not often seen on British soil. Of course, having already conquered most every stadium in the United States, Page was well used to it. "When you're taking about the passion of the fans, the way it manifested... it was simply that the concerts got bigger and bigger," he later told *Classic Rock*. "You could see, by the record sales as well, that the popularity was immense... and that was the manifestation of it, playing bigger shows. The reality of Led Zeppelin, when you look at it, was the audiences just kept swelling, right up to... Knebworth."

Now it was time to get on with it.

Opening with the door-rattling chords of 'The Song Remains The Same', the roar that met Led Zeppelin when they took to the stage at Knebworth was, without exaggeration, truly frightening to behold. Part elongated bellow, part delighted howl, it lasted for at least 10 seconds and shook those making it as much as the band themselves. For some, no doubt, this deep cry amounted to pure relief, the sight of their favourite group now back on the boards after such a prolonged and tortuous absence causing them to lose temporary control of their throat muscles. For many others, however, it was a whoop produced upon seeing Zep in the flesh for the first time, with some in the audience simply too young to have witnessed the little miracles of Birmingham Odeon and Alexandra Palace in 1972 or even Earls Court four years hence. Page wasn't looking for explanations as to the cause, however. He just looked happy to be back.

In truth, Zep's appearance at the Knebworth Festival on August 4, 1979 was not without its fair share of glitches. While there was no doubt it was great to see them onstage again, there were times when the band lacked for match-fitness, their songs sounding sometimes ragged or plain undercooked in the middle. 'No Quarter', particularly, fell into this category. Even trimmed back to 18-odd minutes in length – presumably to accommodate the demands of a leaner, post-punk universe – the tune still meandered terribly in the middle, with Jimmy and JPJ's usually razor-sharp solos now blunt and listless. Robert Plant, too, took some time to find his range as Zep's first three tracks on the night ('The Song...', 'Black Dog' and 'Celebration Day') were all sung in a deeper register than before. Still, given the fact he was working from a standing start after two years offstage, such small problems were eminently forgivable.

When Led Zeppelin did get it right, they were unstoppable. 'Trampled Under Foot', for instance, was full of flair and guile, while 'Since I've Been Loving You' carried the same dual sense of suffering and exhilaration that made it such a live classic on the 1973 tour. 'Over The Hills And Far Away' was also vintage Zep, JPJ and Bonzo tackling all those impossible fills as Page and Plant had fun pulling on the melody line. Even the ever-complex 'Kashmir' was dispensed with real authority, causing *Sounds'* David Hepworth to temporarily abandon pouring cold water on the group in his review of Knebworth to join the side of the yea-sayers. "The twisting Byzantine riff actually raises the spirits rather than riding roughshod over them like pre-Raphaelite boot boys." Given that at least 80% of the British rock press were now actively hostile to Zep in the wake of punk, this was high praise indeed.

As for Jimmy Page, if not quite 1975 all over again, the guitarist still had the power to transport both himself and the audience. Having now consigned those music journalist-baiting dragon and poppy suits to the back of his wardrobe in favour of simple cream trousers and an understated blue shirt, Jimmy was still as thin as a stick and pale as the moon above. But when the violin bow emerged from behind the amp, the cheers that greeted its arrival were as strong as ever.

Accompanied by new special effects that found him standing in the midst of an eerily-glowing, ever-revolving laser pyramid during his solo spot, Page remained the nearest thing that show business had ever produced to a guitar wizard. Soaked in sweat, wracked with concentration and producing the most hellish of sounds from his sunburst Gibson Les Paul, the sight of Zep's leader bathed in green light was still pure, unadulterated rock theatre. "He had a great sense of drama and style, did Jimmy," said Chris Charlesworth. "And if there was ever a guitar player who understood the power of mystery, it was him."

Taking the stage at 9.30 or so on Saturday night and playing for the best part of three and a half hours, Page and Zep's homecoming at Knebworth might have had its hiccups, but for the fans at least, it was all manna from heaven. With the band closing their set on an emotional 'Stairway To Heaven' before a trio of encores ('Rock And Roll', 'Whole Lotta Love' and a lively 'Heartbreaker') properly ended the show, there was nothing left for those gathered beneath the stage but to sing their appreciation. "The first show was very special, because we'd been away for a long time," Page told *Mojo*. "I remember the audience singing 'You'll Never Walk Alone'. [It was] an extremely emotional moment... tears in the eyes, believe me..."

There were also tears for promoter Freddy Bannister. Having narrowly missed the opportunity to book Led Zeppelin for the inaugural Knebworth Festival in 1974 – the headlining slot went to the Allman Brothers instead – Bannister must have been beside himself with joy to have secured their services this time around. Unfortunately, the general air of unpleasantness that had dogged events backstage in sunny Oakland now threatened to return in leafy Hertfordshire when Peter Grant disputed the number of people who had actually attended the show. With a licence granted for 100,000 tickets, Grant was convinced that audience attendance was almost double that figure. Suffice to say, for the group's second performance on August 11 – and reportedly with the full co-operation of Bannister himself – Zep's manager took full control of accounting, using his own staff to man the turnstiles and count the punters in.[211]

With an uneasy atmosphere behind the scenes and fewer fans in attendance[212], 'Knebworth Part Two' was perhaps always fated to have less of an impact, and so it proved. "We always played the best we could," Jimmy later told writer Mick Wall, "... but the first [show] had

---

211 Sadly, the dispute did not end there. Obviously irked by a potential loss of revenue to Led Zeppelin, Grant had aerial photos taken of the crowd at Knebworth sent to a laboratory in New York to ascertain exact attendances for the shows. Reportedly, he believed there were over 200,000 people at the first show and 187,000 at the second (Freddy Bannister claimed a figure of 104,000 for week one). The disagreement between manager and promoter finally saw Bannister's company – Tedoar – forced into liquidation, leaving the Stevenage Borough Council and police force out of pocket to the sum of £2,000 and £50,000 respectively. An unpleasant end, then, to another unpleasant episode.

212 Again, audience attendance figures for Zep's second show at Knebworth remain a matter of some dispute, with some estimates placing the crowd at approximately 180,000, while others have it as low as 50–60,000.

the edge." Following on from a clearly "very refreshed" set from the New Barbarians, Led Zeppelin certainly hit their marks on time and as required, the band making a good fist of 'The Rain Song', 'Sick Again' and a now revitalised 'No Quarter'. Yet, again, the pacing seemed to be a tad off, with tempos either speeding up or dragging, or on occasion coming perilously close to a complete halt. Worse still, the previous week's largely negative press coverage seemed to have genuinely angered Robert Plant who took to publicly defending Zep from the stage. "It rained on us during the week from one or two sources," he told the crowd, "and we're really going to stick it right where it belongs." Nonetheless, by 2005, he was willing to concede that these were not among the group's best appearances. "It didn't work for us," he confirmed to *Uncut*'s Nigel Williamson. "We played too fast and we played too slow and it was like trying to land a plane with one engine. But it was fantastic for those who were there."

As Plant correctly deduced, Led Zeppelin's two-night stand at Knebworth was as much about the fans as the band themselves. As evidenced, for the old guard the gigs represented a chance to once again revel in a key part of their youth, while also showing solidarity to a type of music and approach that had been under threat since the Sex Pistols came knocking in late 1976. For the newer recruits, it was an opportunity to see bona fide legends duck-walking the boards. "Really, we were there," one punter wittily intoned, "to see what all the bloody fuss was about." For Dave Lewis, it was all just two sides of the same coin. "Knebworth was just a terrific show of support for Zeppelin. 200,000-odd people turning up and planting their flag with the band. In a way, they might have been better served playing smaller venues, a few nights at Earls Court, or even a week at The Rainbow, maybe. [But] by then, Peter Grant had become stuck in the mindset of seeing Zep as the biggest band on Earth and therefore they had to play the biggest gigs at the biggest venues. That was Knebworth."

Rough around the edges it might well have been. Yet, Led Zeppelin's return in August 1979 not only ended two years of crippling uncertainty, but also confirmed that whatever the sins and tragedies of the past, there were still four large thrones waiting for the band at any table they wished to sit at. "They'd started calling us demi-gods by then," Jimmy later said, "[but] if they didn't think we played with conviction, they'd be wrong." More, the guitarist was convinced that whatever the music business might have recently thrown up, his own group was still a cut above the rest. "Even if we weren't as good as we might have been at those shows, we were still better than anyone else back then." Ever the optimist, for Jimmy Page at least, Knebworth constituted yet another beginning for both he and Zep, his continuing phrase "Over the top!" now set to resonate well into a new decade. Sadly, Led Zeppelin's Knebworth dates turned out to be more like one last hurrah for the band, with the bar bell soon to call closing time on their marvellous 12-year run.

CHAPTER 28

For Your Life

Quite the family affair, with mothers, fathers, partners and children[213] milling around backstage and another 100,000-odd fans a night front of house, Led Zeppelin's two appearances at Knebworth in August 1979 conclusively proved that the UK at least was still with them in both spirit and, crucially, sheer numbers. But for the recovery to be truly complete, the band had to get the rest of the world on side too. As ever, the easiest way to achieve precisely that was with the release of a new album. In fact, Zep's eighth studio disc was due in shops just before they returned to the stage for their first concert in Hertfordshire on August 4. However, in keeping with several missed deadlines on previous LPs, the record was held up due to production delays with its sleeve. Given the end result, on this occasion, it might have been worth the wait.

Again turning to illustrious design team Hipgnosis to realise their vision, Led Zeppelin asked that their latest album cover portray a "new lick of paint... a return to their roots, but updated with a different twist,"

---

213 In addition to partner Charlotte Martin, Jimmy's parents reportedly attended at least one concert. Robert Plant, too, was accompanied by his wife, Maureen, and their daughter, Carmen, though the couple's baby boy, Logan – then six months old – stayed at home with his grandparents.

this heady combination perhaps meant to symbolise a rebirth of sorts for the group. Having heard their latest songs, Hipgnosis' Aubrey Powell correctly deduced that there was a distinct after-hours feel to the LP and wanted to explore that in any subsequent imagery. Animated by 'Po''s idea, Jimmy Page suggested a late night bar room scenario and the designer duly despatched himself to New Orleans to find one that might well be used for the sleeve. By all accounts, Aubrey found precisely the spot close to Zep's former hang-out of the Royal Orleans Hotel, with The Old Absinthe Bar on 400 Bourbon Street offering the exact sense of shabby grandeur he and Page were after. It was at that point that things got really ambitious. Instead of taking a few simple photographs, Powell and his creative partner, Storm Thorgerson, elected to create a bar of their very own at Elstree's Shepperton Studios. Further, instead of just one cover sleeve, there were now to be six. "Each cover depicted a man in a white suit at a bar[214] taken from the perspective of one of the other six people in the room," Thorgerson told Q in 2003. "The man was burning a piece of paper. You didn't know what it was. Was he destroying evidence or just a painful memory? We really wanted to stretch the listener's imagination."

Obviously on a roll, the duo decided that the six images be produced in sepia tone, but with a brushstroke of pure colour in the middle of each, as if the photograph had actually been wiped by a cloth. "It was like you were looking inside the bar through a dusty window," Thorgerson again told Q, "and the smear was where you'd wiped the pane with your sleeve to peer through." Delighted by Hipgnosis' handiwork thus far, Page was inspired to add a simple, but effective touch of his own to the inner sleeve, suggesting that the two black and white drawings within[215] changed

214 The man in question was 'David H.', a model previously used by Hipgnosis and a friend of Storm Thorgerson. "He had such a great face," Storm later said, "he looked underfed."

215 The black and white line drawings on the LP's inner sleeve depicted a classic 'before and after' scene, with one image showing a full bottle, pack of cigarettes, lighter and ashtray in pristine condition, while the other displayed a smashed glass and partially burnt note with the words 'Dear Jo(hn)' stuffed into a now very full ashtray.

colour when water was added to them. "Jimmy came up with that great idea of using a watercolour on the inner sleeve from one of his daughter Scarlet's books," said Peter Grant. The final conceit was to shrink-wrap the whole package in a brown paper bag, thus making it impossible for prospective buyers to see which of the six album covers they were getting. Perfect pop art or just a brilliant gimmick, the wheeze still fulfilled one of Grant's long-held beliefs about his beloved band. "You could stick a Zep LP in a paper fucking bag and it'd still sell millions."

On August 15, Led Zeppelin put Grant's theory to the test when *In Through The Out Door* was released to the international market. An idiosyncratic yet still beguiling album title, the phrase once again resonated with notions of return. But it also seemed to convey the difficulties involved in re-entering a world where so much had changed in the time Zep had been away. "In through the out door," said Page, "is the hardest way to get back in." Chris Charlesworth saw his point. "That album was a big test for Led Zeppelin, especially in America," he said. "It had been two years since they'd done a gig there and four years since their glory days. We'd had punk, then new wave and during all that time, Zep had really done nothing. Knebworth proved they still had an audience, but there was no real guarantee that would translate into huge world-wide sales. I suspect Jimmy was nervous the day before that one went into the shops."

Ultimately, *In Through The Out Door* turned out to be something of a curiosity all to itself, the strength of the songs veering between two or three stone-cold classics and a smattering of perhaps less distinguished filler material. Dominated by the new writing partnership of John Paul Jones and Robert Plant, the album was also awash with JPJ's Yamaha 'Dream Machine' keyboard, its dreamy tones creating a distinct breakpoint with Zep's previous trademark sound. No bad thing perhaps, as the duo's desire to explore different textures and musical styles at Polar Studios in the daytime absence of Page and Bonham had allowed the band another chance to redefine their boundaries. But with little space given to hard rock, folk or blues, some of the rambunctious energy associated with Led Zeppelin was now lost. For Plant, this was all but inevitable. "Well, we hadn't been in the clamour and chaos for a long time," he later told writer Mat Snow. "In 1977, when I lost my boy, I didn't really want to go swinging around, [so] 'Hey hey mama say the way you move' didn't really have a great deal of import any more. *In Through The Out Door* [was] more conscientious and less animal."

There was also the small, but important matter of Jimmy Page's overall role in the LP. Whereas on *Presence*, the guitarist/producer had all but dominated proceedings, his presence on *In Through The Out Door* felt curiously detached at times. Of course, this was not to say Page was not all over the album. As ever, he was keen to make his mark both in terms of input and innovation. But there remained the distinct feeling on several tracks that Jimmy was almost revisiting his past as a session musician, his guitar entering at speed to create little blasts of havoc or heaven before again withdrawing to the edges of the tune. Indeed, for the first time ever, two of the LP's seven songs bore no writing credit for Page at all.

Like Robert Plant, however, Jimmy offered a sound explanation as to how such changes had come about. "John had [the keyboard] at home and had been working on it, and lo and behold, he's got these songs together," Page told *Radio.com* in 2015. "He'd never written complete songs for Led Zeppelin before. But now he had. It was cool. Because the album before, I'd written it all. It was a guitar driven thing. There [were] keyboards on the first Led Zeppelin album, and [again] over the years. But it made obvious logical sense that if he had numbers that he'd written on this new state-of-the-art keyboard, let's do an album which focuses on the keyboard and features it at the forefront, and that's how it went."

If Jimmy didn't quite inhabit *In Through The Out Door* in the same way as he had *Presence*, the album's first track 'In The Evening' still bore all the hallmarks of a vintage Page performance. Employing a new effects device called a 'Gizmotron'[216] to help create otherworldly drones, rumbling slides and enhanced Arabic scales, Jimmy's sonic trickery at the opening of 'In The Evening' carried the same sense of infernal pleasure one might have expected to hear on his soundtrack to *Lucifer Rising*.

---

216 "It was like a hurdy-gurdy type thing, an electronic wheel," Page later said of the Gizmotron. "You'd hold it near the bridge and depress whichever strings you wanted. Lol Creme of 10cc invented it, (but) I think it never took off and was something of a financial disaster."

Indeed, Page's efforts did not cease at the intro. As the tune powered into life courtesy of Bonzo's lurching bass drum and Robert's chest-beating vocal, Jimmy pulled out the same Lake Placid Blue 1964 Fender Stratocaster employed on the tremolo-heavy 'For Your Life' to add to the overall sense of mayhem. Whether depressing the whammy bar in time with the song's main riff or using it to emulate the sound of a slamming door at the onset of his wigged-out solo, Page was again at his creative best. A feisty way to open any album and, if the rapturous applause that greeted its debut at Knebworth on August 4 was anything to go by, a future live favourite, 'In The Evening' set the bar high for the rest of *In Through The Out Door*.

Unfortunately, said bar immediately dropped a notch or two with 'South Bound Suarez', an amiable, but otherwise inessential ditty written by Plant and Jones while twiddling their thumbs waiting for Page and Bonham to show up at Polar. "We got to rehearsals first and spent a lot of time drinking pints of Pimms waiting for something to happen," Jones later joked. "So, Robert and I wrote a few songs and Jimmy [and Bonzo] added stuff to them." Bouncing along on the piano setting of JPJ's Yamaha GX-1, 'South Bound...''s loose, honky-tonk feel and doo-wop referencing outro were jolly enough, while Jimmy's contrary blast of dissonance certainly added a little extra spice at solo time. Yet, one felt the tune would not even have made the substitute's bench for *Led Zeppelin IV*, *Physical Graffiti* or *Houses Of The Holy*.

The slow-burning 'Fool In The Rain' was thankfully much better. Brilliantly executed by the band – with Bonzo's wrist-snapping rolls and walloping timpani fills worthy of particular praise – the track's undoubted highlight came mid-section when Zep suddenly broke out into a samba, replete with whistles, howls and chugging Latin rhythms[217]. When things eventually righted themselves a minute or so later, Jimmy took his cue

---

217 Zep and Bonham's rude but wondrous samba outburst on 'Fool In The Rain' was actually recorded as a separate track. Also, if rumours are correct, the band's temporary brush with Latin music and rhythms was inspired while watching the 1978 World Cup Finals, which were held in sunny Argentina. The home side won. England, on the other hand, didn't even qualify for the tournament.

and dropped in for a quite formidable solo, its muffled low-octave tones achieved through the use of an MXR 'Blue Box', another effects pedal he had recently experimented with and now made his own.

Then came 'Hot Dog'. Either a wonderfully comedic rockabilly pastiche or complete waste of three minutes and 18 seconds of vinyl depending on which side of the pub table one sat on, 'Hot Dog' really was a tune to divide nations. The only song on *In Through The Out Door* to be credited solely to Page and Plant, like 'South Bound Suarez' before it, one couldn't deny it had a certain sticky charm. Indeed, JPJ's barrel-house piano jabs and Robert's "Elvis Presley via Texas" vocal asides were authentic enough. But however forgiving the ear, its inclusion on the album was as puzzling as the reception the track received when wheeled on for the first time at Knebworth on August 4. Best filed under 'Uninteresting diversion', 'Hot Dog' also had the dubious honour of featuring one of Jimmy's least distinguished guitar parts. Performed in a succession of fits and starts on his brown B-Bender equipped Fender Telecaster, the results were never less than eye-watering.

Thankfully, Page was back to something approximating his best form on 'Carouselambra', a 10-minute tune that heavily recalled the band's first brush with progressive rock on *Houses Of The Holy*. Summoned into existence on Jones' Yamaha Dream Machine during rehearsals at Clearwell Castle in May 1978, Zep had jokingly named it 'The Epic' in honour of both its humungous length and complex musical passages. And epic it indeed was. Full of wind-swept melodies, ever-climbing key changes and rhythmic sleights of hand, 'Carouselambra' also featured a majestic mid-track breakdown that allowed Jimmy to re-acquaint himself with his long-absent Gibson ES-1275 double-neck. Using the guitar's unique timbre to unleash a series of ocean-sized splash chords, Page fair shook the foundations of the track, temporarily dislodging Jones' keyboard part from its position of melodic dominance.[218]

218 Though a key part of his onstage arsenal, Page had never used the Gibson ES-1275 on record before recording 'Carouselambra'. It is also worth noting that Lol Creme's wacky Gizmotron also makes a brief reappearance on 'Carouselambra', its ability to mimic string parts and create strange harmonics put to able use at song's end.

An ambitious enterprise in three distinct parts, 'Carouselambra''s grandiose leanings might well have harked back to a different age, but its sheer sense of ambition could not be faulted.

In subsequent years, *In Through The Out Door* has gained something of a reputation as a moody, even melancholy-sounding album, though in reality many of its tunes were relatively upbeat. The reason for such an assessment must surely be down to the LP's closing tracks: one, a sad-eyed but still uplifting mediation on life and loss; the other, a forlorn midnight blues full of yearning and lust. With 'All My Love', Robert Plant and John Paul Jones conclusively proved their new writing partnership could rival anything penned by – or with – Jimmy Page, the idea for melody and words coming to them "on the spot, even the lyrics". Gently pushed along by JPJ's simple keyboard figure and exquisitely sung by Plant, the song also had a resolutely commercial chorus, so commercial, in fact, that it initially worried Page. "I wasn't really very keen," he told *Guitar World*'s Brad Tolinski in 1993. "I was a little worried about the chorus. I could just imagine people doing 'the wave' and all of that. I just thought 'That's not us'."

Holding his opinion in check, Jimmy again chose to play for the song itself, and just as well, as his contributions turned out to be commendable. Ghosting Robert's almost courtly vocal with a combination of gently clipped chords and country-like figures again courtesy of his B-Bender Telecaster, Page also introduced a beautifully judged acoustic element during his solo, the Spanish guitar's warm, finger-picked tones providing a sweet contrast to the trebly ring of the resolutely electric Fender. Soaked in emotion – Plant was surely in part addressing the death of his son in the lyrics – and showing a new and extremely radio-friendly side to the band, 'All My Love' screamed to be released as a US single[219].

---

219 The band knew 'All My Love' had real commercial possibilities, having already nicknamed it 'The Hook' in honour of its gently insistent chorus. However, for reasons best known to themselves, it was never issued as a 45. That said, for those seeking a '12" version' of the song, an elongated cut of the tune – with a complete ending – does exist and can easily be found on YouTube and at various other web sources.

Yet, it never came, with Zep electing to go instead with the likeable, if inferior 'Fool In The Rain', that particular tune eventually entering the American charts at number 21 in January 1980.

After the gentility and splendour of 'All My Love', Led Zeppelin briefly returned to their earliest inspirations to conclude *In Through The Out Door* with 'I'm Gonna Crawl'. As the title might suggest, a funereally paced blues featuring a vivid string arrangement from JPJ that made one feel as if they were watching an old black and white film as much as hearing a song, '... Crawl''s already melodramatic qualities were amped up by a roaring, Wilson Pickett-approved vocal from Plant and the greasiest, most emotive solo Jimmy had cut since 'Since I've Been Loving You' in 1970. With Bonzo slowly pulling things towards the finish line and Robert surely in need of oxygen by the time they all got there, Jones' final, wavering notes at the close of 'I'm Gonna Crawl' came as blessed relief, allowing the listener to finally step away from the tune while still in one piece.

As with most every Led Zeppelin album before it, *In Through The Out Door* had its share of weaknesses. In addition to the fact that several of the songs lacked for real bite, while conversely, some performances might be construed as being a tad overwrought (see directly above), the LP's production also sounded woolly in places, with Plant's voice occasionally lost in the mix to other instruments. However, ... *Out Door* was by no means a failure, with the likes of 'In The Evening', 'Carouselambra' and 'All My Love' all destined to take their rightful place among the best of Zep's previous work. "We'd had a guitar album," Jimmy later told *In The Studio*. "And now we had a more keyboard-orientated album recorded in a cutting-edge studio that really didn't sound like the others."

Predictably, in the wake of punk, *In Through The Out Door* received a rough ride from some critics, with Zep's veteran status in the music business now used as a stick with which to beat them. "The impressionable first play had everyone in the office rolling around laughing," said *Melody Maker*'s Chris Bohn. "Zep are totally out of touch... displaying the first intimations of mortality. It's time they accepted their fate like men. They squeezed their lemons dry long ago."

Record Mirror was also quick to pick up on the age and irrelevance angle, though, unlike *MM*, it was willing to concede that Zep's collective lemon might have some juice left in it yet. "Yes, Zeppelin are prime targets for the hatchet [and] somehow enormous wealth and longevity is something to be scored. [But] 'Carouselambra' is the sharpest spearhead on the album... magnificent with its flowing mane of keyboards steered and nurtured by John Bonham, [while] 'All My Love' is the peacock of side two... a heroic song couched in the same tones as the opening to 'Stairway To Heaven'."

Surprisingly, it was the new waver's bible *NME* that gave *In Through The Out Door* one of its kindest reviews, as Nick Kent heroically suggested that despite their advancing years, Led Zeppelin remained capable of the odd musical surprise. "Frankly, I came off the lam fully expecting to drive a stake through the heart of this ailing behemoth," he said. "But *ITTOD* is no epitaph. There are potential points of departure that deserve following through. The doctor orders a period of intense activity..."

Though any bouts of intense activity were still some months away, Kent's contention that Led Zeppelin retained at least something of their former potency was soundly confirmed by the sales of *In Through The Out Door*. Reaching number one in the USA in late August 1979, the LP stayed at the top of the American charts for a further six weeks, leading in turn to a new run on the band's back catalogue, all of which re-entered the *Billboard* Top 200 by the end of October, an unprecedented achievement at the time. Of course, punk and new wave had only made a minimal impact on the States so such figures, while surprising (and no doubt delightful for Zep's bank balance), were not reflective of the reception (or lack of it) the group might expect to receive at home. In the end, however, the UK appeared to be as mad about Led Zeppelin as their colonial cousins, with *In Through The Out* Door entering at the top of the British charts and earning itself a platinum disc soon after.

Driven mainly by the penmanship of John Paul Jones and Robert Plant – "God, Jonesy was great," Peter Grant later reasoned, "he put so much effort into [that LP]" – *In Through The Out Door* pulled off the neat trick of not only wrong-footing the post-punk naysayers but also seeing Zep back at the top of the commercial heap just in time for a brand new decade. "It was a chance," JPJ later told *Q*, "to see what else we could do." Nonetheless, Jimmy Page's comparatively diminished role in the enterprise remained surprising. Usually the beating heart at the centre of it all, Page's decision to let Jones and Plant run with the ball was, if not out of character, then certainly poles apart from the man who dragged his band kicking, screaming and, in Robert's case, even wobbling into the studio to complete *Presence*.

But perhaps that was the whole point. Maybe Jimmy wanted to do things differently, at least for a while. "I think after *Presence*, and at the time of *In Through The Out Door*, Jimmy was content enough to go with the flow," reasoned Dave Lewis. "John Paul had come in with some keyboard ideas, Robert was coming back to himself, and John... well, John was John. But that position wasn't going to last long. Jimmy was never going to lose control of Led Zeppelin."

Whatever the reason behind his thinking, *In Through The Out Door's* resounding chart success should have been a time of celebration for Page. But in actuality, there was yet more tragedy for him to contend with. While his colleagues made their hosts at *Melody Maker* eat humble pie by turning up to collect the award for 'Best Group' at the music paper's annual awards, Jimmy was readying himself to provide evidence at an inquest. On October 15, 1979, Philip Churchill Hale, a 23-year-old designer/photographer and friend of Page, had died at the guitarist's house in Plumpton Place, East Sussex. Though any foul play was ruled out, the autopsy did find that Hale carried high traces of both alcohol and cocaine in his bloodstream, the effects of which later led to his death by inhalation of vomit. Inevitably, Philip Hale's sad demise again triggered hearsay concerning Jimmy's own possible drug use, with his lessened contribution to Zep's latest LP now taking on a somewhat different slant. Obviously shaken by events, Page's response was to sell Plumpton Place and buy a new home, though that too would soon hold its fair share of ghosts.

Perhaps the best antidote for his recent loss was work and Jimmy Page found it in spades by the spring of 1980, as Led Zeppelin made preparations for another tour. However, due to Robert Plant's newfound reluctance to revisit their old stomping ground of America, the band were now forced to turn their attentions towards Europe. While losing valuable income Stateside because of Plant's then "difficult frame of mind" was no doubt irritating for manager Peter Grant, it did allow him to explore an idea that had been percolating in Page's brain for many a month. "[He] said 'Let's forget the big lighting rigs and go back to basics.'" As ideas went, it wasn't a bad one. Since December 1978, the group had only really gathered together for Knebworth and that had constituted just two dates. If they were now to return to proper live work, then scaling down the size of their operation and playing more intimate gigs made some sense. "I'm not sure Robert wanted to go back to the States just yet," said Dave Lewis. "It was while there that he'd heard the news about his child and perhaps he wasn't mentally strong enough to face it all again. Also, they didn't feel the time was right for a British tour – the press were still hostile – so going to Europe kind of worked. In fact, it was a tactic they'd employed successfully in Scandinavia in the early days, so why not?"

Buoyed by the prospect of a hassle-free jaunt across the European heartlands, Grant arranged a two-week tour while Page put Zep through their paces at London's Rainbow and New Victoria Theatre, with both halls the perfect size to work up their new small-scale show. Cutting back their lighting rig from a burgeoning 320 lamps to a more modest 120, Bonzo's ornate 'drum throne' was also jettisoned, the sticksman having to make do with a plain old rostrum instead. One thing that didn't greatly change was Zep's seeming resistance to include many new songs in their long-established set. Sticking with the classics, only 'In The Evening', 'Hot Dog' (both of which the band had already debuted live the previous summer), 'All My Love' and a surprise late entrant were deemed worthy of inclusion for the upcoming tour.[220]

Deadly serious about getting it right after the wobbles and shakes of Knebworth a year before, the group extended their rehearsal period from April into May, returning to the very same stage at Shepperton

---

220 Zep had vague plans for 'Carouselambra' to be given a live spin as part of the 1980 tour but, given the complexity and length of the tune, these were soon dropped.

Studios where they had filmed linking passages for *The Song Remains The Same* some six years hence for their final run-throughs. By June 17, they were ready to go and in front of an audience in Dortmund.

Over 14 dates across Germany, Belgium, Holland, Switzerland and Austria throughout June and July of 1980, Page and Led Zeppelin really did make good on their promise to go "back to basics". A far cry from the three-hour plus displays the band had put on in the mid-seventies, Zep's set was now shaved down to a more manageable 120 minutes, with the bloated arrangements and extreme displays of technical virtuosity punk had taken such issue with left well behind in Oakland and Knebworth. Guitar heroics were clipped, drum solos cut back and keyboard explorations mostly absent. They even had the brilliant idea of resurrecting the long deceased 'Train Kept A-Rollin'' as their new set opener[221], its no-nonsense rockabilly twang giving an immediate urgency to the band's newfound sense of attack. That said, Zep's gift for improvisation was still very much present, with encore time used to turn 'Whole Lotta Love' and 'Heartbreaker' into net-free exercises in high-wire musical acrobatics.

"It was a very different Led Zeppelin from the one I'd seen at Knebworth," Dave Lewis continued. "Very scaled down, very tight set list and a real minimum of fuss. Sure, they were a bit rusty at the start, and there was the occasional lapse, but in a way, it was like watching a new Led Zeppelin, a Zeppelin that was trying to take on the eighties and become a working band again. After all the drugs, all the unpleasantness that had surrounded them before, they just wanted to get back to doing things right. Let's not forget, Zeppelin were always at their best when they were working hard."

There were also some changes to onstage etiquette. While Robert remained his good-natured self onstage – cracking jokes about dinosaurs and peppering the set with his new catchphrase "Eye Thank Yew!" (a line actually stolen from veteran British comedian Arthur Askey) – Jimmy broke his usual silence by actually addressing the crowd. Strolling up to

---

221 A delightful surprise on opening night, the last time Led Zeppelin had performed 'Train Kept A-Rollin'' was in Oakland in the late summer of 1970.

the microphone in Dortmund's Westfalenhallen, Page smiled broadly before introducing 'Black Dog' as 'Schwartz Hund' to the delight of the German fans. Obviously pleased with the response, he continued the practice throughout the tour, though for reasons best known to himself, he sometimes changed the song's title to 'Strangers In The Night', thereby drawing many a blank look from those gathered below.

Behind the scenes, there was also much evidence of new brooms and sweeping motions. Unpredictable security advisor John Bindon was no longer a part of the Zep operation, having been sacked by Peter Grant soon after the incident at Oakland. Perhaps more surprisingly, long-time tour manager Richard Cole was also now let go, his descent into full-on heroin addiction making him a liability not only to himself but to the band too. "He had a massive problem," Peter Grant later told Chris Welch, "so I thought the only way to shake him up was to blow him out." Cole's replacement for the tour was Phil Carlo, who Grant and the band knew well through his work with Bad Company. "There were people I didn't take kindly to [at the time]," Plant later said, "I found it very difficult to be a doting father on the one hand, and have to deal with people like Richard Cole[222] on the other."

While the firing of Cole and hiring of Carlo seemed to have the beneficial effect of scaling down the backstage tomfoolery one normally associated with Led Zeppelin tours, not every accident or incident could be managed from the wings. At Nuremberg's Messehalle on June 27, for instance, the group were only three numbers into their set when John Bonham appeared to keel over behind his drums. Minutes later, the curtain was dropped on the show and Bonzo rushed to hospital. Once again, the drug murmuring brigade were on hand with suggestions that Zep's resident force of nature had been felled by a rogue cocktail of toxic pharmaceuticals. The truth was a far less dramatic. Having reportedly eaten a whopping 27 bananas before taking his seat at the kit, the drummer's stomach had simply given up on him.

---

222 Having been sacked by Led Zeppelin, Cole's battle with heroin addiction continued for some time, though he eventually righted by 1986, when he took on a new career as a drug counsellor.

Perhaps more worryingly and certainly a good deal less self-inflicted was Jimmy Page's brush with small explosives at Vienna's Stadthalle the night before. In the midst of his solo piece 'White Summer', the guitarist was struck in the face by a firecracker, causing both he and Zep to vacate the stage immediately. Always a threat at concerts (Aerosmith's Joe Perry almost had his hand blown off by one at Philadelphia's Spectrum Arena in 1977), firecrackers, cherry bombs and M–80s had been lobbed at the group in the States, but the practice was nowhere near as prevalent in Europe. After a long delay during which the concert promoter asked the culprit to own up and apologise to Page backstage, they resumed their set with 'Kashmir'.

Winding on through Zurich, Frankfurt and Mannheim, Led Zeppelin 'Tour Over Europe 1980' finally came to a close at Berlin's Eissporthalle on Monday, July 7. In comparison to events in Munich the previous night – where the quartet had turned in one of their best performances of the tour[223] – the show was somewhat ragged and undisciplined. Indeed, Page broke with Zep's new rule of relative brevity and took a long, expressive solo on 'Stairway To Heaven', stretching the tune out to nearly 15 minutes in length. Obviously unrepentant and now backed up in his crimes by a complicit Robert Plant, a similar trick was pulled on the group's closing number 'Whole Lotta Love', with the duo's vocal vs. Theremin contest almost an aural facsimile of the long, intense battles they had fought onstage during 1973 and 1975. And then, after a witty speech from Plant thanking everyone and anyone within earshot, it was over.

Completed without much in the way of fuss or press intrusion, 'Tour Over Europe 1980' might not have been Led Zeppelin's most debauched or overtly publicised tour, yet it still achieved two principle aims. By allowing the band to musically reengage night after night, a feeling of real possibility was again established among the four, with John Paul Jones later referring to it as "the beginning of a new lease of

---

223 A gig described by Jimmy at the time as "the nearest feeling" he had to Zep's "big American shows" in terms of energy and excitement, the band were also joined at encore time by Bad Company drummer Simon Kirke for a ribald take on 'Whole Lotta Love'.

life". Critically, the European jaunt's low-key success also persuaded Robert Plant that he could finally contemplate returning to America, much to the obvious delight of Jimmy Page and Peter Grant. After the trials and tribulations of 1977, it now appeared that Zep were once again on route to the continent that had played such an enormous role in establishing their legend.

Plant's acquiescence to the cause was not total, however. Unlike the all-conquering campaigns of yesteryear, Zep would not be spending months aboard the Starship in search of cities to ravish this time around. Instead, in line with Robert's wishes, the tour was to be a strict, four-week exercise and then back home to bed. Still for Grant, it at least gave him something to work with. "It was part one of what I hoped would be further visits," he later said. Sensibly, Zep's initial return would concentrate entirely on the Midwest and East Coast of the States and Canada during the late autumn of 1980. A second leg devoted to the potentially dicier West Coast (where promoter Bill Graham still ruled the roost) was tentatively scheduled for the early spring of 1981, with more dates in the UK to follow after that.

For Dave Lewis – whose then new Led Zeppelin fanzine *Tight But Loose* had been cautiously but firmly embraced by the powers that be at Swan Song[224] – this was a perfect opportunity to observe Jimmy Page's love of his band at close quarters. "I remember being allowed into the top floor of Swan Song – hallowed ground that you usually weren't allowed into – and seeing Jimmy behind the desk with a mock-up model of what the stage would look like for the autumn tour of the States," he confirmed in 2015. "There was a huge light show, great use

---

224 "I was lucky enough to be in the right place at the right time, really," Dave said in 2015. "By 1975 and those Earls Court gigs, I knew I wanted to write about Zep, and ironically, taking up that old punk ethos – 'Do it yourself' – I thought about putting together a fanzine, and then just did it. Thankfully, issues one and two of *Tight But Loose* were well received. More, I'd always had a good relationship with Swan Song, especially with Unity MacLean, who did some of the publicity. Soon enough, she brought me in to check various things. My enthusiasm for the band was subsequently noted by Peter Grant and the guys, and instead of opposing it, they saw the value of the fanzine and just let me get on with writing it."

of space, it looked great and Jimmy was really enthusiastic about it. He and the group were ready to do it all again, to go back to America in the autumn and retake their crown."

Rehearsals for what was to be Zep's 12th American tour commenced on September 24, 1980 at Bray Studios, just outside Maidenhead. For Page, the location was reasonably close to the grounds of his new home, purchased for a reported £900,000 (though it might have been closer to £500k) the previous month from British actor and future national treasure Michael Caine. Like Pangbourne before it, the Old Mill House near Windsor was pleasantly close to water, its borders touching the gentle swish and swell of the River Thames. And like Plumpton Place, the building and its grounds were also beautifully rangy, reassuringly solid and delightfully secluded, with six bedrooms and five reception rooms to explore within, and a veritable forest of trees within touching distance outside. In short, another ascetically pleasing paradise for Jimmy to make his own.

Following what appeared to be a short day's work at Bray, the band returned to the Old Mill House where they were all staying. John Bonham was one of the first to bed. Having started drinking early with four large vodkas at a pub pit-stop on the way down to Maidenhead from his home in Worcestershire, the drummer had continued to imbibe throughout rehearsals, his intake steadily propped up by a diet of ham rolls and pizzas. Come midnight, however (and the best part of 40 units drunk), Bonzo was flagging and put to bed by Page's assistant, Rick Hobbs, who propped him on his side with several pillows. Reportedly, Hobbs returned the following morning at eight or so to find him still resting. Nonetheless, by early afternoon Bonham had still not surfaced, causing John Paul Jones and Zep tour manager Benji Lefevre to investigate. They found their friend had died in his sleep, having choked on his own vomit.

In subsequent years, there has been much speculation as to exactly why John Bonham was drinking so much on September 24. Certainly among friends he had expressed concerns about the upcoming tour, his continuing reluctance to leave behind his family coupled with a growing fear of flying and general distaste for American road life all perhaps factoring into a general air of uneasiness around the trip. "It's much easier to play in England," he once said. "You get the motor out of the garage and toddle off and you're so at ease all the time. Whereas, when you're in America, you're all the day in a hotel somewhere having arguments with bloody rednecks and turdheads... and then you've got to go to the gig. [That] does affect you."

Further stories have it that Bonzo was also beginning to doubt his own abilities by 1980, with Zep's recent travels around the stages of Europe convincing him he was losing his touch. Physically out of shape and without much time to do anything about it, again, such matters may have played on his mind and caused him to hit the bottle even harder than usual. Peter Grant thought not. "John just got very nervous in rehearsal situations," he later said. "He tried to overcome his nerves by drinking vodka." In light of such contrasting opinions, then, John Paul Jones' summation of events seems the most logical. Regardless of the psychology of Bonham's drinking or the reasons behind the drummer's possible concerns, the simple truth is that his death was just an unfortunate mishap, albeit at terrible cost. "[It was] because of an accident," Jones later told Chris Welch. "He was lying down the wrong way, which could have happened to anyone who drank a lot. We tried to wake him up. It was... terrible. It just made me feel very angry... at the waste of him."

Within moments of discovering Bonzo, the machinery around Led Zeppelin roared into action. As Jones broke the news to Jimmy and Robert, Benji Lefevre was on the phone to Peter Grant, who in turn had his assistant Ray Washbourne instruct a team to get to the Old Mill House as quickly as possible. A key part of that delegation was security manager Don Murfet, whose links with Grant went back to the mid-sixties, when both men had cut their showbiz teeth working alongside the likes of promoters Vic Lewis and Don Arden.[225] Having seen just about every aspect of what rock'n'roll had to offer, Murfett was still shaken by Bonham's passing. "John was a good friend," he later said. "A walking bag of contradictions... a gentle soul who was nonetheless the epitome of 'the wild man of rock'." Yet, on his arrival in Windsor, it

---

225 In addition to his work with Led Zeppelin, Don Murfet's career included spells running a successful concert security business during the seventies/eighties as well as later managing Adam & the Ants.

459

was Jimmy Page's reaction to the tragedy that most resonated with him. "Jimmy was sitting there by the stairs smoking cigarette after cigarette," Don said in 2000. "He didn't say anything. Not a word. To be honest, he didn't need to. Jimmy just looked... lost."

John Bonham's funeral took place on October 10, 1980 at Rushock Parish Church, the site close to the drummer's own farmhouse in Worcestershire. Fortunately, it was one of the few days that the remaining members of Led Zeppelin and Peter Grant were not bombarded by press enquiries or unwelcome phone calls. Only a week or so after Bonzo's passing, for instance, the *London Evening News* kindly chipped in with the headline story 'Led Zeppelin Black Magic Mystery', presumably written to help the band better deal with their private grief. Full of wild links between Jimmy's interest in the occult and the various calamities that had befallen Zep, it was 1977 all over again – albeit with a sad new angle to now consider. Perhaps even worse than the prodding of tired old coals was the number of rock managers contacting Grant concerning a possible drumming vacancy within Led Zeppelin's ranks. "It was," he later said, "a terrible, terrible time."

Yet, however inappropriate or appallingly mistimed such enquiries were, it was a subject that the group had to face. Though Zep's American tour was immediately cancelled following Bonham's death, the question as to what might happen next still needed to be addressed. Inevitably, the longer they kept their own counsel on the subject, the more the media went into overdrive, with various papers throwing up reams of text concerning who might take over from Bonzo. Some – such as Kiss' Peter Criss – were fanciful at best. Others, like veteran sticksman and then current member of Gillan, Mick Underwood – were based on old associations rather than any real facts[226]. Indeed, one or two names

---

226 A fine drummer, Mick Underwood had been seriously considered by Peter Grant as meriting a place in Led Zeppelin before Jimmy went with John Bonham in July 1968. Then a member of seminal mod-rockers Episode Six – who also boasted singer Ian Gillan and bassist Roger Glover in their ranks before both defected to Deep Purple in 1969 – Underwood again joined up with Gillan a decade later as the vocalist's new, self-titled solo project.

even made some sense, with hard rock journeyman Cozy Powell[227] and former Vanilla Fudge, BBA and Rod Stewart drummer Carmine Appice both certainly capable of attacking the skins in vintage Bonham style. "At the start, it was touch and go as to whether they might carry on, at least from the outside [looking in]," said Chris Welch, "and there were rumours that Carmine would join, along with various others who also threw their hat in the ring."

In the end, it all turned out to be complete rubbish. On December 4, 1980, following a short meeting at London's Savoy Hotel, Led Zeppelin finally put everyone out of their misery with a brief statement to the press. "We wish it to be known that the loss of our dear friend and the deep sense of undivided harmony felt by ourselves and our manager have led us to decide that we could not continue as we were." For one or two, there was still a sense of ambiguity in these words, the phrase "continue as we were" crisp with the possibility that some iteration of the group might rise Phoenix-like from the flames. Other, more cynical types took Zep's words with a pinch of salt. Having been the world's biggest rock band for so long, it was surely only a matter of time before they changed their minds and 'Did a Who', the remaining trio choosing to soldier on with a new drummer. Both viewpoints proved erroneous. "To me," said Robert Plant, "there was no debate."

Realistically, there had never been any behind-the-scenes possibility that Led Zeppelin would carry on in late 1980. Even when Page, Plant and Jones briefly convened on Jersey several weeks after Bonham's passing to discuss any sort of future together, each knew in their own minds it wasn't to be. "When John died, there was a big hole in Zeppelin," JPJ later told *Vanity Fair*'s Lisa Robinson. "The Who and the Stones [were] song-based bands, but Zeppelin wasn't like that. We did things differently every night and we were all tied to each other onstage. I couldn't even think how to do this without John." Robert

---

227 While Powell certainly had the technical goods and established pedigree to try out for Led Zeppelin, there were those who felt the drummer might well have been behind his own candidacy for the job. "Cozy [joining Zep] was probably a rumour started by Cozy Powell," quipped Who bassist John Entwistle.

Plant – so long a friend to Bonham and always his closest ally in the group – was in complete agreement. "After John died, I couldn't deal with any of the old set-ups, the regimes, those knowing nods," he told *The Times'* Will Hodgkinson in 2014. "I'd had enough. When Zeppelin ended, people kept saying to me 'How can you walk away from all that? How can you let it go?' [But] I never wanted to waste a minute on anything that wasn't absolutely real. It had became a chilly little spot, up on that stage."

For Jimmy Page, the feelings were much the same. Having enthusiastically talked up Zep's next LP with Bonzo in the weeks before his death – "[We] had already started discussing plans for a hard-driving rock album... [because] we both felt that *In Through The Out Door* was a little soft" – he was now faced with the loss of "a very close friend. Somebody I felt was the best drummer in the world." Of course, there were other drummers. Yet, Page knew one thing above all else. Despite his original vision and undoubted leadership, Led Zeppelin had always been above all else a band and no amount of true will was going to replace one of its parts.

"Led Zeppelin wasn't a corporate entity," he told *Rolling Stone* in 2014. "Led Zeppelin was an affair of the heart. Each of the members was important to the sum total of what we were. I like to think that if it had been me that wasn't there, the others would have made the same decision. What were we going to do? Create a role for somebody? Say, 'You have to do this, this way?' That just wouldn't have been honest. We'd always had a great deal of respect for each other," he concluded, "and that needed to continue in life or death."

The die firmly cast, Page, Plant, Jones and manager Peter Grant – who like the others, felt "It could never be the same again" – now removed themselves completely from public view, their collective past hermetically sealed, their own futures to be individually contemplated for the first time since 1968. According to Robert Plant, that was to be no easy task. "I think there had to be a period of time that [had] to elapse where you go to your separate corners," Robert later told *Creem*. "[But] whatever then happens in the future is impossible to see. I mean, you really don't know what's going to happen tomorrow or the next day..." Yet, for observers in the music press like Chris Charlesworth, the decision to split – no matter how difficult – was always the right one. "Yes, I think they did the right thing... the dignified thing," he said. "Led Zeppelin were such a tight unit. There'd been no solo albums. No playing outside the pen, so to speak. It had always been Zep and Zep alone. So, when they lost John, it just felt like the bond had been broken and they wouldn't even attempt to carry on with another drummer. The only problem for Jimmy and the others was where next?"

A band of incredible scope, shocking power and wide-ranging versatility, Led Zeppelin had made a mighty noise during their 12-year lifespan. Very possibly the finest rock band ever, they had almost taken on the mantle of gods to millions of fans across the world, their every sound and movement analysed to the point of abstraction. Now, with the sad death of John Bonham, it appeared to be all over. No more concerts, no more records, just a slow climb down from Mount Olympus before taking their place in the history books. As Peter Grant correctly deduced, "A terrible, terrible time." Nonetheless, the future still continued to beckon. While the group itself might have been gone, there were other possibilities to consider – a life outside the bubble, so to speak. For two of the remaining three members of Led Zeppelin, progress in this regard would be slow, but sure. For Jimmy Page, however, the route would be much more difficult, with the next decade bringing its fair share of light, but a great deal of shade, too.

PART 3

IN THE EVENING

"Forget the myths. It was all about the music…"

Jimmy Page

CHAPTER 29

Who's To Blame?

There was to be no 'Stop the clocks' moment in the wake of John Bonham's death. Instead, the machinery around Led Zeppelin would wind down in stages, never for once coming to a complete halt, but showing no obvious signs of movement for months or even years at a time. Like the largest of businesses and brands, the wheels kept going, even if those who originally set it up had long departed the company. That said, after the collective announcement of December 4, 1980, all was effectively silence from the remaining board members, though behind the scenes there were stirrings of definite movement.

Already reeling from years of bad luck and personal tragedy, Robert Plant was reportedly the first to make his future intentions fairly clear to the others. Obviously determined to crack on as quickly as possible, the singer let it be known he was now considering a solo career. "Losing John was criminal, and to be honest, nobody really got over it," Plant later told Malcolm Gerrie. "But you had to strike out again and create a [new] currency... a 'now', if you will. So I made it my business to go out and start again at the age of 32. It was hysterical, really, but I worked and worked [at it]." In this guise as prospective solo artist, Robert also made it plain that striking out meant he would be seeking new management, effectively bringing to an end a 12-year association with Peter Grant.

Though Plant's decision no doubt temporarily hurt Grant, given the circumstances, it was probably the right thing to do. Riven at Bonzo's death and still suffering the psychic traumas of a fairly recent divorce, Peter's health had again begun to deteriorate, his own troubles with drug abuse continuing to weaken both his resolve and need to manage any band or artist, no matter how previously close the client in question. As happy to draw the curtains as Robert was now to open them, Grant soon retreated to his home in East Sussex, turning his moated home Horselunges into a "bleak fortress" from which he would seldom emerge, save for the most essential business. With Plant ready to take flight (even if he didn't exactly know as yet in which form or direction) and Peter Grant's response making his own intentions crystal clear, John Paul Jones was left at his own temporary crossroads. Aware he too had to establish "some sort of career", but as yet unsure what form that might take, JPJ took to his own home to plan a future, with production or film music stirring gently in the corners of his mind.

Captain of the airship for so long, it was perhaps inevitable that John Bonham's passing and the circumstances around it would have a profound effect on Jimmy Page. With Led Zeppelin having been Jimmy's life's blood since 1968, the death of both his friend and the band now led to him feeling completely lost himself. "It took me months upon months to realise that he was [gone]," Jimmy later told *Creem*. "I couldn't believe it. Anyone who has lost a close friend... you always think they're going to walk through the door in the next minute and of course, they don't."

As worryingly, Page had also lost the seeming desire to make music, his usual habit of tinkering away on six strings until inspiration struck having deserted him. "I didn't do anything," he continued. "I just sat there feeling sorry for myself and for the whole situation. Not just for myself, but for everyone involved. I didn't know what I was going to do. It was about nine months that I didn't touch a guitar. When I eventually did, I was in for a shock. I couldn't [even] change chords. If Bonzo were a poltergeist, he'd have kicked me in the arse about it."[228]

Had Page other vested interests at this point, there might have been at least a sense of diversion to his days. But Jimmy's alternative bookshop – Equinox – and record label Swan Song were either now closed or on the verge of it, leaving him to fester on recent events. "[Equinox] obviously wasn't going to run the way it should without some drastic business changes and I didn't really want to agree all that," he had told writer Chris Salewicz in late 1979. "[Besides], I basically just wanted the shop to be the nucleus, that's all. Equinox was never designed to make lots of money – I'd have opened a boutique or something [for that] – but just tick over so it could publish books."

In Swan Song's case, though the kill shot had not yet been fired, by late 1981 the company had grown progressively less active in recent years, with only 10 new, non-Zep album releases in the last five years. As the label's poster boys Bad Company now slunk towards indefinite hiatus and hardy perennial Dave Edmunds' attentions became increasingly focused on his own side-project with singer-songwriter Nick Lowe (the much more successful Rockpile), it was only a matter of time before an increasingly disinterested Peter Grant started the process of winding it all down. "It all really fell apart after Bonzo died," Edmunds later told *Uncut*.

Of course, in previous years Page could have at least taken some comfort at looking at a music scene he had in part helped create, with Black Sabbath, Deep Purple, Aerosmith, Kiss and a thousand other rock bands doffing a grateful cap in the guitarist's direction. Indeed, Jimmy's gifts to the music industry had not ended solely with the invention of

---

228 Another story Page told underlines just how far he had grown away from playing the guitar in 1980–1981. "There was a period after John died when I just didn't touch the guitar for ages. It just seemed related to everything that happened," he later said. "But one day I called up my road manager and asked him to get the Les Paul out of storage. He went to get it and the case was actually empty! It had been borrowed without permission... but when he came back and said 'The guitar's missing', I thought 'That's it, I'm finished! Thank God... it eventually reappeared...'"

hard rock, as the likes of the Eagles and Queen took inspiration from the slow-building orchestral power of 'Stairway To Heaven' and fashioned their own mega-hits 'Hotel California' and 'Bohemian Rhapsody' from it.

However, by early 1981, the game was again changed, with pop 'futurists' Ultravox creating a new type of 'Stairway...' for a new type of audience. Inadvertently plying most of the lessons learned from Zep's most famous tune, but using synthesisers and drum machines rather than acoustic and electric guitars to create the same sense of rising emotion and instrumental melodrama, Ultravox's 'Vienna' was emblematic of the British music scene's then current infatuation with all things European. Instead of embracing American blues and rock'n'roll to form the backbone of their attack as Page had, groups such as Gary Numan & Tubeway Army, Japan, Spandau Ballet and Human League were all indubitably the children of David Bowie[229], their hero's peerless 'Berlin trilogy' acting as an able primer for their own chilly experiments in sound.

If the icy surfaces of the UK 'new romantics' were unfamiliar terrain for Jimmy Page, then America wasn't offering much in the way of succour for him either. Though not yet as obsessed with synthesiser settings and German expressionism as their British counterparts, the States had managed to recently throw up a new six-string hero in his own way every bit as exciting and innovative as Jimi Hendrix, Eric Clapton, Jeff Beck or, indeed, Jimmy himself had been in the late sixties.

With Eddie Van Halen's astounding armoury of flurrying arpeggios, two-handed tapping, deranged tremolo tricks and braying horse noises (all ably demonstrated in his showcase instrumental 'Eruption'), budding

---

229 According to pop folklore, David Bowie was also an avid student of the teachings of Aleister Crowley, having studied the Great Beast's works in the late sixties/early seventies. However, legend has it that when he was confronted with the sight of Crowley expert Jimmy Page at a party in LA sometime in 1975, Bowie quickly exited the building, the singer allegedly unnerved by the 'penetrating stare' and all-pervading 'aura' of Zep's lead guitarist. It is perhaps worth noting, however, that David Bowie was at the height of his addiction to cocaine that year, which might have had a thing or two to do with any of the more fanciful observations he made at the time.

teenage players now had a man they could truly call their own, a "guitar god for the eighties" ready to take the instrument in hitherto uncharted directions. More, Van Halen and his titular band – fronted by the hyperactive, joke-cracking 'Diamond' David Lee Roth – offered the same mix of primal intensity, technical bravado and lithe showmanship Led Zeppelin had in their heyday. Crucially, however, they had also removed the lengthy improvisational aspects of Zep's act and added a real pop sheen instead, making their tunes hummable as well as admirable. In short, Van Halen represented a lean new type of rock for the coming decade and, as such, were a near perfect substitute for the now absent Led Zeppelin.[230] "I can't do it," Jimmy later said of Edward Van Halen's express-train tapping technique to *Guitar World*'s Steve Rosen. "I can't smile like him either." Still, behind the obvious humour, one sensed a man who knew the times were once again changing, though perhaps not in the direction he might have hoped.

With personal and professional woes threatening to engulf him, pop turning ever more towards synthesisers and rock music about to throw up a new legion of guitar virtuosos in the wake of the brilliant Van Halen, these were tough times for Jimmy Page. But somewhat ironically, it was now another veteran rock aristocrat that offered him a potential lifeline. Since the release of their self-titled album in 1969, Yes had been one of the few acts seriously capable of taking on Led Zeppelin at their own game, the prog rockers' peerless musicianship and ability to commandeer elements of folk, blues and even classical music and make it their own proving immensely popular among those fans whose tastes ran more to complex rhythms and elongated structures than Zeppelin's brand of raunch'n'roll. Yet, like Zep, Yes had recently reached some sort of impasse, albeit caused not by losing a member, and

---

230 While Van Halen may have been a new broom on the eighties rock scene, the quartet had been heavily influenced by crisp early seventies hard rockers Montrose, again led by titular guitarist Ronnie Montrose. That said, Montrose in turn had obviously taken several of their own cues from Led Zeppelin, with two of their most famous cuts – 'Space Station No. 5' and 'Rock Candy' – leaning heavily on Zep's own 'Communication Breakdown' and 'When The Levee Breaks' for inspiration.

bassist Chris Squire, a key founding member, was now looking to put together a bold, new project to rival past glories. Who better then than the recently unemployed Jimmy Page to help him do it...

Having met at a party, Squire and Page first talked up the possibility of a new group over Christmas of 1980. Long admirers of each other's work – "Chris was a brilliant bass player," Jimmy later said – the musical attractions were obvious. But according to Squire, at that point at least, Robert Plant was also to be involved. "It was supposed to be with Robert too, but Robert never showed,"[231] the bassist later told *Guitar World*. "I know at the time there were feelings between Jimmy and Robert. Robert had lost his son and John had died, which had all been quite a blow to Jimmy. It sent him into a much 'stricter' mood with himself. So yes, it was a good time to get together with Jim."

Though Plant's involvement obviously came to nought, there were two other potential recruits to Page and Squire's cause by the time things got more serious during the early spring of 1981. Accompanying Chris in the prospective band's rhythm section was former Yes drummer Alan White, the duo having played together since 1972 when White took over from original drummer Bill Bruford. Their other potential conscript was keyboard/synthesiser whizz Dave Lawson, who numbered countless jazz gigs, movie soundtracks and even a spell in art-rock combo Greenslade among his previous credits.[232] A genuinely lovely man and friend of Chris Squire for many a year, Lawson had

---

231 If reports are correct, Plant baulked at the complexity of the material being talked up by Squire and Page, preferring instead to continue with his own solo explorations.

232 Dave Lawson had already contributed to a plethora of acts/artists before hooking up with Chris Squire in 1980. A former student of British jazz great Stan Tracey, Lawson's stints included backing burlesque performers in sixties Soho – "Silly really, playing dance numbers between strippers' sets with long hair, dressed in a black suit and tie" – and a brief tenure with jazz-rock hopefuls Samurai before joining cult act Greenslade. "Samurai were weird jazz... punk stuff with two drummers and an interest in Eastern philosophies. It didn't sell, but it was good fun!" After veering into session and movie soundtrack territory – "Yep, that's me on *The Man Who Fell To Earth*. *Star Wars* too..." – he came to a temporary stop with Squire and Page.

come into the picture when the Yes bassist found himself at something of a low ebb around late 1980. "At the time, Chris had left Yes or the band wasn't together at least and he was floundering a bit," Dave explained in 2015. "He'd got into a certain substance and was only getting up at about three in the afternoon. Basically, he'd lost interest. That's my reading of it, anyway. "

Nevertheless, after several late afternoon conversations at Lawson's home, Squire's interest in music was reactivated. "We'd talk about the musical greats, you know, just chatting," said Dave. "Because I was a non-smoker, I used to make Chris hang out the window to smoke his ciggies! But of course, he had a studio and soon enough we started playing a bit of music over there. I'd just bought a Synclavier, one of the first, so I took it over and again, we started messing around with sounds. He invited me back – no talk about any bands at this point, I must stress – and again, we're just mucking about with settings when Alan White arrives." From there, connecting the dots was admirably easy. "We all got on like a house on fire and, inevitably, we started writing music," Lawson confirmed. "I'd already written a track, Chris had a couple, so we [ended up] working [them up]."

By February 1981 or thereabouts, Page had joined the party and the group even had a name of sorts: 'XYZ', the three letters denoting that Jimmy, Chris and Tony were all either 'eX' 'Yes' or 'Led Zeppelin'. With most of the material provided by Squire – "I wrote all the songs for the band," he later said – and the odd riff courtesy of Page (more of that later), XYZ began committing ideas to tape, the group demoing a pair of then unnamed instrumentals as well as two further tunes arranged and sung by Chris ('Can You See' and 'Mind Secrets'). Nonetheless, it was at this juncture that things started to unravel. "It was going well for a while," Squire told *Guitar World*'s Bud Scoppa in 1986, "but when it started to go [really] well, Jimmy began to get some of his old confidence back, together with a few of his certain 'pleasures'. And at that point," he concluded, "it started to fall apart." As to what exactly these 'pleasures' were, the bassist did not say.

While Dave Lawson was not privy to Squire and Page's differences, he was later led to understand that the project was as much scuppered by the failure of negotiations between Yes manager Brian Lane and an increasingly disengaged Peter Grant as anything else. "I think the respective managers landed in their separate helicopters," laughed Lawson. "Kick-off commenced, the conversation lasted about five minutes and then they returned to their various helicopters and left. So, the band never came to anything."

In the end, the separation between Jimmy, Chris and Alan White proved more amicable than the conversation between Lane and Grant, at least in the short term. With no new band to play in, Squire and White simply remodelled their old one, shaping a new version of Yes with guitarist Trevor Rabin and original singer Jon Anderson. In so doing, they also renewed their acquaintance with international superstardom, with 1984's 'Owner Of A Lonely Heart' topping the US singles chart and its parent album *90125* selling over six million copies. Page, as we will soon learn, also found some projects that would keep him personally busy over the coming months. Regrettably, however, the songs worked up by XYZ did lead to future problems, with issues of authorship and ownership raising their head in later years. "Very interesting, it was... " said a non-too amused Squire.

With Chris Squire and Alan White now bidding their farewells, Jimmy Page was free to throw his lot into two new enterprises he had dabbled with in the past, but which now took on much more concrete significance for him. The first was Mill Studios in Cookham, Berkshire, a large recording facility he had purchased around the same time as he bought Old Mill House in nearby Windsor. Formerly owned by renowned producer Gus Dudgeon[233] – who had built the complex from scratch with the dual aspiration of providing the UK "with a world-class studio" as well as remixing Elton John's back catalogue for proposed

---

233 A proper music biz legend, Gus Dudgeon's career began in the early/mid-sixties when he worked as a sound engineer on the likes of the Zombies' 'She's Not There' and John Mayall's *Bluesbreakers With Eric Clapton*. By the end of the decade, he was a full-blown producer, with credits including David Bowie's ground-breaking 'Space Oddity'. The seventies saw Dudgeon form a fruitful and long-lasting association with Elton John and Rocket Records that lasted until his death in 2002.

ter a period of seclusion following the demise of Led Zeppelin, Jimmy resurfaced at the December 1983
RMS concerts prompted by the plight of Multiple Sclerosis sufferer Ronnie Lane, and designed to raise
oney for MS research. Here Jimmy is flanked by the All Star band that includes, amongst others, Joe Cocker,
aul Rodgers, Jeff Beck, Eric Clapton and Bill Wyman. "At rehearsals," said Beck, "we weren't even sure
mmy was going to make it through."

d Zeppelin reunited without distinction for Live Aid with Tony Thompson and Phil Collins sharing
rcussion duties, JFK Stadium, Philadelphia, July 13, 1985. "Live Aid," Page later said, "was just appalling...
you look at my face on film, you can actually see me going 'Oh my God...'"

Jimmy on stage with Paul Rodgers when the two paired up in the Firm during 1984. "The Firm was put together by Paul and I as a vehicle to get out and tour, to play to audiences," said Jimmy of their short lived group.

Jimmy with David Coverdale, a shot to promote the 1993 album *Coverdale/Page*. Another short lived affair, the duo restricted themselves to one short tour of Japan before Jimmy walked away. "Well," said Robert Plant, "I found it difficult to understand his choice of bedfellow. I just could not get it."

he Unledded project, featuring Jimmy with Robert Plant but not John Paul Jones,
egan as an *Unplugged* show for MTV in August, 1994, and mutated into an album and tour
at featured Middle-Eastern instrumentation and both Western and Egyptian orchestras.
quipped with a variety of guitars, including the impressive Ovation double-neck pictured above,
age's playing took on a new maturity. "You know," he said, "people say I can't play anymore.
) I go out to prove to them that I can."

Jimmy with Robert Plant in 1998 during the *Walking Into Clarksdale* tour that inevitably morphed into a re-hash of Led Zeppelin as it progressed. Eventually Plant pulled the plug, much to Jimmy's chagrin. "All the big trappings," said the singer, "it becomes exasperating."

Jimmy outside Buckingham Palace,
December 14, 2005, having received his
OBE from the Queen in recognition of
his charity work on behalf of Brazilian children.
Around the same time he was made
an honorary citizen of Rio de Janeiro.

The reunification of Led Zeppelin, with John Bonham's son Jason on drums, at London's O2 Arena on December 10, 2007, earned them many awards, including GQ magazine's Band Of the Year in 2008 (above). The heavily oversubscribed concert accelerated the unstoppable growth of the new millennium's 'heritage rock' industry, finally eradicating all traces of generation gaps among fans but at the same time causing a predominar of awards that inevitably devalued them. An exception was Jimmy's acceptance of an honorary doctorate for his services to the music industry from the University of Surrey at Guildford Cathedral on June 20, 2008.

Watched by 91,000 in the stadium and millions more on TV, Jimmy plays 'Whole Lotta Love' at the National Stadium in Beijing during the closing ceremony of the 2008 Olympics, with X-Factor winner Leona Lewis on vocals. "Doing the Olympics with Leona was phenomenal," he said.
"She's really plucky, superb and she sang 'Whole Lotta Love' brilliantly."

Jimmy with U2's the Edge and Jack White, the stars of the film *It Might Get Loud* which premiered in 2008. "It was just fascinating to be that close to Jimmy and see him play," said Edge. "When he went into '...Lotta Love', me and Jack were like two little kids watching with stupid grins on our faces."

Jimmy, Robert Plant and John Paul Jones at the White House on December 2, 2012 when Led Zeppelin received the annual Kennedy Center Honours from President Barack Obama. "Zeppelin grabbed America from the opening chord," said Obama. "These guys also redefined the rock'n'roll lifestyle."

An artists' sketch of Jimmy alongside Robert Plant in a Los Angeles court room in June 2015. The pair, along with John Paul Jones, successfully defended their most famous song 'Stairway To Heaven' against charges of plagiarism brought by a trust representing the late Randy California, lead guitarist of Spirit.

"Forget the myths. It was all about the music."

"Quadraphonic release" on site – the Mill was not only state of the art but also housed in the most beautiful of grounds. Set in a quiet area atop the River Thames, it had been converted from an old watermill, with the studio and accompanying control room in turn giving access across a weir to a residential wheelhouse (nicknamed 'The Attic') that actually sat on its own island. As ever with Jimmy, when it came to eye-catching properties, his taste was impeccable, and the word in the business was that because Dudgeon was in financial difficulties at the time he got it for a song.

Returning the property to its original name – 'The Sol' – Page re-opened the studio's doors for business under his own auspices in late 1980, with early clients including Mick Fleetwood (of Fleetwood Mac fame) and the Rolling Stones' Bill Wyman. "Well, I got involved with the studio over a year ago," he said in 1981, "and it's fully commercial. We've got just about every effects unit that's ever been known!" However, Jimmy's on-site visits to Sol had thus far been sporadic, with much confusion caused when he actually turned up while prog-rock combo Wishbone Ash were busy recording there. "Yeah," Wishbone guitarist Laurie Wisefield later told *International Musician And Recording World*. "[Our bassist] Trevor Bolder nearly threw him out because he thought he was the cleaner!" To make up for Bolder's error, the band offered to make Page a cup of coffee. "We said 'Black or white?' He laughed, then said 'What do you think?'"

Ultimately, it was a knock on the door from a neighbour in London that caused Jimmy to finally take over Sol Studios under his own steam and begin another foray into the world of movie soundtracks. A Marmite-like figure among both critics and audiences, director Michael Winner had long since traded a promising start in the British film industry during the early sixties for a real pop at the Hollywood cherry. And in part, he had succeeded. After a series of middling comedic dramas (1967's *I'll Never Forget What'sisname*), World War II satires (1969's *Hannibal Brooks*) and "piss-weak horrors" (1971's *The Nightcomers*), Winner finally hit pay dirt in 1974 with *Death Wish*.

Part vigilante thriller, part skewed morality tale, *Death Wish*'s story of a quiet soul driven to extreme violence following the murder of his wife and rape of his daughter not only raised uncomfortable questions about the dispensing of justice, but also proved a huge box-office hit. Putting new wind in the sails of veteran actor Charles Bronson (who played *Death Wish*'s kind man turned killer Paul Kersey with his usual grim determination), the flick also established Michael Winner as a "go to" director of action thrillers. Yet, despite the odd modest success during the late seventies, Winner's star had recently begun to dim and he was now after another hit. It didn't take long to strike on the idea of revisiting his biggest success and making a sequel to *Death Wish*. With financing secured via Cannon films, Bronson returning to the fray as the movie's 'vigilante everyman' and a reasonably trouble-free shoot in downtown Los Angeles already behind him, all the pieces were in place for a 1982 theatrical release. The only thing the director needed was a score.

Originally, US soul star and Academy Award winning writer of '(Theme) From Shaft' Isaac Hayes was in the frame to provide Winner with his soundtrack. But then he had a brainwave. "I had lived next door to Jimmy [in Holland Park] for many years," Michael told *Uncut* in 2005. "It was a very bad time for him, his drummer had died and he was in a very inactive period. [So] Peter Grant and I made arrangements for Jimmy to do the *Death Wish II* score." According to the director, Page was not to be paid for his work because "Grant wanted to restore him back to creativity." Further, the music was to be delivered 'tip to toe' in eight weeks.

Nonetheless, when the auteur met the musician sometime in late 1980/early 1981 – "I thought if the wind blows, he'll fall over" – he soon realised all was not going to go his way. After viewing the movie, Jimmy made it clear he would provide a score, but only on his own terms. "Jimmy said to me, 'I'm going to my studio, I don't want you anywhere near me and I'm going to do it all on my own'," Winner told writer Michael Bonner. With little choice but to acquiesce, he provided Page with a video copy of the film (replete with synchronised time code[234]) and crossed his fingers. Jimmy did too. "I walked out of Michael's house after having had a very pleasant afternoon," he later told writer John Tobler, "feeling like a sledgehammer had hit me over the head. Eight weeks..."

Of course, when it came to music and moving images, Jimmy Page obviously had prior experience. As a session man back in the sixties, he contributed to several potential movie projects including Basil Kirchin's 1966 Indian-influenced guitar wig-out *The Wild One,* alongside the ever-present Big Jim Sullivan. Indeed, a year later, among various other commitments to the Yardbirds, Page somehow still found time to work on Brian Jones' soundtrack to *Mord Und Totschlag* (*A Degree Of Murder*), a West German arthouse flick directed by Volker Schlöndorff and featuring the Rolling Stone's then girlfriend Anita Pallenberg. But Jones was long gone[235], and Jimmy hadn't turned his own hand to writing for film since the *Lucifer Rising* debacle of the mid-seventies. As worryingly, Page was also expected to provide a whole album's worth of material as part of a commercial tie-in to the movie. "*Death Wish II* came to me at the right time because I was obviously shattered having lost John. So, it was really good because it kept me focussed creating 45 minutes of music for a 90-minute film," he later told *Classic Rock's* Pete Makowski. "But [then] I was told I was supposed to do an album as well, which was a bit of a shock."

Taking over Sol Studios, Page set about his task with a gusto not seen since the days of *Presence.* Surrounding himself with vintage equipment such as a hollow-bodied Gibson ES5 and its "big brother, an ES Switchmaster," several basses (an Alembic Omega and Fender Precision) and two old acoustics – a Gibson 'Everly Brothers' and his beloved

234 According to Page, using a video copy with a synchronised time code was a novel approach to scoring the soundtrack at the time, with most film composers preferring to employ "The Black Book" method, which measured "frames per second to beats per minute". However, Jimmy wanted to work up "bespoke pieces" that fitted with "the mood of the visuals" on show.

235 A brilliant musician but extremely complex man, Brian Jones drowned in his swimming pool at Cotchford Farm, Sussex on July 3, 1967. He was 27. To this day, claims and theories that he was murdered abound.

Martin D28 – Jimmy also dug out a brand new Roland GR300 guitar synthesiser for added modernity and a few extra 'sounds from space'. "I must admit that guitar synthesisers had stimulated my imagination for quite a long time, but before [the Roland] none of those available would track properly," he told Stuart Grundy in 1981. "But this particular machine is the works and finally gives a guitarist a chance to compete with keyboard players." Obviously, Page had been keeping one eye and two ears on those futurists. However, a similar flirtation with an electronic drum machine did not last as long. "No," said Page's guitar tech Tim Marten at the time. "Jimmy stopped using drum machines when he found it was easier to talk with Dave Mattacks."

Having drifted apart following Led Zeppelin's ascent to mega-stardom in the mid-seventies – "Sadly, I lost contact with Jimmy and John Bonham as Zep got bigger and bigger... at some point, they kind of got untouchable" – an unlikely encounter at a railway station in East Sussex had reintroduced Fairport Convention drummer Dave Mattacks to Page. "Well," he said in 2015, "we were both living in Sussex at the time, me in Haywards Heath and Jim probably in some bloody big castle! But we both bumped into each other at the train station of all places. We struck a conversation, you know, 'How are you, how's the music?' Then he said I'm doing a film score. Do you want to play on it?' I said 'Of course.'"

Now an established session musician as well as Fairport's resident percussionist, Mattacks had more than a passing familiarity both with Sol Studios and its previous owner, Gus Dudgeon. "Jimmy was an absolute sweetheart about it all," he said. "And 'The Sol' was the perfect studio, really. The location was just unbelievable. I knew it well, having done so much work with Gus. Ah, Gus was such a good friend, you know. At one time, I was in danger of getting stuck in a bit of a folk ghetto... the 'go to guy for folk', so to speak. But Gus started calling me for pop sessions, and I was so pleased to get them, because it allowed me to prove there was more to my drumming. But what he went through building that studio. He had a bad accountant who told him whatever he put into the studio would all be written off for tax purposes. But when he finished it, he found out that wasn't true and went through financial hell. Bless him, though. You know, he left me his entire record collection. A real gentleman, was Gus..."

Dave Mattacks now on board, things progressed accordingly, with he and Page soon learning to adapt to each other's working patterns. "A lot of the tracks for *Death Wish II* were done with just the two of us," said Dave. "We'd sit around, then Jimmy would say 'I've just had an idea for this', and then we'd track the guitar and drums together. A relaxed, informal atmosphere, and really easy-going. Also, Jimmy had just got the new Roland guitar synth and I remember he wanted to do an overdub or something, while also changing the pitch. But the [way the synth was set up], he couldn't do it all himself. So, while he's playing the part, I'm down on the floor working the controls! It was early days for guitar synths, though. Things have come on a bit."

Another aspect of their working day was lining up Jimmy's newly written score with Michael Winner's images. "Yeah, sometimes, we'd be working to screen, but it wasn't that sophisticated," said Mattacks. "For instance, when you're working on a film score at a huge studio like Abbey Road now, you have an enormous screen rigged up with a clock count. There was nothing like that at the time. But Jimmy did have the cut synched up on a large TV monitor. Sometimes, we worked to clicks, other times it was a little looser, more free form, but we got there. I remember Jimmy sitting down, just completely concentrated on layering guitar upon guitar." It was this aspect of Page's musicianship that most captivated the drummer.

"Oh, Jimmy was fantastic at orchestrating guitars. I think he started the process as a session man and just honed it to perfection with Zep. He really understood tone. You know, I did an album with John Paul Jones' daughter [Jacinda] a few years ago and Jonesy told me with the old band, stuff could get soaked up – even Bonzo's drums – when Jimmy put 'the army' on it. Pagey would put so many layers on the recordings, but that range of sound – which he understands so well – was right at the heart of Zep. Picking the right frequencies, the right amps, the right guitars, the right tones. Now, that ability to layer is almost a given in the session world... but Pagey was doing it 35, 40 years ago. Visionary stuff."

However, Mattacks did not see Page as some kind of human tone machine or valve-obsessed scientist. Quite the opposite, in fact. "Nah, Jimmy's sloppy good. No, actually, he's sloppy-unbelievably great. The more I think about it, I can see why he and Bonzo worked so well together, because neither of them was machine-precise. They had that tight but loose thing going on. That's a marvellous quality to possess, having that greasy, rolling thing, like Keith Richards. These guys can go in front or behind the beat. Of course, Jimmy could be session man-precise. He'd shown that. But he also had that ability to roll across the beat like a New Orleans jazzer."

With the bedrock of tracks coming together in leaps and bounds, it was time to introduce several other musicians to the project. "If memory serves," said Dave Mattacks, "I think it was me that told Jimmy about Davy Paton." A superb bassist, who had already worked with the likes of Elton John, the Alan Parsons Project, Camel and Pilot[236], Davy Paton proved an astute choice for the *Death Wish II* sessions, adding a melodic flavour to Jimmy's cinematically themed tunes. "Oh yeah," Dave continued. "I'd been working with Davy on some things and mentioned to Jimmy he was really, really good... certainly worth checking out. And of course, Davy contributed some great things to the sessions."

In addition to Paton, pianists David Sinclair Whitaker and Pretty Thing Gordon Edwards were also invited to The Sol to add their own contributions, as was XYZ's Dave Lawson. "I did some keyboard synthesis," Jimmy later revealed, "but when it came down to needing a really proficient player, I got Dave Lawson." Dave was equally complimentary about Page. "I got along great with Jimmy," Lawson recalled in 2015. "We shared a similar approach to music and he was fun to work with. I remember we were working on Chopin's 'Prelude' for a while, building up the arrangement. But I don't know what happened to that because [like *The Man Who Fell To Earth*], I haven't actually seen *Death Wish II* either!" That said, Lawson was impressed with what he

236 Davy Paton was the voice, bass and pen behind Pilot's 1975 mega-hits 'Magic' (co-written with Billy Lyall) and 'January', both of which were produced by Alan Parsons.

heard at the time. "It was a very laid back session, you know, that was being put together as we worked. Jimmy had loads of ideas and that was the really important thing. Sure, he was struggling a bit at times, getting his [guitar playing] chops back together. But make no mistake, he was extremely together when it came to the bill..."

After an additional orchestral session recorded with the GLC Philharmonic, Page was ready to tackle two rock songs specifically written to dovetail the album soundtrack of *Death Wish II*. For these, he needed a brilliant vocalist. He got one. "Oh, Chris Farlowe, come on!" laughed Dave Mattacks. "Who doesn't love Chris Farlowe?" Working with Page for the first time "in donkey's years", Chris Farlowe's arrival in Berkshire added a further touch of class to the whole project. Nonetheless, having finished album and touring stints with the likes of Coliseum and Atomic Rooster, and an additional spell working as an actor on a recent BBC2 drama, his very presence at Sol was a surprise even to him. "Typical Jim," said Farlowe. "He phones me up out the blue, as he does, and said, 'Do you fancy doing this film soundtrack with me?' Well, yes. So off I went to Cookham..."

Written, performed and produced over two gruelling months at The Sol, *Death Wish II: The Original Soundtrack (With) Music By Jimmy Page* was released on March 6, 1982, and pretty good it was too. Full of huge bursts of spiralling synths and *Psycho*-like string squeals ('Hotel Rats And Photostats'), robotic funk rock ('The Chase' and 'Jam Sandwich') and urban hoedowns ('Big Band, Sax And Violence'), Jimmy had certainly captured the drama, danger, tension and release of living in the big city. But there were gentler moments too. 'Carole's Theme' was an impressive case in point, with the massed power of the GLC Philharmonic, Dave Lawson's lilting piano and Page's own bittersweet acoustic fills all combining to create an instrumental of some beauty. 'Prelude' was even better. Based on 'Prelude in E Minor' by the Polish-French composer Frederick Chopin, its winding classical melody, slow, stately guitar (played by Jimmy on his B-Bender brown Fender Telecaster) and inventive bass line (supplied by Davy Paton) provided an elegant diversion amidst all that synthetic mayhem.

For those seeking links with Page's former work, there was also the odd treat. After its dramatic orchestral opening, 'The Release' exploded into a tune that would have sat well on either *Physical Graffiti* or *Presence*, its stacked harmonies, complex chords and bolting rhythms redolent of 'Ten Years Gone' and 'Achilles Last Stand'. 'Shadow In the City' was another track with clear links to Jimmy's past. Built on waves of unsettling harmonics, bowed guitars and sinister Theremin noises, 'Shadow...' had a distinct air of fire and brimstone, its origins surely linked to Page's previous efforts on *Lucifer Rising*[237].

Of the three 'proper songs' on the soundtrack to *Death Wish II*, again it was hard not to think of Zep. With 'City Sirens', Jimmy had written another strutting rocker in the vein of 'In The Evening', Gordon Edwards' impassioned vocal on the track recalling in places a certain lion-haired hip swaggerer. And try as he might, even Chris Farlowe's characteristic "blues boom of a voice" couldn't quite disguise the fact that both 'Who's To Blame' and 'Hypnotising Ways' were begging to be sung by Robert Plant. Still, any such comparisons were moot when considering the main purpose of the overall project. "I hope it's seen for what it is," Jimmy told *International Musician...* at the time, "a soundtrack album – not a solo [or lost Zep] album – it's [music] thought of in context of visuals."

Regrettably, while Page's music sat perfectly well with Michael Winner's images of blazing neon streets, dark foreboding alleyways and sleazy, desperate men doing horrible things to innocent people, *Death Wish II* itself wasn't really much of a film. Excessively violent, "cartoonish in its characterisations" and at times genuinely uncomfortable to watch – like the first movie, it featured an extremely graphic gang rape scene – Winner's attempt at twice capturing lightning in a bottle had failed and then some. "You will have noticed that I've given a 'no stars' rating for *Death Wish II*," wrote respected American critic Roger Ebert in January 1982. "I award 'no stars' only to movies that are artistically

---

237 Indeed, Page has hinted that he did liberate at least one idea from *Lucifer Rising* to inform the soundtrack of *Death Wish II*. By the sounds of it, 'Shadow Of The City' could be the tune.

inept and morally repugnant. So, *Death Wish II* joins such unsavoury company as *Penitentiary II* and *I Spit On Your Grave*." It got worse. "The movie is underwritten and desperately under-plotted, so that its witless action scenes alternate with lobotomised dialogue passages. The movie doesn't contain an ounce of life. It slinks onto the screen, squirms for a while and then it is over." Thankfully for Jimmy, Ebert didn't voice an opinion concerning the film score.

No matter. Despite the many failings of Michael Winner's movie[238], Jimmy Page's soundtrack for *Death Wish II* remained a little gem of its own accord. Crammed with clever ideas and brilliant playing from the likes of Dave Mattacks, Dave Lawson, Davy Paton and Jimmy himself, the score also featured three fine songs that confirmed there was a life outside Led Zeppelin for Page, should he so want it. "I think Jimmy did a marvellous job on that film," said an admiring Robert Plant. "I mean, anyone who can watch a screen for 10 minutes or 10 seconds and actually write to it, really it's remarkable. It requires so much structuring. I know he was very serious about it. He used to start at 10 in the morning and finish at midnight every day. You know, really going for it, [even] writing parts for an orchestra. Jimmy's such a talent, such a remarkable talent. When he does a solo album, it's going to be a really 'Waaa!' thing."

Reaching number 40 and number 50 in the UK and US charts respectively (no mean feat for a film score), *Death Wish II* proved an exhausting enterprise for Page. "At one point," he later joked," I really didn't think I'd get to the end of it." Yet, despite its physical toll, the project had achieved something of real importance for its composer. After months of inactivity, Jimmy was finally back in the studio,

---

238 *Death Wish II* might not have wowed the critics, but it still made bucket loads of money, raking in nearly $45 million worldwide in 1982. A cash cow for the studios, Michael Winner would make one more sequel with Charles Bronson before handing over the franchise to directors J. Lee Thompson and Allan A. Goldstein. The fifth and final movie – 1994's *Death Wish V: The Face Of Death* – ended the series with Bronson throwing a criminal into a large pool of acid before walking into the sunset.

producing themes, writing songs and playing guitar. "It was [meant as] a change that became more of a challenge," he later told writer Dave Green. "[And] It was good in a way to have something to do that necessitated so much discipline. Yet, I hadn't realised just how much was needed to take it on all alone."

Inevitably, having now returned to the fray with a new album (albeit one connected to a movie), the next question begging to be asked was whether Page would form a new band. He sounded unsure. "I'm dying to get out there [but] it'll need some time to get together because I don't want to do anything that isn't 100% terrific," he said in late 1981. "It would be silly to even think about going on with Zeppelin. It would have been a total insult to John. I couldn't have played the numbers and look around to see someone else on the drums. It wouldn't have been an honest thing to do. No, it'll be new ideas, new material and I'm dying to do it."

As the saying goes, 'Pull up a chair'. It was going to be a long wait.

CHAPTER 30

Bird On A Wing

Writing the soundtrack of *Death Wish II* might have got Jimmy Page out of the house, but he was by no means out of the woods just yet. Indeed, much of 1982 and a goodly portion of the following year would find him dealing with various personal and professional difficulties, the guitarist stumbling here and there before things eventually began to right themselves again. "For Jimmy," said Dave Lewis, "the eighties could be described with two words. 'Stop' and 'Start'."

Though little or nothing was said of it in the press, Page's family circumstances underwent some profound changes after the dissolution of Led Zeppelin. First, his parents separated after 40 years of marriage, while Jimmy's father, James Snr. – a quiet attendee at the band's Knebworth shows in 1979 – also reportedly fell ill. More, Page's relationship with Charlotte Martin began to falter, beginning a slow dissolution towards the inevitable. Though Jimmy was linked with several other women during their time together, Martin had proved herself a tenacious partner, the couple's 13-year relationship seeing Jimmy through his entire tenure with Led Zeppelin, while also gifting him with daughter Scarlet, who was now on the cusp of becoming a teenager.

There were other trials and tribulations for Page to contend with, some of which carried potentially serious consequences. In early to mid-1982, he was arrested for possession of cocaine, leading to a subsequent appearance at Inner London Crown Court in October of that year. As a result, previously private matters – albeit ones heavily prone to rumour – were now about to become a matter of public record. On admitting the offence, however, Page was granted a conditional discharge, the attendant judge reportedly noting that a stiffer sentence would result in the loss of millions in expected revenue for the guitarist, given his upcoming tours of the US and Japan in 1983. Perhaps the judge knew something others did not, but there would be no such concerts for Jimmy, at least under his own banner headline, for the next 11 months.

That said, Page did step out under the spotlight at Munich's reassuringly large Sports Arena on May 12, 1982, where alongside Robert Plant he caused paroxysms of delight by joining AOR giants Foreigner onstage for a lively reading of Little Richard's evergreen rock'n'roll belter 'Lucille'. An old friend of the band's lead guitarist/principal songwriter Mick Jones[239], Jimmy was careful when choosing a suitable axe backstage for he and Plant's brief performance, eventually settling on a black Gibson Les Paul[240]. But it was obviously time well spent, with Page's subsequent solo every bit as animated as it had been when tackling the song as part of Neil Christian's Crusaders some 20 years before. "Basically, Jimmy and I just fancied going somewhere to have a break," Robert told *Kerrang!* of the reasons for his and Page's presence in Germany. "He'd been working really hard on the *Death*

239 After a brief spell in cult act Nero & the Gladiators, Mick Jones worked as a session musician in France, where during the mid-sixties, he recorded with the likes of Sylvie Vartan and the 'French Elvis', Johnny Hallyday. It was around this time that Mick met Jimmy, who had also contributed to several tracks by Hallyday. Following stints in Wonderwall and Spooky Tooth, Jones formed Foreigner in 1976, with the band subsequently becoming one of America's best-selling rock acts.

240 As noted earlier, one of Page's favourite early guitars was a 1960 Gibson Les Paul Black Beauty, which he used for many of his sixties sessions. Stolen while in transit at an airport in 1970, it was never recovered. However, the story doesn't end there, as revealed later in this book.

Wish album and I'd been busy with my own [solo album]. But actually, I was petrified. I hadn't walked on a stage that big for ages, but it didn't take more than a few seconds to remember what to do."

With Page and Plant resurfacing onstage in Germany, it took but days for the press to begin working up the possibility of a Led Zeppelin reunion. Though now absent from public view for nearly a year and a half, interest in the group had remained high, especially in the States where punk, new wave and futurism had not yet cleansed the palette of fans' taste for old-school rock theatrics. But this time, there was some truth to these stories of renewed Zep activity although, as would soon become apparent, it was an album rather than a tour that appeared to be on the cards.

Since Zep's speedy, if honourable dissolution in December 1980, Atlantic Records had kept gently, but firmly, insisting that they wanted at least one final LP from the band. By the summer of 1982, they were within spitting distance of finally getting it. "The album was the result of an agreement we struck with Ahmet Ertegun," Peter Grant later told Chris Welch. "It was both to fulfil our long-term album contract and also done as a separate deal. When I [originally] made that deal with Ahmet, we owed him an album or two, but [this] deal was a separate thing. We had a meeting with Jimmy, Robert, John Paul and Pat [Bonzo's widow] to sort it out."

Many ideas were posited as to what exact form the LP would take. One possibility was a compilation of Led Zeppelin's 'greatest hits'. However, with albums by serious rock bands still largely marketed as stand-alone experiences rather than holding pens for potential singles – a policy, lest we forget, originally championed by Zep – the suggestion was quickly pooh-poohed. Elsewhere, some (possibly including Jimmy) argued for a definitive double live set, its contents pulled together from 12 years of concert appearances. Yet again, the proposal soon fell away, with unpleasant memories of *The Song Remains The Same* perhaps still lingering in the background.

In the end, the compromise struck was a career-spanning collection made up of songs that for one reason or another had failed to be included on Zep's previous eight studio albums. Given the working title 'Early Days, Latter Days', Page went to work on finding exactly which tracks to include, turning The Sol into a vast library of old tapes, dusty boxes and vintage recordings. In this enterprise, he was aided and abetted by Stuart Epps, a respected and extremely capable engineer who had worked alongside producer Gus Dudgeon at The Old Mill in the seventies and who had now decided to stay on with Page at The Sol. "Stuart Epps was a lovely man, a fantastic engineer and kept us all on point," said Dave Lawson, who got to know Epps during the recording of *Death Wish II*. "He also kept impeccable track notes... Stuart was the model professional, really." Epps was also extremely respectful of his new employer. "[Jimmy] was an amazing producer, [though] quite a shy guy," he later told BBC Berkshire's Linda Serck. "He played the guitar with a bow and was very inventive with effects... very interesting for me to work with."

Treating the task with typical thoroughness, Page explored an array of old Zep material before settling on eight tunes he deemed worthy of release. Calling in Robert and John Paul to add an overdub here and there, the package was actually completed by the early spring of 1982. Yet rather than compete or clash with Plant's first solo LP – which was due in shops in late June – the album was held back until the end of the year. When it was finally ready to escape from The Sol, all signs pointed at a group still in mourning at the loss of their drummer. Unlike other Zep campaigns, advance publicity around the record was decidedly sparse, with only the odd promotional poster featuring nine small, unexplained discs trailing its arrival. Further, when the album did land in stores on November 22, 1982, its Hipgnosis-designed cover conveyed yet more solemnity. Looking more like an aged tombstone than a celebratory beacon to a once wonderful band, the sleeve's green-grey colour scheme only added to the air of bereavement. But it was the record's title that seemed to say it all. "'Coda'," Jimmy confirmed. "It means a closing repeat at the end of the song. A finale."

Like the vibrant group photographs housed inside the cover, however, *Coda*'s contents revealed a reassuringly energetic and at times surprisingly upbeat collection of songs, all of which highlighted the various facets of what had been Led Zeppelin. Racing into life with the band's cover of Ben E. King and James Bethea's 'We're Gonna Groove', Zep's most reliable early set opener still sounded fresh, feisty and funky, even if the recording itself was made from the back of the Pye mobile truck at the Royal Albert Hall nearly 12 years before. Nonetheless, Jimmy hadn't quite left '... Groove' as he found it. Using The Sol's comprehensive resources, Page had mixed various sub-divider effects in and around the tune, adding a new vibrancy and not inconsiderable amount of low-end 'oomph' to the track. Up next was 'Poor Tom', another tune rescued from 1970, though this time from the sessions for *Led Zeppelin III* held at London's Olympic Studios. Perfectly described by Dave Lewis as a "jugband workout", 'Poor Tom' was written by Page and Plant during their fateful stay at Bron-Yr-Aur, and it sounded like it, the track's melding of folk, Delta blues and old-school country stylistically close to the likes of 'Gallows Pole' and, indeed, 'Bron-Y-Aur Stomp' itself.

Surely the jewel of the album, and again recorded at the RAH in January 1970, 'I Can't Quit You Baby' arguably trounced the version that first appeared on the band's debut LP (no mean feat), and made one remember just how glorious Zep could be when running with the bulls. With Robert simply roaring the lyrics and Page at his frantic, fleet-fingered best, Willie Dixon's lusty blues had seldom been better performed, and at a pre-show rehearsal no less. While not quite on par with 'I Can't...', 'Walter's Walk' had its own peculiar sense of swagger. Originally cut at Stargroves for *Houses Of The Holy* in 1972 with Eddie Kramer at the helm, '... Walk' shared much in common with the odd riffing and screwy time signatures of 'Dancing Days', its bouncing, circular beat and jabbing guitars giving the track a slightly deranged, yet still not unappealing feel.[241]

Perhaps confirming once and for all John Paul Jones' contention that there "Wasn't a lot of [earlier] Zeppelin tracks that didn't go out, we used everything," three of *Coda*'s remaining four songs were taken from the band's sessions at Stockholm's Polar Studios in mid-

---

241 There are plausible rumours that 'Walter's Walk' was substantially re-jigged at The Sol in order to make it onto *Coda*, with Robert Plant's lead vocal added to the tune in 1982 rather than 10 years before.

November 1978. Sliding by mostly on charm, 'Ozone Baby' might not have carried the weight or authority of 'I Can't Quit You Baby' or even 'Poor Tom', but it was hard not to fall for its cycling chord structure, chiming 12-string guitars and fizzy, Nashville-approved solo. Similarly, fifties pastiche 'Darlene' was never going to nudge 'Kashmir' or 'Stairway...' off their grand musical perches, yet again the song had a certain down-home style all its own, with John Paul Jones slyly tickling his piano, Robert channelling his inner Elvis and Page pretending to be James Burton in the background. A step up on 'Hot Dog', at least. 'Wearing And Tearing', on the other hand, was Zep's supposed attempt to beat punk at its own game. In truth, like Queen's 'Sheer Heart Attack' or Aerosmith's 'Bright Light Fright' before it[242], the track was far too professionally rendered to merit inclusion in that particular genre, though given its hurtling pace ('Tearing...' was surely the fastest track Zep had ever recorded), sporadic yelps and yowls from Plant and sudden car-crash ending, the commonalities were glaringly obvious.[243]

Of course, John Bonham's death also cast a huge shadow over *Coda*, and one was simply unable to listen to the album's songs without focusing on his input. As ever, it was enormous. Whether providing the meaty upswing that defined 'Poor Tom', the break-neck snare/bass drum interface at the heart of 'Wearing And Tearing' or the shattering conclusion to 'I Can't Quit You Baby', Bonzo was all over the LP. "Like 99% of the drumming fraternity, I was a huge fan of Bonzo's," said Dave Mattacks. "And I was also lucky enough to know John... a nice guy, you know, but what a drummer. People talk about the

242 Many a rock and pop band had a go at aping the energy and venom of punk, often with decidedly mixed results. Queen's hyper-active 'Sheer Heart Attack' (October 1977) and Aerosmith's combustible 'Bright Light Fright' (December 1977) are two of the better examples of "rockers pulling a punk sneer", though in Queen's case, '... Heart Attack' was actually written in 1974, nearly two years before the Sex Pistols' first gig.

243 'Wearing And Tearing' was to be released as a commemorative single for Zep's appearances at Knebworth in August 1979, though the idea was later shelved due to scheduling issues. Reportedly, acetates of the single do exist and now command up to £600 at collectors auctions.

heaviness of his style, the power, but he swung. I mean, he really did have that swing thing too, like Ringo Starr, like Charlie Watts. He was concise, yes, but he could also stretch the bar, just creating that lovely roll to the beat. So many people think it's all about buying a huge kit and beating the shit out of it, but there was so, so much more to John's style than that."

It therefore came as something of a surprise that the track supposedly highlighting John Bonham was actually one of *Coda*'s weaker moments. Recorded at Mountain Studios in Switzerland during September 1976 when the group were busy avoiding British taxes, 'Bonzo's Montreux' featured a solo performance from the drummer festooned with various electronic effects and sound triggers, some of which were created by Jimmy with a pitch-harmoniser. While a vague melody became discernible courtesy of these treatments (sounding not unlike Trinidadian steelpans), it was more akin to a mouse running across the piano keys than any properly realised tune. One could not argue with the sentiments expressed by including 'Bonzo's Montreux' on the album – "It would be a hard man who questioned the inclusion of this posthumous tribute," Q's James McNair rightly contended in 2003 – but surely there were much better examples of Bonham's undoubted talents hidden among the mountain of tapes gathered by Page at The Sol.

At risk of banging another familiar drum, like the eight LPs that preceded it, *Coda* was not without fault. Aside from '... Montreux', it was easy to see why one or two (or even three or four) of the songs had not made the track listing of the albums they were written for, being either melodically too weak or just too twee for inclusion. Additionally, one of the LP's conceptual strengths – taking tunes from each point in Zep's long career – ironically created another of *Coda*'s principal weaknesses, with the material gathered from various eras sometimes failing to gel together as a cohesive whole. Yet, these were minor failings when faced with the delightful madness of 'Walter's Walk', playful musings of 'Poor Tom' or apocalyptic take on 'I Can't Quit You Baby', all of which would have graced any Zep disc. More, the crash, bang and wallop of 'Wearing And Tearing' confirmed that had it not been for the passing of

Bonham, there was still enough energy and guile left in Jimmy Page and Led Zeppelin's creative engine to carry them forward into the eighties more or less intact. "Anyone who says Jimmy or Zep's work was done, not true," said Dave Lewis. "He, Robert and John Paul had much, much more to give."

For some at least, *Coda* more than fulfilled its brief, allowing fans one last chance to wallow in the legend that was Led Zeppelin. "My only complaint," said *Kerrang!*'s Steve Gett in 1982, "is that *Coda* could have been a double album. In fact, I'm sure that there are plenty of other gems which have been withheld from us. [Still], it's amazing that Zep can put together a compilation of outtakes that sound better than many of today's rock releases." For others, however, there was nothing on the album save for the sound of a barrel being scraped by a very large fork. "Various outtakes all quite without consequence," said *NME*'s Richard Cook at the time. "Idiot blues, folk and the sweating labours of a rock music taken by an agonising bowel disorder. It isn't ABBA who are the most pernicious influence to have blighted popular music," he concluded, "it may still, alas, be this terrible group."

As before, good or bad reviews seemed to have little impact when it came to actual sales, with *Coda* easily climbing into the Top 10 of both the US and UK charts, the album eventually coming to rest at number four in Britain and number six in the States, where its performance gifted Zep their 44th platinum disc. Not quite the numbers one normally associated with the group perhaps, but given the minimal publicity that surrounded its release and a cover best described as 'downbeat', *Coda* had done well enough, especially when taking into account its posthumous circumstances. "*Coda* was released, basically, because there was so much bootleg stuff out," Jimmy later said. "We thought, 'Well, if there's that much interest, then we may as well put the rest of our studio stuff out'."

Back in the charts and still in the game, now might have been a good time for Page to have announced details of a new band or at least another album project. For confirmation of that fact, he only had to look at Robert Plant. Once a nervous young man shyly presenting his favourite albums to Jimmy at Pangbourne in mid-1968, Plant had recently garnered both critical plaudits and firm sales with the release of his first solo effort, *Pictures At Eleven*. A likeable, mature-sounding debut, as with *Coda*, it had taken Robert near the top of the US and UK charts (at number five and number two) and kick-started a promising career for him an artist in his own right. "You've got to remember Robert had been restless in previous years, and he might have just had enough [following the death of John Bonham]," said Dave Lewis. "Though it was terribly, terribly sad for him losing John, it allowed him to reinvent himself as a solo artist... to have a haircut, wear the jumpsuits and change his image. Jimmy, well, less so..."

Less so, indeed. Like Peter Grant, who took the completion and release of *Coda* as a clear sign to finally close the doors on Led Zeppelin and Swan Song[244], and retreat to Sussex until further notice, Page too went to ground. Spending much of 1983 at The Sol and The Old Mill House, the studio's daily business matters continued to engage him to some extent, but it all felt like wasted opportunity. Yet, there remained compelling reasons for his relative seclusion. "My life was Led Zeppelin," Jimmy later told writer Nick Kent. "I lived and breathed Led Zeppelin. When I wasn't touring, I was at home writing music for the group. I could hear John's drumming. I could hear Robert... and John Paul. It was a total obsession for me. And suddenly... it was all over." Still lost at sea, what Page needed was a shunt in the right direction. Mercifully, he was about to get it from two former Yardbirds, "the sixth Rolling Stone" and one Small Face.

The convergence of events that led to Jimmy Page forming a new band probably began on May 24, 1983 when he made a rare trip outside Windsor and Cookham to join Eric Clapton onstage at Guilford Civic Hall. Taking to the boards at encore time alongside Clapton regulars keyboardist Chris Stainton, country guitar wizard Albert Lee, and a guesting Phil Collins on drums, Page's takes on 'Further On Up The Road' and 'Cocaine' may have sounded a tad rusty in comparison to the

---

244 Following *Pictures At Eleven* and *Coda* – both of which were released on the label – Swan Song finally ceased operating in October 1993. It does, however, remain a business outlet for the reissue of previously released material.

tour-hardened Eric, but his very presence at the gig did prove important to future progress.

Like Page, Clapton had been through the wars one way or another since his heady days in the Yardbirds. As already evidenced, a brief, but notable, spell with John Mayall's Bluesbreakers had conferred upon him deity-like status before the formation of Cream in 1966 made the guitarist one of rock music's first genuine superstars. The seventies had been been less kind, however, as drug addiction, alcoholism and some very odd career choices threatened to derail his subsequent progress as a solo artist. That said, Clapton had never really been out of the game. For every lazy album or ill-advised, drunken foray into political commentary[245], there had been hit singles ('I Shot The Sheriff', 'Wonderful Tonight') and million-selling LPs (1977's *Slowhand*) to sustain his profile. More, Eric's recent participation in charitable concerts such as 1981's *Secret Policeman's Other Ball* for Amnesty International had helped partially rehabilitate his standing with younger audiences. And it was in this capacity that Clapton, Jimmy Page and a host of other sixties survivors would soon find themselves working together.

The cause that they would throw themselves behind was a decent one with a touching story to accompany it. While working alongside the Who's Pete Townshend on the album *Rough Mix* in 1977, former Faces and Small Faces bassist Ronnie Lane had been diagnosed with multiple sclerosis. Though he continued to tour into the early eighties, the debilitating nature of the illness forced him to spend more and more time in treatment, where he met doctors, specialists and fellow sufferers as keen as he to find a cure. Taking a positive stance, Lane subsequently

---

245 An obviously very drunk Clapton expressed his support for right-wing politician Enoch Powell's anti-immigration stance onstage in Birmingham in August 1976. In turn, the incident led to the formation of Rock Against Racism, a musical campaign designed to discourage youngsters from supporting racist and fascist causes. Though Jimmy Page always remained cautious about expressing his own political views, he did confirm that he voted for Margaret Thatcher and the Tory party in 1979. "Not just for the lighter taxes, I just couldn't vote Labour," he told writer Chris Salewicz at the time. "They [Labour] actually stated that they wanted to nationalise the media. So, what possible criticism of them could you possibly have?"

set up ARMS (Action for Research into MS) as a blanket charity in order to raise funds towards that aim. Seeking to involve others in the cause, Lane's girlfriend, Boo Oldfield, contacted British promoter Harvey Goldsmith with the idea of staging some type of event drawing support from the larger rock community. With Goldsmith already in the midst of organising Eric Clapton's performance for The Prince's Trust at the Royal Albert Hall on September 21, 1983, he was subsequently able to arrange another concert at the same venue for the night before.

Exactly who extended Page the fateful invitation to perform at the RAH remains a point of some debate. One story has it that Eric called Jimmy to seek his participation soon after the two played together in Guildford, but there is another tale to be told. On June 22 & 23, 1983, at London's Marquee, drummer Jim McCarty, guitarist Chris Dreja and bassist Paul Samwell-Smith reformed the Yardbirds for two reunion shows to celebrate the iconic venue's 35th birthday. "It really was a case of 'why the hell not?'" laughed Dreja. Fronted by new singer John Fiddler and augmented by seasoned guitarist Dzal Martin, the gigs were an unqualified success, leading the original trio to relaunch the band under a new name: Box Of Frogs. "Again, why the hell not?!" laughed McCarty.

But while certain old members of the group had been contacted about appearing at the Marquee and possibly contributing to a new album, Page had not. Seemingly irritated by what appeared to be a snub, Jimmy mentioned it in passing to long-time mate and Rolling Stones tour manager Ian Stewart. "There was sort of a Yardbirds reunion in London [in the] summer," Stewart later told *Rolling Stone*, "and apparently no one asked Jimmy to play on it. I think he was a bit pissed off, really. So, at this party while I was discussing the Ronnie Lane ARMS benefit... Jimmy came up and said 'Nobody ever asked me to play. Why can't I play on it?' So we said 'Step this way'."

Ian Stewart had been discussing the ARMS concert with Jeff Beck before Jimmy joined in the conversation. Like Page and Clapton, Beck's progress since leaving the Yardbirds had been far from trouble-free, though his own travails had less to do with personal tragedies, alcoholism or drug addiction than a sometimes astounding ability to make things as difficult as he could for himself. "I'm an awkward son of a bitch when it comes to doing the expected," he once said. Obviously, one felt for Jeff when Jimmy Page and Led Zeppelin stole a march of his own brand of molten blues rock in 1968, but his subsequent follies were sometimes harder to understand or reconcile.

At the height of a demand for heavy guitar music in the early seventies, at which he would have surely excelled, Beck had turned sharp left into 'the funk' during 1971/2, cutting two albums of "Motown rock" that, while brilliantly quirky and technically dazzling, had left his audience confused and his sales tepid. An even bolder plan to resurrect the classic three-piece 'power rock' format with drummer Carmine Appice and Tim Bogert in BBA might have sold a few more LPs and temporarily deafened half of America, but again Jeff's latest volte-face felt out of time and out of place, things having moved on considerably since the heady days of Cream and the Jimi Hendrix Experience some eight years before.

However, like Eric Clapton, Beck was never once destined for the musical scrapheap. On hearing the rich tonal complexities and dizzying time signatures of John McLaughlin's Mahavishnu Orchestra and Billy Cobham's *Spectrum*, the guitarist decided to completely abandon more traditional models and pursue instrumental jazz rock fusion instead. This time the gamble paid off, as 1976's George Martin-produced *Blow By Blow* and the following year's *Wired* took him into US arenas and the platinum-sellers club. More, he had managed it all without a singer, hit single or nary a hint of real compromise. "There was never an element of showbiz about Jeff, really," said his former manager Simon Napier-Bell in 2010. "I mean, he was happy to get the applause, but he really just wanted to play the guitar. Usually, the people who want to be stars have an overwhelming necessity to be applauded, [but] Jeff didn't have that. Even Clapton found out after years of playing shyly, turning his back to the audience, he wanted to be a star. But obviously, Jeff was different in that area. Instead, he became that rarest of things, a superstar musician."

It appeared that by attaining such million-selling success under his own terms, Jeff Beck had also put aside any festering resentment he still possibly held towards Jimmy Page over similarities between *Truth* and *Led Zeppelin I*. Though there continued to be the odd burst of vitriol towards his old mucker in the music press during the late seventies – "I don't ring him and he doesn't ring me," Jeff growled to *Guitar Player*'s Jas Obrecht – by the time of the impending ARMS concert in the autumn of 1983, the two were very much back on the best of terms. In fact, it was at Beck's show at Hammersmith Odeon on March 10, 1981 that Jimmy had publicly emerged for the first time since the death of John Bonham, the now-former Zep man joining Jeff onstage at encore time for a good-humoured, if ramshackle, take on 'Going Down'. Not having played in front of an audience together since 1966, this was obviously a marker for better things to come between them. But as the Royal Albert Hall shows loomed large, even Beck remained unsure of whether Page had the goods to win the day, let alone carry the night. "At rehearsals," he later said, "we weren't even sure Jimmy was going to make it through."

The pressure on Jimmy Page backstage at the Royal Albert Hall on September 20, 1983 must have been astounding. Having readily agreed to the gig some weeks before when it probably sounded like a good night out for a very good cause, the event had subsequently escalated in terms of both profile and star power. In addition to Page, Clapton and Beck, the line-up now also boasted the Stones' Charlie Watts and Bill Wyman, the Who's Kenney Jones, soul/pop/rock legend Steve Winwood and singer-songwriter (and long-time EC associate) Andy Fairweather Low, as well as a plethora of the finest session musicians in the UK. "All the usual suspects, then," laughed Jeff. Further, the Prince of Wales and his relatively new bride Princess Diana were also in attendance, looking on at the festivities below from a box in the upper tier. "The whole atmosphere was intense," Beck continued. "'Don't shout, don't swear, don't act like hooligans'." None of which were likely in Jimmy's case. "[No]," he later said, "[I was] just a bucketful of nerves..."

Looking not unlike a visiting merchant banker in his pinstriped blue suit and pristine white shirt, Eric Clapton opened proceedings on the night with an equally crisp four-song set that featured long-established crowd-pleasers like 'Lay Down Sally' and 'Cocaine'. Looking relaxed and as ever playing impeccably, EC threw down the gauntlet early for all those to follow. After a short burst of vintage-style rock'n'roll from Andy Fairweather Low ('Man Smart, Woman Smarter') and a brief, if fine set from Steve Winwood (including a crowd-winning 'Gimme Some Lovin''), Jeff Beck picked up Clapton's gauntlet and kicked it several rows into the audience.

Always the most technically accomplished of the the Yardbirds' "big three", Beck could also be the most exciting if his head was in the game, and so it proved here. Whether spraying grace notes from outer space ('Star Cycle'), dispensing lean jazz blues with laughable ease ('Charlie Mingus' 'Goodbye Pork Pie Hat') or upstaging his contemporaries with a hooligan version of his biggest hit/oldest nemesis ('Hi Ho Silver Lining'), Jeff was the unlikely star turn of the night. "There's always been something cool and mean about Becky, though," Eric Clapton later said. "For many months after [ARMS], I began to think of Jeff as probably the finest guitar player I'd ever seen." And now Jimmy Page had to follow him.

Desperately thin, his face partially concealed by a mass of uncombed hair and wreathed in smoke from the cigarette that dangled from his lips, Page looked genuinely startled by the audience's almighty roar as he emerged from the wings. Few present would have placed a fiver on him getting through his first song intact at the Royal Albert Hall, let alone completing a full set. Surrounded by an armed guard of the finest session musicians in the UK, including bassist Fernando Saunders (on loan from Jeff Beck's band), keyboardist Chris Stainton (on loan from EC), percussionist Ray Cooper (of Elton John fame) and Andy Fairweather Low on rhythm guitar, among others, Page could at least lean on a seasoned rock orchestra to cover his tracks should things get a little hairy. And for a moment at least, it looked as if it might. Pacing furiously backwards and forwards while constantly adjusting the sleeves of his pale blue jacket, Jimmy appeared ready to cut and run rather than strike up that all important first note. But then he did. "Same old Jimmy," Jeff later laughed, "hovering on the brink of disaster, then bloody magic..."

Beginning with the soulful tones of 'Prelude' from *Death Wish II* (replete with rich organ accompaniment courtesy of James Hooker), Page slowly eased himself back into the miracles and torments of a live show, albeit one running for only 18 minutes. Hanging onto his Botswana Brown Telecaster for dear life, he looked justifiably nervous but the playing remained surprisingly sturdy nonetheless, with few if any fluffs to speak of. Punching the air with visible relief at tune's end, Jimmy then led guest vocalist Stevie Winwood and the rest of the group into two more tracks from his recent brush with movie soundtracks, as 'Who's To Blame' and 'City Sirens' rang out across the RAH. For the majority of the audience – and, quite possibly, the majority of musicians onstage – Page's decision to construct his set around an album few had really heard might have been baffling, yet he was obviously keen to distance himself from all that had gone before. But only to a point. After the last, stinging chords of 'City Sirens', Jimmy's guitar tech popped up stage right and handed his boss a suspiciously familiar looking double-necked Gibson. There would be no prizes for guessing what came next.

In reality, Jimmy Page's instrumental rendition of 'Stairway To Heaven' was something of a hot mess. After outlining the song's opening chords to the obvious delight of the crowd, Jimmy had expected Jeff Beck to arrive on cue and pluck out Robert Plant's vocal line on his trusty Fender Strat. Unfortunately, Beck was a no-show. "I thought Jeff was going to come out and help me by playing the melody [to 'Stairway...'']," Page later confirmed. "I even said, 'Here he comes, my friend Jeff Beck'. Nowhere. He didn't come on. He didn't think I was being serious about him [doing it]. In the meantime, I've got the double-neck on and everyone's assuming I'm going to play 'Stairway...' I was really in it, [so] I just had to go for it!"

To add to the drama, the man bashing the skins behind him had only begun rehearsing the tune with Jimmy a day or so before. One of the finest drummers to ever pick up two sticks, Simon Phillips' own career had started in West End musicals (*Jesus Christ Superstar*) during the mid-seventies before the likes of Brian Eno and Phil Manzanera came calling for their post-Roxy Music project, 801. Yet, it was Phillips' later association with Jeff Beck on 1980's space metal extravaganza *There And Back* that brought him to the Royal Albert Hall, and at extremely short notice, too. "I touched down at Heathrow Airport and went straight... to Nomis rehearsal studios in Olympia to play with Jeff, [keyboardist] Tony Hymas and Fernando Saunders," he said in 2015. "The next day we went into the Albert Hall for a sound check and right after [that], both Charlie Watts and Kenney Jones came up to me to ask if I'd play Jimmy Page's [set]. I had no previous idea that I'd be playing with him. Just as they left, Jimmy came onstage... and asked me if I would. The reality was that I'd have very little rehearsal time for four or five songs – actually I don't remember how many! – and Jimmy's material was far from straightforward. All I can say is thanks to Steve Winwood for helping me get through it."

While Phillips made an excellent fist of the *Death Wish II* tunes Page chose to perform, things did not go as smoothly on 'Stairway...', with he and Jimmy awkwardly bumping into each other just as things were heading towards the song's dramatic climax. "Playing 'Stairway To Heaven' as an instrumental was the weirdest thing," said Simon. "[It's] such an iconic song where everyone knows the original – except me, ha ha ha! – [and as] I mentioned before, without the vocals it didn't make a lot of sense, and the bridge section was also something that you had to properly rehearse [due to] the time changes there. There was also quite a bit of confusion backstage, [because] both Eric and Jeff were scheduled to come out at the end vamp, and they were looking at me to give them a sign! Even though I got through all the newer material just fine, I really messed up that one. Typical, huh?"

Simon Phillips' minor faux pas really didn't matter much in the scheme of things. With Jimmy Page largely removed from the public eye for so long and Led Zeppelin now ever closer to slipping into fiction, the chance to see 'Stairway To Heaven' performed – even badly – one last time was true bucket-list stuff and the RAH crowd ate it up accordingly. After striking the final chord of Zep's talismanic anthem, an exhausted-looking Page was promptly rewarded with a standing ovation from those in the hall. "It was great, brilliant," he later told *Rolling Stone*, "[and] I played for my life. If only we'd had more time..."

Though Page's scruffy, if heartfelt, rendition of 'Stairway To Heaven' was probably as good a place as any to wind things up, there was one further surprise for those gathered in South Kensington. Following a respectable break in proceedings, Jimmy, Jeff and Eric waltzed back on stage to make a little history for both themselves and those watching expectantly from all corners of the hall. The first time the trio had ever deemed to perform together in public, the prospect of seeing the Yardbirds' 'Holy Trinity' strut their stuff in such close proximity really was akin to guitar nirvana.

Given such weighty expectations, there was no great shock when it all turned out to be a bit of an anticlimax. Backed by a timber-groaning ensemble that included big hitters Watts, Wyman, Jones and just about everyone else bar the audience, Clapton was forced to act both as band leader and master of ceremonies, pulling along a cast of drummers, bassists and keyboardists through his own personal bid for rock immortality – the all-pervading 'Layla' – while simultaneously trying to nail all the guitar parts too. Under-rehearsed and missing cues as they went, only Beck came out of the jam with honour intact, his uncanny ability to swerve a solo out of the tightest of spots marking him out as the true virtuoso of the three. "When he's on," Page once said, "Beck's the best there is."

Perhaps mindful of that fact, Jimmy seemed happy to just sit on the periphery and let Jeff do his thing, the ex-Zep man only really coming forward to provide 'Layla' with its simple, melancholic coda. Nonetheless, when Ronnie Lane stepped out of the shadows to join those gathered onstage for an emotional, last-orders rendition of 'Goodnight Irene', any thoughts of who "wielded the biggest plectrum" quickly went out the window. "I genuinely didn't think I'd get such a huge response," Lane said after the event. "I mean, that was the 'Best of British' out there tonight." A largely ego-free exercise that also made a sizeable sum for ARMS, it wasn't long before someone had the bright idea of taking the show on the road to America. As a result, nine dates were booked at various venues across the States for the early winter of 1983, culminating with a final concert at New York's Madison Square Garden on December 8. "Really," Lane told *Creem* at the time, "I intended it originally to provide a hyperbaric oxygen chamber[246] for London, and that was it. But all the musicians really enjoyed playing with each other, I provided the excuse, and so we [wanted] to put out the same vibe out in America about what ARMS is doing as in England." Assembling much the same crew as before, the only high-profile change for the US concerts came on the vocal front. With Stevie Winwood now committed elsewhere, two top-drawer singers came forward to take his place in the form of Joe Cocker and ex-Free/Bad Company leader Paul Rodgers. Suffice to say, one would play a significant role in Jimmy Page's near future.

Back in 1983, however, Page was still finding his feet after so many years off the road. Spending much of his downtime in the hotel room before gigs, he was also quick to leave after the show concluded, preferring to rest as much as he could between concerts. Though this had been standard practice for him while touring with Led Zeppelin, the guitarist's apparent frailty was still a matter of concern for some of his fellow performers. "Jimmy's probably one of the bravest among us," Kenney Jones told *Rolling Stone*'s Kurt Loder at the time. "He's really put himself on the line here." Eric Clapton concurred. "Jimmy was under pressure at it was, and to have thrown more of that [his way] would have been unfair. He was very nervous... and very frail." Nonetheless, the man behind ARMS was simply glad to have Page along for the ride. "Jimmy's an old buddy of mine," said Ronnie Lane. "He was one of the first people I went to see perform before I could even play. I love Jimmy, you know... he's a very, very sweet man."

Whatever issues Page might have been facing at the time, it did not preclude his efforts to entertain the thousands who turned up each night to see him. Though sticking more or less to the bones of the set he had performed at the RAH, Jimmy had also made some impressive changes here and there in terms of pace and power. 'Prelude', for instance, was a much more dynamic opening number, his ever-developing use of

---

246 Used as one treatment for MS, a hyperbaric oxygen chamber allows air pressure to be increased by three times the normal limit, thus allowing the user's lungs to gather more air than would be possible through ordinary breathing.

the Botswana Telecaster's B-Bender helping wring every ounce of emotion out of its neo-classical melody. Page had also turned 'Stairway To Heaven' into the show-stopper it should have been back in London, with Clapton and Beck now emerging right on cue for a mock guitar war at the song's finale. "There was a little bit of competition there, I suppose," Jeff later said of the trio's nightly shredding, "but we weren't really up there to have a battle. We just traded solos and that was as close as it came."

But surely the biggest change was Page's rapidly developing friendship with Paul Rodgers. Now taking the place of Stevie Winwood as part of Jimmy's makeshift band, "Middlesbrough's answer to Muddy Waters" seemed the perfect fit on tunes such as 'City Sirens' and 'Who's To Blame', his seemingly endless vocal range custom-built for Page's blues-rocking material. It didn't end there either. When Rodgers launched into his own recently written 'Boogie Mama' onstage at Madison Square Garden as part of Page's set, the track sounded immediately at home, with Jimmy breaking out his best Chuck Berry duck-walk in celebration. An even bigger surprise came via a 'new' tune the duo had been working on called 'Bird On A Wing'. Actually a modification of Page's own lost 'Swan Song' – which he had struggled to fully bring to life while in Zep – 'Bird On A Wing' (to put it kindly) still sounded only half-finished. Nonetheless, with Page in full-on Eastern mystical mode and Paul sounding eerily like Robert Plant in places, it didn't take a clairvoyant to figure out where all this might be headed...

Following nine concerts that ranged from wobbly, but spirited (San Francisco and LA) to very much improved (Dallas and New York) the gig at the Garden on 8 December, 1983 marked the end of the ARMS tour. For some at least, it had come all too soon. "No stars and no moods, which came as a bit of a surprise, really," said a cheery sounding Joe Cocker[247]. Jeff Beck felt much the same. "[It was] great fun," he said, "[but] I think it should have gone on for another month." Drummer

---

247 Another old friend of Page's, Joe Cocker was joined onstage each night by the rest of the ARMS ensemble for 'With A Little Help From My Friends', with Jimmy happily recreating his solo from the 1968 original.

503

Simon Phillips summed up the general of air of bonhomie that seemed to surround the whole experience. "I think we all knew [it] was a one-off, so we were happy just to have the experience," he said in 2015. "I think if you asked any of the performers on the tour how they enjoyed it, they'd probably say 'Immensely'. Much more fun than touring with their own bands!"[248]

For Jimmy Page, ARMS had been a roller-coaster ride. At the start of the tour, reviews for his portion of the show made for mostly unpleasant reading. "One of the most overrated guitarists in rock," said the *San Francisco Chronicle*, while *Rolling Stone* concluded he might well be "On another planet." But by the time Page got to the Big Apple and his old playground at the MSG, he genuinely seemed to rally. Ultimately, however, it was the bond that had recently formed with Paul Rodgers that now offered him some real possibility for future progress – if he so wished. Indeed, as Page bade his farewells to the others and headed off for a holiday in Bali, there was only one thing on his mind. "I thought 'If I stop now, I'd be a bloody fool...'"

---

248 A fine enterprise, the ARMS tour raised a tidy sum for research into MS. Sadly, however, Ronnie Lane's condition continued to deteriorate. With long-term issues over royalty payments leaving him little in the way of income, Jimmy Page and his former Faces band mates Rod Stewart and Ronnie Wood continued to help fund Lane's medical care until he died in 1997.

CHAPTER 31

Crackback

Compared with the years that preceded them, both 1984 and 1985 were a hive of activity for Jimmy Page, the guitarist finally shaking off the sense of loss and subsequent inertia that enveloped him following the death of John Bonham. "That whole ARMS thing did me the world of good," he later recalled to Chris Welch. "You cannot imagine. I realised that people did actually want to see me play again." At last, Jimmy was in the mood to duly oblige.

Though fans would have to wait a while longer to hear what he had been up to at London's Nomis Studios at the start of 1984, there was still much to amuse them in the meantime, with a brace of album and live appearances dotted throughout the year. The earliest sighting came in February, when he popped up alongside Eric Clapton, Charlie Watts and the Who's John Entwistle for a jam to mark the occasion of producer Glyn John's 42nd birthday. With any ill feeling between them now long a thing of the past – in fact, it was Johns who helped Harvey Goldsmith organise London's ARMS/Prince's Trust shows in September 1983 – Jimmy just seemed keen to join in the fun. Sporting a brand-new haircut (the shortest seen in nearly two decades), he kept it light and breezy, tearing out a few old blues licks on a stray Gibson SG while Clapton and Entwistle noodled along beside him.

Page was also on hand in early June, when he joined Ian Stewart's Rocket 88 onstage at Nottingham Palais for a tribute concert in honour of Alexis Korner. A veritable legend, whose club nights at London's Marquee in the early sixties had been in part responsible for the British blues boom, Korner had succumbed to lung cancer earlier in the year and his former pupils were now determined to mark his passing in style. Led by pianist Stewart and featuring bassist Jack Bruce, Manfred Mann/Blues Band singer Paul Jones, an ever-present Charlie Watts and soul/R&B vocalist Ruby Turner, Rocket 88 put on quite the show, delivering 14 tunes over the course of two hours.

Jimmy played throughout a set that included old Muddy Waters standards like 'Got My Mojo Working' and 'Hoochie Koochie Man' as well as more ruminative fare such as 'Stormy Monday'. "When I played with Rocket 88... no one's [name] was announced until half way through the second half," he later said. "It was great because I heard people saying, 'That guitarist wasn't bad', and they didn't actually know who I was. That meant more than anything in the world. It really did. I felt, 'That's bloody magic'... it helped put things in proper perspective."

Shortly after a brief appearance with Yes in Germany on June 24[249], the first of several LPs and EPs to feature Page over the next year arrived in shops. Recorded at The Sol during the previous spring, Stephen Stills' new album *Right By You* was a strong return to form from the ex-Buffalo Springfield/CSN&Y songwriter and included Jimmy on three cuts. In the case of the Latin-themed '50/50' and country-rocking 'Flaming Heart', Page's solos arrived at the end of each tune, though his contribution to the bluesy title track was somewhat more substantial. Circling Stills' lead vocal like an angry rat, Jimmy gnawed away at 'Right By You' for three-odd minutes before finally biting down with an almost atonal blast of guitar. Though not quite in the league of 'Leave My Kitten Alone' or 'In The Evening', it was still a pleasure to know

---

249 Reuniting with his former XYZ playmate Chris Squire at Dortmund's Westfalenhallen, Page and the other members of Yes walloped their way through the Beatles' 'I'm Down' at encore time.

that when the urge took him, Page had lost none of his ability to strip paint off the studio walls.

This new penchant for bad-tempered solo flights was also much in evidence on Jimmy's contributions to John Paul Jones' soundtrack for the film *Scream For Help*. Since the dissolution of Led Zeppelin in 1980, not much had been heard from JPJ, though given the character of the man, this was not entirely unexpected. Having been one quarter of the world's biggest rock band for 12 long years, Jones had appeared wholly content to return to relative anonymity after its passing. Following the construction of a 24-track studio in Devon, John Paul went on to teach a course in electronic composition at Dartington College of Arts in 1982 before providing a bass line or three to Paul McCartney's semi-autobiographical musical drama *Give My Regards To Broad Street*. Yet, aside from another quick contribution to 1984's Huddersfield Contemporary Music Festival (this time involving trombones), that had pretty much been it until, of course, director Michael Winner came knocking.

Obviously happy with the work Jimmy Page had provided him with for *Death Wish II*, Winner was now back again, though this time he was willing to give JPJ a try for the soundtrack of his latest thriller, *Scream For Help*. "Well, Michael was the only one who offered me a film, quite honestly, and he'd worked with Jimmy before!" Jones said, laughing, to *Kerrang!*'s Dave Dickson in 1985. Pulling in a "dream team" of contributors that included Yes singer Jon Anderson and soul chanteuse Madeline Bell to aid him with the project, Jones had also thought of Jimmy. One phone call later and he was in the studio. "Getting Jimmy wasn't too bad, actually," Jones continued. "I had an idea for a track – 'Spaghetti Junction' – in the middle of the night and did a quick demo of it the next morning with just a synthesiser and drum machine. When I was listening to it later, I suddenly thought 'What this really needs is a guitar'. And then I thought, 'There's really only one guitarist', so I rang him up."

Though Page was only supposed to provide guitar on one track, the temptation to open things up a little was too hard to resist. "Once Jimmy was in the studio," said JPJ, "[I thought] we might as well do another one, so we concocted 'Crackback'." Needing a drummer for the session, Jones subsequently brought in Graham Ward from the National Youth Jazz Orchestra. It turned out the youngster didn't quite know who he was sharing a studio with. "Graham was only young and didn't recognise either Jimmy or I. [But] I think it slowly dawned on him that it was more than an average session during recording..."

A dizzying concoction of disco, rock, jazz and ballads, with Jones also making his lead vocal debut on the sentimental 'When You Fall In Love', the soundtrack to *Scream For Help*[250] was nonetheless a reasonable enough stab (no pun intended) by JPJ at writing for the screen. "It's a bit of a 'chicken and egg' thing," he later told writer Dave Dickson. "Nobody wants to be the first one to trust you [with a film]. They prefer to go with someone they know. The music might not be perfect, or it might not be the best, but if they go with [an already tested] professional, then they know they'll get a proper job."

Of the tunes featuring Page, both offered a tantalising hint of the direction Led Zeppelin might have taken should things have fallen differently in 1980. Groove orientated and sequencer driven, 'Spaghetti Junction' found Jimmy's lead lines adding a venomous alternative to JPJ's lush keyboard fills while 'Crackback' allowed the guitarist full range to "go a little nuts". As heavy in its own way as anything Zep had recorded – the drums, courtesy of the above-mentioned Graham Ward, were pure Bonzo – Page's Botswana Tele playing on 'Crackback' was both innovative and evil-sounding, his growling tone and physics-defying overbends the work of a man who clearly enjoyed torturing the life out of his guitar.

---

250 While JPJ's soundtrack for Michael Winner's *Scream For Help* was a quiet success, the film itself was not. Billed as a thriller, the end result more resembled a farce. "A hybrid so mind-boggling that viewers may wish to rush back to *Death Wish* [and] reassess [Winner's] hitherto undiscovered comic talent," said *Time Out* in 1985. "The surprise comedy hit of the year so far, [*Scream For Help*] is played to po-faced perfection by its cast of TV soap graduates." Even for the usually thick-skinned Michael Winner, that one must have hurt.

Offering the perfect opportunity to step away from the burden of being 'Jimmy Page – Rock Legend' and return to the considerably less weighty title of 'Little' Jimmy Page - Session Man for Hire', Page's playing seemed positively buoyant on *Scream For Help*. More, the studio date had allowed him to strum away alongside John Paul Jones for the first time in many a moon. "I always want to keep in contact with John and Robert, and the only way you can do that is not by talking on the telephone, but by playing," he said. "That's the only way I can communicate properly – by music. Love-wise and respect-wise, it's all still there. We're all still mates."

That point was substantially drilled home by Page's participation in yet another project he signed up for in 1984, this time with Robert Plant. By now well on his way to solo album number three, Plant's canny transformation from "snake-hipped rock god" to lone-standing, creditable singer-songwriter in the space of just four years was almost complete. Aided and abetted by ex-Silverhead guitarist Robbie Blunt, the singer's sophomore effort – *The Principle of Movements* – had again barged into the US and UK Top 10 when released in July 1983, and even generated an unlikely hit single with the smouldering AOR of 'Big Log'. Shorter of hair, musically lighter of touch and managed by the formidable Bill Curbishley[251], Robert was deliberately distancing himself from the shadow of Led Zeppelin. "To me, Zep didn't exist the moment Bonzo had gone," he once said. "Sometimes I still shout up there at that mass of blue, and say 'That was not a very good trick...'"

Yet, however much artistic and emotional space Robert Plant had placed between himself and his previous life, he remained on excellent terms with Jimmy Page. Further to their German holiday jam with

---

251 A no-nonsense veteran of the music business, Bill Curbishley began his career working for Kit Lambert and old friend Chris Stamp at Track Records, road managing Thunderclap Newman and Golden Earring before taking on a similar role with the Who. Having endeared himself to Roger Daltrey, he took over the management of the Who in 1976 and has remained their manager ever since. Also a film producer of some note (he was the man behind *Tommy*, *Quadrophenia* and *McVicar*), Curbishley was a natural choice to replace Peter Grant as Plant's manager.

Foreigner in May 1982, the two again shared a stage at Hammersmith Odeon a year or so later (December 13, 1983), when Jimmy joined Robert's band for a bluesy take on 'Treat Her Right'. Eight months after that, they performed a short set with Pretty Thing Phil May at Heartbreak Hotel in Ibiza (a regular spot for Jimmy, which we shall return to in due course). But it was a long-gestating side-project of Plant's that the pair had worked on the previous spring which saw them back together on vinyl.

After leaving Zep behind in late 1980, Robert had eased the restless side of his nature by forming an occasional pick-up combo called the Honeydrippers[252]. Named in honour of vintage Arkansas bluesman Roosevelt 'Honeydripper' Sykes, the group allowed Plant to pit his voice against a horn section rather than the usual fire-breathing Les Paul/Marshall amplifier combination, and drew mainly on a set list of old blues, fifties rock'n'roll and R&B tunes for musical sustenance. With a vocalist concentrating on a solo career, the band never really made it much outside of their local Worcestershire pub but, following several prompts from Atlantic's Ahmet Ertegun, Robert began to reconsider things. "Ahmet was always saying to me, 'You're always singing that fifties shit'," he confirmed to Malcolm Gerrie in 2015. "'So why don't you just record it?' That's where the Honeydrippers came from."

Running with the ball, Plant reined in white-hot producer/Chic guitarist Nile Rodgers to oversee the experiment at New York's Atlantic Studios in March 1984. He also made major alterations to their original line-up, bringing in keyboardist Paul Shaffer (later of David Letterman fame), bassist Wayne Pedziwiatr, "super drummer" Dave Weckl and the King Bee Horns to supplement the sound. There were two more guests on hand to help Rodgers with the guitars: Jeff Beck and Jimmy Page. "Good insurance to have," he quipped.

---

252 The original Honeydrippers' line-up consisted of guitarists Robbie Blunt and Andy Silvester, bassist Jim Hickman and drummer Kevin O'Neil. Brass was provided by saxophonist Keith Evans and saxophonist & harmonica player Ricky Cool. One gig with Plant – at Staffordshire's Keele University – took place in 1981.

By winter of the same year, Robert also had a monumental hit on his hands, with the five-track EP *The Honeydrippers: Volume One* reaching number five in the *Billboard* Hot 100 and a break-out single – a cover of Phil Phillips' peerless 'Sea Of Love'[253] – sitting pretty at number three. For Jimmy, who provided the misty-eyed solo on 'Sea...' and a snatch of bottle-neck slide on 'I Get A Thrill', this might have been a time of mild celebration, the 45's success returning him to the upper reaches of the US Top 10 (albeit as the guest on his former singer) some 18 months after the release of *Coda*. But Page seemed more preoccupied with how good Jeff Beck's contributions to the band were rather than his own. "I heard Jeff's performance on 'Rockin' At Midnight' and thought 'Bloody hell, that's good!' That's a beautiful solo. [My solo on] 'I Get A Thrill' is a bit laboured." Sadly, he wasn't wrong.

In fact, Jimmy seemed to take much more satisfaction from another collaboration he involved himself in, having reactivated his friendship with folk rock iconoclast Roy Harper during the spring of 1984. Still blazing a trail uniquely his own, Harper had continued to release albums with varying degrees of artistic, if little real commercial success throughout the seventies. But the new decade seemed to bring only difficulty, as the songwriter lost both his record deal and his farm in Marden due to financial and managerial woes. "I knew I was saying the same stuff as the punk generation," he later told *Mojo*, "[but] punk was the latest phase of youth and it was completely fair I wasn't involved."

However, a new opportunity with independent label Beggars Banquet and a firm offer from Page to temporarily join him on lead guitar offered some hope of reinvigorating both Roy's personal and professional fortunes. "I think Jimmy was being kind, really. To support

---

253 The first single released from Plant's Honeydrippers' enterprise was the actually the salty, up-tempo 'Good Rockin' Tonight'. However, DJs took to its far gentler B-side – 'Sea Of Love' – flipped the record over and Robert had his hit. Unfortunately, having spent the last four years establishing himself as a creditable rock artist, Plant now became worried he would be pigeonholed as "a crooner". Suffice to say, his concern was misplaced. 'Good Rockin'...' was re-released in 1985 and leapt into the US Top 30 of its own accord.

someone who looked like he was having a rough time." According to Page, who had encountered his own fair share of woes trying to find the right vehicle with which to move forward, their partnership cut both ways. "Maybe that's why I played with Roy whenever I could," he later told *Kerrang!*. "Because I knew his stuff and I knew him well."

The two performed together several times throughout 1984, with Jimmy joining Roy both onstage and on record. From a low-key gig at Thetford's May Tree on May 6 to a much higher profile 'double' set at the Cambridge Folk Festival on July 28, Page was there to aid Harper's progress, adding his Botswana Brown Tele and relatively new Ovation acoustic to seasoned, cantankerous classics such as 'Same Old Rock'.[254] Jimmy was also present at the recording of Roy Harper's new album *Whatever Happened To Jugula*, this time contributing broad rhythmic strokes, wild chord flourishes and the odd, fluttering lead to new tunes such as 'Elizabeth', 'Nineteen Forty-Eightish' and the epic-sounding 'Hangman'. Rightfully earning a prominent credit on the cover of the album's Rizla-styled sleeve,[255] Jimmy's presence both live and on tape was surely a defining factor in the LP's mild success, with ... *Jugula* reaching number 44 on the UK charts in March 1985. "I'm really proud of what I played on Roy's album," he later told Chris Welch. "And that's why I was there, to help Roy's album. He's been a really good friend to me and if there was anything I could do to help him, I always would."

Oddly enough, however, it might well be the duo's infamous 14-minute segment on flagship BBC2 rock show *The Old Grey Whistle Test* that sticks in many a mind with regard to Page and Harper's collaboration. A deliberate attempt to do something "a bit different", the piece was filmed halfway up a steep hill on Side Pike near the border of Langdale in Britain's Lake District during the late autumn of 1984. And indeed, Jimmy and Roy's scratchy, somewhat wayward box-top versions of 'Hangman' and '... Rock' perfectly suited the blustery

---

254 Other Page/Harper appearances in 1984 included gigs at the St. Ives Hotel (May 21), Battersea Park (July 29) and Covent Garden's Rock Garden (November 24).

255 Obviously an in-joke on Harper's part, the cover of ... *Jugula* resembled the packaging of Rizla's famed tobacco rolling papers, much favoured for rolling joints.

conditions and surreal setting. But the interview segment between songs with the pair conducted by Mark Ellen was another matter altogether.

It all seemed to being going splendidly until the show's host bluntly asked Page why he been involved in so little music over the last five years. Obviously angered by Ellen's prodding enquiry, the guitarist offered a terse explanation of his emotional state following the death of John Bonham before launching into a withering assessment of the current music scene. "It's still verses and choruses like it was in 1960," growled Jimmy, wine bottle and cigarette juggling for supremacy in his hands. "[But] with all the technology they've got and all the outspoken statements they make, they should come out with something special. They all sound the bloody same to me," he continued, "but [with] different singers. They've all got computers, so why don't they all come out with their batteries?"

When asked about his comments a year later, Page still appeared to be angry. "What Roy wanted to do was to go to the top of [the hill], and get all the fatties from the camera crew to cart all their equipment up there," he told Chris Welch. "We've all had our problems with the BBC and we thought it was a great wheeze. [But] when we got to the top, it was too blowy, so we had to come down a bit." Perhaps so. But by taking the journalistic bait while halfway up said hill, Jimmy had played straight into the stereotype of a grouchy, wine-swilling former rock god predictably bemoaning the lack of any good new bands on the music scene. It was a point not lost on him. "They cut out most of what we said," he later confirmed, "[and] that chap really wound me up on *The Old Grey Whistle Test*."

"That chap" painted a slightly different – and very funny – version of what happened before and after the interview at Side Pike in his own autobiography, 2014's *Rock Stars Stole My Life*. "The *OGWT* sent me to the Lake District where the windswept folk-prophet and his pal from Zep were on a fell-walking excursion," wrote Mark Ellen. "They caroused expansively all evening, enlivened by two favoured pick-me ups: Claret (which they called 'Red tackle') and potent powder ('White tackle'). When told we'd start filming at eight in the morning, they looked aghast and delivered the words to chill the soul of even the hardiest film crew. 'We'll have to stay up all night then!' The interview ended with them impersonating sheep." Indeed it did. "*The Old Grey Whistle Test* with Jimmy and Roy was a bit of a hatchet job," said Dave Lewis. "At the time, it was easy to laugh at those people. By then, Jimmy was starting to be seen as an old rocker. Roy, too. The knives were out."

The *OGWT* interview was not the only uncomfortable conversation in which Page found himself involved during late 1984, though the other was distinctly more one-sided. Stopped by police while travelling through a London train station in early September, Jimmy was again found in possession of cocaine. Given this was his second recorded offence, he now faced the distinct possibility of a jail sentence. Yet, instead of being led away to the cells, Page was issued with another stern warning. "You must realise," argued presiding magistrate Brendan Mitchell in November 1984, "that to dabble with drugs of this nature is entirely wrong... especially when you are associating with other members of the music world, because it may well influence them to take drugs if you yourself use them. [But] I take the view that if a prison sentence is passed, it may well prevent you from pursuing your chosen profession."[256]

The last time a magistrate had shown Page such leniency in pursuing his musical interests, little or nothing had happened, with Jimmy stepping back into the shadows instead of touring America or the Far East as outlined in court. On this occasion, it was all to be very different. After an active year of sporadic gigging, various guest spots, studio visits and dubious interviews in the Lake District, Page at last appeared ready to launch a brand-new group of his very own. "I [wanted] to put a band together so we could get out, play and just really enjoy ourselves," he said. With European dates booked for the end of November 1984, and an LP and US tour also on the way, everything pointed at better horizons ahead. But Jimmy was about to find out that following even in his own illustrious footsteps was a hard trick to pull off.

---

256 Slapped with a £450 fine, Jimmy also agreed to spend time at a health clinic, presumably for treatment relating to his involvement with such 'potent powders'.

CHAPTER 32

You've Lost That Lovin' Feeling

Jimmy Page and Paul Rodgers' plans for a new band had been simmering on the back burner since the autumn of 1983 when the two met at the singer's studio in Surrey. "Jimmy came over to see what I was up to," Paul remembered to *Uncut* in 2009. "I could see that here was someone who needed more than anything to make music." Though Page's "people" were nervous about him being asked to play after such a protracted lay-off, Rodgers proved a persistent host. "I knew that [Jimmy playing] was the way to get it all back together. It was therapeutic."

As already evidenced, Paul was right. Quickly finding "a shared musical vocabulary", he and Page had taken their tentative partnership to America for a string of concerts in support of Ronnie Lane's charity, ARMS. Admittedly, there were times when it all looked desperately uncertain, with Jimmy's frail health and reported drug problems a genuine issue at the start of the tour. But by the last date at New York's Madison Square Garden on December 9, 1983, the signs were there that something more permanent might well be at hand. "Paul and I had been on a nodding 'hello' basis for many years," Page later told *Creem Guitar Heroes*. "[But] we both hadn't been onstage for a while before the ARMS tour. Then people were suggesting that I get together with

Paul. We got together for a few days and played some things, and that's when the embryonic part of the band really happened."

The duo were quick to establish certain ground rules. Though both Page and Rodgers had been in three of the more successful groups of the sixties/seventies, their new project would mine neither Led Zeppelin, Free or Bad Company for stage or album material. "Doing the old stuff wouldn't be fair to anybody," Paul told writer Harold DeMuir. "I think it'd be cheating the kids to bring them in and let them think they're going to hear Led Zeppelin, Bad Company or Free. At this moment in time, we'd like to make the point that [any new] songs [will] stand up on their own two feet, and they don't need propping up [with old tunes]." In short, the weight of history was to be avoided at all costs. "Yeah, [but even] if we did play the oldies," he continued, "[the critics would say] they needed to play X, Y and Z. So, you can't win, really."

Where Page and Rodgers could score a victory was in the choice of players for their band. Booking into west London's Nomis Studios at the start of 1984, the pair took that responsibility seriously, auditioning some fine candidates for the jobs of drummer and bassist. One early hopeful was the Damned's Rat Scabies, who Jimmy had first heard during that tumultuous night back at The Roxy in 1977. For some an unusual choice after the thunderous machinations of John Bonham and Free/Bad Company's Simon Kirke, Scabies was nonetheless a plausible recruit, his high-energy antics and command of the kit certainly impressing Jimmy at the time. "[Rat was] absolutely brilliant, by the way," the guitarist said. "He handled everything brilliantly and he's got a lot of heart. I just loved the Damned." Though it wasn't to be, Scabies sounded as if he had enjoyed the experience. "Page turned out to be a really nice geezer," he later told Dave Lewis. "He looks half-Chinese up close, and a bottle of Grecian 2000 wouldn't go amiss either..."

Another potential nominee for the drum stool following the spirited, but ultimately unsuitable Rat Scabies was Bill Bruford, then seeking gainful employment after his own former glories in Yes, King Crimson and Genesis. "Ha! One extreme to the other," laughed Page. A stunning technician who could easily negotiate his way around rock, jazz, blues and even classical music, Bruford was given serious consideration for the job. But it was Chris Slade that finally caught the ear of Page and especially Rodgers. Brutally loud, yet also capable of great finesse, Slade had earned his stripes as a jobbing session musician, contributing to gigs/ albums by artists as diverse as Tom Jones[257], Gary Numan and Olivia Newton-John, as well as fulfilling a six-year run in Manfred Mann's Earth Band during the mid to late seventies. However, a recent offer to tour with Pink Floyd's David Gilmour (then seeking a much needed break from legal battles within the band) meant that he would not be able to join Jimmy and Paul's new ensemble for four months. They were willing to wait.

Filling the vacant bassist's position was again no easy task. For some time, Page had kept a watchful eye on Pino Palladino, whose ground-breaking fretless bass work with the likes of Tears For Fears and Gary Numan had been much lauded by those in the know. Yet, there were problems securing his services, with Palladino's long-time touring connection with soul/pop singer Paul Young making him unavailable for much of 1984. It was then that Jimmy turned to another fretless wonder he recently encountered while working with Roy Harper.

Though only 22 years old, Tony Franklin had excelled on *Whatever Happened To Jugula*, his ability to find a suitable melody among Harper's multiplex of complex chordings marking him out as a player of real promise. "I did three sessions [with Roy], got on fine, and a week later, he asked me to join the band," Tony told Chris Welch. "It was out of the blue and I became involved with a new circle of musicians." Nonetheless, when Page and Rodgers came calling about a job with them, Franklin was more than happy to take up the offer. "Well, Tony was on the dole," said Jimmy. "He'd been playing on Roy's album. Maybe that's why he was on the dole..."

After finally settling on a solid line-up, a period of intense rehearsals and recording ensued at Nomis and The Sol, albeit one that could accommodate Page's various other commitments with musicians and judiciary alike. There was also the matter of a band name to be sorted

---

257 Chris Slade appeared on Tom Jones' 1967 LP *13 Smash Hits*, which reportedly also featured Jimmy and John Paul Jones.

out. At first, rumour had it that they would call themselves 'The MacGregors', a pseudonym Roy Harper had foisted on Jimmy at their gig in Thetford[258] and which Page had also used when booking time at Nomis. "Too daft," was the overall verdict. Another story had the group toying with 'The Business' and 'The Clan' as possible signifiers. But in the end, it was 'The Firm' that won out. Given Page's previous connection with Zep and the general air of menace that sometimes accompanied them, the name seemed curiously apt.

A rum bunch then, comprising "two aging rockers, a shaven-headed Welsh battering ram and a bassist with the maddest hair in music," the Firm made their live debut at Stockholm's Göta Lejon on November 29, 1984. Just like Zep before them, while an album was already recorded and in the can, the quartet chose to hit the road in advance of its release. "It was a bit unconventional. We did the album first, then [the] live shows," Page told *Kerrang!*. "But the Firm was put together by Paul and I as a vehicle to get out and tour, to play to audiences."

Walking onstage to the strains of Holst's 'The Planets' suite (though obviously not all of it), the Firm's live show proved to be an extension of the duo's ARMS set of the year before, but with a few added extras. Drawing on snippets of *Death Wish II* ('Prelude', 'City Sirens'), material from Paul Rodgers' 1983 solo LP *Cut Loose* ('Boogie Mama', 'Live In Peace') and the odd cover, the group had also banged 'Bird On A Wing' into some kind of usable shape. Now re-titled 'Midnight Moonlight', Page and Rodgers' first joint composition still remained a tad flabby at the edges, but its involved middle-section did allow Jimmy to flash a few snippets of 'White Summer'/'Black Mountain Side' at the crowd, much to their obvious delight. Further, while the Firm had more or less stuck to their promise of 'no LZ/Free/BC material', the ban obviously didn't apply to Page's violin bow, which was given a distinctly 'Dazed And Confused'-like outing during *Death Wish II*'s 'The Chase'. Of the new tunes – of which there were several, and

---

258 For reasons best known to themselves, Harper introduced Jimmy as 'James MacGregor' at the May Three in Thetford. Evidently, the epithet 'S. Flavius Mercurius' had been dropped by then.

which we will return to soon enough – opening number 'Closer' was the obvious stand-out, its funky, circular riff causing severe tapping of the foot by chorus time.

Real trial by fire stuff, the Firm's brave (or extremely foolhardy) decision to hit the road without any product in the stores might well have backfired. Yet, their early shows in Stockholm, Copenhagen and Frankfurt were reasonably well attended, the prospect of seeing what Jimmy Page and Paul Rodgers were now up to simply too much for some European rock fans to miss. Indeed, by the time the group arrived back in London for a two-night stop-over at Hammersmith Odeon on December 8 & 9, 1984, *MTV* was also on the case, the then still new-fangled music channel videotaping the gigs for their American audience. "The band has felt natural from the first gig," drummer Chris Slade told Chris Welch at the time. "I mean, they were standing and screaming in Stockholm, and you know how reserved they can be. The Americans should love it. It's obviously going to be one of the bigger bands around next year. Has to be..."

Or not.

On February 11, 1985, those not in attendance at the quartet's earliest shows were given the opportunity to hear what they had missed, when the Firm's self-titled debut LP was released on Atlantic Records. To say it was something of a disappointment would be kind. Not unlike a large sign with several key letters missing, one could see what the band were getting at, but the urge to give up before finally putting all the pieces back together could be all-pervasive. On the plus side, 'Closer' lived up to its in-concert promise, the addition of a horn section mightily enlivening its already itchy feel. 'Satisfaction Guaranteed' also did pleasant things to the ear, the song's melding of modern pop textures and vintage blues chords both clever and compelling. And after nearly two decades of tortuous gestation, Jimmy had at last managed to salvage something from the bones of the long-lost 'Swan Song', with 'Midnight Moonlight''s epic structure, Arabic/Celtic acoustic interlude and emotive conclusion recalling the sky-rocketing ambition of a certain four-man airship.

Individual performances, too, were hard to fault. In Tony Franklin, Page had found a proper little star, his fretless bass-playing bold and inventive, his synth-work supportive rather than intrusive. Chris Slade was also a granite-like presence, the drummer's power behind the kit pushing his colleagues up many a melodic hill. Indeed, after almost two decades in the game, Paul Rodgers could still sing the hind legs off a donkey, the depth of emotion and accompanying technique he first showed on Free's *Tons Of Sobs* back in 1969 only growing with time. "[Paul's] such a technician, it can be an intimidating problem," said Jimmy. "If I do a guitar solo, I have to warm up. He just goes in there and does it straight off, no problem, note perfect. He seems to have so much control over his voice." As for Page himself, his was no real disgrace either. From the sighing slide guitar of 'Make Or Break' to the Lake Placid Blue Strat tremolo wrangling of 'Satisfaction Guaranteed', Jimmy's relish for smoothing strings or breaking them was still more or less intact.

Yet, from whichever angle one approached the album, *The Firm* was horribly lacking in any great songs, with the likes of 'Money Can't Buy', 'Together' and 'Make Or Break' all melting into one indivisible arena rock-flavoured soup. Worse, the band's cover of The Righteous Brothers' timeless 'You've Lost That Lovin' Feelin'' almost bordered on caricature, its syrupy feel and wall of female backing singers stripping the original tune of all its heart. "A cover version of 'You've Lost That Lovin' Feelin''?" said Dave Lewis. "I mean, really? That wouldn't have happened at Knebworth, would it?"

And that, really, was the problem. Even back in 1979, the Firm's chugging "Man rock grooves" and occasional doffing of the Stetson to Eagles-style West Coast country tunes ('Together') would have sounded a tad passé. But it was now 1985, and things had moved on again, and again, and again. As evidenced, the likes of Van Halen had recently re-electrified hard rock, putting energy, tunefulness and technical guile back into the genre, while glam-metal pups Mötley Crüe, Poison, Ratt and Bon Jovi were now ready to carry on where they had left off.

Meanwhile, over in Nashville, a new brand of authenticity also threatened to return country music to its original roots. Sick of all the overblown arrangements and twee sentimentality that had become increasingly synonymous with the format, songwriters like Steve Earle and Dwight Yoakam were stripping away country's excess fat by feeding it a lean diet of twanging strings, gutsy stories and loud bass drums. Where a band like the Firm sat in this new world of sparkle and sinew was anyone's guess. "The world had turned by 1985," said Chris Charlesworth, "and Jimmy and Paul were still peddling old-school arena stuff and half-cocked country rock. At the point where he and Rodgers needed to deliver something brilliant, something that could compete with all the young guns – something that reminded everyone why we all loved them in the first place – they gave us the Firm."

Too heavy to be neo-country, too soaked in the blues to be glam or pop metal, the Firm were facing a nebulous dilemma and the critics weren't afraid to point it out. "This record stinks, [and] considering who's involved, it's a total outrage," said *Creem*'s Jon Young. "You'd at least expect the Firm to be interesting, and you'd be disappointed. But Page and Rodgers have not struck out in a bold new direction. That [at least], would have been preferable. [Instead], they just rehash too familiar fare."

This 'men out of time' theme was also apparent in Jimmy Page's approach to the promotional video for their first single, 'Radioactive'. Combining staccato chords with an insistent beat and memorable chorus, 'Radioactive' was among the stronger cuts on the album. Indeed, when one added Tony Franklin's wandering, fretless bass fills, a sprinkle or two of Page studio trickery and a spidery solo (actually played by Paul Rodgers), it was also by far the most contemporary-sounding. Yet, one felt Jimmy was distinctly uncomfortable with the demands of the incumbent *MTV* age. "We're going to put out 'Radioactive' as a single, which is new territory for me," he told *Kerrang!* in 1985. "I know in Zeppelin I wouldn't do a single and now I'm doing one and a video for my new band. People might say 'Well, there goes a hypocrite'. But it's not that. The idea is to... show people who've had a lot of faith in me that we're having a go." Nonetheless, while some lines could be crossed, others remained immutable. Eschewing any notion of Duran Duran-like mini-movies, 'Radioactive' was a straight ahead performance-based promo, with Page swinging his trademark Gibson double-neck at the camera whenever it strayed too near. "I don't want to pretend to be an actor [in the video], because I'm not," he said. "When we did our fantasy sequences for *The Song Remains The Same*, nobody was allowed to be around the others while it was being filmed because they'd all take the piss. All you can be is what you are."

Co-produced by Jimmy and Paul Rodgers, and housed in a faux-3D sleeve (designed by Steve Maher), *The Firm* did respectable if not exactly earth-shattering business on its release in February 1985. Entering the UK charts at number 15, it fluttered around for a further four weeks before making its excuses and leaving. Despite Chris Slade's optimistic prediction of American glory and a lengthy tour of the States in support of the album, *The Firm* also failed to ignite in the USA, where it reached number 17 in the *Billboard* Hot 100 before again making its exit. As for 'Radioactive', despite heavy rotation on *MTV*, the 45 could only get as far as number 28, with follow-up single 'Satisfaction Guaranteed' faring even worse at a measly number 73. Not even the sight of Page wielding a violin bow or playing his slide solo with a beer bottle in its steamy, South American bar-set video could save it. "There were two or three good songs on [that record]," Jimmy later said, "but it did have its faults."

While it was too early to write off the Firm on the basis of one album and a pair of underperforming singles, any momentum the band may have been gathering was inadvertently halted in the face of the "global juke box" known as 'Live Aid'. Born out of Bob Geldof's need "to do something" after witnessing the BBC's harrowing footage of the Ethiopian famine, the former Boomtown Rat (and Sol studio user) had pulled together the charity single 'Do They Know It's Christmas?' for 1984's seasonal market. Working alongside co-writer/former Ultravox frontman Midge Ure, Geldof had enlisted the cream of then current British and Irish pop for the song, with U2's Bono, Sting, Paul Young, George Michael, Boy George, Duran Duran and several other groups/ solo artists all singing a line or two, or adding an instrumental part. The result was a runaway train, with Band Aid's 'Do They Know...' becoming the fastest-selling single in UK chart history – shifting over three million units by the first day of 1985, and raising over £8 million for famine relief.

By March of the New Year, the States had answered the call, too, as Harry Belafonte, Michael Jackson, Lionel Richie and producer/arranger Quincy Jones assembled 'USA for Africa'. Comprising Jackson and co., Bob Dylan, Bruce Springsteen, Paul Simon, Stevie Wonder, Ray Charles, Tina Turner, Willie Nelson and a supporting choir of various other pop luminaries, the resulting tune – 'We Are The World' – sold in excess of 20 million copies, making it the first single to be awarded 'quadruple platinum' status.

With a small fortune now raised for Ethiopia, the project might well have stopped there. But Bob Geldof was in no mood to call time just yet. Spurred on by Boy George's suggestion that a themed concert would help bring in even more cash for famine victims, Geldof approached formidable UK promoter Harvey Goldsmith with the idea of staging a "super gig" on both sides of the Atlantic. "[We] wanted the biggest pop event ever staged over a one-day period," he said. Though ludicrously ambitious in terms of scope and scale, the pair somehow managed to get it going, with Goldsmith organising the British side of things while former Zep-nemesis Bill Graham took care of business Stateside. Two stadiums – Wembley Stadium in London and JFK Stadium in Philadelphia – were booked to hold crowds of 72,000 and 90,000 respectively, while the BBC and ABC agreed to televise the whole event[259], with special telephone hotlines also set up allowing viewers to pledge their donations throughout the show. Come July 13, 1985 and Live Aid was finally ready to go.

Beyond the mind-boggling logistics of it all, the central conceit behind the concerts was simplicity itself: "Get the best bands in the world on the stage and let 'em off like fooking fireworks." However, while many acts had bent over backwards to offer their services in advance of the event, others were more difficult to reel in. Both the Who and Black Sabbath, for instance, had to be persuaded by Geldof to put aside their personal and financial differences for the sake of an even bigger cause. Others, like ex-Beatle Paul McCartney (who might well have been

259 In addition to the UK and USA, several other countries organised their own events for famine relief, including the Republic of Ireland, Australia and Germany.

stung by the high expectations and eventual disappointments of charity-themed events before) were convinced to appear by their children or management.

Robert Plant seemed to harbour no such concerns regarding how Live Aid might turn out. Already a strong and very vocal supporter of the idea behind 'Do They Know It's Christmas?', he would have lent his voice to that project had it not been for previous commitments elsewhere. Indeed, when Geldof called to ask for his participation in Live Aid, Plant was reportedly quite happy to say yes to any number of possibilities, including the prospect of a sharing the stage with Eric Clapton. But then the idea of a Honeydrippers-themed set featuring a 'very special guest star' was floated by the vocalist. By all accounts, Geldof was broadly amenable to Robert's suggestion, but the 'guest star' in question – Jimmy Page – was now thinking in bigger terms than fifties jump blues and doo-wop standards. Egged on by Plant, Page wanted to reform Led Zeppelin (or at least three quarters of it) for the day and, what's more, John Paul Jones did too. If Bob had any remaining worries about selling 90,000 tickets at JFK Stadium, they had just been solved.

On the day, Live Aid threw up its fair share of winners and losers. With each major act strictly apportioned just 17 minutes under the lights, the onus was on hitting the ground running, doing as many well-known songs as possible and then heading back into the wings for a celebratory beer. For some, such as David Bowie, Eric Clapton, U2 and Bryan Adams, this format worked out a treat, with each performer tailoring their set accordingly to the time constraints of the show. Others, like Duran Duran, the Who and Paul McCartney, fell prey to stage rustiness, sound problems – or in the case of unlikely trio Bob Dylan, Keith Richards and Ronnie Wood – the quite mad idea of changing their previously agreed set while actually onstage.

If there was one clear victor on the day, however, it had to be Queen. Approaching Live Aid like a well-drilled bomber squadron, the band used their allotted quarter of an hour or so at Wembley to drop hit after hit while frontman Freddie Mercury hammed it up to perfection between tunes. In many ways the direct beneficiaries of Led Zeppelin's creative/business model – though with one eye always fixed on the singles charts, too – Queen guitarist Brian May remained quick to acknowledge his own group's debt to their mighty predecessors. "Zep [were] the model of the way that a band should handle themselves, artistically, management-wise, their attitude to albums and touring, and how they lived," he told *Guitar World*'s Harold Steinblatt. "We used to look at those guys and think 'That's the way it should be done'." Though surely not at Live Aid.

Even before 'Led Zeppelin' took to the boards of JFK Stadium at 8.13 p.m. on 13 July, 1985, there had been definite signs that things might not go as expected. In the absence of John Bonham, Page, Plant and Jones had offered the drummer's stool to former Chic percussionist Tony Thompson, then enjoying a successful spell in the charts with funk rockers the Power Station. Unfortunately, due to a few crammed diaries – Robert was on tour in the US promoting his third solo disc, *Shaken 'N' Stirred*[260] at the time – Thompson only got two hours rehearsal with the band before showtime. That said, he was due to receive some additional assistance from the ubiquitous Phil Collins, who had scheduled to fly out on Concorde from London to Philadelphia following his own set at Wembley to lend the group a hand. Unlike Tony, however, Phil would not get the chance to prepare notes with them beforehand. Still, with luck, it would all hang together perfectly. It didn't. "Live Aid," Page later said, "was just appalling."

Though perhaps not quite as bad as Jimmy would have it, Live Aid did not do the memory of Led Zeppelin any great service. After a whooping introduction from Phil Collins[261], there was almost two minutes of dead air before a note was struck, as roadies desperately ran around the stage trying to find monitors so that the band could actually

---

260 Plant's third solo disc, *Shaken 'N' Stirred* was a huge departure from what came before, with the singer largely abandoning any vestiges of his musical past in favour of a more electronic sound. "I was very inspired by what Peter Gabriel was doing," Robert told Q in 2002, "and wanted to have a crack at something different." While he certainly managed that, sales suffered, with the album peaking at number 19 in the UK charts.

261 Though enthusiastic when introducing the band, Collins was careful not to actually call them 'Led Zeppelin'. Instead, he called out each band member's name individually.

hear themselves. When things did finally get going with 'Rock And Roll', it became immediately apparent that Plant's voice was hoarse, Page's guitar on the verge of going out of tune and drummers Collins and Tony Thompson out of synch with each other. Only the usually unflappable John Paul Jones appeared to be untouched by all the hair and skin flying all around him. Still, with adrenaline levels off the charts and over five years since all three had appeared together onstage, some early nerves were completely understandable.

Regrettably, however, 'Rock And Roll' proved to be the technical highlight of the set. After a few stray riffs from Jimmy (possibly meant to be 'Heartbreaker', but even he sounded unsure), the group launched into a rendition of 'Whole Lotta Love' so ragged it threatened to descend into complete chaos. With Page's Les Paul now tuned to the key of "whatever" and Robert's vocals still the wrong side of grim, it also appeared that neither Thompson nor Collins knew the rhythmic cues to Jimmy's stop/start solo or when to start up again after he had finished playing it. "We'd all been off doing different projects, but still thought we could get it [back] together well enough," Page admitted to *The Guardian* in 2014. "But neither drummer really knew the set, [so] it ended up as wing and a prayer stuff, really. If you look at my face on film, you can actually see me going 'Oh my God...'"

In subsequent years, Phil Collins has come in for some real stick regarding his part in the band's poor set, with the drummer's decision to join them onstage without proper rehearsal causing more problems than it was worth. Yet, according to him, at least some of the blame lay elsewhere. "I thought it was just going to be low-key and we'd all get together and have a play," Collins later told *Q*. "But something happened between that conversation and the day... it became a Led Zeppelin reunion. I turned up and was a square peg in a round hole. Robert was happy to see me[262], but Jimmy wasn't." Realising "this is a mistake" almost as soon as everyone started playing, the chance to get

---

262 At the onset of Plant's solo career, Phil Collins had been enormously helpful to the singer, producing and playing on his debut album *Pictures At Eleven*, while also sitting in as drummer for Robert's 1983 US tour. The two remain firm friends.

out of a difficult situation began ebbing away with every beat. "You could sense I wasn't welcome... Tony was not making life easy [and] if I could have walked off, I would have done," he said. "But then we'd all be talking about why Phil Collins walked off Live Aid, so I just stuck it out. It was a disaster, really," he concluded. "Robert wasn't match-fit with his voice and Jimmy was out of it, dribbling. It wasn't my fault it was crap."

Strangely enough, it was a song that Robert Plant had become increasingly disenchanted with during his time in Led Zeppelin that repaired at least some of the damage at Live Aid. Having co-written one of the most iconic and loved tunes of the seventies, Plant's relationship with 'Stairway To Heaven' had began to sour around the end of that decade, with its singer becoming increasingly reluctant to perform it as part of Zep's live set. "At Knebworth," Peter Grant later said, "he even sang the wrong words to 'Stairway...'. Unforgivable, really." Reportedly embarrassed by what he had grown to consider an idealistic, even naive lyric, intervening years did little to temper Robert's opinion of the song. In fact, he was still throwing darts at 'Stairway...' backstage at Philadelphia. "'Stairway To Heaven' isn't the reason you go on stage together," he reasoned to *Rolling Stone's* Michael Goldberg. "Unfortunately, everyone missed the point with that song. 'Kashmir' was *the* song. It's much more... not ethereal, not aesthetic... but evocative. Really, I have no idea why 'Stairway...' is so popular, no idea at all."[263]

As Jimmy Page plucked the opening chords of 'Stairway...' at Live Aid, Robert Plant's confusion must have only worsened. Deprived of their generation's anthem for so long only to have it now returned, the audience at JFK roared their approval like a pack of wild coyotes, rendering what was happening onstage temporarily inaudible. Curiously,

---

263 Unlike his colleagues, Page's opinion regarding 'Stairway...' had remained remarkably constant. "In America, it's become something of an anthem," Jimmy told Chris Welch in 1985. "They still play it on the radio stations. It's incredible, really. If you're a musician, it's the one thing that you want to do. Leave a mark. Create something that people really relate to. That song is it, for me. I've done everything I wanted to do with that song."

this in turn seemed to have a healing effect on the group, as Plant at last found his voice and Page began playing like it was 1975 all over again. With Thompson and Collins also falling in line and guest bassist Phil Martinez[264] holding down the bottom end while John Paul Jones concentrated on his keyboards, 'Led Zeppelin' (or whatever they might be calling themselves) finally started sounding like a band rather than a collection of stray musicians. Sure, Plant managed to choke off the end of Jimmy's solo by coming in early at the song's end but, by then, nobody really cared anymore. Zep – at least for one night – were back in town. "Say what you want about Live Aid," reasoned Dave Lewis, "they were under rehearsed, Phil Collins didn't suit the style and Jimmy kept getting his bloody scarf caught in his guitar strings, but when that camera pulled away to the crowd during 'Stairway...', they all wanted Zep back. The audience was still there. No one can deny that."

True enough. But for Robert Plant at least, the memory of Live Aid seemed to bring back nightmares long after the event was done. "Live Aid was wonderful, [but] we were awful," he later said. "It was a fucking atrocity for us. It made us look like loonies. I was hoarse, Pagey was out of tune [and] we had no monitors, no nothing."[265] Yet, the numbers at the time didn't lie. Before the band took to the stage, donations stood at £800,000. Sixty minutes after the last chords of 'Stairway...' rang out over Philadelphia, that total had increased to over £2 million. More, thousands of UK Zep fans had stayed up way past their bedtime to watch the show on TV, with the band's set transmitted by the BBC at around one in the morning. Even if they were bad on the night (and 'Stairway...' aside, they really were), the interest was still obviously there. "I'm not ashamed of any of it," said Jimmy of his band's legacy a

---

264 A fine player, Phil Martinez had been drafted in for Live Aid from Robert's own band.

265 Plant, Page and Jones' negative opinion concerning their performance at Live Aid did not change with time. When a 20th anniversary DVD package was being compiled in 2004, all three refused permission for footage from their part of the show to be included, offering instead royalties from several projects they were then involved in to cover any financial loss incurred by its exclusion.

month or so before the show. "Led Zeppelin was magic for me. It was a privilege to play in that band." He was soon afforded the opportunity to try and do so once again.

While Plant may have winced thinking about their performance in Philadelphia, it was not quite enough to stop him joining Page, John Paul Jones and Tony Thompson in the old Roman spa town of Bath during early January 1986. Booked into a village hall not far from Peter Gabriel's Real World Studios in Box Mill near Bath, nobody was precise about what the quartet were doing there, but the inference was fairly clear: a Zep reunion of sorts might at last be on the cards. However, the fates – and several more earthbound irritations – once again conspired against them. On day one, all had looked reasonably promising, with Plant assuming duties on bass guitar while Jones dabbled with his keyboards. According to Robert, "Two or three things" came out of their jams, resembling "a cross between David Byrne and Husker Du." But Jimmy's frail health remained a concern for all, with stories later circulating about his inability to tune up properly. Not so, according to Page. "The second night we got to play, it really started to cook."

Unfortunately, the project was dealt a major blow only hours after the second rehearsal, when Tony Thompson was involved in a motor accident. With their sticksman now out of the picture, Led Zeppelin's original trio soldiered on for a few more days, first putting a roadie behind the kit before resorting to a drum machine. Nonetheless, Robert Plant's patience was beginning to wear thin. Now a band leader in his own right with three successful albums and a million-selling EP under his belt, Plant was in no mood for ifs, buts and maybes. By the end of the week, he – and any hope of a reunion tour or album – were gone. "When Tony went out and got involved in a car crash," said Page, "I thought 'Wait a minute, this just isn't meant to be'." Given Plant's later assessment of the proposed alliance, even if Thompson had remained in the rudest of health, the prospect of Zep reforming was wisp-like at best. "For me to have succeeded in Bath," said Robert, "I would have to have been more patient than I had in years."

Throughout this occasionally tortuous, occasionally hopeful but ultimately skewed enterprise, Page remained connected to the Firm.

Though the original intention had been to cut only one album before going their separate ways, Jimmy and Paul Rodgers decided to give it another shot, now bringing in Australian producer Julian Mendelsohn to help put everyone through their paces. A brilliant technician who had worked with the likes of the Pet Shop Boys, Frankie Goes To Hollywood and Peter Gabriel, Mendelsohn's ability to find hidden treasures within the mix had impressed Page greatly. "We did a 12" remix of 'Radioactive'... with Julian and he was good to work with," he offered by way of explanation. "So [on the second LP], I thought it'd be really good to do it with him." Having already ceded a measure of control by reducing his credit to that of co-producer alongside Rodgers and Mendelsohn, Jimmy also seemed content to leave behind his beloved Sol for part of the project, decamping instead to Trevor Horn's SARM complex in London's Notting Hill to add a tweak or two. "We never saw him, though," Page quipped of the UK's then most lauded pop producer.

Despite all these changes, however, the Firm's second LP *Mean Business* again failed to hit the mark. A moody, sometimes even sombre record filled with wistful pianos and orchestral synths (again courtesy of Tony Franklin), *Mean Business* had at least moved partly away from the more jaded blues and country rock progressions of its predecessor. Indeed, thanks to the new production team of Page, Rodgers and Mendelsohn, the disc sounded genuinely crisp and surprisingly contemporary. But as with the band's debut disc, it still lacked for real intensity and killer tunes, with a glut of filler material overwhelming the few examples of genuine progress on show.

There were exceptions here and there. With 'Live In Peace', the Firm had reworked a track that previously appeared on Paul Rodgers' 1983 solo album *Cut Loose* to their own distinct advantage, considerably slowing down its tempo and adding a strident, searching solo from Jimmy at the finale. "We did 'Live In Peace' on the first tour, but it grew as a number the more shows we did," Page said at the time. "[It was] such a strong song and such a strong lyric." Rodgers' 'All The King's Horses' also had a real sense of drama to it, its melancholic chorus destined to draw the attention of DJs, especially in the States. "One of

Paul's," Jimmy told MTV, "a bit more synthesiser-orientated. Good song."[266] So was Tony Franklin's 'Dreaming'. The bassist's sole song-writing credit with the band, 'Dreaming' was completely at odds with the rest of *Mean Business*, though none the worse for that. A trippy little tune that mixed Hendrix-like guitar with several jazzy chord changes, Page's unexpected but endearing blast of atonal Strat abuse in the midst of it all only helped add to the track's quirky charm.

Another track that captured one's attention – though this time for the wrong reasons – was the cascading rocker 'Fortune Hunter'. Credited to Page and Rodgers on the album's inner sleeve, it transpired that the song might have had its origins in the failed XYZ project of early 1981. Yes bassist Chris Squire certainly thought so. "Interestingly enough, one of the songs I wrote – and I wrote all the songs for [XYZ] – showed up on the last Firm album," Squire later told *Guitar World*. "'Written by Paul Rodgers and Jimmy Page', it said. Very interesting." Nonetheless, Squire didn't seem in any mood to call in the lawyers. Still basking in the warm afterglow of Yes' multi-million selling *90125*, he didn't need the money or the hassle. "It didn't do anything so there was no point making a fuss about it..."[267]

Good in places, but clogged up with more than its fair share of duds ('Cadillac', 'Tear Down The Walls' and 'Free To Live', to name but three), *Mean Business* was the sound of Jimmy Page treading water while Paul Rodgers occasionally tried pushing him towards shore. With his name appearing on only half of the album's eight tracks (and one of those was in some dispute), Page seemed to know he was a more gifted character actor than leading man with the Firm. "It wasn't really meant to be like Led Zeppelin, though," he later told *Classic Rock*. "It was

---

266 Despite being released three times in various formats throughout 1986, 'All The King's Horses' could not quite give the Firm the hit single they were looking for, the band having to make do with number 61 in the *Billboard* Hot 100 (though '... Horses' did make number one in *Billboard*'s 'Album Rock Tracks' chart).

267 Page and Squire had actually jammed together at Ibiza's 'Sun Power' festival on August 28, 1985, several months before the release of *Mean Business*. Presumably, the subject of 'Fortune Hunter' didn't come up at the time...

supposed to be [more] like Free and Bad Company. It was very much Paul's band too."

Released on February 3, 1986, *Mean Business* made a quick stab at the charts, peaking at numbers 22 and 46 in the US and UK respectively, but even a two and half month tour of the States during March–May couldn't stave off the inevitable. By summer, the band had quietly packed it in. "Paul is a technical vocalist, he'll sing with that beautiful quality to his voice, but always within the framework," Jimmy later told *Musician*'s Charles M. Young. "I know when you think of Paul, you immediately think of Bad Company format songs. But I wondered could he stretch from that at all, as I was willing to go his way to a degree. I just wondered if he could stretch into more unusual stuff with that vocal quality. What we did," said Page, "was what we did."

An underperforming experiment cut right down the middle by the reappearance of Led Zeppelin at Live Aid, the Firm still didn't do any real harm to the career paths of those involved. Now established as a bassist of genuine calibre, Tony Franklin almost immediately went on to work with Blue Murder, a power trio put together by former Whitesnake lead guitarist John Sykes and featuring Jimmy's old mate Carmine Appice on drums. Ironically, they had something of Led Zeppelin about them. Chris Slade, too, reaped the benefits of such a high-profile gig, the Welshman soon ending up in the ranks of the glorious AC/DC.

As for Paul Rodgers, it was more a case of 'mission accomplished' than anything else. Eventually returning to a solo career that would see him nicely into the next century[268], Rodgers felt that the Firm had more than achieved its purpose. To wit, the musical re-emergence of Jimmy Page. "We wanted to create original music together," he later told *Uncut*'s Nigel Williamson. "Jimmy felt insecure when we were on tour... if he did four bad gigs no one would want to know him

---

268 Probably the great journeyman vocalist of his generation, Paul Rodgers would lend his name to many a project after the Firm, including the Law (with Kenney Jones, late of the Faces and post-Moon Who), a post-Freddie Mercury Queen and even a reformed Bad Company.

anymore. People who are that much of a genius are very sensitive as to how they will be received. And it's a hard act to follow oneself. But at the end of our time together, he was fully on his feet."

From their hopeful beginnings to their anticlimatic end, the Firm was always going to be obscured by the shadow of Led Zeppelin, and to a lesser extent, Free and Bad Company. But Rodgers did have a point. Before forming the group, Page had been in an extremely dark place, his creative energies in doubt, his physical frailties obvious to all. He was well aware of it. "Well, the Firm isn't the sort of thing where you sign five-year contracts at the age of 41," he said, laughing, in 1985. "I mean, I might not even live to be 46!" Yet, while the band itself proved a disappointment, it had provided Jimmy with new impetus, allowing him back into the studios and concert halls after years spent ruminating on past glories and absent friends. "I just needed to get on with it," he said, and so he had.

Now it was time for Page to prove he could do it all on his own.

CHAPTER 33

The Only One

For Jimmy Page, the dissolution of the Firm meant only one thing: going back to the drawing board. That said, there were now a least a few equations written on it from which to work. "I know Jimmy represented old-school rock by then, but really, the Firm should have succeeded," said Dave Lewis. "I mean, take Paul Rodgers. What's not to like about that voice? Yet the band, well, the band live were nowhere near as authoritative or exciting as Led Zeppelin. The sloppiness at times, the flat repertoire, that cover version of 'You've Lost That Lovin' Feelin'". Still, at least Page was back in the game." Onwards and upwards it was then, though upwards would still take a bit of time.

As had been his wont following the demise of Led Zeppelin in 1980, Page chose to tread slowly as the Firm closed its doors for business, confining his activities to the odd guest appearance or studio date while he worked out his next move. Having missed (or not been asked) to contribute to the Yardbirds reunion some years earlier, Jimmy popped up on the band's second album, 1986's *Strange Land*. Trading under their new name Box Of Frogs[269], the former 'Birds had enlisted a cluster

---

269 As stated in chapter 30, when the Yardbirds scored a new record deal after reuniting in 1983, they decided to change their name to Box Of Frogs. Released a year later, the band's self-titled 'debut' album featured Jeff Beck on four very fine cuts.

of stars to help them out, including Irish blues virtuoso Rory Gallagher, punk/pub rock poet Ian Dury and ex-Genesis guitarist Steve Hackett, among others. For his part, Page offered up a jittery wah solo on the equally nervous-sounding 'Asylum', one of the better tracks on an otherwise patchy LP. "I'm not sure why Jimmy wasn't on the first Box Of Frogs album, really," laughed drummer Jim McCarty, "but he was on the next one!"

Page's next cameo was as uncredited guest on the Rolling Stones' molten 'One Hit (To The Body)', a single drawn from the band's 1986 disc, *Dirty Work*. The shining star of an otherwise risible LP recorded during a personal/professional low point between Mick Jagger and Keith Richards (Keef was miffed with Mick doing a solo album), 'One Hit...' had Jimmy "playing the shit" out of his Botswana Brown Tele on the track's extended outro. "When I was in New York at the end of the Firm tour, I heard from Ronnie and then Keith," Page later explained to MTV. "They were doing their album and invited me along. Well, the first night we had a tremendous time jamming. Keith was doing that Chuck Berry thing and he's like a locomotive. There's no one I know who can do that Chuck Berry thing like Keith. So, the next night I was going to put down some solos for their stuff and Mick was there. It'd been a while since I'd seen him, actually. Anyway, he'd just done a vocal on one of the numbers, and that's the one I played to."[270]

Away from old band mates and feuding friends, Jimmy also made his presence felt at a number of concert halls and clubs throughout 1986, sitting in with various solo performers, living legends and heavy metal comedy acts. The 'mini tour' began on June 9, when Page rocked up in New York to honour Les Paul's 72nd birthday. As evidenced, a

---

270 Before his contribution to 'One Hit (To The Body)', Page had played a tidy little solo on 'These Arms Of Mine', a track featured on Bill Wyman's 1985 all-star album *Willie And The Poor Boys*. Later released as a single, Jimmy (and Paul Rodgers) also made a guest appearance in '...Mine's accompanying video. "We videotaped for almost a whole day at Fulham Town Hall," the Stones bassist later told *Guitar World*, "but then [we] had to shoot footage over. We realised Pagey had his fly open the whole time. Charming to some, I suppose, but also the charm of keeping it off the telly..."

huge fan of Paul since his childhood, and perhaps the most high-profile exponent of his famous electric guitar, Jimmy joined Jeff Beck, Chic's Nile Rodgers, jazz fusion gypsy Al Di Meola and sturdy blues rocker Rick Derringer to pay homage to the 'Wizard of Waukesha' at the Hard Rock Cafe.

"I'd first met Les when he was playing at New York's Fat Tuesdays [jazz club], and he was just a pure delight to hear," Page later told NBC. "He was such a tasteful musician, always was in fact, and it was pure magic listening to him play. Les was the one who really started it all, so yes, I went to the Hard Rock to pay my respects." For Jimmy, though, there had been other guitar dalliances along the way, he always kept returning to his beloved 'No. 1'. "Well, when I discovered the Les Paul, it was so user-friendly, that was it," he confirmed. "Of course, I've had my flirtations with Fender Teles, but from the Custom [Black Beauty] through to the [No. 1] Standard of 'Whole Lotta Love', well, it's been like a marriage for me..."

By early August, Jimmy was back in Ibiza and back onstage, this time appearing as part of an unlikely trio named 'Safe Sex' (more of that later), while a later date on November 9 at London's Hammersmith Odeon found him sending up his rock god status in some style. A charity concert in aid of the NSPCC, Page joined Queen's Brian May and spoof metal act Bad News's lead guitarist Vim Fuego (played to perfection by comedian Adrian Edmondson) for "an axe duel to the death". Sadly, every time Jimmy started into a solo, his amp would mysteriously cut in and out, rendering him for the most part inaudible. His first overt step into comedy (parts of Live Aid notwithstanding), Page was actually quite a good straight man to Edmondson's demented "plank-spanker".

A month later and Jimmy was again under the lights, this time banging out 'Rock And Roll' alongside Robert Plant's Honeydrippers at Stourport Civic Centre for a gig in aid of the late John Pasternak's family. A fine bassist and regular face in the Midlands musical community, Pasternak had also been a member of Plant's old group Band Of Joy, and Robert was determined to mark his passing appropriately. Doing two sets on the night, the singer not only brought Page out for a run-through of their distinguished Zep classic, but also a brace of vintage blues standards. However, for those stupid enough to ask about a possible reunion, the answer remained the same as it had some two years before. "[Getting back with Jimmy] would be like meeting a former wife... going to bed and not making love," Plant had said in 1984. "It's impossible [now], just not appropriate anymore. The combination of personalities has gone." Evidently, Page was as tickled as he was irked by the comparison. "Ooh, that's good!" he laughed. "Maybe he should pay me some alimony then..."

In fact, for the first time in many a year, the state of Jimmy's ongoing 'relationship' with Robert Plant was probably among the very least of his concerns. Having finally broken up with long-term partner Charlotte Martin, Page had found new love with Patricia Ecker, a waitress at a restaurant in New Orleans' French Quarter during the Firm's final 1986 US tour. A cool blonde 24-year-old model born and bred in Metairie, Louisiana, Ecker was working part-time at the eaterie when she caught Jimmy's eye. When Page left America some weeks later for England, so did Patricia, the two soon moving in together at Jimmy's home in Windsor[271]. By December 1986, the couple were married, with a son fairly soon to follow. Born on April 26, 1988, the child was named 'James Patrick III', his distinctive moniker carrying on the Page clan's now long-established tradition of giving the first-born boy the same name as his father.

Marriage and the prospect of a new family seemed beneficial to both Jimmy Page's state of mind and body, with the guitarist removing himself for much of 1987 to play house, make babies and work up material for a proposed solo album, his first after nearly 24 years in the music business. With the Firm a thing of the past, Page was adamant about doing something under his own steam. But as ever with Led Zeppelin, old sins continued to cast long shadows. Some months before, Chicago blues legend Willie Dixon had filed a lawsuit over similarities between 'Whole Lotta Love' and his own 1962 tune 'You Need Love'. It was a problem that needed to be resolved.

271 Before meeting Patricia Ecker in 1986, Page had already sold Plumpton Place, thus finally moving his major base of operations to the Old Mill House and The Sol.

The writer of countless hits for the likes of Muddy Waters (it was actually Muddy who recorded 'You Need Love') and Howlin' Wolf, Dixon had already threatened the band with legal action back in 1972, when he first heard 'Bring It On Home' brazenly parading itself on *Led Zeppelin II*. Essentially a modified version of the song/lyric Dixon had written for Sonny Boy Williamson 10 years earlier – albeit with a brand-new, three-minute electrified rave-up in the middle – Dixon cried foul and Zeppelin settled out of court, adding his name to subsequent pressings of the LP while they were at it. Page wasn't exactly ecstatic about the decision. "The thing with 'Bring It On Home' though, [is] there's only a tiny bit taken from Sonny Boy Williamson's version and we threw that in as a tribute to him," he told *Trouser Press* in 1977. "People say, 'Oh, "Bring It On Home" is stolen.' Well, there's only a little bit in the song that relates to anything that had gone before it, just the end." It mattered not. 'Bring It On Home' could still be seen as Dixon's song simply bookending "the added balls in the middle", and he was now back to contest 'Whole Lotta Love'.

Of course, issues of possible plagiarism around Led Zeppelin had been fizzling away for years. As already stated, from the band's first album onwards, there had been occasional tuts about Zep's somewhat buccaneering approach to copyright, with Yardbird-era updates such as 'Dazed And Confused' solely credited to Page when the exact point of origin may have lain elsewhere. Indeed, the song that first triggered Jimmy and Robert's bromance at Pangbourne – 'Babe, I'm Gonna Leave You' – was classified as 'Traditional arrangement: Page' on the sleeve of *Zep I* until its actual author Anne Bredon rightly came forward to claim it as her own[272]. Other tracks – such as 'How Many More Times' and 'The Lemon Song' (both of which undoubtedly drew a little on existing

272 In fairness to Jimmy, he first come across 'Babe, I'm Gonna Leave You' via Joan Baez, who in turn had listed the song under 'Trad arr: Joan Baez' on her own 1962 album *In Concert Part One*. Assuming it was a traditional tune, Page revamped it for Zep without knowing Anne Bredon to be the true author. When Bredon alerted both Baez and Jimmy to their mistake, the writing credit on both albums was duly changed.

Howlin' Wolf compositions) – were also slowly simmering on the credits back burner, soon to rear their respective heads.

Yet, in the majority of cases, while Page and Led Zeppelin may have cheekily appropriated the odd lyric, title or even riff from the great American blues songbook or British Folk Almanac, as previously touched upon, the eventual results bore little or no relation to their original source material. In fact, they had often been transformed completely. Once a meditative rumination on death rattling around the back of Blind Willie Johnson's throat, 'In My Time Of Dying' had been turned into a veritable blues rock cyclone by Zep, its flailing percussion, roaring vocals and careening guitars simply transcending the song's Delta roots. One could also make much the same case for 'The Lemon Song' and 'How Many More Times'. Again, while the tree was still to be seen in a faraway field, the apples had fallen into a different space-time continuum altogether, with Page and co. performing magical rites to create their own form of modern blues. "We always tried to bring something fresh," Jimmy later told *Guitar World*'s Brad Tolinski. "I always made sure to come up with some variation."

In the case of 'You Need Love', however, Willie Dixon had Led Zeppelin bang to rights. With Robert Plant leaning heavily on passages from Dixon's track to inform his own lyric on 'Whole Lotta Love', even if the quartet had taken the track on a rocket ship to Mars soon after, the damage was done. Dixon reached another out-of-court settlement in his favour, while several other artists (or their estates) began readying their own cases in the wings.[273] "Most of the [song] comparisons rested

---

273 Willie Dixon's legal action seemed to open a door for other performers pursuing such cases against Led Zeppelin. By 1993, Howlin' Wolf's name had been added to the song-writing credits on both 'The Lemon Song' and 'How Many More Times', while 'Dazed And Confused' has carried the explanation 'Jimmy Page – Inspired by Jake Holmes' on Zep albums since 2012. Interestingly, though the Small Faces' 1966 track 'You Need Lovin'' was almost identical to Dixon's own 'You Need Love' – and indeed, probably more inspirational to Page/Plant's eventual writing of 'Whole Lotta Love' – the bluesman chose not to pursue the band in court. However, as the Small Faces had as yet failed to receive a penny in royalties due to bad business dealings (a situation that persisted well into the 1990s), Dixon may have felt it was not worth the bother.

on the lyrics," Page told Tolinski, "and Robert was supposed to change the lyrics, but he didn't always do that, which is what brought on most of our grief. They couldn't get us on the guitar parts or the music, but they nailed us on the lyrics. We did, however, take some liberties, I must say. But never mind. We did pay!"

After nearly a year of laying low, listening to solicitors' grumbles about old blues tracks and quietly making new music of his own, Jimmy Page finally emerged from his Windsor cave in late 1987 to begin another cycle of activity. Predictably enough, it all started with Robert Plant. Since the critical success but relative commercial failure of his third solo album *Shaken 'N' Stirred*, Robert had decided to jettison many of the overt pop flourishes that confused his fans and add a little more rock to the mix. 1988's *Now And Zen* was the result. A smart record, with some fine tunes ('Dance On My Own' and 'Billy's Revenge'), orchestral and even world music undertones, Plant's tweaks did the trick: *Now And Zen* broke into both the US and UK Top 10. Perhaps as crucially (at least for fans of Page and Zep), the disc also featured the symbol 'ZoSo' alongside two of its cuts.

Laid down at the turn of 1987/88, Jimmy's contributions to 'Heaven Knows' and 'Tall Cool One' were both impressive, his flickering guitar on the former as ever a perfect accompaniment to Plant's rich voice, his futuristic lead lines on the latter a delightful surprise after two years of more traditional axe play with the Firm. Additionally, in a sly tribute to their former band, Robert had plastered computerised snippets of 'Custard Pie', 'Whole Lotta Love', 'Dazed And Confused', 'The Ocean' and 'Black Dog' throughout '... Cool One', while also belting out some of the lyrics to 'When The Levee Breaks' whenever the mood took him. Part eighties update on classic Zeppelin, but also something of a two-fingered salute to the sample-friendly likes of rappers the Beasties Boys[274], 'Tall Cool One' made one positively dewy-eyed for the glory days.

---

274 The Beastie Boys' 1986 debut album *Licensed To Ill* had featured unauthorised samples of Zep's 'When The Levee Breaks', 'Custard Pie' and 'The Ocean'.

In another example of their ever-developing 'two steps forward, one step back' relationship, the duo were at it again onstage at Hammersmith Odeon on April 17, 1988, when Page joined his former partner-in-crime's band for an extended three-song workout. Ploughing their way through 'Misty Mountain Hop', 'Trampled Under Foot' and a corking 'St. James' Infirmary (Gambler's Blues)' – which incorporated elements of both 'I Can't Quit You Baby' and 'Since I've Been Loving You' – Page and Plant appeared completely at ease with each other, turning encore time into something akin to a party. Sadly, three weeks later, the pair were at each others' throats backstage in New York.

On May 14, Atlantic Records was scheduled to take over Madison Square Garden to mark the occasion of its 40th birthday. Now one of the most successful and enduring of 'the majors', the show was to be as lavish and star-studded as the label's rich history. In addition to live performances from Foreigner, Crosby, Stills & Nash, Wilson Pickett, Ben E. King, Yes, ELP and Genesis, the concert was to be televised by the Home Box Office channel. Of course, one band above all others had helped enable Atlantic's rise and continued profitability, and boss Ahmet Ertegun was hell-bent on making sure they appeared at his celebration. Making a personal request to Page, Plant and John Paul Jones, Ertegun asked his favourite group to reform for the night. Man by man, they took the bait. "Well," said Jimmy, "I'd hoped the Atlantic Records party would be an opportunity to make amends for Live Aid." Huge gig, huge audience and, in the end, a huge mistake.

The preparations began well enough. Keen not to make the same errors they had in Philadelphia back in July 1985, Jimmy, Robert and JPJ decided to allot themselves some proper rehearsals in advance of the concert. However, with Plant still on tour promoting *Now And Zen*, it was left to Page and Jones to drill their new drummer on the finer points of the Zep back catalogue. Thankfully, he knew it almost as well as they did. It was in his blood.

Almost 21 years old, Jason Bonham had come a long way from bashing away at a mini-Ludwig kit in front of his proud father during the mid-seventies. Now a professional drummer in his own right, Jason's band Virginia Wolf actually supported the Firm on some of their final US dates, with Page keeping a watchful eye on him from the wings. In fact, as time came to show, when Jimmy was looking for someone to play on some new songs at The Sol during the summer of 1987 for his own solo LP, it was Bonham he called in. No great stretch, then, to see Jason now sitting behind his drums, sticks in hand, for Zep's second 'reunion' show. "It's not always easy for other musicians to play [Zep] songs," Page later told Q, "but Jason picked up everything really quickly. It seems like he has a photographic memory for things. He remembers all the arrangement and vocal bits from the album, because I [had] just played it. Jason – as a kid – had listened all the way through on the records."

Various stories have it that at rehearsals a day before their Atlantic anniversary appearance, the modified 'Led Zeppelin' were truly on fire. Bootlegs of the group swinging through their set at soundcheck the next afternoon serve only to confirm that viewpoint. But as with 'the global juke box' before, it all seemed to fall to pieces in front of the TV cameras. This time, however, certain factors may well have put a damp squib on things well before the group had even got out of the backstage area.

In line with their stature, Led Zeppelin were always going to close the Atlantic show. After all, "No offence to anyone else on the bill", trumpeted concert organiser Bill Graham (now obviously back on back-slapping terms with the group) "but nobody could follow them!" Nonetheless, due to various TV production glitches and sets running late, the actual time of their appearance began to seriously slip as the night went on. Called from their hotel rooms 30 minutes before they were due to take the stage at midnight, the quartet would have to wait almost another two hours before the lights hit them. Always jittery in advance of concerts, Page now found himself faced with the prospect of making small talk in a shared dressing room with Crosby, Stills & Nash and Yes (both he and Chris 'Fortune Hunter' Squire must have been delighted). To compound the general sense of misery, Robert Plant chose this moment to inform the rest of the group he was unwilling to perform 'Stairway To Heaven', leading to a backstage shouting match. Page wanted the song in. Robert did not. "Mediocre crap," he later told writer Sylvie Simmons. "I loathed it." In the end, Jimmy had his way. He would live to regret it.

With Jason Bonham no doubt wondering what he had got himself into and an implacable John Paul Jones smiling through it all like a Sidcup Buddha, Zep finally stepped onto the boards of MSG at 1 a.m. or thereabouts to their trademark thunderous applause. Then it all got a bit daft. After a moment or two of opening track 'Kashmir', it became hideously apparent JPJ's keyboards were inaudible[275], leaving Page's Danelectro to carry the song like a Moroccan donkey. With blasts of feedback ringing out around them and Robert appearing to forget the words at least once, the end couldn't come fast enough. Still, only four more numbers to go.

Regrettably, even the appearance of Jimmy's beloved No. 1 guitar couldn't pull the airship up from its fatal nose dive. 'Heartbreaker' saw Page visibly wilt as he struggled to remember the solo, while a heavily modified 'Whole Lotta Love' (first tried out at Knebworth in 1979) failed to provide much in the way of real excitement. Arch hippie anthem 'Misty Mountain Hop' was an immediate improvement, with the group showing the first signs of really motoring, but then came 'Stairway...' and all was lost. Robert's voice cracked (probably more from boredom rather than emotion), Jimmy again tussled with his lead lines and even JPJ appeared to be losing interest. When they finally called time on the set after 30 gruelling minutes, Zep had fluffed their reunion yet again. Jason Bonham, however, had been magnificent. "That show was great for Jason," Page later conceded. "So some good really did come out of it."

It didn't take long for various conspiracy theories to surface. Having fought failing monitors, screeches and hisses from the amps, an intermittent keyboard signal and several faulty effects pedals, some thought the swords were out for Page and co. behind the scenes, with Bill Graham finally taking his revenge for Oakland Coliseum. Others mumbled about old curses and grey churches. The usual nonsense,

---

275 Reportedly, a HBO technician had removed the cable from Jones' keyboard for their own TV feed. Again, the mind fair boggles.

then[276]. Yet, while Jimmy surely didn't subscribe to such points of view, he was nonetheless mystified by the technical gremlins that had plagued Zep's set. "It all got... buggered up," he said, "something happened to my guitar monitor... it was like sabotage or something."

Or just as likely a once mighty group who had somehow lost their mojo, with one of their number now desperate to move on while simultaneously failing to understand why so many people still seemed to care. "Page and I had our usual vibration-filled moment when I didn't want to sing 'Stairway...'" Plant later told Dave Lewis. "He said it was a necessity for the Western world and I said I didn't think it was that important. The rehearsal was good. The soundcheck was good. The previous night was good. But the gig was foul. However," Robert concluded, "I must say that Jason Bonham was stunning." At least he and Jimmy agreed on something.

Mercifully, Jimmy Page didn't have much time to either contemplate the mistakes of May 14, 1988 or Plant's increasingly truculent attitude towards 'Stairway To Heaven'. Instead, the guitarist was now readying a new broom to sweep away at the cobwebs and corners of his own musical career. In a bold move planned some months before, Page had actually kissed goodbye to his association with Atlantic and signed with Geffen instead.

Set up in 1980 by former head of Asylum Records David Geffen, Geffen Records had almost immediately become a major industry player due to the tragic death of John Lennon. Just two weeks after the release of his and Yoko Ono's first album for the label – 1980's *Double Fantasy* – the ex-Beatle had been shot by assailant Mark Chapman outside his home at New York's Dakota Building, resulting in a huge boost in sales

276 Despite his reticence to discuss it, media interest in Page's links to the occult had remained high. However, the Firm's Paul Rodgers seemed to find the right answers on his partner's behalf when addressing such enquiries in 1986. "The press haven't really given Jimmy a fair crack of the whip," he told *Creem's* Harold DeMuir in 1986. "Most people want to talk about all... the mumbo-jumbo shit and mystical meanings to everything. I mean, years ago, some people [said]... that if you played a certain track backwards [probably 'Stairway...'] at three times the speed, there was a message. And Jim said 'Well, I have enough trouble getting it to go forwards.'"

of the LP. With Lennon's final work now selling in the millions, David Geffen was able to use some of the profits to expand his roster, pulling in the likes of Asia, Peter Gabriel, Elton John, Neil Young, Cher and former Eagle Don Henley to help swell the company's artistic standing and financial status.

By the late eighties, Geffen had also begun to establish itself as a new home for hard rock and even 'alternative' acts, with Guns N' Roses, Sonic Youth and Tesla all signing on the dotted line within rapid succession of each other. When one added A&R guru John Kalodner's proven ability to revive the commercial fortunes of seventies titans such as Aerosmith and Whitesnake (both of whom we will return to in due course), Geffen's reputation as an established label with a profitable sideline in career resurrections was complete. For Jimmy Page, who had not had a Top 10 album since 1979's *In Through The Out Door*, the benefits of joining up were fairly obvious.

There were other changes Page had to make around this time that were perhaps less pleasant, however. When Peter Grant disappeared behind the heavy wooden doors of Horselunges in East Sussex in the mid-eighties, Jimmy asked Atlantic Senior Vice President and old friend from Zep days Phil Carson to manage him in the Firm. Also taking on responsibility for the career of Paul Rodgers, Carson had been a loyal servant for almost four years, even joining the band on bass guitar for a hectic rendition of 'Money' at the Firm's last show at Seattle's Centre Coliseum on May 28, 1986[277]. Yet, two years on, and he found his services were no longer required. "Jimmy has to come to terms with the fact he should act like a human being," Phil told author Ritchie Yorke after the fact. Sadly for Carson, Page hadn't really been a mere mortal since late 1968. For the time being at least, then, the running of Jimmy's affairs would fall to Brian Goode, another well-established acquaintance of the guitarist.

277 It was not the first time Phil Carson had joined Jimmy onstage. In 1971, he jammed along to Eddie Cochran's 'C'mon Everybody' with Led Zeppelin at gigs in both Dublin and Osaka, while also playing bass on 'Money' in Frankfurt (June 30, 1980) as part of the group's final European tour.

With these various changes now more or less behind him, it was at last time for Jimmy Page to wheel out the project he had been working on for the last year: his first solo disc, *Outrider*. Put together over the course of nine months in a series of fits, starts and "concentrated bursts" of energy, Page had originally envisaged *Outrider* to be a double album, incorporating "one side of rock'n'roll, one side of blues, one side of acoustic and one side of experimental". But when demo tapes were reportedly stolen from his house in a burglary ("I've got a good idea who did it," he later said), Jimmy hastily reconsidered the notion. "I thought 'For the sake of my sanity, keep it a single.'" That said, he did not skimp on the number of musicians used to help him fulfil his brief, with nine in all contributing to the project. Some, like the Firm's Tony Franklin, were familiar faces. Others, such as session bassists Felix Krish and Durban Laverde, were completely new to his game.

To further aid Jimmy's cause, he had also brought in two drummers. One, Jason Bonham, really was a shoo-in, now being almost like family to Page. "Well, I really wanted to play with Jason," he later told *Musician*. "It was just a natural thing [and] he tends to attack the drums like his father. He's certainly got the power his father had. I'd also say his approach to the artillery is similar." The other was also directly linked to Jimmy's past though, in this case, more because he had appeared on many of the same stages as Led Zeppelin in their heyday. Considered one of the finest percussionists of his generation, Barriemore Barlow had spent nine years criss-crossing the world with folk-rockers Jethro Tull before leaving them at the end of the decade. More or less a free agent at the time of John Bonham's death, some thought he might actually take over Zep's vacant drum stool. Bonzo had certainly rated him. "Barriemore Barlow," Bonham once said, "is the greatest rock drummer England ever produced." As history records, Zep went another way, but Barlow was at last on board with Page, if only for two tracks.

There was also an air of familiarity about Jimmy's remaining recruits, all of whom could more than sing for their supper. Coming back to the table for the first time since *Death Wish II* was Chris Farlowe, whom Page had contacted soon after deciding to press ahead with a solo release in early 1987. "Well, Jimmy's a unique player with his own way of doing things," Farlowe said in 2015. "An extremely talented musician, a great songwriter, the whole bundle, really. So, I was in."

Also more than happy to sign up to Page's little experiment was Geordie John Miles. A talented guitarist/keyboard player also blessed with a throaty blues rock voice, Miles came to prominence in 1976 on the back of his million-selling single 'Music', its soaring harmonies and orchestral splendour earning him an Ivor Novello award for 'Best Song'. "Yes, it did. And very proud of it I am too," he laughed in 2015. However, the hits were somewhat harder to come by after the advent of punk and new wave. "Oh, I enjoyed every minute of it," John said of his early success. "But I think when you get that run of success, you've also got one eye on what's coming next. You're always looking towards what's going on the next album. And of course, when punk hit, that changed everything in Britain. The whole format of radio play literally changed in one day."

Continuing to record and tour throughout the early to mid-eighties, it was while Miles was playing several gigs in Ibiza that he and Jimmy first met. "Well, Phil Carson had a club in Ibiza called Heartbreak Hotel[278], and we were doing a couple of week's worth of dates over there. And while we were there, Jimmy and Robert Plant happened to turn up. Greg Lake from ELP and [briefly] Asia too, as I remember. So, Jimmy and I were introduced, we had a few drinks and then got to talking. He liked to have a good time, you know, but what was also immediately obvious was that he really, really loved music." Some time later, John received "the call". "After a while, I got a phone call from Brian Goode who said that Jimmy had asked if I might pop over, hang out and just play some stuff. So I went down [to Sol], and Jason Bonham and bassist Durban Laverde were already there. I think Jim had already been recording with the guys. Well, we all hit it off, so it was on your marks, get set, go..."

For Page, getting vocalists and musicians of such proven calibre to collaborate on songs made recording the LP all the easier. "I'd actually

278 It was at Phil Carson's club in San Antonio, Ibiza on August 6, 1986 that he, Page and Jason Bonham had formed the temporary trio Safe Sex, jamming their way through a few choice numbers over several sturdy drinks.

jammed with John Miles in Ibiza [and] that's the first time I really met him," Jimmy told MTV at the time. "So, when it came to making the album, I knew that he had a great voice and I thought it'd be worth calling him up to see whether he'd come in. He's extremely versatile within his vocal approach, because the way he sings [on my stuff] is completely different to the sort of work he did with, say, Alan Parsons[279], and even on his own [later] albums." Page was as giving to Chris Farlowe. "I wanted to use Chris because he had such a strong identity to his voice," he confirmed. "After working with someone as immediately identifiable as Robert, I needed to find someone who had their own strength of vocal character." That said, Jimmy hadn't quite let go of Plant just yet. "Well, I did play him a couple of the tracks," he said archly, just before the album's release...

Arriving in shops on 19 June, 1988, *Outrider* proved to be Jimmy Page's most consistently solid, if not fully developed album since the demise of Led Zeppelin. A strange brew of no-nonsense rockers, growling Chicago-style blues, fifties-homaging tear-ups and a trio of weird and wonderful instrumentals, the onus nonetheless remained on one thing and one thing only: guitars, guitars, guitars. "Maybe it took a bit of time to pluck up the courage," he said of the record to writer Mick Wall, "but the time's right now. *Outrider* really is a guitar album, [and] I wanted to give it a real spectrum. Acoustic guitars, electric guitars, blues, folk, all the colours, really." And even if the album was no outright classic, for the most part, Page delivered on that brief.

Lurching out of the gate with the semi-industrial clank of 'Wasting My Time', it was obvious Jimmy had not lost his way around a good riff. A track that might have easily sat well on *Presence* or perhaps side one of *Physical Graffiti*, 'Wasting My Time' had all the cut and thrust of mid-period Zep, with Page's multi-tracked slide guitars battling with John Miles' sore-throated vocals throughout. Sure, the song sounded at times like it had been cut in 1975 at Olympic Studios rather than at The

---

279 John Miles first joined forces with Alan Parsons (of 'Project' fame) in 1975. Parsons subsequently produced Miles' hit singles 'Highfly', 'Music' and best-selling parent album *Rebel*.

Sol more than a decade later. But given that it rocked a good deal harder than almost anything he recorded with the Firm, one had to allow Page his victories here.

That could also be said for the lumbering 'Wanna Make Love'. Constructed around a cyclical, 'dropped D' guitar figure and employing the same mangled use of the tremolo arm that had made 'For Your Life' such fun, the title might have been trite and the lyrical sentiments dated but, again, Jimmy was at least trying to stoke up the fires a bit. "Actually, on 'Wanna Make Love', I think it was me that came up with that riff, while Jimmy [already] had the original riff for 'Wasting My Time'," said John Miles. "But it was the type of situation where we were bouncing riffs off each other, kind of 'Ah, I like that. What about this to go with it?' It was back and forth, a call and response thing." According to Page, 'Wanna Make Love' had another, rather special quality all its own. "I dunno," he later laughed, "I just thought it was super-sleazy…"

Having used Miles' window-rattling roar so effectively on the heavy stuff, Page now turned to Chris Farlowe to take care of the blues side of *Outrider*. A reasonable job he did of it too. On the album's only cover version – an emotive take on Leon Russell's flittering 'Hummingbird' – Farlowe's voice provided a soulful warmth while Jimmy's six strings cried their way through verse and chorus. "Oh, 'Hummingbird' was lovely," Chris later said. "That was completely Jimmy's choice and just a lovely song to sing." 'Blues Anthem' was also an emotional, if excessively sentimental listen. Riding in on a lone acoustic – and, despite the title, a very countrified one at that – the tune soon built into a lighter-waving paean to "heavy loads", "lonely roads" and lost love, with Farlowe singing "all the way to the back of the hall" and Page mimicking a full-blown orchestra courtesy of his guitar synth.

"I stayed over at Jim's for a few days, and one night… well, about four in the morning, I had the idea and started writing it down," Chris said of the song. Nonetheless, while the initial inspiration might have come more or less immediately, he had to wait a while for Page to put the cherry on top of the cake. "I like to get in there. Get the tracks down. But Jim's not quite like that," Farlowe laughed. "His manager might say 'Well, Jim'll be there at eleven to start recording'. But if he was there by two in the afternoon, I'd be lucky. Jim liked to take his time on things."

'Prison Blues' probably did not take quite as much time or effort. "Jim asked me did I have any song ideas, and well...'Prison Blues' was one of them," said Chris. "So, I started singing and he said 'Oh, now I like that.' Anyway, I just made up the lyrics as I went along, Jim started in with the riff and [we] just started to improvise." A ribald, dirty blues in the long-standing tradition of Lucille Bogan's 'Shave 'Em Dry' and Bull Moose Jackson's 'I Want A Bowlegged Woman', 'Prison...''s tale of a sexually frustrated con bemoaning his inability to "climb over the wall" and get back to his "baby" probably wouldn't have won any awards for subtlety. Indeed, at times, Page and Farlowe sounded like a pair of libidinous old goats charging around a locked pen. But with Jason Bonham holding down the sludgy beat, Jimmy nearly tearing the neck off his Les Paul during the solo and Chris' almost primal stuttering – "I'm quite good at scat singing and stuttering," he said, "I learned it when I was young" – one couldn't deny the raw power of it all. "I just said 'Let's do a blues'," Page later told *Musician*, "and [you can really] hear the Les Paul roaring through the Marshall!"

For those offended by Chris Farlowe's risqué banter or deafened by Jimmy's fire-breathing Marshalls, they could at least draw comfort from *Outrider*'s three instrumental cuts, all of which sold themselves on fine-boned melodies and clever time signatures. With 'Writes Of Winter', Jimmy had written another of those complex yet catchy compositions that had made parts of *Death Wish II* such an unexpected pleasure. Full of climbing lead lines and strident rhythm guitar, Page's ever-confident use of his Botswana Brown Tele's B-Bender system allowed him to link major and minor chord progressions together like a seasoned Nashville steel player. "A tour de force instrumental," said *Guitar World* at the time, "'Writes Of Winter' deserves its place in the 'Jimmy Page Hall Of Fame'[280]."

280 Indeed it did. 'Writes Of Winter' was later nominated for a Grammy as 'Best Rock Instrumental'.

While not quite as pleasing, 'Liquid Mercury' also merited its place in *Outrider*'s track listing, with Jimmy's stumbling six-string dragged this way and that by Barriemore Barlow's equally free-form kit work. Yet, it was the poignant 'Emerald Eyes' that was probably the most affecting of Page's vocal-free compositions. Again starting life with a simple acoustic introduction – all minor keys and hesitantly stroked chords – Jimmy was soon activating the tear ducts with a sensitively rendered solo flight reminiscent of his work on Zep's 'Ten Years Gone' or 'All My Love'.

And indeed, it was Page's bug-eyed collaboration with Robert Plant that truly stole the show on *Outrider*. Almost a mirror reflection of Robert's 'Tall Cool One' – but with added wails and a solid wall of electric guitars – 'The Only One' again laid down some big fat hints as to what Led Zeppelin might now have been up to had John Bonham lived. As frenetic and punky as *Coda*'s 'Wearing And Tearing', but with one foot still firmly placed in a fifties-style brothel creeper, 'The Only One' confirmed that whatever the differences between them at times, Page and Plant still brought out the very best in each other.

"I guess it's this temperate thing of working together," Jimmy later told *Kerrang!*. "Robert was really enthused about doing [a song]. He came up with reams of lyrics and we ended up having a great time." On this occasion, Plant wasn't in the mood to argue. "It's so nice to hear a craftsman making a crafted piece of music again," he said of Page's album in *Rolling Stone*. "It's nice to hear him creating what he used to call 'a guitar army effect'." But when the subject of a proper collaboration was again raised, Robert continued to play coy. "The chance of playing together again? Well, I thought we'd try poker first..."

All in all, then, *Outrider* was a commendable effort on Jimmy's part at gathering together his musical thoughts into a neatly wrapped nine-song bundle and presenting them to the world. Yet, as ever before, the album had its faults. 'Blues Anthem', for instance, was simply too cloying for its own good at times, those synthesised orchestral guitar lines at the finale sounding syrupy sweet rather than achingly authentic. More, the likes of 'Prison Blues' really did belong in a different era, one where sniggering references to "weasels in pockets" and "bunny rabbits" disappearing down various holes still sounded daring rather than downright offensive.

Yet, it was an area in which Page had always excelled that the biggest potential drawback to sales now lurked. By choosing to make *Outrider* as live-sounding and unpolished as possible, he was deliberately flying in the face of well-established eighties production values. Whereas two decades before, the sound of frying valves and overdriven amps were deemed radical and new, modern audiences had long grown used to hearing the perambulations of mice between cymbal crashes or pins dropping amidst the loudest of orchestral stabs. Simply put, this was the age of the CD and near-perfect fidelity was all the rage. In comparison with the likes of U2's *The Joshua Tree*, Peter Gabriel's *So* or even Aerosmith's *Permanent Vacation*, *Outrider* sounded, well, a bit old hat. For Jimmy, however, there was nothing to be gained from over-egging his album with various bells and whistles. "*Outrider* was an honest record," he later said. "Not overproduced, as so many discs were during that period. Just... honest."

With its defiant attitude, old-school values and black and white cover photograph capturing a moody-looking, guitar clutching, optically altered Page[281], *Outrider* appeared determined to meet its critics full on. Some were happy to pin the disc to their wall with some pride. Others more likely to test its merits as a Frisbee. "There's been considerable speculation of late as to whether JP has lost it, becoming musically inept through the awesome ravages of time and excess," reasoned *Guitar World*. "[But] *Outrider* suggests that perception is somewhat blurry. Sure, there are a few embers left from the grandiose fire of Led Zeppelin... but Jimmy stills holds his own... his riff-heavy, crashing guitar work remaining solid and adventurous." *Rolling Stone* – now temporarily

---

281 Ever the art student, the blurred front cover image on *Outrider* was Page drawing inspiration from the work of American photographer Robert Mapplethorpe, whose own highly stylised, sometimes time-lapsed black and white images drew critical praise throughout the late seventies/eighties. The shot used on *Outrider* – denoting "energy, movement, flow" as well as Jimmy's fluid relationship with the guitar – was taken by lens man Peter Ashworth. There was also a new logo, with a Celtic-themed 'JP' symbol now taking the place of the long-established 'ZoSo'. Whether this swap in symbolism was for contractual, copyright, aesthetic or other reasons was not explained at the time.

recasting itself as a nay-sayer after a period of relative appeasement with Page and Zep – was considerably less sure of *Outrider*'s value. "*Outrider* is as much a victim of underachievement as of over expectations," reasoned David Fricke. "As a guitar record, [it] proves Page is still the sultan of slash, the Kaiser of krunch. But where he once held the hammer of the gods, he now sounds a bit dazed and confused..."

Billed as the return of one of the original guitar gods, and given a strong push by one of the bigger, better US labels, *Outrider* should have sold by the small truckload. Yet, its commercial performance was tepid rather than feverish. In the UK, the album snuck into the charts at number 27 while only managing one place better across the Atlantic (it finally received a gold disc in the States some months later). By the standards of some fair-to-middling pop or rock acts, these were average numbers. Compared with the multi-platinum sales of Zep, *Outrider* was a bit of a flop. "It didn't do very well," Jimmy later said. "Doesn't matter. But I did go out on tour..."

In fact, if there was any real triumph to be had from *Outrider* for Jimmy Page, it was the shows he did in support of the album's release. Approaching his 1988 world tour as an opportunity to revisit all points of a long and illustrious career, Page announced his intention to play songs not just from *Death Wish II*, the Firm and his latest LP, but also draw from his time with Led Zeppelin and the Yardbirds, too.[282] "I want to go back to the blues, from the Yardbirds through Zep and right into the new stuff," he said in advance of the upcoming dates. "A lot of contrast, really, simple things, complexity, it'll all be there."

Of prime importance to this lofty ambition was assembling the right band to support it. Obviously, Jason Bonham was going to be behind the kit, no questions asked. But the other vacancies were a little more challenging to fill. With Felix Krish, Tony Franklin and Durban Laverde all having done such a bang-up job on *Outrider*, Jimmy was spoiled for choice for potential bassists (their diaries permitting, of

---

282 In this respect, Jimmy was following Robert Plant's lead, who had already begin including select Zep songs ('Misty Mountain Hop', 'Immigrant Song' and 'Trampled Under Foot') in his live set during 1988.

course). In the end, it was Laverde who got the gig, his ability to play hard ('Wanna Make Love') or funky ('Hummingbird') surely a factor in Page's eventual decision. That said, it was finding the right vocalist that was the real pickle. At first, it looked as if Chris Farlowe might be asked to find his passport.[283] But then Jimmy went with John Miles. "Well, I was really chuffed that he asked me to do the tour," John confirmed in 2015. "To be honest though, I wasn't really [thinking] about doing [all] the songs, though there was a huge well he wanted to draw from. The Yardbirds, Zep, the *Outrider* stuff. But I think we all just wanted to get out and get going..."

Slightly delayed when Page was rushed to hospital with abdominal pains (all proved well in the end), Jimmy's first 'solo' tour finally began on September 6, 1988 at Atlanta's Omni Arena. It proved a night of real surprises, with the guitarist actually delivering on his promise of pulling treasures past and present into the live domain. Ably supported by the crack team of Miles, Bonham and Laverde, Page's set found brand-new tracks like 'Writes Of Winter' and 'Wasting My Time' now bumping shoulders with established classics such as 'Custard Pie' and 'Over The Hills And Far Away'. "People can see I'm not avoiding Led Zeppelin," he later told the *Los Angeles Times*. "That's part of my heritage and I'm proud of it."

There was also no holding back on the guitar side of things, either. Employing an arsenal of Les Pauls[284], Telecasters, Danelectros and

---

283 "I don't actually know what happened there," said Farlowe of Page's decision to go with John Miles for the 1988 *Outrider* tour. "One day, the manager rang me up and said 'You're not needed on the tour'. I said 'Fine'. That was it. Short and sweet. But yep, I was pissed off. In fact, I was in America [shortly] afterwards and people were saying to me, 'Why aren't you on the tour, because you're on the album?' I'd say, 'I'm only the singer, mate. Talk to the powers that be'. They got John Miles in though, didn't they? All well. As they say, that's the way the cookie crumbles..."

284 In addition to Page's No. 1 and No. 2 guitars, the *Outrider* tour also saw Jimmy give his 'No. 3' cherry red Gibson Les Paul a fair run out. Originally bought in 1970 as a replacement for his lost Black Beauty, Page had used the guitar on and off up to 1975 when he then mothballed it for a while. However, it reappeared in 1988 (with new B-Bender attached) for a song or two during shows.

double-necks, Jimmy also threw in solo violin bow passages from 'Dazed And Confused' (now, as with the Firm, performed as part of *Death Wish II*'s 'The Chase'), Celtic/Indian drones (a returning 'White Summer'/'Black Mountain Side') and even waves of slide on a big-boned version of 'In My Time Of Dying' (with a snippet of 'Black Dog' in the middle). Facing MTV's cameras after the event, Page could not hide his enthusiasm. "Oh, it was wonderful," he told Mick Wall. "It really went better than I could have expected in my wildest dreams. There's so much work, rehearsal, pre-production that goes into these things before they hit the road and for it to come off, well, that means we got it right."

In fact, the band got better as the tour progressed. With the mighty 'In My Time...' soon becoming a pivot around which the rest of the concert turned, Jimmy was free to contrast the broad charms of 'Prison Blues' and 'Wanna Make Love' with the classical/Flamenco flourishes of 'Prelude' or 'Emerald Eyes', thus providing those present with an A–Z of his various guitar styles. He and the band had also learned to relax come encore time, with the quartet as likely to wheel out a frantic take on 'Train Kept A-Rollin'' as they were *Outrider*'s 'The Only One'.

Of course, the pressure on John Miles to sing everything from old Yardbirds numbers to selected highlights from Zep's back catalogue was immense. "Yes, I felt a lot of pressure having to sing Robert's songs [and] I think Jimmy felt pressured too," the vocalist admitted in 2000. "[And] I actually remember Robert turning up for a gig in Boston. Jimmy didn't want him anywhere near the building, so Robert turned up in a disguise with a baseball cap!" Yet, when it came down to it, Miles learned to cope. "Ah, it wasn't too bad going between these [vocal] styles, you know," he later said. "You just try and keep it natural. And on 'Train Kept A-Rollin'' I got to play harmonica, so I absolutely loved that."

There was one song, however, that Miles was not allowed to sing. As was the case when Jimmy Page performed it on the ARMS tour back in 1983, 'Stairway To Heaven' remained instrumental from start to finish during the *Outrider* shows. "Well, I was always on at Jimmy to let me sing it on that tour," John laughed. "You know the type of thing.

555

'Come on Jim, just let me do it one fucking time!' But he just wasn't having it and I didn't want to push it. Maybe it would have been great, but ah well, it wasn't to be." For Page, it seemed that – royalties aside – 'Stairway...' now belonged as much to the audience as it did anyone else. "Oh, it's much easier to play it as an instrumental when the people who love that song are singing it back to you," he said at the time. "I think the audience will [always] sing it if Robert's not there, [and] I think that's the way it should be." Given that Plant didn't seem to want to sing it ever again, all the better, really.

With over 30 dates performed across America during the autumn of 1988 (including two memorable shows at New York's prestigious Ritz ballroom[285]), Page at last returned home for a quick spray of concerts in England. Kicking off at Birmingham's aptly named 'Hummingbirds' on November 21, Jimmy and the band appeared at Newcastle's City Hall (23) before a two-night stopover at Hammersmith Odeon (24 & 25). "Absolutely everyone was at Hammersmith those nights," said Miles. "And I thought it was only going to be an American tour, so it was really great to come back in front of the home crowd." Following the gigs, Page sounded like a man revitalised, his comments full of energy, his vision locked on the future. "The audience response was fantastic and that's an incredible charge that encourages you to continue... not that it would have stopped me anyway, if it hadn't worked."

But stop it did. After a final concert appearance and after-show party at Manchester Apollo the following night (November 26), Jimmy Page called time on the band and again headed back to Windsor. Whether it was relatively poor album sales or reduced audience numbers – the shows were well attended, but in the main, confined to smaller halls –

---

285 "Ah yeah, The Ritz," said John Miles of Page's New York shows on 12 & 13 November, 1988. "There was probably 1,800, maybe 2,000 people in there for each night. Anyway, there was this guy at the front, and he had a pro-Walkman with a mike in each of his sleeves. He just stood there for the whole gig with his arms in the air, recording away. I've actually got a copy of that, and believe me, it sounds unbelievable. The sound quality is frigging incredible. What would have happened if Peter Grant were there? Ha! Well, he wouldn't have any bloody arms left to record it!"

that were to blame for his subsequent withdrawal is uncertain. Perhaps he simply felt that the experiment had run its course. Yet, once Page downed tools in late 1988 he appeared in no immediate hurry to follow up the album. "The *Outrider* project was fun to do," he later told Dave Lewis. "But looking back, I suppose it was a bit like a glorified demo."

Of course, there might have been another plausible reason Jimmy chose to step back into the shadows once more following *Outrider*. As good as John Miles, Durban Laverde and Jason Bonham had been (and they were a tidy little band[286]), they were no real replacement for the group or frontman that had defined – and, indeed, continued to define – such an important chapter in Page's musical life. "I was actually raring to go after *Outrider*, [to] see that I was alive and kicking," he later confessed to Q. "The trouble was, I didn't have the [right] singer. I waded through loads and loads of demos, but there wasn't anyone who made me feel at all passionate." As ever, when Page talked about 'singers', he probably meant Robert Plant. "Ah well, Jimmy missed Robert, you know," said Chris Welch. "And really, he was always waiting for Robert. Always."

Page would eventually get his wish. But for the time being at least, he'd have to wait just a little while longer.

---

286 Following *Outrider*, Jason Bonham formed his own group, aptly titled 'Bonham', whose two albums and subsequent stage commitments took the drummer nicely into the nineties. Durban Laverde was also involved in several new group projects before eventually returning to sessions. John Miles, on the other hand, became a key member of Tina Turner's touring/recording band as well as a regular contributor to the annual *Night At The Proms* festival. "I considered myself very lucky to get the chance to do this, getting to work with some of my biggest heroes. "Amazing really," he said in 2015. "I've worked with Jimmy and I've worked with Tina. I mean, I used to cover 'Nutbush City Limits' and 'Whole Lotta Love' long before I got the chance to work with either of them, so yeah, I'm a very lucky man..."

CHAPTER 34

Absolution Blues

Creatively at least, the eighties had not been the best of times for Jimmy Page. Having entered the decade in mourning, he spent the first few years both physically frail and artistically uncertain, finding things to do rather than worlds to conquer as he had in the glorious, golden seventies. By the middle of it all, things finally appeared to be on the up. But weak material and the lack of a suitable song-writing partner once again saw the guitarist retreat. Even when he decided to go it alone as a solo artist towards the end of the decade, his progress was stymied by critical dissension and commercial disappointments. Now nearly 46 years old and facing the prospect of doing it all again at the dawn of the nineties, Page must have wondered where and what next. "I'm past middle age," he had said in 1985. "But what do you do when you get to middle age? There was no one for me to look up to who said, 'This is what you do next...'" Strangely, the re-telling of legends, changing fashion and a little bit of luck would do most of the work for him.

In truth, the eighties had been a nervy, uncertain decade for many. With the advent of AIDS, the continued threat of nuclear war, hard-line conservatism, bald-faced greed, miners' strikes and terrifying famines all to contend with, things had swung wildly between blind optimism and bleak prophecy. As ever, such extremities were reflected in the arts, as musicians and filmmakers provided images of aspiration and escapism in line with their audiences' needs. Duran Duran, synthesisers and Madonna. Material Girl, *Working Girl* and *Wall Street*. From the back of the stalls, it really was like the previous two decades had never happened. "Plastic," opined Jeff Beck. "I fucking hated parts of the eighties. It was completely bereft of any music I wanted to be involved in." Yet, even in the midst of this odd little time, the pendulum had begun swinging slowly back in favour of celebrating old gods and their strange practices.

The first real clue came in 1985, with the publication of Stephen Davis' *Hammer Of The Gods: The Led Zeppelin Saga.* A heady page-turner full of teen groupies, roaring drug habits and supposed satanic forces, Davis' tome became statutory reading for those seeking to learn of the blood, thunder and sheer bacchanalian excess of hard rock's biggest group, while selling incredibly well to boot. Predictably, Page, Plant and Jones sniffed at the contents, rubbished the lot (or most of it) and then swiftly moved on. Nevertheless, while its contents may have been an affront to the trio, its impact was significant. "Though the members of the group disdained the book and even claimed not to have read it," wrote Chris Charlesworth, "there can be no question that it enhanced their formidable reputation as intemperate pleasure-seekers, thus glorifying their mystique among more impressionable fans."

Led Zeppelin's legacy, both musical and dissolute, certainly inspired those who sought to fill the vacuum. Following in the footsteps of Aerosmith and Van Halen, glam (aka hair) metallers such as Mötley Crüe, Poison, Cinderella, Ratt and Quiet Riot were all suitably inspired not only by Zep's music, but also their way around a swash and buckle, this third generation of aspiring thrill-seekers finding new and appalling ways to conduct themselves from LA's Sunset Strip to New York's Madison Square Garden. By late 1987, the "most dangerous band in the world" were in on the act too, as Guns N' Roses' Slash doffed his large black top hat in Jimmy Page's very specific direction. For the wild-haired six-stringer, Jimmy Page wasn't just a fine guitarist, brilliant songwriter or innovative producer. "Page," said Slash, "was a fucking legend." This was not what Jimmy – and certainly Robert

Plant[287] – had probably envisaged when writing 'Stairway...', 'Kashmir' or even 'Whole Lotta Love', but such platitudes kept Led Zeppelin's mythological (and commercial) engine running nicely[288].

For British audiences, America's continuing veneration of Led Zeppelin came home to roost throughout 1990, as two US rock giants prostrated themselves before the group's leader on UK soil. On January 10, 1990 at Hammersmith Odeon while performing a gig in aid of music therapy, pop rock king Jon Bon Jovi introduced Jimmy Page from the wings for a whirling run-through of 'Train Kept A-Rollin'' and 'With A Little Help From My Friends'. Barely able to comprehend the fact he was sharing the same stage as his hero, Bon Jovi looked transported with delight when Page tore into the solo he first cut for Joe Cocker some 22 years before. Jimmy, on the other hand, simply appeared happy to be treading the boards again.

The ante was upped considerably on August 18, 1990 when Page found himself facing an audience of 70,000 as the 'special guest' of headliners Aerosmith at Donington Park's 'Monsters of Rock'. After years of explosive inter-band arguments, astounding levels of drug use and rampant alcoholism, Aerosmith's original line-up had finally imploded in 1979 when guitarist Joe Perry walked off into the sunset following one fight too many. Yet, in the most unlikely of career resurrections, the quintet had somehow managed to pull it around

---

287 When glam metal first manifested itself in the mid-eighties, Plant was more than happy to run the other way. "I was inspired by what Peter Gabriel was doing at the time," he told Q in 2002, "[so] I was astounded by poodle rock... Bon Jovi and Mötley Crüe. I thought 'Oh fuck, I can't play that!' So I decided to go off into 'the land of spook'." 1985's *Shaken 'N' Stirred* was the result.

288 There were clear signs that despite their absence for almost a decade, Led Zeppelin's popularity hadn't really abated at all in America. In February 1989, LA radio station KLOS began dedicating an hour of its schedule to Zep each night, while Florida's WKRL played 'Stairway To Heaven' continuously for 24 hours as a prelude to its bold, if slightly flawed plan for an all-Zeppelin format (a month later, and the station had already added Pink Floyd to the playlist). Madness really, but still bold enough pointers to conclude that while the eighties might have finished, the USA's love affair with Led Zeppelin certainly hadn't.

during the eighties, their use of outside song-writers and the support of record label Geffen combining to push them back into the charts and back into the stadiums. But while the drugs and booze had now long gone, the band's love of the Yardbirds, Zep and Page had not. "I bring you one of your fellow countrymen," bellowed singer Steven Tyler from the Donington stage, "who has singlehandedly carved out his place in rock'n'roll's history. Mr..." The rest was drowned out by the opening bars of 'Train Kept A-Rollin''.

Just days later, and Jimmy was back with Aerosmith again, though this time it was in the considerably smaller environs of London's Marquee club for a 'secret' gig in front of an audience of just 300. "Aerosmith are a great band, a really good band to play with," said Page. "Everyone was smiling [after Donington], so they said, 'Look, we're playing The Marquee [on] Tuesday, do you want to come and do it?' I said 'Sure'..." No longer confined to one quick song with the quintet, Page stuck around for nearly half an hour at the Marquee, trading solos with guitarists Perry and Brad Whitford on old Yardbirds tunes such as 'Ain't Got You' and 'Think About It', while also logging Steven Tyler's wide-angle vocal range in his memory bank for future possible use.

In this most intimate of settings, it was clear what time and tide had done to him. No longer the starved whippet of yore, Jimmy was now grey at the temples and fleshier in the face, though his hair remained enviably thick while the Les Paul still hung defiantly an inch or two from his knees. Not quite Keith Richards on the Richter scale of ravaged rock stars, then, but surely a man for whom abstemiousness was a foreign concept.

Still, no one particularly seemed to care what Page looked like. Chanting his name continually between songs, the crowd seemed interested in only one thing: hearing him play a Led Zeppelin tune. After another loose blues jam, Jimmy duly obliged, leading Aerosmith into a storming take on 'Immigrant Song'. Cue flying plastic glasses and the joyful tears of grown men. While no one had been quite sure of the Firm or what to make of *Outrider*, there was little doubting that when it came to Zep, there was still a lot of love in the room both in the USA and UK. It was time for Page to take the hint and give them what they wanted, or at least as close to the real thing as he could.

In line with the explosion of CD sales in the mid to late eighties, Atlantic records had been desperate to get at least some Led Zeppelin-related product onto the market. Yet, without a 'Best Of' collection to draw on – lest we forget, Page and Peter Grant refused to sanction any such compilations within the band's lifetime – the label simply took matters into their own hands and re-released the band's entire back catalogue on shiny disc. Unfortunately, they neglected to inform Jimmy. Appalled by the loss of frequencies and room ambience the straight album-to-disc transfer had caused, he was also furious at the slapdash way certain songs were treated. "They actually cut off the cough at the end 'In My Time Of Dying'," he later grumbled to *Guitar World*. "[That] would irritate any Zeppelin fan." After years spent finding suitable studios and carefully placing microphones at clever angles, this was an affront not only to Page's personal standing as a producer, but also the legacy of his beloved band. Surely there was another way. "Well, I wanted it done properly," he said. "Crisp 'em up and make 'em sparkle." Jimmy decided to do the job himself.

Arriving at New York's Sterling Studios with veteran engineer and old friend George Marino in May 1990, Page spent a week or so upgrading Zep's original tapes to digital quality. A huge project to complete in so short a time, there was little to do but work, though, according to Marino, Jimmy also seemed instinctively to know when to step away from the task. "Jimmy was very professional," the engineer later told *Guitar World*. "He'd put in many hours, but he'd know when to call it a night. He'd know when his ears were getting tired."

Digitally restoring Zep's old masters was one thing. But selling them back to the public in the right format was quite another. As ever among the Yardbirds' 'Holy Trinity', Eric Clapton had helped light the way beforehand. Still somehow managing to find a path through each new twist and turn in the pop game, Clapton continued to score big with audiences during the eighties, as hits like 'Behind The Mask' and 'Forever Man' kept his profile arena-sized at the very least. Unlike so many of his former colleagues, Eric had also somehow managed to inveigle himself onto MTV (and relative latecomer VH1), the guitarist's face regularly peering out between Prince and Peter Gabriel. Therefore, when demand required an epic, career-spanning retrospective set in 1988, he was again at the fore with *Crossroads*, putting out a four-CD, six-LP set that gathered his recordings from the Yardbirds and Cream right through Derek & the Dominos to the present day. Further, the package also included rare cuts, alternative versions of his more famous songs and extensive liner notes. Selling four million copies worldwide (and bagging two Grammys), EC had clearly shown what could be done with a batch of old tunes and a little marketing nous. For the ever-watchful Page, *Crossroads'* success meant only good things for his own project.

With their contents fully sanctioned by Robert Plant and John Paul Jones, *Led Zeppelin* (aka 'Boxed Set') and its companion *Remasters* were foisted upon the world on October 15 and 29, 1990. To no one's great surprise, they were very good indeed. Issued as two separate collections – the 'Boxed Set' comprising a humungous 54-track four-CD/four-cassette/six-vinyl album package, *Remasters* a slightly more manageable 26-track double CD/double cassette/three-album set – this was, as one critic succinctly put it, "Zep to the power of ten". It also smacked of real thought, at least in the majority of places. In keeping with those wonderfully odd Hipgnosis designs of the seventies, both covers[289] bore a cleverly unnerving, computer-manipulated image of an airship's shadow hovering ominously above a huge corn circle. All very mysterious of course, and all very Zep. More, the deluxe 54-track 'Boxed Set' was accompanied by a lavish booklet of rare photographs and supporting essays. Sadly, some stray errors made it by the editor (Live Aid took place in 1985, not 1987), but in the main, it all added to the overall air of collectability.

---

289 *Remasters'* striking cover and insets was overseen by Bristol-based company Mission Control, with Richard Hutchison, Chris Wroe, Jenny Moore and Bill Smith responsible for design co-ordination, imaging/photography and graphic design/artwork.

To his credit, Page boldly re-sequenced songs on the larger collection, chucking caution to the wind by mixing up tracks from various albums as he saw fit. In this new regime, *Zep IV*'s 'Black Dog' now stood proudly next to *Houses'*... 'Over The Hills And Far Away' in the running order, while ...*Out Door*'s 'In The Evening' prefaced *Presence*'s 'Candy Store Rock'. No need to hit shuffle here; Jimmy had done it already. That said, there were certain other oddities among these surprises. For reasons unknown, *Physical Graffiti* was severely underrepresented on both sets, with only 'Kashmir' and 'Trampled Under Foot' making it onto the double CD edition. Given ...*Graffiti*'s place as Led Zeppelin's most completely realised album, such an obvious omission was to say the least strange. For the avid collector – who surely owned most, if not all of Led Zeppelin's previous output – this was all simply window dressing, however. What they wanted was buried treasures. What they actually got (and only on the 'Boxed Set' edition) were a few tasty delights, though perhaps not as many as they were perhaps hoping for. The real jewel turned out to be a pristine restoration of the quartet's free-falling take on Robert Johnson's 'Travelling Riverside Blues'. Originally recorded in June 1969 at the BBC's Maida Vale Studios for John Peel's *Top Gear* radio show, the version that now appeared on the larger edition had been given a real spit and polish by Jimmy, with the producer adding even more gorgeous, sliding guitars to compliment Robert's silky vocal. Of enduring interest to the Zep intelligentsia (Page had been asked repeatedly about the song's whereabouts by US DJs and fans while touring *Outrider*), the emergence of '... Blues' was one less piece in the 'unreleased tunes' puzzle to worry about[290].

'Hey Hey What Can I Do' was also the cause of some excitement. Rescued from a 1970 Island Studios session (and the B-side of a US-only single release of 'Immigrant Song'), 'Hey Hey...'"s breezy feel and easy-going melody harked nicely back to Zep's occasional forays

---

290 To promote the release of 'Boxed Set' and *Remasters*, a video for 'Travelling Riverside Blues' was pulled together from old footage of the band. Distributed to MTV, VH1 and various other networks. the promo became a staple of late-night TV rock shows.

into almost country-style pop. A live take of 'White Summer'/'Black Mountain Side' was perhaps less essential. Part of Zep's *In Concert* performance for the BBC circa June 1969, the show had already been hunted to near-extinction by bootleggers[291], and in all honesty, Jimmy could have probably picked several better highlights from the night in question. The inclusion of 'Moby Dick'/'Bonzo's Montreux' as the final 'bonus cut' was also slightly perplexing. Though Page's idea of amalgamating two of John Bonham's better known drum solos with the aid of a Synclavier programme was novel – and indeed, honoured the drummer's memory appropriately – neither track had ever been among Zep's finer moments. Surely, another live tune with the beast in full bloom was lurking somewhere. On this occasion, Page stuck rigidly to script. "Well, I think Bonzo would be happy with it."

While the relative paucity of unreleased cuts on 'Boxed Set' and *Remasters* threw up questions regarding how much (or how little) Led Zeppelin material was actually left in the can, it didn't harm either collection's pulling power. With the 54-track edition reaching numbers 18 and 48 in the USA and UK respectively (not half bad for a £50 price tag), and the two-CD model hitting number 10 at home – and staying on the charts for a whopping 45 weeks – this was an old-style showing of true star power. "We never tried to think 'Is this radio friendly?' because we didn't really care," Jimmy told *Musician* at the time. "We didn't do television, we didn't do Top 40 radio, we just did what we wanted and that's audible."

Just five years before, Jimmy Page and Led Zeppelin appeared in danger of becoming lost in their own mythology, the band's ever-darkening reputation for excess beginning to define their place in history and culture as much as their music ever had. Yet, 1990's stout collections provided new evidence that behind all the stories about mud

---

291 Despite Peter Grant's best efforts to deter them, bootleggers and Led Zeppelin had gone hand in hand, with a roaring trade in live concerts, radio sessions and studio outtakes flooding the under the counter market during and, indeed, long after the band's 12-year reign ended. Some were so good, Page, Plant and Jones reportedly purchased them for their own private collections.

sharks, cocaine mountains and 'Lori Lightning', there still beat the heart of a planet-straddling band – and one that could still sell in the millions (or four million units for 'Boxed Set' and *Remasters*, to be precise[292]). No wonder, then, after such renewed commercial success, offers for the group to reform only intensified.

In fact, Page, Robert Plant and John Paul Jones had already got back together at least twice since the Atlantic Records debacle of 1988, though only invited guests or close personal friends were present. In November 1989, Jimmy, Robert and JPJ met up in the midst of the Wyre Forest for the 21st birthday party of Plant's daughter, Carmen. Taking the stage after several drinks, they jammed for half an hour or so, playing the likes of 'Trampled Under Foot' and 'Misty Mountain Hop' before a delighted audience. On April 28, 1990, the trio were at it again, this time hogging the boards at Jason Bonham's wedding in Bewdley, Worcestershire. Joined by the groom on drums, 'Led Zeppelin' performed four old favourites, dusting off 'Bring It On Home', 'Sick Again', 'Custard Pie' and 'Rock And Roll' for the 200 attendees.

But it was probably Jimmy's appearance alongside Robert at the Silver Clef winners' charity concert in Knebworth Park on June 30, 1990 that set tongues wagging again about an imminent Zep reunion. Joining a starry cast that included Paul McCartney, Pink Floyd, Dire Straits and Genesis, Plant was scheduled to perform a brief late afternoon set with his own band. But a week or so before the event, rumours began to circulate that he might be joined by Page and Jones. While JPJ proved a no-show, Jimmy did turn up. Again wielding his cherry red

---

292 Due to the huge success of these compilations, another 31-track collection, *Boxed Set II*, was issued in September 1993. A much more eclectic mix featuring deeper cuts such as 'Night Flight', 'Hots On For Nowhere', 'Out On The Tiles' and the previously unreleased 'Baby Come On Home (Tribute To Bert Berns)' from October 1968, Page was again behind the desk for all remastering duties. In the same month, *Led Zeppelin: The Complete Studio Recordings* also hit stores. A cube-shaped box containing all nine Zep albums, an extended version of *Coda* and a 64-page booklet (with a fine essay on the band from former *Rolling Stone* writer – and now film director – Cameron Crowe), this second package sold over two million copies in the US alone.

Gibson Les Paul, the guitarist was in thrilling form, with he and Robert barging their way through their now familiar party piece of 'Rock And Roll' and 'Misty Mountain Hop', while also giving *Coda*'s combustible 'Wearing And Tearing' its live debut before a crowd of over 100,000. Wrapped around each other like a pair of old drunks as they left the stage, surely it was only a matter of time before happy days were here again for Zep fans.

And for a while at least, so it appeared. When 'Boxed Set' and *Remasters*' sales went through the roof in October 1990, Jimmy, Robert and John Paul were reportedly offered a staggering $200 million to reform Led Zeppelin for a new album and world tour. But getting Plant to sign up to the grand plan was considerably harder than it looked. Easily the most commercially successful of the three post-Zep, his fifth solo disc, *Manic Nirvana*, had again cracked the US Top 20 only six months before, leading to yet another round of arena dates. Mindful that after 10 years of hard graft establishing himself as a solo artist he would now have to surrender his independence and again become part of a group he really didn't think needed reforming, the singer remained sceptical about signing on any dotted lines. Further, Plant was allegedly unsure about Jason Bonham being part of any new 'Zep' package[293]. Perhaps concerned about the drummer falling prey to the same problems Bonzo had encountered when engulfed by fame or, as likely, mindful of the 'cheese factor' surrounding such a patently in-house solution, Robert again stepped away. No matter the amount of money, there would be no reunion, no new album and no all-conquering heroes returning to a stadium near you. Flummoxed, flabbergasted and "bloody frustrated", Page's response to Plant's decision was to run off with David Coverdale.

On paper this was perhaps the most bizarre twist yet in Jimmy's now three decade-spanning career. Linking up with Coverdale was actually the idea of Page's manager Brian Goode, who felt the pairing might be

---

293 When Robert was considering a Zep reunion, he suggested that alternative rockers Faith No More's Mike Bordin would be a good replacement for John Bonham. Happy to consider Bordin as a possible option (though he continued to favour Jason), Page studied videos of the drummer in action. In vain, as it turned out...

both creatively inspiring and financially lucrative. Still, given some of the recent history betwixt and between them, this unlikely match still fair took the breath away. According to Jimmy, however, it really wasn't that weird at all. "My manager called and asked if I ever considered working with David," he told *Guitar World*'s Brad Tolinski at the time, "I said 'That's interesting. He's a damn fine singer. Let's see how we get on socially'."

Page was undoubtedly right about David Coverdale. He was a damn fine singer. In fact, one of the very best to ever pick up a microphone when it came to hard and blues rock. A steelworker's son from Saltburn, North Yorkshire, Coverdale had famously been working in a men's clothing shop in 1973 when he saw an ad in *Melody Maker* placed by a group looking for a singer. He sent in his demo tape and was gobsmacked to discover that the group was Deep Purple, who were looking for a new vocalist following the departure of Ian Gillan. He soon found himself fronting one of the biggest acts in rock'n'roll. "I was overweight, wore clothes that looked good in Redcar [but] daft in London," he later told *Q*'s Phil Sutcliffe. "I had a questionable lazy eye and a slumbering caterpillar on my top lip – a very thin moustache touched up with my mother's mascara to look butch. But... you watch what the other people are doing. And I watched, and learned an enormous amount, good and bad."

That he did. As part of Purple's modified line-up[294], David traversed the stadiums and concert halls of the USA and Europe (including a headlining appearance before 200,000 fans at 1974's California Jam) until the group eventually imploded in 1976. Working to the maxim 'You can't keep a good man down', Coverdale then formed his own outfit, Whitesnake, where once again he found success with albums like *Ready An' Willing* and singles such as 'Fool For Your Loving'. Yet, it was when the singer ditched the group's more bluesy inclinations and reinvented Whitesnake as a slinky-hipped, poodle-haired, American-

---

294 After the (voluntary and possibly enforced) departures of singer Ian Gillan and bassist Roger Glover in 1973, Coverdale found himself joining a new, funkier Deep Purple alongside fellow new recruit, bassist Glenn Hughes.

leaning hard rock combo that the multi-platinum sales really arrived. Backed by the marketing nous of Geffen Records and further buoyed by a series of hilariously raunchy promos featuring David's then girlfriend (and soon to be wife, then ex-wife) Tawny Kitaen, Whitesnake's genre-defining album *1987* sold by the bucket load, made a now golden-haired Coverdale a mega-star and also caught the eye of Page.

"When I saw the Whitesnake video (for 'Still Of The Night'), there's the part where the guitarist starts playing with a bow," Jimmy later told *Classic Rock*. "Well, I actually fell around laughing. Literally. I was sitting on the bed watching it and I promise you, I fell on the ground laughing." The source of Page's mirth wasn't just confined to Whitesnake guitarist Adrian Vandenberg's appropriation of his violin bow trick. There were also the marked similarities between 'Still Of The Night' and parts of Zep's own back catalogue that captured Jimmy's – and later, Robert Plant's – ear. In fact, so close in places were Whitesnake to the spirit, sound and voice of prime-period Led Zeppelin on 'Still...' that Robert reportedly began referring to their leader as 'David Cover Version'. Surely, with Page feeling Whitesnake had appropriated several of his stage moves (and indeed, the stop/start swagger of 'Black Dog' on 'Still Of The Night'), the very thought of teaming up with Coverdale would have been anathema to him. Not Jimmy. He was simply intrigued. "I actually liked David's *1987* album and some of the stuff he'd done with Deep Purple," Page later said, "so I thought it would be interesting to see how I got on with him."

Realistically, after the subsequent commercial cooling of Whitesnake in the USA and the failure to relaunch Zep, both men were probably just keen to do something. Anything, in fact. To that end, a meeting was arranged on neutral ground, in this case New York. "We had a glass of wine," Coverdale recalled to *Q*. "Breakfast of champions. Then, we left the powers that be chatting and took a walk around Manhattan. It was, of course, noted we were promenading." By the sound of things, they were also clearing the air. "Jimmy and I have discussed everything that went on," David continued. "We developed a fantastic bond as friends. No, [any past] problem related to Robert, not Jimmy. Jimmy and I had no hatchet to bury. None at all."

Decamping to Vancouver's Little Mountain Studios, the newly formed 'Coverdale/Page' began recording their first album in November 1991. Needing to give their endeavour a contemporary sheen, the duo brought in engineer/producer Mike Fraser whose recent work with the likes of Aerosmith, AC/DC and (relatively new kids on the block) Metallica all pointed towards a man who could translate naked aggression into the firmest of CD sales. Also joining the duo was a strong supporting cast of musicians, including former Babys/Bad English bassist Ricky Phillips, keyboardist Lester Mendez and veteran backing vocalists John Sambataro and Tommy Funderburk. Bringing additional crunch – and an admirable Bonzo impersonation – was ex-Montrose/Heart drummer Denny Carmassi. In common parlance, Jimmy Page was stoked. "It was a really substantial first day," he said. "The stuff was really pouring out."

Over the course of the next several weeks, 'Coverdale/Page' went about the business of recording with due application, while also using any downtime to check out the local area's clubs and hostelries[295]. However, on January 15, 1992, a white-suited Jimmy temporarily set aside his studio duties to fly to New York where he and his fellow former members of the Yardbirds were inducted into the Rock And Roll Hall Of Fame at the Waldorf-Astoria Hotel. A glitzy affair, with a soundtrack of clinking champagne glasses and creaking cigar lighters, the award was yet more proof of just how self-congratulatory the music business had become since the frontier days of the Swinging Sixties.

---

295 Pre- and post recording, Page kept up a fairly busy diary of spontaneous club jams and unannounced appearances. In March 1991, he again joined Les Paul onstage at jazz club Fat Tuesdays, while also popping up in Reno two months later alongside David Coverdale for a sprint through 'Rock And Roll', 'The Rover' and 'Stairway To Heaven' with glam-metallers Poison. At some point during proceedings, Jimmy managed to fall offstage, though no harm was done. When he and Coverdale finally made it to Canada in November, the fun continued, with the two storming Vancouver's Yale Club to perform an impromptu version of 'Dazed And Confused'. Not to be stopped, on December 7, Page played a 30-minute set with his old friend from Blues Incorporated days, Long John Baldry, again in Vancouver. "I love jamming," he once said. This was surely the proof.

Once an act who, by their own admission, were "proto-punks who made it up as we went along", here they now were, being lauded by U2 guitarist The Edge as "inventors of the thing we know today as the rock band", and "sonic pioneers" to a man. True enough, but given the glint of mischief in Jeff Beck's eye as he accepted his award, someone at least had not forgotten that rock'n'roll used to deal in rebellion rather than trophy-gathering. "Somebody told me I should be proud tonight," he said from the stage, "but I'm not. They, this lot, kicked me out. Yes, they did. So," Beck concluded, "fuck them." As the Yardbirds' resident hooligan stepped away from the mike, Page and the band could not stop laughing with him.[296]

By March 15, 1993, Geffen Records was at last ready to release the fruits of two of the label's more high-profile signings. Their A&R department obviously couldn't wait to get the new disc into the shops. "This is totally something Jimmy and David wanted to do for the music," John Kalodner told the *Los Angeles Times*, "[and] it isn't a corporate decision, like an Eagles reunion tour. Jimmy Page couldn't spend all the money he has. It's hard to speak for Jimmy, but I think he wants to show he still has something to say. I think he wants to enjoy being Jimmy Page again." Furthermore, Geffen's huge-bearded master publicist thought that a certain rock god had best beware what else might be headed down the pipe from this most promising of duos. "First off, as a singer, David Coverdale is an improvement on Robert Plant," Kalodner said, throwing down a gauntlet. "Once you hear David do a Led Zeppelin song, there won't be any debate about it..."

Though the chance to hear what David could do with (or to) a Zep tune was still a ways away, at least the album – simply titled *Coverdale/*

---

296 Post-honours, the always ready Page joined Beck, Keith Richards, former Jimi Hendrix Experience drummer/bassist Mitch Mitchell & Noel Redding (among others) onstage for an extended version on 'All Along The Watchtower'. He was still at it a month later, when Page added jazz crooner Harry Connick Jr. to his list of jamming conquests at the Knight Centre in Miami, where further recording for 'Coverdale/Page was taking place at Criteria Studios. (The album was finished at London's Abbey Road.)

Page[297] – was finally here. Housed in a puzzling sleeve that depicted a mysteriously altered road sign popping up in several world-wide locations – "[It signifies] two roads joining to one road," said Coverdale, "try[ing] to express unification or joining together" – the disc also came with a promise of sorts from Jimmy. "I would submit," he said, "that [this] is the best work I've done since Led Zeppelin."

In the main, Page's statement was no idle boast. An accomplished collection of pugnacious rockers, moody ballads and late 20th-century blues, *Coverdale/Page* probably was – a few choice tracks from *Death Wish II* and *Outrider* aside – the best thing in which Jimmy had been involved since 1980. More, David Coverdale's rich voice and ability to climb above and beyond any scale thrown at him also seemed to reactivate something in the guitarist, who in turn produced his most aggressive and feisty playing this side of *Presence*.

There were several genuine moments to savour. On 'Shake My Tree', Page seemed to channel the very spirit of the seventies onto tape, with the song's slow-burning build-up and canny blend of box-tops and Les Pauls recalling his own instrumental navigations with Zep. No great surprise really, as 'Shake My Tree''s peek-a-boo riff was actually born while he was still in the band. "[That riff] was something I presented to Zep during the *In Through The Out Door* sessions," he later told *Guitar World*. "At the time, there was no 'mass enthusiasm' for it. No one except for Bonzo really seemed to understand what to do with it, so I filed it away." Now brought back kicking – and in Coverdale's case, literally screaming – 'Shake My Tree' provided the duo with a suitably explosive way to open their album.

'Pride And Joy' was also brimming over with heat and energy. A fine companion piece to 'Shake My Tree', again making deft use of Jimmy's gift for combining acoustic, electric and even dulcimer textures, its bluesy feel, thumping backbeat and bellicose vocal all combined to keep the listener happily pinned to the wall. It even gave Page a chance to pull out the harmonica for the first time in eons, his steely blasts heard

297 Early indications suggested the album was to be called 'North And South', but then the marketers stepped in.

at regular intervals throughout. "I hadn't played the harp in about 20 years," he laughed. "It was fun, but it took about two hours to recover. I blew so hard, I was seeing stars!" 'Waiting On You', too, provided a lesson in old-school dynamics, with the song's chorus using a dissonant chord motif to add tension and edge. "I called that JP's 'three chord trick'," Coverdale later told writer Greg Di Benedetto. "It was so bizarre, it almost caused me heart failure."

These slow waves of dissonance were at the nub of three more of *Coverdale/Page*'s better tracks: 'It's Over Now', 'Take It Easy' and 'Absolution Blues'. Conveying the same sense of lurching menace that made 'When The Levee Breaks' so compulsively listenable, the stand-out moment of 'It's Over Now' surely came when David commanded Jimmy to "Release the dog of war". Duly complying, Page let fly with an unearthly growl that bit into the track like an Alsatian. "That's probably my favourite effect [on the album]," Jimmy again told *Guitar World*. "I produced that by running my B-Bender Les Paul through an early sixties Vox wah, a Digitech Whammy pedal set deep an old Octavia and one of my old 100-watt Marshall Superleads which I used with Zep. It was easier for me to grab an old pedal because I've used them for years. I mean, they were good in the day, [so] why shouldn't they be good now?"

There was also an air of times past about the haunting, uneasy intros to 'Take It Easy' and 'Absolution Blues'. With 'Take...', Page again played into those areas he had originally uncovered on the likes of 'Friends', as open strings and shifting octaves jarred uneasily against Coverdale's equally complex vocal melody. 'Absolution...', on the other hand, picked up directly where the drones and slivers of 'Kashmir' and 'In The Evening' had left off, as Jimmy's whining Les Paul soloed against a bank of agitated Whammy pedals and hissing echo units.

With the languid sweep of 'Take Me For A Little While' and epic stomp of 'Don't Leave Me This Way', it genuinely looked like Page and Coverdale might have a winner on their hands. But there were a few dead bees among all that honey. With 'Feeling Hot', the duo managed to fall prey to the worst excesses of 'cock rock' (that said, they had probably invented it), the song's coarse riffing and puerile lyricism jarring uncomfortably with its more distinguished peers. "The boys are feeling

573

hot tonight!" bellowed David among all the 'Woah Yeah!" backing vocals and references to "gypsy women" and "backstage passes". Given that Jimmy and David were 49 and 43 years old respectively, their days as 'boys' – hot or not – were long behind them.

'Take A Look At Yourself' was also deeply suspect. Essentially a rewrite of *Outrider*'s 'Blues Anthem' but with even more chords and faux orchestration, sentimentality once again won out over substance. And while there was little doubt that closing track 'Whisper A Prayer For The Dying' had power, snarl and pace to spare, Coverdale's determination to hit notes only detectable by a team of audiologists managed to sully what had been an otherwise impeccably sung collection of tunes. "*Coverdale/ Page* was weird, but you know, it was also really widescreen at times," said Dave Lewis. "David was actually great on that album. Listen to him on 'Shakin' My Tree', an old *In Through The Out Door* riff brought back to life again. I actually think David Coverdale woke Jimmy up and made him think 'God, I can still do this...'"

By no means perfect, but "pretty bloody good" nonetheless, *Coverdale/ Page* proved that despite all the raised eyebrows and suppressed sneers that greeted news of their collaboration, the duo could still deliver the goods when the occasion demanded it. Livelier than the Firm, certainly more assertive than *Outrider* and thanks to some inspired production on the parts of the duo and Mike Fraser, a wily, contemporary update on the classic sounds of both Zep and Whitesnake, there really wasn't much here to dislike. One chap, however, couldn't quite get his head around it all. "Well," said Robert Plant, "I found it difficult to understand his choice of bedfellow. I just could not get it."

Thankfully, others did, with *Coverdale/Page* bounding into the UK and US Top 10 at numbers four and five respectively, the first time Jimmy had achieved such high chart placings since *In Through The Out Door* back in 1979.[298] Geffen's John Kalodner sounded ecstatic on his behalf. "Jimmy is revitalised," said the A&R man. "He's very clear-

---

298 In addition to some admirable album sales, the singles drawn from *Coverdale/Page* also did semi-reasonable numbers, with 'Take A Little While' and 'Take A Look At Yourself' reaching number 29 and number 43 in the UK charts.

headed and enthusiastic, which hadn't always been my experience with him in the past. He seemed highly motivated to make a good record, and [now] go out on tour." Which is where the problems started.

While Page and Coverdale's album had done decent business (in the USA alone, it was already well on its way to platinum), ticket sales for a proposed 45-date American tour were much softer. Having had its own 'Year Zero' in 1991 with the advent of Seattle's 'grunge' movement, the States was now deep in thrall to yet another new generation of rockers, this time wearing plaid shirts, ripped jeans and sporting wonderfully unkempt hair. Some – such as Nirvana and Mudhoney – came from a distinctly punk-leaning ethos.[299] Others, including Pearl Jam, Soundgarden and Alice In Chains, had learned at least some of their musical lessons from the likes of Black Sabbath, early Aerosmith and – no great surprise – Led Zeppelin. Yet, where glam metal had put the emphasis on the buccaneering spirit and general tomfoolery of such hard rock/metal legends, grunge eschewed all such notions of sexism and misogyny, preferring instead to concentrate its philosophical and political thrust on dismantling "the bullshit". It had worked too. By mid-1993, poodle rock was pushing up daisies and Nirvana's Kurt Cobain and Pearl Jam's Eddie Vedder were calling the shots.

Suffice to say, in this atmosphere of challenge and change, ticket demand to see two of rock's older gods strutting their manly stuff around the arenas of the USA was somewhat compromised. Beating a hasty retreat, Page and Coverdale chose instead to concentrate on seven concerts in Japan, where worshipping such deities was still more or less acceptable. Assembling a backing band that included the always impressive Denny Carmassi on drums, session ace Brett Tuggle on keyboards and Guy Pratt on bass, the duo decamped to the East, where Tokyo's legendary Budokan Hall duly awaited them on December 14 & 15, 1993.

299 While Nirvana were undoubtedly on the punk end of the grunge spectrum, frontman/singer Kurt Cobain did pen the tune 'Aero Zeppelin' as a back-handed compliment to both the legacy (and continuing commercial power) of Aerosmith and Led Zeppelin.

On safe ground, Coverdale/Page's Japanese shows proved a delightful, if showy hoot. Deciding to throw caution to the wind, Jimmy and David not only played the majority of their new album, but a goodly number of Zep and Whitesnake tunes too, with 'Kashmir', 'In My Time Of Dying' and even a sly amalgamation of 'Still Of The Night'/'Black Dog' bashed out over the course of their near two-hour set. At first, the concept of hearing 'David Cover Version' rip into such hallowed turf might have seemed positively disrespectful to the memory of Led Zeppelin (or at least Robert Plant's ego). But as John Kaldoner had already intimated, his pipes were more than up to the task.

With two shows at the Bukodan behind them (and two more gigs booked at Tokyo's Olympic Hall to meet public demand in Japan's capital city), the train rolled onto Osaka's Castle Hall (December 20 & 21) before coming to a stop in Nagoya three days before Christmas. Obviously in a cheeky mood, Jimmy chose to make the final night of the tour one to remember by throwing a few stray chords from 'Stairway...' into 'Take Me For A Little While'. Yet, before the sky collapsed, a grinning Page quickly veered the tune back into safer waters. Some things, it appeared, were still sacrosanct.

On paper, of course, it had all looked vaguely ridiculous. But as the Japanese shows so ably demonstrated[300], the improbable pairing of Jimmy Page and David Coverdale had all the makings of a potentially cracking band. If the two could simply see out the commercial changes taking place in America, gather their musical thoughts and push on with another album of strong tunes, there might well be a future for them yet. Or so one might have thought. "So, the stuff with David was actually working," said Dave Lewis. "The album's good, the gigs are good and there's a bit of a buzz in the air. But then in comes the call from Robert..."

And just like that, Jimmy Page was gone in the night.

---

300 As a consequence of their tour, Coverdale/Page reached sales of over 150,000 sales in Japan, with the pair receiving a Sony Music 'In-House' award for their efforts.

CHAPTER 35

Upon A Golden Horse

I t wasn't quite that dramatic.
By mid-1993, Robert Plant had released his sixth solo album, *Fate Of Nations*. Another impressive collection of songs, which this time saw the vocalist revisit some of his sixties musical heroes for inspiration (including Jefferson Airplane, Moby Grape and Tim Hardin), *Fate...* had done well enough but not blindingly so. Reaching number six and number 34 in the UK and USA, it eventually earned a gold disc and even produced a Top 30 single in Great Britain with the breezy '29 Palms'. Yet, in comparison with 1988's *Now And Zen* or even 1990's *Manic Nirvana*, the numbers were down. Robert didn't seem that concerned. "I'm proud of what I attempted to do lyrically on (*Fate Of Nations*)," he said at the time. "I've tried to tell vivid tales that come from a hearty tradition of prose."

Indeed, from the outside looking in, Plant seemed to be wholeheartedly content with his lot. Touring the States alongside soul rocker Lenny Kravitz and southern blues rock revivalists the Black Crowes, he was full of just praise for his compatriots. "I think the Black Crowes' Chris Robinson is the most, eloquent stylistic singer in the mainstream of pop," he told *Guitar World*'s Gary Graff, "and [the group] are pretty sincere retro men, and really, strongly into their music." But when

577

questioned about his old band and its old leader, his remarks turned flintier. "Jimmy's done his best," Robert said of Coverdale/Page, "[but] it's a bit limiting, artistically, to think that's the way it is and that's what's needed." Further, Plant seemed more than a little sniffy about the latest round of Led Zeppelin reissues and Page's continuing desire for a reformation. "I'm a little sceptical they should be... a commercial venture," he told Graff. "And I do find Jimmy's constant commenting about the lack of Led Zeppelin... in festival auditoriums a bit... boring." In short, the line had been drawn again. No Zep albums, no Zep concerts, no Zep anything, period. That said, it wasn't quite over yet.

When in the autumn of 1993, MTV approached Robert Plant with the idea of performing an *Unplugged*[301] show for the network, he at last saw a way that might allow him to team up with Jimmy Page again. Warming to the idea of revisiting Zep's back catalogue – but with a view to radically reinterpreting the songs rather than simply regurgitating them for profit – Plant put in a call to his old friend, albeit via his manager. "I was going to play with David in Japan," Jimmy later told *Classic Rock*, "and I got a call from Robert's management." A summit was called in Boston, where Plant was playing a gig. "Robert said, 'I've been asked by MTV to do an *Unplugged* and I'd really like to do it with you'. I said 'OK'. It gave us a chance to revisit the numbers and use that same picture with a very, very different frame."

As it turned out, none of this might have been possible without the intercession of Plant's manager, Bill Curbishley. Having overseen his charge's business affairs for the best part of a decade, Curbishley was pitifully aware of Robert's desire to avoid anything to do with the dreaded 'Led Zeppelin'. Yet, he also knew that Plant remained open to working with Jimmy, if only in the right circumstances. The trick was setting up a universe in which such a thing could happen. "Robert wasn't unwilling to work with Page," Bill later told *Dave Lewis* and

---

301 First introduced in 1989, MTV's *Unplugged* saw established acts perform stripped down/acoustic versions of their best-known songs in front of a small studio audience. Precursors to the format included Elvis Presley's 1968 'Comeback Special' and the intimate Beatles jams featured in the 1970 movie *Let It Be*.

Talent-PM. "He was unwilling to work with Led Zeppelin because he didn't want to take a backwards step." For Plant, this distinction was crucial. "I was frightened of that bandwagon," he later told *Rolling Stone.* "I saw the Who trundled around the stadiums of America and I found it so dull, obvious and sad. The fact that they carried on without Keith Moon was always a mystery to me, but the fact that they did it again and again, augmenting it with more and more musicians. [I didn't] want to be a part of that aspect of entertainment. I'd played Vegas already."

Taking the view "You two wrote all the songs, so there's no reason why you can't play them," Bill Curbishley subsequently brokered an agreement between Jimmy and Robert that allowed them not only to reconvene for the MTV appearance, but also pave the way for what might come after it. Evidently impressed by Bill's business nous, Page soon threw in his cards with his own manager Brian Goode and came under the umbrella of Curbishley's Trinifold Management group. With his latest venture heading the way of the Dodo (once the Japanese tour was done, so were Coverdale/Page), but now buoyed by the inviting prospect of revitalising his past, Jimmy again began to sound optimistic about the future. "Well, Robert had three or four guitarists with him at that time," he later laughed, "and I just thought 'I can do that with just one!'"

With the business end of their new collaboration in place, Page and Plant wasted little time in testing the water to see if it would work artistically. "We'd only 'rubbed shoulders' in the past 14 years, really," said Jimmy, "so the most important thing was to see how we got on together." To that end, the two booked into "a little dump" in London's Kings Cross in early February 1994 with a microphone, guitar, large PA and several tape loops Robert had commandeered from a French musician/producer/movie-maker of his acquaintance.

"I went to the house of the producer Martin Meissonnier[302] in Paris, and he played me some great loops that were on a film," Robert later told *Talks Music.* "You got the visuals and the sound of the evening.

---

302 An artistic polymath whose career has seen him involved with film, music and journalism, Martin Meissonnier has worked with a plethora of African musicians over the years, including Fela Kuti, King Sunny Adé and Papa Wemba.

I got him to cut some eight-bar sequences from the film, and I thought, wow, these need some tough, oblique Western approach on top to create a song. So, when Jimmy and I reconvened, I played these to him and we got two great tracks." Taking up more or less where they had left off in Morocco 21 years before, the duo set about creating an intriguing stew of North African polyrhythms, subliminal drones, Howlin' Wolf-like riffs and hypnotic wails. The results – 'Wonderful One' and 'Yallah' – would become key to their progress. "Played. Sang. It was great," Page later said. "It was *instant*."

Chemistry suitably restored, the next move was to pull together a band for their upcoming MTV show. Following Plant's original brief of completely overhauling the past for the good of the present, the pair did not skimp on essentials. With arranger/keyboardist Ed Shearmur brought in to oversee the contributions of London's Metropolitan Orchestra (29 players in all) and Hossam Ramzy leading its Egyptian counterpart (11 more), Pakistani singer Najma Akhtar was also invited to sing alongside Plant on 'The Battle Of Evermore' in the absence of Sandy Denny, who had sadly died from a brain haemorrhage in April 1978. As the use of two voluminous orchestras suggested, Page and Plant's core group would be no small affair either. Drafted in from Robert's touring ensemble were nimble-fingered Charlie Jones on bass guitar (also the husband of Robert's daughter, Carmen) and Michael Lee on drums, while newcomers Porl Thompson (ex-Cure), Jim Sutherland and Nigel Eaton brought rhythm guitar/banjo, mandolin/bodhran and hurdy-gurdy with them to the party. A small army, then, but with one glaring omission. "Jimmy and Robert," said John Paul Jones, "just decided to do it without saying anything to me at all."

Even taking into account Plant's stern edict at the start of the project – absolutely no Zep reunions to see here – he and Page's decision not to inform Jones of their intentions seemed even to the casual observer the most bizarre (and unforgivable) of oversights. Having spent the best part of 12 years in the same band – eaten together, travelled together, written 'Black Dog' together, for God's sake – surely a courtesy call was in order. Apparently not. "I thought it was odd behaviour," Jones told *Rolling Stone*. "A bit... discourteous. At least they could say, 'We think you're horrible, so we don't want to use you', or whatever. Nothing. Absolutely nothing. I mean, it's not as if we hated each other or anything."

Yet, according to Robert Plant there was absolutely no slight involved in the decision to leave Jones out of the equation. Instead, it was more a matter on following the clues right in front of them. "Apart from the fact that it would virtually be Led Zeppelin and the next person you start talking about is Jason Bonham, which is so cheesy and ridiculous, the fact is that our thread was this North African thing [and] the Howlin' Wolf riffs," he told *Mojo*. "We focused on those mutual points, so rather than confuse the issue [it was more], 'Let's see what we've still got'. So, it's nothing at all personal. It's just at this point in time, you've got to get a result quickly to know if it's worth it."

Perhaps unsurprisingly, Page concurred. "We were gaining so much momentum from the loops and [then] working with Charlie Jones and Michael Lee, that quite honestly, I for one wasn't thinking about John Paul Jones," he confirmed to Mat Snow in 1994. "I was thinking about what we were getting together between the two of us and the rest of the [new] band. It was its own thing before all of that became an issue." Logical step, bold revisionism or just plain rudeness, John Paul Jones was to take no part in the new regime. "I seem," he laughed, "to have been 'disappeared'." Perhaps so. But based on the final evidence, it took two orchestras and five supporting musicians to replace him.

Following the temporary PR wobble that had threatened to undermine the good news of their collaboration, Page and Plant were quick to regain momentum, the duo popping up here and there throughout the spring and summer of 1994 before *MTV Unplugged* truly came to claim them. On April 17, they at last took "the experiment" out of the rehearsal rooms and put it on the concert stage at Buxton Opera House, performing at a memorial benefit in honour of Alexis 'Blues Incorporated' Korner. Joined by the now well-oiled rhythm section of Jones and Lee, the quartet played a five-song set of both new and old tunes, with two (as yet unnamed) jams hinting at things to come and three established classics – 'Baby, Please Don't Go', 'I Can't Quit You Baby' and 'Train Kept A-Rollin'' – acting as a serviceable reminder of Jimmy and Robert's distinguished past.

581

After yet more preparations, it was onto Morocco on August 9 & 10, where Page and Plant filmed a snippet for their upcoming TV show in the centre of Marrakesh's J'ma el Fna (or 'Square of the Dead'). Seating themselves among the locals, the duo proceeded to bash out 'Yallah' and another new tune – the spinning 'Wah Wah' – to an audience of traders, tourists, stray hippies and bemused children. So delighted was Robert by the reception he and Jimmy received, the vocalist almost didn't notice when one of their PA speakers began slowly travelling around a nearby corner of its own accord. "I loved it. My people!" he guffawed. "[They] weren't stealing hub caps, it was bloody PA speakers!" Suffice to say, the roadies stepped in before this essential piece of kit disappeared forever into the warm Moroccan night.

With Marrakesh behind them, Page and Plant, Jones, Lee, Porl Thompson, Jim Sutherland and Nigel Eaton next popped up among the hills, mountains and valleys of Snowdonia, Wales. Again followed by an MTV film crew, footage for the track 'No Quarter' was shot just outside the village of Dolgoch before the entourage moved on to a slate quarry close to Bron-Yr-Aur. Here, where so much of *Led Zeppelin III* had been written, Robert and Jimmy's latest band performed versions of 'Nobody's Fault But Mine' and 'When The Levee Breaks' while the cameras whirled to the left and right. "I'd been looking forward to working with Robert for so long," said Page of progress thus far, "and [was] looking in that interim period for someone I could have that same rapport with as I had with him. And now," he concluded, "it's certainly come back."

Nearly 14 long years after the fall of Led Zeppelin, Jimmy Page, Robert Plant, their new core group and two full orchestras took over Studio Two of London Weekend's Southbank complex on August 25 & 26, 1994, for the recording of *MTV Unplugged* in front of a (mainly) invited audience.[303] Having experienced the excruciating embarrassment

---

303 Among the musicians crammed into Southbank studios for the Page/Plant extravaganza were Aerosmith drummer Joey Kramer, Depeche Mode singer Dave Gahan, Iron Maiden vocalist Bruce Dickinson and Canadian rocker Bryan Adams. Somewhat surprisingly, punk icons Mick Jones (guitarist with the Clash) and Hugh Cornwall (frontman with the Stranglers) were also part of the audience.

of Live Aid and the even messier failure of the Atlantic Records' 40th Anniversary concert, even if Page and Plant weren't calling themselves 'Led Zeppelin' this time around, the pair were in no mood to screw things up again. Still, backstage, nerves were riding high. "I wanted to call it 'Unhinged'," quipped Plant. There was no real need for worry, however. From the opening bars of the first track, it was obvious that they had it in the bag. "Well, yes," Page later smiled, "people did seem to like it, didn't they?"

Handing over two near-seamless performances where every note, arrangement, paradiddle and crash of the snare had been meticulously planned beforehand, the shows did much to counter any remaining memories of 1985 and 1988. More, they also laid solid foundations for the duo's next steps forward, the sheer breadth and diversity of material on show allowing them several potential avenues to explore should they so wish. If one had to pick the shows' better moments, then surely 'Gallows Pole' was as good a place as any to start. Now more "a musical riot than an actual song", the addition of Nigel Eaton's grinding hurdy-gurdy, Michael Lee's breathless pummelling of his kit and Jimmy's own battering of his Ovation acoustic brought new urgency to an already established classic, with Robert happily racing at the front. That said, there was never a moment where things felt out of control. Weeks of rehearsal had seen to that.

Away from the speed-metal folk of 'Gallows Pole', *Led Zeppelin III's* saddest moment – 'Since I've Been Loving You' – also offered bold and different possibilities for the future. Now benefiting from a lush string arrangement that enhanced the pathos of the original tune, should Page and Plant have wanted to strike out into a new form of orchestral blues, then this was their calling card. Yet, it was probably the radically altered versions of 'Friends' and 'Kashmir' that gave a real indication of where their collaboration might be headed. With the former awash with middle-eastern instrumentation and the latter employing both Western and Egyptian orchestras to deliver its astounding finale, lush sunsets and driving storms again seemed to be calling to Robert and Jimmy. "Morocco is a living, pulsating entity which is changing all the time," Plant later told *Guitar World*. "But there are parts of Marrakech that carry on as they have done for thousands of years, and the music is a reflection of that, of all times and all religions... of all the expectations and conditions of the people who live there. It's amazing, it's pumping, it's furious, it's anxious, it's happy and far more real than anything you'll experience in a Western city."

This fascination was also borne out by the four new compositions premiered as part of the TV package, all of which carried the smell and sounds of North Africa. 'With 'Yallah' (aka 'The Truth Explodes'), Martin Meissonnier's borrowed loop was now covered in effects-laden guitars and Plant's "Muezzin wails", with Page's simple, five-note riff and the ever-thumping drum acting as anchors among all the swirls of sound. 'City Don't Cry' took things even further, with Robert actually singing alongside a sextet of Moroccan Gnaoui devotional musicians led by Brahim El Balkani. "We went to Morocco to try and work with the Gnaoui," he later explained. "Oh, that was great, just great for me to go back to a country that I'm so in love with, a country whose music I so love."

With the similarly themed 'Wah Wah' and drifting, big-skied 'Wonderful One', it was clear that Jimmy and Robert's latest venture was a good deal closer to Plant's work from *Now And Zen* to *Fate Of Nations* than the recent crash, bang, wallop of *Coverdale/Page*. Yet, according to Chris Welch, after years of being his own boss, the singer was unlikely to defer to Jimmy when it came to matters of current (or future) musical direction. "By then, Robert had completely proved himself," said Welch. "He'd had success as a solo artist and could now come back [to Page] on level terms. And we mustn't forget he was a grown man by then, not some young Adonis screaming 'Whole Lotta Love'. He needed to find himself after Zeppelin and find himself he most certainly did."

That Page was suppressing his own musical instincts to placate Plant seems unlikely. In fact, watching the concert footage, Page seemed to be having an absolute ball. Whether delicately plucking the mandolin part of 'The Battle Of Evermore'[304], strumming wildly on his newly

---

304 The mandolin in question was set atop a huge, three-necked (6/12-string) instrument Jimmy actually had to sit down to play.

acquired Ovation acoustic 6/12-string double-neck throughout 'Four Sticks' or dusting off his 'No. 1' Gibson Les Paul for several shivery solos during 'Since I've Been Loving You', Jimmy appeared over the moon and several more stars to boot. More, as 'Kashmir' more than illustrated, he had lost none of his enthusiasm for new technology, the guitarist introducing viewers to his very latest toy: a 'Transperformance' Gold Top Les Paul. Equipped with an in-built electronic self-tuning system, the axe provided Page with 240 different tunings without once having to touch the pegs[305]. "You know," he later said, "people think I can't play anymore. So I go out to prove to them that I can..."

Their two nights' work now joined together into one complete film (with the additional footage shot in Wales and Marrakesh interspersed throughout), the Southbank performance was transmitted by MTV America and MTV Europe under the novel name *No Quarter... Unledded* on October 12 & 17, 1994. Given that John Paul Jones had actually written most of '... Quarter' himself, he was probably overwhelmed with joy by the duo's choice of title. "They're doing Led Zeppelin songs," JPJ said of the 'non-reunion' reunion. "What else would anybody else think it would be?" In reality, the title was probably just an abstraction. Heavily trailed on both networks, *No Quarter...* soon broke Eric Clapton's previous record to become the most watched *Unplugged* session in the show's five-year history.[306] "So live and so exciting," said Page. And soon to be extremely lucrative, too.

On the back of MTV's impressive viewing figures, *No Quarter... Unledded* was released on both CD (and video), the 14-track package climbing to numbers four and seven respectively on the US and UK charts in November 1994. With platinum and gold discs awarded

---

305 The Transperformance's tuning system could be operated either by pressing a specially built electronic board attached to the guitar's body or through the use of a foot pedal. "It really makes peoples' eyes pop out," said Page, proudly.

306 It should be noted that despite *MTV Unplugged*'s previous insistence that only acoustic instrumentation be used on the show, Jimmy Page chose to completely ignore their edict, pulling out several Les Pauls and various amps as and when the situation demanded it. Obviously, no one was brave enough to argue with him.

in those territories – and 255,000 further sales generated in Canada, Australia and South America – only a fool would believe this was to be a one-off event. "The will and eagerness with *Unledded* was fantastic," Plant later told *Uncut*. "Jimmy and I went into a room and it was back." Even the critics wanted more. "The best Led Zeppelin music smacked of serious air miles," said *Q*'s David Cavanagh at the time. "From the cobra-stuffed Kasbahs of 'Kashmir' to the benighted delta of 'When The Levee Breaks'... they certainly got around. [So], while not many rock albums require an atlas as a secondary purchase... this 80-minute burst of electro-acoustic über-Zep is even more peripatetic than *Physical Graffiti*."

But just before Jimmy and Robert could take their wares to the faithful, there was a potentially awkward moment for them to negotiate in New York. On January 30, 1995, after 10 years of existence, The Rock and Roll Hall of Fame finally got around to inducting Led Zeppelin. In a gesture that extended the definition of 'sporting' to new lengths, John Paul Jones joined the duo onstage to accept the award. His short speech was masterfully understated. "Thanks to my friends," said the bassist, "for finally remembering my telephone number..." However, unlike JPJ's brief missive, the applause that greeted it was hearty and sustained. Perhaps there was more to this awards malarkey than first met the eye...

Regardless of what might have been going on behind the scenes at the Waldorf Astoria, the remaining members of Led Zeppelin – plus Jason Bonham, who had come to the Rock and Roll... event to accept the award on behalf of his late father – still managed to take to the stage for a short set. Joined by Aerosmith's Joe Perry and Steven Tyler (who gave their induction speech), it was Page who ended up leading from the front, with the guitarist pushing his cohorts through hard-edged versions of 'For Your Love', 'Bring It On Home' and 'Train Kept A-Rollin'' before veering off into an extended blues jam. After Jason (somewhat inexplicably) stood down behind the kit and drummer Michael Lee took up his sticks, the band – plus special guest/sturdy warhorse Neil Young – belted out a radically reworked version of 'When The Levee Breaks'. According to journalist Steve Sauer, when JPJ asked Jimmy and Robert about the new arrangement for '... Breaks' beforehand, he was given short shrift. "No, we do it a bit differently now," came the reported reply. "You'll catch on..." 15–all it was.

Following yet another gong-show appearance (of sorts) at the American Music Awards on January 30[307], Page and Plant – though certainly not Jones – readied themselves for their longest sustained tour since the days of Led Zeppelin. Scheduled to kick off in Pensacola, Florida on February 26, 1995 and run across America, Europe, South America, Japan and Australia until March 1, 1996, the 115-date jaunt would see them accompanied by not only their now stable group of ...Unledded musos, but also Hossam Ramzy's portable Egyptian mini-orchestra. Further, wherever possible, the troupe would pick up a local string section to augment their already bustling sound, with arranger/keyboardist Ed Shearmur charged with putting these temporary ensembles through their paces before each gig. All in all, ambitious stuff. "I suppose we're trying to reinvent our musical personality," Robert told *Q* in advance of the forthcoming shows, "[though] Jimmy and I have always had a leaning to the East."

Despite the rigorous demands they put upon themselves and their band, the Page/Plant revue surpassed even its own expectations as both crowds and critics seemed to delight in their future/retro-leaning direction. Using the Led Zeppelin back catalogue as a starting point rather than a line in the sand never to be crossed, the duo enhanced, roughed up, cajoled and reinvented everything from 'Dancing Days' and 'Tangerine' to 'In The Evening' and 'The Song Remains The Same', using improvisation and orchestral enhancement to create new sounds for themselves and their audience. Taking a cue from ... Unledded, they were also unafraid to introduce previous material that had been neglected in the live arena, with the likes of 'Custard Pie' and 'Tea For

---

307 Unlike *The Rock and Roll Hall of Fame*, Page and Plant did not attend the American Music Awards in Los Angeles, where Led Zeppelin were named 'Best International Artist'. Instead, they filmed their acceptance speech (again, alongside Jason Bonham) in London, providing an additional clip of their new band performing 'Black Dog', replete with a didgeridoo duo. JPJ, however, did make it to the show, thanking John Bonham and his wife, Mo, in his speech. Jimmy and Robert were not mentioned.

One' joining 'Friends' and 'Four Sticks' under the stage lights. From inspired cover versions and early old favourites (The Doors' 'Break On Through' and Garnett Mimms' 'As Long As I Have You') to mad-haired medleys ('Whole Lotta Love' was often invaded by snippets of 'In The Light' and even 'Down By The Seaside'), this was Jimmy and Robert on the high-wire without a net.[308] "We're a pair of old fuckers who can still do it," laughed Robert, "but we do have a history!"

One of the pair's finer shows came at Wembley Arena on July 25, 1995. The first of two gigs at north London's largest concert venue, Jimmy in particular was on fire. Now 51 summers, but frankly looking healthier than he had in at least a decade, Page's work on '... Loving You', 'The Wanton Song' and 'Black Dog' sounded both vigorous and bold, with nary a sign of the hesitancy that dogged his performances on the ARMS tour of 1983 or occasional laziness he fell prey to during Firm concerts. Weaving his way through endless drones and countless cymbal crashes on 'Kashmir', Jimmy might not have been a man reborn, but he was acting like a kid in a candy shop. "[Teaming up with Robert] was a real challenge," he later told *Mojo*, "but I really wanted to go over those horizons again..."

While the second honeymoon between Page and Plant proceeded apace onstage, behind the scenes there were other challenges to negotiate, some purely logistical, others laced with sadness. Finding ready-made orchestras to fit the bill at each town or city the band visited was proving a nightmare, leading to a more trimmed down instrumental format at certain gigs. Further, in a Zep-style blast from the past, Jimmy brushed with authorities when flying from San Francisco to Portland on May 23. Desperate for a cigarette and possibly the worse for wear after several drinks, he set off the plane's smoke alarm while having a sneaky drag in the toilets. In one report, the guitarist was so drunk, he actually challenged the cabin crew to arrest him. "That would never have happened on the Starship..." someone quipped.

---

308 Astoundingly, Jimmy and Robert even performed a version of 'Shake My Tree' from *Coverdale/Page*, proving that even lion-haired rock gods can change their spots.

Elsewhere, a Led Zeppelin tribute album – *Encomium* – featuring cover versions of old classics by the likes of Duran Duran, Stone Temple Pilots, Rollins and Hootie & the Blowfish was released by Atlantic Records while Page and Plant were still touring in the States. No bad thing in principle (even if did smack of a cash-in on the label's part), the enterprise was severely let down by Robert's own contribution to the disc: a quite awful duet of 'Down By The Seaside' with alternative singer-songwriter Tori Amos. Eight minutes of dreary torture with a whispering Plant playing rudimentary guitar alongside a fluttering Tori, it was the worst track on *Encomium* by a considerable margin. "Bill Curbishley said, 'Don't you think this might be a little self-indulgent,'" the good natured Amos later said, "so we said, 'Well, of course it is. Isn't that the whole point?' I mean, Robert's singing on his own bloody tribute album. C'mon, give me a break. That's vanity if I ever heard it!"[309]

On November 21, 1995, things took on a much darker hue. Just three weeks after Page and Plant had concluded the second leg of their US jaunt at New York's Madison Square Garden, Peter Grant suffered a fatal heart attack. With both Jimmy and Robert in attendance, their former manager was buried two weeks later at St. Peter and St. Paul's church near his home in Hellingly, East Sussex.[310] Grant was 60 when he died. "Wherever Peter is going now," said former Swan Song associate and close friend Alan Callan during his eulogy, "I hope they've got their act together..."

In truth, the last years of Peter Grant's life had seen him become a very different man than the human juggernaut that ruled the offices of Swan Song and stadiums of America with an iron will and the sharpest of tongues during Led Zeppelin's heyday. Following the band's dissolution in 1980, Grant began a long and lonesome retreat behind the doors of Horselunges, distancing himself from what had come before while also

---

309 Released on April 8, 1995, *Encomium* reached number 17 in the US charts and was later awarded a gold disc.

310 Other mourners at Grant's funeral included Jeff Beck, Jim McCarty, Chris Dreja and Paul Rodgers. John Paul Jones reportedly did not attend.

battling drug addiction. Things would get worse before they got better. With relationship woes and health issues already stacking up, Grant now succumbed to diabetes, his physical condition constantly fragile as a result. But by the late eighties, despite a cane to help him walk, Peter rallied. Having finally jettisoned the white powder and an astounding amount of weight, he slowly re-emerged into public view with a new perspective on life. Selling Horselunges, Grant moved to an apartment in Eastbourne, and even became involved in local affairs, judging talent contests in a nearby pub. Indeed, when he was offered a position by the local council as a magistrate, Grant was reportedly flattered, though he was also quick to turn it down.

Above all else, however, Zep's former hurricane seemed keen to reconcile with his own past. Once dubbed "the scariest man in rock'n'roll", Peter now presented himself as an older, kinder and much gentler man: one that realised that while mistakes had been made, they were more often than not for the greater good of his beloved band. "I'd hate to be remembered as a bad person," he later told *Q*. "I've never been a bad person... never meant to be." To this end, perhaps, he also sought to reactivate his friendships with Jimmy Page, John Paul Jones and latterly Robert Plant.

In 1989, he had accompanied Page to a Frank Sinatra concert at the Royal Albert Hall, the two seen hugging each other after the show. And though there had been some financial issues with Robert during the early eighties to contend with[311], Grant was there at Wembley Arena in July 1995 to see his boys play the old songs, albeit in a radically different way. "Peter was a tower of strength as a business partner and a friend," Jimmy said after his passing. "I will miss him and my heart goes out to his family." After his death the Music Manager's Forum instituted the Peter Grant Award in his honour, recognising excellence in this

---

311 According to Peter's son, Warren, his father had been displeased when Plant chose to take his own road after the demise of Led Zeppelin. "I think when Robert did his own solo thing," Warren later told Chris Welch, "he was still under contract to Peter, but then he went off and did his own thing and dad was upset about that. But they buried the hatchet in the end."

most taxing of professions. An industry giant without whom Page could have conceivably built his vast artistic and financial empire, he was once asked why he had walked away from management. "How on earth do you follow Led Zeppelin?" he said. How, indeed...

After nearly 13 months of frenetic travel, brushes with authority and the sad death of an old friend, the Page and Plant touring circus came to rest in Melbourne, Australia on March 1, 1996. Following a three-pronged encore – 'Wonderful One', 'Black Dog' and 'Rock And Roll' – they could now down tools, safe in the knowledge that the grand experiment had worked. It had seen a Top 10 album, some of the best reviews of their career and a huge, well-attended concert experience spanning five continents and 19 countries. As partnerships went – not reunions, never call it a reunion – this was as good as it gets. More, to Robert's evident satisfaction, 'Stairway To Heaven' had not been performed once. According to Jimmy, however, the two were just getting started. "There's still an energy," he told *Uncut*'s Nigel Williamson. "We're still moving things around, still improvising as we always have. That's the thing that keeps us going."

But not, as it turned out, for that much longer.

CHAPTER 36

Blue Train

Come the end of 1996's *Unledded* tour, Robert Plant chose to fill his downtime by travelling the Silk Route through Central Asia. During the seventies, Jimmy Page might well have joined him. Not so now. In fact, he was busy starting another new family.

In what was to be an emotionally turbulent year, Jimmy and wife Patricia Ecker had separated in early 1995, the pair eventually divorcing and Ecker returning to New Orleans with their son James Jr. While the newspapers argued about custody battles and the exact terms of the financial settlement, Page had quietly begun another relationship with Jimena Gomez-Paratcha, whom he had met in Rio de Janeiro while promoting *No Quarter*.... Born in San Francisco to Argentinean parents, Jimena was already an established local community worker when she first encountered Jimmy, the two striking up conversation about the plight of street children in Brazil. Soon to witness genuine unrest between government forces and Rio shantytown locals for himself[312], Page was

---

312 Watching from his hotel window during downtime from promotional duties for *No Quarter...*, Page was reportedly shocked to witness Brazilian military and police forces using tanks and other weapons to quash civil disturbances in Rio's shantytown district (or 'favelas').

subsequently moved to set up a shelter for abandoned kids in the city, called 'Casa Jimmy', calling on Gomez-Paratcha's help while doing so.

Suffice to say, despite an age difference of almost 30 years – Page was 51, Jimena reportedly 23 – romance blossomed, with the couple considerably extending the perimeters of their charitable work together in subsequent years. A dark-eyed brunette who bore more than a passing resemblance to Jimmy's previous LA muse Lori Mattix, Gomez-Paratcha would have two children with Page – Zofia Jade (born in 1997) and Ashen Josan (1999). He also adopted Jimena's daughter, Jana, (born in 1994) from a previous relationship.

Though not quite as important as the life he was now building with his new partner, Jimmy had made several other important changes in intervening years, mainly in the field of property. In 1992, he parted ways with Boleskine. Despite having owned the house and its grounds since the early seventies, the guitarist rarely had time to visit, even after the demise of Zep, and decided to finally let it go. Inevitably, news of the sale briefly raked up old coals concerning Page's abiding interest in the life and work of Aleister Crowley. But whenever it was raised by journalists he was by now a master at changing the subject. "Well, those [old] interviews were a bit hard," he told *Guitar World*'s Joe Bosso. "The questions would be so... I mean, asking me about black magic and Aleister Crowley and whatnot. Gimme a break! It's all so stupid. I'd rather talk about music, you know? It's much better to talk about the music..."

Perhaps more surprisingly – given its practical application to him as a working musician and producer – Page had also sold The Sol at the start of the nineties. For the most part a profitable concern, the studio was regularly used by other acts throughout the previous decade, with Elton John recording two albums there and even Jimmy's old mate Jeff Beck popping in for a visit in 1989 for his own comeback disc, *Guitar Shop*. Like Page, the eighties were a torrid time artistically for the former Yardbird, Beck's eclectic brand of jazz rock and instrumental fireworks proving awkward to market in an age of cold synthesis and chilly samplers. A stab at updating his sound with hit-producer Nile Rodgers – 1985's *Flash* – had largely fallen on deaf ears, but as *Guitar Shop* came to show, like Jimmy, Jeff had a few surprises left in him.

A startling return to form featuring one of the finest displays of guitar playing ever committed to tape (the jaw-dropping 'Where Were You'), *Guitar Shop*'s resultant success put Beck back in the arenas and Odeons after a near 10-year absence. Unfortunately, he had to pay the piper to call the tune in order to do so. "It really hurt knowing Jimmy made all that bread [from us recording at Sol]," he later joked to *Musician*. "I even left my bike behind in his shed, so he got that too!"[313]

While some guitar fans were busy honouring Beck in the concert halls of America and Europe, others were furiously saving their pennies to buy Page's new signature model Gibson guitar. Suffice to say, it did not come cheap, but as the saying goes, 'One pays for luxury'. Based on Jimmy's revered 'No. 2' honeyburst Les Paul (which, like the fabled 'No. 1', had served him well onstage and in the studio since the early seventies), the axe in question featured a gorgeous maple top, 22-fret rosewood neck and gold-painted 'Jimmy Page autograph' on its headstock. Best of all were the 21 different sound combinations the guitar offered, with parallel, out-of-phase and humbucker/single coil options all accessible via its pick-ups, tone knobs and several switches hidden under the cream pickguard. Though there were some teething troubles between Gibson and Jimmy on the way to production – he allegedly threatened to pull out of backing the guitar unless the company rectified certain design specs and paid him a higher percentage on its $6,300 price-tag – the signature Les Paul made it into shops by late 1995, paving the way for several more Page-inspired Gibson designs in subsequent years.[314]

By the spring of 1997 it was back to the grind again, with Jimmy and Robert Plant reconvening in London to begin rehearsals for their first album of wholly new material since *In Through The Out Door*. Some

---

313 As surprising as the sale of The Sol, Page also parted ways with The Old Mill House at around the same time, though he was to buy the property back in subsequent years. That said, it wasn't for too long. By 2006, Jimmy had sold it again.

314 In addition to Page's signature 'No. 2' design, Gibson also worked with the guitarist on several other instruments, including a Custom shop replica of his stolen 1960 'Black Beauty' (with additional improvements suggested by Jimmy), plus inspired recreations of the legendary 'No. 1' 1959 sunburst Les Paul and EDS 'Stairway To Heaven' 6/12-string double-neck.

surprises were in store. Though the duo had benefited greatly by working with an Egyptian orchestra both on *No Quarter...* and their 1995/96 world tour, the musicians' services were now no longer required as Page and Plant made the decision to explore a more "intimate vibe".

This choice was mirrored by the band they would take into the recording studio with them. Stripping back to a core sound of just guitar, vocals, bass and drums (provided by a returning Charlie Jones and Michael Lee), the only additional places on the project were to be filled by Ed Shearmur (occasional programming), Tim Whelan (occasional keyboards) and Lynton Naiff (string arrangements on one track). More, in a massive break with previous protocol, Jones and Lee were to be credited as co-writers alongside Jimmy and Robert on all tracks. Even by the standards of latter-day Led Zeppelin, such equality in the ranks was worth noting.

Perhaps the biggest thunderbolt, however, was their choice of producer. Eschewing more traditional or well-known names, Page and Plant elected to go with Steve Albini, then best known for his pioneering work with grunge kings Nirvana and alternative quartet the Pixies. Preferring to go by the title "recording engineer" rather than anything more grand or 'hifalutin', Albini's style was also decidedly 'minimalist', his stated mission to capture the essential sound of the group rather than drown it in unnecessary frills. For Page, this was a huge bonus. "The greatest problem with a band that plays organically is someone to record it," he told *Q*'s James McNair. "We were fortunate to get Steve because he really knows how to EQ with microphones, that old science of recording." And while Jimmy was watching Steve, Albini was closely observing Page. "Jimmy is an immensely perceptive listener," he later confirmed to *Uncut*. "He can track every bird in the flock, hear through impossibly dense things to small details and intuitively know which are important."

With sessions at London's prestigious Abbey Road Studios due to start in early autumn, news of various other Page/Plant-related product began to break through in the summer months of 1997. The first item to be released was *The Inner Flame*, a benefit album in aid of guitarist Rainer Ptacek, who had played on Robert's 1993 set *Fate Of Nations*. Now suffering from brain cancer, a host of artists – including Emmylou Harris and PJ Harvey – contributed tracks to the cause, with Robert and Jimmy's own cover of Ptacek's tune 'Rude World' resembling a musical trip-hop around North Africa.[315] During this period, the pair also cut a track with the Jimmy Rogers All Stars, a starry ensemble put together to honour Muddy Waters' former guitarist and also featuring Mick Jagger, Keith Richards and Eric Clapton. Duetting with Rogers on John Lee Hooker's '(Boom Boom) Gonna Shoot You Right Down', Page obviously was having a ball, trading vintage licks alongside an old blues master while simultaneously stomping all over his very modern whammy pedal.

That said, it was a new album bearing the name 'Led Zeppelin' that really set fans' hearts a fluttering. Released on November 11, 1997, *Led Zeppelin – BBC Sessions* was a 24-track, two CD-package collecting four 'live'[316] 1969 BBC studio sessions (including the *Top Gear* and *Tasty Pop Sundae* dates referred to in Chapter 15) as well as most of the band's Paris Theatre concert of April 1, 1971.[317] Once meat and potatoes to countless bootleggers, these lost remnants were now housed in a swish set, replete with tasteful black and white cover, a concise written appreciation from journalist Luis Rey and individual transmission dates provided for each song. Whichever way the cake was cut, this really was a chance to travel back in time to the lost kingdom of Zep.

Arguably a much more satisfying collection than the problem-plagued *The Song Remains The Same*, ...*BBC Sessions* presented the group exactly as they were in their pomp: energised, loud, clever and occasionally breathtaking in their musical arrogance. Page – who had personally complied and mastered the tapes – called what he heard "telepathy", and on cuts such as *Top Gear*'s 'Whole Lotta Love', it was hard to argue with him. More immediate and brutal than the version that appeared on

---

315 Though the success of *The Inner Flame* helped cover Rainer Ptacek's medical costs, he sadly died on November 12, 1997.

316 Though the performances were billed as being live, occasional overdubs had been made at the time. "The BBC wanted the best show," Jimmy later said, "so an overdub here and there was fair game."

317 A third CD – collecting radio interviews with the band from 1969, 1976/77 and 1990 – was also part of an early limited edition, but it soon sold out.

Led Zeppelin II, such was the totality of the group's approach that there was little point focusing on any displays of individual brilliance. This was all about the greater whole. "Those performances are surprisingly good," John Paul Jones later said with a degree of understatement, "considering that we were playing in the BBC studios, a pretty sterile environment. There were only about 100 people watching us, so it was hard to generate the same kind of excitement you would have at a real gig."

Alongside the shattering punch of 'Communication Breakdown' – captured at the Playhouse Theatre on 27 June, 1969 and replete with an unhinged mid-section funk-rock interlude – there were also official debuts for Zep's cover of Eddie Cochran's 'Something Else' (disrespectfully good) and their Sleepy Jon Estes adaptation 'The Girl I Love (She Got Long Black Wavy Hair)' (as already discussed, blues, but not quite as we might know it). Further, the band's annexing of the Paris Theatre in 1971 also threw up the chance to again hear 'Stairway To Heaven' before it become the stuff of legend and the subject of many a backstage grumble between Jimmy and Robert. "Led Zeppelin," said Page, "were really moving the music [around] all the time."

This penchant for movement was illustrated by Jimmy's decision to include several alternative versions of various Zep tracks throughout the album. For instance, 'You Shook Me', 'I Can't Quit You Baby' and 'Whole Lotta Love' all appeared twice in the overall running order, while 'Communication Breakdown' hogged three spaces just on disc one. According to Page, such multiple inclusions better allowed listeners to hear the continuous development of the group while also acknowledging its commitment to improvisation. "Led Zeppelin was a band that would change things around substantially each time it played," he told *Guitar Player*. "The two performances of 'You Shook Me' are particularly good examples of what I'm talking about here. I mean, compare our sessions to, say, the BBC recordings of the Beatles. I bet you a cent to a dollar, if they do two or three versions of 'Love Me Do' or whatever, they'll all be identical. That [was] the difference between us and our contemporaries."

As with anything bearing the words 'Led Zeppelin' upon it, *...BBC Sessions* had no problem entering the charts, with the double CD reaching number 23 in the UK and sticking around for six more weeks.

Though perhaps a lower placement than one might have been expecting in Blighty, as ever, the Americans were much more enthusiastic when it came to parting with their cash for Zep collectibles. Pushing the album up to number 12 in the *Billboard* Hot 100, ...*BBC Sessions* would soon shift over two million copies in the States, propelled ever onwards by DJs spinning new takes on 'How Many More Times', 'What Is And Never Should Be' and whatever else tickled their fancy. "We were very young and cocky at the time, very sure of ourselves," said JPJ. And truth be told, frighteningly good, too.

Of course, the belated release of ...*BBC Sessions* only put pressure on Jimmy and Robert's forthcoming album, the pair's latest effort surely destined for comparison with their youthful heyday. Yet, despite the weight of expectation upon their now middle-aged shoulders, Page thought he and Plant's recent decision to jettison the orchestras and scale back their band had generated both new impetus and real clarity. "The most obvious thing for us to do," he told writer Michael Newquist, "was for us to go back to the four piece unit that we knew best and always worked for us. A lot of people thought we were going to carry on with that big extravaganza... but for us it was important to come to terms with the songs."

Completed over the course of 35 days at Abbey Road, *Walking Into Clarksdale* was released on 21 April, 1998. Its title, a clear reference to the geographical, and some might say spiritual, home of the blues, appeared on first hearing to be backwards leaning. But as the cover intimated – a tinted shot of two young boys dressed in angelic white wings by highly regarded rock photographer Anton Corbijn – and the contents confirmed, Page and Plant were not just looking to the Mississippi for inspiration. In fact, *Walking To Clarksdale* was a truly globe-trotting enterprise, with Jimmy and Robert drawing influences from Africa, Brazil, Southern California, film soundtracks and even the London electronica scene[318]. "It is what it is," said Plant at the time, "and the music, well, it's all there to be heard..."

318 In the run-up to ...*Clarksdale*'s release, Page and Plant had name-checked London-based world fusion/electronic act Transglobal Underground as an influence on the album's sound.

Walking Into Clarksdale was not the most comfortable of listens. With ideas "coming fast and furious" and, according to Page, many songs "written on the spot", the album often had a restless edge, its myriad influences flying this way and that without ever truly settling. This was evidenced on ...*Clarksdale*'s opening trio of tunes: 'Shining In The Light', 'When The World Was Young' and 'Upon A Golden Horse'. Pin-wheeling between breathy, ethereal passages that recalled the very best of Jeff Buckley[319], rough-house power chords from Jimmy and spiralling north African-style string arrangements (Lynton Naiff's work on '... Horse'), there was so much to listen to it was almost a struggle to keep up with it. Page and Plant mixed it up even more on 'Heart In Your Hand', a track that walked rapidly between *Pulp Fiction*-style Dick Dale surf guitar and 'Still I'm Sad'-period Yardbirds. Again fascinating. But again hard to hang a hat on.

This eclecticism permeated throughout *Walking Into Clarksdale*. As its title suggested, 'Burning Up' was all irritable, trebly guitars and thumping shifts in rhythm, Michael Lee and Charlie Jones' percussive attack affording Jimmy and Robert the opportunity to rock out circa 1971. But sitting right alongside all this noise was 'When I Was A Child'. Mournful (lost love and emotional vulnerability were a huge theme in Plant's lyrics throughout ... *Clarksdale*), slow-paced and full of tremolo-heavy chording from Page, the contrast was jarring rather than complimentary. 'Sons Of Freedom' was even more out there, Jimmy's de-tuned electrics and Lee's flying kit work not unlike "a soundtrack to the Brazilian martial art of Capoeira".

Yet, in among all the experimental verve and flying instrumental theatrics were also some tunes of proper distinction. 'Walking Into Clarksdale' itself was a wonderfully moody shot of swamp blues, sung with relish by Robert and featuring some genuinely unexpected leaps of faith from Jimmy's guitar. 'Blue Train' also delivered, its gentle

---

319 Page and Plant became huge fans of Jeff Buckley after seeing him in Australia while promoting *No Quarter...* in 1996. Having fallen in love with the singer-songwriter's astounding debut album *Grace*, Jimmy was shaken by Buckley' premature death in May 1997. "That was one of the greatest losses of all, Jeff Buckley," he later said.

chords and unhurried structure at times redolent of Jimi Hendrix's free-floating 'Little Wing'. Closest in terms of composition and feel to Page and Plant's work on *No Quarter...*, 'Most High'[320] took *Walking Into Clarksdale* right into the heart of the Moroccan desert, with Tim Whelan and Ed Shearmur's 'Oriental' keyboard flourishes and string pads cleverly aping the 11-piece orchestra that had brought *Unledded...* so vividly to life back in 1994. But if there was a stand-out track on *...Clarksdale*, it had to be 'Please Read The Letter'. Aptly described by Plant as "the place Roy Orbison meets the Grateful Dead's Jerry Garcia", the song not only showcased Robert's new, breathier vocal style and Charlie Jones' quick-witted bass fills, but also let Jimmy do what he did best: roving across the melody line like a carrion crow, Page picked, plucked, shook and struck at '... Letter', his playing confident, his execution faultless[321].

As baffling in sections as *Houses Of The Holy*, *Walking Into Clarksdale* confused as much as it beguiled. However, it was an album that drew the listener back to it again and again, its sly complexities worthy of re-investigation. The critics concurred. "*Walking Into Clarksdale*'s foundations are vintage Zeppelin – cool eccentricity, vintage folk, Indo-Egyptian exoticism – but the resulting edifice is far more subtle than Zep's big, phallic skyscraper," reasoned *Mojo*'s Sylvie Simmons. "There's no strutting, edgy, monster 'riff-rawk' on this album. Neither is there Zeppelin's sense of violence and danger. [Instead], real life has taken over from mythical landscapes and stairways to heaven, the lyrics are less ego, more first person. And the first person here doesn't seem to want you to squeeze his lemon but read his letter. *Walking Into Clarksdale* is," she concluded, "a complex, elegant, beautiful record."

---

320 Released as a single in May 1998, 'Most High' reached number 26 in the UK charts and also won a Grammy for 'Best Hard Performance' in 1999.

321 As ever, Page drew on a variety of guitars, amps and effects when recording *Walking Into Clarksdale*, using his trusty 'No. 1', EDS 1275 double-neck and Martin acoustic (among others). The biggest surprise, however, was the return of a Gretsch Country Gentleman to his guitar army, the same huge-bodied semi-acoustic he had utilised so efficiently with Neil Christian & the Crusaders in the early sixties.

Uncut's Peter Huxley also found much to enjoy. "The most gratifying aspect of Page and Plant's recent collaborations has been their mutual ability to keep each other's drives in check. [So], together they have produced, in effect, the first new Zeppelin album in 19 years, and the best in over 20 years. An album, which as a whole, should satisfy those who have been waiting... for a worthy sequel to *Physical Graffiti*."

With all tracks democratically credited to Page, Plant, Jones and Lee, and Jimmy happily singing the praises of engineer Steve Albini to anyone within earshot – "I'd love to work with him again," he said – *Walking Into Clarksdale* entered the UK and US charts at numbers three and eight respectively. However, the album did not sell in the millions, instead having to make do with a gold disc (500,000 sales) in America and some excellent reviews from British critics. Obviously, unlike ...*BBC Sessions* or *No Quarter...* before it, ...*Clarksdale*'s contrary nature and moody disposition didn't sit well with some Zep fans who, despite the advice of the critics, chose to reach for their dog-eared copies of *Physical Graffiti* instead. In Robert Plant's mind, they might well have been missing a trick. "The breadth, the access to every different kind of music that is available to people today is phenomenal, [but] most people don't even open their ears," he told *Uncut*. "It's 1998, and we're moving along..."

Jimmy Page had proved Plant's point in some style just two months before the release of *Walking Into Clarksdale* when he accepted an invitation from rapper/business mogul Puff Daddy (aka Sean Combs)[322] to collaborate on the theme tune to the monster movie *Godzilla*. Working through various ideas for a suitably giant-sized track, Daddy had eventually settled on taking the bones of Zep's 'Kashmir' and making it into something even more frightening. "He couldn't get the idea of 'Kashmir' out of his mind because of this huge beast Godzilla," Jimmy later told *Classic Rock*, "[and] he wanted to do something epic

---

322 A former business major who became the mastermind behind Bad Boy Entertainment, Daddy's 1997 debut album *No Way Out* sold 561,000 copies in the first week of its release. A Police-sampling single – 'I'll Be Missing You' – mourning the murder of his close friend Notorious B.I.G. was also the first rap tune to top the *Billboard* Hot 100.

musically." Days later, a phone call was put into Page. "He said, 'I can't get it out of my mind. I come up with some other ideas, but I keep returning to 'Kashmir'. I don't want to sample it... so would you please come and play on it?'"

Offer accepted in principle, Jimmy's already busy schedule meant he couldn't personally join Daddy in the studio, so a compromise was struck. Page would play his part "down a telephone line over the internet". With Puff in Los Angeles, Jimmy in slightly less glamorous Wembley and "massive delays with the audio [feed]", the deed was somehow still done in a matter of hours. Fast-forward several weeks and Page finally heard what had been done to the track when the two hooked up in New York. "It was absolutely epic," laughed the guitarist, "and he played it really loud too!" Fusing two orchestras, a suitably monstrous Bonzo–influenced drum sound and a growling, foul mouthed rap from the man himself to Jimmy's already ornery Les Paul, Puff Daddy had also given 'Kashmir' a new title in line with its new arrangement: 'Come With Me'.

In keeping with the rapper's well-established head for business (and indeed, Jimmy's own nous in that area), promotional activities for the single were ruthlessly efficient. With Page and Puff performing the tune live on *Saturday Night Live* in May 1998 – "He was fantastic," said the guitarist of his co-star, "[he was] doing the vocal in various different ways for each rehearsal, but they were always spot on" – and a strong radio/TV campaign also aiding its release, the duo could reasonably expect a Top 20 hit. But 'Come With Me' surpassed even Page's hopes, as the tune reached number two in the UK and four in USA, and went on to sell over a million copies. "People said 'Oh, you shouldn't have done that', but then you might as well say '[Jimmy], you shouldn't have dabbled in world music'," he later told *Record Collector*'s Pierre Perrone. "Of course I should have. I was doing that as a teenager, so why in heaven's name not? It's all part of the big picture."

While now an honorary member of the Harlem rap community, Jimmy perhaps wisely (or not, as things eventually turned out) chose to stick with Robert Plant in promoting *Walking Into Clarksdale*. Having already played a brief East European tour in February/March 1998 that included visits to Croatia, Bulgaria, Romania and Turkey (as well as a special 'one-off' gig at London's Shepherd's Bush Empire), they now turned westwards again for a new round of dates in America. Setting out their stall in Florida on 19 May, the pair continued to keep things tight on the instrumental front, with keyboardist Phil Andrews the only onstage addition to their now close-knit line-up of guitar, vocals, drums and bass. As before, the set was still heavy with Zep tracks, the likes of 'Rock And Roll', 'Heartbreaker', 'Tangerine' and 'Going To California' all steadily rotated as the show made its way across the States. However, after dipping liberally into the *Walking To Clarksdale* songbook at earlier gigs, Jimmy and Robert soon scaled back on the newer material, choosing to perform just four tracks – 'Walking...', 'Burning Up', 'Heart In Your Hand' and 'Most High' – from the album. Evidently, while "moving along" was eminently desirable for Robert and Jimmy, their audience had established firm limitations on how far they might go.

Come August, and Page and Plant were back in England for a headlining appearance at the Reading Festival. A fulsome night's entertainment that saw Jimmy brandishing his violin bow to rapturous applause during 'How Many More Times' (surely the finest number on ...*BBC Sessions*[323]), it was also a lovely surprise to hear 'Babe, I'm Gonna Leave You' dusted down and given a run out for the benefit of the Reading faithful. Once the track that brought Jimmy and Robert together, its return should have hinted at even better times ahead. Unfortunately, it was the song's title that gave the game away as to what was to happen next.

After a subsequent European trawl running right across the late autumn of 1998, Page and Plant marked the end of their year with a

---

323 Recorded at the Playhouse Theatre on June 27, 1969, the 12-minute version of 'How Many More Times' that appeared on ...*BBC Sessions* featured a heavily improvised middle-section, with snippets of the Yardbirds' 'Shapes Of Things' popping up towards song's end. Indeed, Page's relentless, pummelling 'E' chord at the finale may well have been an influence on David Bowie and guitarist Mick Ronson, who used a similar trick at the conclusion of 1973's 'Jean Genie'.

short but pithy four-song set at Paris' 17,000-seater Bercy stadium in aid of *Amnesty International*. Joining Bruce Springsteen, Peter Gabriel, Radiohead, Tracy Chapman and Alanis Morisette, the duo were all smiles from the stage, their closing number 'Rock And Roll' performed with the same intensity as it had been over the course of 88 gigs in 18 countries throughout the year. Yet, backstage, Robert Plant was starting to feel the burn again. "All the big trappings," he later told *Tight But Loose*, "it becomes exasperating..." 'Babe, I'm Gonna Leave You' it was.

Though plans had already been drawn up for another round of Australian and Japanese shows early in the New Year, Plant had simply had enough. Nonetheless, when the phone call finally came, it was still a shock to his colleagues and manager. "To be honest, by 1998, early 1999, I think Robert was starting to go through the motions," said Dave Lewis. "There were other things on his mind, but again, he was keeping it quiet, so when he did walk away, it was still a surprise. I was actually in Bill Curbishley's office when the news came through he wasn't going to do the tour. I think we were all dumfounded." Despite efforts made to change his mind, Plant was not for turning. "Why?" he later told *Q's* James McNair. "Because I just didn't want to do it anymore. I'd just had enough. There was a spring coming. It was February. The options were to go to Japan and Australia, and then come back through Hawaii. I just thought 'How many more British springs can you see now?'"And that, according to Robert, was that.

By all accounts, Jimmy Page was loathe to let Plant walk away in a hurry. Now five years, two albums and nearly 200 gigs into the experiment, he had not seen things come this far to have them fall away on what might just be a temperamental whim. Locking in the services of drummer Michael Lee, Page reportedly began sending the singer a series of demo tapes in the hope of luring him back. It was all in vain. "I wanted to keep working," Jimmy confirmed to writer Nick Kent in 2003. "But Robert wouldn't hear of it." Indeed, if Page had his way, things might have led to something even more intriguing. "Well, I wanted to eventually bring in John Paul Jones," he said, "but it was hard enough getting two of us together, let alone three." Stripped of any remaining options, Jimmy surrendered to the inevitable. It was done.

But Jimmy wasn't. Having been in similar straits before, the guitarist was in no hurry to return to the torpor and uncertainty that had defined the early eighties for him. Now healthier (certainly wealthier), gig-hardened and still raring to go, if Robert wasn't coming out to play anymore, he'd find someone who would. It turned out to the Black Crowes.

The union started on July 27, 1999, when Page found himself front and centre of an impressively attended benefit show held at London's prestigious Café de Paris. Organised by Jimmy's now wife Jimena and several of her friends and work colleagues, the event was in aid of two specific charities: 'Scream' (Supporting Children through Re-Education And Music) and the ABC Trust (Action for Brazilian Children), the latter of which both Page and his partner had recently established, with Jimmy acting as Founding Patron. A starry night, the Scream/ABC shindig saw the former Zep man performing alongside Michael Lee, bassist Guy Pratt, Aerosmith's Joe Perry and Steven Tyler as well as the Crowes, of whom Page was already an extremely vocal supporter. "The first thing I heard by them was 'Hard To Handle', and I remember thinking 'Jesus, that guy sings good!'" he later told *Classic Rock*'s Mick Wall. "Then I heard something else and I bought the album. And you know, I don't really buy albums by new bands..."

Deep-fried rock'n'roll in the hearty tradition of the Faces, the Stones and the Allman Brothers, the Black Crowes first came to light back in 1990 when their debut album *Shake Your Money Maker* sold in the millions on the back of hit singles 'Hard To Handle', 'She Talks To Angels' and 'Jealous Again'. Led by siblings Chris and Rich Robinson (vocals and lead guitar respectively), the quintet's subsequent penchant for endless jamming and Zep-like instrumental interludes quickly endeared them to a rock community who, in the face of grunge, were starved of old-school dynamics and lusty guitars. With follow-up discs *The Southern Harmony And Musical Companion* and *Amorica* also doing reasonable business worldwide, the group – while never quite becoming stadium-sized – had nonetheless remained a fairly consistent concert draw. Cutting a dash with them on 'Shake Your Moneymaker', 'Woke Up This Morning', Sonny Boy Williamson's off-kilter 'Sloppy Drunk' and 'In My Time Of Dying' at the Café de Paris, Page was obviously enamoured with both the Crowes' sound and attitude. So much so, in fact, that he ended the gig by dragging the Robinson brothers back on stage for a valve-soaked take on 'You Shook Me'. "Such great guys," he later said. "We had such a good time doing what we did."

Watching all this carefully from the wings was the Black Crowes' manager (and former business associate of Van Halen's David Lee Roth), Pete Angelus. Seeing an angle that might work for his clients while also harnessing all the loose energy Page had failed to shake off following Robert Plant's departure for the Priory Of Brion[324], Angelus approached Jimmy about the prospect of both camps teaming up for a series of US dates. Keen to return to the road again, and with his own manager Bill Curbishley gradually warming to the idea – "Well, it's all about enjoyment, isn't it?" Curbishley later told writer Alan di Perna – Page was in. By October 12, 1999, he and the Black Crowes were onstage at the Roseland Ballroom for a three-night stop-off in the Big Apple.

Unlike the massed, multi-cultural exoticism of *No Quarter...* and subsequent North African-themed improvisations on tour with Plant et al., the Led Zeppelin tunes Page performed with the Black Crowes in New York were faithful to their source and knee deep in rock'n'roll and the blues. Feasting heavily on his own back catalogue, Jimmy and his new buddies made tasty work of the likes of 'Sick Again', 'Celebration Day', 'The Lemon Song' and 'Out On The Tiles', while also wrestling 'Hey Hey What Can I Do' and 'What Is And What Should Never Be' from the back of the musical fridge. More, with Page now having access to three guitars onstage instead of just one (in addition to Rich Robinson, the Crowes also boasted rhythm man Audley Freed in their line-up), he could also tackle more challenging Zep fare such as 'Ten

---

324 Soon after leaving Page/Plant, Robert put together a new folk/blues group called the Priory Of Brion with friend and former Band of Joy member Kevyn Gammond. Drawing on a set that included covers of old Love, Tim Hardin and Them songs, the Priory hit the road in July 1999 for a series of small-scale gigs across the UK.

Years Gone'. "It wasn't until I played with the Crowes that I heard all the [guitar] parts to things like 'Ten Years...' live," said Jimmy. "That was such a thrill."

It was also quite thrilling to hear what the Black Crowes made of covering Led Zeppelin. In the main, the results were splendid. Always a bit of a firecracker when it came to vocals, Chris Robinson had few troubles singing his way through 'Your Time Is Gonna Come', 'In My Time Of Dying' or even 'Whole Lotta Love', that soulful drawl lending these old-time classics "a real tang of Otis Redding, Sam Phillips and Rod Stewart". The band themselves were equally a dab hand at negotiating the various curveballs Zep tunes threw at them, with drummer Steve Gorman, keyboardist Ed Harsch and bassist Sven Pipien all ably supporting Jimmy, Rich Robinson and Audley Freed as they took care of the big riffs front of house.

"Anyone can have a crack at a Zeppelin song and plenty do," Page later told Mick Wall. "But to do it properly, especially when someone who partially created those songs is standing there, well, it can't have been easy. But the Black Crowes did it, and with their own identity intact, too. I mean the way Chris sang them... [it was] just amazing." With Page more than happy to contribute to a few Crowes numbers during the set (his work on 'Wiser Time', 'Hard To Handle' and 'Remedy' was exceptional), and a surprise or two thrown in for good measure – the Yardbirds' 'Shapes Of Things' was also removed from its time capsule and given a good airing – the Crowes/Jimmy Page "super team" had all the makings of a tidy little tour. "Musicians playing together," said Chris Robinson, "it's like a conversation, and I want our conversation to be really intriguing, and interesting and beautiful..."

After their three nights at New York's Roseland Ballroom, Page and the Crowes moved quickly up the East Coast to Boston's Centrum hall (October 16). Deep in the heart of Aerosmith country[325], Joe Perry

325 As many already know, and Aerosmith are justly proud to point out, the band have always called Boston their hometown.

again joined the troupe for a stuttering take on 'You Shook Me' and Fleetwood Mac's 'Oh Well', a song that purportedly influenced the stop/start structure of Zep's own 'Black Dog'. Then it was on to Los Angeles for two nights at the Greek Theatre (October 18 & 19), where the shows were taped. Here, the old met neatly with the new as vintage Zep tunes soon found themselves on sale via *musicmaker.com* in February 2000 as part of an internet-only release entitled *Excess All Areas: Jimmy Page & The Black Crowes Live At The Greek*. It hit number seven on *Billboard*'s brand-new 'Internet Albums' chart. Having started his recording career cutting songs on a four-track machine in grimy rooms throughout the back streets of London, Page might have been thrown by the prospect of such progressive technology. Instead, he was almost childlike in his enthusiasm. "The listener at home becomes the A&R man," he told *Guitar World*. "He's the one who chooses the tracks, and that's cool." Not if your name was John Kalodner.

Flush with the success of their internet endeavour – and now with a more standard two-CD package of the Greek Theatre gig in shops to promote[326] – Page and the Crowes were back on the road in the summer of 2000 for a co-headlining US tour alongside Jimmy's old mates the Who. Another band that had clawed their way out of the sixties with popularity largely intact, they had been managed by Bill Curbishley since the mid-seventies, making this three-month double-header across the States both financially appealing and potentially trouble-free.

Yet, by early August, Page's old back problems had re-emerged, leading to the cancellation of several shows and his subsequent bailing out of a European/Japanese tour scheduled for the late autumn. Though no official reason was given as to the actual cause of Jimmy's woes, one didn't have to be a doctor to figure out it might be work

---

326 ...*Live At The Greek* was issued in CD format on 4 July, 2000. For contractual/legal reasons, none of the Black Crowes' own compositions were featured on the album. However, their distinctive avian logo was displayed alongside Jimmy's now proudly returned 'ZoSo' symbol on the cover. The record hit numbers 39 and 64 in the UK/US charts.

related. After decades of hanging heavy Les Pauls and double-necks somewhere around his knees while simultaneously tearing around stadium stages like a Dragon-suited Chuck Berry, there was bound to be a knock-on effect on his body. The doctors ordered a break from touring. For once, the normally cavalier Page took their advice. At nearly 57 years old, the days of self-medicating with lashings of Jack Daniels and various other pain-numbing medications had obviously come to an end.

As had Jimmy Page's time with the Black Crowes. Though there was vague talk of rescheduling the cancelled dates (which included three high-profile nights at Madison Square Garden in October), Page did not return to the fray. "That was a short reincarnation, unfortunately," he later told Q. With benefit of hindsight, however, there was probably no real need for him to come back. After all, the Black Crowes had their own destiny to fulfil[327], and even if Jimmy had committed to another tour, the liaison would soon come to be viewed for what it really was: a Led Zep covers band. A damned good one at that, mind, but a covers band nonetheless.

Besides, according to Page, something far more interesting was around the corner. Having already premiered a moody new instrumental called 'Domino' at Net Aid in New York back in October 1999[328], he had again begun talking up another solo album. "It's still early days and I can't really tell you what it is exactly," he told *Classic Rock* in 2000, "but it's the sort of thing people are going

---

327 Following their break with Page, the Crowes continued to tour and record until 2002 when they took the first of several hiatuses. Despite subsequent reunions, as of 2016, continuing disputes between Chris and Rich Robinson have again rendered the band inactive.

328 An anti-poverty internet initiative transmitted from multiple venues on October 9, 1999, Net Aid pulled together Page and the likes of Bono, Puff Daddy and Sting, where Jimmy premiered a new tune – 'Domino' – onstage at Giants Stadium. The enterprise raised $830,000, setting a new record at the time for an online charity show. A grumbling instrumental played on a baritone 6/12 Jerry Jones guitar, Jimmy was joined for 'Domino' by bassist Guy Pratt and ever-loyal sticksman Michael Lee.

to say 'Thank God, I've always wanted him to do that!'" In spite of losing Robert Plant to the vagaries of artistic wanderlust and a round of concerts to a bad back, Jimmy, it seemed, was reinvigorated, happy and ready to go again. Yet, as time came to show, his future role was to be more connected to past than present, as Page became custodian, guardian and gatekeeper of one of the most illustrious legacies in rock history.

CHAPTER 37

The Ocean

Led Zeppelin had never really gone away. As the success of *Remasters*, *No Quarter...*, *...BBC Sessions* and even *Live At The Greek* proved, the audience for the band – in no matter what form or computation – was still there. Indeed, for some, they remained the yardstick by which all other groups should be judged. "I saw Zep... between their first and second album at the New York State Pavilion," Kiss' Paul Stanley recalled to *Guitar World*. "They were the most astonishing band I've ever seen to this day. There's nothing that even comes close to what I witnessed that night. When it was over... my friend and I looked at each other and said, 'Let's not say anything. Let's not cheapen it'. We never spoke about it, because Led Zeppelin were the perfect marriage of all the elements that made great rock'n'roll. Sexy. Ruthless. And dangerous." And seemingly never to return again. "Led Zeppelin," Robert Plant told Q in 2002, "is preserved in aspic. And that," he concluded, "is the best place for it."

Try as Robert might to pickle the band, nobody was quite willing to let him do it. Back in May 1997, for instance, Led Zeppelin were presented with a 'Lifetime Achievement' gong at the 42nd Ivor Novello Awards in London. On this occasion, all three remaining members attended, with Page, Plant and Jones having squared any differences after the foolishness of *No Quarter...*. Roll on 22 months, and Page and Jones were in New York picking up a 'Diamond' trophy from the Recording Industry Association of America to celebrate sales of 10 and 11 million for *Houses Of The Holy* and *Led Zeppelin II*. By then, the group's biggest seller, 1971's 'Four Symbols', was well on its way to 20 million copies sold. God knows, even the runt of the litter – 1976's *Presence* – had now shifted three million units and counting. These were big numbers, and Page was proud as punch. "Who can complain," he said, "about being so successful after 30 years?"

Yet, for a band so often heard, there was precious little visual evidence of their 12-year life span. "That was the thing, though," said Chris Charlesworth. "While Peter Grant and Jimmy were more than happy to use radio as a promotional tool and have the songs played endlessly over the airwaves – big royalties, after all – they also wanted Zep to retain their mystique. Therefore, TV appearances were usually frowned upon by the band and people had to go and actually see them instead. Brilliant strategy as it turned out, given the amount of money they made and the amount of stadiums they played, but it left precious little camera footage after the event, at least as far we knew. Led Zeppelin were heard, but unless you had a concert ticket or an old video copy of *The Song Remains The Same*, seldom seen." Thankfully, Jimmy Page was about to rectify that.

As evidenced, following his collaboration with the Black Crowes, Page had intimated that a second solo album might be on the way, with the grumbling 'Domino' the first evidence of it. Yet it didn't happen. Instead, Jimmy popped up here and there as the mood took him. Proving that while he and Robert might have gone their separate ways in difficult circumstances back in 1999 there was no bad blood between them, Page joined Plant onstage at the Montreux Festival on July 7, 2001 to celebrate 'A Night Of Sun Records'. With the pair having already contributed a punchy cover of Sonny Burgess' 'My Bucket's Got A Hole In It' for the label's tribute album *Good Rocking Tonight*, Jimmy and Robert's performance in Switzerland was predictably strong on the rockabilly angle. Utilising stand-up bass (courtesy of Big Town Playboy Bill Jennings) and also featuring Mike Watts on skinny drums, the hastily assembled quartet bashed through 'My Bucket...' before veering into *Presence*'s 'Candy Store Rock', Zep's own take on hillbilly swinging. Having been a Sun Records fan as a teenager, this was a little dream come true for Page but, as ever, all the papers wanted to talk about was another possible collaboration with Plant. Within months, the singer silenced them completely by releasing his seventh solo album, the sixties-tinged *Dreamland*.

In the meantime, Jimmy continued to show his face at the odd industry bash or benefit gig. An unlikely team-up with Limp Bizkit frontman Fred Durst and Puddle Of Mudd's Wes Scantlin at the *MTV Europe Awards* in Frankfurt on November 8, 2001 resulted in a surprisingly faithful rendition of Zep's 'Thank You', with nary a nu-metal power chord in sight. Page was also in attendance at London's Royal Albert Hall in February 2002 for a Teenage Cancer Trust charity concert, though the circumstances were a little weird, to say the least. When Robert Plant bounded onto the stage with his new band Strange Sensation for a six-song set that included 'Four Sticks', Jimmy was nowhere to be seen. Ditto, when Page struck into 'Dazed And Confused' alongside various members of the Paul Weller Band and Ocean Colour Scene, Plant, too, was missing in action. Reportedly, there were no issues between them, just unfortunate scheduling. Ultimately, however, it was Jimmy Page's latest enterprise – *DVD* – that would finally allow fans to see what he and Robert looked and sounded like while they were in Led Zeppelin.

As with all serious Zep-related undertakings, the project had actually been in gestation for years, its roots connected to the UK release of 'Whole Lotta Love' as a single in September 1997. Given that Zep had never issued a '45' in Great Britain during their lifetime, this was a bold step at the time and Page was keen to mark it with an impressive promotional video.[329] Trawling through old film footage of the band in his own archives, he soon realised there was enough there to merit a possible "visual document" of Led Zeppelin. With the rise of DVD at

---

329 Released by Atlantic Records in mid-September 1997 – just three weeks before *...BBC Sessions* hit stores – 'Whole Lotta Love' reached number 21 in the UK charts. A CD digipack with a very cool retro-leaning cover, it was backed by 'Baby Come Home' and 'Travelling Riverside Blues'.

the turn of the new century and its radically improved sound/picture quality, Page had a format he deemed truly worthy of the band.

Settling into the task at hand with trademark intensity, Jimmy hired director Dick Carruthers to assist him on the project. A steady hand whose previous work on *The Who's Live At The Royal Albert Hall* three-CD/DVD box set had particularly impressed Page, Carruthers and the guitarist began the painstaking chore of 'ear and eye marking' material for possible inclusion on the disc. While digitally linking visuals with pre-existing audio tapes was a given, ensuring the finished product sounded perfect was just as important. To this end, Jimmy brought in Kevin Shirley to help. Nicknamed 'The Caveman', Shirley had already carved out a notable career engineering/producing bands such as Rush, Aerosmith and Journey during the mid-nineties. Yet, it was his involvement with ...*Live At The Greek* that brought him into Page's orbit. "I think everyone was impressed with it," he later confirmed, "certainly Jimmy said he was." Assuming the role of sound engineer, the South African's keen attention to detail and reputation for "getting it done" again strengthened the pedigree of an already distinguished cast.

By mid-2002, real progress had been made. Though Jimmy's original intention was to concentrate on Zep's 1970 Royal Albert Hall show (to which he had recently acquired the rights), the perimeters of what would become *DVD* were now much more considerable. In addition to the RAH, Page had also accessed both 1979 Knebworth gigs and the original masters of the 1973 New York MSG performances used (in part) for *The Song Remains The Same*. But perhaps the best find of the lot was a crop of footage from the band's Earls Court concerts of May 1975. Still, according to Page, this trove of treasures was not easy to unlock. "I loaded all the live stuff that we had, which isn't that much, surprisingly. I mean, we thought we had three nights recorded from Earls Court or whatever, but then you find out that the recording truck broke down on the first night, the bass drum wasn't being recorded on the second night and all that sort of stuff. Still," he laughed, "it's an epic!"

Now a potentially career-spanning retrospective rather than snapshot of Led Zeppelin circa 1970, Jimmy, Dick Carruthers and Kevin Shirley pulled in the last strands of the package. In addition to the concerts, Zep's frighteningly select TV appearances were now gobbled up from various sources. From France came footage of the pop show *Tous En Scene*, while Denmark provided gorgeous testimony of early Led Zeppelin on black and white film stock. 1969's *Supershow* also threw in a fine performance of 'Dazed And Confused', while a number of press conferences (New York, 1970), TV interviews (Australia, 1972 and UK, 1975) and promos old and new ('Communication Breakdown from 1969, 'Over The Hills...' and 'Travelling Riverside Blues' from 1990) finally completed the set. Carruthers rightly called the process "building a cathedral out of matchsticks". But as ever, Page was building history. "We wanted something that would trace the journey of Led Zeppelin," he said. "In that context, it's a truly historical document."

Encased in a typically inscrutable cover sleeve featuring the burnished sands and towering edifices of the USA's Monument Valley (actually the West and East Mitten Buttes of Navajo Tribal Park), *DVD* was released on May 26, 2003. And though Jimmy's description of its contents might have been rather grandiloquent, he was also essentially correct. A stunning record of Led Zeppelin spanning over a decade of the band's life, *DVD* proved itself a minor revelation, allowing an audience who were not there first time around to now engage with the legend 14 years gone. "*DVD* was a great moment because there were so many new fans who hadn't actually seen Zep in the flesh," said Dave Lewis. "Suddenly they were getting five hours of the closest thing to actually being in the same room as the band."

With the Royal Albert Hall gig of 1970 sounding as fresh and vital as the night they played, and 'In My Time Of Dying' and 'Trampled Under Foot' from Earls Court confirming once and for all that John Bonham truly was "God's own drummer", highlights were many and disappointments almost non-existent. Even Knebworth – at the time considered by many to be a sub-par performance from the band – now took on a charm all its own, with 'Achilles Last Stand' and 'Whole Lotta Love' shattering reminders of Page's abilities with six strings and a pick. For Robert Plant, who like John Paul Jones had given Jimmy his full blessing on the enterprise, *DVD* might have been better still if there had been more cameramen on hand to capture what happened offstage. "How amazing it all looked... [just] frighteningly superb," he later told *Uncut*. "It's just a shame we never had fly on the wall cameras. There's so much missed out. But we never thought of what was happening as important in historical terms that needed to be chronicled. In fact, the other day I found some photos of us in Morocco, and there's Page and me joyously doing a line of coke off the bonnet of some old car with both the moon and the sun in the background. What an image!" Still, given all those stories of strange fish, even stranger women and Herculean drug use, perhaps some things were better left unseen...

Topping the US charts and coming in at number three in the UK, *DVD* sold by the truckload. Breaking the previous BBC sales record for music videos by a margin of three to one, the two-disc set would eventually shift millions of copies worldwide, while also claiming the title of America's highest-selling music DVD for three years in a row. Its release also allowed publications who had held a largely dim view of Led Zeppelin in their prime to now return to the band with fresh ears. "[*DVD*]," said *Rolling Stone*'s Michael Azerrad, "is the Holy Grail of heavy metal, [and] one of the best rock documentaries ever made."

While *DVD* was breaking records left, right and centre, Led Zeppelin's new live album, *How The West Was Won*, seemed to have been caught up in the undertow of it success. Arriving just a day after Zep's new visual extravaganza, the three-CD set comprised two concerts recorded at the LA Forum and Long Beach Arena on 25/27th June, 1972, which Page had come across while searching through his archives for *DVD*. "I discovered two performances which I remember at the time were really good," he told *Guitarist* in 2003. "I'd always wanted to capture what we were doing in LA as we always played at our optimum there. I have memories of that place that somehow just brings something out of you, whether it was the Yardbirds or Zeppelin. LA is always fantastic, so I hope I haven't jinxed myself with that. Each member of the band was playing at their best during those performances and giving like 150 per cent. And when the four of us were playing like that, we combined to make a fifth element. That was the magic, the intangible."

Again, there was little exaggeration here. Another bold testament to the band's live power at (or nearing) their prime, *How The West Was Won* offered 18 tracks of undiluted (and unedited) Zep[330], a fact confirmed by the 19, 23 and 25-minute running times for 'Moby Dick', 'Whole Lotta Love' and 'Dazed And Confused'. Though hideously long when compared with the more abrupt mechanisms of modern rock and pop, there was still no denying that certain passages of *How The West Was Won* retained the ability to move small mountains: Bonham's wilful destruction of his kit during 'Bring It On Home'. Robert's lascivious grunts during 'Black Dog'. JPJ's sublime bass fills all over 'Over The Hills And Far Away', and indeed, Page's mad riff festival on a speedy 'Heartbreaker'. All showboating, sure enough, but it still bashed *The Song Remains The Same* into a cocked hat. "What has been the Achilles heel in Led Zeppelin's otherwise formidable back catalogue?" asked *Rolling Stone*. "The lack of a killer live album... on par with the Who's *Live At Leeds* or the Rolling Stones' *Get Yer Ya Ya's Out!* [Well,] the wait is over. *How The West Was Won*... captures Zep in prime swagger, fresh off their masterpiece *Led Zeppelin IV* and with *Houses Of The Holy* just around the corner."

On its own terms, *How The West Was Won* might well have eclipsed the commercial success of many a Led Zeppelin compilation. And to its credit, the album did reach numbers one and five in the USA and UK in its first week of release, with sales eventually topping a million. Yet, while *DVD* continued to soar commercially, *How The West...* was largely forgotten within months. A shame really, given the fact that as live Zep albums go, this was probably their finest hour. "*How The West Was Won* was a fantastic live album," said Dave Lewis, "but the mistake they made with that was putting it in the shops so close to the release of *DVD*, which let's not forget, got a phenomenal response. As a result, *How The West...* was shoved under the carpet a bit."

330 Like *DVD*, Kevin Shirley was brought on board to oversee engineering duties on *How The West Was Won*, though Eddie Kramer was credited for making the original recording. As ever, Page produced the album.

With all this new Zep activity, the old questions returned. As Page, Plant and Jones did the promotional rounds in support of both *DVD* and *How The West Was Won* throughout the late spring of 2003, journalists continued to ask about the possibility of a reunion. Robert was all smiles, but resolute as ever. "I don't think it could happen in this century," he said. "Zep was a rollercoaster... four guys melding into this great fusion of music. And it's gone." Jones, on the other hand, cited Bonzo's absence as the main impediment to progress: "It just wouldn't be the same." But Jimmy, well, Jimmy was still holding out hope. "I wouldn't discount it," he told *Tight But Loose* at the time. "[But] I just don't know..." For the next four years, Page would stay in the dark about the fate of Led Zeppelin, his main duties now confined to picking up various awards in respect of his charitable efforts and a band it seemed would never see light of day again.

The honour roll began in earnest on February 12, 2005, when Jimmy, John Paul Jones and John Bonham's children Jason and Zoe were the recipients of a 'Lifetime Achievement' crystal trophy at the 47th Annual Grammy Awards. Robert, then preparing for another solo tour, ducked the ceremony, sending a taped message in his place. Angered by what he saw as the singer's impertinence, Jimmy let his feelings be known to the press. "It wouldn't have taken much to pop over and meet everybody, would it? But I'm sure Robert had good reasons..." Plant said nothing. Up next was the bizarre sight of Page ringing the 'opening bell' at New York's Stock Exchange on May 11, 2005. There to acknowledge the public floating of shares for Warners Music – who now owned Jimmy's old label Atlantic – the guitarist also proceeded to knock out the opening chords of 'Whole Lotta Love' to the gathered traders who duly whooped along in support. With Page having made countless millions for Atlantic back in the day, it was the least they could do. Three months later and he was back in London's Piccadilly Circus with his hands covered in cement, becoming the first musician to receive a star on the 'London Walk of Fame'. Actually the second time he had left his prints behind for posterity (on December 7, 1993, Jimmy was honoured with a gold star at Hollywood's 'Rock Walk' by presenter and fan Eddie Van Halen), Page proved humble in his acceptance speech. "If you started putting in all the people I think are deserving," he told the assembled press, "you'd cover the whole of London."

Elsewhere in his life, Page's good deeds did not go unrewarded. In recognition of his charitable works for the city with Action For Brazil's Children's Trust and Task Brazil, Jimmy was made an honorary citizen of Rio de Janeiro in mid-2005 by Paulo Melo, leader of Brazil's Democracy Party. With millions raised through functions, fundraisers, concerts and drives, Page and his wife Jimena had not only enabled street kids and single mothers access to healthcare, shelter and education, but also raised wider public awareness of the problems faced by many in Brazil's beautiful but also troubled conurbations.

By the end of the year, his own nation joined Brazil in bestowing on Jimmy one of its greater honours, as the guitarist was summoned by the Queen to London's Buckingham Palace on December 14 to receive an OBE, or in royal parlance, the 'Order of the British Empire'. Again awarded for his charitable endeavours, Page had met actually Her Majesty nine months before at a dinner acknowledging the achievements of the British music industry. On that occasion, he had been joined by Eric Clapton, Jeff Beck and Queen's Brian May, and the conversation proved droll. When May reportedly pointed out that he had played the national anthem atop a turret at Buckingham Palace as part of the Queen's Golden Jubilee celebrations in 2002, the monarch was said to have replied "Oh, was that you?" She next turned her attention to Eric Clapton. He fared little better. Obviously unaware of Eric's 40 years of preaching the blues, Her Majesty enquired of the guitarist "Have you been playing long?" before moving on to Beck. Ever the comedian, the rooster-haired hoodlum offered a hand and introduced himself with the words "I'm Jeff". Sadly, Page's conversation with Her Majesty went unrecorded.

A year later, and Jimmy was back among his own when Led Zeppelin were inducted into the UK Music Hall of Fame, a new-ish Brit take on the long-established American gong show of a very similar name. Televised in early December 2006, a small legion of admirers all gathered before the cameras to bear testimony on behalf of Page and Zep, who were being inducted alongside the Beach Boys' Brian Wilson, Prince and Rod Stewart, among others. From Queen's Roger Taylor ("There is no better drummer than John Bonham, end of debate!") to Guns N' Roses' Slash and Black Sabbath's Tony Iommi, rock star after rock star sang Zep's praises before Aussie rockers Wolfmother closed proceedings with a brazen cover of 'Communication Breakdown'.

Though it had now been nearly six years since Jimmy had produced any new music to speak of, he still seemed eager to talk up the prospect of solo album number two after the event. According to him, it might finally see light of day sometime in late 2007. "It's an album that I really need to get out of my system... there's a good album in there and it's ready to come out," he confirmed at the time to the BBC. But as ever, the words 'Led' and 'Zeppelin' were also never far from his lips. "Yes, there will be some Zeppelin things on the horizon," Page promised, before adding "I'm not retired yet..."

As if to prove the point, Jimmy had recently turned up on *Last Man Standing*, the latest studio disc from fifties rock'n'roll pioneer Jerry Lee Lewis. A man – as evidenced in chapter four of this book – who could teach most musicians a thing or two about drinking, drugging and questionable teen romances, Lewis was now nearly 70 years old but, like Page, in no mood to throw in the towel just yet. Having somehow outlasted his Sun Records cohorts Elvis Presley, Johnny Cash and Carl Perkins (hence the album's title), Jerry now assembled an impressive roll-call of musicians including Keith Richards, Eric Clapton, Bruce Springsteen, BB King, Ringo Starr and Willie Nelson for album number 39, and Jimmy Page was on it. Accompanying the irascible pianist on a cover of Zep's 'Rock And Roll', Page let fly with a few licks he probably hadn't played since treading the boards with Neil Christian while Lewis rode the keys and hogged the microphone in his unique trademark style. Lovely and lively, Jimmy and Jerry's rendition of 'Rock And Roll' was only surpassed by Mick Jagger's duet with the old master on his own 'Evening Gown', its blend of humour, pathos and honky-tonk piano as pleasurable as a midnight whiskey.

By mid-2007, it became clear that Page's second solo disc would not be released for some while yet, with the guitarist again postponing his own endeavours to gather together yet another Zep compilation.

The sixth such enterprise in 10 years[331], this one was called *Mothership*, and its contents had been specifically chosen by Page, Plant and JPJ. A two-CD set – though deluxe, collector's and vinyl editions were also planned[332] – its release on November 12 was tied into Zep's entire back catalogue being made available in digital format for the first time. All well and good that Zep were ready to enter the iTunes age, of course, but with no new material on the track listing, many a fan was also ready to walk on by. After all, with the band long gone and the archives now seemingly dry, the prospect of hearing it all again – even in re-shuffled form – was hardly that enthralling.

But then in September 2007, something wonderful happened. After so many years occasionally flickering on amber, but mostly stalled at red, the light that had held back Led Zeppelin's reunion for so long suddenly "flashed to green". And, as writer Robert Sandall correctly surmised, "The world went mad." Or at least a little bonkers.

Though soon to be the cause of some celebration, the genesis of Led Zeppelin's 2007 reunion had its roots firmly planted in the death of Atlantic's co-founder Ahmet Ertegun a year before. Described by Robert Plant at the time as "A friend, a sidekick, a true member of Led Zeppelin's entourage", Ertegun's passing on December 14, 2006[333] had also been observed in Jimmy's acceptance speech at the UK Music Hall

---

331 In 1999 and 2000, Led Zeppelin released *Early Days* and *Latter Days*, two CD collections compiling the group's efforts from 1968-1971 and 1973-1979 respectively. Containing some enhanced content of Zep performing 'Communication Breakdown' in 1969 (culled from Swedish TV) and 'Kashmir' (from Earls Court 1975), the discs reached number 71 in the UK and 81 in the USA. While initial chart positions were disappointing, as with most everything band-related, these sets (later combined as *The Best Of Led Zeppelin*) still managed to reach a million sales in due course.

332 Some editions of *Mothership* would contain an addition disc of highlights from 2003's *DVD*.

333 On October 29, 2006, Ertegun had attended a Stones concert at New York's Beacon Theatre. While backstage, he tripped and fell, striking his head on the concrete floor. Rushed to hospital, he at first appeared in stable condition, but later lapsed into a coma, dying six weeks later. He was 83.

of Fame and several subsequent tributes from the remaining members of the band. "Ahmet meant a lot to us all," John Paul Jones later told *Uncut*. "We wanted to be on his label [at the start of Led Zeppelin], so yes, [he] was a very important man to us." Therefore, when Ertegun's widow, Mica, approached Plant with the idea of Led Zeppelin reforming for a 40-minute set in honour of her husband's charity, the Ahmet Ertegun Education Fund[334], Robert's long-seated reservations about putting the band back together were placed to one side. This time, he agreed to do it.

After Robert quietly gave his consent, it all became a matter of getting management behind the idea and the logistics in place. With the press kept firmly in the dark about the reunion, Bill Curbishley was free to approach Jones and Page and gather their opinions. In the case of JPJ, this simply meant lodging a call to his manager Richard Chadwick, the astute and soft-spoken businessman who for several years had overseen John Paul's career, as well as that of King Crimson guitarist Robert Fripp and former Japan singer David Sylvian. With Jimmy, things were now a little more complicated. Though Curbishley had taken care of Page at Trinifold since 1994, the guitarist had recently moved on, his personal affairs first being handled by Swan Song veteran Alan Callan before he switched to Peter Mensch at Q Prime. A tough-talking New Yorker who counted AC/DC, Def Leppard and Metallica among his many distinguished clients, Mensch guarded Page as closely as Jimmy did Zep's back catalogue.

At first, progress on the proposed reunion was slow. Though the subject was touched on at a meeting between Led Zeppelin's big three and their managers[335] in March 2007, no one bit, with Page and JPJ obviously needing time to consider the ramifications of it all. A month later, and there were still no definitive answers. Indeed, when Jones appeared at a private concert in honour of Ertegun at New York's Lincoln Centre on

---

334 Ertegun's fund was dedicated to paying for university scholarships for students in the UK, USA and his native Turkey.

335 According to Q's Robert Sandall, in addition to Page, Plant and JPJ, those attending Zep's annual business meetings included the band's US lawyer George Fearon and accountant Joan Hudson, who was also a trustee of John Bonham's estate.

April 15, while Jimmy and Robert were in attendance, neither joined him onstage. This, it seemed, was more like chess than rock'n'roll.

Then all of a sudden, there was movement on the board. Following another meeting in London, the trio agreed to a short period of rehearsals, or "a testing of the water". In the past, this in turn might have led to furious debate as to who would take up the drummer's stool. But given the potential occasion at hand, there was never any doubt it was going to be Jason Bonham. Having kept his sticks busy with various projects since the dissolution of his own group in the mid-nineties – Paul Rodgers, UFO, blues guitar maestro Joe Bonamassa and his own aunt, Debbie Bonham, were all recent employers – Jason was armed and ready to go.

"For me, it was a dream come true to sit in the drum seat and be treated like an adult by them," he later told writer Steve Rosen. "I didn't feel like a kid anymore. That was monumental." In fact, according to John Paul Jones, Bonham was even more familiar with Led Zeppelin's songs than they were. "Jason was our first choice and he's always fun to have around," he told Q. "In the eighties, we didn't want to draw him into all that Zeppelin stuff... we wanted him to have his own career, but he's in his forties now, and he really knows the songs. He was saying things like 'Do you want to play that like the version you did [live] in 1975?'"

As the quartet continued to dust off the old tunes while still considering whether they actually wanted to reform, tentative preparations for Ahmet Ertegun's benefit concert proceeded apace. Jimmy's old friend and "King of the promoters" Harvey Goldsmith was the man trusted with the responsibility of overseeing the event and helping organise the bill. It was to include Paul Rodgers, Foreigner, Bill Wyman's Rhythm Kings (with a guesting Swan Singer Maggie Bell) and a one-off prog-supergroup comprised of Yes' Chris Squire and Alan White, Bad Company's Simon Kirke and keyboard legend Keith Emerson of ELP. Should Led Zeppelin fail to materialise, Eric Clapton's old band Cream[336] were reportedly on hold to step into the breach. In the end,

336 The progenitors of blues rock, Cream's original line-up of Clapton, drummer Ginger Baker and bassist Jack Bruce had already reunited for four concerts at London's Royal Albert Hall in May 2005.

they were not required. After eight further days of rehearsal spanning late spring to early autumn, Led Zeppelin finally gave the thumbs up. For the first time since 1988 (barring birthdays and weddings), the game was on again.

So it was that on September 12, Harvey Goldsmith met with the press to announce Led Zeppelin's return at London's O2 Arena. The date given was November 26, 2007 and tickets (costing £125 each) were to be made available worldwide via an online lottery system. The response was the first sign of what lay ahead. Shortly after opening for business, *Ahmettribute.com* crashed like a speeding car as human demand for Zep's appearance at the O2 completely outstripped the technology employed to deal with it. With a (very) conservative estimate of over one million fans vying for fewer than 20,000 tickets, it was probably inevitable. That said, the sheer number of hits still shocked Page to his boots. "Nobody, I mean *nobody* thought for a moment that there would be such an intense and overwhelming response," he later said. "The [demand] went beyond my wildest dreams."

Now committed to what some journalists were calling "the most anticipated rock concert of the decade", Zep knuckled down to the task at hand. Obviously determined not to blow it, three more weeks of rehearsals were deemed necessary, with Surrey's Shepperton film studios also booked for final tweaks and stage/lighting demands.[337] Page was justifiably nervous, reportedly visiting the O2 Arena well in advance of the gig to check out its acoustics. He also appeared somewhat more uncomfortable than usual when addressing the media. With Robert Plant deciding not to talk about anything other than his latest album with Alison Krauss – the excellent *Raising Sand*[338] – it was now left to Jimmy and JPJ to fill in the dots. "You have to ask Robert," he said of Plant's reticence to speak of the reunion. "He doesn't want to." Now within touching distance of bringing his beloved band back into the

337 At final rehearsals, both *In Through The Out Door*'s 'Fool In The Rain' and 'Carouselambra' were tried on for size, though neither song made the final cut.
338 A fine collaboration featuring country, bluegrass and folk flavours, Plant and Krauss' *Raising Sand* sold over a million copies while also winning five Grammy awards.

light, Page had no intention of seeing it slip away it at the last minute by putting words in the singer's mouth.

However, for one brief moment at least, it looked like it might all be off. On November 1, less than four weeks before showtime, Page took a tumble in the garden, fracturing the little finger of his left hand. A potentially awkward injury for any guitarist, breath was held and prayers said. In the end, the accident was not as severe as first thought, though to be on the safe side, the concert was put back to December 10. More time for rehearsals, then, but also more time to think. "To be honest, it's not the gig I find daunting," he told Robert Sandall in the run up to O2. "It's all the backstage nonsense you get at a Led Zeppelin show. The people milling around, the security, the general madness, which [is] worse now that Peter Grant's not around. [But] we should be able to have a laugh..."

On December 10, 2007, before an audience of over 18,000 fans and a large boat's worth of rock stars and other celebrities[339], Led Zeppelin took to the stage at London's O2 Arena at 9 p.m. sharp to put Page's theory to the test. They opened the show with 'Good Times Bad Times', the first number on their first album, as fine a place as any to start. Without announcement, 'Ramble On' quickly followed, even incorporating a snippet from 'What Is And What Should Never Be' as it flew by. Both songs were performed brilliantly, yet something was missing. It was as if the band onstage and the crowd could not quite believe either were actually there. Then Robert sang 'Hey Hey Mama...', Led Zeppelin locked into JPJ'S snaking riff, 'Black Dog' took off like a rocket and the last 27 years peeled back like an onion. "We'd paced ourselves for this

---

339 In addition to the near 20,000 fans gathered at O2 from around the world, musicians attending the show included Paul McCartney, Mick Jagger, Jeff Beck, Queen's Brian May, Pink Floyd's Dave Gilmour, U2's The Edge, Peter Gabriel, the Foo Fighters' Dave Grohl, the Red Hot Chili Peppers' Chad Smith, Heart's Ann Wilson, Oasis' Noel and Liam Gallagher, the Stone Roses' John Squire, Manic Street Preacher James Bradfield and Marilyn Manson, among others. A number of models and actors were also at the gig, with Jerry Hall, Kate Moss, Naomi Campbell, Priscilla Presley, Juliette Lewis, Paris Hilton and David Boreanaz all putting in an appearance. Crown Prince Frederik of Denmark was the sole royal.

concert," Jimmy later told *Uncut*. "We'd given it our total commitment and nothing – not even broken fingers – was going to get in the way of it..."

Nothing did. With group and audience now locked in synch, over the course of the next two hours Led Zeppelin played one of the finer sets of their career. At times, such as with 'The Song Remains The Same' and 'Nobody's Fault But Mine', they sounded planet-sized, the noise coming offstage genuinely threatening to engulf the arena and surrounding buildings. At others, such as on 'No Quarter' and 'Stairway To Heaven' (no complaints for Robert on this occasion), Zep seemed to be playing more for themselves than anyone else, the nods, glances and shy smiles between them travelling no further than each other.

Indeed, each musician could feel genuinely proud of their night's work. Still "the quiet man at the back", John Paul Jones was nonetheless key to O2's success. Whether providing the spooky orchestral lines on 'No Quarter', shooting in and out of the beat on 'The Song...' or riding his bass pedals while his fingers simultaneously jabbed at the keys on 'Trampled Under Foot', Jones' worth to Led Zeppelin remained immeasurable. "If you watch John Paul onstage at the O2 during 'Trampled Under Foot'," said Dave Lewis, "you'll realise right there that Zep just couldn't have happened without him."

Similarly, Robert Plant could still command a stage like few other frontmen. Cracking odd jokes, making the front rows swoon (at 58 years old, no less), and ever capable of going from a scream to a sigh in the space of a millisecond, Plant remained the 'Golden God on vacation from Mount Olympus', happy to be among us sure enough, but enjoying the adulation, too. And while he may have been suspiciously quiet about Zep's reunion in advance of the event, he was also dutifully honest about the risks of doing it afterwards. "The potential for failure was great," he said, "because nobody knew what it was going to be like... but I really enjoyed it. Our profit on the night was... metaphysical."

In many ways, Jason Bonham was the real star of the show. Stepping behind a kit that was once home not only to one of rock's greatest ever drummers but his own father to boot, he was playing a high-stakes game which could have gone very wrong indeed. Yet, his performance at the

O2 showed few signs of nerves, as he punctuated every vocal inflection, riff and solo within an inch of its life. "Jason performed marvellously," Page later said. "His father would have been so proud of him." For Bonham himself, taking up his father's mantle in London at last earned him a place at the grown-ups' table. "When I lost my dad," he later told *Ultimate Guitar*'s Steve Rosen, "he was still on a pedestal, and I wanted... reassurance. I wanted him to go 'That's fine, you're doing good'. So I think my entire life has been in search of that. To get it from [Led Zeppelin], well, if I can't get it from my dad, then the closest thing to him was the band."

And in the midst of it all, of course, was Jimmy. Ever the clothes horse in long black frock coat, shades and shiny leather shoes, Page looked immaculate when he took to the stage, the trademark Gibson Les Paul – despite previous doctor's orders – still hanging 'just so' above his knees. Even his hair, now chalk white and free of the dye that had coloured it for so many years, appeared elegant, stately and thoroughly befitting of such an occasion. "I loved that new look," laughed Paul Rodgers. "Overnight, white hair was *the look* for guitar players." Yet, just nine songs later, the same man was stripped to a white shirt, soaked in sweat and seemingly oblivious to anything other than his solo on 'Since I've Been Loving You'. "I didn't really see the audience," he confirmed to Allan Jones. "I was just getting lost in the music."

Lost, but as it turned out, also deliriously happy. Grinning, gurning and grimacing his way through the set, Jimmy Page gave everything he had at the O2, as double-necks were donned ('Stairway...' and 'The Song...'), whammy pedals mangled ('Nobody's Fault...') and whammy bars pushed to breaking point (a live debut for *Presence*'s 'For Your Life') over the course of 120 minutes. Indeed, when it came to his long-established set piece, the always intense 'Dazed And Confused', Page was at the very top of his game. With the stage now bathed in green light and the guitarist contained within an eerie laser pyramid (very Knebworth), the violin bow he had wielded like a magic wand since 1967 was once more summoned to call the four winds back into the arena. Pure unadulterated theatrics, one might say. But only the most cynical among us would deny 'ZoSo' his due that night.

627

Yet as good as Jimmy's individual performance was, by his own admission Led Zeppelin had always been above all else a band, and set closer 'Kashmir' was the best evidence of it. As a deep turquoise sun streamed white light on the huge backdrop behind them, Zep transported the crowd back to 1975, which remained a place where "yellow desert streams" flowed freely and Robert's personal Shangri-La could still be found beneath "the summer moon". A grand take on a now legendary song, Led Zeppelin's 'Kashmir' at O2 was damn near perfect, and they hadn't even got to the encores yet. "They had a lot to lose, no doubt about it," said Dave Lewis. "And nobody knew that more than Jimmy. But it turned out to be a wonderful night, a night that Jimmy *needed*. Actually, they all needed it. Robert was the golden god all over again, John Paul his usual, impeccable self and Jason, well, he truly rose to the occasion. But it was Jimmy's [gig] really. He was in his element and he was simply outstanding."

Back in 1969, Zep couldn't buy a good review. Four decades later, and they couldn't get away from them. "Led Zeppelin were quite magnificent," said *The Guardian*'s Kitty Empire. "Yes, reunions are staid, venal affairs that seek to make a noxious heritage industry out of rock. But this one is worth all the hyperbole." *The Telegraph*'s David Cheal was also quite impressed. "'Dazed and Confused'! 'Since I've Been Loving You'! 'Stairway to Heaven'! They were fantastic. Better than I expected, [and] it was a joy and a privilege to be there." For those joining in the fun from across the Atlantic, the response was much the same. "The failed gigs of the nineteen-eighties and nineties have been supplanted by a triumph," said the *New York Times*' Sacha Frere-Jones, "and the band should be pleased to have done Ahmet Ertegun proud with such a spirited performance." But it was *NME* that really pointed to the question on everyone's lips. "What Led Zeppelin have done here tonight is proof that they can still perform to the level that originally earned them their legendary reputation. We can only hope this isn't the last we see of them."

In the end, that decision lay not with the press or fans, but with each member of the band. Weeks before the show, John Paul Jones had hinted that something might be on the horizon post O2 – "I guess the door has been left slightly ajar" – though he was equally quick to add a caveat before any fireworks exploded. "[But] we'll have to see," the bassist cautioned, "how we feel about it afterwards." Nearly three years later, Jason Bonham also let it be known that he had been up for the challenge of continuing onwards. "I felt like I'd pulled the sword from the stone," he laughed to Steve Rosen. Yet, as the dust began to settle after the concert itself, even promoter Harvey Goldsmith wasn't sure what would happen next. "Well, I only asked them to do 30 minutes but they came back after a week's rehearsals and said they wanted to do the full show," he told *Classic Rock* at the time. "So, you have to take one step at a time, but I certainly hope they do something else. If something materialises after this show, that'll be fantastic."

As ever, there was no doubt as to where Jimmy Page hoped all this might lead. "I'd like to keep this going," he told *Q* before the show. "I've got things I've been working on for the last four years that I'm proud of and some of the songs I've got ready are as good as anything I've done in the past. I wouldn't necessarily save them for my solo career." So, with all eyes now firmly planted in his direction, it was up to a certain lion-haired vocalist to settle the 'will they, won't they?' debate once and for all. "I felt like it was a job done," said Robert Plant, "that we were friends, strong and good."

That didn't quite sound like a 'Yes'.

CHAPTER 38

In The Evening

In the immediate aftermath of O2, Led Zeppelin again appeared to go their separate ways, the question of any continuing reunion left for journalists to mull over rather than the band to actually confirm. Still, as before, Jimmy Page continued to hold out hope for better days ahead. "[To carry on playing after O2] seemed the right thing to do," he told *Mojo* in early 2008. Indeed, according to Dave Lewis, Page's plans for the band were never likely confined to just one gig. "[I'm sure] in Jimmy's mind, that wasn't going to be it," he said. "In a perfect world, there should have been at least 10 more dates. Three more in London, three in LA, three in New York. Tokyo, Europe, Australia, maybe. Who knows?"

With four year's worth of songs in his back pocket now ready to go, Page was surely gunning for a studio album as well as more live dates. Yet, the answer to whether Zep would or would not proceed still seemed to lie in Robert Plant's hands. As before, he sounded mighty unsure. "That's the trouble with... Led Zeppelin," Robert told *Uncut*'s Allan Jones the spring of 2008. "It was always bigger than the beauty of what we had in mind." Now revelling in the huge commercial wins of *Raising Sand* with Alison Krauss and about to cart home five Grammy awards as a result, Plant's need to revisit his past was surely lessened[340]. "Robert's parallel project has been successful," Jimmy admitted at the time, "which I suppose means he doesn't have time for Led Zeppelin at this point." With Plant again appearing to withdraw, Jimmy would soon find himself, John Paul Jones and Jason Bonham discussing possible singers who might fill the void.

In the meantime, there were other things to occupy his days and nights – some connected to the mighty works of his past, others highlighting his increasingly important role as custodian of Zep's legacy and elder statesman for British rock and pop. Occasionally, these honours carried humour with them, as was the case when Page received a 'Living Legend' award from *Classic Rock* in late 2007. "Jimmy wore the clothes," said Aerosmith's Steve Tyler, while paying tribute to his teenage hero in London. "He had the hair. He smoked the cigarettes. He got the girls. He wrote the songs. He produced them. He did every fucking thing. Jimmy Fuckin' Page!" (They would meet again in less ebullient circumstances within a year.) Elsewhere, the atmosphere was somewhat more formal, such as when Jimmy was awarded an honorary doctorate for his services to the music industry from the University of Surrey at Guildford Cathedral on June 20, 2008. Decked out in the necessary vestments of office – to wit, a multi-coloured gown and soft felt cap – Page still managed to look as dapper as ever.

This contrast between rock'n'roll theatrics and more hifalutin engagements continued to play itself out across the year. In fact, just a week or so before Jimmy accepted his doctorate in Guildford, he was bashing out Led Zeppelin tunes with the Foo Fighters and John Paul Jones at Wembley Stadium. The brainchild of former Nirvana

---

340 While Zep's appearance at O2 surely didn't hurt Plant's profile and the sales of *Raising Sand*, it did Led Zeppelin no great harm either. Released some four weeks before the show, the band's sixth compilation album *Mothership* went to number four and seven in the UK and USA. In addition to *Mothership*, *The Song Remains The Same* was also reissued on DVD on November 20, 2007. Containing 40 minutes of bonus footage – including unseen performances of 'Celebration Day' and 'The Ocean' – its contents were again overseen by Page, with Kevin Shirley providing a new mix of the original 1973 MSG concerts.

drummer Dave Grohl, the Foo Fighters' anthemic blend of melody and muscle had recently seen them graduate from large halls to full-blown football grounds, and the band's frontman wanted to mark that passing in the best possible way. A "mega fan" of Zep – and once (erroneously) rumoured to be in the running for the vacant drum stool at O2 – Grohl had personally invited Page and Jones to perform in north London and they did not let him down. With the Foo's own drummer, Taylor Hawkins, taking the vocals to 'Rock And Roll' and Dave doing his best Robert Plant impersonation on 'Ramble On', Grohl looked more like a hyperactive teenager than a jobbing rock star as Jimmy and JPJ played on behind him.

Page's next stop was a supposedly more formal occasion, though not by the time he'd finished with it. Having flown to Beijing, he was at the National Stadium on August 23 to perform at the closing ceremony of the 2008 Olympics. Often spectacular if stuffy events, with choreographed dancers and acrobats doing back flips as choirs warbled good-naturedly in the background, Jimmy and former *X Factor* winner Leona Lewis obviously had different ideas as to how these things should go.

Stunning the gathered crowd with a shockingly loud rendition of 'Whole Lotta Love', Jimmy riffed away on his Les Paul before Lewis, who was raised 20-odd feet above his head on a hydraulic metal platform. As the song drew to a close, David Beckham appeared on an adjoining platform alongside a violist and cello player, who joined in the fun. "I'd be very sincere if I said doing the Olympics with Leona was phenomenal," he later told *Uncut*. "She's really plucky, superb and she sang 'Whole Lotta Love' brilliantly. We managed to do the full length [version]. It wasn't edited. It was so cool the way she approached it. For that audience, and the fact we didn't fuck it up, that was important. It was a Led Zeppelin number, but it took on another persona." Watched by 91,000 people in the stadium itself and at home on TV by 250 million more, Page called his Beijing experience "One of the highpoints of my career." Given that towering platform, it was a highpoint for Leona Lewis, too...

It was again in honour of Page's role as 'Grand Father of the Riff' that the next project with which he involved himself came to him. In late

2007, director Davis Guggenheim met with Jimmy in a London hotel to discuss a new movie he was working on. Unlike his most notable film – 2006's head-turning essay on global warming, *An Inconvenient Truth* – Guggenheim wanted this time to explore the guitar and the creative (and often eccentric) qualities of both the instrument and those who played it. As the conversation expanded, Page thought this might be something worth sinking his teeth into. "It became apparent that Davis wanted to capture that spark when creativity happens among guitarists or writers," he later told *Mojo*.

There was another conceit to Davis' idea that further intrigued Jimmy. As well as seeking Page's participation, the moviemaker wanted to involve two more generations of guitarist, notably U2's multi-effects texturalist The Edge and blues/garage revivalist Jack White from the White Stripes. Further, Guggenheim did not want them to meet beforehand. Instead, they would all gather before the cameras at a designated 'summit' (actually Warner Bros. film studios in LA) and simply talk, play, while at the same time try to unravel the creative secrets of the guitar. "The whole point about [the film] is that you've got three unschooled musicians, all self-taught," said Jimmy. "They've all been self-taught, they're all character players, so they're all bound to be a bit eccentric with it. Davis wanted to capture that actual moment we all saw each other, and we stuck to it."

Though Page was happy to follow Guggenheim's brief and avoid talking with White or The Edge before their mutual appointment in LA, he had actually met them both before. In White's case, their paths had crossed at the odd show and photo session, while Jimmy was introduced to the man formerly known as Dave Evans when he inducted the Yardbirds into the Rock and Hall of Fame way back in 1992. However, that hardly made them all friends. "I didn't know much that wasn't outside the printed page," he said, "so it was really good to learn how [they] ticked."

The end result – entitled *It Might Get Loud* – saw Guggenheim get within touching distance of his original intention, as Page, The Edge and White individually and collectively pontificated on guitars, music and what made it all tick. Interspersed with footage of each player's journey to stardom and the landmarks on the way (in an enjoyable reveal, Jimmy actually travelled back to hallowed Headley Grange with a camera crew in tow), it was also interesting to see how much the younger men deferred to the wisdom of their grey-haired superior. Like children gathered at their father's feet while he slowly unfolded a magic trick before them, both The Edge and Jack White gobbled up the sight of Page running through the riffs to 'Kashmir' and 'Whole Lotta Love' with big, green, greedy eyes. "It was just fascinating to be that close to Jimmy and see him play," Edge later told *Mojo*. "When he went into '... Lotta Love', me and Jack were like two little kids watching with stupid grins on our faces." Ending with the trio performing a (rather bad) rendition of the Band's old classic 'The Weight', and featuring two new short instrumental compositions from Jimmy – the snaking 'Embryo Number 1' and 'Embryo Number 2' – *It Might Get Loud* premiered to positive reviews at the Toronto Film Festival on September 5, 2008.

Sadly, there was bad news for Page to contend with at the end of the year, as his former drummer Michael Lee suddenly passed away. Just 39 years old, Lee – who suffered from epilepsy – was found dead at his flat following a seizure. A fine percussionist with a probing musical nature and jackhammer approach to the kit, Lee had added much to *No Quarter* and *Walking Into Clarksdale*[341], and Jimmy was among his mourners at Darlington Crematorium on December 3. In the midst of the floral tributes was also a message from Robert Plant. "What a waste. Too soon. I'm so sorry, I always enjoyed your enthusiasm and ideas. Robert P".

The mood had lightened considerably by April 2009 when Page found himself back at the Rock and Roll Hall of Fame for the third time, though on this occasion he was presenting the honours rather than receiving them. After five decades of relentless invention, career turns that would shame a job adviser and some of the finest guitar solos ever committed to tape, vinyl or compact disc, Jeff Beck was finally getting his own moment in the sun. "I'd listen to Jeff along the way, and I'd think 'He's getting really, really good,'" said Page at Cleveland Public

---

341 In addition to his work with Page and Plant, Lee had also drummed with Little Angels, the Cult, Ian Gillan, Echo & the Bunnymen and the Tea Party's Jeff Martin.

Hall on April 4. "Then you'd hear him a few years later and he just kept getting better and better and better. And he's still getting better now. He leaves us mere mortals wondering, [with] sounds and techniques totally unheard of before. An amazing feat and I'm just honoured to be here to induct him." Beck was almost teary-eyed with all the compliments. "I didn't know Jimmy was doing the speech," he later said. "Amazing, a complete surprise, and he said such nice things."

Having bonded over James Burton solos in the fifties, shared the same stages with the Yardbirds in the sixties and – despite a slight wobble in the seventies – remained close ever since, Beck and Page marked their continuing friendship onstage at Cleveland in the most delightful way. As Jeff's band soared through their version of 'Beck's Bolero' for the crowd, Jimmy suddenly emerged from the wings with the same Fender XII electric he had used on the original. Then, right on cue, the quintet switched gears and went into a blazing take on Zep's 'Immigrant Song', replete with Beck aping Robert Plant's Viking howls on his own white Fender Strat. After two-odd minutes of casual mayhem, they all then switched back to '... Bolero' as if nothing had happened.

"It was [Beck bassist] Tal Wilkenfeld's idea," Jeff later told *... Talks Music*. "She said 'Why don't we come out of '... Bolero' and go into 'Immigrant Song' in the middle? I ended up playing Robert's vocal part on guitar... no rehearsal, but it worked perfectly!" In time-honoured fashion, Beck and Page's performance at the RARHOF[342] re-stoked the old idea that the former Yardbirds might cut an album together. Not the worst idea, really, and one talked up often in previous years. But Jimmy had been far too busy trying to put Led Zeppelin – or at least an iteration of it – back together for that little miracle to happen.

By the summer of 2008, it was clear that Robert Plant had absolutely no intention of returning to Led Zeppelin any time soon. Happy to have honoured Ahmet Ertegun's memory, but also apparently happy to walk away from Zep afterwards, Plant was still committed to another album

---

342 In addition to their performance of 'Beck's Bolero'/'Immigrant Song' at the RARHOF, Beck and Page also jammed along on a version of 'Train Kept A-Rollin'' with Aerosmith's Joe Perry, and Metallica's James Hetfield and Kirk Hammett.

with Alison Krauss[343], while also giving serious thought to revisiting his sixties roots with a new Band Of Joy. "From my angle, the get together was really well-thought out, professionally put together and a beautiful night," he later said of his O2 experience. "[But] the weight of expectation and what it does to you when you're in the middle... well, we didn't start off like that when we were kids."

For Plant, any notion of stepping back in time to reclaim his youth just did not appeal. Now over 60 years old, comfortable in his own skin and with a creditable solo career that allowed him to merrily pursue any musical direction he damn well pleased, the thought of donning low-slung jeans and singing 'Black Dog' till the cows came home was just not on the cards. "We're old guys now," he said, "and we're not supposed to be hip-shrugging teenage idols anymore." Embarrassed by some of his contemporaries chasing around the stage like it was still 1969, the last thing he wanted Led Zeppelin to be was "a bunch of bored old men following the Rolling Stones around".

One might debate some of the reasoning. Indeed, there were worse things than simply giving the fans what they wanted. But say what you will, there was also a genuine nobility to Plant's argument. "Robert just didn't need it anymore, the pay check, the hassle, any of it, really," said Chris Charlesworth." I also think he's a bit embarrassed, singing 'Stairway...' 40-odd years after the fact. I'm sure he was happy to do the gig in honour of Ahmet, his widow, and indeed, for Atlantic Records. More, after the muck-up at Live Aid and the first Atlantic tribute, there was a sense of wanting to get it right, to truly honour the memory of Led Zeppelin one last time. But after the O2, I think he just wanted to leave it there."

Jimmy Page felt very differently. And this time, he had allies pushing him along. "Robert didn't want to do it," John Paul Jones later told *Classic Rock*, "[but] me, Jim and Jason had worked so hard together, I thought 'Let's start a different band, a totally different band...'"

That journey had actually begun shortly after O2 when, after Plant opted to continue exploring fresh fields, JPJ suggested that he, Page

---

343 Despite further rehearsals/recording sessions, Plant and Krauss chose to go their separate musical ways in 2009.

and Jason Bonham band together for another series of rehearsals. "We had no singer in mind... to bring on board though," Jimmy later told *Mojo*. "I felt it was somewhat like putting the cart before the horse... bringing an unknown into an environment of three known elements. I thought it would be premature, because we were coming up with so much material that was really vibrant, urgent... it was scary. It wasn't scaring the pants off me, it was inspiring me." In addition to the songs the trio were now exploring, they had also tried their hand at lesser known gems from Zep's latter days. Having already played around with some tunes from *In Through The Out Door* during the run-up to the O2 concert, 'Carouselambra' was put through its paces for a second time, Jones again pulling double-duty on bass pedals and keyboards. With these new tracks and deep cuts sending "shivers" down Jimmy Page's spine, it wasn't long before the band started looking outside their own three walls for someone to sing the songs.

Though a blanket of secrecy was thrown up at the time as to exactly who and who did not audition, two names managed to escape through the stitches. In the case of 39-year-old Myles Kennedy, the signs were promising. An old acquaintance of Jason Bonham, Kennedy was at the time singing with American rockers Alter Bridge, whose then latest album, 2007's *Blackbird*, had more than a little Zep about it. With a vocal range to rival Robert Plant and a fine guitar player too, Myles fulfilled certain of the criteria Page and co. were looking for. Yet, despite rehearsing with the group, working on their new songs and even getting a reported thumbs up from Jones, Kennedy went back to his day job in Alter Bridge. "I am not singing in Led Zeppelin or any offshoot of Led Zeppelin, but I did have a great opportunity and it was something that I'm very grateful for," he told DJ Eric Blair in early 2009. "But Alter Bridge will go on and that's that."[344]

---

344 Formed by guitarist Mark Tremonti in 2004 from the ashes of his former group Creed, Alter Bridge persist to this day, their line-up unchanged. In fact, when Myles Kennedy first posited the idea of joining up with Page, JPJ and Bonham, Tremonti gave his blessing, proving the old adage "You always get more with honey than salt."

Enter Aerosmith's Steven Tyler. "Yardbirds freak", Zeppelin "nut" and friend of Jimmy's from "way back when", there was no disputing either Tyler's pedigree as a singer or his closeness to Page. Indeed, the pair had jammed or met so many times before – onstage at Donington, the Marquee, the Hall of Fame, the list was near endless – and Steven had in many ways been auditioning for the job since at least 1990. However, there was also the not inconsiderable fact that "the demon of screamin'" was also the frontman of one of the biggest bands in American rock history and, as such, was well used to doing things his way. This may have been a factor in why the Tyler/Zep interface didn't come off.

According to various reports, when Steven arrived in London (probably in late September 2008) to meet with the trio, he had a bad cold, which meant pushing back the first jam with Jimmy, JPJ and Jason Bonham by a day or so. When it did take place, things went at best 'OK', but Tyler then reportedly suggested they work on some material he and occasional song-writing partner Marti Frederiksen[345] had tried out back in the States. In at least one account of the story, this did not sit well with the man who had co-authored 'Whole Lotta Love', 'Stairway To Heaven' and 'Kashmir', and Steven left for America soon afterwards. However, Tyler later offered his own take on what happened when talking with 'Shock Jock' Howard Stern. "I'm in Aerosmith. [Jimmy's] in the biggest band in the world, and I'm in a band like that. I've [got] such an allegiance to my band. [So] when it came time for [him] to say 'You want to write a record with me?' I looked Jimmy in the eyes and I went 'No'."[346]

---

345 A professional songwriter with a list of credits as long as his arm, Frederiksen had composed or co-written songs with Aerosmith, Mick Jagger, Def Leppard, Ozzy Osbourne and Meatloaf, among others.

346 In his 2014 autobiography *Rocks*, Aerosmith's Joe Perry disputes several previously published accounts of the Tyler/Page tale, claiming that he did not know his 'Toxic Twin' had even auditioned until after the event. "I was pissed, not because Steven was trying out for another band, but because he had done it behind my back." Painting a very different picture of events from an Aerosmith perspective, Perry's account is worth a read.

In the end, Page, Jones and Jason Bonham did not find a singer. Any singer, in fact. Despite reports that a tour was definitely in the offing for 2009/10, the band would dissolve before a single venue had been booked. Obviously irritated by the failure of his client's latest enterprise, Jimmy's manager Peter Mensch sounded not unlike a policeman moving traffic by the side of an accident when dealing with the press. "They tried out a few singers and no one worked out," he told *Musicradar* in early 2009. "That was it. The thing is over now."

But the theories persisted. Some argued that concert promoters were distinctly underwhelmed by the thought of anyone other than Robert Plant fronting the group – whether they were called 'Led Zeppelin' or not – thus leading to less interest in the tour than first anticipated. Others suggested that that the whole thing was little more than a ruse to get Plant jealous, the thought of another vocalist taking his place in Zep (by any other name) causing him to rethink his plans and return to the fold. "Sounds like rubbish," said Chris Charlesworth, and according to JPJ he was absolutely right. "I don't think Jimmy's heart was ever really in it," Jones later confirmed to *Mojo*. "I did feel we should do something, anything. But it fell apart." Whatever the original motivations, replacing Robert was obviously not going to fly. With the still band singer-free and stymied as a result, John Paul Jones moved on to ventures new (and soon to be returned to), Jason formed 'Jason Bonham's Led Zeppelin Experience' with his friend Jason Dylan[347] and Page packed up his songs in a metaphorical kit bag for use on another day.

For a while, it looked like the songs would not have to wait too long for a public airing, as Jimmy announced to *Sky News* in December 2009 that he might tour with a new band the following year. With stories already circulating about the possibility of Page solving his vocalist dilemma by getting several singers to contribute to a solo album as guitarist Carlos Santana had successfully done with *Supernatural* in 1999, things at last seemed to be on the move. Yet, 2010 came and

---

347 A live celebration of the music of Zep and his late father, Bonham's 'Zep Experience' continue to tour the US. Since 2009, Jason has also worked with Heart, Glenn Hughes and Sammy Hagar, among others.

went without new music from him, though it did bring the consolation prize of a pictorial autobiography. "I've been approached on quite a number of occasions to do an autobiography," Jimmy told *The Times*, "which I've never wanted to do, because to sell a book you can bet your life it's stoked up in a sensational furnace. But, you know, I've had a substantial career and I thought it would be interesting to do a photographic autobiography."

Ornate, handcrafted and released by Genesis Publications in a limited edition print-run of just 2,150 copies at the end of 2010, *Jimmy Page By Jimmy Page* was a pictorial jaunt through the life of one of rock's more private characters. Taking up the story with a photo of Page as an angelic-looking choir boy at St. Barnabas' Church in fifties Epsom and running the gamut of his adventures with Neil Christian, studio sessions, the Yardbirds, Zep and all thereafter, the book was light on words but loaded with rare images: Jimmy onstage with Red E Lewis & the Red Caps back in 1960 (or thereabouts); Page in Bron-Yr-Aur with Robert, circa 1970; Jimmy smiling to camera while standing in front of the Sphinx in Egypt in May 1977; Page gently strumming his gorgeous antique harp guitar in 1993. All interesting glimpses into the artist's life and some seldom, if ever, seen before.

Of course, pictorial evidence of the guitarist enjoying the attentions of the lovely Miss Pamela from 1973, photographic proof of what allegedly went on under the stage of the LA Forum while John Bonham bashed out 'Moby Dick' in 1975, or even a blurry negative of Jimmy playing cards with the devil at the crossroads in Clarksdale, was lacking. But according to its author, the autobiography was never intended to be a voyeur's paradise. "I wanted to do a book that showed the career rather than concentrate on hearsay and colourful stories."[348]

That said, there were other moments dotted throughout 2010 that confirmed conclusively that while Page was now a long way from the excesses of his 'colourful' past, he was still being honoured for the music that went with it. On June 11, Jimmy joined the ranks of previous

---

348 *Jimmy Page By Jimmy Page* was subsequently re-published by Genesis in 2014. By then, Jimmy's own official website, *JimmyPage.com*, was also long up and running.

winners James Brown, the Doors and Elton John when he and Led Zeppelin were inducted into *Mojo*'s 'Hall of Fame'. Making reference to the fact that Zep had recently topped the Beatles in terms of popularity in a BBC poll, the magazine's editor Phil Alexander's induction speech also proudly stated that Jimmy "set the standard by which all other musicians are measured". Wearing a crisp black suit and with his hair now pulled back in a pigtail (it was a style that he would stick with in subsequent years), Page's own acceptance speech was brief, but essentially accurate. "I've taken some chances in the past," he said, "and hopefully I'll do so in the future..."

There were more honours to accept and give away. Having already received the first ever 'Global Peace Award' from the United Nations' *Pathways To Peace* organisation the previous April – "We're doing this because musicians have a global impact on the world, said the UN's Rick Garson"[349] – Page found himself back at *Classic Rock* in November 2010 handing over a prize to post-punk legends Killing Joke. Long a friend of the band and their mercurial frontman Jaz Coleman, Jimmy was keen to underline the Joke's special qualities at a ceremony held at Camden Town's Roundhouse. "They're really tribal, really intense," he told journalist Liz Barnes. "[And it] was just good to hear something like that during the eighties when it was all haircuts and synthesisers."

Among the fellow guests at the 2010 *Classic Rock* Awards was John Paul Jones, who was undergoing a renaissance of his very own. Though the slowest out of the starting gates after the original demise of Led Zeppelin back in 1980, Jones had spent subsequent decades furiously playing catch-up. Following his brush with soundtracks on 1985's *Scream For Help*, JPJ had turned his hand to production, with the bassist overseeing albums by acts as diverse as the Mission, the Butthole Surfers, Heart and the Datsuns, as well as arranging the orchestral backing on four tracks on R.E.M.'s mega-selling 1992 album *Automatic For The People*. Then, after a bright-eyed collaboration with avant-garde performance artist Diamanda Galas in 1994 (*This Sporting Life*), Jones

---

349 Page was also one of several performers who had agreed to appear in Beijing on 10 October, 2010 at a planned 'Show of Peace' concert.

spun the wheel again, with two subsequent solo albums *Zooma* (1999) and *The Thunderthief* (2001) leading to several American tours and some exceedingly fine reviews. But it was what came in the wake of he and Page's attempts to restart/re-fashion Zep in 2008/9 that had truly surprised and, indeed, pushed him back into the charts. Forming a 'rock supergroup' called Them Crooked Vultures alongside Foo Fighters' Dave Grohl and Queens Of The Stone Age frontman Josh Homme, the band's self-titled 2009 debut album had sailed into the US and UK charts at numbers 12 and 13, and even won them a Grammy for 'Best Hard Rock Performance' with the tune 'New Fang'. "Who'd have thought, eh?" Jones might have said at the time. If only Jimmy Page were so lucky in finding singers.

Despite more vague promises at the end of the year, 2011 went by without any new music from Page, though he did make the odd concert appearance here and there. On June 11, Jimmy travelled one and a half miles up the road from his gothic home in Holland Park to join folk troubadour Donovan onstage at the Royal Albert Hall. Unsurprisingly, the pair performed 'Sunshine Superman', the hit to which Page contributed a few hippie-sounding licks way back in 1966. In mid-July, he again traversed across the capital, this time making a slightly longer journey to the Shepherd's Bush Empire where he jammed along with the Black Crowes. Then in the midst of a 20th anniversary tour, they still proved a good fit for the guitarist, with Jimmy's brisk solo on 'Shake Your Moneymaker' nicely stirring up an already enthusiastic crowd.

By November 11, he was back at the RAH and shaking hands onstage with another old friend. Ever the iconoclast, Roy Harper was celebrating his 70th birthday with a concert at London's most distinguished venue and Jimmy was never going to miss it. Drawing up two tall stools and two acoustic guitars, the duo set to work on Harper's signature tune 'Same Old Rock', though this time there was no *Old Grey Whistle Test* presenter asking awkward questions from the sidelines. "He's one of my oldest friends and I treasure him a lot," Roy said of Jimmy in his introduction. If Page were wearing a hat, he'd have probably taken it off.

If 2011 had been defined by a relative lack of activity on Jimmy's part, then 2012 saw him returning to the fray, if not actually the stage.

On March 16, an announcement was made via his own website (*JimmyPage.com*) that Page's long-buried soundtrack to *Lucifer Rising* was to be made available as a limited edition vinyl set in just four days: the exact date, in fact, of the Spring Equinox. "The collection," the announcement confirmed (rather archly), "has been exhumed and is now ready for public release." In addition to the standard vinyl package, there was also a separate run of 418 copies, of which the first 93 would be signed by Jimmy himself. As *Mojo*'s Phil Alexander later explained, "This use of numerology pointed to [the] qabalistic numbers associated with Aleister Crowley's *The Book Of The Law*, a cornerstone of his Thelemic philosophy."

Though now nearly 40 years old, Page's soundtrack to Kenneth Anger's ill-fated film still managed to sound remarkably contemporary, the near-endless drones and oscillating, electronic nature of several tracks closer to the timeless work of German composer Klaus Stockhausen than anything Jimmy had attempted with Led Zeppelin. "I'm pleased that came out, because [it's] really flirting with the avant-garde," he told *Classic Rock*. "It's the sort of stuff I could never have done in Led Zeppelin. But I was thinking that way as much as I was thinking rock'n'roll. It's sort of like a mad scientist at home in his laboratory." Indeed, the laboratory metaphor was extremely apt when listening to the likes of 'Incubus', 'Damask' and 'Lucifer...' itself, as tablas, synthesisers, Mellotrons and phantom 12-string guitars floated in and out of the mix. "The fact I got involved with Kenneth Anger and *Lucifer Rising*," Jimmy said in subsequent liner notes, "was really just a step along the road in my interest in the extreme and alternative."[350]

Given the fact that Page's original involvement with Anger had stirred up a hornet's nest of controversy, one or two articles again asked

---

350 In 2015, Page followed up *Lucifer Rising And Other Soundtracks* with *Soundtracks*, a four-CD/vinyl set that collected *Lucifer...* (and its unreleased 'Early Mix') as well as Jimmy's work on *Death Wish II* (again including various unreleased musical extras). A comprehensive history of his involvement with film music, the collection also included a 36-page booklet containing rare photos and a series of short essays from Page.

questions about the composer's exact relationship to the occult. Yet, like the soundtrack to *Lucifer...* itself, Jimmy's previous remarks on the subject stood the test of time well enough. "I'm interested in all theology," he had said in the seventies. "I really did in-depth psychology and studied the religions of the world... that was relevant to the 20th century. I read Nietzsche as well, and that's not very acceptable these days. However," he added firmly, "I've never practised black magic before in my life." And that was as far as he would go. Though some of Zep's previous work had flirted heavily with aspects of mysticism, and Page's own persona had always hinted at deeper mysteries still, the exact nature of the guitarist's beliefs remained as inscrutable as his symbol ZoSo. One might ask, but never was an answer given. So be it.

Thankfully, there were no arcane-themed questions asked of Page regarding *Celebration Day*. Five years in coming – "Five years is like one year in Zeppelin time," quipped JPJ. "I'm actually amazed it's come out so quickly..." – Dick Carruthers' filmed record of Zep's historic gig at London's O2 Arena on December 10, 2007 often proved to be as inspiring as the concert itself. Using 16 cameras to capture every nook and cranny of the stage, and Jimmy on hand to ensure the movie's sound quality ran at optimum efficiency[351], the director presented Zep as few had seen them before. From those sly nods between JPJ and Jason Bonham to the smiles and giggles shared between Plant and Page, this was as close as one might reasonably get to pulling up a chair alongside the group. More, the songs were as often as explosive on film as they had been in the arena, with the likes of 'In My Time Of Dying', 'Trampled Under Foot' and 'Kashmir' all enjoying a robust second life on screen. "You get the sense [from the film] that everyone was listening to each other," Jimmy told *Mojo* at the time, "and we're really attentive. It goes into another sort of zone, really."

Premiered at cinemas in London, Los Angeles, New York City, Berlin and Tokyo on October 13, 2012, with a limited theatrical run soon after, *Celebration Day* drew both Zep and Dick Carruthers another set of

---

351 Despite a "few small fixes", Page did not alter what was played on the night. "It is," he said, "what it is."

fine reviews. "*Celebration Day*," said *The Telegraph*, "is a celebration of rock'n'roll at its most moving, magical and magnificent." The DVD was pretty good, too. Released on November 17 and containing a second disc of the band's pre-gig rehearsals at Shepperton Studios on December 6, 2007 (all filmed on one camera), this behind-the-scenes look at Zep going through their paces showed just how much blood, sweat, tears and the odd laugh had gone into creating the final show.

Two further events bookended Led Zeppelin's secondary triumph with *Celebration Day*, bringing light and shade to the end of Page's year. On October 2, 2012, Jimmy's old session companion Big Jim Sullivan died at the age of 71 from complications stemming from diabetes and heart disease. A musician for whom the epithet "unsung hero" might well have been created, Sullivan had played on over 750 recordings throughout the course of his career, 54 of them going to number one. Later a regular in Tom Jones' touring band and then a prominent fixture in the James Last Orchestra, it was almost impossible to find anyone with a bad word to say about him. "Big Jim was on our first couple of records and part of that great session [scene]," John Carter, of Carter-Lewis, confirmed. "Just a fantastic player, a lovely guy and always very interested in what you were doing." For an 18-year-old Jimmy Page, Sullivan was also a gift from the gods. After all, when the young guitarist had stumbled while trying to read the sheet music for 'Diamonds'/ '...Hully Gully' on his first real session in late 1962, it was Big Jim that picked up the lead line and rescued him. Though it would be idle speculation to suggest things might have gone differently for Page but for that intercession, Jimmy never forgot Sullivan's act of kindness. "Big Jim Sullivan was a perfect gentleman..."

2012 came to a formal but glittery end for Page, Robert Plant and John Paul Jones on December 2 when Led Zeppelin received the annual Kennedy Center honours from President Barack Obama at a White House ceremony in Washington, DC. The highest award given to those who had influenced US culture through the arts, POTUS noted the band's unique qualities in a surprisingly informal and, at times, genuinely funny speech. "Zeppelin grabbed America from the opening chord," he said, before focusing on the group's now legendary offstage activities. "These guys also redefined the rock'n'roll lifestyle. We do not have video of this, but there were some hotel rooms thrashed and mayhem all around, so it's fitting we're doing this in a room with windows about three inches thick with secret service all around. So guys," he then suggested to Jimmy, Robert and JPJ, "just settle down. After all, these paintings are valuable..."

With a personal fortune estimated at £75 million in the *2012 Sunday Times Rich List*, Jimmy Page could have easily taken 2013 off. Having re-conquered the world with another near-million sales for *Celebration Day*, and now wearing more badges, hats and gongs than the most decorated of generals[352], Page had fulfilled several lifetime's worth of ambition and was one of the wealthiest rock stars on the planet as a result. Respected by his peers and still worshipped by the fans, should he have chosen never to lift another finger again, no one would really blame him. "Jimmy had already done so much, influenced so many bands, created such a body of work as a guitarist, songwriter, musician and producer, that if he decided to never get out of bed again, well, that's his business," said Dave Lewis. "I mean, what else does he need to prove?" Yet, Page appeared to have a compulsion to keep going. "This time last year," he said at the end of 2012, "I intended to be actually playing by now in a live outfit. So that will have to be postponed into... the tail end of [2013]. But I definitely want to be doing that..." In the end, he didn't do any of it, though the alternative path he chose wasn't bad either.

For years, Page had hinted there was more left in the Led Zeppelin archives than anyone actually realised. But with John Paul Jones having already gone on record to say the band had used up most of their material on previous albums, and with Jimmy's own private collection of tapes diminished considerably following a burglary in the mid-eighties, hopes weren't high. However, the 2014–2015 'Reissues' programme did much to rectify that.

---

352 Page's list of honours would again grow in May 2014 when he was presented with a second 'Honorary Doctorate Degree', this time by Berklee College of Music. He noted at the time the "profound effect" American music had over the course of his life.

Perhaps geed on by the success of Pink Floyd and the Beatles in the expansion and remastering of their own back catalogues, Page again approached Zep's recorded history with new ears, searching for treasures and artefacts that could explain and enhance albums that saw light of day decades before. But the "good idea" soon became "an epic task", as he found himself revisiting every corner of his musical history. "When I started what became this project," Jimmy later told DJ Nicky Horne, "I was... going through my whole archive, It went back to me being a teenager with a tape recorder at home, doing what a lot of musicians did, writing songs – really embarrassing stuff! [But] I wanted to hear them, I wanted to see what they were [and] I wanted to make an inventory of them. It goes through all of that to the Yardbirds and my contribution, and then it [got] to Led Zeppelin. I was listening to all of this stuff. You can listen to it [and] not have any idea of the things that are really important... [but] you also know instinctively when something is right to do and you just jolly well do it."

While Jimmy chose not to share with the world his teenage recordings (some of which must have been made in his parents' front room in Miles Road, Epsom), the Zep stuff would get an airing. Working right across 2013, Page's efforts were arduous but ultimately fruitful as he listened to vintage studio tapes, commandeered old bootlegs and set to work on creating definitive versions of each Led Zeppelin album. Further, by providing "a companion disc" for each release, his hope of offering listeners a better understanding of Led Zep's back catalogue and what went into it grew substantially. "Each of the companion discs will be like looking through a portal and seeing where we were at during that particular stage," he told *Classic Rock*. "It's a mirror image of the tracks as you know them – some were reference mixes for us, others completely different in approach."

Offered to the world in a steady stream of releases over the course of 2014/15, Led Zeppelin's 'Deluxe Reissue' campaign was further proof of how fine a curator Page had become of his band's past, even if the phrase irked him somewhat. "No, I'm not," he had told *Uncut* back in 2008, "but I've certainly tried to make sure there wasn't a rape and pillage of it." While it would take another small book to do justice to each and every reissued album, suffice to say, Jimmy had done his homework and provided fans with enough in the way of studio outtakes, rough mixes and new material to keep them satisfied for a few years yet.

Starting slowly, the debut *Led Zeppelin* album contained the least in the way of extras, though Page's addition of a live disc 'At the Paris Olympia, 1969' (replete with rumbling rendition of 'You Shook Me') was extremely welcome all the same. Similarly, *Led Zeppelin II* did not come particularly laden with new thrills, even if an alternative guitar solo on 'Heartbreaker', a drum solo-less 'Moby Dick' and recently found instrumental (the folky 'La La') all made one want to re-examine the album with fresh ears. *Led Zeppelin III* offered much more. Reflecting the quartet's then growing interest in acoustic textures, 'Gallows Pole (Rough Mix)' was beautiful in stripped down form, while the combination of the much bootlegged 'Jennings Farm Blues' (incorporating the main riff from 'Bron-Y-Aur Stomp') and raw take on 'Out On The Tiles' again made the case for electricity. The best of the bunch thus far, 'Deluxe III' also included one of Jimmy's favourite discoveries: the first recording of 'Since I've Been Loving You'. "I knew it existed," he said, "but to hear it afresh after all those years was wonderful. The performance from everybody was just magnificent."

In comparison, the legendary 'Four Symbols' was actually a bit of a let-down. Arriving replete with alternate mixes for each and every track, expectations were suitably high, but aside from the novelty of hearing 'Stairway To Heaven' in a slightly different way (more or less the same, but with warmer 12-string guitar sounds), there wasn't much to get excited about. *Houses Of The Holy* fared better, as Page plied on never-heard-before guitar parts for 'The Song Remains The Same' and a hard-edged, more energetic take of 'Dancing Days'. Mercifully, *Physical Graffiti* also benefited from the upgrading process. Sounding even fresher and sharper than it did in 1975, the three-disc set also provided a seriously weird run-through of 'Sick Again', crystal clear alternative mix of 'Trampled Under Foot' (now titled 'Brandy & Coke', in honour of its original nickname) and a version of 'In The Light' (aka 'Everybody Gets Through') that might actually have been recorded in a parallel universe. 'Driving Through Kashmir (Rough Orchestra

Mix)', however, did not improve on the original. "[*Physical Graffiti*] is a favourite with fans, and there's so much character work on it," Jimmy told the BBC. "And one thing about Led Zeppelin was that it wasn't a format band, and it wasn't about replication."

For some, the 'black sheep' of the Zep canon (though certainly not for Page), *Presence* again failed to stun in deluxe format, though Jimmy's feisty reference mix on 'Achilles Last Stand' (now called 'Two Ones Are Won') and JPJ's achingly short instrumental – the newly uncovered 'Ten Ribs And All...' – were worth investigating. Released like the original LP in a paper bag, *In Through The Out Door* had always carried the stigma of being Zep's worst-produced LP, with Sweden's Polar Studios somehow dialling down the band's overall energy levels (though drugs and drink might have been the culprit for two members of the group). But Page had worked hard to turn that round as ...*Out Door* now took on a more lively air. He was also not averse to injecting a bit of humour into proceedings, restoring the alternative takes of 'Carouselambra', 'All My Love' and 'I'm Gonna Crawl' to their working titles of 'The Epic', 'The Hook' and 'Blot', respectively.

Of all these handsome new packages, *Coda* benefited best. More sad afterthought than enduring monument to "rock's great lost group" on its original release, Jimmy seemed determined to eradicate any such sour memories here by filing its three discs with unheard jewels and unexpected gems. 'St. Tristan's' Sword' was a fitting example. Missing in action since 1970, this funky little tune – full of raw riffs from Page and dancing rhythms from JPJ and Bonzo – might not have been an easy fit for *Led Zeppelin III*, but it worked beautifully on the reconstructed *Coda*. The same could be said for 'Sugar Mama'. Oft bootlegged, but never given an official run-out by the group, the 1968 track – while raw as an uncooked potato – earned its place on Bonham's drums alone. From the Headley Grange wallop of 'Desire' ('The Wanton Song' in a slightly different shape) to the extremely anticipated retrieval of Jimmy and Robert's Bombay Sessions from the hands of "the bootleg brigade", *Coda* had come from the back to win the race.

An enjoyable trawl through past glories that added at least a dozen new bites to savour beyond the group's already established catalogue,

'Deluxe Reissues' again put Zep back into the charts, with all nine sets reaching the US Top 20 and several Top 10 placings in the UK. "These remasters aren't asking you to extend your idea of the Led Zeppelin canon but retract it," said *Uncut*'s John Robinson of Zep *I–III*, "to realise why these albums have the power and mystery that they do. And the reason that there aren't [even] more songs is because control – over quality, over everything – was, and is, very high." There was one man, however, who didn't rate Page's reissues series too highly. "What you're hearing there is mostly work-in-progress stuff," Robert Plant told *Billboard*. "Things on their way to completion, and maybe there's some little quirk or something that led to an 'either/or' moment. But it's nothing relevant. Not to me, at least."

Then in the midst of promoting his tenth (and it should be said, pretty good) solo album *Lullaby And The Ceaseless Roar*, Plant wasn't usually this blunt or scathing when it came to Zep product. But then, he and Jimmy Page had recently put aside their previous rules of engagement to conduct a highly unproductive, though still entertaining, sparring match in the pages of the press. No prizes for guessing the subject. "I was told last year that Robert Plant said he is doing nothing in 2014, and what do the other two guys think?" Page growled to *The New York Times* in the spring of that year. "Well, he knows what the other guys think. Everyone would love to play more concerts for the band. He's just playing games and I'm fed up with it, to be honest with you. [But] I don't sing, so I can't do much about it." Plant, who had reportedly offered Page an olive branch in previous months by suggesting an acoustic collaboration – "I said 'If you've got anything acoustic, let me know, I'll give it a whirl'" – was quick to respond and equally waspish in his rhetoric. "I think he needs to go to sleep," the singer told *The National*, "have a good rest, and think again. We have a great history together... like all brothers we have these moments where we don't speak on the same page. But that's life..."

By the autumn of 2014, the undignified exchange between the 'brothers' appeared to cool, with Robert now choosing less inflammatory ways of expressing his viewpoint. "I feel for the guy," he told *NME*. "He knows he's got the headlines if he wants them. But I don't know what he's trying to do, so I feel slightly disappointed and baffled." Jimmy, on the other hand, still sounded slightly aggrieved. "I can't be bothered anymore," he told *Rolling Stone*. "I don't think it's fun, so I'll say nothing." However, by the end of the year, he was willing to offer a little more. "Sometimes I raise my eyebrows at the things [Robert] says, but that's all I can say about it," he confirmed to *GQ* in December 2014. "I don't make a point to read what he says about Zeppelin. But people will read me things he has said, and I'll usually say, 'Are you sure you're quoting him correctly?' It's always a little surprising. But I can't answer for him. I have a respect for the work of everyone in the band. I can't be dismissive of the work we did together. I sort of know what he's doing. But," he concluded, this time with more confusion than ire, "I don't fully understand it."

So, there it was again. Page wanted to reform Led Zeppelin and Robert, as ever, didn't. Two contrasting opinions, seemingly immutable, that had come to define their relationship ever since the mighty airship first departed for the stars nearly 35 years before. Chris Welch, so long an ear to the original band, understood the dilemma better than most. "*Unledded* and *...Clarksdale* had been a pact between Jimmy and Robert to do something new and fresh," he said in 2015. "That really appealed to Robert and, of course, the hardcore Zep fans wholly approved. But beyond that, Jimmy's past was so illustrious, and Led Zeppelin had been his biggest achievement. I'm sure he didn't want to run from it, but actually *run to it*. After all, wouldn't you?"

CODA

The Fourth Life Of Jimmy Page

June 2016

On June 15, 2016, Jimmy Page once again found himself embroiled in issues of alleged plagiarism, this time appearing alongside Robert Plant in a Los Angeles courtroom to defend their most famous song, 'Stairway To Heaven'. Arriving with his old sparring partner in tow, Page was there to hear a case brought against the band by a trust set up to manage the legacy and affairs of the late Randy Craig Wolfe, better known to rock fans as 'Randy California', lead guitarist of Spirit[353].

The issue that brought Page and Plant back to LA was the claim that the opening bars of Spirit's 1968 instrumental track 'Taurus' were similar to 'Stairway...'. Defending Zep's famous duo was lawyer Robert

---

353 A gifted guitarist, Randy drowned in 1997 after rescuing his son, Quinn, from a rip current in Molokai, Hawaii. He was 45 years old. Before he died, however, California did leave behind an opinion regarding the similarities between 'Taurus' and 'Stairway...'. "Well, if you listen to the two songs, you can make your own judgement," he told *Classic Rock*. "I'd say it was a rip-off. Maybe some day their conscience will make them do something about it. There's funny dealings between record companies, managers, publishers and artists. But when artists do it to other artists... there's no excuse for that."

Anderson who was emphatic his charges "created 'Stairway To Heaven' independently without resort to 'Taurus' or without copying anything in 'Taurus'." Anderson was also keen to point out that the similarity in question – a "descending chromatic line" – was "something that appears in all kinds of songs", a "commonplace musical device" dating back centuries and, as such, not protected by copyright nor actually owned by the plaintiff. However, Randy California's lawyer, Francis Malofiy, took a different view, arguing the case could be reduced to just six words. "Give credit," he said, "where credit is due."

It is worth noting that nobody was denying that Page or Plant were unfamiliar with California or Spirit. In fact, as already stated in these pages, Zep had opened for the band and Vanilla Fudge at a concert in Denver in late 1968. Further, there were no issues that Zep had performed a section of Spirit's tune 'Fresh Garbage' in their own early sets, a song that, like 'Taurus', was featured on the band's debut LP[354]. But what they were denying in the strongest possible terms was that when Jimmy and Robert sat down together in Bron-Yr-Aur in 1970 to write 'Stairway...', 'Taurus' was no kind of influence at all. And for good reason, too. Aside from the potential damage to their credibility and reputation, Page and Plant's "masterpiece" had earned them a reported $58.5 million. With Wolfe/California's trust seeking "royalties and other compensation of around $40m", losing the case would not only be a blot on their artistic standing, but also extremely expensive. No matter how difficult a relationship Robert might previously have had with 'Stairway...', this was something worth fighting over. And indeed, by 24 June, it was all over. After a week or so of testimony from both sides – and an appearance from John Paul Jones to provide evidence on their behalf – the jury found in Page and Plant's favour, with 'Stairway To Heaven' deemed "not intrinsically similar"

---

354 Indeed, as part of his testimony, Jimmy confirmed he owned a copy of Spirit's debut LP, though he was "surprised" to find it in among his collection. "To be honest," he told the court, "I could have bought it or been given it." To further illustrate how it might have been overlooked, Page confirmed ownership of 4,329 LPs and 5,882 CDs.

to Spirit's 'Taurus'. In a brief statement, the pair celebrated the court's decision, saying that it "put to rest questions about (the song's) origins... (while also) confirming what we have known for 45 years." 'And that, any possible appeals notwithstanding, appeared to be that.'

Given their own apparent falling out in 2014, the 'Stairway To Heaven' case was perhaps not the kindest or most flattering way to get Jimmy Page and Robert Plant back together. But at least the two seemed to have resolved any differences in the run-up to the case, their bouts of sniping in the press now behind them. For Dave Lewis, this apparent rapprochement was all part of the rich, if occasionally tangled, relationship that had always existed between the two. "The relationship between Page and Plant has always been very complex," he confirmed. "At the start, they just got each other. Robert immediately understood all those years ago at Pangbourne what Jimmy was aiming for. He just got it. More, the synergy was there from the start, that shorthand, if you will. They also had a shared respect for each other's talents. But they were also markedly different in terms of where they were and what they'd done. Robert was this young guy down from the Midlands in jeans and a T-shirt while Jimmy's walking around his own rather nice place dressed in mock-Edwardian clothes with antique art hanging off his walls. There was a bit of catching up to do for Robert. But make no mistake, Plant was a quick study." And, as time had come to show, a man who seldom, if ever, wished to revisit the past just for the sake of it.

Of course, Jimmy Page had grown well used to Robert Plant's reluctance about refloating Zep, even if this reluctance still occasionally rankled him. "Well, it's his journey, isn't it?" he sighed at the end of 2014. And Page had one to make of his own, too. In the wake of their temporary spat and the Zep reissues that had occupied so much of his time, the guitarist had ended his own 2014 by discussing that ever-elusive second solo album and the prospect of another solo tour. "I haven't put [the musicians] together yet," he confirmed at the time, "but I'm going to do that next year. If I went out to play, I'd play material that spanned everything from my recording career right back to my very, very early days with the Yardbirds. There would certainly be some new material in there as well." Page's commitment to championing new acts was also apparent, his recent name-checking of nu-folk singer Laura Marling and Brighton's Royal Blood proving he could still spot good sounds when he heard them.

But it was not so much new music as neighbourhood disputes and fledgling romances that kept Page's name in the headlines over the course of the next year. In the spring of 2015, Jimmy lodged yet another complaint with Kensington & Chelsea Council over his new neighbour's plans to refurbish and extend his home. The neighbour in question was former Take That singer Robbie Williams, who in turn had purchased Michael Winner's old mansion – Woodland House, next door to Page's Tower House in Holland Park – for £17.5 million after the film director passed away in 2013.

Already consisting of 46 rooms, Williams' bold plans for his new property reportedly included removing a swimming pool and gym, altering flooring layouts, installing new air conditioning and a recording studio, while also replacing the garage. Jimmy, who had been living at the historic, Grade 1 listed Tower House beside Woodland House since 1972, was worried such extensive work would not only shake the foundations of his own home but also grant the public a better chance to see into it. Lodging a complaint stating Robbie's alterations were "extremely unfortunate in architectural terms", he backed his concerns with supporting letters from conservation architects, engineers and lawyers. Nonetheless, council authorities appeared to side with Williams, who was given the go ahead to make his improvements in July 2015, subject to certain criteria.[355]

Though Page might have been concerned with the extent of Robbie Williams' ambitions for Woodland House, he could at least take succour in another country home he had acquired in previous years. Like Pangbourne Boathouse, Plumpton Place and the Old Mill before,

---

355 The issue appeared to rumble on into early 2016, with other of William's neighbours reportedly joining Page in his original efforts to halt the work. However, by June of this year (2016), press coverage seems to have gone quiet and Robbie's work on Woodland House proceeds apace. Vibration monitors are possibly being used to ensure Page's Tower House will be unaffected by the proposed improvements.

Jimmy's Deanery Garden (or The Deanery) in the village of Sonning, a few miles east of Reading in Berkshire, had history as well as beauty to commend it. Designed by renowned Victorian architect Edwin Lutyens – who also had a hand in aspects of Plumpton Place – and built between 1899 and 1901 for Edward Hudson (the founder of *Country Life* magazine) as a show home, the house's high walls and secluded grounds afforded Page all the privacy he feared losing in Kensington. Among his neighbours in Sonning are the actor George Clooney and the illusionist Uri Geller.

Normally the most discreet of men away from the stage, Page's family and personal affairs now also seemed to follow his neighbourly disputes into the public domain. In the case of his daughter Scarlet, this was all for the good. A well-respected music photographer – who had made Jimmy a grandfather back in October 2007 with the birth of her first child, Martha[356] – Scarlet Page had been capturing musicians, rock stars and bands on film since the early nineties, initially under the guidance of the noted rock photographer Ross Halfin, himself a member of Jimmy's inner circle. But her 2014/15 exhibition *Resonators* saw her pointing a lens specifically at guitarists. First staged at the RAH in conjunction with Teenage Cancer Trust (and later, Crouch End's Arthouse), *Resonators* captured six-string legends such as Jeff Beck, Brian May, Slash, Albert Lee, Wilko Johnson, Blur's Graham Coxon, and not to mention her dad, in a series of relaxed and un-showy poses, the mock heroism usually associated with the genre for the most part absent. "I really wanted to do a charity project and Teenage Cancer Trust, with its incredible musical pedigree, and the amazing work it does, seemed ideal,"[357] she said.

However, while Jimmy was surely proud to see his daughter receiving positive reviews for her latest work, continuing press coverage of his new relationship with Scarlett Sabet must have been much less welcome. Page had always done much to keep his private affairs precisely that,

356 Sadly, Page's own mother Patricia passed away in 2015.
357 A book of Scarlet Page's portraits – also called *Resonators* – was published in December 2015.

with his divorce from Jimena Gomez-Paratcha in 2008 a strong case in point. Cruising under the radar at the time, few had known of the couple's separation, and it was only when Page himself reportedly let slip that he was single in an interview during 2011 that matters came to light. Unfortunately, there were few ways to manage the same trick with Sabet, who became the subject of some scrutiny over the course of 2015/16.

A poet, actress and film director based in London and of Iranian/French heritage, Scarlett Zoreh Sabet had won a drama scholarship to distinguished theatre school Hurtwood House as a teenager and subsequently acted in a number of British TV series, including *Peep Show*, *Skins* and *Life's Too Short*. According to reports, it may have been when her first book of verse, *Rocking Underground*, was launched at Chelsea Art Club in the winter of 2014 that she met first Jimmy. As striking as his previous partners and sporting a lustrous mane as burgundy as her forename suggested, Sabet's entrance into Page's life would probably have been less interesting to the press had it not been for the fact that she was 25 years old, some 46 summers younger than her new boyfriend. Inevitably, given their age difference, photographers were soon following the couple around in small droves, leading to an unlikely snap of multi-millionaire Page and his beau emerging from a branch of Nandos, the popular high street chicken restaurant chain, located near his sumptuous Kensington pile. "Why," asked the *Daily Mail* in 2015, "has a middle-class girl of 25 fallen for 71-year-old Jimmy Page?"

As was the case with his interest in the arcane, it was easy to link Jimmy's current romantic circumstances with the exploits of the past, as media coverage again fixated on his relationships in the seventies, and especially Jimmy's time with Lori Mattix.

Page, as ever, kept his counsel on the matter, though Zep biographer Barney Hoskyns did offer an opinion of his own concerning the other, less salubrious side of Zep's history. '[Jimmy] has always liked young girls," he said. "Like other rock stars of the time he was involved in a scene with young girls, particularly in LA. It was a particular period, which does not excuse it. But when a powerful older man takes up with

657

someone who is so much younger than them it does suggest immaturity. You have to ask if you can have a real relationship with someone young enough to be your granddaughter."

Again, these were questions only Page could answer, but he appeared in no hurry to do so. For the guitarist, his side of the Led Zeppelin story would have to wait until he was long gone. "I'd do a book that would be published posthumously," he told Channel 4 in 2015, "and I say that for a good reason. I wouldn't want to get caught up in legal wranglings. I just want to be able to do a book, say it how it was and that's it. I don't want to be bogged down in unpleasantness. I'd just like to tell the real story."

In early 2016, the focus of attention again swung back to Page and music, when rumours began to circulate that he and a reunited Led Zeppelin might headline the Glastonbury festival. With the Stones having got Pilton Farm off their bucket list in 2013 and Jimmy already appearing there alongside Robert Plant in 1995, the idea carried some logic. But as was the case so many times before, it came to nought. "Oh, I find that all really amusing," he once said of such tittle-tattle. "Will they, won't they join the dance..." Indeed, as the years go by, the idea of ever seeing Led Zeppelin on a stage again becomes ever more unlikely, though some continue to hold out shy hopes. "Oh, one more shake of the dice, I think!" laughed Chris Welch. "A semi-unplugged, perhaps, or even another 'time capsule' performance as a gesture to the fans. Just do it properly. No tours, no misleading expectations. Just one last shot for history's sake."

It is that notion of history and the enduring weight it carries that has become progressively more important in the story of Jimmy Page. As a teenager, like so many of his generation, he became obsessed with rock'n'roll, its power pulling at him until, in turn, he was powerless to do anything other than surrender to it. "At the end of the day, it really is all about the music," he told Mick Wall in 2000, "because I'm a fan of it. And that's what I really am. A fan." Nonetheless, unlike those content to just listen, Page wanted to actively participate, the mysterious guitar he found at his parents' house in Epsom beginning the journey for him.

By the early sixties, he was standing alongside Neil Christian and his fellow Crusaders, pipe-cleaner thin, but now in the words of John Hawken, "head and shoulders above everybody else on that stage. Just stunningly brilliant on guitar". And it was that gift with the guitar that got him into the London session scene, where he again prospered quickly. "Jimmy learned to read the parts, improvise, and take – or make – suggestions from the other players," said Dave Berry. "So, yes, Jimmy was way ahead of the game." The leap from studio player to pop star also seemed admirably easy for him, though there were casualties in the ranks afterwards. "Jimmy had an eye on the future in the Yardbirds," said Chris Dreja in 2010, "and there was friction [between him and Jeff Beck], even though they were great friends. It was a bit like a ménage a trois. Jeff, Jimmy but really, only one guitar. It wasn't going to work." But in the end, it was Beck's departure that set the scene for all that was to come. "Jimmy and Peter Grant really hit it off from the start," said Jim McCarty. "They were both 'into' and 'of' the business. And of course, Jimmy and Peter were very keen to carry on when the band broke up." Led Zeppelin were the result of that desire.

It is easy to be hagiographic about Jimmy Page and Led Zeppelin. Indeed, this author probably has been. But given the sheer scope of their achievements, Page and the band surely deserve much of their praise. From brash hard rock and searing blues to wistful folk, progressive whimsy and pioneering Sahara sounds, Zep always made a beguiling racket. "Aside from the music – which was sometimes just stunning – and the personalities involved, there was also a sense of real mystery to Led Zeppelin, a certain mystique that they created around themselves," said Chris Charlesworth. "Plus, there's also that very tidy catalogue, nine studio albums and out. All lean meat with no extra fat to wade through. By doing that, Zep presented an almost perfect package. Music, mystery, honour and endeavour. And Jimmy sat right on top of it."

No doubt about that. The driver behind the wheel, Jimmy Page's creativity and work rate in Zep cannot be underestimated. As lead guitarist, producer and principal songwriter, Page led by example, creating a band that would be astoundingly successful and shockingly influential, the prototype, in fact, for countless other groups to follow.

"People think of me as just a 'riff' guitarist, but I think of myself in broader terms," Jimmy told *Mojo* in 1996. "As a musician, my greatest achievement has been to create unexpected melodies and harmonies within a rock framework. As a producer, I'd like to be remembered as someone who was able to sustain a band of unquestionable individual talent and push it to the forefront during its working career."

That said, there were mistakes made on the way, and not all of them easily forgotten. At times, Led Zeppelin could appear avaricious, the constant crowing about the group's financial success and Peter Grant's determination to grasp every cent owed them probably alienating sections of the American press and leading to years of bad reviews as a result. The violence and sense of menace surrounding the band's latter years was also hard to conscience, as some in Zep's camp lost the run of themselves, leading to needless injury and tarnished reputations. Again, the sticky habit of not initially giving credit to the blues artists that inspired them tends to rankle, especially when one considers the sums of money made.

Still, there is always the music. Still vibrant, still alive and, for millions of rock fans, still untouchable. Following his time with Led Zeppelin, Jimmy Page tried to recreate some of the band's magic and, on occasion, he came close: parts of *Death Wish* and *Outrider*, a track here and there on *Coverdale/Page* and certainly his later work with Robert Plant all glistened with new promise, some tunes even touching the hem of Led Zeppelin's all-pervasive garment. But nothing came quite close enough to what had come before, which in turn led Page to return again and again to the band that he made and that ultimately made him. *Remasters*, *DVD*, *How The West Was* Won, and the deluxe reissues of 2014/15. All were examples of Jimmy re-examining the source material, often reframing it for the better and, in so doing, restoring much of its original power and potency for old and new fans alike.

And it is the care he has shown for his previous work with Led Zeppelin that will probably define Jimmy Page's fourth life. While he may not greatly care for the term, he has become – in the words of *Uncut*'s Allan Jones – the "curator of Led Zeppelin's heritage", and proved himself very good at it. Curator, but guardian and gatekeeper too, Page is now largely responsible not only for how future generations might engage with the band, but also the terms of that engagement. "In its own way, it's sad," said Chris Charlesworth. "By achieving so much so young, Jimmy's almost held to his past. But it's a glorious past, and one that would be almost impossible to top. God, he's like Churchill, isn't he? This towering figure forever defined by the victories of one glorious era. But Jimmy's also been very canny. He's learned to administrate that past and make it work for him. In interviews, he'll avoid certain questions he's uncomfortable with or plead ignorance on others that might 'shake the legend', like Oakland. I suspect he learned a lot from Mick Jagger in that area. But there's a reason for it. Throughout it all, Jimmy has kept the flag flying for Led Zeppelin and he now knows what he has to do to keep it from blowing away during any unexpected storms."

It is easy to lose sight of Jimmy Page in the mystique and myths, or at least the ones he is willing to share. However, as he has always said, "It's the music that counts", and ultimately, it is the music he leaves behind by which he will be judged. "If you compare Jimmy to his peers, Eric Clapton, Jeff Beck, even David Gilmour, no disrespect to them, but he towers above them all in terms of his persona, and what he's achieved," said Dave Lewis. "Jimmy has an aura that's always been there, that separates him from the others. And that won't change. As the years go by, Led Zeppelin and their music are becoming more important, more revered, more loved. And that's been helped by Jimmy's work as a custodian of the legend and keeper of the flame. He knew what he had all those years ago and how important it was. His life's work has made a massive impact on millions of people. If the 17-year-old Jimmy Page met his 72-year-old self, what would he think, I wonder? I suspect he'd think he'd done pretty well..."

It is unlikely that Jimmy Page is finished with music or that music is finished with him. In fact, seldom does a month pass by without more rumours of albums, collaborations and tours. As in previous years, most of it turns out to be unlikely or fanciful, but occasionally there is enough to the story to make the pulse race. Whether we have seen the last of Led Zeppelin is equally uncertain. Despite the wishes of some, as ever that decision lies in the lap of the golden gods. But stranger things have happened. Until then, there is enough music to be getting on with. Page has seen to that. "Have I done enough?" he was once asked. His answer said much. "Well, you can never do enough. But I don't care. It doesn't matter. It is what it is."

It is what it is, then.

JIMMY PAGE

A Selected Discography

What follows is a selected discography of Jimmy Page's work as a session musician, band leader and collaborator. While not detailing each and every release he has involved himself with over the last six decades, this discography nevertheless covers the majority of Page's recordings, covering the years 1963 to 2015.

1) Sessions
It would take a brave man to categorically state which tracks Jimmy Page played on during his tenure as a session musician. In fact, he has freely admitted that it is impossible even for him to remember every song and studio date. The number surely runs to hundreds. What follows then, are selected highlights from Page's session back catalogue (1963–1968), plus a number of additional singles, EPs and album tracks he contributed to either during his time with Led Zeppelin and thereafter.

January 1963: Diamonds/Hully Gully - Jet Harris and Tony Meehan
June 1963: Hey Josephine/Road Runner - Wayne Fontana & the Mindbenders
July 1963: The Worryin' Kind/Come To Me - Brian Howard & the Silhouettes

July 1963: A Little Bit Of Something Else/Get A Load Of This
 - Neil Christian & the Crusaders
September 1963: The Feminine Look/Shame On You Boy - Mickie Most
November 1963: Secret Love/You Have To Want To Touch Him
 - Kathy Kirby
December 1963: Roll Over Beethoven/Is It Love? - Pat Wayne With The
 Beachcombers
January 1964: My Baby Left Me/Hoochie Coochie Man - Dave Berry
March 1964: Skinnie Minnie/Easy To Cry - Carter-Lewis & the
 Southerners
March 1964: Little Child/Never A Mention - Jackie Lynton
April 1964: Shout/Forget Me, Baby - Lulu & the Luvers
April 1964: Pills/Hush Your Mouth - Mickey Finn & the Blue Men
May 1964: Hold Me/The Tips Of My Fingers - PJ Proby
May 1964: Honey Hush/One For The Money - Christian's Crusaders
July 1964: The Crying Game/Don't Give Me No Lip Child
 - Dave Berry
July 1964: It's Only Make Believe/Honey What You Want Me To Do
 - Billy Fury
July 1964: Heart Of Stone/What A Shame - The Rolling Stones
July 1964: Bye Bye Baby/She's Fallen In Love With The Monster Man
 - Screaming Lord Sutch
August 1964: Is It True?/What'd I Say - Brenda Lee
August 1964: Together/Sweet And Tender Romance - PJ Proby
September 1964: I'll Cry Instead/Those Precious Words - Joe Cocker
September 1964: Walk Tall/Only The Heartaches - Val Doonican
October 1964: A Certain Girl/Leave My Kitten Alone - First Gear
October 1964: Downtown/You'd Better Love Me - Petula Clark
October 1964: Good Morning Little Schoolgirl/I'm Gonna Move...
 - Rod Stewart
October 1964: Terry/The Boy Of My Dreams - Twinkle
November 1964: Baby Please Don't Go/Gloria - Them
November 1964: Don't Turn Your Back On Me/Be Good Baby
 - Jackie DeShannon
November 1964: Sweet And Tender Romance/That Lonely Feeling
 - The McKinleys

February 1965: Come And Stay With Me/What Have I Done Wrong
- Marianne Faithfull

March 1965: I Pity The Fool/Take My Tip - Mannish Boys

April 1965: After A While/You Know - Brian Poole & the Tremeloes

April 1965: Masters Of War/Castin' My Spell - Talismen

May 1965: What The World Needs Now Is Love/Be Good Baby
- Jackie DeShannon

June 1965: Let The Water Run Down/I Don't Want To Hear It Anymore
- PJ Proby

July 1965: This Strange Effect/Now - Dave Berry

July 1965: The Monkey Time/Chocolate Rolls, Tea And Monopoly
- Golden Apples Of The Sun

August 1965: The Last Mile/I'm Not Sayin' - Nico

September 1965: I'm Your Witchdoctor/Telephone Blues - John Mayall &
Eric Clapton

October 1965: Someday/(We're) Wasting Time - Jimmy Tarbuck

November 1965: Mary Anne/Like Grains Of Sand - Glyn Johns

November 1965: To Whom It May Concern/It's Up To You Now
- Chris Andrews

January 1966: The World Keeps Going Round/Not The Same Anymore
- Lancastrians

March 1966: The Pied Piper/Sweet Dawn, My True Love - Crispian St. Peters

June 1966: Out Of Time/Baby Make It Soon - Chris Farlowe

August 1966: The Elf/Turn Into Earth - Al Stewart

September 1966: You Must Be The One/Why Treat Me This Way
- Tommy Vance

November 1966: Shapes In My Mind/Blue Sands - Keith Relf

March 1967: Hi Ho Silver Lining/Beck's Bolero - Jeff Beck

April 1967: A Degree Of Murder (Soundtrack album) – Brian Jones

May 1967: Barrelhouse Woman/Under Your Hood - Champion Jack Dupree

December 1967: Garden Of My Mind/Time To Start Loving You
- Mickey Finn

January 1968: The Maureeny Wishful Album – John Williams, Jimmy Page,
Big Jim Sullivan

May 1968: Hurdy Gurdy Man/Teen Angel - Donovan

July 1968: Paint It Black/I Just Need Your Loving - Chris Farlowe

September 1968: With A Little Help From My Friends/Something's Coming On - Joe Cocker

October 1968: The Day Lorraine Came Down/Mary Hopkins... - PJ Proby

January 1969: Knick Knack Man/A Penny For The Sun - Cartoone

September 1969: The Love Chronicles (Album) - Al Stewart

June 1970: Election Fever/Rock The Election - Screaming Lord Sutch

May 1971: Same Old Rock (from the album *Stormcock*) - Roy Harper

March 1975: If You Don't Know (from the album *Suicide Sal*) - Maggie Bell

July 1984: 50/50/Flaming Heart/Right By You - Stephen Stills

October 1984: Sea Of Love/I Get a Thrill - The Honeydrippers

March 1985: Spaghetti Junction/Crackback (from the album *Scream For Help*) - John Paul Jones

April 1985: These Arms Of Mine/Slippin' And Slidin' - Willie & the Poor Boys

March 1986: Asylum (from the album *Strange Land*) - Box Of Frogs

May 1986: One Hit To The Body/Fight - The Rolling Stones

February 1988: Tall Cool One/White, Clean and Neat - Robert Plant

July 1998: Come With Me/Apollo Four Forty Remix/S.S.O. Remix - Puff Daddy

September 2006: Rock And Roll (from the album *Last Man Standing*) - Jerry Lee Lewis

Session Compilations

There are a number of CDs collecting various session appearances by Jimmy Page during the sixties, some good, some less so. For anyone looking to find a proper anthology that captures both the variety and spirit of Jimmy's work as a guitarist/producer, then *Hip Young Guitarslinger* does the job nicely enough. Stand advised, however; there remains some dispute as to whether Page actually plays on all featured tracks. Anyway, please find details below.

Jimmy Page – Hip Young Guitarslinger

Disc One: Who Told You (Carter Lewis & the Southerners)/Angie/Please Believe Me (Gregory Phillips)/Somebody Told My Girl/Skinnie Minnie (Carter Lewis & the Southerners)/Kelly/See You Later Alligator (Wayne Gibson)/Revenge/Bald Headed Woman (The Kinks)/A Certain Girl/Leave My Kitten Alone (First Gear)/Help Me/Let Them Tell (The Primitives)/We'll Sing In The Sunshine/Was She Tall (The Lancastrians)/You Said/How Do You Feel (The Primitives)/The

'In' Crowd/Gotta Make Their Future Bright (First Gear)/The Bells
Of Rhymney/Just Like Anyone Would Do (The Fifth Avenue)/I'm
Not Sayin'/The Last Mile (Nico)/Down In The Boondocks/That's
The One (Gregory Phillips)/She Belongs To Me/Taken My Love (The
Masterminds)

Disc Two: I'm Your Witchdoctor/Telephone Blues/On Top Of The World
(John Mayall & the Bluesbreakers featuring Eric Clapton)/Moondreams/
Wait For Me (Les Fleur De Lys)/The World Keeps Going Round/Not
The Same Anymore (The Lancastrians)/Can't Go Home Anymore/
My Love (The Factotums/Circles/So, Come On (The Fleur De Lys)/
Sittin' On A Fence/Step Out Of Line (Twice As Much)/Moanin' (Chris
Farlowe)/Choker/Freight Loader/Miles Road/Draggin' My Tail (Jimmy
Page & Eric Clapton)/L.A. Breakdown/Down in The Boots (The All
Stars with Jimmy Page)/Snake Drive/West Coast Idea/A Tribute To
Elmore (Eric Clapton)/Chuckles/Stealin' (The All Stars with Jeff Beck)/
Piano Shuffle (The All Stars with Nicky Hopkins)/Not Fade Away (Cyril
Davies's Rhythm & Blues All Stars)

Castle NEE CD 486 CD August 2000

2) The Yardbirds

Singles

Happening Ten Years Time Ago/Psycho Daisies
Epic DB 8024 7" October 1966

Little Games/Puzzles
Epic DB 8165 7" April 1967

Ha Ha Said The Clown/Tinker, Tailor, Soldier, Sailor
Epic 10204 72 June 1967

Ten Little Indians/Drinking Muddy Water
Epic 10248 7" October 1967

Goodnight Sweet Josephine/Think About It
Epic/Columbia DB 8368/10303 7" March 1968

LPs

Little Games

Little Games/Smile On Me/White Summer/Tinker, Tailor, Soldier, Sailor/
    Glimpses/Drinking Muddy Water/No Excess Baggage/Stealing, Stealing/
    Only The Black Rose/Little Soldier Boy

Columbia/Epic LN 24/BN 26 313 LP August 1967

Live Yardbirds

Train Kept A-Rollin'/You're A Better Man Than I/I'm Confused/My Baby/
    Over, Under, Sideways, Down/Drinking Muddy Water/Shapes Of Things/
    White Summer/I'm A Man

KE KE 30615 LP September 1971

3) Led Zeppelin – Studio, Live, Collections

Led Zeppelin were always an albums band and it suited them well. Therefore,
this discography ignores the few singles that did escape the mothership over
the course of its 12-year voyage, and concentrates instead on the big guns,
including recent reissues (Deluxe Editions) with additional tracks.

Studio Albums

Led Zeppelin

Good Times Bad Times/Babe, I'm Gonna Leave You/You Shook Me/
    Dazed And Confused/Your Time Is Gonna Come/Black Mountain Side/
    Communication Breakdown/I Can't Quit You Baby/How Many More
    Times

Atlantic 588 171 LP January 1969

Led Zeppelin (2 CD Deluxe Edition)

Disc One: Good Times Bad Times/Babe, I'm Gonna Leave You/You Shook
    Me/Dazed And Confused/Your Time Is Gonna Come/Black Mountain
    Side/Communication Breakdown/I Can't Quit You Baby/How Many
    More Times

Disc Two (Companion Audio): Live at The Olympia, Paris 1969): Good
    Times Bad Times/Communication Breakdown/I Can't Quit You Baby/
    Heartbreaker/Dazed And Confused/White Summer–Black Mountain
    Side/You Shook Me/Moby Dick/How Many More Times

Atlantic 8122 796 457 CD June 2014

Led Zeppelin II
Whole Lotta Love/What Is And What Should Never Be/The Lemon Song/
  Thank You/Heartbreaker/Living Loving Maid (She's Just A Woman)/
  Ramble On/Moby Dick/Bring It On Home
Atlantic 588 188 LP October 1969

Led Zeppelin II (2 CD Deluxe Edition)
Disc One: Whole Lotta Love/What Is And What Should Never Be/The
  Lemon Song/Thank You/Heartbreaker/Living Loving Maid (She's Just A
  Woman)/Ramble On/Moby Dick/Bring It On Home
Disc Two (Companion Audio): Whole Lotta Love (Rough Mix With Vocal)/
  What Is And What Never Should Be (Rough Mix With Vocal)/
  Thank You (Backing Track)/Heartbreaker (Rough Mix With Vocal)/Living
  Loving Maid (She's Just A Woman) (Backing Track)/Ramble On (Rough
  Mix With Vocal)/Moby Dick (Backing Track)/La La (Intro/Outro Rough
  Mix)
Atlantic 8122 796 453 CD June 2014

Led Zeppelin III
Immigrant Song/Friends/Celebration Day/Since I've Been Loving You/
  Out On The Tiles/Gallows Pole/Tangerine/That's The Way/Bron-Y-Aur
  Stomp/Hats Off To (Roy) Harper
Atlantic 2401 002 LP October 1970

Led Zeppelin III (2 CD Deluxe Edition)
Disc One: Immigrant Song/Friends/Celebration Day/Since I've Been Loving
  You/Out On The Tiles/Gallows Pole/Tangerine/That's The Way/Bron-Y-
  Aur Stomp/Hats Off To (Roy) Harper
Disc Two (Companion Audio): The Immigrant Song (Alternate Mix)/
  Friends (Track – No Vocal)/Celebration Day (Alternate Mix)/Since I've
  Been Loving You (Rough Mix)/Bathroom Sound (Track – No Vocal)/
  Gallows Pole (Rough Mix)/That's The Way (Rough Mix)/Jennings
  Farm Blues (Rough Mix)/Keys To The Highway–Trouble In Mind
  (Rough Mix)
Atlantic 8122 796 449 8 CD June 2014

Led Zeppelin IV
Black Dog/Rock And Roll/The Battle Of Evermore/Stairway To Heaven/
Misty Mountain Hop/Four Sticks/Going To California/When The Levee
Breaks
Atlantic K50008 LP November 1971

Led Zeppelin IV (2 CD Deluxe Edition)
Disc One: Black Dog/Rock And Roll/The Battle Of Evermore/Stairway To
Heaven/Misty Mountain Hop/Four Sticks/Going To California/When
The Levee Breaks
Disc Two (Companion Audio): Black Dog (Basic Track With Guitar
Overdubs)/Rock And Roll (Alternate Mix)/The Battle Of Evermore
(Mandolin/Guitar Mix From Headley Grange)/Stairway To Heaven
(Sunset Sound Mix)/Misty Mountain Hop (Alternate Mix)/Four Sticks
(Alternate Mix)/Going To California (Mandolin/Guitar Mix)/When The
Levee Breaks (Alternate UK Mix)
Atlantic 8122 796 446 7 CD October 2014

Houses Of The Holy
The Song Remains The Same/The Rain Song/Over The Hills And Far
Away/The Crunge/Dancing Days/D'Yer Mak'er/No Quarter/The Ocean
Atlantic K50014 LP March 1973

Houses Of The Holy (2 CD Deluxe Edition)
Disc One: The Song Remains The Same/The Rain Song/Over The Hills
And Far Away/The Crunge/Dancing Days/D'Yer Mak'er/No Quarter/
The Ocean
Disc Two (Companion Audio): The Song Remains The Same (Guitar
Overdub Reference Mix)/The Rain Song (Mix Minus Piano)/Over The
Hills And Far Away (Guitar Mix Backing Track)/The Crunge (Rough Mix
– Keys Up)/Dancing Days (Rough Mix With Vocal)/No Quarter (Rough
Mix With JPJ Keyboard Overdubs – No Vocal)/The Ocean (Working Mix)
Atlantic 8122 795 827 5 CD October 2014

Physical Graffiti
Custard Pie/The Rover/In My Time Of Dying/Houses Of The Holy/
Trampled Under Foot/Kashmir/In The Light/Bron-Yr-Aur/Down By

The Seaside/Ten Years Gone/Night Flight/The Wanton Song/Boogie
With Stu/Black Country Woman/Sick Again
Swan Song SSK 89400 LP February 1975

Physical Graffiti (3 CD Deluxe Edition)
Disc One: Custard Pie/The Rover/In My Time Of Dying/Houses Of The
   Holy/Trampled Under Foot/Kashmir
Disc Two: In The Light/Bron-Yr-Aur/Down By The Seaside/Ten Years
   Gone/Night Flight/The Wanton Song/Boogie With Stu/Black Country
   Woman/Sick Again
Disc Three (Companion Audio): Brandy & Coke (Trampled Under Foot –
   Initial/Rough Mix)/Sick Again (Early Version)/In My Time Of Dying
   (Initial/Rough Mix)/Houses Of The Holy (Rough Mix With Overdubs)/
   Everybody Makes It Through (In The Light – Early Version/In Transit]/
   Boogie With Stu (Sunset Sound Mix)/Driving Through Kashmir (Kashmir
   – Rough Orchestra Mix)
Atlantic 8122 795 794 0 CD February 2015

Presence
Achilles Last Stand/For Your Life/Royal Orleans/Nobody's Fault But Mine/
   Candy Store Rock/Hots On For Nowhere/Tea For One
Swan Song SSK 59402 LP March 1976

Presence (2 CD Deluxe Edition)
Disc One: Achilles Last Stand/For Your Life/Royal Orleans/Nobody's Fault
   But Mine/Candy Store Rock/Hots On For Nowhere/Tea For One
Disc Two (Companion Audio): Two Ones Are One (Achilles Last Stand)/For
   Your Life/Ten Ribs & All–Carrot Pod Pod (Pod)/Royal Orleans/Hots On
   For Nowhere (Reference Mixes Of Work In Progress)
Atlantic 8122 795 573 1 CD July 2015

In Through The Out Door
In The Evening/South Bound Suarez/Fool In The Rain/Hot Dog/
   Carouselambra/All My Love/I'm Gonna Crawl
Swan Song 59410 LP August 1979

In Through The Out Door (2 CD Deluxe Edition)
Disc One: In The Evening/South Bound Suarez/Fool In The Rain/Hot
 Dog/Carouselambra/All My Love/I'm Gonna Crawl
Disc Two (Companion Audio): In The Evening/South Bound Piano (South
 Bound Suarez)/Fool In The Rain/Hot Dog/The Epic (Carouselambra)/
 The Hook (All My Love)/Blot (I'm Gonna Crawl) (Rough Mixes Of
 Work In Progress)
Atlantic 8122 795 5793 CD July 2015

Coda
We're Gonna Groove/Poor Tom/I Can't Quit You Baby/Walter's Walk/
 Ozone Baby/Darlene/Bonzo's Montreux/Wearing And Tearing
Swan Song 790051 LP November 1982

Coda (3 CD Deluxe Edition)
Disc One: We're Gonna Groove/Poor Tom/I Can't Quit You Baby/Walter's
 Walk/Ozone Baby/Darlene/Bonzo's Montreux/Wearing And Tearing
Disc Two (Companion Audio): We're Gonna Groove (Alternate Mix)/If It
 Keeps On Raining (When The Levee Breaks – Rough Mix)/Bonzo's
 Montreux (Mix Construction In Progress)/Baby Come On Home/Sugar
 Mama (Mix)/Poor Tom (Instrumental Mix)/Travelling Riverside Blues
 (BBC Session)/Hey, Hey What Can I Do
Disc Three (Companion Audio): Four Hands (Four Sticks–Bombay
 Orchestra)/Friends (Bombay Orchestra)/St. Tristan's Sword (Rough Mix)/
 Desire (The Wanton Song – Rough Mix)/Bring It On Home (Rough
 Mix)/Walter's Walk (Rough Mix)/Everybody Makes It Through (In The
 Light – Rough Mix)
Atlantic 8122 795 584 7 CD July 2015

Live Albums
The Soundtrack From The Film 'The Song Remains The Same'
Rock And Roll/Celebration Day/The Song Remains The Same/The Rain
 Song/Dazed And Confused/No Quarter/Stairway To Heaven/Moby
 Dick/Whole Lotta Love
Swan Song 89402 LP October 1976

The Soundtrack From The Film 'The Song Remains The Same' (Reissue)
Disc One: Rock And Roll/Celebration Day/Black Dog (inc. Bring It On
Home)/Over The Hills And Far Away/Misty Mountain Hop/Since I've
Been Loving You/No Quarter/The Song Remains The Same/The Rain
Song/The Ocean
Disc Two: Dazed And Confused/Stairway To Heaven/Moby Dick/
Heartbreaker/Whole Lotta Love
Swan Song R2 328 52 CD November 2007

Led Zeppelin – The BBC Sessions
Disc One: You Shook Me/I Can't Quit You Baby/Communication
Breakdown/Dazed And Confused/The Girl I Love (She Got Long Black
Wavy Hair)/What Is And What Should Never Be/Communication
Breakdown/Travelling Riverside Blues/Whole Lotta Love/Something
Else/Communication Breakdown/I Can't Quit You Baby/You Shook Me/
How Many More Times
Disc Two: Immigrant Song/Heartbreaker/Since I've Been Loving You/Black
Dog/Dazed And Confused/Stairway To Heaven/Going To California/
That's the Way/Whole Lotta Love/Boogie Chillun'/Fixin' To Die/That's
All Right Mama/Thank You
Atlantic 7567 83061 2 CD November 1997

How The West Was Won
Disc One: LA Drone/Immigrant Song/Heartbreaker/Black Dog/Over The
Hills And Far Away/Since I've Been Loving You/Stairway To Heaven/
Going To California/Bron-Yr-Aur Stomp
Disc Two: Dazed And Confused/Walter's Walk/The Crunge/What Is And
What Should Never Be/Dancing Days/Moby Dick
Disc Three: Whole Lotta Love/Boogie Chillun'/Let's Have A Party/Hello
Marylou/Going Down Slow/Rock And Roll/The Ocean/Bring It On
Home
Atlantic 7567 83587 2 CD May 2003

Celebration Day
Disc One: Good Times Bad Times/Ramble On/Black Dog/In My Time Of
Dying/For Your Life/Trampled Under Foot/Nobody's Fault But Mine/
No Quarter

673

Disc Two: Since I've Been Loving You/Dazed And Confused/Stairway To Heaven/The Song Remains The Same/Misty Mountain Hop/Kashmir/Whole Lotta Love/Rock And Roll

DVD (Disc): Good Times Bad Times/Ramble On/Black Dog/In My Time Of Dying/For Your Life/Trampled Under Foot/Nobody's Fault But Mine/No Quarter/Since I've Been Loving You/Dazed And Confused/Stairway To Heaven/The Song Remains The Same/Misty Mountain Hop/Kashmir/Whole Lotta Love/Rock And Roll

Swan Song/Atlantic 8122 CD/DVD 796788 2

Collections

Led Zeppelin Box Set (Four Disc Edition)

Disc One: Whole Lotta Love/Heartbreaker/Communication Breakdown/Babe, I'm Gonna Leave You/What Is And What Never Should Be/Thank You/I Can't Quit You Baby/Dazed And Confused/Your Time Is Gonna Come/Ramble On/Travelling Riverside Blues/Friends/Celebration Day/Hey Hey What Can I Do/White Summer–Black Mountain Side

Disc Two: Black Dog/Over The Hills And Far Away/Immigrant Song/The Battle Of Evermore/Bron-Y-Aur Stomp/Tangerine/Going To California/Since I've Been Loving You/D'Yer Mak'er/Gallows Pole/Custard Pie/Misty Mountain Hop/Rock And Roll/The Rain Song/Stairway To Heaven

Disc Three: Kashmir/Trampled Under Foot/For Your Life/No Quarter/Dancing Days/When The Levee Breaks/Achilles Last Stand/The Song Remains The Same/Ten Years Gone/In My Time Of Dying

Disc Four: In The Evening/Candy Store Rock/The Ocean/Ozone Baby/Houses Of the Holy/Wearing And Tearing/Poor Tom/Nobody's Fault But Mine/Fool In The Rain/In The Light/The Wanton Song/Moby Dick–Bonzo's Montreux/I'm Gonna Crawl/All My Love

Atlantic 75677821441 CD September 1990

Remasters (Two Disc Edition)

Disc One: Communication Breakdown/Babe, I'm Gonna Leave You/Good Times Bad Times/Dazed And Confused/Whole Lotta Love/Heartbreaker/Ramble On/Immigrant Song/Celebration Day/Since I've Been Loving You/Black Dog/Rock And Roll/The Battle Of Evermore/Misty Mountain Hop/Stairway To Heaven

Disc Two: The Song Remains The Same/The Rain Song/D'yer Mak'er/No
   Quarter/Houses Of The Holy/Kashmir/Trampled Under Foot/Nobody's
   Fault But Mine/Achilles Last Stand/All My Love/In The Evening
Atlantic 7567804152 CD October 1990

Led Zeppelin – Boxed Set Two (Two Disc Edition)
Disc One: Good Times Bad Times/We're Gonna Groove/Night Flight/That's
   The Way/Baby Come On Home/The Lemon Song/You Shook Me/
   Boogie With Stu/Bron-Yr-Aur/Down By The Seaside/Out On The Tiles/
   Black Mountain Side/Moby Dick/Sick Again/Hot Dog/Carouselambra
Disc Two: South Bound Suarez/Walter's Walk/Darlene/Black Country
   Woman/How Many More Times/The Rover/Four Sticks/Hats Off To
   (Roy) Harper/I Can't Quit You Baby/Hots On For Nowhere/Living
   Loving Maid (She's Just A Woman)/Royal Orleans/Bonzo's Montreux/
   The Crunge/Bring It On Home/Tea For One
Atlantic 82477 CD September 1993

The Best Of Led Zeppelin (Volume One) – Early Days
Good Times Bad Times/Babe, I'm Gonna Leave You/Dazed And Confused/
   Communication Breakdown/Whole Lotta Love/What Is And What Never
   Should Be/Immigrant Song/Since I've Been Loving You/Black Dog/
   Rock And Roll/The Battle Of Evermore/When The Levee Breaks/
   Stairway To Heaven
Atlantic 832 68 1 CD November 1999

The Best Of Led Zeppelin (Volume Two) – Latter Days
The Song Remains The Same/No Quarter/Houses Of The Holy/Trampled
   Under Foot/Kashmir/Ten Years Gone/Achilles Last Stand/Nobody's Fault
   But Mine/All My Love/In The Evening
Atlantic 832 78 2 CD March 2000

Mothership
Disc One: Good Times Bad Times/Communication Breakdown/Dazed And
   Confused/Babe, I'm Gonna Leave You/Whole Lotta Love/Ramble On/
   Heartbreaker/Immigrant Song/Since I've Been Loving You/Rock And
   Roll/Black Dog/When The Levee Breaks/Stairway To Heaven

Disc Two: The Song Remains The Same/Over The Hills And Far Away/D'Yer Mak'er/No Quarter/Trampled Under Foot/Houses Of The Holy/ Kashmir/Nobody's Fault But Mine/Achilles Last Stand/In The Evening/ All My Love

Swan Song/Atlantic 8122 79961 5 CD November 2007

4) Jimmy Page – Singles, Soundtracks, Solo Album
Singles
She Just Satisfies/Keep Moving
Fontana TF 533 7" February 1965

Soundtracks
Death Wish II
Who's To Blame/The Chase/City Sirens/Jam Sandwich/Carole's Theme/ The Release/Hotel Rats And Photostats/Shadow In The City/Jill's Theme/ Prelude/Big Band, Sax And Violence/Hypnotising Ways (Oh Mamma)
Swan Song SSK 594 15 LP February 1982

Lucifer Rising And Other Soundtracks
Disc One: Lucifer Rising (Main Track)/Incubus/Damask/Unharmonics/ Damask-Ambient/Lucifer Rising (Percussive Return)
Disc Two: Lucifer Rising Early Mix/Sonic Textures 1 – Earth/Sonic Textures 2 – Air/Sonic Textures 3 – Fire/Sonic Textures 4 – Water/Sonic Textures 5 – Ether
Disc Three (*Death Wish II*): Who's To Blame/The Chase/City Sirens/Jam Sandwich/Carole's Theme/The Release/Hotel Rats And Photostats/ Shadow In The City/Jill's Theme/Prelude/Big Band, Sax And Violence/ Hypnotising Ways/Main Title
Disc Four (*Death Wish II* Expansion): Jill's Orchestral Theme/Alternate Jill's Theme/9MI/City Sirens/Baby I Miss You So/Hey Mama–Swinging Sax/ Carole's Theme–Strings/Prelude/Country Sandwich/A Minor Sketch
JP RCD BX1 CD March 2012

Solo Album
Outrider
Wasting My Time/Wanna Make Love/Writes Of Winter/The Only One/ Liquid Mercury/Hummingbird/Emerald Eyes/Prison Blues/Blues Anthem

Geffen 924 188 2 CD June 1988

Collaborations/Notable Appearances
Roy Harper (Featuring Jimmy Page)
Whatever Happened To Jugula?
Nineteen Forty-Eightish/Bad Speech/Hope/Hangman/Elizabeth/Frozen
   Moment/Twentieth Century Man/Advertisement (Another Intentional
   Irrelevant Suicide)
Beggars Banquet BEGA 60 LP March 1985

The Firm
Closer/Make Or Break/Someone To Love/Together/Radioactive/You've
   Lost That Loving Feeling/Money Can't Buy/Satisfaction Guaranteed/
   Midnight Moonlight
Atlantic 781 2392 81239 CD February 1985

Mean Business
Fortune Hunter/Cadillac/All The King's Horses/Live In Peace/Tear Down
   The Walls/Dreaming/Free To Live/Spirit Of Love
Atlantic 781 628 2 81628 CD February 1986

Coverdale/Page
Shake My Tree/Waiting On You/Take Me For A Little While/Pride And Joy/
   Over Now/Felling Hot/Easy Does It/Take A Look At Yourself/Don't
   Leave Me This Way/Absolution Blues/Whisper A Prayer For The Dying
EMI/Geffen 0777 7 81401 22 CD March 1993

No Quarter: Jimmy Page & Robert Plant Unledded
Nobody's Fault But Mine/Thank You/No Quarter/Friends/Yallah/City
   Don't Cry/Since I've Been Loving You/The Battle Of Evermore/
   Wonderful One/Wah Wah/That's The Way/Gallows Pole/Four Sticks/
   Kashmir
Fontana 526 362 2 CD Fontana October 1994

Walking To Clarksdale
Shining In The Light/When The World Was Young/Upon A Golden Horse/
   Blue Train/Please Read The Letter/Most High/Heart In Your Hand/

Walking Into Clarksdale/Burning Up/When I Was A Child/House Of
Love/Sons Of Freedom/Whiskey From The Glass (Bonus Track, Japanese
Edition)
Mercury 558 025 2 CD April 1998

Jimmy Page And The Black Crowes – Live At The Greek
Disc One: Celebration Day/Custard Pie/Sick Again/What Is And What
Should Never Be/Woke Up This Morning/Shapes Of Things To Come/
Sloppy Drunk/Ten Years Gone/In My Time Of Dying/Your Time Is
Gonna Come
Disc Two: The Lemon Song/Nobody's Fault But Mine/Heartbreaker/Hey
Hey What Can I Do/Mellow Down Easy/Oh Well/Shake Your Money
Maker/You Shook Me/Out On The Tiles/Whole Lotta Love
TVT 2140 2 CD February 2000

5) Films/DVDs
Led Zeppelin – The Song Remains The Same
Mob Rubout/Mob Town Credits/Country Life (Autumn Lake)/Bron-
Yr-Aur/Rock And Roll/Black Dog/Since I've Been Loving You/No
Quarter/Who's Responsible/The Song Remains The Same/The Rain
Song/Fire And Sword/Capturing The Castle/Not Quite Backstage Pass/
Dazed And Confused/Strung Out/Magic In The Night/Gate Crasher/No
Comment/Stairway To Heaven/Moby Dick/Country Squire Bonham/
Heartbreaker/Grand Theft/Whole Lotta Love/End Credits
Warner Bros. October (Film) 1976

The ARMS Concert (1983)
Eric Clapton – Everybody Oughta Make A Change/Rita May/Lay
Down Sally/Ramblin' On My Mind/Cocaine/Andy Fairweather-Low
– Man Smart, Woman Smarter/Steve Winwood (with Eric Clapton) –
Roadrunner/Slowdown Sundown/Take Me To The River/Gimme Some
Lovin/Jeff Beck – Star Cycle/The Pump/Goodbye Pork Pie Hat/Led
Boots/Hi Ho Silver Lining/Jimmy Page – Prelude/City Sirens (with Steve
Winwood)/Who's To Blame (with Steve Winwood)/Stairway to Heaven
(Instrumental)/Ronnie Laine Ensemble – Tulsa Time/Layla/Goodnight,
Irene
VAP Video 2004 03 DVD September 2008

DVD

Disc One: Live At the Royal Albert Hall, 1970 – We're Gonna Groove/I Can't Quit You Baby/Dazed And Confused/White Summer/What Is And What Should Never Be/How Many More Times/Moby Dick/Whole Lotta Love/C'Mon Everybody/Something Else/Bring It On Home

Extras: Communication Breakdown Promo/Danmarks Radio/Supershow/ Tous En Scène

Disc Two: Immigrant Song, 1972/Madison Square Garden, 1973 – Black Dog, Misty Mountain Hop/Since I've Been Loving You/The Ocean/Earls Court, 1975 – Going To California/That's The Way/Bron-Yr-Aur Stomp/ In My Time Of Dying/Trampled Under Foot/Stairway To Heaven/ Knebworth, 1979 – Rock And Roll/Nobody's Fault But Mine/Sick Again/Achilles Last Stand/In The Evening/Kashmir/Whole Lotta Love

Extras: NYC Press Conference/Down Under/The Old Grey Whistle Test/ Promos

Warner Music Vision 0349701982 DVD May 2003

No Quarter: Jimmy Page & Robert Plant Unledded

No Quarter/Thank You/What Is And What Should Never Be/The Battle Of Evermore/Gallows Pole/Nobody's Fault But Mine/City Don't Cry/The Truth Explodes (Yallah)/ Wah Wah/When The Levee Breaks/ Wonderful One/Since I've Been Loving You/The Rain Song/That's The Way/Four Sticks/Friends/Kashmir

Bonus: Black Dog (live at the ABC American Music Awards)/Moroccan Montage/Most High/Interviews

Warner Music Vision 0349 70324 2 DVD October 2004

Celebration Day

DVD (Disc): Good Times Bad Times/Ramble On/Black Dog/In My Time Of Dying/For Your Life/Trampled Under Foot/Nobody's Fault But Mine/No Quarter/Since I've Been Loving You/Dazed And Confused/ Stairway To Heaven/The Song Remains The Same/Misty Mountain Hop/ Kashmir/Whole Lotta Love/Rock And Roll

Swan Song/Atlantic 8122 796788 2 CD/DVD (The DVD/Blu Ray package also comes with two CDs recorded at the O2 concert of November 2007.)

Acknowledgements
& Source Notes

There are many people to thank.

In the course of researching this biography, I consulted the following television/radio networks, organisations, magazines, newspapers, websites and weeklies (some of which have now ceased publication). In some cases, I extracted previously published/broadcast material. For this, I remain truly grateful to *60 Minutes Australia, Achilles Last Stand, A-Zeppelin, Ancestry.co.uk,* the *BBC, Beat International, Billboard, Blogcritics.com, Business Week, Channel 4, Circus, Creem, Daily Mail, Disc, DMME.net, DollyRockerGirl.com, Epsom & Ewell History Explorer, Finding ZoSo: Discovering The Music Of Jimmy Page, General Registry Office, Gibson.com, GQ, GroundGuitar.com, The Guardian, Guitar, Guitar Classics, Guitar For The Performing Musician, Guitar Greats, Guitar Heroes, Guitar International, The Guitar Magazine, Guitar Presents..., Guitar One, Guitar Shop, The Hollow Verse, Kerrang!, The Independent, International Musician And Recording World, JimmyPage.com, JimmyPage. co.uk, JohnBonham.co.uk, Led Zeppelin Official Forum, Los Angeles Times, LZhistory.com, Making Music, Melody Maker, Modern Guitars, MTV, Much Music, Musician,* Music Radar, *The National, The New York Times,*

NME, *The Northern Echo*, *The Observer*, *Oz*, *Perfect Sound Forever*, *Q*, *The Quietus*, *RareRecordCollector.com*, *Reality Sandwich*, *Record*, *Record Collector*, *Record Mirror*, *Retrorock.co.uk*, *Rocklopedia.com*, *ShadyOldLady. com*, *Singapore Sixties*, *Sky.com*, *Sounds*, *Talent/PM*, ... *Talks Music*, *The Times*, *Trouser Press*, *UltimateClassicRock.com*, *UltimateGuitar.com*, *Variety*, *VH1* and *YouTube* (including those who posted rare Yardbirds/Zep/ Page clips online).

I must offer a particular debt of gratitude to the following publications that in recent years have printed reams of quality journalism dedicated to Jimmy Page and Led Zeppelin. These articles were extremely useful in providing valuable research material and selected quotes for this biography. (Please see 'Sources' for a list of other articles used.) An abundance of thanks, then, to those at *Classic Rock*, *Guitarist*, *Guitar Player*, *Guitar World*, *Mojo*, *Q*, *Rolling Stone* and *Uncut*. And, of course, a big thumbs up for the magnificent fanzine, magazine and now excellent website *Tight But Loose*. Hats off to you, Mr. Lewis. Thanks for the interview and writing so many great books about Zep, all of which greatly helped in the course of this project.

For providing additional source material, I'd like to offer my appreciation to the following journalists/authors and one or two moonlighting rock stars: Owen Adams, Andy Aledort, Marcel Anders, Adrian Ashton, Martin Aston, Leslie Baldock, Liz Barnes, Max Bell, Johnny Black, Mark Blake, George Bodnar, Mick Bonham, Michael Bonner, Alison Boshoff, Joe Bosso, Kathryn Bromwich, David Cheal, Chuck Closterman, Nick Coleman, Chris Cornell, David Dalton, Stephen Davis, John Dekel, Adrian Deevoy, Dave DeMartino, Harold DeMuir, Liz Derringer, Greg Di Benedetto, Dave DiMartino, Dave Dickson, Peter Doggett, Tom Doyle, Sian Edwards, Paul Elliot, Kitty Empire, Gavin Esla, Jerry Ewing, Michael Feeney-Callan, Hugh Fielder, Mike Figgis, Andy Fyfe, Vic Garbarini, Malcolm Gerrie, Steve Gett, Simon Goddard, Michael Goldberg, Patrick Goldstein, Joe Gore, Gary Graff, Dave Green, Russell Hall, Michael Hann, Nick Hasted, Will Hodgkinson, Nicky Horne, Rob Hughes, Allan Jones, Sacha Frere-Jones, Max Kay, Nick Kent, Martin Kielty, Christopher Knowles, Joe Lalaina, Nick Logan, Kurt Loder, John McDermott, Alistair McKay,

Pete Makowski, Jason Mankey, Toby Manning, Richard Marcus, Perry Margouleff, Neville Marten, Julian Marszalek, John Mendelson, Howard Mylett, HP Newquist, Jas Obrecht, Simon Pallet, Ed Park, Pierre Perrone, Joe Perry, Tom Pinnock, Lauren Pyrah, Mark Radcliffe, Alex Reisner, Matt Resnicoff, Steven William Rimmer, Alan Robinson, Johnny Rogan, Jordan Runtagh, Chris Salewicz, Sydelle Schofield, David Schulps, Bud Scoppa, Will Shade, David Sinclair, Mat Snow, Peter Stanford, Harold Steinblatt, Phil Sutcliffe, Fiona Talkington, Paul Trynka, Jaan Ubelszki, Gary Valentine, Susan Whitall, Colin Wilson (RIP), Bill Wyman, Andy Young, Charles M. Young, Jon Young, Rob Young and absolutely anybody that I've accidentally missed.

I must also make special mention of several writers, authors and editors whose previous work on Jimmy Page and Led Zeppelin provided both inspiration and selected quotes for this book. All thanks, then, to Phil Alexander, George Case, David Cavanagh, Alan di Perna, David Fricke, Stuart Grundy, Barney Hoskyns, Richard Mann, Robert Sandall, Sylvie Simmons, John Tobler, Brad Tolinski, Mick Wall and the fine work of Nigel Williamson. I must also pay respectful thanks to the mighty Chris Welch, whose own book – *Peter Grant: The Man Who Led Zeppelin* – proved extremely helpful when researching sections of this biography.

Much gratitude, too, to Steve Rosen. A great writer and nice guy, Steve's previous work not only provided several quotes on this project, but was also a fine source of information and a number of useful quotes for another of my books *Hot Wired Guitar: The Life Of Jeff Beck*. Steve, many thanks, I genuinely appreciate your help.

Last but not least, a huge thank you to the people who kindly gave up their time and thoughts by allowing me to interview them for this biography: Chris Andrews, Dave Berry, John Carter, Chris Charlesworth, Mick Dines, Manja Dolan, Chris Farlowe, John Hawken, Nigel Kerr, Dave Lawson, Dave Lewis, Dave Mattacks, Jim McCarty, John Miles, Don Murfet (RIP), Simon Phillips, PJ Proby, Rani Sharma, Jim Taggart, Shel Talmy, Chris Welch and Ian Whitcomb. For those who wished their contributions to remain 'behind the scenes', I also remain extremely grateful.

When researching my book, *Hot Wired Guitar: The Life Of Jeff Beck*, I was fortunate enough to interview the Yardbirds' Chris Dreja, the band's second manager Simon Napier-Bell, guitar effects genius Roger Mayer and Tridents guitarist Mike Jopp. Sadly, due to various circumstances, we were unable to meet up on this occasion, so I have used extracts from previous interviews concerning their work with Jimmy Page, the Yardbirds and the Tridents here. Upmost thanks, then, to Chris, Simon, Roger and Mike.

Several honourable mentions: first (as always), a special thanks to Chris Charlesworth, whose reserves of patience on this project have surely granted him a place in heaven. Chris, working with you over the last 20 years has been an absolute pleasure. Roll on the memoirs... Thanks also to Lucy Beevor for immaculate proofing. As ever, to Anthony Cutler, Ben Davis, David Kelly, Stephen Joseph and Andrew Robinson – gentlemen, thanks for listening. A special mention, too, for absent friends. Mr. Stewart, all the best, wherever you are. And of course, I mustn't forget Trish. Thank you for getting me over the line.

There remains one last debt of gratitude: Thank you, Mr Page, for providing over five decades of fine music. We all look forward to the sixth.

Sources

In addition to the sources named above, below is a further list of magazine articles, books and DVDs – ranging from the late seventies to 2015 – that were again particularly helpful when gathering additional information and various quotes for *No Quarter*.... I remain grateful to these authors, editors, journalists, magazines and publishers for all their endeavours.

Magazine Articles

'Jimmy Page' – Steve Rosen. *Guitar Player,* July 1977
'The Page Memoirs' – Nick Kent. *The Best Of Creem,* spring 1978
'Led Zeppelin Redux...' – Chris Salewicz. *Creem,* November 1979
'Guitar Hero In Transition' – Jas Obrecht. *Guitar Player,* October 1980
'Back Pages And New Pages' – Chris Welch. *International Musician & Recording World,* January 1982

'Robert Plant – A World Exclusive' – Steve Gett. *Kerrang!*, May 1982

'Taking Root In The 80s' – Susan Whitall. *Creem*, October 1982

'Hits The Road' – Dave DeMartino. *Creem*, October, 1983

'The Guitars Of Jimmy Page' – Ed Park. *Guitar Heroes*, November 1982

'Blunt Instrument' – Steve Gett. *Guitar Heroes*, June 1983

'Beck, Clapton & Page' – Perry Margouleff. *Guitar Player*, January 1984

'Rock Of Ages' – Kurt Loder and Michael Goldberg. *Rolling Stone*, January 1984

'Page Onstage 1985' – Chris Welch. *Creem*, April/May 1985

'The Day The World Rocked' – Michael Goldberg. *Rolling Stone*, August 1985/1987

'Mission Confirmed/Holding Firm' – Chris Welch. *Kerrang!*, December 1985

'Jimmy Page – The Legend' – Liz Derringer and Sydelle Schofield. *Creem Guitar Heroes*, 1986

'Standing Firm, Kinda...' – Harold DeMuir. *Creem*, July 1986

'Jimmy Page: The Ulitmate Guitar Hero' – Steve Rosen, Joe Lalaina and various others. *Guitar World*, August 1986

'Jimmy Has A Play' – George Bodnar. *Guitar World*, September 1986

'Led Zeppelin: First US Tour' – Various. *Rolling Stone*, August 1987

'Turn Of The Page' – Mick Wall. *Kerrang!*, June 1988

'Jimmy Page's True Will' – Charles M. Young. *Musician*, July 1988

'Just Say No' – David Sinclair. Q, October 1989

'In Through The Out Door' – Matt Resnicoff. *Musician*, November 1990

'Glory Days/Steady Rollin' Man/Studio Masters' – Joe Bosso, Alan di Perna. *Guitar World*, January 1991

'Debunking The Myths' – Joe Gore. *Guitar Player*, January 1992

'Who'd Have Thought?' – Phil Sutcliffe. Q, April 1993

'Days Of Heaven/The Reel Story' – Brad Tolinski, Greg Di Benedetto, John McDermott. *Guitar World*, December 1993

'Back Pages: A Celebration' – Richard Mann, Adrian Ashton. *The Guitar Magazine*, January 1995

'Peter Grant – Obituary' – Johnny Rogan. Q, January 1996

'Deep Blue' – Paul Trynka. *Mojo*, February 1996

'Enormo!' – Mat Snow. *Mojo*, May 1996

'Stalingrad Meets Laura Ashley' – Nick Coleman and Dave Lewis, Q *Special Edition*, 1996

'The Real Seventies' – Various. Q, April 1998

'From Our Own Correspondent' – Sylvie Simmons/Mat Snow. *Mojo*, May 1998

'The 100 Greatest Guitar Solos Of All Time' – Various. *Guitar World*, September 1998

'Blow By Blow' – Alan di Perna. *Guitar World*, May 1999

'The Last Hurrah' – Mick Wall & Dave Lewis. *Mojo*, August 1999

'Pleased To Meet You...' – David Dalton, Gary Valentine, Paul Trynka & Mick Wall. *Mojo*, September 1999

'The Crowe's Nest/Good Times, Bad Times' – Alan di Perna & Mick Wall. *Classic Rock*, May 2000

'Led Zeppelin – Q Special Edition' – Various. *Q*, March 2003

'Jimmy Page: 100 Guitar Heroes' – Chris Welch. *Guitarist*, 2004

'Hats Off' – Jerry Ewing. *Classic Rock*, 2004

'The Guvnors' – Charles Shaar Murray. *Mojo*, August 2004

'Good Times, Bad Times/Forget The Myths' – Nigel Williamson. *Uncut*, May 2005

'Graffiti Art' – Mark Blake. *Guitar World*, May 2005

'Four Play' – Mick Wall. *Metal Hammer – 1970s Special*, 2006

'Sympathy For The Devil' – Christopher Knowles. *Classic Rock*, summer 2006

'Living Legend' – Pete Makowski. *Classic Rock*, January 2008

'The Q Interview' – Robert Sandall. *Q*, January 2008

'Led Zeppelin Rising' – Brad Tolinski. *Guitar World*, January 2008

'100 Guitar Songs – Jimmy Page' – David Fricke. *Rolling Stone*, June 2008

'The Real Jimmy Page' – Michael Bonner, David Cavanagh, Nick Hasted, Rob Hughes, Allan Jones & Alistair McKay. *Uncut*, January 2009

Led Zeppelin: 40th Anniversary – Alan di Perna and various others. *Guitar World*, March 2009

'Loud And Proud' – Sian Edwards. *Guitar & Bass Magazine*, November 2009

'Up Close And Personal' – Phil Alexander. *Mojo*, February 2010

'House Of the Unholy' – David Cavanagh. *Uncut*, March 2011

'When All Is One And One Is All' – Barney Hoskyns. *Classic Rock*, August 2011

'Jeff Beck – Living Legend' – Max Bell. *Classic Rock*, December 2011

'For One Night Only?' – Phil Alexander. *Mojo*, December 2012

'You Never Say Never' – Marcel Anders & Rob Hughes. *Classic Rock*, January 2013

'The Man Zep Called Merlin' – Martin Aston. *Mojo*, October 2013

'I Was Listening To Everything...' – Phil Alexander. *Mojo*, December 2013

'Over The Hills And Far Away' – Jaan Ubelszki. *Classic Rock*, January 2014

'The Wild Ride...' – Various. *Q*, April 2014

'Led Vault' – Brad Tolinski. *Guitar World*, July 2014

'The Only Way To Fly'/'Divide And Conquer' – Chris Dreja, Phil Alexander. *Mojo*, July/August 2014

'The Fourth Album? It's Good, Isn't It?' – Paul Elliot. *Classic Rock*, October 2014

'Ascension!' – Phil Alexander. *Mojo*, April 2015

'Led Get Physical' – Pierre Perrone. *Record Collector*, April 2015

Led Zeppelin: The Ultimate Music Guide – Various. *Melody Maker/Uncut*, August 2015

Books

Bonham, Mick. *John Bonham: The Powerhouse Behind Led Zeppelin* (Southbank Publishing, 2005)

Case, George. *Jimmy Page: Magus, Musician, Man* (Hal Leonard, 2007)

Clapton, Eric. *Eric Clapton: The Autobiography* (Century, 2007)

Davis, Stephen & Aerosmith. *Walk This Way: The Autobiography Of Aerosmith* (Avon, 1997)

Davis, Stephen. *Hammer Of The Gods* (Sidgwick & Jackson, 1985)

Davis, Stephen. *Old Gods Almost Dead* (Broadway, 2001)

Frame, Pete. *Rock Family Trees* (Omnibus Press, 1993)

Hoskyns, Barney. *Trampled Under Foot: The Power And Excess Of Led Zeppelin* (Faber & Faber, 2012)

Lewis, Dave. *Led Zeppelin: A Celebration* (Omnibus Press, 1990)

Lewis, Dave. *Led Zeppelin, A Celebration Two – The Tight But Loose Files* (Omnibus Press, 2003)

Lewis, Dave. *The Complete Guide To The Music Of Led Zeppelin* (Omnibus Press, 1994)

Lewis, Dave & Pallet, Simon. *Led Zeppelin: The Concert File* (Omnibus Press, 2005)

Mylett, Howard. *Tangents Within A Framework* (Omnibus Press, 1983)

Page, Jimmy. *Jimmy Page By Jimmy Page* (Genesis, 2010)

Perry, Joe with Ritz, David. *Rocks: My Life In And Out Of Aerosmith* (Simon & Schuster, 2014)

Reddin, Frank. *Sonic Boom: The Impact Of Led Zeppelin* (Enzeppolopaedia, 2011)

Room, Adrian (Ed.). *Brewster's Dictionary Of Phrase And Fable: Fifteenth Edition* (Cassell, 1996)

Stanford, Peter. *The Devil: A Biography* (Mandarin, 1996)

Tobler, John & Grundy, Stewart. *The Guitar Greats* (BBC Publications, 1983)

Wall, Mick. *Led Zeppelin: When Giants Walked The Earth* (Orion, 2008)

Welch, Chris. *Peter Grant: The Man Who Led Zeppelin* (Omnibus Press, 2001)
Wilson, Colin. *Aleister Crowley: The Nature Of The Beast* (Aeon, 2005)
Wyman, Bill. *Bill Wyman's Blues Odyssey* (Dorling & Kindersley, 2001)
Yorke, Ritchie. *Led Zeppelin: The Definitive Biography* (Virgin – revised edition, 1993)

Films/DVDs
The Song Remains The Same, Led Zeppelin (1976)
DVD, Led Zeppelin (2003)
Red, White & Blues – A Film By Mike Figgis (2003)
No Quarter: Jimmy Page & Robert Plant Unledded (2004)
Celebration Day (2007)
The ARMS Concert (1983) (2008)
It Might Get Loud – Davis Guggenheim (2009)

Index

Page numbers with an n indicates a footnote

689

Index